Routledge Handbook of Maritime Regulation and Enforcement

With advances in technology and maritime transport, human use of the ocean now extends beyond the traditional activities of navigation and fishing. Emerging activities such as bioprospecting, deep seabed mineral and hydrocarbon exploration and exploitation, offshore renewable energy developments and marine scientific probes of deep sea areas challenge the applicability of maritime law and policy in new ways.

This handbook examines current regulatory and enforcement instruments and mechanisms for different sectors of maritime activity. Covering various jurisdictions, its specially commissioned chapters are authored by some of the world's foremost authorities on maritime law, and offer unique perspectives on maritime law, policy and practice.

This highly relevant collection is organised into four parts:

- International law considerations in maritime regulation and enforcement
- Role of states and other international actors in maritime regulation and enforcement
- Regulation and enforcement in different maritime sectors
- Current issues and future challenges

This comprehensive reference work will be of interest to scholars and students of maritime law, practitioners and non-lawyers interested in the regulation of offshore areas, as well as policy-makers.

Robin Warner is Professor at the Australian National Centre for Ocean Resources and Security. She was formerly the Assistant Secretary of the International Crime Branch of the Criminal Justice Division in the Commonwealth Attorney General's Department from 2002 to 2006. Previously she served with the Royal Australian Navy as a legal officer.

Stuart Kaye is Director and Professor of Law within the Australian National Centre for Ocean Resources and Security (ANCORS) at the University of Wollongong. He was formerly the Dean of Law at the University of Western Australia having been appointed Winthrop Professor of Law in July 2010. He held a Chair in Law at the University of Melbourne from 2006 to 2010 and was Dean and Professor of Law at the University of Wollongong between 2002 and 2006.

Routledge Handbook of Maritime Regulation and Enforcement

Edited by
Robin Warner and Stuart Kaye

LONDON AND NEW YORK

First published 2016
by Routledge

2 Park Square, Milton Park, Abingdon, Oxfordshire OX14 4RN
711 Third Avenue, New York, NY 10017

Routledge is an imprint of the Taylor & Francis Group, an informa business

First issued in paperback 2018

Copyright © 2016 Robin Warner and Stuart Kaye

The right of Robin Warner and Stuart Kaye be identified as editors of this work has been asserted by them in accordance with sections 77 and 78 of the Copyright, Designs and Patents Act 1988.

All rights reserved. No part of this book may be reprinted or reproduced or utilised in any form or by any electronic, mechanical, or other means, now known or hereafter invented, including photocopying and recording, or in any information storage or retrieval system, without permission in writing from the publishers.

Notice:
Product or corporate names may be trademarks or registered trademarks, and are used only for identification and explanation without intent to infringe.

British Library Cataloguing in Publication Data
A catalogue record for this book is available from the British Library

Library of Congress Cataloging-in-Publication Data
Routledge handbook of maritime regulation and enforcement.
    pages cm
  Includes bibliographical references and index.
  1. Maritime law.   2. Marine resources development—Law and legislation.
I. Warner, Robin, editor.   II. Kaye, Stuart, editor.
  K1150.R68 2015
  343.09'6—dc23
  2015011923

ISBN: 978-0-415-70445-8 (hbk)
ISBN: 978-1-138-61439-0 (pbk)

Typeset in Bembo
by Apex CoVantage, LLC

Contents

Contributors ix
Abbreviations xix
Foreword by Marie Jacobsson xxv

    Introduction xxvii
    Robin Warner and Stuart Kaye

PART A
International Law Considerations in Maritime Regulation and Enforcement   1

    1. A Zonal Approach to Maritime Regulation and Enforcement   3
       Stuart Kaye

    2. The High Seas Regime: a Model of Self-regulation?   16
       Robin Warner

    3. The Use of Force   27
       Cameron Moore

PART B
Role of States and Other International Actors in Maritime Regulation and Enforcement   41

    4. The Role of Flag States   43
       Sam Bateman

    5. The Role of Coastal States   59
       Lowell Bautista

Contents

6. The Role of Port States   71
  Rosemary Rayfuse

7. The Role of Global Organisations   86
  J. Ashley Roach

8. The Role of Regional Organisations   106
  Kerry Tetzlaff

9. The Role of Courts and Tribunals in Maritime Regulation and Enforcement   122
  Dale Stephens

PART C
Regulation and Enforcement in Different Maritime Sectors   **137**

10. Fisheries Enforcement and the Concepts of Compliance and Monitoring, Control and Surveillance   139
  Mary Ann Palma-Robles

11. Shipping: Safety of Life at Sea   161
  Anthony Morrison

12. Shipping: Vessel-source Pollution   176
  Erik J. Molenaar

13. Regulation of Offshore Hydrocarbon Exploration and Exploitation under International Law   193
  Youna Lyons

14. The Regulation of Marine Scientific Research: Addressing Challenges, Advancing Knowledge   212
  Harriet Harden Davies

15. Deep Seabed Mining: Key Obligations in the Emerging Regulation of Exploration and Development in the Pacific   231
  Robert Makgill and Ana P. Linhares

16. Transnational Crime   262
  Douglas Guilfoyle

17. Combating Piracy and Armed Robbery at Sea: from Somalia to the Gulf of Guinea   277
  Clive Schofield and Kamal-Deen Ali

PART D
Current Issues and Future Challenges   **293**

18. Regulation of Marine Renewable Energy   295
    Anne Marie O'Hagan

19. The Potential to Regulate Bioprospecting for Marine
    Genetic Resources: Two Case Studies   324
    Julia Jabour

20. Ocean Acidification: Scientific Surges, Lagging Law and Policy Responses   342
    Katja Fennel and David L. VanderZwaag

21. Use of Technology in Maritime Regulation and Enforcement   363
    Chris Rahman

22. Cooperative Maritime Surveillance and Enforcement   378
    Warwick Gullett and Yubing Shi

23. Developing New Regulatory Paradigms for the Conservation
    and Sustainable Use of Marine Biodiversity in Areas beyond
    National Jurisdiction   394
    Robin Warner

Index   409

Contributors

Sam Bateman retired from the RAN as a Commodore and is now a Professorial Research Fellow at the Australian National Centre for Ocean Resources and Security (ANCORS) at the University of Wollongong in Australia, and an Adviser to the Maritime Security Programme at the S. Rajaratnam School of International Studies (RSIS) at the Nanyang Technological University in Singapore. His naval service included four ship commands ranging from a patrol boat to guided-missile destroyer. He has written extensively on defence and maritime issues in Australia, the Asia-Pacific and Indian Ocean, and was awarded his PhD from the University of NSW in 2001 for a dissertation on "The Strategic and Political Aspects of the Law of the Sea in East Asian Seas". Co-authored reports for the Australian Strategic Policy Institute (ASPI), include *Our Western Front: Australia and the Indian Ocean* (2010), *Staying the Course: Australia and Maritime Security in the South Pacific* (2011), *Making Waves: Australian Ocean Development Assistance* (2012) and most recently, *Terms of Engagement – Australia's Regional Defence Diplomacy* (2013). He has also co-authored policy papers for RSIS including *ASEAN and the Indian Ocean* (2011). His recent co-edited publications include *Maritime Challenges and Priorities in Asia – Implications for Regional Security* (Routledge, 2012).

Lowell Bautista is a Lecturer at the School of Law and a Staff Member at the Australian National Centre for Ocean Resources and Security (ANCORS), Faculty of Law, Humanities and the Arts, University of Wollongong. He is a lawyer with more than ten years of experience in legal and policy research, litigation and consultancy. He holds Bachelor of Arts in Political Science (cum laude) and Bachelor of Laws (LL.B.) degrees from the University of the Philippines, a Master of Laws (Marine and Environmental Law) degree from Dalhousie University in Canada, and a Doctor of Philosophy (PhD.) in law from the University of Wollongong. His areas of research include territorial and maritime boundary issues in the Asia-Pacific, the South China Sea, Philippine maritime and territorial issues, maritime piracy and terrorism, international humanitarian law, underwater cultural heritage, and international environmental law, on which topics he has also published. Dr Bautista has participated in numerous research and consultancies, as well as in the preparation of submissions, opinions, and reports for government department and agencies in Australia and in the Philippines, as well as for regional and international organisations. On numerous occasions, Dr Bautista has provided confidential advice and opinions on matters pertaining to offshore oil and gas resources, the law of the sea, the South China Sea, maritime boundary delimitation and public international law to the Philippine Government, and to private companies in the Philippines and Australia.

Contributors

Kamal-Deen Ali is the Legal Director of the Ghana Navy and concurrently Director of Research at the Ghana Armed Forces Command and Staff College. He previously held several appointments including deployments in the United Nations Peacekeeping Missions in the DR Congo and Sierra Leone. He is the Executive Director of the Centre for Maritime Law and Security Africa. He is also a Fellow of the Australian National Centre for Ocean Resources and Security (ANCORS), University of Wollongong, Australia, an Associate of the Corbett Centre for Maritime Policy, United Kingdom, and a Fellow of Africa Security Dialogue and Research (ASDR). Commander Ali earned a PhD from the University of Wollongong, Australia. His previous academic qualifications include a Master of Laws degree in international maritime law and Master of Arts degree in international relations. He has, since 2006, been extensively involved in maritime security capacity-building and policy-shaping in the Gulf of Guinea. He has published significantly including a book chapter titled "African States and the Law Sea: Have the Benefits Been Realized?" in *Ocean Yearbook 2012*, and a seminal article "The Anatomy of Gulf of Guinea Piracy," *Naval War College Review, 2015*. He has an upcoming book "Maritime Security Cooperation in the Gulf of Guinea: Prospects and Challenges," (Brill/Martinus: 2015).

Katja Fennel is Associate Professor in the Department of Oceanography at Dalhousie University in Halifax, Canada and holds the Canada Research Chair in Marine Prediction. As head of the Marine Environmental Modeling Group (http://memg.ocean.dal.ca) she leads the development of marine ecosystem and biogeochemical models at Dalhousie. For the past two decades Dr Fennel has developed and applied numerical models of marine ecosystems and biogeochemistry with particular focus on continental shelf systems and the assimilation of observations into these models in order to improve their predictive capabilities. She has authored and co-authored more than 60 publications in the peer-reviewed literature, and collaborated in several major national and international research projects including the NSF North Atlantic Bloom experiment; the NSERC Ocean Tracking Network; the US IOOS Coastal and Ocean Modeling Testbed (COMT); and the Marine Environmental Observation, Prediction and Response (MEOPAR) Network of Centers of Excellence. She served as theme leader for the Ocean Tracking Network and is currently project leader for projects within COMT and MEOPAR. Dr Fennel serves as co-editor-in-chief of the journal *Biogeosciences*, is a member of the editorial boards of the journals *Frontiers in Ocean Observation* and *Ocean Modelling*, and has served on several international science advisory bodies including the IMBER/LOICZ Continental Margins Task Team and the CLIVAR Working Group on Ocean Model Development. She is presently a member of the international GODAE OceanView science team and co-chairs the GODAE Marine Ecosystem Analysis and Prediction Task Team.

Douglas Guilfoyle is an Associate Professor at the Faculty of Laws, Monash University. He is the author of *Shipping Interdiction and the Law of the Sea* (CUP, 2009) and numerous articles on maritime security and law enforcement, naval warfare and Somali piracy. He was previously a Reader in Law at University College London and has acted as a consultant to the Contact Group on Piracy off the Coast of Somalia (Working Group 2), the Foreign Affairs Committee of the House of Commons and the UN Office on Drugs and Crime. He also acted as an adviser to the government of Mauritius in the *Mauritius v UK* case before the Permanent Court of Arbitration. He holds a PhD and LLM from the University of Cambridge, where he was a Chevening and Gates Scholar, and undergraduate degrees in law and history from the Australian National University. Prior to graduate study he worked as a litigation solicitor and as a judge's associate in Australia.

Contributors

Warwick Gullett is Professor and Dean of Law at the University of Wollongong and former Deputy Director of the Australian National Centre for Ocean Resources and Security (ANCORS) at the University of Wollongong. His research interests focus on legal protection of the marine environment and the international law of the sea. He is the author of *Fisheries Law in Australia* (335pp, LexisNexis Butterworths, 2008) and co-editor of *Marine Resources Management* (359pp, LexisNexis Butterworths, 2011). Professor Gullett is on the Editorial Committee of the *Environmental and Planning Law Journal* and the *Australasian Journal of Natural Resources Law and Policy* and was Editor of the *Australian Journal of Maritime and Ocean Affairs* for 2007–2010. Professor Gullett has written extensively on laws regarding the marine environment, in particular focusing on fisheries law, marine protected areas, marine resource management and jurisdictional issues.

Harriet Harden Davies is a PhD candidate at the Australian National Centre for Ocean Resources and Security (ANCORS), University of Wollongong. The main focus of Harriet's research is the governance of marine genetic resources in areas beyond national jurisdiction, with a particular focus on non-monetary benefit sharing. Harriet has a keen interest in the linkages between science, law and policy, and particularly the role of science in informing new approaches to global ocean governance. Prior to joining ANCORS Harriet was the Policy and Projects Manager at the Australian Academy of Technological Sciences and Engineering (ATSE), where she was responsible for the delivery of a number of research projects and activities relating to the role of technological innovation in improving governance across a range of priority areas. Harriet has contributed to projects for international organisations including the Organisation for Economic Cooperation and Development and the Intergovernmental Oceanographic Commission of UNESCO. Previously, Harriet was at the UK Royal Society's Science Policy Centre, working on projects relating to geoengineering governance, international scientific collaboration and marine science policy. She holds a BSc (Hons) Marine Biology with Oceanography from the University of Southampton.

Julia Jabour is a member of the Ocean & Antarctic Governance Research Program at the Institute for Marine and Antarctic Studies (IMAS). She has been researching, writing, and lecturing on polar governance for 20 years. Most of her teaching and research is interdisciplinary and multidisciplinary, involving examining current scientific and technical developments, determining their utility to the policy and law-making processes, and translating that information into user-friendly knowledge for uptake by non-specialist audiences. Julia has visited Antarctica six times, and been an adviser to the Australian Government at Antarctic Treaty Consultative Meetings on three occasions.

Stuart Kaye is Director and Professor of Law within the Australian National Centre for Ocean Resources and Security (ANCORS) at the University of Wollongong. He was formerly the Dean of Law at the University of Western Australia having been appointed Winthrop Professor of Law in July 2010. He held a Chair in Law at the University of Melbourne from 2006 to 2010 and was Dean and Professor of Law at the University of Wollongong between 2002 and 2006. He holds degrees in arts and law from the University of Sydney, winning the Law Graduates' Association Medal, and a doctorate in law from Dalhousie University. He is admitted as a Barrister of the Supreme Courts of New South Wales, Tasmania and Queensland. He has an extensive research interest in the law of the sea and international law. He has written a number of books, including *Australia's Maritime Boundaries* (2001), *The Torres Strait* (1997), *International*

Fisheries Management (2001), *Freedom of Navigation in the Indo-Pacific Region* and almost 90 other books, articles and chapters. He was appointed to the International Hydrographic Organization's Panel of Experts on Maritime Boundary Delimitation in 1995 and in 2000 was appointed to the List of Arbitrators under the Environmental Protocol to the Antarctic Treaty. He was chair of the Australian International Humanitarian Law Committee from 2003 to 2009, for which he was awarded the Australian Red Cross Society Distinguished Service Medal. He was elected a Fellow of the Royal Geographical Society in 2007 and a Fellow of the Australian Academy of Law in 2011.

Ana Paula Linhares is a doctoral researcher and legal consultant working in Robert Makgill's Chambers, who specialises in natural resources, carbon trading, international environmental law and law of the sea. She has undertaken postgraduate studies in New Zealand and the UK, and worked in a number of environmental think-tanks within those jurisdictions and Brazil. Ana Paula is fluent in a number of languages, and experienced in the practice of both civil and common law. Her doctoral research is presently concerned with transboundary resource development, while her consultancy largely focuses on the interface between international environmental law and its application within domestic jurisdictions.

Youna Lyons is a bilingual former French litigator with more than 12 years of international practice in Asia and Europe. Passionate about the ocean, Youna later studied marine sciences and holds a Masters in Marine Affairs from the University of Washington. She is currently pursuing a PhD with the Australian National Centre for Ocean Resources and Security (ANCORS) at the University of Wollongong titled: "Defining and mapping valuable and sensitive marine environments in the South China Sea". Youna's dual expertise in law and marine sciences uniquely position her to integrate these fields for marine policy-making purposes and has led her to spearhead and coordinate several multidisciplinary research projects at CIL including: the prospects for re-use of obsolete offshore installations as artificial reefs in Southeast Asia, sensitivity mapping for Singapore in the context of oil spill preparedness and response and the mapping of shallow features in the South China Sea. She is bilingual French and English, has worked across Europe, the US and Asia and, besides her Masters in Marine Affairs, holds an LLM and two Bachelors from La Sorbonne respectively in international public and private law and in procedural law.

Robert Makgill is a Barrister who specialises in environmental, natural resources and public law. He regularly appears as legal counsel before the Environment Court and courts of general jurisdiction in New Zealand. In 2005 Robert was awarded a doctoral scholarship though the Maritime Institute, Department of Public International Law, Ghent University, Belgium. In 2010 he was legal counsel in the International Law for the Sea Tribunal's (ITLOS) historic advisory opinion on deep sea mining in the High Seas. In 2011 he chaired the legal working group for the International Seabed Authority's international workshop on "Environmental Management Needs for Exploration and Exploitation of Deep Sea Minerals", and represented the New Zealand Law Society before the Parliamentary Select Committee during the enactment of the Exclusive Economic Zone and Continental Shelf (Environmental Effects) Act 2012. In 2012 he advised the Secretariat of the Pacific Community (SOPAC) on the European Union funded deep sea minerals project, which aims to establish deep sea regulatory frameworks for Pacific Island member States. He has provided on-going advice to SOPAC on the regulation of deep sea mining in the Pacific. In 2013 he was appointed an Exclusive Economic Zone (EEZ) Hearing Commissioner for the New Zealand Environmental Protection Authority, and assisted in advising a party to the ITLOS advisory proceedings on illegal fishing activities within the EEZs of third party States. In 2014 he was legal counsel for the commercial fishers in successful opposition to the first public hearing into an application to undertake deep seabed mining in New Zealand's EEZ. Robert is a doctoral researcher at the University of Ghent, and research fellow with the Faculty of Environment, Society and Design at Lincoln University, New Zealand.

Erik J. Molenaar is Deputy Director of the Netherlands Institute for the Law of the Sea (NILOS) at Utrecht University and Professor with the K.G. Jebsen Centre for the Law of the Sea (JCLOS) at the University of Tromsø. After completing his PhD on "Coastal State Jurisdiction over Vessel-Source Pollution" in 1998, he broadened his research field with international fisheries law and the international law relating to the Antarctic and Arctic. In addition to fundamental research, he has also provided juridical advice to, *inter alia*, various shipping and fishing companies, Netherlands and Norwegian Ministries, the European Parliament, the European Commission, and UNEP and FAO. His research has led to his participation in various diplomatic conferences and other intergovernmental meetings, including the meetings of several regional fisheries management organisations. Since late 2013 his research has had a specific focus on participation, allocation and the ecosystem approach to polar fisheries.

Cameron Moore is a Senior Lecturer in the School of Law at the University of New England (UNE), Armidale, NSW. He is also an Adjunct Senior Lecturer at the Australian National University and an Honorary Fellow of the Australian National Centre for Ocean Resources and Security at the University of Wollongong. He has previously been the Academic Master of Robb College at UNE. His publications include the book *ADF on the Beat: A Legal Analysis of Offshore Enforcement by the ADF* (2004) and other articles and chapters on the Australian Defence Force and maritime security. Between 1996 and 2003, Cameron was a Royal Australian Navy Legal Officer. His legal experience includes service at sea as well as advising at the strategic level on a number of ADF deployments, ongoing fisheries and border protection operations and the TAMPA incident. Cameron is still an active Navy reservist and has worked closely with Border Protection Command. He had a brief deployment to Afghanistan in 2010. He has recently completed a PhD thesis through the Australian National University on the Australian Defence Force and the Executive Power.

Anthony Morrison is a Research Fellow at the Australian National Centre for Ocean Resources and Security. Dr Morrison came to ANCORS after having spent over 30 years as a lawyer in private, corporate and public practice as a Legal Officer in the Royal Australian Navy, a lawyer in private practice, Legal Counsel and Claims Manager for an insurance company and, for the 20 years prior to coming to ANCORS, a senior lawyer and company secretary for the Maritime Service Board of New South Wales (MSB) and its various successor bodies. During this latter period, he undertook various roles including Legal Manager of the MSB, General Counsel and Deputy Secretary of the MSB until its abolition in 1995, acting General Counsel and Deputy Secretary of the Sydney Ports Corporation, Corporate Secretary of the Port Kembla Port Corporation, General Counsel to the Office of Marine Administration and finally General Counsel to the NSW Maritime Authority. Dr Morrison's research interests include Law of the Sea, marine environmental law, maritime security, legal regulation of shipping and ports, marine insurance and commercial maritime law. Dr Morrison is the author of *Places of Refuge for Ships in Distress: Problems and Methods of Resolution* (Martinus Nijhoff, 2012) and has contributed a number of articles in the areas of legal regulation of shipping and environmental law.

Contributors

Anne Marie O'Hagan has over 15 years of experience in coastal and marine research and is currently a Senior Research Fellow in the MaREI Centre, University College Cork (Ireland). Her present research focuses on the law, policy and environmental aspects of ocean energy development and how these can be accommodated in planning and management systems. Dr O'Hagan qualified in environmental science before undertaking a PhD on the legal framework for coastal management in Ireland. She subsequently completed a degree in law whilst working full-time on Law of the Sea projects in the National University of Ireland, Galway. Dr O'Hagan moved to University College Cork in 2007 where she worked initially on national and European projects on coastal management and adaptation to climate change in coastal areas. In 2009, she took up a position under the prestigious Science Foundation Ireland (SFI)-funded, Charles Parsons Energy Research Award, a government initiative designed to build capacity in key research areas. She continues to be involved in multidisciplinary projects including those focused on aquaculture, spatial planning, environmental assessment and most recently risk-based consenting for offshore energy. Dr O'Hagan is a recognised expert on national and European coastal and marine legislation and policy and represents MaREI on several working groups (IEA-OES, EC Ocean Energy Forum and ICES) and national industry association (MRIA). She has published her research on coastal, marine and energy topics in numerous papers and has presented her findings at several international conferences.

Mary Ann Palma-Robles obtained her Doctor of Philosophy from the University of Wollongong, Australia. She completed the Master of Marine Management at Dalhousie University in Canada and a Bachelor of Arts in Public Administration from the University of the Philippines. Mary Ann is a Visiting Senior Fellow at the Australian National Centre for Ocean Resources and Security (ANCORS), University of Wollongong and holds an Adjunct Senior Research Fellow position at the Centre for Sustainable Tropical Fisheries and Aquaculture (CSTFA), College of Marine and Environmental Sciences, James Cook University. Her research interests include international fisheries law and policy, ocean policy and management, maritime security and regional marine governance. She has published widely on these topics, including a co-authored book, *Promoting Sustainable Fisheries: The International Legal Framework to Combat Illegal, Unreported and Unregulated Fishing* (Brill, 2010). Mary Ann has undertaken research on fisheries law and policy funded by international organisations, Australian government agencies, foreign governments and international non-government organisations. Her most recent research includes the impact of IUU fishing regulations on international fish trade, combating transnational crime in fisheries, and exploring fisheries cooperation in the Indo-Pacific region.

Chris Rahman is Senior Research Fellow in Maritime Strategy and Security at the Australian National Centre for Ocean Resources and Security (ANCORS), University of Wollongong. He is an academic strategist, with a research focus on maritime strategy, strategic theory, Australian defence policy, China and the strategic relations of the Indo-Pacific region; as well as contemporary issues in maritime security, including technology applications such as vessel tracking. He is currently coordinating a major project on the history of the Pacific Patrol Boat Program and manages the ANCORS Vessel Tracking Initiative in collaboration with industry and Australian government partners.

Rosemary Rayfuse is a Professor of International Law in the Faculty of Law at UNSW Australia and holds a conjoint appointment as Professor in the Faculty of Law, Lund University and a visiting appointment at the University of Gothenburg. She is a member of the IUCN Commission on Environmental Law and the ILA Committee on Sea Level Rise and International Law. Her research focuses primarily on protection of the marine environment in areas beyond national jurisdiction and on the normative effects of climate change adaptation and mitigation responses, including climate engineering, on international law. She is the author of *Non-Flag State Enforcement in High Seas Fisheries* (Martinus Nijhoff, 2004) and editor of a number of books including the *Research Handbook on International Marine Environmental Law* (Edward Elgar, 2015) and (with S. Scott) *International Law in the Era of Climate Change* (Edward Elgar, 2012).

J. Ashley Roach (Captain JAG Corps US Navy Ret.) was an attorney adviser in the Office of the Legal Adviser, U.S. Department of State, from 1988 until he retired at the end of January 2009, responsible for law of the sea matters. He has taught, advised and published extensively on national maritime claims and other law of the sea issues, including the Arctic. He has negotiated, and participated in the negotiation of, numerous international agreements involving law of the sea issues. Since retiring he has concentrated on piracy, Arctic and island-dispute issues. The third edition of his book (with Dr Robert W. Smith), *Excessive Maritime Claims*, was published by Nijhoff in August 2012. He chairs the International Law Association Committee on Baselines under the International Law of the Sea dealing with straight baselines (2013–2016). He is a Global Associate and Senior Visiting Scholar (2014–2015), Centre for International Law, National University of Singapore. He received his LL.M. (highest honours in public international law and comparative law) from the George Washington University School of Law in 1971 and his J.D. from the University of Pennsylvania Law School in 1963.

Clive Schofield is Professor and is Director of Research at the Australian Centre for Ocean Resource and Security (ANCORS), University of Wollongong (UOW). He is also the Leader of the University's Sustaining Oceans and Coastal Communities research theme within the UOW Global Challenges Program. He is a past Australian Research Council (ARC) Future Fellow and QEII Senior Research Fellow. He holds a PhD (geography) from the University of Durham, UK and an LLM from the University of British Columbia, Canada. Clive's research interests relate to international boundaries and particularly maritime boundary delimitation and marine jurisdictional issues. He has published over 200 scholarly publications including 22 books and monographs (including edited works) on these issues as well as geo-technical aspects of the law of the sea and maritime security. Clive serves as an International Hydrographic Office (IHO)-nominated Observer on the Advisory Board on the Law of the Sea (ABLOS). He has also been involved in the peaceful settlement of boundary and territory disputes, for example through the provision of technical advice and research support to governments engaged in boundary negotiations and in dispute settlement cases before the International Court of Justice (ICJ) and in international arbitration cases and has been appointed as a Peacebuilding Adviser on behalf of the United Nations and World Bank.

Yubing Shi is Associate Professor at the South China Institute, Xiamen University, China. He is also a visiting fellow at Australian National Centre for Ocean Resources and Security. He obtained his PhD from ANCORS, University of Wollongong (UOW) in 2014. Before that, he received a Master of Transnational Crime Prevention (M.TCP) from UOW and a Master of Laws degree (LL.M) from Beijing Technology and Business University. Dr Shi served as a senior lecturer at Beijing College of Politics and Law from 2003 to 2011, and then he was employed as a sessional lecturer by Law School of UOW during his PhD candidature. He has over ten years of experience in teaching various international law and business law related courses for Chinese and Australian students. Dr Shi's research interests are international law, the law of the sea and international environmental law. To date he has published over 30 Journal articles or book chapters in his research fields. He is a member of China Law Society and the deputy secretary-general of Beijing Association for Transnational Crime Prevention. The peer reviewed Journals that he has published with include the *International Journal of Marine and Coastal Law*, *Journal of East Asia and International Law* and *Yearbook of International Environmental Law*. Dr Shi has received various scholarships and awards, such as the Global Challenges PhD Scholar Award by UOW (2014), University Postgraduate Award (2011–2014), International Postgraduate Tuition Award (2011–2014), Australian AusAid Award (2006), Chinese Government Award for Outstanding Self-financed PhD Students Abroad (2014), Best Paper Award (2014), and Beijing Outstanding Youth Teacher (2008).

Dale Stephens spent 20 years as a legal officer in the Royal Australian Navy. In February 2013, Captain Stephens RAN transferred to the Navy Reserve and took up a full time position as an Associate Professor at the University of Adelaide Law School where he is currently located. His operational deployments include East Timor in 1999 and 2000, as well as Iraq in 2005 and 2008. In 2004, Dr Stephens completed a Master of Laws degree at Harvard University Law School. In February 2014 he completed his Doctor of Juridical Science at Harvard Law School. His dissertation topic was "Lawfare or Law Fair? The Role of Law in Military Decision Making". During his time in the Australian Defence Force, Dr Stephens was involved in providing legal advice regarding numerous operational, disciplinary and administrative law issues, including fisheries, customs and immigration matters within Australia's maritime zones, combined operations with other military forces, UN Peace Operations, drafting Rules of Engagement, implementation of international treaties including the International Criminal Court Convention as well as numerous weapons reviews. In the early 2000's Dr Stephens was part of the Australian delegation to UNESCO negotiating the Underwater Cultural Heritage Convention. In the mid-2000's he taught at the U.S. Naval War College located in Newport, Rhode Island as a faculty member of the International Law Department. In 2010 was seconded to the Department of the Prime Minister and Cabinet as a senior advisor on Afghanistan. He is currently Head of the SA Navy Legal Reserve Panel and also Director of the Adelaide University Research Unit on Military Law and Ethics.

Kerry Tetzlaff is currently a Research Fellow at the Faculty of Law, University of Auckland, New Zealand. Prior to this, she was Director of the Environmental Law Programme at the School of Law, University of the South Pacific, where she taught law of the sea and international fisheries law. Kerry has also taught law at the University of Cambridge, University of Auckland and University of Trier. Kerry is a legal advisor to various Pacific states on issues of the environment, resource management, fisheries, deep sea mining, law of the sea and climate change. She is on the Board of Advisors for the Fisheries Law Centre, Canada, and a Member of the Academic Advisory Group of the Resource Management Law Association of New Zealand. Kerry is also a member of the IUCN Commission on Environmental Law (Specialist Group on Oceans, Coasts and Coral Reefs) and consults for governments, organisations and companies on issues of international and environmental law. She has published extensively in international journals and spoken at conferences and/or given lectures in the United States, Canada, United Kingdom, Norway, Italy, New Zealand, Vanuatu and the Cook Islands. Kerry's research interests include international environmental law, resource management law, law of the sea, fisheries law, deep sea mining law, international law, and small island developing states. Kerry studied law at the University of Cambridge, Harvard University, University of Auckland as well as the European University Institute and, prior to the move to academia, practiced corporate and resource management law in New Zealand.

David L. VanderZwaag holds the Canada Research Chair (Tier 1) in Ocean Law and Governance at Dalhousie University, Halifax, Canada. He teaches international environmental law and is the past Co-director of Dalhousie's interdisciplinary Marine Affairs Program and the past Director of the Marine & Environmental Law Institute. Dr VanderZwaag is currently a member of the IUCN's World Commission on Environmental Law (WCEL) and Co-chair of the WCEL's Specialist Group on Oceans, Coasts & Coral Reefs. He is an elected member of the International Council of Environmental Law. Dr VanderZwaag has authored over 150 papers in the marine and environmental law field. His most recent book publications include: *Polar Oceans Governance in an Era of Environmental Change* (edited with Tim Stephens) (Cheltenham, UK: Edward Elgar, 2014); and *Recasting Transboundary Fisheries Management Arrangements in Light of Sustainability Principles: Canadian and International Perspectives* (edited with D.A. Russell) (Leiden: Martinus Nijhoff, 2010). Professor VanderZwaag's educational background includes: PhD (1994, University of Wales, Cardiff), LL.M. (1982, Dalhousie Law School), J.D. (1980, University of Arkansas Law School), M.Div. (1974, Princeton Theological Seminary), and B.A. (1971, Calvin College).

Robin Warner is Professor at the Australian National Centre for Ocean Resources and Security. She was formerly the Assistant Secretary of the International Crime Branch of the Criminal Justice Division in the Commonwealth Attorney General's Department from 2002 to 2006. During that period Dr Warner led 12 Australian delegations to bilateral and multilateral delegations on transnational crime and criminal justice cooperation issues. Previously she served with the Royal Australian Navy as a legal officer. During her Defence Force legal career, Captain Warner occupied a wide range of positions including Director of International Law for the Australian Defence Force and Deputy Director of Naval Legal Services. She graduated as a PhD from the University of Sydney in November 2006. Her doctoral research concerned the international law framework for protection of the marine environment and conservation of marine biodiversity beyond national jurisdiction. She is the author of *Protecting the Oceans Beyond National Jurisdiction: Strengthening the International Law Framework* (Martinus Nijhoff Publishers, Leiden, 2009), editor (with Simon Marsden) of *Transboundary Environmental Governance: Inland, Marine and Coastal Perspectives* (Ashgate Publishers, Farnham, Surrey, 2012), editor (with Clive Schofield) of *Climate Change and the Oceans: Gauging the Legal and Policy Currents in the Asia Pacific and Beyond* (Edward Elgar Publishers, Cheltenham, UK, 2012) and editor (with Stuart Kaye) of *Routledge Handbook on Maritime Regulation and Enforcement* (Routledge Publishers, UK, 2015). She has also published numerous articles in international peer reviewed journals and chapters in books on international law and policy.

Abbreviations

ABNJ	areas beyond national jurisdiction
AFMA	Australian Fisheries Management Authority
Area	seabed, ocean floor and subsoil beyond the outer limits of national jurisdiction
ASEAN	Association of Southeast Asian Nations
ATCM	Antarctic Treaty Consultative Meeting
ATCP	Antarctic Treaty Consultative Party
ATS	Antarctic Treaty System
BBNJ	Ad Hoc Open-ended Informal Working Group on conservation and sustainable use of marine biological diversity in areas beyond national jurisdiction
BCN	biological, chemical and nuclear
BMP	best management practice
BOEM	Bureau of Ocean Energy Management
CBD	Convention on Biological Diversity
CCAMLR Convention	Convention on the Conservation of Antarctic Marine Living Resources
CCAMLR	Commission for the Conservation of Antarctic Marine Living Resources
CDEM	construction, design, equipment and manning
CDS	catch documentation scheme
CEP	Committee for Environmental Protection
CHM	common heritage of mankind
CITES	Convention on International Trade in Endangered Species of Wild Fauna and Flora
CLC	International Convention on Civil Liability for Oil Pollution Damage
CLCS	Commission on the Limits of the Continental Shelf
CMS	Convention on the Conservation of Migratory Species of Wild Animals
cooperating NCP	cooperating non-contracting party
COP	Conference of the Parties
DOALOS	Division for Ocean Affairs and the Law of the Sea
DSM	deep sea mining
EA	environmental assessment
EBSA	ecologically and biologically significant areas
ECA	emission control areas

Abbreviations

ECCAS	Economic Community of Central African States
EEDI	Energy Efficiency Design Index
EEZ	exclusive economic zone
EIA	environmental impact assessment
EIS	environmental impact statement
EM	electronic monitoring
EPA	Environmental Protection Authority
EPPR	emergency prevention preparedness and response
EU	European Union
FAL	Facilitation Committee of the IMO
FAO	Food and Agriculture Organization
FONSI	finding of no significant impact
Frontex	European Agency for the Management of Operational Cooperation at the External Borders of the Member States of the European Union
FSA	Fish Stocks Agreement
FOC	flag of convenience
FSI	Flag State Implementation Sub-Committee
GAIRS	generally accepted international rules and standards
GATT	General Agreement on Tariffs and Trade
GHG	greenhouse gases
GT	gross tonnage
H&S	health and safety
HRA	high risk area
IACS	International Association of Classification Societies
ICAO	International Civil Aviation Organization
ICCAT	International Commission on the Conservation of Atlantic Tunas
ICCPR	International Covenant on Civil and Political Rights
ICES	International Council for the Exploration of the Sea
ICPC	International Cable Protection Committee
ICS	International Chamber of Shipping
ICJ	International Court of Justice
ICRW	International Convention for the Regulation of Whaling
IEA	International Energy Agency
IGO	inter-governmental organisation
IHO	International Hydrographic Organization
ILC	International Law Commission
ILO	International Labour Organization
ILR	*International Law Review*
IMB	International Maritime Bureau
IMCO	International Maritime Consultative Organization (now IMO)
IMO	International Maritime Organization
IOC	Intergovernmental Oceanographic Commission
IOPA	International Plans of Action
IOPC	International Oil Pollution Compensation Funds
IPCC	Intergovernmental Panel on Climate Change

IPOA-IUU	International Plan of Action to Prevent, Deter and Eliminate Illegal, Unreported and Unregulated Fishing
ISA	International Seabed Authority
ISF	International Shipping Federation
ISO	International Organization for Standardization
ISPS Code	International Ship and Port Security Code
ISSC	International Ship Security Certificate
ITF	International Transport Workers' Federation
ITLOS	International Tribunal for the Law of the Sea
IUCN	International Union for Conservation of Nature
IUU Fishing	illegal, unreported and unregulated fishing
IWC	International Whaling Commission
JDZ	joint development zone
LME	large marine ecosystem
London Convention	Convention on the Prevention of Marine Pollution by Dumping of Wastes and Other Matter
London Protocol	1996 Protocol to the London Convention
LOSC	1982 United Nations Convention on the Law of the Sea
M	Nautical Mile according to the International Hydrographic Organization
MARPOL	International Convention for the Prevention of Pollution by Ships
MBM	market-based measure
MCS	monitoring, control and surveillance
MDA	maritime domain awareness
MEPC	Marine Environment Protection Committee (IMO)
MGR	marine genetic resources
MLC	Maritime Labour Convention
MOP	meeting of the parties
MOU	memorandum of understanding
MOU	mobile offshore unit
MPA	marine protected area
MRE	marine renewable energy
MSC	Maritime Safety Committee (IMO)
MSP	Marine Spatial Planning
MSR	marine scientific research
MSY	maximum sustainable yield
NEAFC	North-East Atlantic Fisheries Commission
NGO	non-governmental organisation
nm	nautical miles
NPT	nuclear non-proliferation treaty
OCCS	offshore carbon capture and storage
OCS	Outer Continental Shelf
OPRC	International Convention on Oil Pollution Preparedness, Response and Cooperation
OR	open registry

Abbreviations

OTEC	ocean thermal energy conversion
PMSC	private maritime security company
PPMV	parts per million by volume
PSC	port state control
PSI	Proliferation Security Initiative
PSSA	particularly sensitive sea area
RAC	Regional activity centre
RCU	Regional coordinating unit
REZ	renewable energy zone
RFMO	regional fisheries management organisation
RO	recognised organisation
RSC	Regional Seas Convention
RSO	regional seas organisation
RSP	Regional Seas Programme
SAR	search and rescue
SBSTTA	Subsidiary Body on Scientific, Technical and Technological Advice
SCAR	Scientific Committee on Antarctic Research
SEEMP	Ship Energy Efficiency Management Plan
SIDS	small-island developing states
SIPRI	Stockholm International Peace Research Institute
SLOC	sea lanes of communication
SOLAS	International Convention for Safety of Life at Sea
SPREP	Secretariat of the Pacific Regional Environment Programme
SPRFMO	South Pacific Regional Fisheries Management Organisation
SUA	1988 Convention on the Suppression of Unlawful Acts against the Safety of Maritime Navigation
SUCBAS	Sea Surveillance Cooperation Baltic Sea
TAC	total allowable catch
TOC	UN Convention against Transnational Organized Crime
TSS	traffic separation scheme
UK	United Kingdom of Great Britain and Northern Ireland
UN	United Nations
UNCED	United Nations Conference on Environment and Development
UNCLOS I	First United Nations Conference on the Law of the Sea
UNCLOS III	Third United Nations Conference on the Law of the Sea
UNDOALOS	United Nations Division on the Law of the Sea
UNEP	United Nations Environment Programme
UNEP RSP	UNEP's Regional Seas Programme
UNESCO	United Nations Educational Scientific and Cultural Organization
UNFCCC	United Nations Framework Convention on Climate Change
UNGA	United Nations General Assembly
UNICRI	United Nations Interregional Crime and Justice Research Institute
UNODC	UN Office of Drugs and Crime
UNSCR	United Nations Security Council Resolutions
UNTOC	United Nations Convention against Transnational Organized Crime
US	United States of America

USCG	United States Coast Guard
VIMSAS	Voluntary IMO Member State Audit Scheme
VME	vulnerable marine ecosystem
VMS	vessel monitoring systems
VOC	volatile organic compound
WCPFC	Western and Central Pacific Fisheries Commission
WTO	World Trade Organization
WFF	World Wide Fund for Nature

Foreword by Marie Jacobsson

With the advent of UNCLOS in 1982, the idea that a coastal State could have jurisdiction and sovereign rights over vast geographical areas in which it did not have sovereignty was formalised to an extent that was unprecedented. The solution was the result of a compromise – or a political *non liquet* and an associated lack of legal clarity – on the status of the Exclusive Economic Zone (EEZ). No one knew how this would work and how it would be developed.

Not only did UNCLOS introduce this notion, it also accentuated the idea of different kinds of jurisdiction in the various maritime zones. Admittedly, coastal States already had the right to exercise the control necessary to prevent and punish infringement of their customs, fiscal, immigration or sanitary regulations within its territory or territorial sea, in an area contiguous to their territorial seas. They also had certain regulatory rights in fishery zones as well as sovereign rights for the purpose of exploring and exploiting natural resources on their continental shelves. In addition, UNCLOS redefined the area of continental shelf, widened the territorial sea and the contiguous zone and introduced the concepts of the EEZ, archipelagic waters and the Area. The vast areas of the high seas were left to be regulated by flag States, albeit with an encouragement to States to cooperate. Certain activities on the deep seabed beyond national jurisdiction were to be administered by the International Sea-Bed Authority.

UNCLOS introduced a complex pattern of sovereignty, sovereign or exclusive rights, levels and forms of jurisdiction and control that was unprecedented. The right to legislate was not always followed by a right to enforce. Occasionally enforcement measures were restricted or conditional, as with enforcement of fisheries offences where no imprisonment or corporal punishment is permitted. Sometimes competing jurisdictions were foreseen creating inherent tensions between flag State and coastal State exercise of regulatory and enforcement powers. So even if the world had been frozen in time since the advent of UNCLOS in 1982, there would have been uncertainties regarding the rights of regulating and enforcing regulations against the background of the legal map provided by this seminal convention.

But time has not been frozen. As the editors point out: advances in technology, transport and human activities in all parts of the ocean and the deep seabed are steadily increasing. Furthermore human rights and the rule of law at international and national levels can no longer be neglected. Perceptions of what is acceptable from a human rights and environmental perspective have changed. There is an increasing awareness of the consequences of climate change, sea-level rise and possible "environmental refugees". UNCLOS and sustainable development are now equally important in the international system and the situation of small island developing states poses new challenges. The implications of the right of the individual to enjoy full respect for his or her human rights at all times and irrespective of where the individual is located, are yet to be addressed. Protection of the rights of seafarers can no longer be neglected.

The decades that have passed have shown that States have developed national, regional and multilateral implementation and approaches to the various challenges they face. At the multinational level, we recall the examples of the Agreement relating to the Implementation of Part XI of UNCLOS and the United Nations Fish Stocks agreement, the increasing number of regulations to increase both safety and security adopted by the IMO and the welcome addition to international labour law through the adoption of the ILO Maritime Labour Convention, as well as the measures taken under the auspices of the United Nations Security Council to fight piracy and armed robbery off the coast of Somalia. Regional cooperation includes not only the establishment of RFMOs, but also initiatives and measures taken by ASEAN, the EU, CCAMLR and the Arctic Council on a variety of maritime matters. Initiatives such as the Proliferation Security Initiative, regional measures aimed at cooperation to combat drug crimes and trafficking in human beings as well as measures to respond to migrants at sea are other examples. All such initiatives and measures will have to take international law, including law of the sea, into account in determining regulatory and enforcement measures.

Underlying all these efforts are national legislation, regulations, rules of operation and engagement. National courts have had to interpret the rules and so have international courts and tribunals, as well as regional courts. A web of case law at the domestic and international level has already emerged and more is to be expected.

All this takes place against a somewhat uncertain "territorial" background and the basic international law rule that land dominates the sea. As maritime disputes are not solved, tensions between States increase as they attempt to assert their jurisdiction or regulatory measures over disputed areas.

All these issues are addressed in the present volume. It is a modern, well composed, informative and analytical work, but it is not uncontroversial – the authors do not shy away from taking positions on sensitive questions. The Handbook is a comprehensive and welcome contribution for all of us that are trying to navigate the legal maritime domain.

The diverse array of maritime regulatory and enforcement issues addressed in this volume demonstrates the many areas of international law relevant to the sea. International law is a legal system and the challenge facing the international community is to move ocean governance gradually into a more integrated and cross-sectoral system. This process is still evolving and steadily growing in importance for the international community.

Introduction

Robin Warner and Stuart Kaye

Objectives and scope

With advances in technology and maritime transport, the spectrum of human activities in all parts of the ocean and the deep seabed is steadily increasing. A combination of factors such as the depletion of fisheries within national jurisdiction, the expansion in global maritime trade, the quest for renewable and non-renewable energy sources and scientific interest in the deep sea has led to greater usage of offshore areas. Human uses of the ocean now extend beyond the traditional activities of navigation and fishing to new and emerging activities such as bioprospecting for marine genetic resources, deep seabed mineral and hydrocarbon exploration and exploitation, offshore renewable energy developments and marine scientific probes of deep sea areas. The range of actors with interests in the maritime domain has diversified considerably to include not only flag, coastal and port States but transnational corporations, intergovernmental and non-governmental organisations, coastal communities and the marine scientific research community. The cornerstone of the international law framework for regulating activities at sea is the 1982 United Nations Convention on the Law of the Sea (LOSC) but in the three decades since its adoption, this jurisdictional blue print for the oceans has been augmented with a burgeoning array of more specific laws and regulations governing activities at sea and accompanying enforcement mechanisms. These derive from fields as diverse as international environmental law, international fisheries law, transnational criminal law, maritime security law and international trade law.

The objective of this *Handbook* is to examine current regulatory and enforcement instruments and mechanisms for different sectors of maritime activity in the various zones of maritime jurisdiction. It is a collection of short chapters by experts in their particular fields on the regulatory and enforcement regimes applicable to a variety of activities and actors in the maritime domain. It addresses the prescriptive and enforcement powers of coastal States, ports States and flag States and the rights and freedoms of flag States in different zones of ocean space. The regulatory powers of global and regional organisations in a range of maritime sectors are discussed as well as their emerging enforcement powers and interrelationships. The *Handbook* also examines maritime regulation and enforcement in the wider context of international law and policy including the relevance of maritime regulation and enforcement to national, regional and global events. Although the *Handbook* traverses multiple developments in the law of the sea, international environmental

Introduction

law and the maritime elements of transnational criminal law in the course of discussing maritime regulation and enforcement, it does not purport to provide a comprehensive treatment of any of these bodies of law. Rather the various chapters explore gaps in the maritime and regulation enforcement fabric and identify future challenges in regulation and enforcement at sea.

Organisational structure of the *Handbook*

This *Handbook* brings together authors from a variety of disciplines with specific expertise in the diverse aspects of maritime regulation and enforcement within a structure that provides an integrated perspective on the topic. Part A of the *Handbook* adopts the zonal approach taken by the LOSC to maritime regulation and enforcement analysing the key provisions of the 1982 Convention on the Law of the Sea (LOSC) and their application to the full spectrum of maritime zones and marine areas beyond national jurisdiction. Relevant legal and policy considerations in the development and enforcement of maritime jurisdiction are also addressed including the use of force and international environmental law principles. Part B of the *Handbook* examines the role of States in their various capacities as flag States, port States and coastal States and the role of other actors such as global and regional organisations in maritime regulation and enforcement.

Part C of the *Handbook* analyses regulatory and enforcement frameworks for traditional ocean activities such as fisheries and shipping as well as regulatory and enforcement developments related to new and emerging activities such as hydrocarbon exploitation, deep seabed mining, bioprospecting for marine genetic resources and ocean energy generation. This part of the *Handbook* also reviews developments in regulation and enforcement measures to combat transnational crime at sea and piracy and armed robbery at sea. Finally Part D of the *Handbook* investigates emerging issues and future challenges for maritime regulation and enforcement including cooperative maritime surveillance and enforcement, the use of technology in maritime surveillance and enforcement and maritime regulation and enforcement in marine areas beyond national jurisdiction particularly in the context of conservation and sustainable use of marine biodiversity.

The opening chapter of Part A by Stuart Kaye examines the prescriptive and enforcement powers of coastal States in maritime zones under national jurisdiction including internal waters, territorial waters, the contiguous zone, the exclusive economic zone, archipelagic waters and above the continental shelf. It emphasises the inherent complexity of maritime regulation and enforcement due to the fact that no State has sovereignty over the majority of the world's oceans and concurrent jurisdiction frequently arises over an activity depending upon the basis for the exercise of jurisdiction. Noting the fundamental importance of the zonal approach in the regulatory and enforcement options available to a coastal State, it also acknowledges other key bases for maritime jurisdiction under international law such as flag State, port State and nationality.

Robin Warner's chapter in Part A traces the development of the high seas regime from Grotius early treatise on Mare Liberum through to the codification of the regime in the 1958 Geneva Convention on the High Seas and the LOSC. It evaluates the efficacy of the flag State model of jurisdiction as the predominant mode of maritime regulation and enforcement on the high seas and the need for supplementary forms of jurisdiction which take into account the broader interests of the international community in conservation and sustainable use of marine resources and biodiversity. Some emerging collaborative forms of regulation and enforcement are also addressed in this chapter.

Cameron Moore's chapter in Part A explores international law principles and constraints on the use of force in regulating activities at sea and enforcement practice. It draws on international judicial decisions, conventional international law and domestic law to give an indication of state practice. Although it highlights the myriad potentially overlapping jurisdictions and different national and international approaches to the use of force in law enforcement, the derivation of principles on the use of force in law enforcement at sea from the *Saiga Case*, international human rights law, and a representative selection of relevant international instruments is still considered possible. The common denominator emerging from these sources is that the general principles applicable to the use of force in national regulation and enforcement at sea are adherence to minimum force and minimum interference in law enforcement action.

Sam Bateman's opening chapter in Part B examines the pivotal role of flag States in regulating and enforcing the activities of their flag vessels in all areas of the ocean and relevant provisions of the LOSC on flag State responsibilities. It also discusses the deficiencies in the flag State system particularly the phenomenon of flags of convenience and global initiatives to strengthen flag State responsibility. Bateman concludes that while the flag State regime remains at the core of the system of maritime regulation and enforcement, it is no longer the traditional system of absolute control of the flag State over ships flying its flag. Rather flag State responsibility is now discharged through a complex system of administrative arrangements, including different types of ship register, company structures and classification societies. He acknowledges that significant problems remain with the flag State system such as substandard shipping and reflagging which are unlikely to be fully remedied by the mandatory audit scheme being introduced by the International Maritime Organisation (IMO). In the longer term, he posits that the exclusivity of flag State jurisdiction on the high seas may be qualified by a more integrated approach to ocean governance involving more collaborative forms of regulation and enforcement.

Lowell Bautista's chapter in Part B discusses the general jurisdictional competence of coastal States and their regulatory and enforcement powers in maritime zones under their jurisdiction. He outlines the wide array of regulatory challenges and enforcement issues confronting coastal States in their offshore zones including illegal fishing, piracy and armed robbery at sea, illicit traffic in narcotic drugs and psychotropic substances, illegal traffic in hazardous wastes and other substances, smuggling of migrants, management of marine resources and preservation of the marine environment compounded by the adverse impacts of climate change. He notes the lack of regulatory and enforcement expertise and capacity that besets many coastal States in implementing their obligations under the LOSC.

Rosemary Rayfuse's chapter in Part B discusses the concept of port State jurisdiction and its parsing into the dual functions of port State control and enforcement. It also examines the increasing adoption of port State measures aimed at ensuring compliance by foreign-flagged vessels with both national and international regulatory efforts to enforce marine pollution, safety of life at sea and fisheries laws. She concludes that port State jurisdiction is an important complement and essential adjunct to flag State jurisdiction, particularly in situations where a flag State, for whatever reasons, is either unwilling or unable to effectively control its vessels. In common with Sam Bateman, she foresees that the exclusivity of flag State jurisdiction is likely to be tempered by other forms of jurisdiction in particular the increasingly global coverage of port State control and enforcement regimes.

J. Ashley Roach's chapter in Part B surveys the many global organisations which play a role in regulating and enforcing maritime activities, key regulatory and enforcement instruments and measures emerging from these bodies and the linkages between different organisations. At the apex of these organisations is the IMO but other relevant organisations include the Food and Agriculture Organisation (FAO) for fisheries, the International Seabed Authority (ISA), the Intergovernmental Oceanographic Commission and cultural sector of UNESCO, the UN Office of Drugs and Crime (UNODC), the UN Environment Programme (UNEP) and the International Whaling Commission. He concludes that for the most part, the global organisations responsible for regulating and enforcing maritime activities continue to meet their obligations and to work closely with each other, however, he identifies a prominent omission in relation to hydrocarbon exploration and exploitation in marine areas under national jurisdiction. This is the failure of the IMO to establish global rules, standards and recommended practices and procedures to prevent, reduce and control pollution of the marine environment arising from or in connection with seabed activities subject to national jurisdiction, as required by Article 208(5) of the LOSC.

Kerry Tetzlaff's chapter in Part B reviews the critical role of regional organisations in implementing maritime regulation and enforcement measures in different spheres of maritime activity. In particular, she discusses the regulatory and enforcement role of regional fisheries management organisations (RFMOs) in conserving and managing fish stocks and regional seas organisations (RSOs) in protection and preservation of the marine environment. She assesses that under the UN Fish Stocks Agreement (UNFSA), the regulatory role of RFMOs in the conservation and management of fish stocks has been significantly developed into a comprehensive framework while the regulatory role of RSOs in protecting and preserving the marine environment under Part XII of the LOSC has been implemented to a much lesser extent through the UNEP Regional Seas Programme. She acknowledges that both RFMOs and RSOs still face considerable hurdles in relation to implementing regional enforcement frameworks for marine resource and biodiversity conservation and management measures. Finally, she foresees a central role in the evolution of regional marine governance for RFMOs and RSOs in the development of new frameworks for ocean governance including ecosystem-based management on the scale of large marine ecosystems as well as a comprehensive integrated approach to conservation and sustainable use of marine ecosystems in areas beyond national jurisdiction.

Dale Stephen's chapter concludes Part B with an examination of the role played by courts and tribunals in maritime regulation and enforcement. He outlines the dispute resolution provisions of the LOSC and then focuses on themes relevant to maritime regulation and enforcement in the jurisprudence of the International Court of Justice (ICJ) and ITLOS. He comments that while freedom of navigation is a theme that has been frequently articulated and reinforced by the ICJ, ITLOS has been both strident and decisive in its determination of exacting limits on the use of force in law enforcement at sea. Finally he analyses the interaction between international and Australian domestic jurisprudence on law maritime enforcement matters highlighting rifts that are emerging between these two bodies of law and comments on attempts to reconcile the two.

In the opening chapter of Part C, Mary Ann Palma-Robles analyses the increasingly complex matrix of regulatory and enforcement measures which apply to fisheries both within and beyond national jurisdiction including measures to address illegal unreported and unregulated (IUU) fishing as well as issues such as bycatch and vulnerable marine ecosystems. Her chapter focuses on the enforcement of fisheries regulations, particularly the rights and obligations of States under international law and provides examples of State practice. It examines the fisheries enforcement framework under the LOSC and other global fisheries agreements in zones of sovereignty, zones under sovereign rights, and on the high seas. The chapter analyses the concept of monitoring, control and surveillance (MCS) as a central concept in fisheries enforcement and contrasts it with the element of fisheries compliance. She concludes that although the LOSC provides the basic framework for fisheries regulation and enforcement in the different maritime zones, the adoption of international agreements post LOSC has strengthened the regulatory and enforcement powers of States. The negotiation of bilateral, subregional and regional agreements on MCS, compliance and enforcement have further enabled States to tackle IUU fishing.

The next two chapters of Part C address some key regulatory and enforcement issues associated with international shipping. The first part of Anthony Morrison's chapter analyses customary international law principles and international law instruments relevant to safety of life at sea highlighting the gaps that exist in the regulatory framework. The second part of his chapter examines

Introduction

some current issues and factors affecting the enforcement of obligations under the international legal regime. He explores the question of whether coastal States are obliged under international law to permit entry of ships in distress into their territory where there is a humanitarian risk involved and if so whether they are obliged to allow disembarkation of persons from the rescuing ship. Although he finds that the different aspects of international law relevant to these issues do not provide definitive answers to these questions, he concludes that the best way to resolve the problems inherent in the saving of life at sea regime is by regional cooperation so that a number of countries agree to spread the load. Erik Molenaar's chapter focuses on the international law that has been developed at global and regional levels to prevent, reduce and control pollution of the marine environment by merchant ships. His chapter is divided into two sections the first examining substantive international rules and standard relating to vessel-source pollution, and the second, international mechanisms such as audits and harmonised inspections aimed at ensuring compliance with these rules and standards. He comments on the steady expansion of international efforts to combat vessel-source pollution from an initial focus on oil pollution to a broader range of impacts of merchant shipping on the marine environment including emissions, anchoring, ballast water and sediments, anti-fouling systems, ship recycling, ship strikes on cetaceans and noise. He notes the trajectory of IMO compliance mechanisms beyond the more 'traditional' reporting requirements towards the mandatory audit scheme for flag States and characterises this scheme as being on the softer side of compliance mechanisms because it lacks a response or enforcement component.

Youna Lyon's chapter in Part C focuses on the obligations of States under international law for hydrocarbon exploration and exploitation activities taking place in waters under their national jurisdiction. The first part of the chapter reviews relevant LOSC provisions and general rules of international law relevant to such activities and discusses the failure of the international community to agree on global rules for offshore hydrocarbon activities and its consequences. The second part examines other international treaties that apply to offshore hydrocarbon activities while the third part discusses the remaining legal gaps with respect to the control of pollution of the marine environment from offshore hydrocarbon activities. She analyses the fragmentary international law regime applicable to offshore hydrocarbon activities and notes that despite major disasters with transboundary impacts such as the Deep Water Horizon oil spill in the Gulf of Mexico and the Montara oil spill in the Timor Sea, the prognosis is not good for developing global best practice standards to regulate the offshore hydrocarbon industry.

Robert Makgill's and Ana Paula Linhare's chapter in Part C examines the LOSC provisions for regulation and enforcement of deep seabed mining activities in the Area and in particular the key obligations identified for States sponsoring exploration contractors in the Area by the Seabed Disputes Chamber of the International Tribunal for the Law of the Sea (ITLOS) in its February 2011 Advisory Opinion. They focus on how these obligations have been adopted in the Pacific region as regulatory prerequisites to deep sea mining exploration and development. As well as analysing relevant legislative provisions from Tonga, the Cook Islands and New Zealand they discuss how best practice environmental safeguards have been developed in the European Union and Secretariat of the Pacific Community Regional Legislative and Regulatory Framework for Deep Sea Minerals Exploration and Exploitation.

Harriet Harden Davies' chapter in Part C analyses the international framework for the regulation of marine scientific research including the relevant LOSC provisions and complementary instruments that also contain provisions on the regulation of marine scientific research including the Antarctic Treaty, the Convention on Biological Diversity, the London Convention and London Protocol as well as voluntary codes of conduct. She notes that while the LOSC provides a regime for the conduct of marine scientific research that emphasises international cooperation, capacity building and technology transfer, and balancing freedom of marine scientific research with coastal State jurisdictional control, there is no agreed definition of marine scientific research leading to doubt over which activities fall under the LOSC regime for marine scientific research. She cites examples arising in the marine scientific sphere that could cause contention such as the manipulation of the marine environment by geoengineering, the sharing of benefits from marine genetic resources and the protection of jurisdictional rights from roaming ocean observing systems.

Douglas Guilfoyle's chapter in Part C examines the key provisions of international instruments relevant to combating transnational crime at sea. He assesses that the LOSC provides a broad backdrop for enforcement powers at sea and then multilateral treaties such as the Suppression of Unlawful Acts against the Safety of Maritime Navigation (SUA) Convention, the Vienna Narcotics Convention or the Migrant Smuggling Protocol to the UN Convention against Transnational Organised Crime establish frameworks for sectoral cooperation. Rather than relying on these sectoral frameworks, he notes that States have often preferred to negotiate bilateral or regional treaties or arrangements to combat transnational crime at sea. While these arrangements may provide solutions tailored to a particular region or situation, they remain ad hoc in nature. Guilfoyle comments on the multiple challenges confronting enforcement at sea including the need to obtain flag State consent, its logistical complexity, potential danger and prohibitive cost.

Clive Schofield's and Kamal Deen-Ali's chapter in Part C analyses the issue of combating the threat of piracy and armed robbery at sea through the prism of case studies off the Horn of Africa, where incidents of piracy are now in decline, and in the Gulf of Guinea, which has witnessed a surge in piracy and armed robbery at sea in recent years. It first evaluates the adequacy of the current international law framework in combating piracy and armed robbery at sea with particular reference to the relevant LOSC provisions and the application of the SUA Convention. It draws a range of lessons from the two case studies emphasising the need for a combination of regulatory and enforcement tools to combat particular incidences of piracy and armed robbery at sea. These include robust governance and the rule of law in the proximate coastal States, effective legal regimes, patrols and enforcement, regional cooperation and global support.

Part D surveys a selection of the multiple challenges in contemporary maritime regulation and enforcement and some of the solutions States have devised to address these problems. It opens with Anne Marie O'Hagan's chapter on the regulation of marine renewable energy (MRE) comprising offshore wind, wave, tidal and current energy. She notes that while there is a general legal basis for MRE activities in the EEZ provisions of the LOSC, proponents of such activities are frequently subject to more detailed regulation in a range of relevant instruments and measures at global, regional and national levels. She assesses that regulatory systems for MRE are still in the developmental stages in many national jurisdictions. Offshore wind has triggered the formation of a more appropriate consenting system in some jurisdictions but in others the regulatory system could be described as more reactive responding to project demand. She suggests that governments need to take a more proactive regulatory approach in dealing with MRE proposals drawing from the example of Scotland where there has been strategic level marine planning down to site level guidance on applicable procedures.

Julia Jabour's chapter follows with an analysis of the benefits and drawbacks of a new regulatory regime for accessing and sharing the benefits to be derived from marine genetic resources in areas beyond national jurisdiction (ABNJ). It presents two case studies both drawn from the Antarctic on the difficulties of accessing marine genetic resources in ABNJ and sharing the benefits of their development, while also protecting biodiversity generally through implementing suitable environmental safeguards in areas which are outside the control of a State. She contests the utility of such a regime with the existing paucity of scientific knowledge on MGRs in ABNJ and the lack of enforcement assets to monitor compliance with access restrictions and environmental safeguards. Katja Fennel's and David VanderZwaag's chapter explores the complex and seemingly intractable regulatory issues posed by ocean acidification. They point to the urgent need to minimise and address the impacts of ocean acidification highlighted in recent UN General Assembly resolutions, and new Sustainable Development Goals agreed to in 2014. The first part of the chapter reviews the basic chemistry of ocean acidification referring to the extensive scientific information regarding biological effects and ecosystem-level responses and the numerous scientific uncertainties and information gaps still remaining. The second part analyses five different aspects of international law and policy relevant to ocean acidification: the LOSC; the UN climate change regime; marine pollution control instruments; the Convention on Biological Diversity and relevant UN General Assembly resolutions and processes. It concludes that the most likely regulatory responses to curbing ocean acidification would emerge from the UN Framework Convention on Climate Change regime. These could include a pH level target for the global oceans, the establishment of a fund or funding priority under the climate change framework to support States in conserving critical coastal sinks for carbon such as mangroves, saltmarshes and seagrass beds or through setting a benchmark for carbon dioxide in the atmosphere that would address both climate change and ocean acidification concerns.

Chris Rahman's chapter in Part D is solution oriented, demonstrating how a growing number of technological applications have emerged for both maritime regulation and enforcement. He draws a distinction between technology used for regulation and that used for enforcement at sea. Under the regulatory category, he addresses firstly, examples of regulations that prescribe the application of specific technologies and secondly, regulations that promote the application of non-specified technologies to achieve regulatory goals. The first set of examples concern vessel tracking systems used in the fisheries management sector and shipping sector to enhance ship safety, security and marine environmental protection. The second set of examples concern suites of technological measures adopted to reduce harmful atmospheric emissions from port related activities in California. He also discusses vessel tracking and surveillance technologies that can be employed to enable enforcement actions including unmanned aerial, surface and underwater vehicles.

Warwick Gullett's and Yubing Shi's chapter in Part D highlights the critical need for more cooperative maritime surveillance and enforcement arrangements particularly at the regional level to combat illegal activities at sea. It discusses the nature and scope of maritime law enforcement challenges and examples of cooperative surveillance and enforcement arrangements in Europe, the South Pacific, the Southern Ocean and East Asia. It proposes that States facing common threats can adopt a progressive approach to maritime surveillance and enforcement cooperation, termed a "scaffold" approach, from initial activities focused on building understanding and trust between counterpart government officers, through to the sharing of intelligence data, and then joint operations at sea.

The final chapter in the *Handbook* by Robin Warner is prospective in nature exploring the potential development of new paradigms for maritime regulation and enforcement in ABNJ. It explores key features of the maritime regulation framework for ABNJ and its applicability to the conservation and sustainable use of marine biodiversity, gaps and disconnects in that framework and ongoing global efforts to develop more effective regulation systems for these vast areas of the ocean. It discusses some of the options which have been considered in the UN Ad Hoc Informal Open-ended Working Group to study issues related to the conservation and sustainable use of marine biodiversity in areas beyond national jurisdiction (BBNJ Working Group) to evolve the

Introduction

legal and institutional framework for conservation and sustainable use of marine biodiversity in ABNJ and their current and future relevance for maritime regulation in ABNJ. In the face of growing threats and pressures on the marine environment of ABNJ and its biodiversity, she concludes that it is timely to promote a new convergence of the modern conservation principles, measures and tools developed under international marine environmental law with the law of the sea. A more integrated regulatory and enforcement framework involving elements such as area based management measures and global standards for environmental impact assessment of activities in ABNJ represent steps toward this objective.

Emerging themes

Each of the chapters in the *Handbook* has a distinctive subject matter and reflects the author's own views, however a number of more general themes can be discerned in the *Handbook* as a whole.

- The need for enhanced cooperation in maritime surveillance and enforcement between all actors in the maritime domain is a fundamental theme throughout the *Handbook*. This extends beyond traditional bilateral and multilateral cooperation between States to the establishment of close links between global and regional organisations with interests in maritime activities and between regulatory and enforcement authorities and representative bodies for industries such as shipping, fisheries and offshore hydrocarbon exploitation
- A number of contributors comment on the inherent flaws in the concept of flag State jurisdiction and the need for supplementary mechanisms such as port State control and regional boarding and inspection regimes to enhance the efficacy of maritime regulation and enforcement.
- In analysing regulatory and enforcement frameworks for different activities, many contributors note that the pace of regulation far outstrips the resources and capacity of States and regional organisations to enforce compliance particularly at sea.
- Several contributors identify gaps in the regulation and enforcement fabric relating to the establishment of global best practice standards and environmental safeguards for maritime activities. These activities include offshore hydrocarbon exploration and exploitation, marine renewable energy projects and marine geo-engineering.
- The increasing quantity, diversity and complexity of activities at sea have led some contributors to comment on the need for regulatory and enforcement regimes tailored to the nature of the activity and the geographic and geopolitical circumstances of the relevant region. This is certainly the case with piracy, armed robbery at sea and other forms of transnational crime that require multifaceted regulatory and enforcement solutions with both land and sea components. This also applies to new and emerging activities such as bioprospecting for marine genetic resources which involves the collection of small samples of marine organisms followed by lengthy laboratory processes and cannot be regulated in the same way as the harvesting of fish stocks or the large extractive processes of deep seabed mining or offshore hydrocarbon activities.
- Many of the contributors refer to the increasing primacy of conservation concerns in regulatory models and the need for a precautionary approach to activities with the potential for significant adverse effects on the marine environment in the majority of marine areas particularly ABNJ where knowledge of the marine environment and biodiversity is still developing.

- Several contributors comment on the utility of innovative technology to reduce the need for risky, protracted and costly surveillance and enforcement at sea. This will entail greater incorporation of elements such as enhanced communications, vessel tracking, exchange of voyage data and unmanned surveillance units in regulatory and enforcement frameworks.
- Finally, a number of contributors refer to the potential negotiation of a multilateral agreement on conservation and sustainable use of marine biodiversity in ABNJ and the opportunities this presents for developing a more integrated approach to ocean governance including maritime regulation and enforcement in these vast areas of ocean. Integral to these aspirations is a potent concern for the long term sustainability of the marine biodiversity in ABNJ against a rising backdrop of human activities with the potential for adverse impacts on the marine environment.

The collection of contributions in this *Handbook* demonstrates emphatically the increase in and complexity of activities at sea and the risks this poses for the environmental integrity of the oceans. The LOSC represented an important starting point in the development of a balanced maritime and regulatory system for the oceans attempting as it did to balance the multiple actors and interests in the maritime domain. Since then many other law and policy regimes have emerged to regulate the burgeoning human uses of the oceans. As we prepare to negotiate a further agreement on the conservation and sustainable use of marine biodiversity in ABNJ, it is timely to reflect on the different dimensions of maritime regulation and enforcement and whether they reflect an equitable and sustainable mix of environmental, economic and social interests.

Part A
International Law Considerations in Maritime Regulation and Enforcement

1

A Zonal Approach to Maritime Regulation and Enforcement

Stuart Kaye

Introduction

This chapter will examine the prescriptive and enforcement powers of coastal states in maritime zones under national jurisdiction as described in the United Nations Convention on the Law of the Sea (LOSC).[1] These zones are internal waters, territorial waters, the contiguous zone, the exclusive economic zone, archipelagic waters and the continental shelf. There will also be consideration of special regimes for archipelagic waters, and for safety zones around offshore installations.

Jurisdiction is essentially the ability of a State to validly make laws over activities. Where a State possesses jurisdiction, it has the power to regulate and sometimes to enforce its laws. In the ordinary course of events, a coastal State possesses uncontested and complete jurisdiction over matters that take place within its land territory. The situation becomes more complex on the ocean, where vessels of all States can more directly interact, and more than one State may possess jurisdiction to regulate and enforce.

Jurisdiction can take on different forms, and be generated in different ways. States may possess prescriptive and enforcement jurisdictions. In the case of the former, a State may possess the ability to regulate an activity – to prescribe the manner in which the activity is undertaken. This prescriptive jurisdiction can exist independent of any ability on the part of the State to enforce its laws, and may extend to activities taking place upon the territory of another State. On the other hand, enforcement jurisdiction is the ability of the State to actively enforce its laws, through the actions of those exercising its authority, such as police or coast guard officials. A State's enforcement jurisdiction is not always present where the State possesses prescriptive jurisdiction. Enforcement jurisdiction cannot be exercised where another State has sovereignty, such as within the land territory or internal waters of another State.[2]

On the ocean, greater complexity arises because no State has sovereignty over the vast bulk of the world's oceans, and accordingly more than one State may possess enforcement jurisdiction over an activity at the same time, depending upon the basis for the exercise of jurisdiction. A coastal State possesses jurisdiction over certain activities in parts of the ocean, proximate to its coast, but a flag State may also possess jurisdiction over the same activities, by virtue of its jurisdiction over ships flying its flag.

Coastal State jurisdiction is derived from proximity to the territory of the coastal State. The LOSC organises maritime jurisdiction under a series of maritime zones, where the extent of jurisdiction increases the closer the relevant zone is to the coastal State. For example, the waters closest to the coastal State, internal waters enclosed by bays, fringing islands or in ports or roadsteads, give the coastal State a jurisdiction that almost equates to that of jurisdiction on land.[3] On the other hand, in the waters of the exclusive economic zone, the coastal State's jurisdiction is limited to specific activities only, and boarding of vessels for enforcement purposes would be limited to those purposes.[4]

Before considering jurisdiction in each of the maritime zones, it is important to note that some vessels are exempt from the operation of coastal State law, regardless of which maritime zone the vessel is in. Warships and government vessels engaged in non-commercial service are described as being sovereign immune, and not subject to enforcement action under the law of the coastal State, even if present in internal waters or the territorial sea. In the event such a vessel contravenes the laws of the coastal State, it may be asked to leave the territorial sea, but the only other recourse a coastal State has, is to make a claim against the flag State.[5]

Maritime zones

The maritime zones available under the LOSC radiate outwards from a coastal State's territory, as illustrated in Figure 1.1 below. The rule of thumb is that the rights and extent of coastal State jurisdiction increase as one approaches the coast. As such, the two innermost zones, those of internal waters and the territorial sea, are subject to the sovereignty of a coastal State, and therefore are not subject to the enforcement jurisdiction of any other State. Further out, the jurisdiction of the coastal State attenuates, which allows for other enforcement jurisdiction to be undertaken.

An important issue to be considered, having looked at the relevant maritime zones, is what is needed to generate each of these zones? The obvious answer is land, although precisely what features will qualify as land is sometimes a difficult question. In addition to vast continental land masses like Africa or Australia, or large islands like Madagascar or Tasmania, there are features like the small sand cays of the Coral Sea, or small rocky outcrops like Rockall in the North Atlantic Ocean. When one considers that an isolated outcrop alone in the ocean has the potential to generate a vast circular exclusive economic zone (EEZ) over 125 000 square miles in area, determining exactly which features are entitled to produce such zones becomes an economically significant question.

The answer is to be found in Article 121 of the Law of the Sea Convention which provides that all islands are entitled to generate the full range of maritime zones.[6] An island is defined as being a naturally formed area of land, surrounded by water that is above water at high tide.[7] This potentially could have allowed small isolated outcrops to generate vast areas, so the Article contains a qualification which states: "Rocks which cannot sustain human habitation or an economic life of their own shall have no exclusive economic zone or continental shelf".[8]

The qualification has not resolved the debate as to which outcrops will be entitled to an EEZ and continental shelf for two reasons. First, there is no definition of the term "rock" in the text and this has led to two different interpretations by various scholars. Some take the view that a "rock" is literally simply just that, and accordingly the exception embodied in Article 121(3) therefore does not apply to features which are not "rocky"; that is sand cays and coral atolls are exempt from the qualification.[9]

The alternative approach is that "rock" is simply a description of a feature that is too small to be an island, and that it is irrelevant to consider the geological make-up of the feature to determine whether it falls within Article 121(3). This is the view of Hodgson and Smith, and it has much to recommend it, in that it would seem to be more in accord with the spirit of the article, and is consistent with pre-existing nomenclature for referring to physical features.[10]

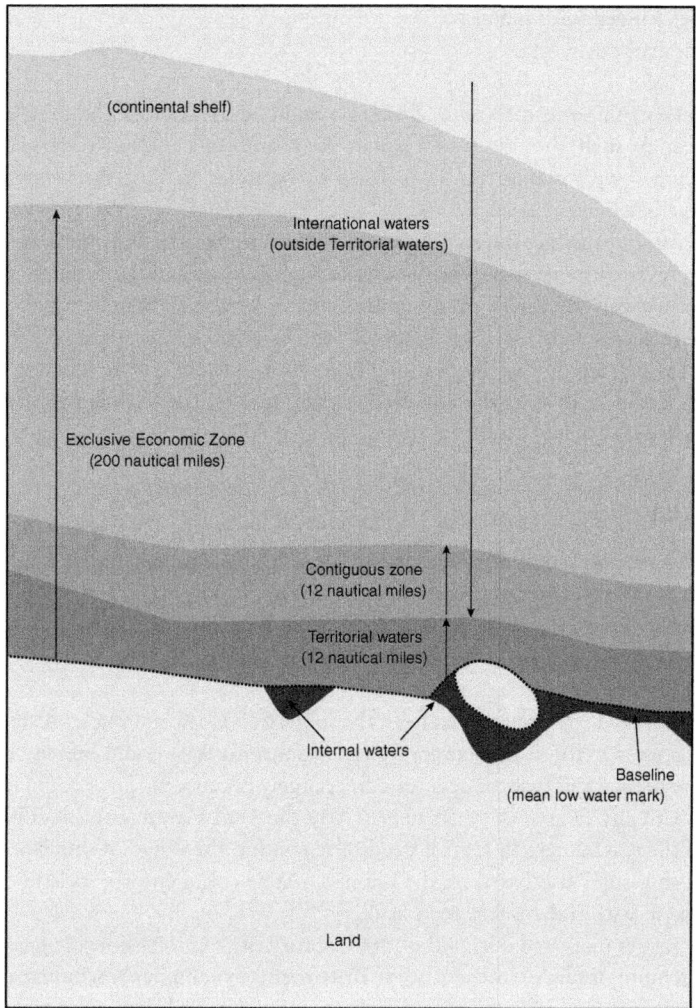

Figure 1.1 Maritime Zones

The second difficulty is what is meant by the terms "capable of human habitation" and an "economic life of its own". Interpretations of these terms differ considerably, for instance as to the level of outside support that may disqualify a rock from qualifying for the full ambit of zones. There is no consensus among States as to what is meant by these terms, and State practice varies widely.

Internal waters

Internal waters are those waters on the landward side of territorial sea baselines. Such baselines are used to measure other maritime zones, such as the territorial sea, and can be employed in certain circumstances permitted under the Law of the Sea Convention. These circumstances can include:

- bays,
- rivers,
- deeply indented coastlines,

- coastlines fringed with islands,
- ports and harbour works.[11]

The presence of these features will allow, in certain circumstances, the drawing of territorial sea baselines. As such, the waters of a bay or the mouth of a river or waters that are deeply indented or fringed with islands can be enclosed by baselines, making the waters on the landward side of the baselines internal waters.

In jurisdictional terms, the internal waters of a State are treated as equivalent to land. They are part of the sovereignty of the coastal State and foreign vessels in these waters have no guaranteed right of navigation, save in circumstances where the coastal State would be able to close off access where access rights were guaranteed, such as across an international strait. Vessels in internal waters which are not sovereign immune are subject to the full jurisdiction of the coastal State, although traditionally coastal States do not apply laws related to the internal economy and operation of foreign vessels.[12]

Territorial sea

The territorial sea is the oldest of the maritime zones in international law. It is an area of water adjacent to land, and the airspace above and seabed below that water,[13] over which the coastal State may assert its sovereignty is largely unfettered by the actions or rights of third States. Sovereignty over the territorial sea is only limited by the obligation on a coastal State to permit innocent passage of vessels through its territorial sea.[14]

The breadth of the territorial sea has been the subject of debate among scholars for centuries. It had been suggested in the 17th Century by Grotius that no State could exercise its sovereignty over part of the oceans and that the seas were free, largely because no State could impose its will over the seas with any degree of permanence.[15] By the 18th Century, this had been modified to freedom of the seas, except in a small band of sea within the range of shore-based cannon.[16] This "cannon-shot rule" was based on the premise a State could enforce its laws on those areas of sea which were within the range of its artillery.

As artillery ranges increased during the 19th Century, the cannon-shot rule gradually evolved into a more definite distance. In the case of Britain and its colonies (including the Australian colonies) this distance was arbitrarily fixed at three nautical miles.[17] However other States chose different distances; for example the Scandinavian countries preferred a distance of 4 nautical miles, and the Soviet Union, when it came into existence after World War I, elected to have a territorial sea of 12 nautical miles.[18]

The lack of consensus on the breadth of the territorial sea proved a major stumbling block in the development of the Law of the Sea. Three major international conferences in 1930, 1958 and 1960 were greatly hampered by the question of how wide the territorial sea ought to be. Being uncertain as to the width of the zone, States were reluctant to consider their rights and obligations within and outside it.

The issue was ultimately only resolved at the Third United Nations Conference on the Law of the Sea (UNCLOS III), where the bulk of the international community accepted a 12 nautical mile territorial sea. Article 3 of the Law of the Sea Convention, which was adopted at the conclusion of UNCLOS III, sets a maximum breadth of the territorial sea at 12 nautical miles.

The territorial sea is also under the sovereignty of the coastal State, but a foreign vessel may not necessarily be subject to the complete jurisdiction of the coastal State. This is because foreign vessels have a right of innocent passage through the territorial sea, and coastal State jurisdiction over such vessels is restricted to specific subject areas. These vary depending on the type of jurisdiction and the matter the coastal State wishes to regulate, and are considered individually below.

The coastal State always retains a "right of protection" to prevent passage through its territorial sea that is not innocent, and to ensure vessels bound for its internal waters do not breach their conditions of entry. This right is dealt with under Article 25 of the Law of the Sea Convention, and it appears to legitimise efforts by a coastal State to remove vessels from its territorial sea if their passage is not innocent.[19] In addition, the coastal State may impose laws relating to innocent passage. These may be directed at the following areas under Article 21:

(a) the safety of navigation and the regulation of maritime traffic;
(b) the protection of navigational aids and facilities and other facilities or installations;
(c) the protection of cables and pipelines;
(d) the conservation of the living resources of the sea;
(e) the prevention of infringement of the fisheries laws and regulations of the coastal State;
(f) the preservation of the environment of the coastal State and the prevention, reduction and control of pollution thereof;
(g) marine scientific research and hydrographic surveys;
(h) the prevention of infringement of the customs, fiscal, immigration or sanitary laws and regulations of the coastal State.

Criminal jurisdiction can be exercised by the coastal State in the territorial sea in relation to a vessel passing through the territorial sea, but is restricted to a number of defined circumstances. Article 27 of the LOSC provides for the exercise of criminal jurisdiction by the coastal State:

1. The criminal jurisdiction of the coastal State should not be exercised on board a foreign ship passing through the territorial sea to arrest any person or to conduct any investigation in connection with any crime committed on board the ship during its passage, save only in the following cases:
   (a) if the consequences of the crime extend to the coastal State;
   (b) if the crime is of a kind to disturb the peace of the country or the good order of the territorial sea;
   (c) if the assistance of the local authorities has been requested by the master of the ship or by a diplomatic agent or consular officer of the flag State; or
   (d) if such measures are necessary for the suppression of illicit traffic in narcotic drugs or psychotropic substances.

As criminal jurisdiction can be awakened where the coastal State is requested to provide assistance, whether by the flag State, or by the master of the ship, there is potentially no restriction as to the subject matter of the jurisdiction. The coastal State is also able to impose measures on vessels in its territorial sea that have been within its internal waters under Article 27(2) of the LOSC. There is a restriction however that criminal jurisdiction can only be applied to offences that have occurred in the territorial sea, and not prior to entry in it, providing the ship is foreign and is proceeding from a foreign port without entering internal waters.[20]

A more restrictive regime from the perspective of a coastal State operates in those portions of its territorial waters that are within an international strait. Such straits are areas of territorial sea which must be transited by foreign vessels to sail from one part of the EEZ or high seas to another, without a route of similar convenience being available. The regime of transit passage, as opposed to innocent passage, is available to shipping, and notably, also to aircraft. Within such straits, the coastal State's jurisdiction diminishes over transiting vessels, being restricted to the following subjects:

(a) the safety of navigation and the regulation of maritime traffic, as provided in Article 41;
(b) the prevention, reduction and control of pollution, by giving effect to applicable international regulations regarding the discharge of oil, oily wastes and other noxious substances in the strait;
(c) with respect to fishing vessels, the prevention of fishing, including the stowage of fishing gear;
(d) the loading or unloading of any commodity, currency or person in contravention of the customs, fiscal, immigration or sanitary laws and regulations of States bordering straits.

This means the jurisdiction of the coastal State is reduced in an international strait as compared to the remainder of its territorial sea.

Contiguous zone

Beyond the territorial sea, a coastal State may also claim a contiguous zone,to a distance of 24 nautical miles. The contiguous zone has its origins in the "hovering acts" used by Britain and the United States in the 19th and 20th Centuries to combat smuggling.[21] Coastal States have enhanced jurisdiction over customs, fiscal, immigration and sanitary matters, although it would be incorrect to assume that the contiguous zone gives a State complete jurisdiction over these matters. Article 33 of the LOSC provides:

1. In a zone contiguous to its territorial sea, described as the contiguous zone, the coastal State may exercise the control necessary to:
   (a) prevent infringement of its customs, fiscal, immigration or sanitary laws and regulations within its territory or territorial sea;
   (b) punish infringement of the above laws and regulations committed within its territory or territorial sea.

It is significant that Article 33 only gives a State jurisdiction to *prevent* infringement of customs, fiscal, immigration and sanitary law within its territory or territorial sea. As Shearer points out, this may be sufficient to give a coastal State the right to engage in warnings or inspections of an infringing vessel, but not sufficient to be able to take enforcement action against an infringing vessel.[22] Whether prevention could be stretched to permit a boarding is a moot point, but it seems clear that such a boarding ought not to lead to the arrest of a vessel and its crew without the ship having entered the territorial sea at some point, at least from a literal reading of the text of the LOSC.

In practice, many coastal States have not concerned themselves with the adoption of a contiguous zone, while those that have taken the trouble have not sought to distinguish between prevention and punishment as discussed above.

Exclusive economic zone

The EEZ is the most recent of the maritime zones permitted in the Law of the Sea, with its origins arising out of the practice of States in Latin America in the 1940s and 1950s[23], and the term

"EEZ" being first used at the Organisation of African Unity Meeting in Yaoundé in 1972.[24] The basic principles associated with the EEZ, that it gave an exclusive right of economic exploitation of the seabed and the super-adjacent water column, including fisheries, to a coastal State out to a distance of 200 nautical miles, were established relatively quickly. At UNCLOS III, there was widespread agreement that the concept should be adopted, and although there was some concern raised by land-locked and geographically disadvantaged States, and the distant water fishing nations (DWFNs), the basic concept remained largely unaltered in the LOSC.

Beyond the territorial sea, to a maximum distance of 200 nautical miles, a State may claim an EEZ. Within the EEZ, the coastal State has jurisdiction over economic activities in the water column and on the seabed, environmental protection and installations and artificial islands. The coastal State can undertake enforcement action in support of these areas.[25]

The provisions relating to the EEZ are to be found in Part V of the LOSC. A coastal State is given jurisdiction over all resource-related activities in the EEZ, whether concerned with exploitation, conservation or management, and whether in the waters or on the seabed and its subsoil, for living or non-living resources.[26] Jurisdiction is also given for marine scientific research,[27] artificial islands,[28] and protection and preservation of the marine environment.[29] Article 57 sets the breadth of the EEZ at 200 nautical miles, while other provisions modify the above rights in respect of seeking optimum utilisation of fisheries,[30] rights for landlocked and geographically disadvantaged States,[31] conservation of fish stocks straddling the EEZ and the high seas,[32] marine mammals[33] and highly migratory fish species.[34]

In the context of marine living resources, the coastal State's rights of enforcement are contained in Article 73 of the LOSC. The coastal State has a right to board, inspect and arrest vessels as necessary to ensure compliance with its laws operating in the EEZ. Limitations on the rights relate to guarantees that vessels and crews arrested should be able to be released on the posting of a reasonable bond, and that crews, in the absence of an agreement with the flag State, ought not to be liable to imprisonment.[35]

The Convention also imposes certain regulatory duties upon States, and wider obligations on some other States. For example, the coastal State is obliged to set catch limits for stocks based upon certain criteria, essentially derived from the fisheries management concept of maximum sustainable yield, with some qualification for economic and social factors.[36]

Jurisdiction over environmental matters in the EEZ also gives the coastal State an enforcement jurisdiction in certain circumstances over foreign flagged vessels in these waters. There is a specific provision dealing with enforcement against ocean dumping by vessels, as well as a more general provision. To deal with the specific provision dealing with ocean dumping first, Article 216 of the LOSC provides that laws and regulations implemented in accordance with the Convention and applicable international standards can be enforced by the coastal State with respect to dumping in its territorial sea, EEZ or on its continental shelf. While this provision gives a coastal State a wide reach, it also specifically empowers the flag State with the same jurisdiction, and notes that once proceedings have begun in one State, the other State cannot take action. As such, flag States could limit the ability of a coastal State to take action by doing so themselves.

With respect to more general environmental protection in the EEZ, enforcement is pursuant to Article 220 of the LOSC. It in part provides:

3. Where there are clear grounds for believing that a vessel navigating in the exclusive economic zone or the territorial sea of a State has, in the exclusive economic zone, committed a violation of applicable international rules and standards for the prevention, reduction and control of pollution from vessels or laws and regulations of that State conforming and giving effect to such rules and standards, that State may require the vessel to give information

regarding its identity and port of registry, its last and its next port of call and other relevant information required to establish whether a violation has occurred.
4. States shall adopt laws and regulations and take other measures so that vessels flying their flag comply with requests for information pursuant to paragraph 3.
5. Where there are clear grounds for believing that a vessel navigating in the exclusive economic zone or the territorial sea of a State has, in the exclusive economic zone, committed a violation referred to in paragraph 3 resulting in a substantial discharge causing or threatening significant pollution of the marine environment, that State may undertake physical inspection of the vessel for matters relating to the violation if the vessel has refused to give information or if the information supplied by the vessel is manifestly at variance with the evident factual situation and if the circumstances of the case justify such inspection.
6. Where there is clear objective evidence that a vessel navigating in the exclusive economic zone or the territorial sea of a State has, in the exclusive economic zone, committed a violation referred to in paragraph 3 resulting in a discharge causing major damage or threat of major damage to the coastline or related interests of the coastal State, or to any resources of its territorial sea or exclusive economic zone, that State may, subject to section 7, provided that the evidence so warrants, institute proceedings, including detention of the vessel, in accordance with its laws.
7. Notwithstanding the provisions of paragraph 6, whenever appropriate procedures have been established, either through the competent international organization or as otherwise agreed, whereby compliance with requirements for bonding or other appropriate financial security has been assured, the coastal State if bound by such procedures shall allow the vessel to proceed.

This means that different scope for coastal State enforcement action will arise based on an assessment of the severity of the pollution incident. A violation that is rated as causing or threatening significant pollution permits the coastal State to undertake a physical inspection of a vessel if the vessel has failed to provide adequate information in the circumstances. Only what is considered major pollution damage or a pollution threat will entitle a coastal State to detain a polluting vessel. The subjectivity in assessing what will constitute major damage to some extent vitiates, from a coastal State's point of view, the restriction in this case.[37]

Continental shelf

Unlike the development of the territorial sea, which can be traced back over centuries, the concept of a State having rights to its adjacent continental shelf is relatively recent. It is usually accepted that the concept had its origin in State practice, beginning with the proclamation by President Truman in 1945.[38] In fact, the first instance of the delimitation of two State's continental shelves occurred in 1942, between Great Britain and Venezuela.[39] However, President Truman's proclamation had a profound effect on State practice, particularly in Latin America, so it is still perhaps the best starting point.

The Truman continental shelf proclamation stated that "the exercise of jurisdiction over the natural resources of the subsoil and sea bed of the continental shelf by the contiguous nation is reasonable and just".[40] The basis for this was that "the continental shelf may be regarded as an extension of the land-mass of a coastal nation".[41] This is essentially the notion of natural prolongation which the International Court of Justice (ICJ) fixed upon in the *North Sea Continental*

Shelf Cases[42] more than twenty years later. The proclamation also said that where opposite or adjacent shelves met, they should be delimited in accordance with "equitable principles".[43]

In the years following the Truman Proclamation, dozens of States declared continental shelves, but there was no international agreement on the precise definition of the term, and therefore no agreement on how far the continental shelf extended. Through the 1950s, the International Law Commission (ILC) debated what the nature of the continental shelf was, and ultimately produced two definitions: one based upon water depth, setting an arbitrary limit of 200 metres as the limit of the shelf; and the other based upon exploitability.[44] That is to say if the seabed can be exploited by a State, then it is part of its continental shelf. At the time these rules were formulated, 200 metres was well below what could be feasibly exploited, although technological advances suggested that it would be surpassed in the future. In 1958, at the First United Nations Conference on the Law of the Sea (UNCLOS I), the delegates present adopted the dual test proposed by the ILC. It became embodied in Article 1 of the Convention on the Continental Shelf.[45]

The remainder of the Convention indicated the rights which a coastal State enjoyed over its adjacent continental shelf. These rights have not been significantly altered in the LOSC so they may profitably be examined here. Essentially the coastal State had an exclusive right to explore and exploit the seabed of the adjacent continental shelf[46] (as defined by the Convention). This included all the mineral and other non-living resources of the seabed and its subsoil, as well as any sedentary creatures living on the sea bottom.[47] The exclusive rights to this area were not dependent upon any effective occupation, but accrued by virtue of the State's sovereignty to the land. This was evidenced by the fact a State automatically had such rights, whether it chose to proclaim them or otherwise.[48]

Through the 1960s, States became increasingly dissatisfied with the existing 200 metres/exploitability definition of the continental shelf, in part due to the vagueness of the concept of exploitability.[49] Accordingly at UNCLOS III, there was a serious attempt to revise and redefine the concept of the continental shelf. This proved a difficult task, that continued over many sessions of the Conference, but ultimately a complex consensus definition was arrived at.

The continental shelf is defined in Article 76 of the LOSC as:

(1) All of the seabed, regardless of depth, to a distance of 200 nautical miles from the baselines of the territorial sea; or
(2) Beyond 200 nautical miles if the shelf meets either of the following criteria:
    (i) where the thickness of the sedimentary rocks on the seabed is at least one percent of the distance from such a point to the foot of the continental slope;[50] or
    (ii) a point not more than 60 nautical miles from the foot of the continental slope.
(3) The criteria in (2) are qualified by an absolute limit of no more than 350 nautical miles, or 100 nautical miles beyond the 2500 metre isobath.

This definition is inherently complex, imposing a substantial obligation upon coastal States in the collection of data to substantiate their claim to areas of continental shelf beyond 200 nautical miles. Further, the LOSC provides for a mechanism to test the adequacy of a coastal State's data in support of the possession of a continental shelf beyond 200 nautical miles by the provision of a referral process to a body established under the LOSC, the Commission on the Limits of the Continental Shelf. A large number of States are wending their way through the Commission's processes at the time of writing.

Regulation on the continental shelf overlaps considerably with that of the EEZ, both literally and figuratively. In jurisdictional terms, the continental shelf gives a coastal State regulation and enforcement powers over the exploration and exploitation of the natural resources of the seabed, whether living or non-living, by virtue of Article 77 of the LOSC. The EEZ gives an almost identical jurisdiction over the seabed, with the exception of sedentary living resources which are not subject to the same regulations as for fish and other marine living resources. The EEZ and continental shelf both give jurisdiction over the seabed where it is within 200 nautical miles of the coastal State. The continental shelf may extend beyond 200 nautical miles as noted above.

Archipelagic waters

A special regime exists for waters within an archipelago that meet particular conditions under the LOSC. Under the LOSC, an archipelago is defined to include not merely the islands and reefs of a geographical group, but also the waters in between the islands.[51] A State consisting entirely of one or more archipelagos is entitled to draw baselines around the archipelago, provided they meet certainly carefully defined criteria. The baselines are then used as a basis for the calculation of the territorial sea and other maritime zones, while the waters inside these baselines are given the status of archipelagic waters.[52]

The regime for archipelagic States was adopted during UNCLOS III after the efforts of a number of States led by Indonesia and the Philippines. It was designed to give archipelagic States greater rights over the waters between their constituent islands, while at the same time guaranteeing rights of navigation through the archipelago for other States.[53]

Archipelagic waters are under the sovereignty of a coastal State, as is the territorial sea, and in many cases the rights with respect to regulation and enforcement are similar. This is because vessels passing through most of an archipelagic State's waters are subject to the regime of innocent passage, the same regime as is applicable in much of the territorial sea. Those waters which are treated differently, are those within an archipelagic sea lane, where the rights of a coastal State are more restrictive, as they are with the transit passage regime within international straits.[54]

Safety zones

Special rules also exist for safety zones around structures built on the sea, as an exception to the coherence of the regime of maritime zones. All States have a right to construct structures on the high seas (although at the time of writing none had actually done so), and coastal States possess the exclusive right to build installations upon their continental shelves. Any installation constructed at sea is entitled to have a 500 metre safety zone around it, wherein unauthorised navigation is prohibited.[55]

A coastal State's rights in the safety zone are analogous to those possessed in internal waters, as entry into the safety zone is prohibited without the authorisation of the coastal State.[56] However, it would be wrong to equate the safety zone with a small belt of internal waters, as the zone may be hundreds of miles from the nearest land – particularly if the structure was located upon the seabed beyond national jurisdiction. Nevertheless, as the presence of the structure is entirely dependent upon the authorisation of a State, it may mean that jurisdiction within the safety zone is not dissimilar to that of a State utilising port State control, as failure to comply with the State's rules could mean exclusion from the safety zone.

Hot pursuit

An exception to the zonal approach of the LOSC can be found in the concept of hot pursuit, described in Article 110 of the LOSC. This exception provides that in certain circumstances, jurisdiction over a vessel can be maintained while pursuing the vessel, even when the vessel leaves the relevant maritime zone. The LOSC sets requirements with respect to the commencement of the pursuit, requiring it to be initiated by a visual or auditory signal at a distance which enables it to be seen or heard by the offending vessel when the offending vessel is within a maritime zone where the coastal State has jurisdiction, and for it to be continued without interruption. Further the pursuit must cease if the offending vessel enters its own flag State's territorial sea, or the territorial sea of a third State. On this last point, at least two coastal States have reached agreement on waiving this last requirement.[57]

Conclusion

The use of a zonal approach to maritime jurisdiction is one of the hallmarks of the LOSC. The breadth of the matters codified in the EEZ and continental shelf provision of the LOSC indicate the extent of a coastal State's legal competence to regulate and enforce its laws in these offshore zones beyond the territorial sea. The impact this change has had is profound, given the volume of natural resources States take from these adjacent waters as compared to the oceans as a whole.

On the other hand, it is important to recognise that regulation and enforcement are by no means limited to the applicable maritime zones. Jurisdiction based upon nationality, be it personal or flag State, applied to a ship by its State of registration, is also very important. Regulation by port States, where a vessel comes along side in internal waters, is also of growing importance, recognising the limitations in territorial jurisdiction based on maritime zones, and flag State jurisdiction. However, the codification of the zonal approach in the Law of the Sea Convention is still an essential and fundamental component of the regulatory and enforcement options available to a coastal state in dealing with its offshore interests.

Notes

1 United Nations Convention on the Law of the Sea, 10 December 1982, 1833 UNTS 3 [hereinafter LOSC].
2 D.R. Rothwell, S. Kaye, A. Akhtarkhavari and R. Davis, *International Law*, Melbourne: Cambridge University Press, 2014, p. 370.
3 See Part II, Section 2, LOSC.
4 Part V, LOSC.
5 Article 30 and 31, LOSC.
6 Article 121(2) LOSC.
7 Article 121(1) LOSC.
8 Article 121(3) LOSC.
9 See the discussion in J.M. Van Dyke and R.A. Brooks, 'Uninhabited Islands: Their Impact on the Ownership of the Oceans' Resources', *Ocean Development and International Law*, 1983, vol. 12, p. 265 at p. 283; see also H. Dipla, *Le Régime Juridique des Îles dans le Droit International de la Mer*, Geneva: Presse Universitaire de France, 1984, pp. 82–85.
10 R.D. Hodgson and R.W. Smith, 'The Informal Single Negotiating Text (Committee II): A Geographical Perspective', *Ocean Development and International Law*, 1976, vol. 3, p. 225 at p. 230.
11 See Articles 10, 9, 7 and 11, LOSC.
12 *Patterson v The Eudora* (1903) 190 US 169.
13 Article 2, LOSC.

14 Part II Section 3, LOSC.
15 H. Grotius, *Mare Liberum*, Oxford: Oxford University Press, 1916 (translation by R. van D. Magoffin). This work, published in 1608, touched off a storm of academic debate in Europe, notably in Selden's *Mare Clausum*, published in 1635: see R.P. Anand, *Origin and Development of the Law of the Sea*, The Hague: Martinus Nijhoff, 1982, pp. 100–103; R.R. Churchill and A.V. Lowe, *The Law of the Sea*, Manchester: Manchester University Press, 1988, pp. 3–4.
16 This rule was suggested by Bynkershoek in 1702: J. Colombos, *The International Law of the Sea*, London: Longmans, 1967, p. 92; D.P. O'Connell (I.A. Shearer (ed.)), *The International Law of the Sea*, Oxford: Clarendon Press, 1982, vol.1, pp. 126–127.
17 This was established by the *Territorial Waters Jurisdiction Act* 1878 (UK).
18 See *American Journal of International Law*, Special Supplement, 1930, vol.23, p. 250.
19 See I.A. Shearer, 'Problems of Jurisdiction and Law Enforcement against Delinquent Vessels', *International and Comparative Law Quarterly*, 1986, vol.35, p. 320 at p. 325.
20 Article 27(5), LOSC.
21 See Colombos, op. cit., pp. 136–140; M.S. McDougall and W.T. Burke, *The Public Order of the Oceans: A Contemporary International Law of the Sea*, New Haven: New Haven Press, 1987, pp. 585–603.
22 Shearer, op. cit., p. 437.
23 Publicists often trace back the origins of the EEZ to the Santiago Declaration in 1947, which was itself a reaction to the Truman Proclamation in 1945: D.J. Attard, *The Exclusive Economic Zone in International Law*, Oxford: Clarendon Press, 1987, pp. 3–9; F. Orrego Vicuña, *The Exclusive Economic Zone: A Latin American Perspective*, Boulder: Westview Press, 1984, pp. 20–25.
24 Attard, op. cit., pp. 20–25.
25 Article 73, LOSC.
26 Article 56, LOSC.
27 Article 56(1)(b)(ii), LOSC.
28 Articles 56(1)(b)(i) and Article 60, LOSC.
29 Article 56(1)(b)(iii), LOSC.
30 Articles 61 and 62, LOSC.
31 Articles 69 and 70, LOSC.
32 Article 63, LOSC.
33 Article 65, LOSC.
34 Article 64, LOSC.
35 Articles 73(2) and 73(3), LOSC.
36 Article 61(3), Law of the Sea Convention.
37 Article 226, Law of the Sea Convention.
38 Proclamation by the President of the United States of America, 28 September 1945; reprinted in S.H. Lay, R. Churchill and M. Nordquist, *New Directions in the Law of the Sea*, Dobbs Ferry: Oceana, 1973, vol.1, pp. 106–107. Note that O'Connell discusses the writings of a number of authors prior to World War II, pointing out that the concept of a continental shelf in international law is not as recent as a number of authors would claim. However, he notes that the development of offshore drilling in the late 1920s and 1930s provided the practical impetus for developments in the 1940s; O'Connell, op. cit., pp. 467–470.
39 Treaty between His Majesty in Respect of the United Kingdom and the President of the United States of Venezuela relating to the Submarine Areas of the Gulf of Paria, 20 February 1942, 205 LNTS 121; O'Connell, op. cit., pp. 470–471; M.D. Evans, *Relevant Circumstances and Maritime Delimitation*, Oxford: Clarendon Press, 1989, p. 1; M.L. Jewett, 'The Evolution of the Legal Regime of the Continental Shelf', *Canadian Yearbook of International Law*, 1984, vol.22, p. 153 at pp. 162–163.
40 Lay, Churchill and Nordquist, op. cit., p. 106.
41 Ibid.
42 ICJ Reports 1969, p. 3.
43 Lay, Churchill and Nordquist, op. cit., p. 107.
44 These debates can be found in the *Yearbook of the ILC* for the years 1949–56.
45 29 April 1958, 499 UNTS 311.
46 Article 77(1), LOSC.
47 Article 77(4), LOSC.
48 Articles 77(2) and 77(3), LOSC.

49 For example see the debate in United Nations, *Third United Nations Conference on the Law of the Sea. Official Records*, New York: United Nations, 1975, vol.2, pp. 142–171.
50 The LOSC defines the foot of the slope to be, in the absence of evidence to the contrary, the point with the maximum change in the gradient at the base of the continental slope: Article 76(4)(b), LOSC.
51 "Archipelago" means a group of islands, including parts of islands, interconnecting waters and other natural features which are so closely interrelated that such islands, waters and other natural features form an intrinsic geographical, economic and political entity, or which historically have been regarded as such: Article 46(b), LOSC.
52 Article 49, LOSC.
53 See M. Nordquist (ed.), *United Nations Convention on the Law of the Sea 1982: A Commentary*, Dordrecht: Martinus Nijhoff, 1993, vol.2, pp. 399–404.
54 See Article 54, LOSC.
55 Article 60(4) and 60(5), LOSC.
56 Article 60(6), Law of the Sea Convention.
57 Agreement on Cooperative Enforcement of Fisheries Laws between the Government of Australia and the Government of the French Republic in the Maritime Areas Adjacent to the French Southern and Antarctic Territories, Heard Island and the McDonald Islands, 8 January 2007, Aust. TS 2011, No.1.

2
The High Seas Regime: a Model of Self-regulation?

Robin Warner

Introduction

The high seas as an international law concept is generally considered to have originated in the doctrine of the freedom of the seas advocated by the seventeenth century Dutch jurist, Hugo Grotius in his treatise *Mare Liberum*, published in 1609.[1] Grotius drew a distinction between the "inner sea" which was surrounded on all sides by the land and thus susceptible to human occupation and the "outer sea, the ocean" which he described as "immense ... infinite, bounded only by the heavens" which could neither be "seized or inclosed."[2] His fundamental premise that the sea may not be subjected to the sovereignty of individual States survived in Article 89 of the United Nations Convention on the Law of the Sea (LOSC). *Mare Liberum* also introduced the principles of freedom of navigation and fishing which remain an integral part of the present high seas regime codified in Part VII of the LOSC.[3]

The doctrines Grotius expounded in *Mare Liberum* were in part a reaction against sovereignty claims by Spain and Portugal to vast areas of ocean space for the purpose of monopolising the trade routes to the New World and the East Indies.[4] An opposing juridical position of *mare clausum* or the "closed sea" continued to be popular with British and European rulers building their colonial empires and establishing naval dominance at sea during the seventeenth and eighteenth centuries. States' sovereignty over large areas of ocean space was defended by English jurists such as Welwood, Selden and Coke in the decades following the publication of Grotius' *Mare Liberum*.[5] The principles contained in *Mare Liberum* did not gain ascendancy until the nineteenth century when they were used to support the expansion of free trade between European countries and their distant empires.[6] In jurist's writings and state practice, however, a modified version of coastal State sovereignty over the maritime belt adjacent to land territory developed in parallel to the doctrine of the freedom of the seas.[7] The extent of a coastal State's dominion over its adjacent waters was considered by most jurists to relate to its capacity to exercise sovereignty over these areas by means of guns or cannon.[8] The three nautical mile distance which subsequently gained currency as the customary international law breadth for the territorial sea, was related to the maximum range of these weapons. These parallel developments in legal treatises and state practice in relation to the maritime belt adjacent to the coastline of a State and the open or high seas, introduced a basic spatial differentiation in the law of the sea between areas of water subject to coastal State sovereignty or jurisdiction and the residual areas of ocean space which were effectively a global commons.

The conventional international law codification of the high seas regime began in the early twentieth century with the efforts of non-government bodies such as the International Law Association, the Institut de Droit International and the Harvard Research in International Law to distil customary international law principles from state practice and the writings of jurists.[9] Early draft conventions by these bodies emphasised the invalidity of States' claims to sovereignty over the high seas and the free and full use of the sea by all States without impediment.[10] Later codifications of the high seas regime in the 1958 High Seas Convention and the 1958 Convention on Fishing and Conservation of the Living Resources of the High Seas (High Seas Living Resources Convention) and Part VII of the LOSC reiterated these principles but recognised the need to balance the unfettered exercise of high seas freedoms with the discharge of certain international responsibilities such as the policing of international and transnational crime and the conservation and management of the living resources of the high seas.[11]

Invalidity of sovereign claims over the high seas

The fundamental principle that no State is capable of exercising territorial sovereignty over the high seas appears as a core element in successive international law codifications of the high seas regime. In its 1956 Report on the Law of the Sea, which formed the basis for deliberations by States at the First United Nations Conference on the Law of the Sea (UNCLOS I), the International Law Commission commented that "the principle generally accepted in international law that the high seas are open to all nations governs the whole regulation of the subject" and "that no state may subject any part of the high seas to its sovereignty ... or exercise jurisdiction over any stretch of water."[12] The unoccupied status of the high seas was reinforced by the retention of an almost identical formulation in Article 2 of the High Seas Convention and Article 89 of the LOSC which provides that "No State may validly purport to subject any part of the high seas to its sovereignty." The High Seas Convention and the LOSC do not expand on the juridical status of the high seas although many commentators have speculated on the juridical nature of these areas of ocean space and the appropriate management regime which should apply to the high seas.[13] The precise juridical nature of the high seas remains an open question. Any presumption that the high seas is a jurisdictional vacuum, however, is qualified by other provisions in the High Seas Convention and the LOSC which refer to the concept of flag State jurisdiction which applies to ships transiting the high seas and some collective obligations of States to exercise certain shared responsibilities on the high seas.[14] All States are required to cooperate to the fullest extent possible in the repression of piracy, the slave trade and illicit traffic in narcotic drugs and psychotropic substances and in the suppression of unauthorised broadcasting from the high seas.[15] States are also required to cooperate in the conservation and management of the living resources of the high seas.[16] These responsibilities of the international community in relation to the high seas imply that any measures taken in exercise of these duties, particularly those involving restrictive measures in particular areas of the high seas, should be globally endorsed. The need to incorporate mechanisms conferring such global endorsement is important in considering further development of maritime regulation and enforcement in the high seas.

Freedoms of the high seas

In Grotius doctrine of the freedom of the seas, the corollary principle to the invalidity of sovereign claims over the sea was the free and open use of the seas by all nations. Grotius identified the principal freedoms of the sea as navigation and fishing.[17] The content of this principle evolved to encompass new uses of the high seas in later codifications of the law of the sea. The draft article on the freedom of the high seas in the 1956 ILC Report on the Law of the Sea (ILC Report) identified four freedoms of the high seas considered to be the most prevalent uses of the high seas at the time of drafting the report.[18] The freedom to lay submarine cables and pipelines and the freedom to fly over the high seas were added to the long-standing customary freedoms of navigation and fishing. These four freedoms were retained in Article 2 of the High Seas Convention. The ILC Report specifies that these four freedoms are not an exhaustive categorisation of the freedoms of the high seas and refers to other freedoms such as the freedom to undertake scientific research and the freedom to explore or exploit the subsoil of the high seas.[19] There is also an explicit recognition of the need to regulate the exercise of high seas freedoms in the interests of the entire international community.[20] In this connection, the International Law Commission (ILC) notes the right of individual States to exercise their sovereignty on board ships flying their flag on the high seas, the exercise of certain policing rights by States on the high seas and the rights of States relative to the living resources of the high seas.[21] All these rights are the subject of subsequent articles in the High Seas Convention, the High Seas Living Resources Convention and the LOSC and underscore the need for individual and collaborative action by States to regulate the adverse impacts of human uses of the high seas.[22]

The high seas regime was also considered in the work of the Committee on the Peaceful Uses of the Seabed and the Ocean Floor beyond the Limits of National Jurisdiction (Sea-Bed Committee) established prior to the Third United Nations Conference on the Law of the Sea (UNCLOS III). In a statement by the Indonesian representative to the 12th meeting of Sub-Committee II of the Sea-Bed Committee there is an early recognition of the need to protect and preserve the marine environment of the high seas. He notes that the freedoms of the high seas formulated in the High Seas Convention should be "coupled with certain responsibilities" and that their exercise should not "endanger the ecology and environment of the oceans."[23] The debate on the freedom of fishing on the high seas was the most contentious in the deliberations of Sub-Committee II. The Venezuelan representative highlighted the division of opinion among delegations at the 47th meeting of Sub-Committee II, referring to the widely divergent views of delegations that on the one hand, there should no longer be any freedom of fishing on the high seas and that it should be strictly regulated and on the other, that the freedom of fishing should be maintained.[24]

Similar debates on the qualifications which should be made to high seas freedoms continued throughout the UNCLOS III negotiations. The potentially harmful effects of the unregulated exercise of high seas freedoms on the marine environment is recognised in general terms in the statements of delegates to informal meetings of the Second Committee of UNCLOS III and proposals received from States for draft articles on the high seas. In a statement to the 31st meeting of the Second Committee on 7 August 1974, Mr. Galindo Pohl (El Salvador) commented that "the regulations concerning navigation, overflight and the laying of submarine cables and pipelines were still relevant to contemporary conditions, though they would need adjusting to ensure that such operations did not adversely affect the marine environment."[25] At the same meeting of the Second Committee, Mr. Arias Schreiber (Peru) commented that a future regime for the high seas "should contain adequate provisions for the control and elimination of pollution which endangered the ecological balance in the oceans."[26] Some delegates to the Second Committee such as Mr. Pollard (Guyana) were in favour of extending the competence of the International Seabed Authority to the water column and its resources as well as the deep seabed.[27]

During the UNCLOS III negotiations, many delegates were already concerned about the over exploitation of high seas fisheries by vessels from a limited number of distant water fishing nations and the lack of international regulations governing such activities. El Salvador's representative at the 31st meeting of the Second Committee commented that "Fishing in the high seas must be governed by regulations that would meet the new circumstances created by current technological development with its threat of exhausting species."[28] His concerns were echoed by Mr. Warioba (Tanzania) who noted that "Fishing on the high seas had become piracy and plunder . . . urgent and effective international action was needed. . . and management of the living resources of the high seas must be placed under effective international control."[29] The Peruvian and Senegalese representatives noted the need to formulate regulations to "ensure proper international control over fisheries in order to preserve the renewable resources in the international sea" and that fisheries commissions should "genuinely represent the interests of the international community with regard to the protection of the resources in the high seas."[30]

Statements in favour of more extensive regulation of activities on the high seas were balanced in the Second Committee by strong advocacy on the part of delegates from Western nations and distant water fishing nations for the retention of unfettered freedoms of navigation, overflight and fishing. Mr. Anderson (UK), at the 31st meeting of the Second Committee, commented that while "freedom of the seas has always been subject to qualifications", his delegation "attached particular importance to the freedom of navigation and overflight" and "favoured the retention of as much as possible of the existing freedom of the high seas in the area beyond the territorial sea."[31] Mr. Movchan (USSR) expressed his delegation's preference for "a firm regime of the high seas which would prevent any interference with the freedom of the high seas" and rejected proposals that "would divide the ocean into two parts, one part under national jurisdiction and the other under international jurisdiction."[32]

In a working paper prepared for the Second Committee in the early stages of the UNCLOS III negotiations, which reflected the main trends emerging from proposals submitted to the Seabed Committee and UNCLOS III, there was a draft provision 149 which read:

> "All States shall be obliged to comply with international regulations designed to prevent, reduce or eliminate any damage or risks arising from pollution or other effects detrimental or dangerous to the ecological system of the international seas, water quality and use, living resources and human health."[33]

Later informal proposals to the Second Committee removed this draft provision noting that "the preservation of the marine environment of the high seas is being dealt with in the Third Committee." The US, in one draft article for inclusion in the chapter on the high seas, proposed that explicit reference be made to the provisions of the Convention on the protection of the marine environment, modifying the regime of the high seas.[34] In the final text of Part VII of the LOSC, however, there is no specific recognition of the need to protect and preserve the marine environment of the high seas.

Two additional freedoms are included in the non-exhaustive list of freedoms of the high seas in Article 87 of the LOSC, the freedom to construct artificial and other installations permitted under international law and the freedom of scientific research. Four of the freedoms in

Article 87, the freedom to lay submarine cables and pipelines, the freedom to conduct artificial islands and other installations, the freedom of fishing and the freedom of scientific research, are made subject to other sections and parts of the LOSC recognising the balance which needed to be struck between the exercise of these freedoms and other activities occurring in marine areas within national jurisdiction and providing some indication as to how these freedoms might be exercised.[35] The freedoms of navigation and overflight remain unqualified in Article 87.

Flag state jurisdiction

In the absence of any global authority governing the high seas, the flag State model of jurisdiction has become the predominant method of regulating high seas activities. Linking ships with the nationality of their flag State automatically imports a system of rights and obligations under national and international law into the high seas domain. Although Grotius doctrine of the freedom of the high seas did not incorporate the notion of flag State jurisdiction or propose that ships possess a nationality, later jurists such as Ortolan were convinced of the indispensable character of this mode of jurisdiction if the activities of multiple vessels on the high seas were not to descend into chaos.[36] The system of flag State jurisdiction was a logical, if not perfect, device to impose a measure of order on ships activities in marine areas beyond national jurisdiction. The ascription of nationality to the flag vessels of sovereign States also accorded with the customary international law principles of the sovereign equality of States.[37]

The High Seas Convention and Part VII of the LOSC, together with other global and regional instruments on marine living resource exploitation and maritime transport, create a framework within which States can regulate the activities of their flag vessels on the high seas. The articles contained in these instruments specify certain minimum rights and obligations which States must comply with in relation to their flag vessels but allow considerable discretion in implementing these requirements. The codification of this framework began with the ILC's 1955 and 1956 Reports on the Law of the Sea which formed the basis for the relevant articles in the High Seas Convention. The right of every State to sail ships under its flag on the high seas was described by the ILC in its 1956 Report on the Law of the Sea as one of the essential adjuncts to the principle of the freedom of the high seas.[38] This comment reinforces an earlier comment in this report that certain rules are necessary to safeguard the exercise of high seas freedoms.[39] While allowing States to fix the conditions for the registration of their ships, draft Article 5 of the high seas articles in the ILC's 1955 Report on the Law of the Sea was quite prescriptive in enumerating the conditions for recognition of a ship's national character by other States. To be accorded recognition as a flag vessel of a particular State, ships were required to:

"1. Be the property of the State concerned; or
2. Be more than half owned by:
    (a) Nationals of or persons legally domiciled in the territory of the State concerned and actually resident there; or
    (b) A partnership in which the majority of the partners with personal liability are nationals of or persons legally domiciled in the territory of the State concerned and actually resident there; or
    (c) A joint stock company formed under the laws of the State concerned and having its registered office in the territory of that State."[40]

In commenting on this draft article, the ILC noted that there must be a minimum national element in the conditions for granting flag ship status "since control and jurisdiction by a State over ships flying its flag can only be effectively exercised when there is in fact a relationship between the State and the ship other than that based on mere registration."[41] The formulation proposed in draft Article 5 was not retained after negative comments from Governments. Instead, the vaguer formulation of a 'genuine link' was drawn from the 1955 judgment of the International Court of Justice in the *Nottebohm* case and applied by analogy to the grant of flag ship status.[42] In a revised draft Article 29 on nationality of ships in its 1956 Report on the Law of the Sea, the ILC adopted the 'genuine link' formula without defining its specific content or prescribing relevant sanctions such as non-recognition of a ship's nationality if a 'genuine link' between a State and its flag vessels did not exist.[43] The ILC was obviously uneasy about the imprecision of the genuine link concept, emphasising in its commentary to draft Article 29 that the grant of a flag to a ship cannot be "a mere administrative formality with no accompanying guarantee that the ship possesses a real link with its new State."[44] The final version of Article 5 of the High Seas Convention specified very general indicia of the existence of a genuine link between a State and its flag vessel providing that:

> "There must exist a genuine link between the State and the ship; in particular, the State must effectively exercise its jurisdiction and control in administrative, technical and social matters over ships flying its flag."

The genuine link concept was retained in Article 91(1) of the LOSC and the provisions on the flag State's duty to effectively exercise its jurisdiction and control over ships registered in its territory was augmented. A working paper on the high seas submitted by nine Western European States to the Second Committee set out a catalogue of flag state obligations in draft Article 6 bis which, while mainly connected with safety of navigation, required flag States to take the necessary measures to ensure that the master and officers were fully conversant with and were required to observe the applicable international regulations concerning the prevention and control of marine pollution.[45] Flag States were also required to cause an enquiry to be held into every marine casualty or incident of navigation on the high seas involving ships flying their flags where serious damage was caused to the marine environment.[46] These draft articles were retained in Article 94(4)(c) and (7) of the LOSC. The content of Article 94 was influenced by the work of the International Maritime Consultative Organization (IMCO), as it then was, which had submitted a summary of its activities to the Second Session of UNCLOS III on 20 June 1974.[47] As IMCO had already sponsored some international conventions and subsidiary regulations on the prevention, reduction and control of marine pollution such as the 1973 International Convention for the Prevention of Pollution from Ships, Article 94 of the LOSC incorporated by reference relevant provisions from those conventions which applied to flag vessels on the high seas. The incorporation in Article 94 of "generally accepted international regulations, procedures and practices" concerning marine pollution and other matters such as safety of life at sea and the prevention of collisions reflected a trend towards more detailed sectoral regulation of human activities on the high seas.

Economic and organisational factors in the shipping and maritime transport industry have had a profound impact on the standard of flag State compliance with and enforcement of the obligations relating to safety of life at sea and protection of the high seas marine environment from vessel source pollution in Part VII of the LOSC.[48] Although the majority of flag States have implemented the LOSC provisions and IMO regulatory conventions such as the London

Convention and MARPOL 73/78 Annexes I and II in their domestic legislation, this is not always accompanied by a competent maritime administration which oversees compliance with these laws for flag vessels.[49] In practice, the genuine link required by Article 92 of the LOSC between the flag State and the operations of its flag vessels in administrative, technical and social terms is frequently lacking, especially in States which operate flags of convenience registries.[50] Some flag States have abrogated their responsibility for certification and survey of vessels, relying entirely on non-government bodies such as classification societies to fulfil these functions. Economic pressures have led ship owners to limit their expenditure on maintenance of vessels and qualified crew to gain short-term competitive advantage in the maritime transport industry.[51] Poor investigation of ship casualties by some flag States has also led to the continued operation of unsafe flag vessels which present a potent threat to the marine environment within and beyond national jurisdiction.[52] The decentralised nature of flag state responsibility and the lack of sanctions under international law for recalcitrant flag States militate against adequate protection of the increasingly vulnerable high seas environment.

Conservation of the living resources of the high seas

Concern for the effects of marine living resource exploitation on the high seas marine environment emerged in the discussions of the Sea-Bed Committee prior to UNCLOS III. A draft Ocean Space Treaty prepared by Malta envisaged that, in international ocean space, a Council of State Parties would "manage the living resources . . . in such a manner as to secure the maximum sustainable yield taking into due account the need to preserve the ecological balance of ocean space."[53] The decisions of the Council would be based on scientific findings. The theme of conservation and management decisions which would take into account environmental factors and would be based on scientific findings was also present in two proposals submitted by the US to the 1971 and 1972 sessions of the Sea-Bed Committee.[54] The environmental protection element of the high seas fisheries provisions was further developed in States' proposals to the Second Committee at UNCLOS III. A US Proposal included in the Main Trends working paper required States to adopt measures on "the best evidence available designed to maintain or restore populations of harvested species at levels which can produce the maximum sustainable yield, as qualified by relevant environmental and economic factors including the interdependence of stocks."[55] They were also required to take into consideration the effects on species with a view to maintaining or restoring populations of such associated or dependent species above levels at which their reproduction may become seriously threatened.[56] This proposal introduced a precautionary element into the draft provisions requiring States to adopt conservation measures even where the best scientific evidence might not be present as a basis for such measures.[57] It also introduced an obligation to maintain or restore associated or dependent species affected by high seas fisheries.[58] This proposal was the basis for Article 119 of the LOSC which adopts the maximum sustainable yield objective for determining the allowable catch but qualifies that objective with broader environmental protection considerations. Under Article 119(1)(a) and (b), States must take conservation and management measures for high seas living resources based on the best scientific evidence available as qualified by relevant environmental factors such as the interdependence of stocks and taking into consideration the effects on associated and dependent species with a view to maintaining their populations above levels at which their reproduction may be seriously threatened. Article 119 of the LOSC and the associated Articles 117 and 118, which require States to take unilateral and cooperative measures to conserve the living resources of the high seas, have been further implemented in the Agreement for the Implementation of the Provisions of the United Nations Convention on the Law of the Sea of 10 December 1982 relating to the Conservation and Management of Straddling Fish Stocks and Highly Migratory Fish Stocks (UN Fish Stocks Agreement)[59] and in the provisions of some regional fisheries management agreements.

Enforcement jurisdiction over activities on the high seas

Flag State jurisdiction is central to the majority of enforcement activities on the high seas. Other bases for interdicting non-sovereign immune vessels on the high seas are very limited and confined to vessels suspected on reasonable grounds of being engaged in piracy, the slave trade or being without nationality.[60] In most other multilateral regimes which apply to the high seas, interdiction to enforce international obligations is based on the consent of the flag State. Flag State consent is required to interdict vessels suspected of drug trafficking on the high seas under the 1988 Vienna Convention against Illicit Traffic in Narcotic Drugs and Psychotropic Substances (Vienna Convention).[61] The UN Fish Stocks Agreement moves further in the direction of collaborative enforcement by permitting States Parties enforcement vessels under the auspices of a relevant regional fisheries management organisation (RFMO) to board and inspect not only their own flag vessels but also vessels of other flags in high seas areas covered by the RFMO in question whether or not the flag States of those vessels are party to the UN Fish Stocks Agreement.[62] Where there are clear grounds for suspecting a violation of the RFMO's conservation and management measures, inspecting States still need to contact the flag State to obtain its authorisation to proceed further with enforcement, but if the flag State fails to take action within three days and there are clear grounds for believing that a serious violation has taken place, the inspecting State may bring the offending vessel to port for further investigation. There are also examples of more collaborative enforcement arrangements for counter drug operations in some high seas areas based on standing agreements among flag States which authorise enforcement of their relevant laws by other States enforcement vessels without referral to the flag State of the interdicted vessel on each occasion. Counter-drug operations by the US Coastguard in the Caribbean are a case in point.[63] Clearly, development of more collaborative enforcement regimes on the high seas which go beyond individual flag State enforcement, will continue to rely to a large extent on the development of regional capabilities. Strong incentives will also be required for such regional cooperation to occur such as the depletion of a valuable fishery or the adverse impacts of transnational criminal activities such as drug trafficking and people smuggling on regional security.

Conclusion

The LOSC confirms the customary international law principle that the high seas is a global commons, and specifies that freedom of the high seas may be exercised by all States whether coastal or landlocked.[64] Importantly, the LOSC specifies that the freedoms of the high seas are exercised under the conditions set out in the LOSC and by other rules of international law.[65] With this qualification, the LOSC recognises the need to balance the unfettered exercise of high seas freedoms with the discharge of certain international responsibilities. For example high seas freedoms must be exercised subject to the general obligation to protect and preserve the marine environment in Article 192 of the LOSC. Additionally, a core high seas freedom, the freedom of fishing, is subject to the duty to cooperate in conserving and managing the living resources of the high seas codified in Article 118 of the LOSC. This obligation has been implemented through the UN Fish Stocks Agreement and the many conservation and management measures adopted by RFMOs that are binding on their member States. These include measures directed at conserving ecosystems that are associated or dependent on fisheries resources.[66]

The flag State model of jurisdiction has become the predominant method of regulating high seas activities. Part VII of the LOSC specifies certain obligations which States must comply with in relation to their flag vessels. Among the flag State's duties is the requirement to ensure that the master, officers and crews of its flag vessels are fully conversant with and observe the applicable international regulations concerning the prevention, reduction and control of marine pollution.[67] These regulations are contained in an array of conventions developed by the International Maritime Organization such as the 1973 International Convention for the Prevention of Pollution from Ships (MARPOL 73/78) with its detailed technical annexes.[68] Economic and organisational factors in the shipping and maritime transport industry have had a profound impact on the standard of flag State compliance with and enforcement of these obligations, particularly as they relate to the protection of the high seas marine environment.[69] In practice, the genuine link between the flag State and the operations of its flag vessels in administrative, technical and social terms, required under Article 91 of the LOSC, has often been missing. This has led to the continued operation of unsafe and delinquent flag vessels which represent a potent threat to the marine environment both within and beyond national jurisdiction. To remedy this situation, additional cooperative measures at the regional and global levels need to be developed together with economic incentives for shipping and fisheries industry compliance. States may combine to develop international rules and standards on safety of life at sea or protection of the marine environment but implementation of these rules is largely dependent on individual flag States rather than on global and regional authorities or any multinational enforcement mechanism. The emphasis on global and regional efforts to protect the marine environment in the general articles of Part XII is also at odds with the relative freedom of States and non-state actors to engage in a range of activities on the high seas without prior assessment or monitoring of their impacts on the environment. The current system of high seas regulation and enforcement under the LOSC, which is largely dependent on individual flag State implementation, does not reconcile this tension. This tension will continue to play out in global efforts to develop a further implementation agreement under the LOSC to address the conservation and sustainable use of marine resources and biodiversity in these vast areas of the ocean.[70]

Notes

1 Hugo Grotius, *The Freedom of the Seas or the Right which Belongs to the Dutch to Take Part in the East Indian Trade* (translation and revision of the text of 1633 by Ralph Van Deman Magoffin) (Oxford University Press, New York, 1916); D.P. O'Connell (with I.A. Shearer ed.), The International Law of the Sea (Clarendon Press, Oxford, 1984), Vol II, pp. 792–793; J.H. Verzijl, International Law in Historical Perspective (Sijthoff, Leiden, 1971), pp. 31–35; United Nations Office for Ocean Affairs and the Law of the Sea (DOALOS), Navigation on the High Seas: Legislative History of Part VII, Section 1 (Arts 87, 89, 90–94, 96–98) of the United Nations Convention on the Law of the Sea (1989) p. 8.
2 Grotius, supra note 4, p. 37.
3 Ibid, pp. 7 and 32.
4 Verzijl, above note 1, p. 30; Thomas W. Fulton, *The Sovereignty of the Sea* (Blackwood, Edinburgh, 1911), pp. 338–339.
5 Fulton, above note 4, pp. 352–357; DOALOS Navigation on the High Seas, above note 1, p. 8.
6 Hersch Lauterpacht (ed.), Oppenheim's International Law. A Treatise (8th Ed.) (Longmans, London, 1955), pp. 585–587.
7 Verzijl, above note 1, p. 31; Lauterpacht, above note 6, p. 586 ; Fulton, above note 4, pp. 537–575.

8 Fulton, above note 4, p. 549.
9 DOALOS Navigation on the High Seas, above note 1, p. 8.
10 Ibid, pp. 8–9.
11 High Seas Convention, Articles 13–23; 1958 Convention on Fishing and Conservation of the Living Resources of the High Seas, 559 UNTS 285 (High Seas Living Resources Convention); LOSC, Articles 116–119.
12 Official Records of the General Assembly, Eleventh Session, Supplement No. 9, UN Doc A/3159, Chapter III, Part II, Article 27 commentary, para 1.
13 D.P. O'Connell, The International Law of the Sea, above note 1, pp. 792–793.
14 High Seas Convention, Article 4; LOSC, Article 90.
15 High Seas Convention, Article 14; LOSC, Articles 100, 108 and 109.
16 High Seas Living Resources Convention; LOSC, Articles 116–119.
17 Grotius, above note 1, pp. 7 and 32.
18 Official Records of the General Assembly, above note 12, para 2.
19 Ibid.
20 Ibid, para 5.
21 Ibid.
22 Above note 11.
23 Report of the Twelfth Meeting of Sub-Committee II of the Sea-Bed Committee, UN Doc A/A.138/SC.II/SR.12, p. 111.
24 Report of the Forty Seventh Meeting of Sub-Committee II of the Sea-Bed Committee, UN Doc. A/A.138/SC.II/SR.47, p. 95.
25 Official Records of the Third United Nations Conference on the Law of the Sea, Vol II, Second Committee, 31st Meeting (7 August 1974), para 49.
26 Ibid, para 76.
27 Ibid, para 66.
28 Ibid, para 53.
29 Ibid, paras 61–62.
30 Ibid, paras 70 and 76.
31 Ibid, para 69.
32 Ibid, paras 74 and 75.
33 Official Records of the Third United Nations Conference on the Law of the Sea, UN Doc A/CONF.62/C.2/WP.1, Draft Provisions, Part VII (15 October 1974), Provision 149.
34 Official Records of the Third United Nations Conference on the Law of the Sea, UN Doc A/CONF.62/C.2/Blue Paper No. 9 (16 April 1975), Provision 149.
35 The freedoms to lay submarine cables and pipelines, to construct artificial islands and other installations permitted under international law, to fish and to conduct scientific research are all made subject to other parts of the LOSC in Article 87(1)(c), (d), (e) and (f).
36 O'Connell, above note 1, pp. 750–751; Verzijl,, above note 1, p. 40.
37 Verzijl, above note 1, p. 40, n.36 comments: "It would be possible, in theory, to regulate jurisdiction over sea-going vessels in a different way, *inter alia*, by organizing a system of control by the international community, or by way of mutual acquiescence in concurrent jurisdiction. The first solution, however, is unrealistic and would be too cumbersome; the second would be unacceptable to sovereign states, save as far as the suppression of extremely grave crime is concerned, in which latter case the system has worked (piracy, slave-trade)."
38 Official Records of the General Assembly, above note 12, Article 30 commentary, para 1.
39 Ibid, para 5.
40 Yearbook of the International Law Commission, Vol II (1955) UN Doc A/2934, Chapter II, Article 5.
41 Ibid, Article 5 comment.
42 Nottebohm (Second Phase) Case (Lithuania v. Guatemala) [1955] ICJ Rep 4.
43 Official Records of the General Assembly, above note 12, Article 29.
44 Ibid, Article 29 commentary, para 3.
45 Official Records of the Third United Nations Conference on the Law of the Sea, UN Doc A/CONF.62/C.2/L54 (12 August 1974) Article 6 bis (2)(g).
46 Ibid, Article 6 bis (2)(e).
47 DOALOS, Navigation on the High Seas, supra note 1, p. 53.

48 H. Scheiber 'Economic Uses of the Oceans and the Impacts on Marine Environments: Past Trends and Challenges Ahead' in D. Vidas and P.J. Schei (eds) The World Ocean in Globalisation (Martinus Nijhoff Publishers, Leiden, 2011), pp. 65–66; E. Molenaar, Coastal State Jurisdiction over Vessel Source Pollution (Kluwer Law International, the Hague, 1998), pp. 25–26.
49 Ibid; P. McGrath and M. Julian, 'Protection of the Marine Environment from Shipping Operations: Australian and International Responses' in D. Rothwell and S. Bateman (eds), *Navigational Rights and Freedoms and the New Law of the Sea* (Martinus Nijhoff, The Hague, 2000), pp. 192–193.
50 Molenaar, above note 48, pp. 30–31.
51 McGrath and Julian, above note 49, pp. 192–193.
52 McGrath and Julian, above note 49, p. 194.
53 Proposal by Malta at the 1971 Session of the Sea-Bed Committee, UN Doc. A/AC.138/53, Article 138, para 2(a).
54 Proposal by the US at the 1971 Session of the Sea-Bed Committee, UN Doc. A/AC.138/SC.II/L.4 and Corr.1, Article III, para 2, sub-paras A and B; Proposal by the US at the 1972 Session of the Sea-Bed Committee, UN Doc. A/AC.138/SC.II/L.9, Article IV.
55 Official Records of the Third United Nations Conference on the Law of the Sea, Main Trends Working Paper (15 October 1974), UN Doc. A/CONF.62/WP.1, Provision 156, Formula C, para 2(a).
56 Ibid, para 2(b).
57 Ibid, para 2(a).
58 Ibid, para 2(b).
59 1995 Agreement for the Implementation of the Provisions of the United Nations Convention on the Law of the Sea of 10 December 1982 relating to the Conservation and Management of Straddling Fish Stocks and Highly Migratory Fish Stocks, 2167 UNTS 3 (UN Fish Stocks Agreement).
60 LOSC, Article 110(1).
61 Vienna Convention, Article 17.
62 UN Fish Stocks Agreement, Article 21.
63 See Chapter 16 in this volume.
64 LOSC, Articles 89, 87.
65 Ibid, Article 87(2).
66 1995 Agreement for the Implementation of the Provisions of the United Nations Convention on the Law of the Sea of 10 December 1982 relating to the Conservation and Management of Straddling Fish Stocks and Highly Migratory Fish Stocks, Article 6.
67 LOSC, Article 94(4)(c).
68 Annex I entered into force 2 October 1983, Annex II entered into force 6 April 1987, Annex III entered into force 1 July 1992, Annex IV entered into force 27 September 2003, Annex V entered into force 31 December 1988, Annex VI entered into force 19 May 2005.
69 Scheiber, above n 48, 90.
70 See Chapter 23 in this volume.

3
The Use of Force

Cameron Moore

Introduction

At the heart of the issue of the use of force by warships and government law enforcement vessels engaged in maritime regulation and enforcement is the risk to life, limb and property. In any area of the law the use of force is usually subject to a great deal of regulation and discussion. It might be surprising then that the *Law of the Sea Convention* (LOSC) itself does not deal with the use of force much at all. There are some references to fisheries and environmental investigations[1] but there is no reference to powers in areas such as customs and immigration. In this sense the LOSC is an orthodox instrument of international law that governs relations between States and, through the concept of the flag state, their vessels. International human rights law provides some guidance on the relationship between states and private individuals subject to their jurisdiction, but does not specifically address the use of force at sea. The use of force at sea is therefore primarily a matter of customary international law[2] as well some limited conventional international law on specific matters, such as fisheries, or of a regional or bilateral character. Other than this the conduct of boarding officers is very much the domain of domestic law, whether it be the law of the nationality of the boarding officer or the law of the flag state of the vessel subject to the boarding. This chapter will therefore look at international judicial decisions and such conventional international law as there is, as well as some domestic law to give an indication of state practice.

This chapter will not address the law of naval warfare as, by its nature, it is a matter of warfare and not maritime regulation and enforcement. It is therefore outside of the scope of this book.[3] This chapter will also not address hot pursuit as it is the subject of other chapters. While hot pursuit can be a preliminary action to the use of force, it does not of itself necessarily involve the threat or use of force. Questions of enforcement jurisdiction are for other chapters in this book so it is important to note that the focus of this chapter is not so much on the jurisdictional basis to use force, except in so far it affects the level of force that may be permissible in a particular circumstance.

This chapter will consider the use of force across a number of specific sectors mainly because this is how the law is to be found. This will allow for some comparison of use of force provisions intended for different law enforcement purposes. These sectors will include enforcement of United Nations Security Council Resolutions, narcotics, weapons of mass destruction, violence at sea, people smuggling and fisheries. This chapter will also address the extreme case of possible destruction of a civilian vessel at sea or civilian aircraft in the air in a situation of national self-defence or necessity. This is at the margins of what might be considered maritime regulation and enforcement, but it could also be below the threshold of armed conflict and therefore not regulated by the law of naval warfare.

It is important to keep in mind the various purposes of the use of force at sea in maritime regulation and enforcement. It might be for the purpose of compelling a vessel to go to a particular place without boarding, such as into port for a fisheries investigation, or simply away from the coastal state to prevent people smuggling. Alternatively, the use of force might be to board a vessel to divert, investigate or apprehend it. The use of force might also be to destroy a civilian vessel at sea or civilian aircraft in the air in a situation of national self-defence or necessity. Upon boarding, the use of force might occur in defence of the boarding officers themselves or those that they find on board. The use of force might also occur in the conduct of the investigation of an offence or, on the other hand, to restrain potential illegal immigrants while moving them away from the coastal state.[4]

It is not possible within the scope of this chapter to address the detail of matters such as arrest, detention, search and so on. Its aim instead is to discern the extent to which, in the absence of specific provision in the LOSC, there are still international law principles which can guide the use of force in maritime regulation and enforcement generally. This chapter argues that there is enough law and state practice to establish that there are such principles.[5] These principles are the use of minimum force and minimum interference, while maintaining the ability to enforce the law and the right of self-defence. Specifically, there must be efforts to ensure that life is not endangered, including a particular restraint on the use of force against civilian aircraft. There might be variations in emphasis between areas of regulation, such as between narcotics, fisheries and people smuggling probably due to the perceived risk of death or injury: however the principles remain essentially the same. The circumstances of destruction of vessels and aircraft in national self-defence stand as an exception to these principles, although destruction of vessels in cases of environmental necessity does not.

The *Saiga* principles

The more common use of force at sea is in the context of national regulation and enforcement. As the LOSC is silent on the question of firing at or into a vessel and is very limited in respect of the use of force at all,[6] there are two significant cases referred to most by writers in this field, the *I'm Alone* and the *Red Crusader*.[7] There are other cases worth noting but it is these two that the International Tribunal on the Law of the Sea considered in the *Saiga Case*[8] in 1999, the most authoritative consideration of the question. Papastavridis describes this case as the *locus classicus* of the law on the use of force in interception operations[9] and Guilfoyle sees it as restating 'the general international law on the use of force to effect interdictions'.[10]

The *I'm Alone*[11] case involved the pursuit of a Canadian registered schooner by two US Coastguard vessels in 1929. After a long chase the US ships fired into *I'm Alone* and sank her with loss of life. The case raised a number of questions including the right of hot pursuit. On the use of force however, a Joint Canadian and American Commission found that the use of force had been excessive. It was acceptable to fire into a vessel to compel it to stop. If it sank as an incidental result then this was also acceptable. It was not acceptable however to fire into the vessel for the purpose of sinking it:

> ...the intentional sinking of the vessel...could not be justified by any principle of international law.[12]

The *Red Crusader Case* saw the pursuit of a British trawler by a Danish fisheries vessel, the *Neils Ebbesen*, in 1961.[13] The *Red Crusader* had two members of the Danish vessel's crew onboard when she fled. The Danish vessel directed machine gun and 40 millimetre calibre gun fire into the mast, radar scanner and lights, then the stem, of the *Red Crusader* after the initial use of warning shots from the ship's 127 millimetre calibre gun. An Anglo-Danish Commission of Enquiry found that the Danish vessel:

> Exceeded legitimate use of armed force on two counts:
>
> (a) firing without warning of solid [as opposed to explosive] gunshot;
> (b) creating danger to human life on board the Red Crusader without proved necessity, by the effective firing at the Red Crusader...
>
> The Commission is of the opinion that other means should have been attempted, which if duly persisted in, might have finally persuaded Skipper Wood to stop and revert to the normal procedure.[14]

The International Tribunal on the Law of the Sea came to consider these matters in the case of the MV *Saiga*.[15] In that case, a Guinean patrol boat opened fire on a St Vincent and the Grenadines registered tanker upon suspicion that it was bunkering fishing vessels contrary to Guinean customs law. The tribunal found that the Guinean patrol boat fired without warning. The tribunal considered a number of questions but particularly considered the use of force to apprehend vessels at sea. It considered the *I'm Alone* and *Red Crusader* cases as well as the use of force provision in art 22(1)(f) of the *United Nations Fish Stocks Agreement*,[16] discussed below. The essence of the Tribunal's decision on this point is that,

> It is only after appropriate actions fail that the pursuing vessel may, as a last resort, use force. Even then, the appropriate warning must be issued to the ship and all efforts should be made to ensure that life is not endangered.[17]

The LOSC also specifies that states shall not impose custodial penalties for fishing offences so it is unlikely that use of potentially lethal force, merely in order to stop a vessel to board it, would be consistent with international law.[18]

From these considerations it would appear that the international law principles regarding firing into vessels require:

- That such action must be a last resort. It must be absolutely necessary evidenced by patiently exhausting all less forceful means available, including warning shots, unless an urgent threat to life demands otherwise.
- That it must follow an explicit warning that shots are to be fired into the vessel.
- That all efforts are made to ensure that life is not endangered. Any appreciable risk to life would render the use of direct fire unlawful. A death would not necessarily render the

action unlawful in itself provided that the risk of death from direct fire was extremely unlikely and mitigated against.[19]

As to the use of force in enforcement at sea generally, the Tribunal also usefully stated:

> Although the Convention does not contain express provisions on the use of force in the arrest of ships, international law, which is applicable by virtue of article 293 of the Convention, requires that the use of force must be avoided as far as possible and, where force is unavoidable, it must not go beyond what is reasonable and necessary in the circumstances.[20]

The Tribunal, citing its *Saiga* decision, restated these principles in 2014 in the *MV Virginia G Case*[21] concerning the apprehension of a Panamanian flagged bunkering vessel in the exclusive economic zone (EEZ) of Guinea-Bissau.[22] In applying the *Saiga* principles it found that 'the use of force [by Guinea-Bissau] did not go beyond what was reasonable and necessary in the circumstances.'[23]

Consistent with this, the ad hoc tribunal in the *Guyana/ Suriname* arbitration of 2007 stated:

> ... in international law force may be used in law enforcement activities provided that such force is unavoidable, reasonable and necessary.[24]

(It is worth noting that in this case, the tribunal considered that the threat of the use of force by Surinamese warships against platforms in a disputed maritime area was not law enforcement but a threat of military action.[25] For this reason this chapter will not address this case further.)

International law enforcement instruments

It comes then to consider the extent to which the *Saiga* principles reflect state practice in the use of force in maritime regulation and enforcement. A survey of a variety of instruments collected in Lowe and Talmon's *The Legal Order of the Oceans*[26] provides a representative, even if not exhaustive, view of international law instruments which either reflect these principles or provide a little more guidance on the use of force at sea. While some of these are instruments of a regional rather than global character, it is still possible then to consider to what extent the principles which may be drawn from the *Saiga Case* represent customary international law.

Narcotics

The *United Nations Convention Against Illicit Traffic in Narcotic Drugs and Psychotropic Substances*[27] contemplates boarding of vessels with the consent of the flag state under art 17. It also states that actions taken under that article:

> shall take due account of the need not to endanger the safety of life at sea, the security of the vessel and the cargo or to prejudice the commercial and legal interests of the flag state or any other interested state.

This goes to considerations of reasonableness and necessity which involve broader considerations than the risk to life. Its statement of the 'need not to endanger ... life' is very close to the words of the *Saiga Case*, even though the *Saiga Case* of 1999 did not refer to this *Convention* of 1988.

The 1995 *Implementing Agreement*[28] to this *Convention*, at art 12 and titled 'Operational Safeguards', restates the form of words regarding use of force under the *Convention* itself but goes on to elaborate that parties shall take into account that there are dangers in boarding at sea and that boarding could be more safely done at a vessel's next port of call. It also draws attention to minimising interference with legitimate commercial activities and unduly detaining or delaying a vessel. More importantly it states 'the need to restrict the use of force to the minimum necessary' but with the additional words 'to ensure compliance with the instructions of the intervening State'. These latter words emphasise the law enforcement character of the use of minimum force provision, which is absent from the *Saiga* principles but still consistent with them. The overall effect is still firmly a minimum force and minimum interference, but nevertheless a law enforcement, approach.

Moving to a regional perspective, an agreement of 2002 between the United States and Panama[29] on counter-narcotics enforcement uses the same formulation of words at art XV of the *United Nations Convention Against Illicit Traffic in Narcotic Drugs and Psychotropic Substances*, titled the 'Conduct of Law Enforcement'. It adds requirements to 'observe the norms of courtesy, respect and consideration for persons on board the suspect vessel' and 'not endanger the lives of persons on board and the safety of civil aircraft'. Article XVIII directly addresses the use of force. While explicitly preserving the 'inherent right of self-defense', it states that the use of force otherwise

> shall be in strict accordance with applicable laws and policies of that Party and shall in all cases be the minimum necessary in the circumstances, except that neither Party shall use force against civil aircraft in flight.

It is consistent with the *Saiga* principles while building upon them to emphasise a minimum force law enforcement model, which also excludes the use of force against civil aircraft.

It is interesting to compare the 2002 US/ Panama Agreement to the 2003 *Agreement Concerning Co-operation in Suppressing Illicit Maritime and Air Trafficking in Narcotic Drugs and Psychotropic Substances in the Caribbean Area*.[30] These agreements are closely related in terms of subject matter, time and area of geographical concern. This *Agreement* therefore unsurprisingly also uses the same form of words with respect to the use of force as used in the US/ Panama Agreement and art XV of the *United Nations Convention Against Illicit Traffic in Narcotic Drugs and Psychotropic Substances*. It adds the provisions found in the 1995 *Implementing Agreement* concerning the safety of boarding in port instead of at sea and unduly detaining or delaying a vessel. It does not at this point restate the provisions concerning legitimate commercial activity or minimum force. It does instead, at art 22, provide a much more detailed minimum force provision as follows:

1. Force may only be used if no other feasible means of resolving the situation can be applied.
2. Any force used shall be proportional to the objective for which it is employed.
3. All use of force pursuant to this Agreement shall in all cases be the minimum reasonably necessary under the circumstances.
4. A warning shall be issued prior to any use of force except when force is being used in self-defence.
5. In the event that the use of force is authorised and necessary in the waters of a Party, law enforcement officials shall respect the laws of that Party.

6. In the event that the use of force is authorised and necessary during a boarding and search seaward of the territorial sea of any Party, the law enforcement officials shall comply with their domestic laws and procedures and the directions of the flag State.
7. The discharge of firearms against or on a suspect vessel shall be reported as soon as practicable to the flag State Party.
8. Parties shall not use force against civil aircraft in flight.
9. The use of force in reprisal or as punishment is prohibited.
10. Nothing in this Agreement shall impair the exercise of the inherent right of self-defence by law enforcement or other officials of any Party.

Despite the extra detail, these provisions are still essentially consistent with those outlined in the other narcotics instruments discussed above. They reinforce an approach of minimum force and minimum interference and a general restraint on the use of force against civil aircraft, whilst still pursuing a law enforcement objective and maintaining rights of self-defence. This approach by the US and Caribbean flag states provides a good indication of state practice on the use of force in intercepting vessels. Guilfoyle addresses each of these rules separately in order to ascertain the extent to which they reflect customary international law. Without repeating that analysis, he usefully considers rules 1 to 5 and 8 together, concluding that together they are a restatement of the customary international law put forward in the *Saiga Case*.[31]

Weapons of mass destruction

A further US agreement worth mentioning in this survey is the 2004 *Agreement Between the Government of the United States of America and the Government of the Republic of Liberia Concerning Cooperation To Suppress the Proliferation of Weapons of Mass Destruction, Their Delivery Systems, and Related Materials By Sea*.[32] Without using exactly the same form of words as already discussed, art 8 of this Agreement, titled 'Safeguards', addresses similar concerns as follows:

1. Where a Party takes measures against a vessel in accordance with this Agreement, it shall:
   a. take due account of the need not to endanger the safety of life at sea;
   b. take due account of the security of the vessel and its cargo;
   c. not prejudice the commercial or legal interests of the Flag State;
   d. ensure within available means, that any measure taken with regard to the vessel is environmentally sound under the circumstances;
   e. ensure that persons on board are afforded the protections, rights and guarantees provided by international law and the boarding State's law and regulations;
   f. ensure the master of the vessel is, or has been, afforded the opportunity to contact the vessels' owner, manager or Flag State at the earliest opportunity.
2. Reasonable efforts shall be taken to avoid a vessel being unduly detained or delayed.

A key development here is the addition of the regard for the environment, which echoes art 225 of the LOSC as discussed below. This agreement is also significant because the US entered into similar agreements with a large number of flag states during the first decade of this century, covering 60% of the world's shipping by tonnage.[33] It therefore represents a significant example of state practice with respect to the use of force in maritime regulation and enforcement. Even if it uses different wording to that appearing in the instruments dealing with narcotics, it relies upon the same principles of minimum force and minimum interference.

The Use of Force

Violence against ships and platforms

The Protocol of 2005 to the Convention for the Suppression of Unlawful Acts Against the Safety of Maritime Navigation, also known as the 2005 *SUA Protocol*,[34] at art 8 *bis* (10), uses very similar wording to that in the agreements relating to weapons of mass destruction. The *Protocol* concerns boarding operations to counter violence against shipping and platforms. Despite the different subject matter, the approach to the use of force is essentially the same. This lends weight to principles of minimum force and minimum interference underlying this form of words, even if not the words themselves, being principles of general application to the use of force at sea in maritime regulation and enforcement.

People smuggling

Continuing the point about instruments on different subject matter relying upon similar provisions, the *Protocol Against the Smuggling of Migrants by Land, Sea and Air Supplementing the United Nations Convention on Transnational Organised Crime*, adopted by the General Assembly of the United Nations in 2000,[35] is relevant. It uses essentially the same form of words as used in the instruments on weapons of mass destruction and violence against shipping and platforms, with the notable additional requirement to ensure the safety and humane treatment of the person on board. This requirement precedes the other requirements. Papastavridis is of the view that there is less scope for the use of force in regulating people smuggling given the threat to the human cargo.[36] This would indicate a different emphasis within the principles of minimum force and minimum interference, which would suggest that the acceptable levels of force should be lower because of the context but not because there is a fundamentally different principle.

Fisheries

The use of force in the regulation of fisheries has a markedly understated approach, although still broadly consistent with the minimum force and minimum interference approach discussed above. The *United Nations Fish Stocks Agreement* art 22(1)(f), to which the International Tribunal for the Law of the Sea referred in the *Saiga Case*, states that an inspecting state shall ensure that its inspectors:

> avoid the use of force except when and to the degree necessary to ensure the safety of the inspectors and where the inspectors are obstructed in the execution of their duties. The degree of force used shall not exceed that reasonably required in the circumstances.

This maintains a law enforcement approach but is much less detailed than the provisions discussed above.

Guilfoyle suggests that fisheries law is more restrained in respect of the use of force because of a common perception it is not as serious as drug smuggling and fishermen are not dangerous criminals. He then cites the Australian experience of violence on fishing vessels towards boarding parties to suggest that this perception is misplaced.[37] Even so, the *Pacific Fisheries Treaty*[38] is a fisheries instrument which seeks to avoid the use of force at all and perhaps exemplifies this perception, the last few lines of Part 5 of art 1 of which state,

> Such boarding and inspection shall be conducted as much as possible in a manner so as not to interfere unduly with the lawful operation of the vessel. The operator and each member

of the crew shall facilitate and assist in any action by an authorised officer of a Pacific Island party and shall not assault, obstruct, resist, delay, refuse boarding to, intimidate or interfere with an authorised officer in the performance of his or her duties.

The provision is cast in terms of duties rather than rights. In terms of ascertaining the extent to which there are general principles for the use of force in maritime regulation and enforcement, this example indicates that there are approaches to enforcement which eschew force almost completely. This does not deny that there can be general principles when there is provision for the use of force. It does demonstrate that provision for the use of force in an enforcement instrument is not always considered appropriate. This would lend weight to the principle that any use of force in maritime regulation and enforcement, where it is accepted as appropriate, should be the minimum necessary. It also suggests that what minimum force means can vary depending on the sector being regulated.

The LOSC and the use of force

As to the LOSC itself, art 225 provides a general guideline as to the extent of force to be used in enforcement against foreign vessels:

> In the exercise under this Convention of their powers of enforcement against foreign vessels, States, shall not endanger the safety of navigation or otherwise create any hazard to a vessel, or bring it to an unsafe port or anchorage, or expose the marine environment to an unreasonable risk.

Whilst the language in art 225 is prohibitive, it implies measures including force by expressly limiting the potential damage enforcement could cause. Article 225 is to be found in Part XII of the LOSC which deals with 'Protection and Preservation of the Marine Environment'. Whilst it refers to the exercise of powers 'under this Convention' it is curious that this provision does not appear together with the articles concerning the rights of coastal states or the articles concerned with the high seas. This suggests that art 225 is primarily concerned with the preservation of the marine environment and much less with the use of force against vessels.[39] It is nonetheless consistent with a minimum force and minimum interference approach.

Human rights law at sea

Moving to more general international law, human rights law has little to say directly about maritime regulation and enforcement. It is relevant however because it provides some guidance on the general relationship between those who exercise authority and those who are subject to it. As national approaches to this question vary considerably, for example China is not a party to the *International Covenant on Civil and Political Rights* (ICCPR),[40] human rights provisions are useful mainly as sources of principle to guide interpretation more than being rules of law applicable *de jure*. Further, it is a question as to whether, for the purpose of the application of human rights law, a person on a vessel subject to a boarding is 'subject to jurisdiction' of the flag state conducting the boarding.[41] However, as the International Tribunal for the Law of the Sea stated in the *Saiga Case*,[42] 'Considerations of humanity must apply in the law of the sea, as they do in other areas of international law'.[43]

The ICCPR could be considered to embody customary international law.[44] It states that 'rights derive from the inherent dignity of the human person' and is probably the starting point for legal interpretation of phrases such as 'human dignity'.[45] In particular, the rights that the ICCPR recognises which may be relevant to maritime regulation and enforcement would also often be subject to domestic legal sanction in any event such as the right to life in art 6, the right not to be subject to arbitrary arrest and detention as well as the right to *habeas corpus* (to seek release from unlawful detention) in art 9. Further, art 7 concerns the right not to be subject to cruel, inhuman or degrading punishment, and art 10 concerns the dignity of those deprived of their liberty. This *Convention* therefore embodies principles which inform and underpin the principles of minimum force and minimum interference applicable to the use of force at sea in maritime regulation and enforcement.

Destruction

Turning from the routine to the exceptional, the destruction of vessels at sea and aircraft in the air over the sea is at the highest end of the spectrum of the use of force at sea. There are situations where this can occur outside of armed conflict and this chapter will discuss them as a means of bounding its consideration of the issue.

The destruction of aircraft in flight is the most dramatic example of the use of force at sea and has been controversial. Article 2 of LOSC makes clear that airspace over the territorial sea is part of the coastal state's sovereignty and therefore is national, rather than international, airspace. Unlike ships, aircraft have no right of innocent passage in another state's airspace over the territorial seas.[46] The International Civil Aviation Organisation moved to limit the possibility of the use of force against civilian airliners after an incident involving the shooting down of a Korean civilian airliner by the Soviet Union, after it apparently strayed into national airspace in 1983.[47] The *Chicago Convention*[48] regulates overflight by civilian aircraft and its 1984 Protocol[49] set requirements for intercepts in art 3 bis (a) as follows:

> ... every State must refrain from resorting to the use of weapons against civil aircraft in flight and that, in case of interception, the lives of persons on board and the safety of the aircraft must not be endangered. This provision shall not be interpreted as modifying in any way the rights and obligations of States set forth in the Charter of the United Nations.

The International Civil Aviation Organisation's 'Rules of the Air' set out detailed rules for the conduct of intercepts.[50]

Since then, civilian aircraft have become seen as a legitimate threat in themselves after their use as weapons to attack the World Trade Center, New York City and the Pentagon building, Washington DC, in the US on September 11th 2001. This draws attention to the last sentence of art 3 bis (a), which indicates that it does not affect the right of self-defence by states under art 51 of the *United Nations Charter*. The non-state and isolated character of the September 11th 2001 attacks did not amount to a situation of armed conflict. However it was considered to be an armed attack within the meaning of art 51, which gave rise to a right of national self-defence.[51] It is on the basis of self-defence then that a state might use force against an aircraft in flight.

The precise circumstances of when this might be lawful are difficult to ascertain, as reflected in the decision of the German Constitutional Court to find German legislation which authorised the use of force against aircraft unconstitutional. This was partly on the basis that it was contrary to the fundamental right to life.[52] On the other hand, Australian legislation provides for the use of force against civilian aircraft without being too prescriptive about what factual circumstances might justify this. The legislation is directed towards high level security threats, rather than just law enforcement, which would suggest that it would most likely only be relied upon in situations of national self-defence.[53] Given that the use of force against civilian aircraft has a high likelihood of having lethal consequences, it should only be available in exceptional circumstances of national self-defence.

There is less law or precedent with respect to destruction of vessels at sea in situations of national self-defence. The same Australian legislation provides for this to occur in essentially the same circumstances as for aircraft.[54] The main difference is that practically speaking there can be alternatives to destruction in the case of vessels as they are normally slower and operate on the surface. It still may be however that the threat which the vessel poses is such that boarding, for example, is not a realistic option. A threatening vessel might be well defended, present a dangerous chemical, biological, radiological or nuclear risk or simply be too fast or manoeuverable to board. In situations amounting to national self-defence, destruction of such vessels could be within the right of states under art 51 of the *United Nations Charter*.[55]

It is not only national self-defence that might justify the destruction of a vessel at sea. Circumstances of necessity might also justify such action. It is much less likely to authorise the use of lethal force however. For this reason it is unlikely to justify the destruction of aircraft. In 1967 the United Kingdom's Royal Air Force had to bomb the abandoned and stricken tanker MV *Torrey Canyon* to prevent the wreck foundering upon the British coast and also to break up the oil slick.[56] This incident led to the *Intervention Convention*,[57] art I of which provides that parties 'may take such measures on the high seas as may be necessary to prevent, mitigate or eliminate grave and imminent danger to their coastline ... from ... pollution of the sea by oil'. The 1973 *Protocol*[58] to the *Convention* extends this to protection from substances other than oil, which it defines very broadly.[59] Article V of the *Convention* states that measures, which would presumably include the use of force, must be proportionate to the damage 'actual or threatened' and 'shall not go beyond what is reasonably necessary'. In assessing proportionality, this article requires account to be taken of the damage which would occur if the measures were not taken, whether the measures would be effective and the damage which the measures themselves might cause. The *Convention* and *Protocol* together therefore provide potentially far reaching authority for the use of force where necessity justifies it in circumstances of environmental peril. For non-parties, or in analogous circumstances not contemplated in the *Convention*, this would indicate that necessity alone might still justify destruction of vessels under customary international law.

Destruction of vessels and aircraft at sea would be quite exceptional events, so it is not straightforward to apply general principles to them which might apply to other uses of force in maritime regulation and enforcement. They might apply more readily to situations of necessity however than of national self-defence.

United Nations Security Council Resolutions

It is also worth considering the use of force at sea to enforce international law itself. There is some limited precedent for United Nations Security Council Resolutions (UNSCR) to authorise the use of force at sea.[60]

This first occurred in 1966 in respect of Rhodesia's unilateral declaration of independence from the United Kingdom. UNSCR 221[61] called upon the United Kingdom 'to prevent, by *use of force if necessary*' the arrival of oil at the port of Beira in then Portuguese Mozambique, which would then be transported overland to Rhodesia. In 1990, in respect of Iraq's invasion of Kuwait, UNSCR 665[62] authorised member states 'to use such *measures commensurate to the specific circumstances as may be necessary* under the authority of the Security Council to halt all inward and outward maritime shipping' in order to enforce sanctions laid down in UNSCR 661.[63] In 1992, in respect of the break up of Yugoslavia, UNSCR 787[64] authorised member states to 'use such *measures commensurate with the specific circumstances as may be necessary* to halt all inward and outward maritime shipping...' (including on the Danube River) to enforce this and earlier resolutions. UNSCR 820[65] in 1993 subsequently sought 'to prohibit all commercial maritime traffic from entering the territorial sea of the Federal Republic of Yugoslavia (Serbia and Montenegro) except where authorised ... or in case of force majeure'.

Later operations moved to a more direct form of words. In 1994 UNSCR 917[66] in respect of Haiti authorised member states to use 'all necessary means' to enforce the embargo on that country. Subsequently, in 2008, UNSCR 1816[67] used the same language. It authorised 'States cooperating with the TFG in the fight against piracy and armed robbery at sea off the coast of Somalia', to:

(a) Enter the territorial waters of Somalia for the purpose of repressing acts of piracy and armed robbery at sea, in a manner consistent with such action permitted on the high seas with respect to piracy under relevant international law; and
(b) Use, within the territorial waters of Somalia, in a manner consistent with action permitted on the high seas with respect to piracy under relevant international law, *all necessary means* to repress acts of piracy and armed robbery;

In 2011, UNSCR 1973[68] in respect of the embargo on Libya also used the 'all necessary means' formulation. The words 'all necessary means' escalated the language from the UNSCR discussed in the previous paragraph to be consistent with that used in forceful land operations, such as that authorised in Somalia in 1992 by UNSCR 775[69] and East Timor in 1999 by UNSCR 1264.[70]

The broad language of these authorisations indicate that they operate at the strategic level and provide scant operational or tactical level direction. It is useful to be aware of the terminology favoured by the Security Council when authorising force in case of future similarly worded UNSCR, but otherwise the UNSCR cited really turn on their own circumstances.

Conclusion

As stated above, the use of force by boarding officers is not a subject which the LOSC addresses. This makes the issue one primarily for customary international law, some international enforcement instruments which address particular regulatory sectors, the domestic law of the flag states of warships and government law enforcement vessels conducting interceptions, as well as the flag states of the vessels subject to them. On the face of it, this creates a bewildering array of potentially overlapping jurisdictions and different national and international approaches to the use of force in law enforcement. Situations of national self-defence or enforcement of United Nations Security Council Resolutions at sea do not really assist in ascertaining these principles. Even so, it is possible to derive principles from the *Saiga Case* international human rights law, and the representative selection of relevant international instruments discussed above.

The *Saiga* principles essentially provide that the general principles applicable to the use of force in national regulation and enforcement are the use of minimum force and minimum interference whilst still permitting law enforcement action. These principles do not detract from the inherent right to self-defence, but extend to a firm rule prohibiting the use of force against civil aircraft for law enforcement purposes. A number of international instruments dealing with specific regulatory sectors bear this out. The use of common wording on the use of force indicates a broad acceptance of the principles, whether in the form common to a number of narcotics instruments, or in the different form of words common to quite different instruments dealing with weapons of mass destruction, violence at sea or people smuggling. The less detailed and restrained approach in some fisheries enforcement instruments still rests upon principles of minimum force and minimum interference, but indicates that the regulatory context can alter perceptions of what minimum force might mean. Arguably then, the *opinio juris* and state practice are therefore sufficient to establish the *Saiga* principles as customary international law.

As to whether this is an area that requires reconsideration in the form of new treaties or amendment to the LOSC, this is probably unnecessary. The *Saiga* principles are reasonably clear and not apparently subject to serious dissent. Their manifestation in more precise or detailed but quite varied form in a range of enforcement instruments indicates a wide degree of support for them. The best way to develop these principles would be for future sectoral instruments to try to adopt similar wording to that already adopted, although with the liberty to make relevant adaptations as required. This would reinforce the general principles whilst permitting flexibility to address the particular concerns at hand.

Notes

1 For example, LOSC arts 73 and 226.
2 D. Rothwell and T. Stephens appear to share this view in *The International Law of the Sea*, Oxford: Hart, 2010, p. 419; see also I. Shearer 'Problems of Jurisdiction and Law Enforcement Against Delinquent Vessels', *International and Comparative Law Quarterly*, 1986, vol. 35, p. 341; M. Tsamenyi and K. Mfodwo 'Enforcing Fisheries Jurisdiction in the EEZ: Some Legal and Policy Considerations' in D. Mackinnon and R. Sherwood (eds) *Policing Australia's Offshore Zones: Problems and Prospects*, Centre for Maritime Policy, University of Wollongong 1997, pp. 257, 259–260 and 262–264.
3 For this reason this chapter will not address the Israeli enforcement of a blockade of Gaza. Whether the law of naval warfare authorised the boarding of the *Mavi Marmara* in 2010 or not, the incident is inseparably connected with the hostilities between Israel and Gaza. It is not possible within the confines of this chapter adequately to analyse the complex legal questions involved. See the discussion in J. Kraska and R. Pedrozo, *International Maritime Security Law*, Martinus Nijhoff, Leiden, 2013, pp. 895–901.
4 These examples are discussed below.
5 A position for which Papastavridis and Guilfoyle also argue. E. Papastavridis, *The Interception of Vessels on the High Seas: Contemporary Challenges to the Legal Order of the Oceans*, Oxford: Hart, 2013, pp. 81–82. D. Guilfoyle, *Shipping Interdiction and the Law of the Sea*, Cambridge: Cambridge University Press, 2009, p. 266.
6 See discussion in Shearer, op. cit. pp. 349–352.
7 Primary references cited with discussion of each case below. See D.P. O'Connell, *The Influence of Law on Sea Power*, Manchester: Manchester University Press, 1975 pp. 65–69; Guilfoyle, op. cit., 271 and 277; Rothwell and Stephens, op. cit. 420–422.
8 The *'M/V Saiga' (No.2) Case* International Tribunal for the Law of the Sea, Year 1999, (Saint Vincent and the Grenadines v. Guinea).
9 Op. cit., 69.
10 Op. cit., 277.
11 '*Claim of the British Ship "I'm Alone" v United States*, Joint Interim and Final Reports of the Commissioners, 1933 and 1935', *American Journal of International Law*, 1935, vol. 29, p. 326.
12 At 330. See discussion in Kraska and Pedrozo, op. cit., 760–762.

13 35 *International Law Reports* 485 (1962) pp. 497–499, see discussion in Kraska and Pedrozo, op. cit., pp. 762–763.
14 ILR, ibid, p. 499.
15 Op. cit.; see discussion in Kraska and Pedrozo, op. cit., pp. 763–766.
16 *Agreement for the Implementation of the Provisions of the United Nations Convention on the Law of the Sea of 10 December 1982 Relating to the Conservation and Management of Straddling Fish Stocks and Highly Migratory Fish Stocks 1995*, done 4 December 1995, 2167 UNTS 88, entered into force 11 December 2001.
17 *Saiga* para 156.
18 LOSC art 73(3).
19 Kraska and Pedrozo, op. cit., p. 549, state that the *Saiga* principles are similar to those in the *Basic Principles on the Use of Force and Firearms by Law Enforcement Officials*, adopted by the Eighth United Nations Congress on the Prevention of Crime and the Treatment of Offenders, Havana, Cuba, 1990.
20 *Saiga* para 155.
21 The *'M/V Virginia G' Case* International Tribunal for the Law of the Sea, Year 2014, (Panama v Guinea-Bissau).
22 Ibid, para 48.
23 Ibid, para 361.
24 (2008) 47 *International Law Materials* 164 at para 445. Discussed in Papastavridis, op. cit., p. 70; Guilfoyle criticises the ambiguity of this distinction, op. cit., 275–276.
25 *ILM*, ibid.
26 A.V. Lowe and S.A.G. Talmon, *Basic Documents on the Law of the Sea: The Legal Order of the Oceans*, Oxford: Hart, 2009.
27 Done 20 December 1988, 1582 UNTS 165, entered into force 11 November 1990.
28 *Agreement on Illicit Traffic by Sea, Implementing Article 17 of the United Nations Convention Against Illicit Traffic in Narcotic Drugs and Psychotropic Substances*, done 31 January 1995, 2136 UNTS 81, entered into force 1 May 2000.
29 *Supplementary Arrangement between the Government of the United States of America and the Government of the Republic of Panama for Support and Assistance from the United States Coast Guard for the National Maritime Service of the Ministry of Government and Justice*, done 5 February 2002, entry into force 5 February 2002, cited in Lowe and Talmon, op. cit., p. 443.
30 Done 10 April 2003, not yet in force, cited in Lowe and Talmon, op. cit., p. 789.
31 Guilfoyle, op. cit., 282 and 278–294 more generally.
32 Done 11 February 2004, entered into force 8 December 2004, cited in Lowe and Talmon, op. cit., p. 805.
33 Kraska and Pedrozo, op. cit., p. 788. The 'safeguards' article is very similar across the various agreements. The flag states concerned are Antigua and Barbuda, Bahamas, Belize, Croatia, Cyprus, Liberia, Malta, Marshall Islands, Mongolia, Panama (building on the agreement discussed above) and St Vincent and the Grenadines. See http://www.state.gov/t/isn/c27733.htm for the text of the agreements.
34 Done 14 October 2005, 1678 UNTS 304, not yet in force. Discussed by Guilfoyle, op. cit., at p. 266.
35 UN Doc. A/RES/55/25 (2000) of 15 November 2000, entered into force 28 January 2004.
36 Papastavridis, op. cit., p. 301.
37 Guilfoyle, op. cit., pp. 290–291.
38 *Agreement among Pacific Island States Concerning the Implementation and Administration of the Treaty on Fisheries between the Governments of Certain Pacific Island States and the Government of the United States of America of 2 April 1987*, done at Port Moresby on 2 April 1987, *Australian Treaty Series* 1988 No.42, entered into force 15 June 1988.
39 See Rothwell and Stephens, op. cit., pp. 419–420.
40 *International Covenant on Civil and Political Rights* done 19 December 1966, 999 UNTS 171, entered into force 23 March 1976.
41 *[First] Optional Protocol to the International Covenant on Civil and Political Rights*, done 16 December 1966, 999 UNTS 171, entered into force 23 March 1976, art 1. See discussion in Papastavridis, op. cit., pp. 242–243, who is of the view that the 'preponderant view' is that such persons are under the jurisdiction of the flag state conducting the boarding. Whilst this author is inclined to agree with Papastavridis on this point, it is not necessary to argue a decided position in this chapter, nor is there is space to. Guilfoyle's view is consistent with that of Papastavridis, op. cit., p. 268.
42 Op. cit.

43 Para 155.
44 See Guilfoyle, op. cit. p. 268.
45 *ICCPR* Preamble.
46 A plain reading of art 17 shows that the LOSC is silent on whether aircraft have a right of innocent passage, from which it can be inferred not to exist. Article 19 states that launching, landing or taking aboard any aircraft is not innocent passage (but does not expressly prohibit overflight).
47 P. Grier, 'The Death of Korean Airlines Flight 007', *Air Force Magazine*, 2013, vol. 96(1), p. 62.
48 Properly titled the *Convention on International Civil Aviation* done 7 December 1944, 15 UNTS 295, entered into force 4 April 1947.
49 *Protocol relating to an Amendment to the Convention on International Civil Aviation* done 10 May 1984, *Select Documents on International Affairs* No.32 (1984) 2.
50 Being Annex 2 to the *Chicago Convention*, see specifically chapters 5, 6, 8 and 9.
51 See discussion of this issue in Daniel Bethlehem, 'Self-Defense Against Imminent or Armed Attack by Nonstate Actors', *American Journal of International Law*, 2012, vol. 106(4), p. 769.
52 Bundesverfassungsgericht (BVerfG – Federal Constitutional Court) 59 *Neue Juristische Wochenschrift* (NJW) 751 (2006) discussed in O. Lepsius, 'Human Dignity and the Downing of Aircraft: The German Federal Constitutional Court Strikes Down a Prominent Anti-terrorism Provision in the New Air-transport Security Act' *German Law Journal*, 2006, vol. 7(9), p. 761.
53 *Defence Act* (Cth) s 51SE, discussed in S. Bronitt and D. Stephens, '"Flying Under the Radar" – The Use of Lethal Force Against Hijacked Aircraft: Recent Australian Developments', *Oxford University Commonwealth Law Journal*, 2007, vol. 7, p. 265.
54 Ibid.
55 See discussion in Papastavridis, op. cit., 148–154.
56 Rothwell and Stephens, op. cit., 364.
57 Ibid; *International Convention Relating to Intervention on the High Seas in Cases of Oil Pollution Casualties*, done 29 November 1969, 1975 UNTS 212, entered into force 6 May 1975.
58 *Protocol Relating to Intervention on the High Seas in Cases of Pollution by Substances Other than Oil*, done 2 November 1973, 1313 UNTS 4, entry into force 30 March 1983.
59 Art I.
60 Kraska and Pedrozo discuss this issue at some length, op. cit., pp. 903–921. See also R. McLaughlin, 'United Nations Mandated Naval Interdiction Operations in the Territorial Sea?', *International and Comparative Law Quarterly*, 2002, vol. 51(2), p. 249.
61 UN SCOR, 1277th mtg UN Doc S/Res/221 (1966).
62 UN SCOR, 2938th mtg UN Doc S/Res/665 (1990).
63 UN SCOR, 2932nd mtg UN Doc S/Res/661 (1990).
64 UN SCOR, 3137th mtg UN Doc S/Res/787 (1992).
65 UN SCOR, 3200th mtg UN Doc S/Res/820 (1993).
66 UN SCOR, 4987th mtg UN Doc S/Res/917 (1994).
67 UN SCOR, 5902nd mtg UN Doc S/Res/1816 (2008).
68 UN SCOR, 6498th mtg UN Doc S/Res/1973 (2011).
69 UN SCOR, 3110th mtg UN Doc S/Res/775 (1992).
70 UN SCOR, 4045th mtg UN Doc S/Res/1264 (1999).

Part B
Role of States and Other International Actors in Maritime Regulation and Enforcement

4
The Role of Flag States

Sam Bateman

The role of flag States in exercising effective jurisdiction and control over administrative, technical and social matters on ships flying their flag lies at the heart of the international system of maritime regulation and enforcement. As other chapters in this book discuss, that system is now a multi-faceted and collaborative one involving flag, port and coastal States both individually and collectively. This chapter addresses specifically the role played by flag States in the system.

While ship owners have primary responsibility for the safe operation of their ships and the safety and welfare of their crews, the flag State plays a critical role by ensuring that the owners of ships flying its flag act in accordance with their international obligations. This chapter will seek to answer the following questions: What precisely are the responsibilities of flag States? How do flag States discharge their responsibilities? How effective is the system of flag State responsibility in providing for good order at sea? What is being done to overcome apparent shortcomings in the system? While the chapter mainly addresses issues of flag State responsibility in commercial shipping, some consideration is also given to related issues in the fishing industry where the flag States of fishing vessels have a major role in combating illegal, unreported and unregulated (IUU) fishing.

After first describing relevant aspects of international shipping, the main section of the chapter assesses how well flag States are discharging their responsibilities. Flag States have exclusive jurisdiction over ships flying their flag on the high seas, but some adopt a very lax attitude with respect to their international obligations under the 1982 United Nations Convention on the Law of the Sea (LOSC) and other relevant international maritime conventions. This is shown by the way in which some flags figure more prominently in accidents at sea; are more prone to pirate hijacking or being used for illegal activities at sea; and are regularly included on the 'black' and 'grey' lists of the more effective regional systems of Port State Control (PSC). Reference will be made to what the International Maritime Organization (IMO) is doing to make the system of flag State responsibility more effective through the introduction of flag State audits and the work of the Flag State Implementation (FSI) Sub-Committee. The latter committee has the mandate to deal with the implementation of IMO instruments by port, flag and coastal States and related matters.[1]

Sam Bateman

International shipping

International shipping is the classic globalised industry with ships often under the flag of one country, owned by a company in another country, which in turn might be a subsidiary of a company in yet another country, and crewed by seafarers of many different nationalities. Cargo owners might come from other countries, and the various insurance policies required by a ship might represent the interests of even more countries. It is a highly competitive industry with ship owners under continual pressure to reduce costs. Many opportunities exist for disreputable practices, including corruption, false certification, and the abuse of the seafarers that crew ships engaged in international trade.[2] An unscrupulous ship owner can follow a 'cheap skate' policy of attempting to get a quick profit by buying a ship cheaply, operating it cheaply, skimping on maintenance and safety measures, registering it in a country with a lax regulatory regime, and in a worst case scenario when repairs become too expensive, abandoning the ship and its crew in some obscure port from which the owners cannot be easily traced.[3]

Ownership of the world shipping fleet is highly concentrated. Table 4.1 shows that ship owners from just three countries – in order of decreasing tonnage, Greece, Japan and China – together account for 41 per cent of the world tonnage. Greece remains the world's largest ship owning nation. China is the fastest growing ship owning nation with 11.8 per cent of world tonnage in early 2013 up from 8.6 per cent just two years earlier.

In terms of vessel numbers, owners from Germany, Japan and China each have more ships than Greek owners, mainly because in the case of China and Japan, these countries have large

Table 4.1 Twelve major ship-owning countries as of 1 January 2013

Country	Number of Vessels			Deadweight Tonnage ('000 dwt)			Foreign & International Flag (dwt) as % of Total	Total (dwt) as % of world
	National Flag	Foreign Flag	Total	National Flag	Foreign Flag	Total		
Greece	825	2 870	3 695	69 645	175 206	244 851	71.56	15.17
Japan	738	3 253	3 991	17 216	206 599	223 815	92.31	13.87
China	2 665	2 648	5 313	66 936	123 143	190 079	64.79	11.78
Germany	396	3 437	3 833	16 642	109 137	125 779	86.77	7.79
Republic of Korea	764	812	1 576	16 625	58 471	75 096	77.86	4.65
Singapore	1 090	798	1 888	32 711	31 442	64 153	49.01	3.98
US	768	1 175	1 943	8 672	49 606	58 278	85.12	3.61
UK	415	822	1 237	10 448	39 857	50 305	79.23	3.12
Norway	414	1494	1 908	2 190	43 802	45 992	95.24	2.85
Taiwan	102	712	814	3 311	40 949	44 260	92.52	2.74
Denmark	45	946	991	69	40 646	40 715	99.83	2.52
Bermuda	4	206	210	210	32 686	32 896	99.36	2.04

Sources: UNCTAD Review of Maritime Transport 2013, Table 2.4
Note: Vessels of 1 000 GT and above, ranked by deadweight tonnage

domestic fleets, including some relatively small vessels. In terms of nationally flagged and nationally owned tonnage, the Greek fleet continues to be the world's largest, accounting for nearly 70 million dwt, closely followed by the Chinese owned and flagged fleet which accounts for about 67 million dwt. In terms of vessel numbers, China is by far the world's largest ship-owning country with 5,313 ocean-going merchant ships of which about half fly the national Chinese flag.

From a registration perspective, all of the top ten ship-owning countries, with the exception of Singapore and China to a small extent, use foreign flags for well over half of their tonnage. Using a flag of convenience (FOC) – or what the IMO calls an open registry (OR) to avoid giving offence to its larger member States[4] offers benefits by avoiding heavy tax liabilities and expensive labour standards in the ship owner's own country. The International Transport Workers' Federation (ITF) defines FOCs as 'Where beneficial ownership and control of a vessel is found to lie elsewhere than in the country of the flag the vessel is flying, the vessel is considered as sailing under a flag of convenience'.[5] The ITF currently lists 34 flags as FOCs.[6]

Major ship owning countries, such as Greece, Japan, the United States and China have a high percentage of their fleets registered with ORs. Some ORs have excellent safety records while some closed registers have poor ones.[7] Some countries, including Norway, operate international registries catering mostly for owners from their respective countries, albeit under conditions that are more favourable than those of the more classic national registries, which, for example, place stricter limitations on the employment of foreign seafarers. The flag State remains the responsible authority with both international and national registries.

Table 4.2 shows the largest flags of ship registration as at 1 January 2013. However, the flag of a ship is no indication of the true nationality of its owners. In January 2013, a historically high record of about 73 per cent of the world's tonnage was 'flagged out' in that the nationality of the vessel's owner was different from the flag under which the ship was registered.[8] This percentage has been steadily increasing from about 40 per cent in 1989.[9]

Important reasons for ship owners choosing a foreign flag include gaining a more favourable tax treatment and the possibility of employing foreign seafarers who can be paid a lower pay than national seafarers. In doing so, a reputable ship owner will also look to a flag that offers a solid institutional framework and enjoys a good compliance record.[10] Conversely a flag State can make a conscious decision not to exercise some of its authority as a flag State so as to attract ships to its flag that either do not or cannot conform to acceptable international standards.[11]

Among the top 20 registries, eight are 'national' registries, used largely by owners from the same country who own more than 90 per cent of the total national fleet by tonnage. These are the flags of China, Germany, Greece, India, Indonesia, Italy, Japan and the Republic of Korea.[12] Seven of the top 20 registries (Panama, Liberia, Marshall Islands, Bahamas, Malta, Isle of Man, and Antigua and Barbuda) could be considered purely open as less than 2 per cent of the ships flying their flags belong to owners from the same country. Many national flag States have introduced second registers, or registration in dependent territories (e.g. the UK has additional registries – Isle of Man, Bermuda), in order to allow advantages, such as employing lower cost crews, while the ships remain under the national maritime law of the mother State.[13]

The flag State regime

The LOSC provides the overarching framework governing the flag State regime. It asserts that the flag State is the principal authority responsible for ensuring that vessels flying its flag are in compliance with international laws and regulations, particularly in areas beyond national

Table 4.2 Twelve largest flags of registration (as at 1 January 2013)

Flag	No. of Vessels	Share of World Total (no. of ships)	DWT '000 dwt	Share of World Total (dwt)	National Ownership (per cent)	Per Cent growth dwt 2012–2013
Panama	8.580	9.87	350 506	21.52	0.14	5.03
Liberia	3.144	3.62	198 032	12.16	0.01	5.83
Marshall Is.	2.064	2.37	140 016	8.60	0.11	11.08
Hong Kong (China)	2.221	2.55	129 806	7.97	12.15	16.87
Singapore	3.339	3.84	89 697	5.51	36.60	16.62
Greece	1.551	1.78	75 424	4.63	92.60	5.13
Bahamas	1.446	1.66	73 702	4.52	1.18	1.44
Malta	1.794	2.06	68 831	4.23	0.35	8.18
China	3727	4.29	68 642	4.21	98.18	9.83
Cyprus	1030	1.18	31 706	1.95	19.51	7.61
Isle of Man	422	0.49	22 629	1.39	0.00	9.32
UK	1.343	1.54	21 095	1.30	49.88	6.99

Source: UNCTAD, *Review of Maritime Transport 2013*, Table 2.6, p. 56

jurisdiction. Key articles from LOSC establishing the flag State regime and the responsibilities of these States are listed in the Appendix. The duties of the flag State are conveniently summarised in the Code for the Implementation of Mandatory IMO instruments agreed by IMO resolution A.973(24) in 2005.[14]

A ship requires a nationality to identify it for legal and commercial purposes.[15] This is obtained by registering the ship with the administration of a national flag. A ship has the nationality of the State whose flag it is entitled to fly but this does not necessarily mean it has the same nationality as its owner or operator. A vessel without a flag is subject to the exercise of jurisdiction and control by all nations.[16]

Under LOSC Article 94, the flag State is under a duty to exercise effective jurisdiction and control over administrative, technical and social matters on their ships on the high seas. The regulatory regime for the responsibilities of flag States extends to ship safety and construction standards, crew training and certification requirements relating to marine pollution, maritime security, and seafarer welfare. Jurisdiction includes the right to prescribe laws and regulations that are to apply onboard a particular vessel, the right to enforce those laws and regulations, and an implied right to 'interfere' with the vessel to the extent necessary to exercise that jurisdiction.[17] Flag States are responsible for ensuring that ships flying their flag comply with generally accepted international standards, and are operated safely, including ensuring vessels are seaworthy and manned by appropriately qualified seafarers. They are thus the first line of defence in eliminating sub-standard ships. While responsibility for security arrangements onboard ships is not mentioned specifically in Article 94, this has become a flag State responsibility under the International Ship and Port Facility Security (ISPS Code).[18] A more recent requirement of flag States is the need to have proper standards for private maritime security company (PMSC) personnel and armed security guards on their flagged ships. While the IMO has published interim guidance to PMSCs, this is not legally binding.[19]

States may enact legislation applicable to vessels flying their flag, regardless of their location. There is much variation in the requirements set by different flag States for ships to register under their flag. Some require a vessel to be owned wholly or partly by a national citizen or entity, but others have no nationality requirement. Most ship registers allow the registration of ships without requiring the identification of the beneficial owners. This is very often hidden under the veil of incorporation and the use of corporate structures spread over a number of jurisdictions.[20]

Limitations on flag State jurisdiction

When a vessel leaves the high seas and enters the maritime zones of a coastal/port State, the flag State's jurisdiction over that vessel remains in force but is no longer exclusive.[21] While a warship or other duly authorised ship clearly marked and identifiable as being on government service may board a ship flying its own flag, or believed to be of the same nationality as the warship, on the high seas or in an exclusive economic zone (EEZ), it would be restricted in its ability to exercise that jurisdiction once the ship entered the territorial sea of another State. The flag State is only able to exercise its jurisdiction over its own flag vessels in the territorial sea of another State with the consent of that State to enter its waters for that purpose.

Only the flag State may exercise jurisdiction over a vessel on the high seas with very limited exceptions.[22] The United States in implementing the Proliferation Security Initiative (PSI) overcame this difficulty by ship-boarding agreements with various ship registries that pre-authorise boarding of vessels suspected of carrying weapons of mass destruction or related materials with the proviso that the flag State initially has two hours to respond to a boarding request.[23] UN Security Council Resolution 1874, which strengthened sanctions on North Korea, had called on member states to inspect vessels on the high seas 'with the consent of the flag State', if they believe them to be carrying conventional arms, nuclear- and missile-related goods and technologies or other banned goods to or from North Korea.[24]

Discharging flag State responsibilities

Under the framework provided by the LOSC, the flag State regime is established by the IMO and the International Labour Organization (ILO), as well as by classification societies. The IMO and ILO provide the international instruments which either should be complied with by flag States, or which should guide them in the discharge of their responsibilities. The classification societies set the technical standards of design, construction and maintenance of mercantile and non-mercantile shipping. The role of classification societies as recognised organisations (ROs), however, has increased over the years and they now assist the regulators in making laws with a technical, human or environmental focus.

The process of vessel registration is a key component in the implementation of flag State responsibilities. It presents an opportunity for flag States to verify compliance with national and international laws and to prevent the flagging of vessels with a history of non-compliance. Most flag States discharge their responsibilities through a national maritime administration that manages the national ship register and develops the national legislation and regulations to fulfil the nation's responsibilities as a flag State. With an OR, the role of the flag State may be discharged by some entity outside the flag State itself which simply collects part of the fee for a ship using its flag. Classification Societies also offer their services to Governments to perform statutory surveys on ships registered under their flags on their behalf. More and more flag States are delegating most of their technical duties to these societies although many registries still use their own inspection units to conduct many, if not all, the necessary inspections.

UNCLOS Article 91 requires that there be 'a genuine link' between a State and the ships entitled to fly the flag of that State. However, because the flag State can define the nature of this link, in practice it can register any ship it chooses without a tangible link to the ship.[25] The UN Convention on Conditions for Registration of Ships, adopted in 1986, would have set some requirements for participation by nationals of a flag State in owning and manning vessels flying its flag thus establishing a genuine link, but it has never entered into force.

The lack of a genuine link between the ship and its flag is an unequivocal sign of an OR.[26] There is nothing inherently unusual in an international ship registry system in which the owner of a ship may be located in a country other than the State whose flag the ship flies, but a balance has to be struck between the commercial advantages of selecting a particular flag and the need to discourage the use of flags that do not meet their international obligations. It remains a key interest of the international community to develop policies to eradicate flag registries that do not ensure that ships flying their flags do not put at risk both lives and goods at sea, as well as the marine environment.[27]

The ILO plays a leading role in setting international standards for working, living and welfare conditions for seafarers.[28] The Maritime Labour Convention (MLC) adopted in 2006 consolidates earlier labour conventions and provides for PSC oversight of seafarer conditions onboard ship. It is supported by the ILO Guidelines for Flag State Inspections under the Maritime Labour Convention (2009).

Effectiveness of the regime

The report of the UN Secretary-General submitted to the 58th session of the UN General Assembly found that 'many shipping accidents and resulting loss of life and marine pollution are not the result of inadequate regulation at the global level, but are due to ineffective flag State implementation and enforcement'.[29] Similar reports over the years have noted how some flag States regularly fail to comply with the LOSC and other relevant international instruments and agreements. Marking the annual observance of World Maritime Day in 2014, the UN Secretary-General Ban Ki-moon urged 'all concerned to strengthen their efforts to achieve the full and effective implementation of all IMO conventions'.[30]

Sub-standard ships

Current measures to ensure compliance with relevant international instruments have not succeeded in reducing the number of sub-standard ships to an acceptable level.[31] While the primary responsibility for ensuring that ships are not sub-standard rests with the flag State, it 'has been clear for many years that quite a number of flag States are either unable or unwilling to take the necessary action to ensure such compliance'.[32] PSC has become the main international system to counter sub-standard vessels, but some PSC regimes are ineffective. This is the case with the Indian Ocean Memorandum of Understanding (MOU) on PSC, which is less effective than the Paris and Tokyo MOUs.[33] Some important shipping countries in the region are not parties to the MOU, and some parties fall well short of fulfilling their inspection commitments. Even the Tokyo MOU, which is regarded as one of the most effective regimes, includes some members that make little or no contribution to the inspection effort.[34]

Sub-standard ships, their owners, and by implication, the flag States that register such vessels are threats to maritime safety and security. A study by the Stockholm International Peace Research Institute (SIPRI) found that ships involved in trafficking in destabilising commodities, such as destabilising military equipment, dual use goods and narcotics, when the owner, commercial operator or ship's officers appear to have been complicit in the activity, had an average age of more than 27 years with poor PSC records.[35] They were vessels repeatedly identified as poor performers in PSC inspections carried out by European or North American authorities for at least seven of the past eleven years.[36]

Sub-standard ships also appear to be at greater risk of successful attack by pirates. Research has shown that sub-standard ships were more likely to be successfully hijacked by Somali pirates than quality vessels.[37] While well-operated and maintained vessels will follow the best management practice (BMP) guidelines recommended by the IMO and ship owner associations to avoid attack, poor quality vessels are less likely to do so. Of the 54 commercial vessels hijacked by Somali pirates in 2010 and 2011, 23 vessels, or about 42 per cent of the total hijacked, could be assessed as being sub-standard by virtue of age and their PSC record.[38]

Assessing the performance of flag States

The performance of flag States is largely assessed through the PSC regime. The first PSC regime was established in Europe in 1982 following the *Amoco Cadiz* oil spill off the coast of northern France. The introduction of this regime was, in effect, saying that flag States could not be trusted to fulfil the obligation to perform effective safety oversight and compliance with international regulations.[39] The PSC regime involves the inspection of foreign ships entering port by the authorities of the port State to verify that the condition of the ship and its equipment comply with the requirements of international regulations and that the ship is manned and operated in compliance with these rules. The regime is based on the principle that a port State is entitled to set conditions for the entry of ships into its ports.

The international shipping organisations, International Chamber of Shipping (ICS) and the International Shipping Federation (ISF), publish an annual Flag State Performance Table.[40] This collates various data available in the public domain, such as the collective PSC record of ships flying a particular flag (based on the flag's record with three principal PSC authorities: the Paris MOU, the Tokyo MOU and the United States Coast Guard (USCG)), whether or not the country has ratified relevant international maritime conventions,[41] and the age of the fleet under the particular flag. In 2011 the USCG decided to include a new factor in their risk-based ratings: the fact a flag had been voluntarily audited by IMO.[42]

The Performance Table serves two purposes: it gives shipping companies an overview before they choose to register vessels under a particular flag and provides companies with a reason to put pressure on a country to improve its performance as a flag State.[43] It helps strike a balance between the commercial advantages of selecting a particular flag and the need to discourage the use of flags that do not meet their international obligations. Only eleven flag States (Denmark, France, Germany, Greece, Isle of Man, Japan, Liberia, Marshall Islands, Netherlands, Russia and the UK) achieved top ranking in the 2013–14 Performance Table by meeting all the performance criteria. A ship flying a flag on the 'white-list' of one of the major PSC MOUs, or enrolled in the Qualship 21 programme of the USCG,[44] is less likely to be inspected. In a competitive ship registry market, this fact could influence a ship owner in choice of register.

In 2013, 33 flags were targeted for special attention by one or more of the major PSC authorities – the Paris MOU, the Tokyo MOU or the USCG.[45] Tables 4.3 and 4.4 provide

49

Table 4.3 Flags with greater than a 10 per cent detention rate in 2013 – Paris MOU

Flag	No. of inspections	No. of detentions	% of detentions per inspections
Belize	197	22	11.17
Saint Kitts and Nevis	103	12	11.65
Cambodia	135	16	11.85
Comoros	90	11	12.22
Albania	31	4	12.90
Algeria	30	4	13.33
Moldova	198	28	14.14
Togo	129	20	15.50
Cook Is.	107	18	16.82
Dominica	23	4	17.39
Tanzania	107	21	19.63

Source: Paris MOU Annual Report 2013
Note: Only includes flags whose vessels were inspected more than 20 times

Table 4.4 Flags with greater than a 10 per cent detention rate in 2011–2013 – Tokyo MOU

Flag	No. of inspections 2011–2013	No. of detentions 2011–2013	3-year rolling average detention %
Kiribati	614	64	10.42
Saint Kitts and Nevis	126	16	12.70
Bangladesh	137	18	13.14
Egypt	51	7	13.73
Indonesia	531	79	14.88
Cambodia	4 996	769	15.35
Sierra Leone	764	131	17.15
Mongolia	408	70	17.16
DPRK	593	110	18.55
Georgia	42	9	21.43
Tanzania	73	18	24.66

Source: Tokyo MOU Annual Report 2013
Note: Only includes flags whose vessels were inspected more than 40 times during the three-year period

an indication of poorly performing flag States based on data from the Paris MOU and Tokyo MOU respectively. A poorly performing flag is one with a detention rate of more than 10 per cent in the timeframe indicated (i.e. more than one in ten of ships flying that flag were detained as a result of serious deficiencies in seagoing ability). The flags with the worst performance tend to be those with the weakest regulatory frameworks as indicated by the number of relevant

IMO conventions that the flag State has ratified. A weak regulatory framework may be attractive to ship owners who find the regulatory burden of well-established and reputable ORs too burdensome.[46]

Vetting regimes

Verification that flag States are ensuring that ships flying their flag are following required levels of safety and security is attempted through various types of inspection. These are both mandatory and non-mandatory. As well as inspection by PSC authorities, mandatory ones are normally performed by classification societies on behalf of the maritime administrations of flag States to issue and maintain certificates required by the IMO and to ensure that ships comply with minimum international standards. Classification societies were originally established to apply technical standards related to the design, construction and survey of ships and other offshore facilities, but have now taken over all aspects of ship operations. The International Association of Classification Societies (IACS) represents the ten major classification societies, such as Lloyd's Register, the American Bureau of Shipping and Det Norske Veritas, but there are many other classification societies that are not members of IACS.[47] A sub-standard ship is more likely to be classified by a non-IACS member.

Non-mandatory inspections are those performed by industry. Industry vetting regimes have been established to allow cargo owners and ship charterers to assess whether a ship is suitable for its purpose. For example, RightShip is a vetting regime based in Australia for vetting dry bulk carriers and oil tankers. Its ship vetting procedures involve sourcing data on ships and evaluating potential risks such as the ship's structural integrity, competence of owners, managers and crew, past casualties and incidents.[48] Industry inspections are much more extensive than PSC inspections, especially those for oil tankers.

Improving flag State effectiveness

The IMO has undertaken much work over the years to improve the effectiveness of flag State jurisdiction notably through a system of flag State audits. However, restoring faith in the flag State system of regulating safety in shipping is proving to be a long and slow process.[49] The old adage of 'think globally, act regionally and nationally' applies to the failure to implement international instruments effectively at the national and regional levels.

Flag State audits

IMO established the Voluntary IMO Member State Audit Scheme (VIMSAS), in 2005 to address the problem of delinquent flag States.[50] VIMSAS was based on the approach of the International Civil Aviation Organization (ICAO) to monitor safety standards in the aviation industry.[51] The scope of VIMSAS includes the flag, port and coastal State obligations of a country in relation to the mandatory IMO instruments to which it has acceded, including how they have been incorporated into national legislation and the capacity of the national maritime administration. The audit is part of IMO's response to the criticism of the flag State system that led to the development of PSC and is aimed at improving compliance by flag States.

During the voluntary the phase of VIMSAS from 2005 to 2013, 66 audits were conducted, involving 58 IMO Member States, two Associate Members and five dependent territories.[52] Those flags that have been through the process are rewarded for their commitment to raising standards.

The Paris MOU now produces a separate and shorter list of low-risk flags whose registered ships are eligible for exemption from inspections. This whiter-than-white list has two criteria: inclusion on the main white list and evidence of an IMO audit. The US Coast Guard's Qualship 21 program has a similar arrangement with 23 flags qualified as Qualship 21 flags in 2014 and three others would have been included but for their failure to supply the required VIMSAS information.[53] Typical shortcomings revealed in the audits undertaken included a lack of co-ordination among the different government agencies involved in implementing IMO regulations; a lack of resources; a lack of training programmes; and the absence of documented procedures.[54]

Despite sensitivity within IMO, mainly from developing countries and the large flag States, both of which are concerned about the costs of such a system, the IMO is now moving towards a mandatory audit system. The IMO Assembly at its 28th session adopted key resolutions and amendments relating to the Organization's mandatory audit scheme, paving the way for the scheme to come into effect by 2016 once amendments to mandatory instruments have entered into force.[55] Sensitivities remain, however, and it is still not clear whether IMO member states will decide whether to make the results public or not.

Flag States and fisheries management

The responsibilities of flag States for their fishing vessels with respect to safety and security are broadly similar to those for commercial ships. However, differences arise as a consequence of the obligations of flag States for responsible fisheries management, the sustainable use of fishery resources and the conservation of the marine environment in which those resources are found. These obligations give flag States a key role in combating IUU fishing.[56] The basic obligation with regard to the duty of flag States to take measures as may be necessary for the conservation of the living resources of the high seas is set out in LOSC Article 117 and has been supplemented by later agreements.

Other key flag State responsibilities are established by two instruments: the *Agreement to Promote Compliance with International Conservation and Management Measures on the High Seas 1995* (the Compliance Agreement) and the *United Nations Agreement for the Implementation of the Provisions of the United Nations Convention on the Law of the Sea of 10 December 1982 relating to the Conservation and Management of Straddling Fish Stocks and Highly Migratory Fish Stocks 1995* (the UN Fish Stocks Agreement). However, these agreements have a much lower level of ratification and acceptance than the LOSC itself. The UN Fish Stocks Agreement had 82 parties and the Compliance agreement 39 parties as at 3 October 2014.[57]

These Agreements enunciate a range of flag State duties that give specific practical effect to the obligation to ensure effective jurisdiction and control in relation to the activities of fishing vessels.[58] Article III of the Compliance Agreement sets out the responsibility of the flag State for fishing vessels flying its flag. The UN Fish Stocks Agreement establishes in Articles 5 and 6, and Annex 1 and 2 a range of obligations related to the conservation and management of high seas fisheries, the collection of data and the application of the precautionary approach. Articles 18–22 elaborates a series of flag State duties with respect to authorising vessels to fish on the high seas and in relation to compliance and enforcement. Flag States must ensure that they can exercise their responsibilities with respect to vessels entitled to fly their flag before they register a vessel and, in the context of high seas fishing, before they authorise the use of a vessel for fishing on the high seas. Article 18 requires States parties to maintain a national record of fishing vessels authorised to fish on the high seas.

With regard to flag State performance, the UN General Assembly has urged States and regional fisheries management organisations (RFMOs) to develop appropriate processes to assess the performance of States and has encouraged further work, including that by the Food and Agriculture Organization of the UN (FAO), on the development of guidelines on flag State control of fishing vessels.[59] Fishing vessel owners have incentives to use poorly performing flags, or, as they are sometimes described in the fisheries sector 'flags of non-compliance'. The IMO has adopted over the years several international instruments to establish the responsibilities of a flag State for fishing vessels flying its flag, but so far none have entered into force.[60]

Whilst the issues in fisheries are often different from those in maritime transport, the questions of accountability and performance are similar. A report to the World Wide Fund for Nature (WWF) in 2008 raised concerns over the persistent flag State offenders associated with IUU fishing.[61] It found that according to Lloyd's Register, 318 large-scale fishing vessels were registered to Cambodia, Georgia, Mongolia, North Korea, Sierra Leone and Togo, but based on a review of the information available from relevant RFMOs, none of those countries had any vessels authorised to fish in any of the areas on the high seas regulated by these organisations. On the contrary, fishing vessels from five of these six countries were currently 'blacklisted' by RFMOs for having engaged in IUU fishing.

Conclusion

While the flag State regime remains at the core of the system of maritime regulation and enforcement, it is no longer the traditional system of absolute control of the flag State over ships flying its flag. While formally flag States hold the responsibility, it is now discharged through a complex system of administrative arrangements, including different types of ship register, company structures and classification societies all of which means that a flag State can be 'at arm's length' from vessels flying its flag. Indeed the motives behind using a non-national flag could eventually result in the role of the flag State being largely ignored.[62]

Looking to the future, the concept of exclusive flag State jurisdiction over vessels on the high seas may come to be undermined by increasing regulation of activities on the high seas. This would reflect, for example, developing moves towards integrated governance of high seas areas.[63] It is also evident in the implementation of PSI with some flag States granting de facto approval for ships flying their flag to be boarded on the high seas. In another prospective example, a report for the European Union in 2007 recommended that the LOSC should be amended to allow ships of any flag to be stopped and searched, even on the high seas, if it was thought that they were carrying illegal immigrants.[64]

Significant problems remain with the flag State regime. Sub-standard ships still ply the seas threatening the marine environment, other shipping and the safety of their crews. PSC as the major alternative means of ensuring that ships are complying with international regulations remains less than fully effective in many parts of the world. The ability of vessels to consistently re-flag with less and less vigilant registers further undermines the effective operation of flag State jurisdiction.[65] It remains to be seen how effective the mandatory audit system will be. It will not be fully transparent and with a limited number of auditors, it will take time to audit all IMO member states and may not have the desired effect of restoring faith in the flag State system.[66]

Lastly, effective regulation of international shipping can also be stifled by conflicts of interest. Flag States and ship owners hold much power and influence at the IMO, and can be slow to support new regulations that might lead to increased costs for ship owners. Because the IMO is funded by membership fees based on the size of the respective fleets, flag States provide most of the organisation's financial support and are able to exercise influence at the technical committees where the real power of the IMO lies.[67] The FSI which has to deal with issues of flag State responsibilities and the different perspectives of members has been described as 'inevitably the most political of IMO committees'.[68]

Appendix – Key LOSC Articles establishing the flag State regime

Article 91 – Nationality of ships

1. Every State shall fix the conditions for the grant of its nationality to ships, for the registration of ships in its territory, and for the right to fly its flag. Ships have the nationality of the State whose flag they are entitled to fly. There must exist a genuine link between the State and the ship.
2. Every State shall issue to ships to which it has granted the right to fly its flag documents to that effect.

Article 92 – Status of ships

1. Ships shall sail under the flag of one State only and, save in exceptional cases expressly provided for in international treaties or in this Convention, shall be subject to its exclusive jurisdiction on the high seas. A ship may not change its flag during a voyage or while in a port of call, save in the case of a real transfer of ownership or change of registry.

Article 94 – Duties of the flag State

1. Every State shall effectively exercise its jurisdiction and control in administrative, technical and social matters over ships flying its flag.
2. In particular every State shall:
    (a) maintain a register of ships containing the names and particulars of ships flying its flag, except those which are excluded from generally accepted international regulations on account of their small size; and
    (b) assume jurisdiction under its internal law over each ship flying its flag and its master, officers and crew in respect of administrative, technical and social matters concerning the ship.
3. Every State shall take such measures for ships flying its flag as are necessary to ensure safety at sea with regard, *inter alia*, to:
    (a) the construction, equipment and seaworthiness of ships;
    (b) the manning of ships, labour conditions and the training of crews, taking into account the applicable international instruments;
    (c) the use of signals, the maintenance of communications and the prevention of collisions.

Article 98 – Duty to render assistance

1. Every State shall require the master of a ship flying its flag, in so far as he can do so without serious danger to the ship, the crew or the passengers:
    (a) to render assistance to any person found at sea in danger of being lost;
    (b) to proceed with all possible speed to the rescue of persons in distress, if informed of their need of assistance, in so far as such action may reasonably be expected of him

Article 117 – Duty of States to adopt with respect to their nationals measures for the conservation of the living resources of the high seas

All States have the duty to take, or to cooperate with other States in taking, such measures for their respective nationals as may be necessary for the conservation of the living resources of the high seas.

Article 211 – Pollution from vessels

2. States shall adopt laws and regulations for the prevention, reduction and control of pollution of the marine environment from vessels flying their flag or of their registry. Such laws and regulations shall at least have the same effect as that of generally accepted international rules and standards established through the competent international organization or general diplomatic conference.

Article 217 – Enforcement by flag States

1. States shall ensure compliance by vessels flying their flag or of their registry with applicable international rules and standards, established through the competent international organization or general diplomatic conference, and with their laws and regulations adopted in accordance with this Convention for the prevention, reduction and control of pollution of the marine environment from vessels and shall accordingly adopt laws and regulations and take other measures necessary for their implementation. Flag States shall provide for the effective enforcement of such rules, standards, laws and regulations, irrespective of where a violation occurs.
2. States shall, in particular, take appropriate measures in order to ensure that vessels flying their flag or of their registry are prohibited from sailing, until they can proceed to sea in compliance with the requirements of the international rules and standards referred to in paragraph 1, including requirements in respect of design, construction, equipment and manning of vessels.
3. States shall ensure that vessels flying their flag or of their registry carry on board certificates required by and issued pursuant to international rules and standards referred to in paragraph 1. States shall ensure that vessels flying their flag are periodically inspected in order to verify that such certificates are in conformity with the actual condition of the vessels. These certificates shall be accepted by other States as evidence of the condition of the vessels and shall be regarded as having the same force as certificates issued by them, unless there are clear grounds for believing that the condition of the vessel does not correspond substantially with the particulars of the certificates.

Notes

1 John N K Mansell, *Flag State Responsibility – Historical Development and Contemporary Issues* (Springer, 2010) 135.
2 Some case studies of disreputable practices in international shipping are provided in Alastair D Couper, *Voyages of Abuse – Seafarers, Human Rights and International Shipping* (Pluto Press, 1999).
3 Richard Goss, 'Social responsibility in shipping' (2008) 32 *Marine Policy* 143.
4 Mansell, above n 1, 101.

5. International Transport Workers' Federation (ITF) 'Improving conditions for seafarers – the ITF FOC campaign', *FOC Leaflet* (2012) <http://www.itfglobal.org/files/extranet/-1/36479/FOC_leaflet_2012.pdf>
6. ITF, *Flags of Convenience campaign* (2014) <http://www.itfglobal.org/flags-convenience/index.cfm>
7. Francisco J M Llacer, 'Open registers: past, present and future' (2003) 27 *Marine Policy* 521.
8. UN Conference on Trade and Development (UNCTAD), *Review of Maritime Transport 2013*, UN Doc. UNCTAD/RMT/2013 (2013) 55.
9. Ibid., Figure 2.7.
10. Ibid., 55.
11. Mansell, above n 1, 2.
12. UNCTAD, above n 8, Table 2.6.
13. Mansell, above n 1, 103.
14. Ibid., 5.
15. Martin Stopford, *Maritime Economics*, 3rd ed. (Routledge, 2009) 667.
16. A J Norris, 'The "Other" Law of the Sea', (2011) 64(3) *Naval War College Review* 80.
17. Ibid.
18. This Code includes a mandatory section (Part A) and a recommendatory section (Part B). Part A requires ships to have security assessments and plans, ship security officers and certain onboard equipment, as well as permanent ship identity markings and a Continuous Synopsis Record recording ship ownership. Ships will have to carry an International Ship Security Certificate (ISSC) indicating that they comply with the requirements of SOLAS and the ISPS Code. The ISSC is subject to port State inspections.
19. IMO, 'Interim Guidance to Private Maritime Security Companies Providing Privately Contracted Armed Security Personnel onboard Ships in the High Risk Area', MSC.1/Circ.1443 (2013).
20. Stopford, above n 15, 673–674.
21. Norris, above n 16, 81.
22. The exceptions are those in LOSC Article 110, notably if there are reasonable grounds for suspecting that a ship is engaged in piracy.
23. Song Yann-huei, 'The U.S.-Led Proliferation Security Initiative and UNCLOS: Legality, Implementation, and an Assessment' (2007) 38(1–2) *Ocean Development & International Law* 106.
24. Hugh Griffiths and Michael Jenks, 'Maritime Transport and Destabilizing Commodity Flows', *SIPRI Policy Paper 32* (Stockholm International Peace Research Institute, 2012) 33–34.
25. Stopford, above n 15, 664.
26. Llacer, above n 7, 519.
27. Ibid., 522.
28. Mansell, above n 1, 109.
29. United Nations General Assembly (UNGA), *Oceans and the law of the sea – Report of the Secretary-General*, UN Doc A/58/65 (3 March 2003) paragraph 36.
30. UN News Centre, 'On World Maritime Day, UN urges ratification of conventions to protect global seaways'(25 September 2014) <http://www.un.org/apps/news/story.asp?NewsID=48867#.VDWWh9Jxkrw>
31. Robin Churchill, 'From Port State to Court State? International Litigation as a Possible Weapon to Combat Sub-standard ships' in Yafsir Malick Ndiaye and Rudiger Wolfrum (eds), *Liber Amicorum Judge Thomas A. Mensah: Law of the Sea, Protection of the Marine Environment and Settlement of Disputes* (Martinus Nijhoff, 2007) 901.
32. Ibid., 903.
33. Sam Bateman, 'Maritime security and port state control in the Indian Ocean Region' (2012) 8(2) *Journal of the Indian Ocean Region* 197.
34. Churchill, above n 31, 903.
35. Griffiths and Jenks, above n 24, 29.
36. Ibid.
37. Bateman, above n 33, 193–194.
38. Ibid., 194.
39. Andrew Guest, 'Finding faith in flags', *BIMCO News* (5 December 2012) <https://www.bimco.org/News/2012/12/05_Feature_Week_49.aspx>
40. The 2013–14 table is available at: http://www.ics-shipping.org/docs/flagstateperformancetable.

41 The core international conventions are: the International Convention for the Safety of Life at Sea, 1974 as amended, including the 1988 Protocol, the International Safety Management (ISM) Code and the International Ship and Port Facility Security (ISPS) Code (SOLAS 74); the International Convention for the Prevention of Pollution from Ships,1973 as modified by the Protocol of 1978, including Annexes I – VI (oil, bulk chemicals, dangerous packaged goods, sewage, garbage and atmospheric pollution) (MARPOL 73/78); the International Convention on Load Lines, 1966, including the 1988 Protocol (LL 66); the International Convention on Standards of Training, Certification and Watchkeeping for Seafarers, 1978 as amended, including the 1995 amendments (STCW 78); the Maritime Labour Convention, 2006 (ILO MLC); the International Convention on Civil Liability for Oil Pollution Damage, 1992, and the International Convention on the Establishment of an International Fund for Compensation for Oil Pollution Damage, 1992 (CLC/Fund 92).

42 United States Coast Guard (USCG), Foreign & Offshore Compliance Division, *QUALSHIP 21 Initiative* (2014) <http://www.uscg.mil/hq/cgcvc/cvc2/safety/qualship.asp>

43 Maritime International Secretariat Services Ltd, *Shipping Industry Guidelines on Flag State Performance*, 2nd ed. (2006) <www.marisec.org/flag-performance>

44 QUALSHIP 21 is an initiative by the USCG to eliminate substandard shipping, to enforce compliance with international and U.S. standards, and to reward high-quality ships with incentives to encourage quality operations.

45 Equasis, *The world merchant fleet in 2013 — Statistics from Equasis*, Annex II (2014) <http://www.equasis.org/Fichiers/Statistique/MOA/Annual%20Statistics/Equasis%20Statistics%20-%20The%20world%20fleet%202013.pdf>

46 Tony Alderton and Nik Winchester, 'Flag states and safety 1997:1999' (2002) 29(2) *Maritime Policy and Management* 159.

47 A discussion of the role of classification societies is available in Alan E. Branch, *Elements of Shipping*, 8th ed. (Routledge, 2007) 132–135.

48 RightShip, 'Shipping can be a risky business' (2014) <http://site.rightship.com/services/ship-vetting/>

49 Guest, above n 39.

50 IMO, *Voluntary Member State Audit Scheme* (2011) <http://www.imo.org/blast/mainframe.asp?topic_id=841>

51 Mansell, above n 1, 145–147.

52 IMO, *IMO Member State Audit Scheme (IMSAS)* (7 January 2015) <http://www.imo.org/ourwork/msas/Pages/default.aspx>

53 USCG, above n 42.

54 Guest, above n 39.

55 IMO, 'IMO Assembly adopts mandatory audit scheme' *IMO Press Briefing: 54* (5 December 2013) <http://www.imo.org/MediaCentre/PressBriefings/Pages/A-28-ends-.aspx>

56 Camille Goodman, 'The Regime for Flag State Responsibility in International Fisheries Law – Effective fact, creative fiction, or further work required?' (2009) 23 *Australia and New Zealand Maritime Law Journal* 157.

57 <http://www.un.org/depts/los/reference_files/chronological_lists_of_ratifications.htm#Agreement for the implementation of the provisions of the Convention relating to the conservation and management of straddling fish stocks and highly migratory fish stocks; and: http://www.fao.org/fileadmin/user_upload/legal/docs/1_012s-e.pdf>

58 Goodman, above n 56, 162.

59 UNGA, 'Sustainable fisheries, including through the 1995 Agreement for the Implementation of the Provisions of the United Nations Convention on the Law of the Sea of 10 December 1982 relating to the Conservation and Management of Straddling Fish Stocks and Highly Migratory Fish Stocks, and related instruments', *Resolution 65/38 adopted by the General Assembly on 7 December 2010*, UN Doc A/RES/65/38 (2010), paragraphs 44 and 58.

60 The last of these is the Cape Town Agreement of 2012 on the Implementation of the Provisions of the 1993 Protocol relating to the Torremolinos International Convention for the Safety of Fishing Vessels, 1977.

61 Matthew Gianni, *Real and Present Danger: Flag State Failure and Maritime Safety and Security* (World Wide Fund for Nature and International Transport Workers' Federation, June 2008).

62 Bevan Martin, *Port State Jurisdiction and the Regulation of International Merchant Shipping* (Springer, 2014) 231.

63 Rosemary Rayfuse and Robin Warner, 'Securing a sustainable future for the oceans beyond national jurisdiction: The legal basis for an integrated cross-sectoral regime for high seas governance for the 21st Century' (2008) 23 *The International Journal of Marine and Coastal Law* 399–421.
64 Justin Stares, 'Brussels pushes for change in UNCLOS', *Lloyd's List* (London), 4 June 2007.
65 Goodman, above n 56, 159.
66 Guest, above n 39.
67 William Langewiesche, *The Outlaw Sea: A World of Freedom, Chaos and Crime* (North Point Press, 2004) 87.
68 Mansell, above n 1, 136.

5
The Role of Coastal States

Lowell Bautista

Introduction

The Coastal State plays a central role in global maritime regulation and enforcement. The role of the Coastal State complements, supplements, and counter-balances those of the Port State, the Flag State, international organisations, and other entities that enforce maritime rules, regulations and standards.[1] The systemic feature of international law as having no central enforcement body necessitates that States, and in some instances, international organisations, are conferred significant enforcement powers on behalf of the international community of States.[2] The powers, duties and responsibilities exercised by the Coastal State in respect of maritime regulation and enforcement, which are conferred and limited by customary international law and treaty law, are of paramount importance in ensuring safety and good order at sea, including the protection of the marine environment and the conservation of the ocean's living and non-living resources.

The *1982 United Nations Convention on the Law of the Sea (LOSC)*,[3] universally recognised as the 'constitution for the oceans', constitutes the principal legal framework governing the role of the Coastal State in maritime regulation and enforcement.[4] However, international maritime law, not much different from law of the sea as a branch of public international law, is also governed and subject to customary international law,[5] and a wide array of general and specific international agreements that regulate the legal regime of maritime areas,[6] regulations relating to the safety of navigation,[7] and other conventions intended to protect the marine environment.[8] Nevertheless, the LOSC remains to be the overarching, fundamental framework that ties together the rules of international law relating to the scope and limits of the powers of Coastal State in the various maritime areas with other subsequent conventions especially those within the International Maritime Organisation (IMO) on the technical aspects of shipping, safety at sea and environmental protection.[9]

The assertion of Coastal State jurisdiction and control over natural resources and activities over expanses of waters surrounding their coasts has been a persistent feature of the law of the sea.[10] The enduring tension between Coastal States and maritime States, principally Flag States, is carefully balanced and preserved in LOSC.[11] The predominant role of the Flag State has traditionally been established and confirmed in customary international law and confirmed in treaties.[12] The primacy of Flag State jurisdiction is reflected in the rule conferring exclusive Flag State jurisdiction on the high seas.[13] On the other hand, foreign ships and vessels voluntarily present in ports, are subject to the jurisdiction of the Port State.[14] However, the competencies of the Coastal State over activities within their territorial sea and in the other maritime zones, are well established in international law, especially as prescribed in the LOSC.[15] This sharing of enforcement powers amongst these categories of States – Coastal, Port and Flag – is essentially positive and complimentary, and a central feature of the delicate balances codified in the LOSC.[16]

This chapter examines the role of the Coastal State in maritime regulation and enforcement. It will be divided into four sections. The first will discuss the general jurisdictional competence of Coastal States in order to provide a basic contextual information to the chapter. The second will examine the enforcement and regulatory powers of the Coastal State in the various maritime zones of jurisdiction. The third will discuss contemporary challenges and enforcement issues. The final section will be the conclusion, which will provide some final observations and recommendations.

The jurisdictional competence of Coastal States

The general competence of the Coastal State to exercise jurisdiction and to enact legislation and lawfully enforce them is an aspect of sovereignty.[17] This competence flows from the sovereignty it exercises over its land territory and internal waters to the territorial sea,[18] and for limited and specified purposes over the other maritime zones.[19] This is recognition of the inherent right of Coastal States to protect their coasts. The Coastal State may exercise enforcement in-port or at sea, for violations within its maritime zones.[20]

Coastal State jurisdiction, it must be emphasised, complements the jurisdiction of the Port and Flag State.[21] In some instances, it is a response over the inadequacy of Flag State regulation of vessels.[22] It is clear that the rights of the Coastal State are not absolute. In particular, international law provides for some general limitations on enforcement against foreign ships.[23] It is clearly beyond the scope of this chapter to examine and analyse all of the provisions of LOSC applicable to Coastal States. However, a summary of the relevant provisions in respect of enforcement and regulatory powers of the Coastal State in the various zones of maritime jurisdiction will follow in the next section.

Enforcement and regulatory powers of Coastal States in the various maritime zones of jurisdiction

This section, following a zonal approach, will discuss the enforcement and regulatory powers of the Coastal State in the various maritime zones of jurisdiction.

Internal waters

The powers of the Coastal State are complete and absolute over its internal waters.[24] Internal waters refer to waters lying landward of the territorial sea baseline and normally include bays, lakes, canals and river mouths, estuaries, harbours and ports.[25] The Coastal State exercises complete prescriptive and adjudicative jurisdiction over criminal and civil matters in this maritime zone.[26] Since internal waters have same status as the State's land territory, the Coastal State's power is virtually unhampered within this maritime zone and these waters are not subject of detailed regulation under the LOSC.[27]

The full sovereignty and jurisdiction exercised by the Coastal State over its internal waters carries the competence and the right to control and even exclude foreign vessels from entering its internal waters, specifically its ports.[28] However, in practice, a Coastal State grants access to its ports as a reciprocal condition for its own merchant vessels to be allowed access to other ports. In any case, the Coastal State may deny access to its ports if its peace, good order or security is endangered or when the merchant vessel is sailing under the flag of a country with which it is at war.[29]

The LOSC allows the Coastal State to set conditions for entry into its internal waters.[30] The right of innocent passage does not exist in internal waters, except in exceptional cases provided under Article 8(2), LOSC, where the establishment of a straight baseline under Article 7, LOSC, has the effect of enclosing as internal waters areas not previously considered as such.[31]

The power of the Coastal State to regulate access to its internal waters is uncontested.[32] This includes the power to enforce its laws over the ship and over property or persons on board the vessel, subject to rules that apply to sovereign and diplomatically immune vessels such as warships.[33] However, commonly, the Coastal State does not enforce its laws in cases solely concerning internal affairs of the ship, unless such affects the Coastal State.[34] Furthermore, the Coastal State will intervene or assert jurisdiction when its intervention is requested by the captain or the consul of the Flag State, or in cases involving a non-crew member.[35] The Coastal State will also exercise jurisdiction and enforce its laws such as those concerning pollution, pilotage and navigation, against a foreign vessel, including the arrest of ships in the course of civil proceedings in the Coastal State.[36] This is evidently articulated in Article 220 (1), LOSC, which gives the Coastal State the enforcement powers over vessels voluntarily within its port or an off-shore terminal, to institute proceedings for any violation of its national laws, regulations adopted in accordance with LOSC or applicable international rules and standards on vessel source pollution committed in the territorial sea or the exclusive economic zone (EEZ).[37] This gives the Coastal State wide latitude to enforce marine environmental laws over foreign vessels exercising innocent passage in these zones.[38]

Territorial sea

The rights and duties of the Coastal State including its legislative and enforcement jurisdiction over the territorial sea are inherent in the sovereignty it exercises over the territorial sea.[39] The powers of the Coastal State whilst broad, expansive and almost absolute within the territorial sea,[40] need to be interpreted within the context of other provisions of the LOSC and relevant international law such as IMO conventions dealing with shipping and vessel-source pollution.[41]

The principal limitation on the exercise of Coastal State jurisdiction is the right of innocent passage.[42] The right of innocent passage through the territorial sea is enjoyed by ships of all States.[43] This right is founded on the principle of freedom of navigation to ensure freedom of trade.[44] The navigational regime of innocent passage within the territorial sea is subject to certain constraints which set the limits of Coastal State sovereignty over the territorial sea.[45] The Coastal State may adopt laws and regulations, in conformity with the LOSC and other rules of international law, that relate, *inter alia*, to safety of navigation, maritime traffic and facilities or installations, living resources including fisheries, marine scientific research and hydrographic surveys, protection of cables and pipelines, preservation of the environment, and customs, fiscal, immigration or sanitary matters.[46] However, such laws and regulations need to be given due publicity,[47] and shall not apply to the design, construction, manning or equipment of foreign ships unless they are giving effect to generally accepted international rule or standards.[48]

The Coastal State has the right to take necessary steps in the territorial sea to prevent passage which is not innocent.[49] The list of activities which are considered prejudicial to the peace, good order or security of the Coastal State, and therefore non-innocent, are listed in Article 19 (2) of LOSC.[50] These include any threat or use of force, weapons exercise of any kind, spying, any act of propaganda, fishing, research or survey activities, among others.[51] The list is considered non-exhaustive and refers to activities, and not to the mere presence or passage of ships.[52] The right to exclude vessels not engaged in passage is recognised in customary international law.[53]

In addition, the Coastal State cannot enact laws that hamper[54] or levy charges on vessels exercising the right of innocent passage.[55] The Coastal State may levy charges against foreign vessels passing through the territorial sea for specific services rendered such as rescue and pilotage but without discrimination.[56]

The Coastal State may temporarily suspend innocent passage in specified areas of the territorial sea for the protection of its security, including weapons exercises, but only after due publicity and without discrimination.[57] The Coastal State may designate or prescribe sea lanes and traffic separation schemes,[58] including requiring tankers, nuclear-powered ships and ships carrying noxious or inherently dangerous substances to confine their passage to such lanes,[59] and for such vessels to carry documents and observe special precautionary measures established by international agreements.[60]

The LOSC specifies the rules applicable when Coastal States may exercise criminal and civil jurisdiction to enforce its laws upon merchant vessels and government ships operated for commercial purposes. The Coastal State may only exercise criminal jurisdiction to arrest a person on board or conduct an investigation in connection with a crime committed on board a foreign ship passing through the territorial sea for severe cases whose consequences extend to the Coastal State.[61] The civil jurisdiction of the Coastal State in relation to foreign ships in the territorial sea is even more limited and restricted to civil liability arising out of obligations incurred by the ship in the course of its voyage through the territorial sea.[62] There are also rules under the LOSC which regulate the exercise of Coastal State jurisdiction over warships and other government ships operated for non-commercial purposes which follow and respect immunities enjoyed by these vessels.[63] However, the LOSC gives the Coastal State the right to require such ships to leave immediately upon non-compliance with its laws and regulations concerning passage after a request is made,[64] and for the Flag State of such vessels to assume international responsibility for any loss or damage to the Coastal State resulting from such non-compliance or other rules of international law.[65]

Archipelagic waters

The archipelagic State exercises sovereignty over its archipelagic waters, which includes the subjacent seabed and subsoil, and the superjacent airspace.[66] As such, the archipelagic State has powers of maritime regulation and enforcement over these waters. However, the sovereignty that the archipelagic State exercises over its archipelagic waters is subject to the condition that the archipelagic State respect existing agreements with other States, including traditional fishing rights and other legitimate activities of the immediately adjacent neighbouring States,[67] and respect existing submarine cables laid by other States passing through its waters without making a landfall.[68]

Furthermore, the archipelagic State has the power to control and regulate the right of innocent passage enjoyed by other States, similar to the powers of the Coastal State over its territorial sea.[69] This includes the right to temporarily suspend the right of innocent passage in specified areas of its archipelagic waters for the protection of its security, and after due publicity.[70] In addition to the right of innocent passage enjoyed by all ships in archipelagic waters,[71] foreign ships and aircraft enjoy the right of archipelagic sea lanes passage in sea lanes and air routes designated by the archipelagic State in consultation with the IMO.[72] In the absence of such designation, the right of archipelagic sea lanes passage may be exercised through routes normally used for international navigation.[73]

In relation to enforcement powers over vessel-sourced pollution within archipelagic waters or those relating to enforcement powers in relation to the protection and preservation of the marine environment, the archipelagic State seems to possess less enforcement jurisdiction over foreign vessels than those exercised by a non-archipelagic State over its territorial sea or straits.[74] However, over the archipelagic State's territorial sea beyond the limits of its archipelagic baselines, an archipelagic State possesses the same rights as other Coastal States in regulating vessel-source pollution within this area.[75]

Contiguous zone

The Coastal State exercises limited powers of maritime regulation and enforcement over the contiguous zone as provided for under Article 33, LOSC. In the contiguous zone, the Coastal State exercises the right to prevent infringement of its customs, fiscal, immigration or sanitary laws and regulations within its territory or territorial sea, for inward-bound vessels;[76] and to punish infringement of its customs, fiscal, immigration or sanitary laws and regulations committed within its territory or territorial sea, for outward-bound vessels.[77]

These limited powers are consistent with the *sui generis* nature of the contiguous zone and the fact that the Coastal State does not exercise sovereign rights over this zone although it is coterminous with the EEZ and continental shelf.[78] In this regard, the rights of the Coastal State over the contiguous zone need to be interpreted in light of the navigational freedoms which exist on the high seas and in the EEZ up to edge of the territorial sea.[79]

The extension of Coastal State legislative and enforcement powers over the contiguous zone to cover security issues, has been met with opposition and has been considered a threat to the freedom of navigation.[80] Another area of contention is whether the Coastal State has the right within the contiguous zone to tow foreign ships to deter them from approaching the territorial sea, especially in cases of vessels carrying asylum seekers intending to enter the territorial sea of the Coastal State.[81] In such instances, international law protects the safety of the people on board the vessel and prohibits the towing of unseaworthy vessels from the contiguous zone to be abandoned at sea.[82]

Rothwell and Stephens opine that such actions need to be 'consistent with the respect for the safety of life at sea'.[83]

Exclusive economic zone

The Coastal State exercises sovereign rights over the natural resources in the EEZ, which is a zone beyond and adjacent to the territorial sea extending to a maximum distance of 200 nautical miles from the baseline.[84] Over the EEZ, the Coastal State has sovereign rights to explore, exploit, conserve and manage the living and non-living resources of the seabed, subsoil and superjacent waters.[85] On the other hand, third States enjoy the freedom of navigation, overflight by aircraft and the laying of submarine cables and pipelines.[86] It is well to remember that the rights and duties of the Coastal State over the EEZ are not only *sui generis* in nature, and only those specifically specified under the LOSC,[87] but also that they relate primarily to resources in the EEZ.[88] In the EEZ, the LOSC imposes upon the Coastal State the general duty to 'have due regard to the rights and duties of other States' and to 'act in a manner compatible with the provisions of this Convention.'[89]

Under the LOSC, in the EEZ, the Coastal State has legislative and enforcement competence with regard to the protection and preservation of the marine environment,[90] which is expanded in Part XII of the LOSC.[91] This includes the power to regulate pollution in the EEZ from sea-bed activities,[92] from the dumping of wastes,[93] and other forms of pollution from vessels.[94] The powers of the Coastal State in respect of operational vessel-source pollution are more limited and legislation passed by the Coastal State that applies to the EEZ must conform with generally accepted international rules and standards such as those set within the framework of the IMO.[95] Furthermore, the LOSC provides that the enforcement against foreign vessels within the EEZ for marine environmental infringement can only be exercised by officials or by warships, military aircraft, other ships or aircraft clearly marked and identifiable as being on government service and authorised to that effect.[96] The Coastal State shall be liable for damage or loss arising from unlawful or excessive enforcement measures.[97]

In addition to the jurisdiction over the protection of the marine environment, the Coastal State also possesses jurisdiction over the establishment and use of artificial islands,[98] and marine scientific research (MSR).[99] The Coastal State has the power to regulate MSR in the EEZ under a consent regime regulated in Part XIII of the LOSC.[100]

In the EEZ, the high seas freedoms of navigation and overflight enjoyed by third States are similar to those on the high seas.[101] However, there are other provisions in the LOSC that give extensive regulatory powers to the Coastal State. These include the power to board, inspect, arrest and institute judicial proceedings against fishing vessels and their crews to ensure compliance with fisheries laws adopted in conformity with LOSC.[102] The arrested vessels and their crews are to be released promptly after the posting of a reasonable bond.[103]

The issue of 'creeping jurisdiction' over the increasing assertion of Coastal State jurisdiction in the EEZ over matters which are not essentially of a resource or environmental character, has been flagged by commentators.[104] For instance, the power of the Coastal State to regulate marine pollution has been interpreted by some States to extend to require 'prior notification' and even 'prior informed consent' which may amount to a denial of passage through the EEZ.[105] Another area of contention is the assertion by Coastal States of security jurisdiction in the EEZ including polarising debates over assertions to carry out surveillance and other military activities, including weapons exercises, in the EEZ, as part of high seas freedoms guaranteed under the LOSC.[106]

High seas

In the high seas, in contrast to the extensive powers of the Coastal State to regulate activities and resources within waters that encircle their coasts, the legal regime of the high seas is traditionally the domain of exclusive Flag State jurisdiction and traditional high seas freedoms, namely, freedom of navigation, overflight, laying of submarine cables and pipelines, and fishing.[107] The high seas are open to all States and cannot be subject to the sovereignty of any State.[108] Churchill and Lowe regards this rule of customary international law, the very 'cornerstone of modern international law.'[109] On the high seas, every State has the right to its flag,[110] and exercise the non-exhaustive list of high seas freedoms enumerated in Article 87, LOSC, subject to the 'due regard obligation' to protect the interests of other States exercising the same freedoms and also other rights under the LOSC in respect of activities in the Area.[111]

On the high seas, the general rule is that the Flag State exercises exclusive legislative and enforcement jurisdiction over ships that fly its flag.[112] However, exclusive Flag State jurisdiction is not absolute and is subject to several recognised exceptions in customary international law, codified in the LOSC, where the Coastal State legislative or enforcement jurisdiction, or both, with the Flag State. These exceptions include piracy,[113] unauthorised broadcasting on the high seas,[114] illicit traffic in narcotic drugs and psychotropic substances,[115] and slave trade.[116] In specific instances listed in Article 110 of the LOSC, States also has the right to visit and enforce their laws against their own ship or against ships of uncertain nationality, or stateless ships.[117]

The Coastal State may also assert the right of hot pursuit to pursue a foreign ship which has violated its laws and regulations within its internal waters or territorial sea and to arrest it on the high seas.[118] The right of hot pursuit ceases the moment the ship being pursued enters its own territorial sea or of a third State.[119] Customary international law also allows the Coastal State the right to arrest foreign ships which have committed offences within the territorial sea whilst remaining on the high seas, under the doctrine of constructive presence.[120] Another recognised exception to exclusive Flag State jurisdiction is the right of Coastal States to take and enforce measures to protect their coastlines from actual or threatened damage from pollution following a maritime casualty.[121] In any event, and in exceptional circumstances, Coastal States find justification to lawfully exercise jurisdiction over foreign ships on the high seas on grounds of self-defence or necessity,[122] or as conferred under special treaties.[123]

Contemporary challenges and enforcement issues

There are many contemporary challenges faced by Coastal States in ensuring that the oceans remain secure, safe and environmentally protected. The deteriorating state of the global marine environment alongside increasing pressures on marine resources and ecosystems brought about by a constantly expanding global population present formidable challenges that are both urgent and large-scale. Threats include, among others, piracy and armed robbery, illicit traffic in narcotic drugs and psychotropic substances, illegal traffic in hazardous wastes and other wastes, smuggling of migrants, management of marine resources and preservation of the marine environment, and far-reaching challenges associated with climate change.[124] The transnational nature of many of these issues necessitate that measures need to be undertaken at the global and regional levels requiring multilateral cooperation and capacity-building to assist Coastal States in undertaking maritime regulation and enforcement measures.

The increasing demand upon Coastal States, along with Flag States, Port States and international organisations, to ensure safety and security at sea through obligations imposed under the LOSC and other international agreements, are often onerous and Coastal States need financial and technical support in order to discharge them. For instance, the LOSC establishes detailed deposit and due publicity obligations for its parties.[125] However, many coastal States have yet to deposit charts or lists of geographical coordinates with the Secretary-General.[126] The importance of this seemingly innocuous obligation cannot be overemphasised as an essential component of maritime regulation and enforcement. In fact, clearly defined and duly publicised limits of maritime zones will not only provide jurisdictional certainty for enforcement purposes but more importantly for the exploration and exploitation of the Coastal State's waters and the resources therein.

There are other challenges which are more complex, such as the consistency of 'multilateral hot pursuit' with the LOSC when two or more Coastal States are engaged in the hot pursuit resulting in the arrest of a delinquent vessel,[127] or the lawful extent of use of force of Coastal States to enforce its constabulary or policing functions,[128] or military uses of the sea during peacetime, including military activities, exercises or manoeuvres or the deployment of military installations in the EEZ.[129] On the other hand, there are issues which are of an enduring nature such as the persistent issue of creeping Coastal State jurisdiction already addressed above, or the still largely unsettled ambiguity in the operation of Part V of the LOSC including the uncertainty over the juridical nature of the EEZ as a *sui generis* and *sui juris* maritime zone.[130] These are very important issues but cannot be addressed in detail in this chapter. However, it can be safely assumed that widespread divergence in State practice will remain, and even the possibility of new norms or rules of international law emerging to address these challenges.

Conclusion

The list of contemporary and emerging issues that need to be dealt with by Coastal States will continue to grow both in complexity and urgency. Whilst the relevance of the LOSC as a framework instrument dealing with all ocean-related issues will remain, it cannot be denied that many of these issues were not contemplated or discussed in detail at the time the LOSC was negotiated. Some of these issues include bioprospecting of marine genetic resources, the deployment of offshore wind farms for energy development, even the pressing concern over the pivotal role of the oceans in climatic processes. In addition, new international agreements, rules and standards are now in place which expands and supplements many of the obligations of Coastal States under the LOSC. In order to ensure safety of ships and navigation, it is crucial that Coastal States participate, and effectively implement these relevant international agreements alongside their obligations under the LOSC.

Whilst the law of the sea remains one of the most stable fields of international law, radical progress in maritime technology and the multiplicity and in fact overlapping jurisdictional competencies of international treaties and organisations have all made maritime regulation and enforcement quite complex. Cooperative initiatives to address various maritime security threats will need to be undertaken at a multilateral level and following an integrated approach. However, it can be securely asserted that maritime security will remain a global priority and the role of the Coastal State in maritime regulation and enforcement will remain important.

Notes

1 Patricia Birnie and Alan Boyle, *International and the Environment* (Oxford University Press, 1992) 253.
2 Doris Konig, 'The Enforcement of the International Law of the Sea by Coastal and Port States' (2002) 62 *ZaoRV* 1, 2–3.
3 *United Nations Convention on the Law of the Sea*, opened for signature 10 December 1982, 1833 UNTS 3 (entered into force 16 November 1994). Hereinafter, LOSC.
4 Myron Nordquist (ed), *United Nations Convention on the Law of the Sea 1982: A Commentary* (Martinus Nijhoff, 1985) Volume I, 11.
5 Rene-Jean Dupuy Daniel Vignes, *A Handbook on the New Law of the Sea* (Martinus Nijhoff, 1991) 60–61; Donald Rothwell and Tim Stephens, *The International Law of the Sea* (Hart Publishing, 2010) 22.

6 These include, the LOSC, the *1958 Convention on the Territorial Sea and the Contiguous Zone*, the *1958 Convention on the High Seas*, the *1958 Convention on the Continental Shelf*, among others.
7 These include the *1974 International Convention for the Safety of Life at Sea* (SOLAS), and subsequent Amendments and Protocols, the *1969 International Convention on Tonnage Measurement of Ships*; the *1972 International Convention on the International Regulations for Prevention Collision at Sea* with subsequent Amendments; the *1978 International Convention on Standards of Training, Certification and Watching for Seafarers* (STCW), including the 1995 and 2010 amendments; the *1979 International Convention on Maritime Search and Rescue* (SAR), among others.
8 The most important of which include, the *International Convention for the Prevention of Pollution from Ships* (MARPOL) and subsequent protocols and amendments; the *1969 International Convention Relating to Intervention on the High Seas in Cases of Oil Pollution Casualties* (INTERVENTION), the *1972 Convention on the Prevention of Marine Pollution by Dumping of Wastes and Other Matter* (LC), 1972 (and the 1996 London Protocol), the *1990 International Convention on Oil Pollution Preparedness, Response and Co-operation* (OPRC), *2000 Protocol on Preparedness, Response and Co-operation to pollution Incidents by Hazardous and Noxious Substances* (OPRC-HNS Protocol), the *2001 International Convention on the Control of Harmful Anti-fouling Systems on Ships* (AFS), the *2004 International Convention for the Control and Management of Ships' Ballast Water and Sediments*, and the *2009 Hong Kong International Convention for the Safe and Environmentally Sound Recycling of Ships*, among others.
9 Robin Churchill and Vaughan Lowe, *The Law of the Sea* (Manchester University Press, 1999) 23.
10 Rothwell and Stephens, above n 5, 27. This gradual encroachment or assertion of jurisdiction over their adjacent maritime domain has been referred to as 'creeping jurisdiction' or 'territorialisation' of the oceans. See for example, Barbara Kwiatkowska, 'Creeping jurisdiction beyond 200 miles in the light of the 1982 Law of the Sea Convention and state practice' (1991) 22 *Ocean Development & International Law* 153–187, and Stuart Kaye, 'Freedom of Navigation in a Post 9/11 World: Security and Creeping Jurisdiction' in David Freestone, Richard Barnes and David M. Ong (eds), *The Law of the Sea: Progress and Prospects* (Oxford University Press, 2006), 347–364.
11 Erik Jaap Molenaar, *Coastal State Jurisdiction over Vessel-Source Pollution* (Kluwer Law International, 1998) 30.
12 Myron Nordquist (ed), *United Nations Convention on the Law of the Sea 1982: A Commentary* (Martinus Nijhoff, 1985) Volume VII, 126.
13 Article 92 (1), LOSC.
14 Article 218, LOSC. See generally, George Kasoulides, *Port State Control and Jurisdiction: Evolution of the Port State Regime* (Martinus Nijhoff, 1993).
15 Article 2, LOSC. See also, Articles 21, 24, 25 and 30, on the powers of the Coastal State in the territorial sea; see Article 56, on the rights, jurisdiction and duties of the Coastal State in the EEZ; see Article 77, on the rights of the Coastal State over the continental shelf; see Article 142, on the rights and legitimate interests of Coastal States over the Area; and Articles 220 and 248, on the enforcement powers of the Coastal State for the protection of the marine environment.
16 Christopher P. Moorandian, 'Protecting "Sovereign Rights": The Case for Increased Coastal State Jurisdiction over Vessel-Source Pollution in the Exclusive Economic Zone' (2002) 82 *Boston University Law Review* 767, 773–774.
17 Ian Brownlie, *Principles of Public International Law* (Oxford University Press, Seventh Edition, 2008) 105.
18 Article 2, LOSC.
19 Haijiang Yang, *Jurisdiction of the Coastal State over Foreign Merchant Ships in Internal Waters and the Territorial Sea* (Springer, 2006) 112.
20 Erik Jaap Molenaar, *Coastal State Jurisdiction over Vessel-Source Pollution* (Kluwer Law International, 1998) 92–93.
21 Kasoulides, above n 14, 115.
22 Camille Goodman, 'The Regime for Flag State Responsibility in International Fisheries Law – Effective Fact, Creative Fiction, or Further Work Required' (2009) 23 *Australia and New Zealand Maritime Law Journal* 157, 160.
23 Yang, above n 19, 38–39.
24 Churchill and Lowe, above n 9, 61.
25 Article 8 (1), LOSC. Churchill and Lowe clarify that foreign ships may seeks access to international rivers which flow through the territory or constitute the boundary of more than one State. Churchill and Lowe, above n 9, 64.

26 Yang, above n 19, 90.
27 Churchill and Lowe, above n 9, 61.
28 Kasoulides, above n 14, 20–21.
29 Kasoulides, above n 14, 21.
30 Article 25(2), 211 (3) and 255, LOSC.
31 Also in Article 5(2), *Convention on the Territorial Sea and the Contiguous Zone*, opened for signature 29 April 1958, 516 UNTS 205 (entered into force 10 September 1964).
32 Kasoulides, above n 14, 23.
33 Churchill and Lowe, above n 9, 65. The LOSC exempts sovereign immune vessels from the legal regime of jurisdiction over vessel-source pollution (Article 236, LOSC). However, the Flag State of sovereign immune vessels may be held liable for any loss or damage to Coastal States (Articles 31, 42(5) and 54).
34 Churchill and Lowe, above n 9, 66; Kasoulides, above n 14, 23–26; Yang, above n 19, 90–97.
35 Churchill and Lowe, above n 9, 67.
36 Churchill and Lowe, above n 9, 67. See also, Articles 2 and 3, *International Convention on Arrest of Ships*, opened for signature 12 March 1999, 2801 UNTS Doc. A/CONF.188.6 (entered into force 14 September 201), for the conditions and qualifications where a ship may be arrested.
37 Article 220 (1), LOSC.
38 Yang, above n 19, 112.
39 Article 2, LOSC. Brownlie, above n 17, 186. Churchill and Lowe, above n 9, 95.
40 Yang opines that 'coastal States can in principle adopt rules in respect of any activities and matters of foreign ships in the territorial sea, as long as there is no express prohibition in international law.' Yang, above n 19, 186.
41 Rothwell and Stephens, above n 5, 70.
42 Yang, above n 19, 185.
43 Article 17, LOSC.
44 Yoshifumi Tanaka, *The International Law of the Sea* (Cambridge University Press, 2012) 85.
45 Articles 17 to 26, LOSC.
46 Article 21, LOSC.
47 Article 21(3), LOSC.
48 Article 21(2), LOSC.
49 Article 25(1), LOSC.
50 See Churchill and Lowe, above n 9, 85.
51 Article 19(2), LOSC.
52 Churchill and Lowe, above n 9, 85.
53 Churchill and Lowe, above n 9, 87.
54 Article 24(1), LOSC.
55 Article 18(2), LOSC.
56 Article 26, LOSC.
57 Article 25(3), LOSC.
58 Article 22 (1), LOSC.
59 Article 22(2), LOSC.
60 Article 23, LOSC.
61 Article 27(1), LOSC.
62 Article 28, LOSC.
63 Article 32, LOSC.
64 Article 30, LOSC.
65 Article 31, LOSC.
66 Article 49, LOSC.
67 Article 51(1), LOSC. See also Article 47(6), LOSC.
68 Article 51(2), LOSC.
69 Article 52(1), LOSC.
70 Article 52(2), LOSC.
71 Article 52(1), LOSC.
72 Article 53, LOSC.
73 Article 53(12), LOSC.

74 Churchill and Lowe, above n 9, 127–128, who opine that this 'seems anomalous, and undesirable, and may possibly be an oversight in drafting.'
75 Rothwell and Stephens, above n 5, 426.
76 Article 33(1)(a), LOSC.
77 Article 33 (1)(b), LOSC.
78 Rothwell and Stephens, above n 5, 427.
79 Articles 58(1) and 87, LOSC.
80 Churchill and Lowe, above n 9, 138.
81 Rothwell and Stephens, above n 5, 427.
82 Rothwell and Stephens, above n 5, 428.
83 Rothwell and Stephens, above n 5, 428.
84 Article 56(1) and 57, LOSC.
85 Article 56(1)(a), LOSC.
86 Article 58(1), LOSC. See Churchill and Lowe, above n 9, 170–174.
87 Article 55, LOSC.
88 Churchill and Lowe, above n 9, 166.
89 Article 56(2), LOSC.
90 Article 56(1)(b)(iii), LOSC.
91 Churchill and Lowe, above n 9, 169.
92 Articles 208 and 214, LOSC.
93 Articles 210(5) and 216, LOSC.
94 Articles 211(5–6), 220, 234, LOSC.
95 Rothwell and Stephens, above n 5, 92.
96 Article 224, LOSC.
97 Article 232, LOSC.
98 Article 56(1)(b)(i) and Article 60, LOSC.
99 Article 56(1)(b)(ii), LOSC.
100 Article 246, LOSC.
101 Article 58(1) in relation to Article 87, LOSC.
102 Article 73(1), LOSC.
103 Article 73(2), LOSC.
104 Erik Franckx, 'The 200-mile Limit: Between Creeping Jurisdiction and Creeping Common Heritage?' (2007) 3 *George Washington International Law Review* 467, 476.
105 Rothwell and Stephens, above n 5, 94.
106 Rothwell and Stephens, above n 5, 95.
107 Churchill and Lowe, above n 9, 203.
108 Articles 87 and 89, LOSC.
109 Churchill and Lowe, above n 9, 204.
110 Article 90, LOSC.
111 Article 87(2), LOSC; Churchill and Lowe, above n 9, 206.
112 Article 92(1), LOSC.
113 Article 100, LOSC.
114 Article 109, LOSC.
115 Article 108, LOSC.
116 Article 99, LOSC.
117 Churchill and Lowe, above n 9, 213–214.
118 Article 111, LOSC.
119 Article 111 (3), LOSC.
120 Churchill and Lowe, above n 9, 215.
121 Article 221, LOSC.
122 Churchill and Lowe, above n 9, 216–217.
123 Churchill and Lowe, above n 9, 218–219.
124 See for instance, discussion of these issues in United Nations General Assembly, Oceans and the law of the sea Report of the Secretary-General, A/69/71/Add.1, 1 September 2014.
125 Articles 16 (2), 47 (9), 75 (2) and 84 (2), LOSC. See also Articles 21 (3) and 42 (3), LOSC.

126 United Nations General Assembly, Oceans and the law of the sea Report of the Secretary-General, A/69/71/Add.1, 1 September 2014, para. 14.
127 See for example, Warwick Gullett and Clive Schofield, 'Pushing the Limits of the Law of the Sea Convention: Australia and French Cooperative Surveillance and Enforcement in the Southern Ocean' (2007) 22 *International Journal of Marine and Coastal Law* 545.
128 Rothwell and Stephens, above n 5, 418–421.
129 Churchill and Lowe, above n 9, 421–430.
130 Rothwell and Stephens, above n 5, 97.

6
The Role of Port States

Rosemary Rayfuse

Introduction

It is often said that a vessel is subject only to the jurisdiction of its flag state. Indeed, traditionally, exclusivity of flag state jurisdiction has been considered a fundamental principle of the law of the sea. However, historically the principle has always been tempered by the ascription of certain jurisdictional rights to other states. As now articulated in the Law of the Sea Convention (LOSC),[1] the exclusivity of flag state jurisdiction is tempered by the jurisdictional rights given to coastal states, which enjoy full sovereignty, including enforcement jurisdiction, in their internal waters and, subject to the right of innocent passage, within their territorial sea.[2] Beyond the territorial sea and within the contiguous zone, coastal states may exercise the control necessary to prevent infringements of their customs, fiscal immigration or sanitary laws by inbound vessels. Additionally, within the exclusive economic zone (EEZ) coastal states enjoy sovereign rights over, and enforcement jurisdiction in respect of, the exploration and exploitation of the living and non-living natural resources of the EEZ.[3] Likewise, coastal states enjoy a measure of enforcement jurisdiction in respect of certain activities on the extended continental shelf.[4]

While it is possible to conceive of a coastal state that is not a port state, by definition, in the law of the sea context, all port states are coastal states. They thus enjoy the rights associated with coastal state jurisdiction. However, in addition to coastal state jurisdiction, port states have historically enjoyed certain jurisdictional rights over foreign flagged vessels within their ports derived from their sovereignty over their territory and internal waters. Whether a port state exercised that jurisdiction was a matter for the port state to determine and, in practice, they rarely did so except in cases where the peace and tranquillity of the port had been disturbed.[5] Today, however, these jurisdictional rights have been parlayed into the concepts of 'port state control' and 'port state enforcement' whereby port states are not merely entitled, but may even be obliged, to adopt measures aimed at ensuring compliance by foreign-flagged vessels with both national and international regulatory efforts. Thus the exclusivity of flag state jurisdiction is also increasingly tempered by port state jurisdiction.

The rationale for enlisting port states in support of maritime regulation and enforcement is simple. As Molenaar puts it, ports are 'an obvious place to verify if visiting foreign ships are in compliance with certain types of national or international technical standards or if they have engaged in illegal behaviour in the port state's own maritime zones, in the maritime zones of other states or on the high seas. The costs and difficulties of enforcement at sea also mean that, despite its shortcomings, in-port enforcement is often the preferable or, perhaps, the only option.[6] Port state jurisdiction is thus an important complement and essential adjunct to flag state jurisdiction, particularly in situations where a flag state, for whatever reasons, is either unwilling or unable to effectively control its vessels.

This chapter examines the rights and responsibilities of port states to enforce international maritime standards, particularly in the areas of marine pollution, safety of life at sea and international fisheries law. It begins with a discussion of the concept of port state jurisdiction and then discusses the development of the concepts of port state control and port state enforcement. It then examines the manner in which the international community has sought to ensure the efficacy of port state jurisdiction through developing the role of port states in the shipping and high seas fishing contexts, before concluding with some thoughts on the future of port state control and enforcement.

Port state jurisdiction

Port state jurisdiction refers to the jurisdiction a state may exercise over vessels visiting its ports. It is based, first and foremost, on the principle of territoriality. When in port, a vessel is within the territory of the port state and hence subject to its jurisdiction. Pre-dating the concept of coastal state jurisdiction, since ancient times it has been generally accepted that a state is entitled to exercise jurisdiction over a foreign merchant ship lying in its port and over persons and goods on board.[7]

Traditionally, the concerns of port states, over which they would exercise their jurisdiction, related to the safety and welfare of the state such as health and quarantine requirements as well as immigration and security restrictions.[8] Economic and commercial factors were also relevant, with states seeking to reap the advantages of customs duties and other fees collected from vessels visiting their ports. However, in general, it was the cargo and persons on board rather than the vessel per se that the port authorities were interested in.[9] Thus, quarantine and customs regulations applying to incoming vessels were commonplace for centuries while regulations relating to the safety of vessels, crews and passengers only started to emerge in the 19th century.

Historically, port state jurisdiction was exercised over activities taking place within only a narrow strip of coastal waters. Today port states exercise jurisdiction in respect of behaviour that takes place within the maritime zones adhering to the territory of the state: internal waters, archipelagic waters, and the territorial sea. Moreover, by virtue of the sovereign rights afforded to coastal states over the exclusive economic zone and the continental shelf by the LOSC, port state jurisdiction can now also be exercised over certain events occurring within these areas. In this case the jurisdiction is 'quasi-territorial' in nature. In addition, in certain circumstances, port states can now exercise jurisdiction over a vessel in respect of events occurring in areas beyond national jurisdiction or in areas under the jurisdiction of another state. In such cases, jurisdiction is based on the principle of extra-territoriality and is dependent on the existence of treaty rights or other customary jurisdictional rules such as the principle of universal jurisdiction.

Of course, in order to physically exercise port state jurisdiction it is first necessary for a vessel to be in port. Whether all vessels of all states have a right of entry into the maritime ports of all states has been a much debated issue throughout the history of the law of the sea. A basic presumption, which arises as a natural and necessary corollary of the freedom of the seas, is that the ports of a state are open to all. However, extensive analyses of state practice and *opinio juris* confirm that in customary international law no general right of access exists.[10] As noted by the International Court of Justice in the *Nicaragua* case, 'by virtue of its sovereignty . . . the coastal state may regulate access to its ports'.[11] Port states are therefore entitled to exclude foreign vessels from entering their ports subject only to exception in situations of distress (*force majeure*) or in situations specifically agreed to in treaties.[12] Port states are also free to set conditions for port access and may nominate ports for use by foreign vessels or even close their ports entirely to protect their interests.[13] The right of exit is likewise subject to the right of the port state to condition departure and to arrest vessels in port for breaches of its laws, in accordance with its normal legal processes.[14] As confirmed by the International Tribunal for the Law of the Sea (ITLOS) in the *MV Louisa* case, the freedom of navigation does not give a vessel 'a right to leave the port and gain access to the high seas notwithstanding its detention in the context of legal proceedings against it'.[15]

As Marten puts it, 'there is a potentially limitless number of policies that port states may devise and translate into laws impacting on international shipping. Some of these will be expressly directed at foreign vessels, while others will have no specifically maritime character, but be drafted in such a way that foreign vessels fall within their scope'.[16] Port state jurisdiction is not, however, unlimited. Maintenance of the public order of the oceans, premised as it is on the concepts of freedom of navigation and flag state jurisdiction, presupposes that restriction of access to ports will be done on a non-discriminatory basis and will only be done in respect of interests recognized by the international community as appertaining either generally or specifically to the port state.[17] Generally recognized interests include the customary rights to safeguard peace, security and the good order of the state through the adoption and enforcement of laws pertaining to subjects such as health, immigration, customs and revenue and security, or for the purposes of displaying political displeasure.[18] Specific interests include the rights and duties accepted by states in treaties to which they are party. In this case, port states may implement standards into their domestic legislation to which they have agreed in a treaty thereby making those treaty standards a condition of access to their ports. In the shipping context, these interests largely fall within the remit of the International Maritime Organization (IMO) relating to 'maritime safety, efficiency of navigation and prevention and control of marine pollution from ships'[19] and the International Labour Organization (ILO) relating to crew working conditions. In the high seas fisheries context, expression of the collective interests of states is embodied in the United Nations Fish Stocks Agreement[20] (FSA), the treaties adopted under the auspices of the Food and Agriculture Organization (FAO), and the treaties establishing regional fisheries management organizations (RFMOs) with competence to adopt conservation and management measures for high seas fisheries.

The internationally agreed standards embodied in these treaties are, however, generally considered only minimum standards; the lowest common denominator on which all states parties could agree.[21] Unless otherwise prohibited by treaty, a port state remains free to exercise its residual jurisdiction to adopt more stringent measures as a condition of access to its ports.[22] In the environmental context well known examples include the unilateral adoption by the United States of double hull requirements for oil tankers in the light of the *Exxon Valdez* disaster,[23] and the controversial adoption by Australia of a compulsory pilotage regime for the Torres Strait, the failure to comply with which would result in prosecution and non-custodial penalties against a vessel when next in port in Australia.[24] In the high seas fisheries context, a number of states have adopted legislation unilaterally prohibiting foreign vessels from landing in their ports catches taken in high seas fisheries.[25]

This is not to suggest that all unilateral assertions of port state jurisdiction have gone uncontested. Staunch protests from the United States, Singapore and others resulted in Australia watering down the compulsory pilotage requirement in the Torres Strait to refer only to a 'risk' of prosecution and, in fact, no prosecution has even been taken pursuant to the measure.[26] In the *EC-Chile Swordfish case*[27] the EC (as it then was) objected to Chile's unilateral application of its domestic fisheries regulations and denial of port access to Spanish vessels fishing for swordfish in the high seas of the Southeast Pacific. At issue was the question of whether these particular access denials fell foul of the GATT/WTO provisions (Articles V(3) and IX) regarding freedom of transit and the prohibition of arbitrary or discriminatory trade restrictions. The issue was left unresolved when the proceedings were suspended and eventually terminated. In a similar vein, the issue was again left unresolved in 2013 when Denmark (in respect of the Faroe Islands) instituted proceedings in the WTO against the EU contesting the closure of EU ports to Faroese vessels and various other economic measures as being inconsistent with the GATT.[28] The proceedings were terminated when agreement was reached by the parties on the underlying irritant issue of the allocation of Atlanto-Scandian herring.

Nevertheless, while the prevailing preference may be to discourage unilateralism,[29] there is no doubt, as Boyle notes, that 'some of the most important developments in the law of the sea since 1945 have been the product of unilateral actions by a single state or a small group of states'.[30] These developments have taken shape in the adoption of treaties embodying not only internationally agreed standards but also internationally agreed mechanisms for their enforcement. It is through this medium that port state jurisdiction has been developing, not to replace or challenge, but rather to supplement traditional flag state jurisdiction.

The development of the concept of port state control

A natural corollary of the right to exercise jurisdiction is the right not to exercise jurisdiction. The lucrative nature of port servicing facilities and the dictates of reciprocity and friendly relations have provided ample excuse for reluctance on the part of many states to exercise their jurisdiction over vessels in port for the purpose of enforcing internationally agreed standards. The concept of port state control has thus developed as the principal mechanism to ensure the exercise of port state jurisdiction in support of internationally agreed shipping standards and conservation and management measures relating to high seas fisheries.

The notion of empowering and encouraging, indeed obliging, port states to act in support of specific treaty obligations emerged as a response to growing labour and environmental awareness and the need to deal with substandard shipping and the problem of flags of convenience.[31] In particular, during the 1960s and 1970s, measures providing for port state control, particularly aimed at reducing vessel source pollution, were incorporated into a number of conventions adopted by the IMO and the ILO relating, *inter alia*, to ship design, construction and crewing conditions, safety of life at sea, operating procedures and marine pollution.[32] Early conventions like that on the Safety of Life at Sea (SOLAS),[33] required flag states to issue certificates to their ships stating that they complied with the agreed standards. Port states were then entitled to verify that the certificate was valid and that the condition of the vessel substantially accorded with the particulars stated in the certificate. Any discrepancy was to be reported to the flag state. Later conventions such as MARPOL[34] allowed for port state verification of certificates but any deficiencies were to be reported to the flag state unless there were clear grounds for believing that the conditions on board the vessel did not conform with the certificate. In such a case the port state was empowered to prevent the vessel from sailing until necessary repair work had been carried out. Where evidence of a pollution violation at sea was found it was to be sent to the flag state which remained responsible for any prosecution.[35] In short, these conventions allowed for port states to inspect, require rectification and, thereby, 'control' the condition of ships visiting their ports. These conventions did not, however, allow the port state to take enforcement action in respect of breaches. Powers of enforcement and sanction remained with the flag state.[36]

When the LOSC was adopted in 1982 the practice developed in these other treaty regimes was recognized and essentially incorporated into its provisions. Articles 94(3)-(5) of the LOSC require flag states to adopt, and enforce, legislation relating to construction, equipment, seaworthiness, and crewing standards (commonly referred to as construction, design, equipment and manning, or CDEM, standards) and labour standards, which conform with the 'generally accepted international regulations, procedures and practices' adopted in the IMO and ILO Conventions. To ensure their observance, where a port state has reason to believe these rules have been violated, pursuant to Article 95(6), it may report this to the flag state which is then obliged to investigate and, if appropriate, take action to remedy the situation. Ultimate prosecutorial discretion is, however, left to the flag state with no sanction should it fail to act.

The LOSC goes even further in respect of pollution offences by requiring states to adopt legislation relating to dumping and vessel source pollution which must 'at least have the same effect as that of generally accepted international standards established through competent international organizations or diplomatic conference'.[37] In doing so the LOSC implicitly reinforces the customary position regarding port state jurisdiction by recognizing the right of port states to adopt particular requirements for the prevention, reduction and control of pollution of the marine environment, over and above any generally accepted international standards, as a condition for entry into their ports or internal waters.[38] In addition, Article 219 allows, indeed requires, port states to prevent foreign-flagged vessels within their ports from sailing when those vessels are in violation of applicable international rules and standards relating to seaworthiness and constitute a threat to the marine environment. Such vessels are only to be allowed to proceed to the nearest shipyard for repair and removal of the causes of the violation.

The rationale for the difference in treatment between CDEM and environmental standards is based on the nature and character of shipping. CDEM standards are regarded as 'static' standards that follow a ship throughout its voyage. Compliance with different standards in every state through whose waters a vessel sails would place unduly complicated and expensive burdens on shipping. Global standardization on the basis of 'generally accepted international regulations, procedures and practices' therefore assures the unhindered movement of shipping.[39] Environmental protection requirements, however, vary depending on physical conditions and location. Thus while flag states may be obliged to adopt regulations that, at a minimum, reflect internationally agreed standards, they may also be obliged to comply with particular regulations adopted by the port state in its capacity as a coastal state.

Despite the customary right of port states to control access to their ports, the development of the concept of port state control has not been entirely uncontroversial. Where flag states are not party to the relevant international conventions, it could be argued that port state attempts to enforce domestic legislation incorporating those convention provisions violates the *pacta tertiis* rule whereby a treaty is binding only on its parties. However, in truth, any such violation is illusory as it is not the convention being enforced but rather the domestic law of the port state.[40] A more fundamental objection relates to the extent of 'general acceptance' of the 'generally accepted' international rules and standards being invoked and the criteria by which this 'general acceptance' is to be judged. Where interested states have not participated in the development of, or have otherwise objected to, the application of these standards and rules, the extent of their acceptance and the ability to enforce them may be in doubt.[41] Nevertheless, while this concern may affect the application of port state control in particular circumstances, it has not affected the spread of the concept into the broader context of the law of the sea, in particular, in the high seas fisheries context.

There is no mention of the concept of port state control in Articles 116–119 of the LOSC which deal with high seas fishing. By the 1990s, however, the potential promise of the exercise of port state jurisdiction to assist in the fight against illegal, unreported and unregulated (IUU) fishing on the high seas had not gone unnoticed. In the fisheries context, the concept of port state control appears to have made its specific debut in the 1989 Convention for the Prohibition of Fishing with Long Drift-nets in the South Pacific[42] (the Wellington Convention). Article 3(2) of the Convention provides for both restriction of access to ports and to use of service facilities in the ports of parties for foreign-flagged vessels involved in drift-net fishing. In the global context, port state control was not included in the original draft text of the FAO Compliance Agreement,[43] an omission which attracted some criticism and was partially rectified.[44] Article V(2) of the Compliance Agreement requires a port state to promptly notify a flag state when a fishing vessel is voluntarily within its ports and it has reasonable grounds for believing that the fishing vessel has been used for an activity that undermines the effectiveness of international conservation and management measures. Arrangements regarding investigatory measures are to be made between the two states although in the absence of such arrangements, notification remains the only avenue of redress.

Despite protests from a number of distant water fishing states that port state control could not be applied outside the CDEM and pollution contexts provided for in the LOSC,[45] port state measures were specifically provided for in the FSA when it was adopted in 1995. Pursuant to Article 23 port states have both the right and the duty, on a non-discriminatory basis, to 'take measures to promote the effectiveness of subregional, regional, and global conservation and management measures'. When vessels are voluntarily within its ports, the port state may, *inter alia*, inspect documents, fishing gear and catches. Port states may also adopt regulations prohibiting landings and transshipments where it has been established that the catch has been taken on the high seas in violation of subregional, regional or global conservation and management measures on the high seas. Importantly, these powers are not dependent on prior agreement with the flag state.

In truth, these provisions may reflect nothing more than the customary position that port states are free to adopt conditions for port ingress and egress and to close their ports to foreign vessels subject to any treaty obligations not to. However, when adopted into the FSA, international law had not yet specifically addressed the right of port state control in support of high seas fisheries conservation and management measures and the extent of that right was unclear.[46] In particular, the provision allowing states to prohibit landings and transshipments was seen by some states as going far beyond the customary right to control access. However, as Orrego Vicuña notes, Article 23 must be read as merely supplementary to, and not a derogation from, the recognized right of states to control access to their ports.[47]

Port state control vs port state enforcement

As Kasoulides points out, implementation of international conventions through port state control 'does not imply an extension of the port state's enforcement authority over violations on the high seas or in foreign coastal waters' but only control over the various aspects covered in the conventions such as ships and their equipment, discharge at sea, crew competence and working conditions. 'The rectification of these conditions,' he says, 'is well within the jurisdiction of the port state' since it relates to matters occurring while a vessel is 'present' in the port state's waters.[48] In other words, the port state is only enforcing domestic legislation which just happens to incorporate internationally agreed standards in respect of breaches of that legislation committed by non-nationals that have occurred within its territory.

Port state enforcement, however, refers to the power of the port state not only to police and control but also to exercise judicial or administrative jurisdiction to prosecute and punish non-compliance by foreign-flagged vessels.[49] While historically the port state, has enjoyed enforcement powers in respect of violations occurring within its waters, no right of sanction has applied in respect of activities that took place on the high seas or within the maritime zones of other states before a vessel entered a port state's waters. However, with the adoption of the LOSC, international law specifically recognized a right of port state enforcement in respect of vessel source pollution occurring on the high seas and in the maritime zones of other states.

The provision for port state enforcement in respect of high seas activities is found in Article 218 of the LOSC which provides that where a vessel is voluntarily in a port the port state may not only investigate but may also institute proceedings in respect of any discharge from that vessel which has occurred outside the area of waters under the port state's jurisdiction in violation of applicable international rules and standards. In other words, the port state is exercising extra-territorial universal jurisdiction to enforce internationally agreed standards in respect of breaches of international standards committed by foreign-flagged vessels that occurred outside its territory. The rationale for port state enforcement in this context rests on the acceptance that environmental degradation is contrary to the interests – both political and economic – of all states. Admittedly primary competence for environmental protection has been given to coastal states through the medium of the EEZ. Nevertheless, as Article 218 makes clear, states also recognize the need for regulation of activities on the high seas and within the waters of other states in order to make this protection wholly effective. Where such regulation cannot or will not be effected by flag states, port states may intervene. The collective effect of this is to create a new legal basis for port state enforcement in response to what was, and remains, a pressing problem,[50] although it should be noted that the right remains subject to the right of flag state pre-emption provided for in Article 228.

Regarded as a radical development when the LOSC was adopted, whether port state enforcement could be extended to situations involving the violation of conservation and management measures adopted by regional fisheries management organizations (RFMOs) in respect of high seas fisheries was one of the most contentious issues during the FSA negotiations.[51] The Revised Negotiating Text prepared by the Chairman of the negotiations at the third session would have allowed port state detention pending flag state action.[52] In the end, however, the FSA very specifically avoided use of the term 'port state enforcement' or reference to the power of the port state to detain or prosecute the vessel.[53] The best that could be achieved was Article 23 which, as noted above, confirms both the right and the duty of port states to 'take measures in accordance with international law, to promote the effectiveness of subregional, regional and global conservation and management measures', but does not assist in delineating what the relevant internationally lawful measures might be. Guidance is provided by allowing that port states may inspect documents and catch when foreign fishing vessels are voluntarily within their ports and may adopt regulations prohibiting landings and transshipments of fish that has been taken in a manner which undermines the effectiveness of regional, subregional or global conservation and management measures on the high seas. However, beyond that, the nature and scope of the measures permitted is unclear. As noted by the International Court of Justice (ICJ) in the *Fisheries Jurisdiction* case (Spain v Canada),[54] the terminology of 'measures' is 'descriptive not normative'. It refers to any act, step or proceeding and 'imposes no particular limit on [the measures'] material content or on the aim pursued thereby'.[55] Thus, it should be sufficient that the purpose of the measure is to promote the effectiveness of regional, subregional or global conservation and management measures and that it is taken in accordance with international law.[56] In this respect it is important to note the savings clause in Article 23(4) by which nothing in Article 23 affects the exercise by port states of their sovereign rights under international law. In other words, the residual jurisdiction of a port state to take stricter measures remains.

Clearly, the FSA does not settle the issue of the possibility of port state detention and sanction against foreign-flagged vessels for violations of conservation and management measures adopted by RFMOs. As suggested by Orrego Vicuña, the inclusion of the term '*inter alia*' in Article 23 in referring to the actions a port state may take does appear to leave open the possibility of detention and prosecution.[57] This interpretation is reinforced by reference to the negotiating history of the LOSC during which the Drafting Committee took the position that 'adopt' should be used to refer to 'laws' while 'take' should refer to 'measures'.[58] This has been interpreted by the ICJ as meaning that the obligation to 'take' measures is broader than the obligation merely to 'adopt' and also encompasses the obligation to enforce those measures.[59] However, in 2003 the FAO Expert Consultation to Review Port States Measures to Combat Illegal, Unreported and Unregulated Fishing[60] expressly excluded the possibility of detention of vessels although it did consider refusal of a right of egress pending consultation with the flag state to be an appropriate action. The 2009 FAO Agreement on Port States Measures to Prevent, Deter and Eliminate Illegal, Unreported and Unregulated Fishing[61] (PSM Agreement) retreats even further from the concept providing only for an obligation to deny port entry or to deny use of port facilities and services.[62] Admittedly, nothing in the PSM Agreement prevents the port state from taking additional measures that are in conformity with international law.[63] Moreover, it is always open to a port state to request the cooperation of a flag state, or a flag state the cooperation of a port state, in allowing the port state to sanction. However, it would seem that international law does not yet recognize a general right of port state enforcement in the high seas fisheries context.[64] As Molenaar puts it 'it is unfortunate that an opportunity was missed to progressively develop international law by explicitly empowering port states to impose punitive measures modelled on Article 218 of the LOSC'.[65]

Making port state control effective

Today many of the IMO technical conventions contain provisions for ships to be inspected when they visit foreign ports in order to ensure that they meet IMO requirements[66] and many RFMOs have adopted port control schemes. Even allowing, however, for the possibility of control measures being adopted and implemented by individual port states it is clear that a harmonized regional or global approach to the cooperative exercise of port state control is necessary in order to avoid the problem of 'port hopping' to 'ports of convenience' and to enhance uniformity and consistency in the struggle against 'substandard ships' and IUU fishing. Various mechanisms have therefore been developed to ensure the cooperative exercise of port state control to enforce commonly agreed standards.

Shipping

In the shipping context, the first such regional mechanism was developed in Europe largely in response to the grounding of the *Amoco Cadiz* and the belief that international shipping was not complying with internationally accepted safety standards. The Hague Memorandum on Port State Control, which was adopted in 1978,[67] provided for surveillance of ships in port to verify compliance with the requirements of the various IMO, ILO and other international agreements listed in its Preamble, and to ensure on-board conditions were not hazardous to health or safety.[68] The Hague Memorandum was replaced in 1982 by the more stringent and more expansive Paris Memorandum of Understanding on Port State Control (the Paris MOU)[69] which calls for the inspection of 25% of all foreign merchant ships calling at each European port on a non-favoured basis to ensure compliance with internationally accepted pollution, design, construction and crewing, health and safety standards. In other words, all vessels, whether flying the flag of parties to these agreements or not, are subject to the possibility of inspection and, ultimately, detention for failure to comply with these recognized international standards.

The Paris MOU was a cooperative agreement between port administrators. While certainly not a failure, it was not the total success its supporters would have liked[70] and it was eventually supplemented by the adoption of the legally-binding EC Directive on Port State Control which came into force on 1 July 1996.[71] Port state control in Europe is now based on mandatory inspection requirements supported by sophisticated IT tools for selecting ships to be inspected and assessing their risk profile on a daily basis. MOUs based on the Paris MOU model have been adopted in Latin America,[72] the Asia Pacific (the Tokyo MOU),[73] the Caribbean,[74] the Mediterranean,[75] the Indian Ocean,[76] West and Central Africa,[77] the Black Sea[78] and the Persian Gulf.[79] However, in these regions, port state control is still based on these non-binding administrative coordination arrangements which merely provide some target as to the percentage of ships that should be inspected.

Taken together these port state control schemes provide near global coverage. However, as Molenaar notes, 'mere geographical coverage' does not necessarily mean that all schemes achieve the same levels of performance.[80] In particular performance in some regions has been affected by a lack of alacrity on the part of the port states in legislatively adopting and physically implementing the underlying treaty obligations.[81] Whether a result of inability or unwillingness on the part of the port state, the result is the same; it encourages port-hopping and undermines efforts to eliminate sub-standard shipping. Efforts to enhance the coordinated implementation of these MOUs have therefore been pursued in the IMO through, for example, the establishment of international harmonized minimum standards for the conduct of port state control.[82] Bi-annual workshops for Secretariats and Database Managers of the regional MOUs provide a forum for the exchange of information thereby facilitating harmonized approaches.[83] Further enhancement of inter-MOU cooperation is provided by agreements on joint inspection efforts and the reciprocal granting of observer status.[84]

Fishing

In the fisheries context, the adoption of port control schemes by RFMOs is a more recent practice. With the exception of the post-FSA agreements, provisions calling for the establishment of port control schemes are not generally found in the constituent treaties of RFMOs. This led to the argument articulated by Japan in the International Commission on the Conservation of Atlantic Tunas (ICCAT) that absent a treaty obligation to do so, no such scheme can be adopted.[85] Nevertheless, the right of an RFMO to adopt and the obligation of contracting parties to implement such schemes has been inferred from provisions calling for establishment of management, control and enforcement measures. Unfortunately, as these schemes are not required by treaty but derive from the power to manage, not only are they subject to the vagaries of implementational will but they are also subject to objection and opt-out procedures within RFMOs, thus potentially compromising their general applicability.[86]

Reciprocal port inspection schemes have been adopted in a number of RFMOs, although in some cases the scheme is optional, inferior to the unilateral port control schemes already existing in a number of member states, or applies only to vessels of non-contracting parties.[87] Nevertheless, the essential function of these schemes is four-fold. First, they seek to condition access in respect of activities that have occurred on the high seas. Second, they attempt to achieve harmonization of a minimum standard in this regard. Third, they operate to ensure reciprocity and fair competition as between the contracting parties. Finally, they are intended to operate as a deterrent to port-hopping, at least as between the ports of member states.

No RFMO scheme goes so far as to provide for port state enforcement. In all cases, prosecution and the right of sanction is left to the flag state. Likewise measures banning landings and transshipments appear to provide as their only recourse the right of denial of access rather than a right of sanction. However, if denial of access is the only remedy then port-hopping is precisely what will occur. In such cases, RFMOs are dependent on the goodwill of non-member port states to adopt port control measures incorporating the port control requirements adopted by RFMOs and banning landings and transshipments of IUU fish.

While parties to the FSA and members of RFMOs may be obliged as a matter of treaty law to exercise port state jurisdiction, there is no general treaty or customary obligation on *all* port states to apply port controls to all foreign fishing vessels for the purpose of ensuring compliance with measures adopted by RFMOs of which they are not members.[88] However, the practice within RFMOs of adopting port control schemes has provided both content to and the impetus for the adoption of a broader obligation of port state control. In 2001 the FAO adopted the International Plan of Action to Prevent, Deter and Eliminate Illegal, Unreported and Unregulated Fishing (IPOA-IUU)[89] which includes detailed provisions on port state measures. Although not legally binding, these provisions provide evidence of developing consensus on global minimum standards for port state control in the high seas fisheries context.

Building on the IPOA-IUU, and taking inspiration from the approach adopted in the IMO, in 2005 the FAO adopted a Model Scheme on Port State Measures[90] which was intended to promote, reinforce and harmonize the implementation of port state measures through their adoption via harmonized regional arrangements. This non-binding instrument further laid the groundwork for the adoption in 2009 of the PSM Agreement[91] which establishes global minimum standards for port state control in the high seas fisheries context. These standards include the obligation to cooperate with RFMOs, to take port control measures in support of conservation and management measures adopted by RFMOs and to deny entry where the port state has sufficient proof that a vessel has engaged in IUU fishing or related activities, particularly where the vessel is listed on an RFMO IUU vessel list.[92] The objective of this global, legally binding, agreement is to level the playing field both within and among regions, by ensuring a minimum of controls are enforced in the ports of all states. Incidentally, its negotiation may also be regarded as evidence of state practice and *opinio juris* in support of a more general customary obligation on port states to take measures in support of RFMO conservation and management measures. The Agreement, however, is not yet in force.[93]

Conclusion

Port states are playing an increasing and increasingly important role in maritime regulation and enforcement. Once considered an optional jurisdiction to be exercised only in limited circumstances, port state jurisdiction is moving, in the words of Molenaar, 'towards comprehensive, mandatory and global coverage'.[94] It is an open question as to how far port states might go in the future in unilaterally invoking their residual prescriptive and enforcement jurisdiction, including their right of extraterritorial jurisdiction in respect of activities taking place in areas beyond national jurisdiction, to protect their interests in maritime safety, security and the marine environment. However, regardless of unilateral actions, achievement of a truly level playing field and the elimination of the possibility of ports of convenience will require a collective commitment on the part of all port states to adhere to multilateral port control and enforcement regimes and to exercise their jurisdiction in support of, at the very least, internationally agreed standards. The paucity of practice under Article 218 of the LOSC and the current state of the PSM Agreement provide reason to pause. Nevertheless, given their current trajectory, there is every reason to believe that global and regional efforts to ensure both the reality and the efficacy of the exercise of port state jurisdiction will continue. That 'old chestnut', the fundamental principle of exclusivity flag state jurisdiction, looks set to be tempered even further by port state jurisdiction.

Notes

1 United Nations Convention on the Law of the Sea (adopted 10 December 1982, entered into force 16 November 1994) 1833 UNTS 397 (LOSC).
2 LOSC Arts 2 and 17–19.
3 LOSC Art 56.
4 LOSC Arts 76 and 77.
5 David Anderson, 'Port States and Environmental Protection' in David Freestone and Alan Boyle (eds), *International Law and Sustainable Development: Past Achievements and Future Challenges* (Oxford: Oxford University Press, 1999), 325–344, 326.
6 Erik Jaap Molenaar, 'Port State Jurisdiction: Towards Mandatory and Comprehensive Use' in David Freestone, Richard Barnes and David Ong (eds) *The Law of the Sea: Progress and* Prospects (Oxford: Oxford University Press, 2006) 192–209, 192.
7 For an overview of historical positions see, Bevan Marten, *Port State Jurisdiction and the Regulation of Merchant Shipping* (Springer International Publishing Switzerland, 2014) 37–42.
8 Ibid., 38.
9 Ibid., 39.
10 George C. Kasoulides, *Port State Control and Jurisdiction: Evolution of the Port States Regime* (Dordrecht: Martinus Nijhoff, 1993).
11 *Military and Paramilitary Activities in and Against Nicaragua* (Nicaragua v United States of America) (Judgment) [1968] ICJ Reports 14, para. 213.
12 A.V. Lowe, 'The Right of Entry into Maritime Ports in International Law' (1977) 14 *San Diego Law Review* 597, 622.
13 Ibid.

14 R. Churchill and A.V. Lowe, *The Law of the Sea* (3rd edn) (Manchester: Manchester University Press, 1999), 64.
15 *MV Louisa (Saint Vincent and the Grenadines v Spain)*, (Judgment) International Tribunal for the Law of the Sea (ITLOS) (28 May 2013), para. 109.
16 Marten, above n 7, 49.
17 Churchill and Lowe, above n 14, 61–65.
18 *ARA Libertad (Argentina v Ghana)* (Provisional Measures) [2012] ITLOS Reports 21, para. 95.
19 Convention on the International Maritime Organization, 6 March 1948, entry into force, 17 March 1958, 289 UNTS 48, Art 1(a).
20 Agreement for the Implementation of the Provisions of the United Nations Convention on the Law of the Sea of 10 December 1982 relating to the Conservation and Management of Straddling Fish Stocks and Highly Migratory Fish Stocks, 1995, 2167 UNTS 3.
21 Richard A. Legatski, 'Port State Jurisdiction over vessel-Source Marine Pollution' (1997) 2 *Harvard Environmental Law Review* 448.
22 Erik Jaap Molenaar, 'Port State Jurisdiction: Towards Comprehensive, Mandatory and Global Coverage' (2007) *Ocean Development and International Law* 225–243, 231.
23 Oil Pollution Act 1990, 46 USC 3703a. For discussion see Marten, above n 7, 53.
24 See, Julian Roberts, 'Compulsory Pilotage in International Straits: The Torres Strait PSSA Proposal' (2006) 37 *Ocean Development and International Law* 93–112; Robert Beckman, 'PSSAs and Transit Passage – Australia's Pilotage System in the Torres Strait Challenges the IMO and UNCLOS' (2007) 38 *Ocean Development and International Law* 325–357; Donald K Anton, 'Does Australia Make or Break the International Law of transit Passage? Meeting Environmental and Safety Challenges in the Torres Strait with Compulsory Pilotage' in David D Caron and Nilufer Oral (eds) *Navigating Straits: Challenges to International Law* (Leiden: Brill, Martinus Nijhoff, 2014) 49.
25 The United States, for example, denies access to its ports to all foreign vessels fishing on the high seas. Canada denies access to vessels that undermine conservation measures by fishing contrary to conservation regimes established by RFMOs of which Canada is a member. Norway denies access to vessels that have taken part in an unregulated fishery on the high seas. Russia, too, denies access to foreign vessels fishing in the high seas enclave in the Sea of Okhotsk. For more information see, FAO, *Implementation of the International Plan of Action to Prevent, Deter and Eliminate Illegal, Unreported and Unregulated Fishing*, FAO Technical Guidelines for Responsible Fisheries, No. 9, (Rome, FAO, 2002), 41–46. See also, Terje Lobach, *Port State Control of Foreign Fishing Vessels*, FAO Fisheries Circular No. 987, FIP/C987 (Rome: FAO, 2003); Erik Franckx, *Fisheries Enforcement, Related Legal and Institutional Issues: National, Subregional or Regional Perspectives*, FAO Legislative Study 71 (Rome, FAO, 2001).
26 Erik Jaap Molenaar, 'Port and Coastal States' in Donald R. Rothwell, Alex G. Oude Elferink, Karen N. Scott and Tim Stephens (eds), *Oxford Handbook of the Law of the Sea* (Oxford: Oxford University Press, 2015) 280–303, 289.
27 *Chile – Measures Affecting the Transit and Importation of Swordfish*, EC request for Consultations, WT/DS193 (19 April 2000).
28 *European Union – Measures on Altanto-Scandian Herring*, Denmark Request for Consultations, WT/DS469 (4 November 2013).
29 See, eg, Michael R. M'Gonigle, 'Unilateralism and International Law: The Arctic Waters Pollution Prevention Act' (1976) 34 *University of Toronto Faculty Law Review* 180; John Warren Kindt, 'Vessel Source Pollution and the Law of the Sea' (1984) 17 *Vanderbilt Journal of Transnational Law* 287; David Allan Fitch, 'Unilateral Action versus Universal Evolution of Safety and Environmental Protection Standards in Maritime Shipping of Hazardous Cargoes' (1979) 20 *Harvard International Law Journal* 127; Sergei Vonogradov, '"Tightening the Regulatory Web": Issues and trends in Navigation Regimes' in Davor Vidas and Willy Østreng (eds), *Order for the Oceans at the Turn of the Century* (The Fridtjof Nansen Institute, Oslo, 1999); Veronica Frank, 'Consequences of the Prestige sinking for European and international Law' (2005) 20 *International Journal of Marine and Coastal Law* 1; Henrik Ringbom, 'Global Problem – Regional Solution? International Law Reflection on an EU CO_2 Emissions Trading Scheme for Ships' (2011) 26 *International Journal of Marine and Coastal Law* 613.
30 Alan Boyle, 'EU Unilateralism and the Law of the Sea' (2006) 21 *International Journal of Marine and Coastal Law* 15, 15.
31 Sir Anthony Clarke, 'Port State Control or Sub-Standard Ships: Who is to Blame? What is the Cure?' (1994) *Lloyd's Maritime and Commercial Law Quarterly* 202, 205.

32 For an extensive study see Kasoulides, above n 10.
33 1929 International Convention on the Safety of Life at Sea, UKTS No. 34, Cmd. 4198, replacing the 1914 Convention on the Safety of Life at Sea, adopted in the aftermath of the sinking of the Titanic. See discussion in Anderson, above n 5.
34 1973 International Convention for the Prevention of Pollution from Ships (1973) 12 *International Legal Materials* 1319. Before this Convention entered into force it was modified by the 1978 Protocol Relating to the Convention for the Prevention of Pollution form Ships (17 February 1978, entered into force 2 October 1983), (1978) 17 *International Legal Materials* 246. Collectively the conventions are generally referred to either as MARPOL or as MARPOL 73/78.
35 MARPOL Arts 5 and 6.
36 For discussion see, eg, Kasoulides, above n 10, 43. See also Richard W.J. Schiferli, 'The Memorandum of Understanding on Port State Control: Its History, Operation and Development', (1993) 25 *Law of the Sea Institute Proceedings* 434; P.B. Payoyo, 'ILO Convention no. 147, Port State Control, and the Human Element in Shipping' (1993) 68(1) *Philippine Law Journal* 62; and T. Keselj, 'Port State Jurisdiction in Respect of Pollution from Ships: The 1982 United Nations Convention on the Law of the Sea and the Memorandum of Understanding (1990) 30 *Ocean Development and International Law* 127.
37 LOSC, Arts 210, 211, 216, 217, 218, 220.
38 LOSC, Art 211(3).
39 Allan Khee Jee Tan, 'The Regulation of Vessel Source Marine Pollution: Reconciling the Maritime and Coastal State Interests' (1997) 1 *Singapore Journal of International and Comparative Law* 355, 374–376.
40 Rosemary Rayfuse, *Non-Flag State Enforcement in High Seas Fisheries* (Leiden: Martinus Nijhoff, 2004), 68.
41 Rayfuse, ibid. See also, Budislav Vukas, 'Generally Accepted International Rules and Standards' in A.H.A. Soons, (ed) *Implementation of the Law of the Sea Convention Through International Instruments* (1990) 405; Henrik Ringbom, 'Preventing Pollution from Ships: Reflections on the "Adequacy" of Existing Rules' (1999) 8 *Review of European Community and International Environmental Law* 21, 22.
42 24 November 1989, entered into force 17 May 1991, 29 *International Legal Materials* 1449 (1990).
43 1993 Agreement to Promote Compliance with International Conservation and Management Measures by Fishing Vessels on the High Seas (24 November 1993, entered into force 24 April 2003), 2221 UNTS 120 (Compliance Agreement).
44 Patricia Birnie, 'Reflagging of Fishing Vessels on the High Seas' (1993) 2(3) *Review of European Community and International Environmental Law* 270.
45 See Francisco Orrega Vicuña, *The Changing International Law of High Seas Fisheries* (Cambridge: Cambridge University Press, 1999), 259–264.
46 André Tahindro, 'Conservation and Management of Transboundary Fish Stocks: Comments in Light of the Adoption of the 1995 Agreement for the Conservation and Management of Straddling Fish Stocks and Highly Migratory Fish Stocks' (1997) 28 *Ocean Development and International Law* 1, 41.
47 Orregi Vicuña, above n 45, 264.
48 Kasoulides, above n 10, 110.
49 Rosemary Rayfuse, 'To Our Children's Children's Children: Achieving Compliance in High Seas Fisheries' (2005) 20(3/4) *The International Journal of Marine and Coastal Law* 509–532, 512.
50 See Ted L. McDorman, 'Port State Enforcement: A Comment on Article 218 of the 1982 Law of the Sea Convention' (1997) 28(2) *Journal of Maritime Law and Commerce* 305, David Anderson, 'Port States and Environmental Protection' in Alan Boyle and David Freestone (eds) *International Law and Sustainable Developments: Past Achievements and Future Challenges* 325 (1999) and P. Birnie and A. Boyle, *International Environmental Law* (2nd edn) (2002) at 376.
51 Orrego Vicuña, above n 45, 261.
52 Revised Negotiating Text, Prepared by the Chairman of the Conference, UN Doc. A/CONF.164/13/Rev.1 (30 March 1994), Art 38.
53 For discussion see, Lobach, above n 25, para 4.7.2.
54 *Fisheries Jurisdiction* case (Spain v. Canada), (jurisdiction and admissibility), (1998) ICJ Reports 432.
55 Ibid., para. 66. There the court was referring to 'conservation measures'.
56 *Ibid.*, para. 70.
57 Orrego Vicuña, above n 45, 261.
58 Myron H. Nordquist, Satya N. Nandan and Shabtai Rosenne (eds), *United Nations Convention on the Law of the Sea 1982: A Commentary*, vol. III, 294.

59 *Fisheries Jurisdiction* case, above n 55, para. 84.
60 FAO, Report of the Expert Consultation to Review Port States Measures to Combat Illegal, Unreported and Unregulated Fishing, FAO Fisheries Report No 692 (Rome: FAO, 2002) para. 18.
61 Adopted 22 November 2009. Not yet in force. Text available at http://www.fao.org/fileadmin/user_upload/legal/docs/1_037t-e.pdf (PSM Agreement).
62 PSM Agreement, Arts 9, 11, 18.
63 PSM Agreement, Art 18(3).
64 Rayfuse, above n 40, 355.
65 Erik Jaap Molenaar, 'Port State Jurisdiction to Combat IUU Fishing: The Port State Measures Agreement' in D.A. Russell and D.L. VanderZwaag (eds), *Recasting Transboundary Fisheries Management Arrangements in Light of Sustainability Principles. Canadian and International Perspectives* (Leiden: Martinus Nijhoff, 2010) 369–386, 386.
66 See, www.imo.org/OurWork/Safety/Implementation/Pages/PortStateControl.aspx.
67 Reproduced in the House of Commons Paper 105-III (1978–9), Measures to Prevent Collisions and Strandings of Noxious Cargo Carriers in Waters Around the United Kingdom, 91–99.
68 For discussion, see, Kasoulides, above n 45, 142–143.
69 (1982) 21 *International Legal Materials* 1. See Kasoulides, above n 45, 149–182 for discussion and evaluation of the Paris MOU. See also, Gerhard Kiehne, 'Investigation, Detention and Release of Ships under the Paris Memorandum on Port State Control: A View from Practice' (1996) 11(2) *International Journal of Marine and Coastal Law* 217, 218.
70 Roberto Salvarani, 'The EC Directive on Port State Control: A Policy Statement' (1996) 11(2) *International Journal of Marine and Coastal Law* 225. See also P.B. Payoyo, *Port State Control in the Asia-Pacific: An International Legal Study of Port State Jurisdiction* (1993) ch 4.
71 For detailed discussion see Erik Jaap Molenaar, 'The EC Directive on Port State Control in Context' (1996) 11(2) *International Journal of Marine and Coastal Law* 241 (1996). The text of the Directive is reproduced therein at 269–288. See also, P. Boisson, 'Classification Society Cooperation With Port State Control: A Move Towards the End of Substandard Practices' (1996) 24(8) *International Business Lawyer* 352.
72 Latin American Agreement on Port States Control, 5 November 1992.
73 Memorandum of Understanding on Port State Control in the Asia-Pacific Region, 1 December 1993. See P.B. Payoyo, *Port State Control in the Asia-Pacific: An International Legal Study of Port State Jurisdiction* (1993).
74 Memorandum of Understanding on Port State Control in the Caribbean Region, 9 February 1996, (1997) 36 *International Legal Materials* 231 (1997).
75 Memorandum of Understanding on Port State Control in the Mediterranean Region, 11 July 1997.
76 Memorandum of Understanding on Port State Control for the Indian Ocean Region, 5 June 1998.
77 Memorandum of Understanding on Port State Control for the West and Central African Region, 5 June 1998.
78 Memorandum of Understanding on Port State Control in the Black Sea Region, 7 April 2000.
79 Riyadh Memorandum of Understanding on Port State Control in the Gulf region, 30 June 2004.
80 Molenaar, above n 26, 292.
81 Henrik Ringbom, 'Vessel Source Pollution' in R. Rayfuse (ed) *Research Handbook on International Marine Environmental Law* (Cheltenham: Edward Elgar, 2015) forthcoming.
82 See, eg, IMO Assembly Res A. 1052(27), Procedures for Port State Control (30 November 2011).
83 See, eg, IMO Doc PSCWS6/11, Record of Recommendations (9 July 2013).
84 See, eg, the Joint Declaration on inter-regional action to eliminate substandard shipping signed by the representatives of the parties to the Paris and Tokyo MOU's at Vancouver, Canada on 24–25 March 1998. The 'Vancouver Declaration', entitled 'Tightening the Net: Inter-Regional Action to Eliminate Sub-standard Shipping' commits the parties to 'strengthen[ing] compliance with International Labour Organization (ILO) and IMO standards by enhancing the application of port state control in both regions so as to maximise its deterrent effect'. More generally see also J. Hare, 'Port State Control: Strong Medicine to Cure a Sick Industry' (1997) 26 *Georgia Journal of International and Comparative Law* 71; J. Hoppe, 'Port State Control – an update of IMO's work' (2000) 1 *IMO News* 1.
85 Rayfuse, above n 40, 175.
86 Ibid., 351.

87 Ibid., 352. See also, K. von Kostowski et al, *Port State Performance: Putting Illegal, Unreported and Unregulated Fishing on the Radar* (Pew Environment Group Online 2010) available at www.portstateperformance.org.
88 Rayfuse, above n 40, 355.
89 FAO, International Plan of Action to Prevent, Deter and Eliminate Illegal, Unreported and Unregulated Fishing (FAO Rome 2001) adopted by consensus by FAO's Committee on Fisheries on 2 March 2001 and endorsed by FAO Council on 23 June 2001, available at http://www.fao.org/docrep/003/y1224e/y1224eoo.htm.
90 FAO, *Model Scheme on Port State Measures to Combat Illegal, Unreported and Unregulated Fishing* (FAO Rome 2007); reproduced in Report of the Technical Consultation to review Port State Measures to Combat Illegal, Unreported and Unregulated Fishing, FAO Fisheries Report No 759 (2004), Annex E.
91 For a comprehensive history of the FAO efforts see, David J. Doulman and Judith Swan, *A Guide to the Background and Implementation of the 2009 FAO Agreement on Port State Measures to Prevent, Deter and Eliminate Illegal, Unreported and Unregulated Fishing*, FAO Fisheries and Aquaculture Circular No 1074 (Rome, FAO, 2012).
92 PSM Agreement Arts 6 and 9(4).
93 As of January 2015 only 11 states are parties to the Agreement; 25 are required to bring it into force. See, http://www.fao.org/fileadmin/user_upload/legal/docs/6_037s-e.pdf.
94 Molenaar, above n 22.

7
The Role of Global Organisations

J. Ashley Roach

Introduction

This chapter surveys the global UN specialized agencies, UN programmes and research institutes, intergovernmental organizations and non-governmental organizations that play a role in regulating and enforcing maritime activities. This chapter also surveys the key regulatory and enforcement instruments and measures emerging from these bodies. It also surveys the linkages between the organizations.

The UN specialized agencies reviewed include the International Maritime Organization, the Food and Agricultural Organization, the International Labor Organization, the International Civil Aviation Organization, the UNESCO Cultural Sector and the Intergovernmental Oceanographic Commission of UNESCO. UN programmes and research institutes reviewed include the UN Office of Drugs and Crime, the UN Environment Program and the UN Interregional Crime and Justice Research Institute. The role of the International Whaling Commission, a non-UN international organization, is reviewed. The non-governmental organization reviewed is the International Standards Organization. The special roles of the UN Secretariat's Legal Office Division of Ocean Affairs and the Law of the Sea are reviewed. The roles of the independent bodies established by the Law of the Sea (LOS) Convention,[1] the International Seabed Authority and the International Tribunal for the Law of the Sea, and role of the International Court of Justice, are examined.

Global entities

International Maritime Organization

The International Maritime Organization (IMO), headquartered in London, England, was established in 1948 when an international conference in Geneva adopted a convention formally establishing IMO. The IMO Convention entered into force in 1958 and the new Organization met for the first time the following year.[2]

The purposes of the Organization, as summarized in article 1(a) of the Convention, are "to provide machinery for cooperation among Governments in the field of governmental regulation and practices relating to technical matters of all kinds affecting shipping engaged in international trade; to encourage and facilitate the general adoption of the highest practicable standards in matters concerning maritime safety, efficiency of navigation and prevention and control of marine pollution from ships". The Organization is also empowered to deal with administrative and legal matters related to these purposes.[3]

As IMO instruments have entered into force and been implemented, developments in technology and/or lessons learned from accidents have led to changes and amendments being adopted.[4]

Food and Agricultural Organization

The Food and Agricultural Organization (FAO), headquartered in Rome, Italy since 1951, is a specialized agency of the United Nations, established in 1945.[5] Article I(1) of FAO's Constitution provides that "The Organization shall collect, analyse, interpret and disseminate information relating to nutrition, food and agriculture. In this Constitution, the term "agriculture" and its derivatives include fisheries, marine products, forestry and primary forestry products."[6]

International Seabed Authority

The International Seabed Authority is an autonomous international organization established under the LOS Convention and the 1994 Agreement relating to the Implementation of Part XI of the United Nations Convention on the Law of the Sea.[7] The Authority is the organization through which States Parties to the Convention, in accordance with the regime for the seabed and ocean floor and subsoil thereof beyond the limits of national jurisdiction (the Area) established in Part XI and the Agreement, organize and control activities in the Area, particularly with a view to administering the resources of the Area.

The Authority came into existence on 16 November 1994 upon the entry into force of the LOS Convention. The Authority became fully operational as an autonomous international organization in June 1996, when it took over the premises and facilities in Kingston, Jamaica previously used by the United Nations Kingston Office for the Law of the Sea.[8]

International Labor Organization

The International Labor Organization (ILO) was founded in 1919 to pursue a vision based on the premise that universal, lasting peace can be established only if it is based on social justice. The ILO became the first specialized agency of the UN in 1946. The unique tripartite structure of the ILO gives an equal voice to workers, employers and governments to ensure that the views of the social partners are closely reflected in labor standards and in shaping policies and programmes.[9]

The Maritime Labor Convention, 2006, was adopted by government, employer and worker representatives at a special ILO International Labor Conference, in February 2006, to provide international standards for the world's first genuinely global industry. The comprehensive Convention sets out in one place seafarers' rights to decent conditions of work on almost every aspect of their working and living.[10]

International Civil Aviation Organization

The International Civil Aviation Organization (ICAO), a specialized agency of the United Nations, was created in 1944 to promote the safe and orderly development of international civil aviation throughout the world.[11] It sets standards and regulations necessary for aviation safety, security, efficiency and regularity, as well as for aviation environmental protection. The Organization serves as the forum for cooperation in all fields of civil aviation among its 191 Member States.[12]

Aircraft in transit passage over straits used for international navigation and in archipelagic sea lanes passage over archipelagic waters are required to:

(a) observe the Rules of the Air established by the International Civil Aviation Organization as they apply to civil aircraft; state aircraft will normally comply with such safety measures and will at all times operate with due regard for the safety of navigation; [and]
(b) at all times monitor the radio frequency assigned by the competent internationally designated air traffic control authority or the appropriate international distress radio frequency.[13]

United Nations Educational, Scientific and Cultural Organization

The United Nations Educational, Scientific and Cultural Organization (UNESCO), headquartered in Paris, France, is another specialized agency of the UN. Its Culture Sector is the implementing body for the 2001 Convention for the Protection of Underwater Cultural Heritage.[14]

The Intergovernmental Oceanographic Commission (IOC) of UNESCO promotes international cooperation and coordinates programmes in marine research, services, observation systems, hazard mitigation and capacity development in order to better manage the nature and resources of the oceans and coastal areas.[15]

The IOC provides the international forum for implementation of LOS Convention Part XIII, Marine Scientific Research, and Part XIV, Development and Transfer of Marine Technology.[16]

International Whaling Commission

The International Whaling Commission (IWC) is the global intergovernmental body charged with the conservation of whales and the management of whaling. It is set up under the 1946 International Convention for the Regulation of Whaling.[17] The IWC has a current membership of 88 Governments from countries around the world.[18]

International Organization for Standardization

The International Organization for Standardization (ISO), a non-governmental organization headquartered in Geneva, Switzerland, develops International Standards. It was founded in 1947, and since then has published more than 19,500 International Standards covering almost all aspects of technology and business. International Standards give state of the art specifications for products, services and good practice, helping to make industry more efficient and effective.[19]

ISO is assisting in the drafting of rules for the use of force in the UN's counter-piracy effort.[20]

UN Division for Ocean Affairs and the Law of the Sea

The UN Secretariat's Office of Legal Affairs Division for Ocean Affairs and the Law of the Sea (DOALOS) at UN Headquarters in New York City provides to States and intergovernmental organizations a range of legal and technical services, such as information, advice and assistance as well as conducting research and preparing studies, relating to the LOS Convention, the Agreement relating to the implementation of Part XI of the LOS Convention and the Agreement for the implementation of LOS Convention relating to the Conservation and Management of Straddling Fish Stocks and Highly Migratory Fish Stocks (UN Fish Stocks Agreement)[21] with a view to promoting a better understanding of the Convention and implementing Agreements, their wider acceptance, and uniform and consistent application and effective implementation.[22]

The UN Office of Drugs and

Crime

The UN Office of Drugs and Crime (UNODC), a specialized UN agency headquartered in Vienna, Austria, is a global leader in the fight against illicit drugs and international crime. Established in 1997 through a merger between the United Nations Drug Control Program and the Centre for International Crime Prevention, UNODC operates in all regions of the world through an extensive network of field offices.[23]

In relation to maritime matters, UNODC supports counter-narcotics,[24] counter-piracy,[25] and counter-migrant smuggling efforts.[26]

United Nations Interregional Crime and Justice Research Institute

The United Nations Interregional Crime and Justice Research Institute (UNICRI), headquartered in Turin, Italy, is a United Nations entity established in 1967 to support countries worldwide in preventing crime and facilitating criminal justice.[27] The Institute is an autonomous institution of the UN, and is presently ruled by the Statute adopted by ECOSOC.[28] UNICRI operates within the framework of the United Nations Crime Prevention and Criminal Justice Program Network.[29]

UNICRI is mandated to assist intergovernmental, governmental and non-governmental organizations in formulating and implementing improved policies in the field of crime prevention and criminal justice.

UNICRI assists in the UN's counter-piracy effort.[30]

United Nations Environment Programme

The mission of the UN Environment Program (UNEP) is to provide leadership and encourage partnership in caring for the environment by inspiring, informing, and enabling nations and peoples to improve their quality of life without compromising that of future generations.[31] UNEP is headquartered in the United Nations Office in Nairobi (UNON), Kenya.

International Court of Justice

The International Court of Justice (ICJ) is the principal judicial organ of the United Nations. It was established in June 1945 by the Charter of the United Nations[32] and began work in April 1946. The seat of the Court is at the Peace Palace, The Hague, Netherlands.

The Court's role is to settle, in accordance with international law, legal disputes submitted to it by States and to give advisory opinions on legal questions referred to it by authorized United Nations organs and specialized agencies.

The Court is composed of 15 judges, who are elected for terms of office of nine years by the United Nations General Assembly and the Security Council. It is assisted by a Registry, its administrative organ. Its official languages are English and French.[33]

The ICJ has decided some 30 maritime cases, many dealing with sovereignty disputes and maritime boundaries.[34]

International Tribunal for the Law of the Sea

The International Tribunal for the Law of the Sea is an independent judicial body established by the LOS Convention[35] to adjudicate disputes arising out of the interpretation and application of the Convention. The Tribunal, headquartered in Hamburg, Germany, is composed of 21 independent members, elected for a term of nine years from among persons enjoying the highest reputation for fairness and integrity and of recognized competence in the field of the law of the sea.[36]

The Tribunal has jurisdiction over any dispute concerning the interpretation or application of the LOS Convention, and over all matters specifically provided for in any other agreement which confers jurisdiction on the Tribunal (Statute, article 21). The Tribunal is open to States Parties to the Convention (i.e., States and international organizations which are parties to the Convention). It is also open to entities other than States Parties, i.e., States or intergovernmental organizations which are not parties to the Convention, and to state enterprises and private entities, "in any case expressly provided for in Part XI or in any case submitted pursuant to any other agreement conferring jurisdiction on the Tribunal which is accepted by all the parties to that case" (Statute, article 20).[37]

To date the Tribunal has rendered judgments in 21 cases, mostly dealing with prompt release of vessels.[38] It decided its first maritime boundary case in 2012.[39] The Seabed Disputes Chamber issued its first advisory opinion in 2011.[40] The first request to the full tribunal for an advisory opinion is pending.[41]

Law of the Sea Convention

The LOS Convention contains many provisions on the regulation and enforcement of maritime activities. Many of these provisions require implementation by other organizations and States party to the LOS Convention.[42] The sections that follow briefly describe what the LOS Convention has to say about each topic and what has been done to implement them.

Maritime safety

IMO's first task was to adopt a new version of the International Convention for the Safety of Life at Sea (SOLAS), the most important of all treaties dealing with maritime safety. This was achieved in 1960,[43] and revised in 1974.[44] IMO then turned its attention to such matters as the facilitation of international maritime traffic,[45] load lines[46] and the carriage of dangerous goods,[47] while the system of measuring the tonnage of ships was revised.[48]

On 1 February 1997, the 1995 amendments to the International Convention on Standards of Training, Certification and Watchkeeping for Seafarers, 1978[49] entered into force. They greatly improve seafarer standards and, for the first time, give IMO itself powers to check Government actions with Parties required to submit information to IMO regarding their compliance with the Convention. A major revision of the STCW Convention and Code was completed in 2010 with the adoption of the Manila amendments to the STCW Convention and Code.[50]

In 1994 and 2006 the IMO adopted amendments to SOLAS and MARPOL providing for port state control on operational requirements[51] and is developing an international code for ships operating in ice-covered waters (Polar Code).

Marine pollution[52]

Part XII of the LOS Convention sets out a comprehensive international framework for the protection and preservation of the marine environment. By addressing all sources of marine pollution, Part XII promotes continuing improvement in the health of the world's oceans. Compliance with Part XII's environmental obligations is subject to compulsory dispute settlement procedures.

Part XII was developed at the same time that the IMO was adopting detailed treaties for the prevention of pollution of the marine environment from vessels. Accordingly it is no surprise that the provisions of the LOS Convention mirror the work of the IMO in pollution prevention. Indeed, Section 11 of Part XII (article 237) provides that the obligations of Part XII are without prejudice to the specific obligations assumed by States under special conventions and agreements concluded in the past and future relating to the protection and preservation of the marine environment.

Article 1(4) of the LOS Convention defines "pollution of the marine environment" as follows:

> "pollution of the marine environment" means the introduction by man, directly or indirectly, of substances or energy into the marine environment, including estuaries, which results or is likely to result in such deleterious effects as harm to living resources and marine life, hazards to human health, hindrance to marine activities, including fishing and other legitimate uses of the sea, impairment of quality for use of sea water and reduction of amenities.

Of greatest relevance to this Handbook, Section 5 of Part XII (articles 207–212) sets out international rules and requires national legislation to prevent, reduce and control pollution of the marine environment. Section 6 (articles 213–222) details the enforcement regime for those rules and legislation. Section 9 (article 235) addresses responsibility and liability.

Other sections of Part XII address general provisions (Section 1, articles 192–196), global and regional cooperation I (Section 2, articles 197–201), technical assistance (Section 3, articles 202–203), monitoring and environmental assessment (Section 4, articles 204–206), safeguards (Section 7, articles 223–233), ice-covered areas (Section 8, article 234) and sovereign immunity (Section 10, article 236).

Pollution by dumping

Articles 1(5), 210 and 216 of the LOS Convention address pollution by dumping. Article 1(5) of the LOS Convention defines "dumping" as follows:

(a) "dumping" means:
   (i) any deliberate disposal of wastes or other matter from vessels, aircraft, platforms or other man-made structures at sea; [and]
   (ii) any deliberate disposal of vessels, aircraft, platforms or other man-made structures at sea.
(b) "dumping" does not include:
   (i) the disposal of wastes or other matter incidental to, or derived from the normal operations of vessels, aircraft, platforms or other man-made structures at sea and their equipment, other than wastes or other matter transported by or to vessels, aircraft, platforms or other man-made structures at sea, operating for the purpose of disposal of such matter or derived from the treatment of such wastes or other matter on such vessels, aircraft, platforms or structures; [or]
(ii) placement of matter for a purpose other than the mere disposal thereof, provided that such placement is not contrary to the aims of this Convention.

The Convention on the Prevention of Marine Pollution by Dumping of Wastes and Other Matter 1972 (the London Convention)[53] was one of the first global conventions to protect the marine environment from human activities and has been in force since 1975. Its objective is to promote the effective control of all sources of marine pollution and to take all practicable steps to prevent pollution of the sea by dumping of wastes. Currently, 87 States are Parties to this Convention.[54]

In 1996 the London Protocol was adopted to modernize the Convention and, eventually, replace it.[55] The London Protocol entered into force in March 2006 and currently has 45 Parties. Under the Protocol all dumping is prohibited, but Parties may issue permits to allow the dumping of the following specified materials, subject to certain conditions: dredged material; sewage sludge; fish wastes; vessels and platforms; inert, inorganic geological material (e.g., mining wastes); organic material of natural origin; bulky items primarily comprising iron, steel and concrete; and carbon dioxide streams from carbon dioxide capture processes for sequestration.

Article 210 of the LOS Convention addresses the legislative obligations of States while article 216 requires enforcement by coastal States and flag States.

Pollution from seabed activities subject to national jurisdiction

Article 208(1) of the LOS Convention requires coastal States to "adopt laws and regulations to prevent, reduce and control pollution of the marine environment arising from or in connection with seabed activities subject to their jurisdiction and from artificial islands, installations and structures under their jurisdiction". Article 214 requires States to enforce their laws in this regard. Article 208(5) requires the IMO to establish "global and regional rules, standards and recommended practices and procedures to prevent, reduce and control pollution of the marine environment referred to in paragraph 1." The Member States of the IMO have been unwilling to do this, and thus have not been able to comply with the requirement of article 210 to implement these international rules and standards, relying rather on national legislation.[56]

Pollution from activities in the Area

Articles 209 and 145 of the LOS Convention require the International Seabed Authority to establish international rules, regulations and procedures to prevent, reduce and control pollution of the marine environment from activities in the Area. Article 209 also requires States to adopt laws and regulations to prevent such pollution. The ISA has adopted such rules and regulations for exploratory activities in the Area and is developing them for exploitation in the Area.[57]

Pollution from vessels

The growth in the amount of oil being transported by sea and in the size of oil tankers was of particular concern and the Torrey Canyon disaster of 1967, in which 120,000 tons of oil was spilled, demonstrated the scale of the problem.

During the next few years IMO introduced a series of measures designed to prevent tanker accidents and to minimize their consequences. It also tackled the environmental threat caused by routine operations such as the cleaning of oil cargo tanks and the disposal of engine room wastes – in tonnage terms a bigger menace than accidental pollution.

The most important of all these measures was the International Convention for the Prevention of Pollution from Ships, 1973, as modified by the Protocol of 1978 relating thereto (MARPOL 73/78).[58] It covers not only accidental and operational oil pollution but also pollution by chemicals, goods in packaged form, sewage, garbage and air pollution (added by the Protocol of 1997). It continues to be updated with relevant amendments.

MARPOL has greatly contributed to a significant decrease in pollution from international shipping and applies to 99% of the world's merchant tonnage.

Other treaties address anti-fouling systems used on ships,[59] the transfer of alien species by ships' ballast water[60] and the environmentally sound recycling of ships.[61]

Pollution from or through the atmosphere

In 1997 a new annex was added to the International Convention for the Prevention of Pollution from Ships (MARPOL).[62] The Regulations for the Prevention of Air Pollution from Ships (Annex VI) seek to minimize airborne emissions from ships (SOx, NOx, ODS, VOC) and their contribution to local and global air pollution and environmental problems. Annex VI entered into force on 19 May 2005 and a revised Annex VI with significantly tightened emissions limits was adopted in October 2008 which entered into force on 1 July 2010.

In 2007 international shipping was estimated to have contributed about 2.7% to the global emissions of carbon dioxide (CO_2). IMO has adopted mandatory technical and operational energy efficiency measures which will significantly reduce the amount of CO_2 emissions from international shipping. The growth of world trade in the future represents a challenge to meeting a target for emissions required to achieve stabilization in global temperatures and so IMO continues to work on the development of market-based measures as a complimentary means of achieving the required target for emissions.

Land-based sources of marine pollution

Article 207(1) of the LOS Convention requires States to "adopt laws and regulations to prevent, reduce and control pollution of the marine environment from land-based sources, including rivers, estuaries, pipelines and outfall structures, taking into account internationally agreed rules, standards and recommended practices and procedures." Article 213 requires States to enforce their laws and regulations adopted in accordance with article 207. Article 207(4) requires States acting through competent international organizations or diplomatic conference to "endeavour to establish global and regional rules, standards and recommended practices and procedures to prevent, reduce and control pollution of the marine environment from land-based sources. . . ." In 1995 the Global Plan of Action for the protection of the marine environment from land-based activities was adopted.[63]

Liability and compensation

Article 235(3) of the LOS Convention requires States to

> cooperate in the implementation of existing international law and the further development of international law relating to responsibility and liability for the assessment of and compensation for damage and the settlement of related disputes, as well as, where appropriate, development of criteria and procedures for payment of adequate compensation, such as compulsory insurance or compensation funds.

Over the years, the IMO has put in place a comprehensive set of regulations covering liability and compensation for damage caused by oil transported by ship, through which the shipping industry (in conjunction with oil importers) provides automatic cover of up to US$1 billion for any single incident, regardless of fault. This tiered system of compensation includes the International Convention on Civil Liability for Oil Pollution Damage (CLC)[64] and the International Oil Pollution Compensation (IOPC) Funds,[65] including the 2003 Supplementary Fund,[66] which collectively provide more coverage than ever before to those affected by oil spills.

The International Convention on Civil Liability for Bunker Oil Pollution Damage entered into force in November 2007, extending the liability and compensation regimes to damage caused by spills of oil when carried as fuel in ships' bunkers.[67]

The International Convention on Liability and Compensation for Damage in connection with the Carriage of Hazardous and Noxious Substances by Sea, 1996, would serve to complete this framework by establishing a regime to cover spills involving hazardous and noxious substances.[68] A Protocol aimed at addressing the issues that were widely viewed as barriers to ratification of Convention was adopted in April 2010, with the hope that this would accelerate the entry into force of the Convention, providing the much-needed compensation scheme for spills involving HNS.[69]

Marine living resources

Fishing

The LOS Convention authorizes the coastal State to take a broad range of measures to enforce its fishery laws, including boardings and inspections, requirements for observer coverage and vessel position reports, and arrests and fines (articles 62(4) and 73). The Convention requires that vessels arrested in the exclusive economic zone (EEZ) and their crews must be promptly released upon posting of a bond or other security. A foreign fisherman charged with a criminal violation of fisheries law may post bail.

Under the LOS Convention, penalties for violations of fisheries laws in the EEZ may not include imprisonment, unless the States concerned agree to the contrary, or any other form of corporal punishment (article 73(3)). The Convention does not preclude imprisonment of those who assault officers, resist arrest, or violate other non-fishery laws.[70]

Marine mammals

The Law of the Sea Convention has two articles on marine mammals, 65 for the EEZ and 120 applying article 65 to marine mammals found in the high seas. Article 65 recognizes the right of a coastal State or the competence of an international organization, as appropriate, to prohibit, limit or regulate exploitation of marine mammals more strictly than is required in the case of other living marine resources. Article 65 also requires States to cooperate with a view to conserving marine mammals and, in the case of cetaceans (e.g., whales), to work in particular through appropriate international organizations.

The International Whaling Commission adopted a commercial whaling moratorium in 1986 and other measures that strictly protect marine mammals.[71] The legality of the Japanese scientific whaling programme has been addressed by the ICJ.[72]

Deep sea mining

See the discussion above regarding pollution from activities in the Area.

Submarine cables and pipelines

There is no intergovernmental organization dealing with submarine cables and pipelines. The International Cable Protection Committee (ICPC), based in London, is a private organization composed of representatives of submarine cable owners, submarine cable maintenance authorities, submarine cable system manufacturers, cable ship operators, submarine cable route survey companies and governments.[73] ICPC now has over 140 members from 60 countries.

Submarine cables have become key facilitators of modern life. Telecommunication cables form the backbone of the global communications network, indeed the Internet itself could not function without them. Submarine power cables have enabled the bulk import and export of electric power for commercial benefit and to cover peak loads. ICPC's aim is to foster a team-working relationship with other seabed users, so that submarine telecommunications and power cables can operate in harmony with other seabed activities.[74]

Submarine cables were first addressed internationally in the 1884 Submarine Cable Convention.[75] Portions of this treaty were included in the 1958 Geneva Convention on the Continental Shelf[76] and the Convention on the High Seas.[77] Those provisions were incorporated in the 1982 Law of the Sea Convention.[78] The COLREGS contain some protections for cable laying ships.[79]

Maritime law enforcement

Maritime security

In 1988, following the MS *Achille Lauro* hijacking,[80] a diplomatic conference convened by the IMO adopted the Convention for the Suppression of Unlawful Acts (SUA) against the Safety of

Maritime Navigation, and the Protocol for the Suppression of Unlawful Acts against the Safety of Fixed Platforms Located on the Continental Shelf.[81]

Following the attacks of 11 September 2001, in 2005 IMO adopted amendments to the SUA Convention and its related Protocol, which among other things, introduced procedures for the right of a State Party that desires to board a ship flying the flag of another State Party when the requesting Party has reasonable grounds to suspect that the ship or a person on board the ship is, has been, or is about to be involved in, the commission of an offence under the Convention.

Also following 9-11-01, the IMO focused on maritime security, with the entry into force in July 2004 of a new, comprehensive security regime for international shipping, including the International Ship and Port Facility Security (ISPS) Code, made mandatory under amendments to SOLAS adopted in 2002.[82]

Narcotics[83]

The three major international drug control treaties, the Single Convention on Narcotic Drugs of 1961 (as amended in 1972), the Convention on Psychotropic Substances of 1971, and the United Nations Convention against Illicit Traffic in Narcotic Drugs and Psychotropic Substances of 1988, are mutually supportive and complementary.

An important purpose of the first two treaties is to codify internationally applicable control measures in order to ensure the availability of narcotic drugs and psychotropic substances for medical and scientific purposes, and to prevent their diversion into illicit channels. They also include general provisions on illicit drug trafficking and drug abuse.

The 1988 United Nations Convention against Illicit Traffic in Narcotic Drugs and Psychotropic Substances extends the control regime to precursors, and focuses on establishing measures to combat illicit drug trafficking and related money-laundering, as well as strengthening the framework of international cooperation in criminal matters, including extradition and mutual legal assistance.

The three conventions attribute important functions to the Commission on Narcotic Drugs and to the International Narcotics Control Board.[84]

Article 17 of the 1988 Convention provides the framework for international cooperation in the suppression of drug trafficking at sea.

Smuggling of migrants

In 1993, the UN General Assembly[85] and the IMO[86] adopted resolutions setting forth the steps that States should take to prevent and deter the smuggling of aliens by ships. These steps included the following:

- cooperate in order to prevent the illegal transport by smugglers of third country nationals through their territory, and in the interest of safety of life at sea, to increase their efforts to prevent the smuggling of aliens on ships and to ensure that prompt and effective action is taken against the smuggling of aliens by ship;
- take all feasible steps to prevent those vessels from engaging in the transport of passengers in violation of SOLAS 74/78, including monitoring suspects and suspect vessels, preventing fishing and cargo vessels from being refitted for alien smuggling, denying registration to vessels and licensing of masters engaging in alien smuggling, and preventing any such

vessel in their port from sailing that does not meet the SOLAS standards for carrying passengers;
- authorize maritime law enforcement officials from other countries to board any vessel claiming registry in its country that is suspected of engaging in unsafe practices associated with alien smuggling for the purposes of verifying the claim of registry and of inspecting the vessel for evidence of compliance with SOLAS requirements, to detain any such vessel found to be engaged in alien smuggling, and to report the results of the boardings to the flag State for appropriate action; and
- if it is not already a crime under local law, to amend criminal laws to encompass the smuggling of aliens.[87]

Flag states should also allow the entry of ships and smuggled aliens apprehended in international waters for disposition in accordance with standards that ensure protection of bona fide refugees and safe treatment for all migrants.

In 2000 the UN General Assembly adopted a protocol on the smuggling of migrants to the UN Convention against Transnational Organized Crime (TOC), section two of which dealt with the smuggling of migrants by sea.[88] The objectives of the UNGA and the IMO in 1993 were thus addressed in the TOC Convention and its migrant smuggling protocol.

Piracy[89]

The IMO took the lead in galvanizing UN and international support to suppress piracy off the coast of Somalia.[90] It provides leadership in the implementation of the Djibouti Code of Conduct. It is taking a similar role in combatting piracy off the west coast of Africa, particularly in the Gulf of Guinea.[91]

UNODC has an active counter-piracy programme, particularly in the Horn of Africa.[92]

UNICRI in partnership with the IMO have established a database on court decisions related to piracy off the coast of Somalia.[93] UNICRI is also developing an initiative related to the use of private security contractors on board commercial vessels with a view to preparing a set of guidelines and standards which may be considered and a code of conduct which may guide private contractors, funded by the Government of Italy.[94]

ISO has developed an international model set of maritime rules for the use of force by privately contracted armed security personnel on board ships.[95] These rules are under consideration by ISO subcommittee CD 28007–2 of Technical Committee 8, Ships and Marine Technology, for development of guidelines on the use of force.[96]

Fisheries

Within maritime areas under the jurisdiction of the coastal State (i.e., internal waters, the territorial sea and EEZ) it has exclusive rights to manage, conserve and enforce fishing. On the high seas, there is freedom of fishing for all States subject to the conditions laid down in articles 116–120 of the LOS Convention. The international community, acting through the FAO, has acted to deal with overfishing within these constraints.

In 1995 the UN adopted the Fish Stocks Agreement.[97] To promote long-term sustainable fisheries, in 1995 the FAO Conference adopted the FAO Code of Conduct for Responsible Fisheries.[98]

In 1999 the FAO adopted three International Plans of Action (IOPA): (1) for Reducing Incidental Catch of Seabirds in Longline Fisheries,[99] (2) for the Conservation and Management of Sharks, and (3) for the Management of Fishing Capacity.[100]

In 2001 the FAO adopted a fourth IOPA, to Combat Illegal, Unregulated and Unreported (IUU) Fishing.[101] In 2009 the FAO adopted the Agreement on Port State Measures to Prevent, Deter and Eliminate IUU Fishing.[102]

Underwater cultural heritage

The LOS Convention has two limited provisions regarding archaeological and historical objects found at sea. Article 149 requires that all such objects found in the Area (i.e., the seabed beyond the limits of national jurisdiction) be preserved or disposed of for the benefit of mankind as a whole, "particular regard being paid to the preferential rights of the State or country of origin, or the State of cultural origin, or the State of historical and archaeological origin."

Article 303 provides:

1. States have the duty to protect objects of an archaeological and historical nature found at sea and shall cooperate for this purpose.
2. In order to control traffic in such objects, the coastal State may, in applying article 33 [contiguous zone], presume that their removal from the seabed in the zone referred to in that article without its approval would result in an infringement within its territory or territorial sea of the laws and regulations referred to in that article.
3. Nothing in this article affects the rights of identifiable owners, the law of salvage or other rules of admiralty, or laws and practices with respect to cultural exchanges.
4. This article is without prejudice to other international agreements and rules of international law regarding the protection of objects of an archaeological and historical nature.

The Convention has no provisions regarding such objects found on the continental shelf.

To fill that gap, in 2001 UNESCO adopted the Convention for the Protection of Underwater Cultural Heritage.[103] Unfortunately this treaty does not recognize the continuing ownership rights of flag States in their sunken warships. Further, the treaty extends coastal State rights to such objects located on the continental shelf notwithstanding the LOS Convention limits those rights to natural resources.

Settlement of disputes

Part XV of the LOS Convention provides detailed provisions for the peaceful settlement of disputes, including compulsory procedures entailing binding decisions (Section 2, articles 286–296) and limitations and exceptions to the applicability of Section 2 (Section 3, articles 297–299). For Part XV to be applicable, any dispute must concern the interpretation or application of the LOS Convention.

Where no settlement has been reached through other peaceful means the dispute can be submitted by any party to the dispute to the court or tribunal having jurisdiction.[104] These are the International Court of Justice, the International Tribunal for the Law of the Sea, an arbitral tribunal constituted in accordance with Annex VII, or a special arbitral tribunal constituted in accordance with Annex VIII for one or more of the categories of disputes there specified. Annex

VII is the default choice when the parties to the dispute have not agreed on a forum to hear the dispute.[105]

The UN treaty office maintains the list of arbitrators available to serve in Annex VII arbitrations.[106]

The IMO maintains the list of experts in the field of navigation, including pollution from vessels and by dumping, available to serve as arbitrators under LOS Convention Annex VIII, Special Arbitration.[107] The FAO maintains the list of experts in the field of fisheries available to serve as arbitrators under Annex VIII.[108] The IOC-UNESCO maintains the list of experts in the field of marine scientific research available to serve as arbitrators under Annex VIII.[109] UNEP maintains the list of experts in the field of the protection and preservation of the marine environment available to serve as arbitrators under Annex VIII.[110]

Parties to the Convention have the option to exclude certain categories of disputes concerning the interpretation or application of the Convention with regard to the exercise by a coastal State of its sovereign rights or jurisdiction provided for in the Convention.[111]

Conclusions

This survey reveals that, for the most part, the global organizations responsible for regulating and enforcing maritime activities continue to meet their obligations and to work closely with each other to that end. These institutions have been, and will continue to be, particularly active in the areas of maritime safety, maritime security, maritime law enforcement, marine pollution, conservation and management of living resources, development of the natural resources of the seabed beyond the limits of national jurisdiction, and dispute settlement.

The one glaring omission is the failure of the International Maritime Organization to establish global rules, standards and recommended practices and procedures to prevent, reduce and control pollution of the marine environment arising from or in connection with seabed activities subject to national jurisdiction, as required by article 208(5) of the LOS Convention. Fortunately a number of regional organizations have acted to meet their similar obligations under that article.

In another area, efforts to protect underwater cultural heritage have not been in complete conformity with the provisions of the LOS Convention, and consequently have not been as successful as they might otherwise have been.

Work is ongoing in another area, that of marine biological diversity in areas beyond national jurisdiction (not discussed in this chapter). Its results remain to be seen.

Notes

1 United Nations Convention on the Law of the Sea, Montego Bay 10 Dec. 1982, entered into force 10 November 1994, UN Doc. A/CONF.62/122, 21 ILM 1621–1354 (1982), 1833 UNTS 397, *available at* http://www.un.org/Depts/los/convention_agreements/texts/unclos/unclos_e.pdf (last accessed 14 August 2013) (hereafter LOS Convention).
2 Convention on the Intergovernmental Maritime Consultative Organization, Geneva 6 March 1948, entered into force 17 March 1958, 289 UNTS 3, *available at* http://treaties.un.org/doc/publication/UNTS/Volume%20289/v289.pdf (last accessed 19 August 2013). The original name, the Inter-Governmental Maritime Consultative Organization, or IMCO, was changed in 1982 to IMO.
3 *See further* the IMO's website http://www.imo.org/About/Pages/Default.aspx (last accessed 13 August 2013), from which the foregoing was adapted.

4 For details *see* the IMO website About IMO *available at* http://www.imo.org/About/Conventions/Pages/Home.aspx (last accessed 19 August 2013).

5 Constitution of the United Nations Food and Agriculture Organization, Quebec 16 October 1945, entered into force 16 October 1945, as amended to 1957, 12 UST 980, TIAS 4803, as amended at 2013 *available at* http://www.fao.org/legal/home/basic-texts/en (last accessed 13 August 2013).

6 FAO, Basic Texts, vol. I, p. 3 (2013), *available at* http://www.fao.org/legal/home/basic-texts/en/ (last accessed 16 August 2013).

7 LOS Convention, Part XI Section 4, The Authority, as amended by the 1994 Agreement. The text of the 1994 Part XI Agreement is *available at* http://daccess-ods.un.org/access.nsf/Get?Open&DS=A/RES/48/263&Lang=E (last accessed 17 August 2013).

8 *See* the website of the Authority, http://www.isa.org.jm/en/home (last accessed 12 August 2013).

9 *See* the ILO's website at http://www.ilo.org/global/about-the-ilo/lang—en/index.htm (last accessed 13 August 2013).

10 Maritime Labor Convention, 2006, Geneva 7 Feb. 2006, entered into force 20 August 2013, UNTS, *available at* I-51299-080000028006822e.pdf *and* http://www.ilo.org/ilolex/english/convdisp1.htm (last accessed 9 October 2014 and 13 August 2013). *See further* the ILO MLC website, http://www.ilo.org/global/standards/maritime-labour-convention/lang—en/index.htm (last accessed 13 August 2013).

11 Convention on International Civil Aviation, Chicago 7 Dec. 1944, entered into force 4 April 1947, 61 Stat. 1180, TIAS 1591, 3 Bevans 944, 15 UNTS 295, *available at* http://www.icao.int/publications/Pages/doc7300.aspx (last accessed 13 August 2013).

12 *See* the website of ICAO, http://www.icao.int/Pages/default.aspx (last accessed 13 August 2013).

13 LOS Convention, articles 39(3) and 54.

14 Convention on the Protection of the Underwater Cultural Heritage, Paris 2 Nov. 2001, entered into force 9 January 2009, 2562(I) UNTS 3, *available at* http://portal.unesco.org/en/ev.php-URL_ID=13520&URL_DO=DO_TOPIC&URL_SECTION=201.html (last accessed 15 August 2013). *See further* the Cultural Sector's website, http://www.unesco.org/new/en/culture (last accessed 17 August 2013) and text *infra* accompanying note 105.

15 http://www.unesco.org/new/en/natural-sciences/ioc-oceans/ (last accessed 19 August 2013). The IOC has adopted "Guidelines for the implementation of resolution XX-6 of the IOC Assembly regarding the deployment of profiling floats in the high seas within the framework of the Argo Programme," IOC EC-XLI.4 doc, *available at* http://ioc3.unesco.org/iocraib/files/locaribe_C/IOC-XLI%20Adopted_Res_e.pdf. For a discussion of the various forms of marine data collection, most of which are not marine scientific research, *see* Roach, "Marine Data Collection: U.S. Perspectives," Nordquist et al. (eds.), *Global Challenges and Freedom of Navigation* 283–300, Leiden/Boson: Nijhoff, 2014, and sources cited therein.

16 *See* the *IOC Criteria and Guidelines on the Transfer of Marine Technology, 2005*, *available at* http://www.scor-int.org/CB_Summit/IOC_Tech_Transfer.pdf (last accessed 17 August 2013).

17 International Convention for the Regulation of Whaling, with schedule of whaling regulations, Washington 2 Dec. 1946, entered into force 10 Nov. 1948, 62 Stat. 1716, TIAS 1849, 4 Bevans 248, 161 UNTS 72, *available at* http://treaties.un.org/doc/Publication/UNTS/Volume%20161/v161.pdf (last accessed 19 August 2013).

18 *See* the IWC's website, http://iwc.int/home (last accessed 16 August 2013). *See further* text accompanying note 71 *infra*.

19 *See* ISO's website, http://www.iso.org/iso/home.html (last accessed 13 August 2013).

20 *See infra* notes 95 and 96 and accompanying text.

21 *See infra* note 70 and accompanying text.

22 For additional functions of DOALOS *see* http://untreaty.un.org/ola/div_doalos.aspx?section=doalos (last accessed 19 August 2013).

23 *See* the website of UNODC, http://www.unodc.org/ (last accessed 13 August 2013).

24 *See infra* note 84 and accompanying text.

25 *See infra* note 92 and accompanying text.

26 *See infra* note 88 and accompanying text.

27 UNICRI was established by the Economic and Social Council (ECOSOC) following Resolution 1086B (XXXIX), 1968, which urged an expansion of United Nations activities in crime prevention and criminal justice.

28 ECOSOC Resolution No. 1989/56 of 24 May 1989, Resolutions and Decisions of the Economic and Social Council Official Records 1989, Supplement No. 1, at 41–3, UN doc. E/1989/89, *available at* http://daccess-ods.un.org/TMP/4671152.8301239.html (last accessed 16 August 2013).
29 *See* the website of UNICRI, http://www.unicri.it/institute/ (last accessed 13 August 2013).
30 *See infra* notes 93–96 and accompanying text.
31 http://unep.org/Documents.Multilingual/Default.asp?DocumentID=43 (last accessed 13 August 2013).
32 Charter of the United Nations with the Statute of the International Court of Justice annexed thereto, San Francisco 26 June 1945, entered into force 24 Oct. 1945, 59 Stat. 1031, TS 993, 3 Bevans 1153, *available at* http://www.un.org/en/documents/charter/index.shtml (last accessed 19 August 2013).
33 *See* the website of the ICJ, http://www.icj-cij.org/homepage/index.php (last accessed 13 August 2013).
34 *See* the list of all ICJ cases *available at* http://www.icj-cij.org/docket/index.php?p1=3&p2=2 (last accessed 14 August 2013).
35 LOS Convention, Annex VI, Statute of the International Tribunal for the Law of the Sea.
36 *Id.* articles 2 & 4. *See* the website of ITLOS, http://www.itlos.org/ (last accessed 13 August 2013).
37 *See further* the ITLOS website, http://www.itlos.org/index.php?id=15, from which the foregoing is adapted.
38 *See* the list of cases at http://www.itlos.org/index.php?id=35&L=1%2525252F (last accessed 16 August 2013).
39 Dispute concerning delimitation of the maritime boundary between Bangladesh and Myanmar in the Bay of Bengal (Bangladesh/Myanmar), Case No. 16, *available at* http://www.itlos.org/index.php?id=108&L= (last accessed 14 August 2013).
40 Responsibilities and obligations of States sponsoring persons and entities with respect to activities in the Area, Case No. 17, *available at* http://www.itlos.org/index.php?id=109&L=0%2FoOpensinternal linkincurrentwindo (last accessed 14 August 2013).
41 *See* http://www.itlos.org/index.php?id=252&L=1%27%60%28[{^~, and Becker, "Sustainable Fisheries and the Obligations of Flag and Coastal States: The Request by the Sub-Regional Fisheries Commission for an ITLOS Advisory Opinion," ASIL Insight, vol. 17 issue 19, 23 August 2013, *available at* http://www.asil.org/insights130823.cfm (last accessed 23 August 2013).
42 For a table listing the sources and implementation of the LOS Convention, *see* Nordquist et al. (eds.), VII *UNCLOS 1982 Commentary: Supplementary Documents* 905–909, Leiden/Boston: Martinus Nijhoff, 2012. For a table listing the comparable provisions of the 1958 Geneva Conventions on the Law of the Sea, *see id.* 911–916. For a detailed study of the IMO's role under the LOS Convention, *see* IMO Secretariat, *Implications of the United Nations Convention on the Law of the Sea for the International Maritime Organization*, IMO doc. LEG/MISC.6, 10 Sept. 2008, *in id.* 741–883.
43 International Convention for the Safety of Life at Sea (with annexed Regulations), London 17 June 1960, entered into force 26 May 1965, 16 UST 185, TIAS 5780, 536 UNTS 27, *available at* http://treaties.un.org/doc/Publication/UNTS/Volume%20536/volume-536-I-7794-English.pdf (last accessed 20 August 2013).
44 International Convention for the Safety of Life at Sea, London 1 Nov. 1974, entered into force 25 May 1980, 32 UST 47, TIAS 9700, 1184 UNTS 278, *available at* http://treaties.un.org/doc/Publication/UNTS/Volume%201184/volume-1184-I-18961-English.pdf *and* http://www.austlii.edu.au/au/other/dfat/treaties/1983/22.html (both last accessed 20 August 2013).
45 Convention on Facilitation of International Maritime Traffic, with annex, London 5 April 1965, entered into force 5 March 1967, 18 UST 410, TIAS 6251, 591 UNTS 265, *available at* http://treaties.un.org/doc/Publication/UNTS/Volume%20591/v591.pdf (last accessed 20 August 2013).
46 International Convention on Load Lines, London 5 April 1966, entered into force 21 July 1968, 18 UST 1857, TIAS 6331, 640 UNTS 133, *available at* http://treaties.un.org/doc/Publication/UNTS/Volume%20640/volume-640-I-9159-English.pdf (last accessed 20 August 2013).
47 International Convention for Safe Containers (CSC), Geneva 2 December 1972, entered into force 6 September 1977, 1064 UNTS 25, *available at* http://treaties.un.org/doc/Publication/UNTS/Volume%201064/volume-1064-I-16198-English.pdf (last accessed 20 August 2013).
48 International Convention on the Tonnage Measurements of Ships, 1969, with annexes, London 23 June 1969, entered into force 18 July 1982, TIAS 10490, 1291 UNTS 3, *available at* http://treaties.un.org/doc/Publication/UNTS/Volume%201291/volume-1291-I-21264-English.pdf (last accessed 20 August 2013).

49 International Convention on Standards of Training, Certification and Watchkeeping for Seafarers, with Annex (STCW) London 7 July 1978, entered into force 28 April 1984, 1361 UNTS 75, *available at* http://treaties.un.org/doc/Publication/UNTS/Volume%201361/volume-1361-I-23001-English.pdf *and* http://www.admiraltylawguide.com/conven/stcw1978.html (last accessed 20 August 2013). A Conference of Parties to the Convention adopted on 7 July 1995 amendments to chapters I-VIII of the Convention and the STCW Code.

50 A Conference of Parties to the International Convention on Standards of Training, Certification and Watchkeeping for Seafarers, 1978, held in Manila, the Philippines, June 2010, adopted, by resolutions 1 and 2 respectively, amendments to the annex to the Convention and to the STCW Code (the Manila amendments). *See* http://www.stcw.org/ *and* http://www.imo.org/About/Conventions/ListOfConventions/Pages/International-Convention-on-Standards-of-Training,-Certification-and-Watchkeeping-for-Seafarers-%28STCW%29.aspx (last accessed 20 August 2013).

51 SOLAS regulation XI/4 and MARPOL regulations I/11, II/16.9 and V/8. MARPOL regulation IV/13 was adopted in 2006.

52 For a comprehensive treatment of the global rules for the protection of the marine environment from shipping activities *see* C. de la Rue and C.B. Anderson, *Shipping and the Environment*, London: Informa, 2nd ed., 2009.

53 1977 UNTS 138. The definition of dumping is identical in both the London Convention (Article III(a)) and the LOS Convention. The 1996 Protocol expanded the definition of dumping to include waste storage on the seabed and abandonment of platforms.

54 *See* the website of the London Convention and Protocol, http://www.imo.org/OurWork/Environment/SpecialProgrammesAndInitiatives/Pages/London-Convention-and-Protocol.aspx (last accessed 9 October 2014).

55 Protocol to the Convention on the Prevention of Marine Pollution by Dumping of Wastes and other Matter, 1972, London 7 Nov. 1996, entered into force 24 March 2006, 36 ILM 7 (1997), *available at* http://www.admiraltylawguide.com/conven/protodumping1996.html, *and as amended in 2006 at* http://www.imo.org/blast/blastData.asp?doc_id=13203&filename=PROTOCOL%20Amended%202006.doc (both last accessed 19 August 2013).

56 *See further* Roach, "International Standards for Offshore Drilling," in Nordquist et al. (eds.), *The Regulation of Continental Shelf Development: Rethinking International Standards* 105–150, Leiden/Boston: Martinus Nijhoff, 2013. Regional conventions are set out on pages 124–150.

57 Regulations 7 and 31–32 on prospecting and exploration for polymetallic nodules in the Area, doc. ISBA/6/A/18, 20 July 2000; Regulations 5 and 33–37 on prospecting and exploration for polymetallic sulphides in the Area, doc. ISBA/16/A/12/Rev.1, 7 May 2010, *available at* http://www.isa.org.jm/files/documents/EN/Regs/PolymetallicSulphides.pdf; and Regulations 5 and 33–35 on Prospecting and Exploration for Cobalt-rich Ferromanganese Crusts in the Area, ISBA/18/A/11, 27 July 2012. The three regulations are reprinted in *UNCLOS 1982 Commentary: Supplementary Documents* 115–279. *See* "Environmental Management Needs for Exploration and Exploitation of Deep Sea Minerals," Technical Study No. 10, 2012, *available at* http://www.isa.org.jm/files/documents/EN/Pubs/TS10/index.html, *and* "Recommendations for the Guidance of the Contractors for the Assessment of the Possible Environmental Impacts Arising from Exploration for Polymetallic Nodules in the Area," ISBA doc. ISBA/16/LTC/7, 2 Nov. 2010, regulations 31–34, *available at* http://www.isa.org.jm/files/documents/EN/16Sess/LTC/ISBA-16LTC-7.pdf. *See also* "Towards the Development of a Regulatory Framework for Polymetallic Nodule Exploitation in the Area," Technical Study No. 11, 26 Feb. 2013, *available at* http://www.isa.org.jm/files/documents/EN/Pubs/TStudy11-Final.pdf (study does not deal with the specifics of an environmental regime for exploitation as that is being considered separately within ISA but does specify key environmental components that will have to be developed and included in an overall exploitation framework) (each last accessed 15 August 2013).

58 International Convention for the Prevention of Pollution from Ships, 1973/1978, London 17 Feb. 1978, entered into force 2 Oct. 1983, 12 ILM 1319 (1973), 1340 UNTS 61, *available at* http://treaties.un.org/doc/Publication/UNTS/Volume%201340/volume-1340-A-22484-English.pdf (1978 text) *and* http://www.austlii.edu.au/au/other/dfat/treaties/1988/29.html (text as amended in 1985 and 1985) (both last accessed 19 August 2013).

59 International Convention on the Control of Harmful Anti-Fouling Systems on Ships, 2001, London 5 Oct. 2001, entered into force 17 Sept. 2008, IMO doc. AFS/CONF/26, *available at* http://www.uscg.mil/hq/cg5/cg522/cg5224/docs/Antifouling.pdf (last accessed 19 August 2013).

60 International Convention for the Control and Management of Ships' Ballast Water and Sediments, 2004, London 13 Feb. 2004, not in force, IMO doc. BWM/CONF/36, *available at* http://water.epa.gov/type/oceb/oceantreaties.cfm, http://www.ecolex.org/server2.php/libcat/docs/TRE/Multilateral/En/TRE001412.pdf *and* http://www.tematea.org/?q=node/178 (each last accessed 19 August 2013).

61 Hong Kong International Convention for the Safe and Environmentally Sound Recycling of Ships, 2009, Hong Kong 15 May 2009, not in force, IMO doc. SR/CONF/45, *available at* http://www.cfr.org/environmental-pollution/hong-kong-international-convention-safe-environmentally-sound-recycling-ships/p20627 (last accessed 19 August 2013).

62 Protocol of 1997 to amend the International Convention for the Prevention of Pollution from Ships, 1973, as modified by the Protocol of 1978 relating thereto (adding Annex VI), London 26 Sept. 1997, entered into force 19 May 2005, TIAS, UNTS, *available at* http://www.admiraltylawguide.com/conven/protomarpol1997.html *and* http://water.epa.gov/type/oceb/oceantreaties.cfm (both last accessed 19 August 2013).

63 *See* UNEP, Global Plan of Action for the Protection of the Marine Environment from Land-based Activities, *available at* http://www.gpa.unep.org/ (last accessed 18 August 2013).

64 International Convention on Civil Liability for Oil Pollution Damage, Brussels 29 Nov. 1969, entered into force 19 June 1975, 973 UNTS 3, UKTS No. 106 (1975), 9 ILM 45 (1970), 64 Am. J. Int'l L. 481, *available at* http://treaties.un.org/doc/Publication/UNTS/Volume%20973/v973.pdf; Protocol to the International Convention on Civil Liability for Oil Pollution Damage, 1969, London 27 Nov. 1992, entered into force 30 May 1996, 1956 UNTS 255, *available at* http://treaties.un.org/doc/Publication/UNTS/Volume%201956/v1956.pdf (both last accessed 19 August 2013).

65 International Convention on the Establishment of an International Fund for Compensation for Oil Pollution Damage, Brussels 18 December 1971, entered into force 16 October 1978, 1110 UNTS 58, *available at* http://treaties.un.org/doc/Publication/UNTS/Volume%201110/volume-1110-I-17146-English.pdf *and* http://www.admiraltylawguide.com/conven/oilpolfund1971.html; Protocol to the International Convention on the Establishment of an International Fund for Compensation for Oil Pollution Damage, 1971, London 19 November 1976, entered into force 22 November 1994, 1862 UNTS 509, *available at* http://treaties.un.org/doc/Publication/UNTS/Volume%201862/v1862.pdf; Protocol of 1992 to amend the International Convention on the establishment of an international fund for compensation for oil pollution damage, London 27 November 1992, entered into force 30 May 1996, 1953 UNTS 330, *available at* http://treaties.un.org/doc/Publication/UNTS/Volume%201953/v1953.pdf *and* http://www.admiraltylawguide.com/conven/protocivilpol1992.html (each last accessed 19 August 2013).

66 Protocol of 2003 to the International Convention on the Establishment of an International Fund for Compensation for Oil Pollution Damage, 1992, London 16 May 2003, entered into force 3 March 2005, UNTS, *available at* http://www.jus.uio.no/english/services/library/treaties/06/6-04/imo_iopc_supplementary_fund.xml (last accessed 19 August 2013).

67 International Convention on Civil Liability for Bunker Oil Pollution Damage, 2001, London 23 March 2001, entered into force 21 November 2008, UNTS, IMO doc. LEG/CONF.12/19, *available at* http://www.official-documents.gov.uk/document/cm66/6693/6693.pdf (last accessed 19 August 2013).

68 International Convention on Liability and Compensation for Damage in Connection with the Carriage of Hazardous and Noxious Substances by Sea, 1996, London 3 May 1996, not intended to enter into force, *available at* http://www.hnsconvention.org/Documents/HNS%20Convention%201996.pdf (last accessed 19 August 2013).

69 Protocol of 2010 to the International Convention on Liability and Compensation for Damage in connection with the Carriage of Hazardous and Noxious Substances by Sea, 1996, London 30 April 2010, not in force, IMO doc. LEG/CONF.17/10, *available at* http://www.hnsconvention.org/Documents/2010%20HNS%20Protocol.pdf. The consolidated convention text is *available at* http://www.hnsconvention.org/Documents/2010%20HNS%20Convention%20Consolidated%20text.pdf (both last accessed 19 August 2013).

70 Commentary – The 1982 United Nations Convention on the Law of the Sea and the Agreement on Implementation of Part XI, Senate Treaty Doc. 103–39, pp. 45–46, *available at* http://www.jag.navy.mil/organization/documents/Senate_Transmittal.pdf.

71 *See* the website of the International Whaling Commission, http://iwc.int/home (last accessed 15 August 2013).

72 *Whaling in the Antarctic* (Australia v. Japan: New Zealand intervening), judgment 31 March 2014, *available at* http://www.icj-cij.org/docket/files/148/18136.pdf (last accessed 9 October 2014).
73 *See* the ICPC's website, http://www.iscpc.org/ (last accessed 9 October 2014).
74 *See* D.R. Burnett et al. (eds.), *Submarine Cables: The Handbook of Law and Policy*, Leiden/Boston: Martinus Nijhoff, 2013.
75 Convention on the Protection of Submarine Cables, Paris 14 March 1884, entered into force 1 May 1888, 24 Stat. 989, TS No. 380, as amended 25 Stat. 1414, TS Nos. 380 1 and 380 2, 380 3, 1 Bevans 89, 112, 114, *available at* http://cil.nus.edu.sg/wp/wp-content/uploads/2009/10/Convention_on_Protection_of_Cables_1884.pdf (last accessed 19 August 2013).
76 Article 4 of the Convention on the Continental Shelf, Geneva 29 April 1958, entered into force 10 June 1964, 15 UST 471, TIAS 5578, 499 UNTS 311, *available at* http://untreaty.un.org/ilc/texts/instruments/english/conventions/8_1_1958_continental_shelf.pdf (last accessed 19 August 2013).
77 Articles 26–29 of the Convention on the High Seas, Geneva 29 April 1958, entered into force 30 Sept. 1962, 13 UST 2312, TIAS 5200, 450 UNTS 82, *available at* http://untreaty.un.org/ilc/texts/instruments/english/conventions/8_1_1958_high_seas.pdf (last accessed 19 August 2013).
78 LOS Convention articles 79, 87(1)(c), 112–115, *supra* note 1.
79 E.g., Convention on International Regulations for Preventing Collisions at Sea, 1972, Rules 3(g)(i) and 27, London 20 Oct. 1972, entered into force 15 July 1977, 28 UST 3459, TIAS 8587, 1050 UNTS 17, *available at* http://www.dft.gov.uk/mca/mcga07-home/shipsandcargoes/mcga-shipsregsandguidance/marinenotices/mcga-mnotice.htm?textobjid=383C9CC4873C5108 (1996), http://www.dft.gov.uk/mca/mcga07-home/shipsandcargoes/mcga-shipsregsandguidance/marinenotices/mcga-mnotice.htm?textobjid=51D567940828B3D6 (correction), and http://www.dft.gov.uk/mca/mcga07-home/shipsandcargoes/mcga-shipsregsandguidance/marinenotices/mcga-mnotice.htm?textobjid=249AC37C42801743 (amendment) *and* http://treaties.un.org/doc/Publication/UNTS/Volume%201050/volume-1050-I-15824-English.pdf (original text). *See also* http://www.imo.org/OurWork/Safety/Navigation/Pages/Preventing-Collisions.aspx (each last accessed 19 August 2013).
80 *See* 'Achille Lauro hijacking,' *available at* http://en.wikipedia.org/wiki/Achille_Lauro_hijacking (last accessed 20 August 2013).
81 Convention for the Suppression of Unlawful Acts against the Safety of Maritime Navigation, Rome 10 March 1988, entered into force 1 March 1992, 27 ILM 672 (1988), UN, LOS Bull., No. 11, July 1988, at 14, 1678 UNTS 221, and Protocol for the Suppression of Unlawful Acts against the Safety of Fixed Platforms located on the continental shelf, Rome 10 March 1988, entered into force 1 March 1992, 27 ILM 685 (1988), UN, LOS Bull., No. 11, July 1988, at 24, 1678 UNTS 221, *available at* http://treaties.un.org/doc/db/Terrorism/Conv8-english.pdf (last accessed 20 August 2013).
82 A Conference of Contracting Governments to the SOLAS Convention adopted on 12 December 2002, in accordance with article VIII(c)(ii) of the Convention, amendments to the Annex of the Convention (Chapters V, XI and new Chapter XI-2) regarding the ISPS Code.
83 LOS Convention, article 108, and United Nations Convention Against Illicit Traffic in Narcotic Drugs and Psychotropic Substances, Article 17, Vienna 20 December 1988, entered into force 11 November 1990, 1582 UNTS 95, 28 ILM 497 (1989), *available at* http://www.unodc.org/unodc/en/treaties/illicit-trafficking.html. *See* http://www.unodc.org/unodc/en/drug-trafficking/index.html (both last accessed 16 August 2013).
84 *See further* UNODC's website on drug trafficking, https://www.unodc.org/unodc/en/drug-trafficking/legal-framework.html (last accessed 16 August 2013), from which the foregoing is adapted.
85 UNGA Res. 48/102, 20 December 1993, Prevention of the smuggling of aliens, *available through link at* http://www.un.org/Docs/journal/asp/ws.asp?m=A/RES/48/102 (last accessed 19 August 2013).
86 IMO Res. A.773(18), 4 November 1993, Enhancement of safety at sea by the prevention and suppression of unsafe practices associated with alien smuggling by ships, *available at* http://www.imo.org/blast/blastData.asp?doc_id=9808&filename=A%20773%2818%29.pdf. *See also* IMO Res. A.867(20), 27 Nov. 1997, Combating Unsafe Practices Associated with the Trafficking or Transport of Migrants by Sea, *available at* http://www.imo.org/blast/blastData.asp?doc_id=9895&filename=A%20867%2820%29.pdf (both last accessed 19 August 2013).
87 *See* 11 Italian Y.B. Int'l L. 2001, at 273–276 (2003).
88 Protocol against the Smuggling of Migrants by Land, Sea and Air, supplementing the United Nations Convention against Transnational Organized Crime, New York 15 November 2000, entered into force 28 January 2004, 40 ILM 384 (2001), 2241 UNTS 507, *available at* http://treaties.un.org/doc/Pub

lication/UNTS/Volume%202241/v2241.pdf *and* https://www.unodc.org/pdf/crime/a_res_55/res5525e.pdf. *See* the UNODC website on migrant smuggling, https://www.unodc.org/unodc/en/human-trafficking/smuggling-of-migrants.html?ref=menuside (last accessed 16 August 2013).

89 LOS Convention, articles 100–108, 110. *See* http://www.unodc.org/unodc/en/piracy/index.html?ref=menuside (last accessed 13 August 2013).
90 See Roach, "IMO Policies and Actions regarding Piracy," in David Caron and Nilufer Oral (eds.), *Navigating Straits: Challenges for International Law*, Leiden/Boston: Brill Nijhoff, 2014, pp. 241–267.
91 *See* IMO, Piracy and armed robbery against ships, *available at* http://www.imo.org/OurWork/Security/PiracyArmedRobbery/Pages/Default.aspx (last accessed 16 August 2013). For an analysis of piracy in the ASEAN region, *see* Robert C. Beckman and J. Ashley Roach (eds.), *Piracy and International Maritime Crimes in ASEAN*, Cheltenham UK/Northampton MA: Edward Elgar, 2012.
92 *See* UNODC's website on piracy, https://www.unodc.org/unodc/en/piracy/index.html?ref=menuside (last accessed 17 August 2013).
93 *See* http://www.unicri.it/topics/piracy/database/ (last accessed 13 August 2013).
94 *See* http://www.unicri.it/topics/piracy/security_contractors/ (last assessed 13 August 2013), http://www.iso.org/iso/home/store/catalogue_tc/catalogue_detail.htm?csnumber=63166, and IMO doc MSC 93/16/2, 11 March 2014 (ISO) (ISO PAS 28007 accreditation study).
95 ISO, An International Model Set of Maritime Rules for the Use of Force (RUF), 3 May 2013, *available at* http://www.100seriesrules.com/ (last accessed 14 August 2013). *See also* IMO doc. MSC 92/INF.14, 9 April 2013, and MSC 92/26, 30 June 2013, paras. 18.13–18.14.
96 http://www.iso.org/iso/home/store/catalogue_tc/catalogue_detail.htm?csnumber=63166 (last accessed 9 October 2014).
97 The text of the Fish Stocks agreement is *available at* http://www.un.org/Depts/los/convention_agreements/texts/fish_stocks_agreement/CONF164_37.htm (last accessed 17 August 2013).
98 *See* http://www.fao.org/fishery/code/en (last accessed 18 August 2013).
99 *See* http://www.fao.org/fishery/ipoa-seabirds/en (last accessed 18 August 2013).
100 *See* http://www.fao.org/fishery/ipoa-capacity/en (last accessed 18 August 2013).
101 *See* http://www.fao.org/fishery/ipoa-iuu/en (last accessed 18 August 2013).
102 Rome 22 Nov. 2009, not in force, *available through link at* http://www.fao.org/fishery/topic/166283/en (last accessed 18 August 2013).
103 *See* note 17 *supra*.
104 LOS Convention, article 286.
105 *Id.*, article 287.
106 The official list of arbitrators nominated under article 2 of annex VII to the Convention can be found on the web site of the United Nations Treaty Section of the Office of Legal Affairs, http://treaties.un.org/Pages/ViewDetailsIII.aspx?&src=TREATY&mtdsg_no=XXI~6&chapter=21&Temp=mtdsg3&lang=en (last accessed 17 August 2013).
107 LOS Convention, Annex VIII, article 2. The list is *available at* http://www.un.org/Depts/los/settlement_of_disputes/expertsunclosVIIIimo.pdf (last accessed 13 August 2013).
108 *Ibid*. The list is *available at* http://www.fao.org/fileadmin/templates/legal/docs/fish_experts.pdf (last accessed 13 August 2013) *and* http://www.un.org/Depts/los/settlement_of_disputes/expertsunclosVIIImar2012fao.pdf (last accessed 14 August 2013).
109 *Ibid*. The list is *available at* http://www.un.org/Depts/los/settlement_of_disputes/expertsunclosVIII may2011iocunesco.pdf (last accessed 13 August 2013).
110 *Ibid*. For this list of experts *see* http://www.un.org/Depts/los/settlement_of_disputes/expertsunclos VIIInov2002unep.pdf (last accessed 13 August 2013).
111 *Id.*, article 297. The declarations of States exercising this right are *available at* the website of the UN Treaty Section of the Office of Legal Affairs, *supra* note 81 (last accessed 14 August 2013).

8

The Role of Regional Organisations

Kerry Tetzlaff

Introduction

Regional organizations have increasingly become the preferred instrument for the regulation and enforcement of maritime activities especially when concerned with straddling fish stocks and highly migratory fish stocks as well as the protection and preservation of the marine environment. In this chapter, the regulatory and enforcement roles of regional fisheries management organizations (RFMOs) in the conservation and management of fish stocks and the role of regional seas organizations (RSOs) in the protection and preservation of the marine environment will be reviewed and a number of critical issues and themes discussed.

The role of regional fisheries management organizations in the conservation and management of fish stocks

The role of RFMOs[1] in fisheries management has evolved gradually over the course of the twentieth century from the initial allocation of fish stock quotas and gathering and analysis of data to the development of basic management systems such as mesh size limits and closed areas to present day conservation, management and enforcement measures, which include international observer and inspection programmes at sea and in port, satellite-based vessel monitoring systems and catch and trade documentation schemes.[2]

The framework provisions relating to the regulatory and enforcement role of RFMOs in the conservation and management of fish stocks are provided in the United Nations Convention on the Law of the Sea (LOSC).[3] These provisions have been considerably developed in relation to straddling fish stocks and highly migratory fish stocks under the 1995 Agreement for the Implementation of the Provisions of the United Nations Convention on the Law of the Sea of 10 December 1982 relating to the Conservation and Management of Straddling Fish Stocks and Highly Migratory Fish Stocks (UNFSA).[4]

United Nations Convention on the Law of the Sea

The LOSC[5] contains framework provisions for the management of fish stocks and, to this end, makes reference to "competent international organizations, whether subregional, regional or global",[6] "subregional or regional organizations",[7] "international organizations",[8] "regional organizations"[9] and "subregional or regional fisheries organizations".[10] These terms are not defined and will all be assumed as meaning RFMOs in this chapter.

Within the Exclusive Economic Zone (EEZ), the role of RFMOs extends to cooperation with coastal states. In Article 61(2), "competent international organizations, whether subregional, regional or global" shall cooperate as appropriate with coastal states to ensure that the "maintenance of the living resources in the exclusive economic zone is not endangered by over-exploitation". In Article 61(3), measures taken by the coastal state must take into account "fishing patterns, the interdependence of stocks and any generally recommended international minimum standards, whether subregional, regional or global". It follows that RFMOs will be a major source of such information for the high sea areas adjacent to the EEZ and can also provide information on any regional and subregional minimum standards developed by the RFMO. A further role for RFMOs under Article 61(5) is to receive and exchange available scientific information, catch and fishing effort statistics and other data relevant to the conservation of fish stocks.

With regard to straddling fish stocks and highly migratory fish stocks, the LOSC assigns RFMOs the role of an optional forum for the development of conservation measures. Under Article 63, where straddling fish stocks occur in the EEZs of two or more coastal states, a RFMO may be used as a forum for such states to seek to agree on measures necessary to coordinate and ensure the conservation and development of such stocks.[11] Where straddling fish stocks occur in the EEZ of a coastal state and in the area beyond and adjacent to the EEZ, a RFMO may be used as a forum for the coastal state and states fishing for such stocks in the adjacent area to seek to agree on measures necessary for the conservation of these stocks in the adjacent area.[12] For highly migratory stocks, RFMOs may be used as a forum for the coastal state and other states, whose nationals fish in the region for such stocks, to cooperate with a view to ensuring conservation and promoting the objective of optimum utilization of highly migratory stocks throughout the region within and beyond the EEZ.[13]

Article 65 affirms any established competence of an RFMO to "prohibit, limit or regulate the exploitation of marine mammals more strictly than provided for in this Part [V]". In the case of cetaceans, states shall "in particular work through the appropriate international organizations for their conservation, management and study".[14]

The last reference to the role of RFMOs under the provisions for the EEZ is in Article 66(5), which provides that the state of origin of anadromous stocks and other states fishing for such stocks shall make arrangements for the implementation of the provisions of Article 66, where appropriate, through regional organizations.

The high seas provisions of LOSC contain similar roles for RFMOs. Under Article 118, states "shall, as appropriate, cooperate to establish subregional or regional fisheries organizations" for the conservation and management of living resources of the high seas. Article 119 on the conservation of the living resources of the high seas contains several relevant provisions. Firstly, Article 119 (1)(a) requires that "any generally recommended international minimum standards, whether subregional, regional or global" be taken into account by states when determining the allowable catch and establishing conservation measures for the living resources of the high seas. This would include any generally recommended international minimum standards developed by RFMOs. Secondly, Article 119(2) provides a role for RFMOs as a clearinghouse for "available scientific information, catch and fishing effort statistics, and other data relevant to the conservation of fish stocks". Finally, Article 120 extends the role of RFMOs found in Article 65 to the high seas.

United Nations Fish Stocks Agreement

The Agreement for the Implementation of the Provisions of the United Nations Convention on the Law of the Sea of 10 December 1982 relating to the Conservation and Management of Straddling Fish Stocks and Highly Migratory Fish Stocks (UNFSA)[15] focuses on implementing LOSC provisions regarding the conservation and management of straddling fish stocks and highly migratory fish stocks. The UNFSA develops the LOSC principle of cooperation to ensure that conservation and optimum utilization of fisheries resources are achieved on both sides of the EEZ. To this end, it calls for the development of RFMOs.

It has been stated that the "value of the approaches [the UNFSA] takes is such that it is likely to be regarded, in situations where it is not binding, as a charter for . . . the conservation and management of straddling and highly migratory fish stocks".[16] The UNFSA is also "bound to influence international relations concerning conservation and management of fish stocks to which the [UNFSA] does not apply and which also occur in areas beyond the exclusive jurisdiction of states".[17] As such, it is an important source when considering the role of RFMOs in the conservation and management of all fish stocks.

Whilst the LOSC contains no preference as to whether cooperation should take place directly between states or through RFMOs, UNFSA proceeds on the basis that RFMOs will be the preferred mode of cooperation and provides particulars regarding the role and functions of RFMOs. Article 13 provides that states shall cooperate to strengthen existing RFMOs "in order to improve their effectiveness in establishing and implementing conservation and management measures" for straddling fish stocks and highly migratory fish stocks and, to this end, UNFSA also provides specific direction.

Article 5 contains a number of general principles and is the starting point for strengthening RFMOs. General principles include:

- the adoption of fisheries and conservation measures to ensure long-term sustainability of straddling fish stocks and highly migratory fish stocks and to promote optimum utilization of stocks;
- measures are to be based on best scientific evidence to maintain or restore stocks at levels capable of producing maximum sustainable yields;
- the application of the precautionary principle;
- the protection of biodiversity of the marine environment;
- the collection and distribution of data on fishing activities and from research programmes;
- the promotion and conduct of scientific research and development of technology to support fisheries conservation and management; and
- the implementation and enforcement of conservation and management measures through effective monitoring control and surveillance.

While these principles are directed at coastal states and states fishing on the high seas, it is clear that implementation of most of these principles can be most efficiently undertaken by cooperative action within RFMOs.

The precautionary approach is defined under Article 6 and assumes a similarly cooperative action by states to ensure that the precautionary approach is included in decision-making regarding fisheries and conservation and management. While RFMOs are not specifically mentioned, it appears to be assumed under Annex II Guidelines for the Application of Precautionary

Reference Points in Conservation and Management of Straddling Fish Stocks and Highly Migratory Fish Stocks that RFMOs will play a principal role in applying the precautionary approach to stock specific fish quotas and management strategies.

Article 7 introduces the requirement that fisheries conservation and management measures established for the high seas and those adopted for areas under national jurisdiction be compatible to ensure the conservation and management of straddling fish stocks and highly migratory fish stocks in their entirety.[18] This has been termed the compatibility principle. The role of RFMOs is mentioned on a number of occasions in Article 7. In particular, under Article 7(1)(a) with respect to straddling fish stocks, relevant states shall "seek, either directly or through the appropriate mechanisms for cooperation provided for in Part III, to agree upon the measures necessary for the conservation of these stocks in the adjacent high seas area". Notably, this is almost identical wording to Article 63(2) of LOSC directing relevant states to cooperate either directly or through "appropriate subregional or regional organisations". Part III focuses on the development of the role and functions of RFMOs. This makes it clear that RFMOs are the "mechanism for cooperation provided for in Part III". In a similar manner, Article 7(1)(b) is essentially an import of Article 64 of LOSC focusing on highly migratory fish stocks substituting "appropriate international organisations" under Article 64 of LOSC with "appropriate mechanisms for cooperation provided for in Part III". It is clear that, with regard to straddling fish stocks and highly migratory fish stocks, the basic concepts of "subregional or regional organisations" and "appropriate international organisations" referred to under LOSC have been further developed into a detailed structure and role for RFMOs under UNFSA.

Part III on Mechanisms for International Cooperation Concerning Straddling Fish Stocks and Highly Migratory Fish Stocks is central to the development of the regulatory and enforcement role of RFMOs in the conservation and management of straddling fish stocks and highly migratory fish stocks. Part III develops the duty to cooperate for the conservation and management of such fish stocks; stipulates criteria for states to agree on prior to the establishment of a new RFMO; sets out a number of functions of RFMOs; provides a list of considerations for RFMOs to take into account when considering the nature and extent of participatory rights for new members of an RFMO; highlights the importance of transparency in RFMO activities; calls for states to cooperate in strengthening existing RFMOs to improve effectiveness in establishing and implementing conservation and management measures; and addresses the collection and provision of information and cooperation in scientific research.

Article 8 develops the duty to cooperate for the purposes of conservation and management of straddling fish stocks and highly migratory fish stocks. Article 8(1) first outlines the general duty for states to "pursue cooperation" either directly or through RFMOs to ensure effective conservation and management of such stocks. Article 8(3) requires relevant coastal states and states fishing for the stocks on the high seas to give effect to their duty to cooperate by becoming members of, or participants in, the relevant RFMO or by agreeing to apply the fisheries conservation and management measures established by the RFMO. States with a real interest in the fisheries concerned may become members of, or participants in, such RFMO. The terms of participation must not preclude such states from membership or participation and nor may they be applied in a manner which discriminates against any state with a real interest in the fisheries concerned. Article 8(4) provides that only states that are members of, or participants in, an RFMO or that agree to apply the fisheries conservation and management measures of the RFMO shall have access to the fishery resources to which those measures apply. Article 8 reflects the primacy of the role of RFMOs in the conservation and management of fish stocks under UNFSA.

While not directly outlining roles of RFMOs, Article 9(1) provides a list of subject matter, which must be agreed on by states wishing to establish a RFMO. This includes the stocks to which conservation and management measures apply, the area of application, the relationship between the work of the new RFMO and the role of any relevant and existing fisheries management organization, and the mechanisms by which the RFMO will obtain scientific advice and review the status of stocks (including a possible scientific advisory body). These provisions all point to roles a RFMO will play in the conservation and management of fish stocks.

Article 10 contains a comprehensive list of the regulatory and enforcement roles of RFMOs in the conservation and management of straddling fish stocks and highly migratory fish stocks. These functions include:

- the development of conservation and management measures to ensure the long term sustainability of straddling fish stocks and highly migratory fish stocks;
- the development of participatory rights such as allocations of allowable catch and levels of fishing effort;
- the adoption and application of any generally recommended international minimum standards for the responsible conduct of fishing operations;
- the procurement and evaluation of scientific advice, the review of the status of the stocks and the assessment of the impact of fishing on non-target and associated or dependent species;
- the development of standards for the collection, reporting, verification and exchange of data on fisheries for the stocks;
- the compilation and dissemination of accurate and complete statistical data (as described in Annex I);
- the promotion and conduct of scientific assessments of the stocks and relevant research and dissemination of the results;
- the establishment of appropriate cooperative mechanisms for effective monitoring, control, surveillance and enforcement;
- the development of means by which the fishing interest of new members or new participants will be accommodated;
- the development of decision-making procedures which facilitate the adoption of conservation and management measures in a timely and effective manner;
- the promotion of peaceful settlement of disputes in accordance with Part VIII;
- the procurement – through member states – of full cooperation of relevant national agencies and industries in the implementation of recommendations and decisions of the RFMO; and
- the publication of all conservation and management measures established by the RFMO.[19]

UNFSA also provides guidelines for the determination of the nature and extent of participatory rights for new members and new participants of a RFMO. The diverse considerations under Article 11 include the status of the straddling fish stocks and highly migratory fish stocks and the existing level of fishing effort in the fishery; the respective interests, fishing patterns and fishing practices of new and existing members or participants; the respective contributions of new and existing members or participants to conservation and management of the stocks, to the collection and provision of accurate data and to the conduct of scientific research on the stocks; the needs of coastal fishing communities dependent on fishing for the stocks; the needs of coastal states whose economies are mainly dependent on the exploitation of marine living resources; and the interests of developing states from the region (or subregion) in whose areas of national jurisdiction the stocks also occur. Such criteria must be taken into account as RFMO member states decide on the nature and extent of participatory rights for new members and new participants.

The issue of transparency has been a recurring one in RFMOs and UNFSA addresses this in Article 12 by requiring RFMOs to be transparent in decision-making processes and other activities as well as permitting observers at meetings and timely access to records and reports subject to the procedures of the RFMO.

Article 17 demonstrates the primacy and centrality of the role of RFMOs in the conservation and management of straddling fish stocks and highly migratory fish stocks. A state, which is not a member of, or a participant in, a RFMO and which does not agree to apply the fisheries conservation and management measures established by the relevant RFMO, still has a duty to cooperate in the conservation and management of the relevant fish stocks.[20] Such a state shall not authorize vessels flying its flag to engage in fishing operations for the stocks, which are subject to fisheries conservation and management measures of the RFMO.[21] RFMO member states must exchange information regarding any fishing vessels of such states located in the RFMO area.[22] RFMO member states "shall take measures consistent with this Agreement and international law to deter activities of such vessels which undermine the effectiveness of subregional or regional conservation and management measures".[23] Thus, it would appear that the role of an RMFO in the regulation and enforcement of conservation and management measures for straddling fish stocks and highly migratory fish stocks in a particular area may be considered comprehensive for all state parties to UNFSA.

RFMOs also have roles in relation to developing states under Part VII. These include to "provide assistance to developing states",[24] "to enhance the ability of developing states . . . to conserve and manage straddling fish stocks and highly migratory fish stocks and to develop their own fisheries for such stocks",[25] to assist them to participate in high seas fisheries for straddling fish stocks and highly migratory fish stocks and to facilitate their participation in RFMOs.[26]

UNFSA also develops an enforcement role for RFMOs. Part VI on compliance and enforcement is based on the requirement established in Article 8(3)-(4) and repeated in Article 19(1) that states ensure their vessels comply with fisheries conservation and management measures established by competent RFMOs regardless of whether the states concerned are members of the same RFMOs. States have the option to cooperate through RFMOs to ensure compliance with and enforcement of fisheries conservation and management measures[27] including the conduct of investigations into alleged violations of conservation and management measures.[28] Members of, and participants in, an RFMO may

> take action in accordance with international law, including through recourse to subregional or regional procedures established for this purpose, to deter vessels which have engaged in activities which undermine the effectiveness of or otherwise violate the conservation and management measures established by that organisation or arrangement from fishing on the high seas in the subregion or region until such time as appropriate action is taken by the flag state.[29]

To this end, Article 21 contains an innovative feature in international fisheries law. Under this article, a state party to UNFSA which is also a member of, or participant in, the relevant RFMO may board and inspect fishing vessels flying the flag of another state party to UNFSA in any high seas area covered by the RFMO whether or not the second state party is also a member of the relevant RFMO for the purpose of ensuring compliance with fisheries conservation and management measures established by the relevant RFMO.[30] RFMOs must establish procedures for boarding and inspection in accordance with Articles 21 and 22 of UNFSA. They may also specify further serious violations in addition to those listed in Article 21(11)(a)-(h), which activate the enforcement measures provided in Article 21(8).[31] Additionally, RFMOs may establish "an alternative mechanism" to discharge the obligation under UNFSA of its members and participants to ensure compliance with conservation and management measures established by the RFMO.[32]

Article 30(1) of UNFSA adopts the dispute settlement mechanisms set out in Part XV of LOSC regardless of whether states parties are also parties to LOSC. These mechanisms apply also to any dispute between states parties to UNFSA concerning the interpretation or application of a subregional, regional or global fisheries agreement relating to straddling fish stocks or highly migratory fish stocks to which they are parties, including any dispute concerning the conservation and management of such stocks.[33] RFMOs may even influence the outcome of courts and tribunals due to the fact that such courts and tribunals are mandated to apply LOSC, UNFSA, relevant subregional, regional and global fisheries agreements as well as generally accepted standards for the conservation and management of marine living resources and other rules of international law.[34] This could include standards in conservation and management of marine living resources developed by RFMOs.

In summary, UNFSA develops the general duty of states to cooperate either directly or through relevant international organizations under LOSC by placing RFMOs at the centre of international cooperation and developing a comprehensive framework for the regulatory and enforcement roles of RFMOs in the conservation and management of straddling fish stocks and highly migratory fish stocks.

The role of regional seas organizations in the protection and preservation of the marine environment

The framework provisions pertaining to the regulatory and enforcement role of regional seas organizations (RSOs) in the protection and preservation of the marine environment are provided for in Part XII of LOSC. Numerous references are made to "competent international organizations" and the need to adopt regional rules, standards and recommended practices and procedures to prevent, reduce and control pollution of the marine environment. This has been achieved primarily through regional arrangements under the umbrella of the United Nations Environment Programme's Regional Seas Programme together with a number of independent RSOs.

United Nations Convention on the Law of the Sea

All states have a general duty to protect and preserve the marine environment.[35] This includes areas both within and beyond national jurisdiction.[36] States also have a duty to take – individually or jointly – all measures necessary (consistent with LOSC) to prevent, reduce and control pollution of the marine environment from any source.[37] Furthermore, states have a duty to:

> cooperate on a global basis and, as appropriate, on a regional basis, directly or through competent international organizations, in formulating and elaborating international rules,

standards and recommended practices and procedures consistent with this Convention, for the protection and preservation of the marine environment, taking into account characteristic regional features.[38]

Competent international organizations, which include global and regional seas organizations, are to be notified by states in cases where the marine environment is in imminent danger of being damaged or has been damaged by pollution.[39] Such organizations must cooperate – to the extent possible – with states in the area affected in eliminating the effects of pollution and preventing or minimizing the damage and must develop and promote contingency plans for responding to pollution incidents.[40] Competent international organizations are also to promote studies, undertake programmes of scientific research and facilitate the exchange of information and data about pollution of the marine environment.[41] States must endeavour to participate actively in regional (and global) programmes to acquire knowledge for the assessment of the nature and extent of pollution, exposure to it, and its pathways, risks and remedies.[42] With this knowledge, states have a duty to cooperate either directly or through competent international organizations to establish scientific criteria for the formulation and elaboration of rules, standards and recommended practices and procedures for the prevention, reduction and control of pollution of the marine environment.[43]

Further, states shall, directly or through competent international organizations, provide scientific, educational, technical and other assistance to developing states for the protection and preservation of the marine environment as well as the prevention, reduction and control of marine pollution.[44] Such assistance may include training of scientific and technical personnel, facilitating participation in relevant international programmes, provision of equipment and facilities and enhancing capacity to manufacture such equipment as well as advice on developing facilities for research, monitoring, educational and other programmes.[45] In addition, states, either directly or through competent international organizations, shall provide "appropriate assistance" to developing states both for the minimization of the effects of major incidents, which may cause serious pollution of the marine environment, as well as for the preparation of environmental assessments.[46] International organizations shall also grant preference to developing states in the allocation of appropriate funds and technical assistance and the utilization of their specialized services for the purposes of prevention, reduction and control of pollution of the marine environment or minimization of its effects.[47]

With regard to monitoring and environmental assessment, further roles for competent international organizations include the observation, measurement, evaluation and analysis of the risks or effects of pollution of the marine environment[48] and the dissemination to all states of reports of such activities.[49]

Competent international organizations also have a role to play in the development of international rules to prevent, reduce and control pollution of the marine environment. In relation to pollution from land-based sources, states are encouraged to act "especially through competent international organizations" to establish "global and regional rules, standards and recommended practices and procedures to prevent, reduce and control pollution of the marine environment from land-based sources".[50] States must also endeavour to harmonize their own policies at the appropriate regional level.[51] They have similar obligations with regard to pollution from seabed activities subject to national jurisdiction,[52] pollution by dumping,[53] pollution from vessels[54] and pollution from or through the atmosphere.[55]

Finally, LOSC contains a number of provisions relating to the enforcement of regional rules, standards and recommended practices to prevent, reduce and control pollution of the marine environment. While enforcement by individual states – as flag states, port states and/or coastal states – is the generally preferred mode of enforcement, a role for competent international organizations is mentioned in Article 223 in which it is envisaged that such organizations may be involved in proceedings instituted under Part XII through the provision of witnesses and evidence.

Thus, it is clear from the framework provisions of LOSC that RSOs have important roles to play in the protection and preservation of the marine environment. These roles have been further developed mainly through regional arrangements under the umbrella of the UNEP's Regional Seas Programme together with a number of independent RSOs.

United Nations Environment Programme's Regional Seas Programme

The UNEP's Regional Seas Programme (UNEP RSP) was established in 1974 to promote the preservation and protection of the marine environment. The UNEP RSP provides a framework for regional cooperation and coordination through a network of Regional Seas Programmes, which implement action plans – often supported by regional seas conventions – to address the specific environmental issues of each region.[56]

Currently, more than 143 states participate in one or more of the 13 Regional Seas Programmes covering the Black Sea,[57] Wider Caribbean,[58] Eastern Africa,[59] East Asian Seas,[60] South Asian Seas,[61] ROPME Sea Area,[62] Mediterranean,[63] North-East Pacific,[64] North-West Pacific,[65] Red Sea and Gulf of Aden,[66] South-East Pacific,[67] South Pacific,[68] and West and Central Africa.[69] In addition, there are five independent partner programmes for the Antarctic, Arctic, Baltic Sea, Caspian Sea and North-East Atlantic regions.[70]

In addition to its role as coordinator of the Regional Seas Programmes, the UNEP RSP also directly administers six of the Regional Seas Programmes, namely Wider Caribbean, East Asian Seas, Eastern Africa, Mediterranean, North-West Pacific and Western and Central Africa.[71] For the remaining seven Regional Seas Programmes, namely, Black Sea, North-East Pacific, Red Sea and Gulf of Aden, ROPME Sea Area, South Asian Seas, South-East Pacific Region and South Pacific, a regional organization hosts or provides the secretariat and implementing services and financial and budgetary services (trust funds) are managed by the programme.[72] Each Regional Seas Programme has a secretariat or Regional Coordinating Unit (RCU), which is often assisted by a Regional Activity Centre (RAC). The RCU oversees the implementation of the action plan and associated programmes of work, strategies and policies.[73]

The UNEP Governing Council originally defined the role of Regional Seas Programmes as follows:

- Promotion of international and regional conventions, guidelines and actions for the control of marine pollution and for the protection and management of aquatic resources;
- Assessment of the state of marine pollution, of the sources and trends of this pollution, and of the impact of the pollution on human health, marine ecosystems and amenities;
- Co-ordination of the efforts with regard to the environmental aspects of the protection, development and management of marine and coastal resources; and
- Support for education and training efforts to make possible the full participation of developing countries in the protection, development and management of marine and coastal resources.[74]

The UNEP Regional Seas Strategic Directions 2013–2016 identify the Regional Seas Programmes as fulfilling an important role in "implementing the international agenda on marine and coastal issues" and providing "valuable regional frameworks for assessing the state of the marine environment; addressing key developments (e.g. socio-economic activities, coastal settlements, land-based activities) that interact with the marine environment; and agreeing on appropriate responses in terms of strategies, policies, management tools and protocols".[75]

Independent regional seas organizations

There are also a number of independent RSOs whose mandate is the protection and preservation of the environment. In particular, there are five organizations covering the Antarctic,[76] Arctic,[77] Baltic Sea,[78] Caspian Sea[79] and North-East Atlantic[80] regions. All five organizations collaborate with the UNEP RSP as "partner programmes", participate in global meetings and implement the UNEP Regional Seas Strategic Directions. This contributes to increased uniformity of roles across all RSOs in the regulation and enforcement of the protection and preservation of the marine environment

Regional fisheries management organizations and conservation of biodiversity

Notably, the role of RFMOs has developed under UNFSA to include a duty to protect biodiversity in the marine environment. This is part of a broader duty to conserve and manage straddling fish stocks and highly migratory fish stocks and give effect to the duty to cooperate under LOSC.[81] The Western and Central Pacific Fisheries Commission was the first post-UNFSA RFMO to be established and reflects this wider mandate in Article 5(f) of the Convention on the Conservation and Management of Highly Migratory Fish Stocks in the Western and Central Pacific Ocean.[82]

Critical issues and themes

It is a pivotal time in the development of regional marine governance. As momentum grows towards a comprehensive integrated approach to the conservation and sustainable use of marine ecosystems, RFMOs and RSOs have a unique opportunity to contribute to and, indeed, lead the development of new frameworks for integrated regional governance in this endeavour.

RFMOs already have a history of transformation from initial resource allocation organizations to organizations focused on the conservation and management of fish stocks. Many RFMOs have adopted the wider mandate and roles prescribed under UNFSA. There remain issues with enforcement of fisheries conservation and management measures and illegal, unreported and unregulated fishing activities. There also needs to be greater coordination and collaboration between RFMOs as well as between RFMOs, RSOs, coastal states and other relevant actors.[83]

RSOs have been noted for their flexibility in addressing developing environmental concerns through the use of action plans, conventions and associated protocols for specific issues, their level of cooperation and coordination with other organizations and their "strong integrative tendency, while addressing the particular ecological circumstances of individual regions".[84] Despite this, there is a need for greater cooperation and coordination between RSOs and other interested actors to adequately address growing environment concerns.[85] Notably, action plans are not legally binding and enforcement is largely left to the goodwill and capacity of member states.

The UNEP Regional Seas Strategic Directions 2013–2016 identifies a number of issues and encourages Regional Seas Programmes to, *inter alia*, apply ecosystem-based management; strengthen national marine governance to enable coherence with systems such as the Large Marine Ecosystem approach, RFMOs, and River Basin Organizations; and strengthen collaboration mechanisms to address common regional objectives and coordinated regional implementation of multilateral environmental agreements and global and regional initiatives.[86]

In recognition of the need for a comprehensive integrated approach to conservation and sustainable use of the marine ecosystem in areas beyond national jurisdiction (ABNJ), several RSOs have extended activities into ABNJ and created marine protected areas (MPAs).[87] Under the Mediterranean Regional Seas Programme, the Pelagos Sanctuary for Mediterranean Marine Mammals (Pelagos Sanctuary), which is partly located in high seas, has been recognized as a Specially Protected Area of Mediterranean Importance.[88] In the North-East Atlantic, the OSPAR Commission established the world's first network of MPAs in 2010 with management measures contained in non-binding OSPAR Recommendations (reflective of limited competence over ABNJ).[89] In the Southern Ocean, CCAMLR established the first MPA in ABNJ in 2009 for the South Orkney Islands southern shelf and is negotiating to create a circumpolar network of MPAs.[90] The Secretariat of the Pacific Regional Environment Programme's (SPREP) mandate extends to ABNJ with possibilities to create MPAs in these areas.[91]

While the special legal framework that exists in the Mediterranean and Southern Ocean may not be replicable elsewhere, it may be possible to extend activities into ABNJ in other areas using similar approaches such as that of the OSPAR Commission (non-binding recommendations) and the original parties to the Pelagos Sanctuary (creation of obligations among themselves that were later recognized and adopted by the Mediterranean Regional Seas Programme). Problematic issues in this respect are likely to include a lack of competence of RSOs over ABNJ, non-universal participation in RSOs and the capacity of existing RSOs to fulfill an expanded role in ABNJ.[92]

Under UNFSA, RFMOs have a mandate to conserve and manage fish stocks on the high seas as well as to conserve biodiversity in the marine environment. As such, there is clearly a role for RFMOs in creating an integrated approach to conservation and sustainable use of marine ecosystems in ABNJ. This could be further strengthened through coordination and collaboration with relevant RSOs (as well as other RFMOs). One such example is the collaboration between the North-East Atlantic Fisheries Commission (NEAFC) and the OSPAR Commission. NEAFC is responsible for the conservation and management of fish stocks in the region while the OSPAR Commission manages a network of MPAs in ABNJ. In 2009, NEAFC closed certain areas to bottom trawling. These areas coincided to a large degree with OSPAR's MPAs. To coordinate management efforts for selected areas in ABNJ, OSPAR and NEAFC have concluded a "Collective Arrangement".[93] Other competent organizations are encouraged to participate in the arrangement to pursue an integrated approach to the conservation and sustainable use of the marine ecosystem in ABNJ.[94]

In addition, whilst establishment of CCAMLR's MPA may have been made possible by the unique framework of the Antarctic Treaty System and CCAMLR's mandate, the CCAMLR model could still serve as a valuable example of how RFMOs could develop mandates to conserve marine biodiversity through ecosystem based management particularly in areas managed solely by an RFMO.[95]

In developing an integrated approach to conservation and sustainable use of marine biodiversity in ABNJ, both RSOs and RFMOs also have an opportunity to play an important role in current international discussions regarding the possibility of an international instrument under LOSC.[96] Their contributions are vital to the development of the role of RSOs and RFMOs under such an instrument. The discussions of the Ad Hoc Open-ended Informal Working Group to Study Issues Relating to the Conservation and Sustainable Use of Marine Biological Diversity Beyond Areas of National Jurisdiction so far have identified and promoted options for RSOs and RFMOs to engage in the conservation and sustainable use of marine biodiversity in ABNJ and the negotiation process is likely to further clarify those options.[97]

Conclusion

This chapter has reviewed the regulatory and enforcement roles of RFMOs in the conservation and management of fish stocks and RSOs in the protection and preservation of the marine environment. Under UNFSA, the role of RFMOs in the conservation and management of fish stocks has been developed into a comprehensive framework while RSOs have played a significant role in beginning to implement the duty to protect and preserve the marine environment under LOSC. Both RFMOs and RSOs face difficulties with enforcement and coordination with third party states and other global and regional organizations. At this critical stage in the evolution of regional marine governance, RFMOs and RSOs have the opportunity to play an important role in the development of new frameworks for integrated regional governance including ecosystem based management on the scale of large marine ecosystems as well as a comprehensive integrated approach to conservation and sustainable use of marine ecosystems in areas beyond national jurisdiction.

Notes

1 For the purpose of this chapter, this term will be used to denote all entities comprising "subregional and regional fisheries management organizations and arrangements" referred to in the Agreement for the Implementation of the Provisions of the United Nations Convention on the Law of the Sea of 10 December 1982 Relating to the Conservation and Management of Straddling Fish Stocks and Highly Migratory Fish Stocks (UNFSA). UNFSA does not differentiate between the roles of "organizations" and "arrangements".

2 There are now more than 30 regional fisheries organizations worldwide, many of which do no more than provide advice to member states. Sixteen of these regional fishery bodies have the competence to establish conservation and management measures with varying degrees of authority and resources to assess quantities of fish stocks, set catch quotas, and inspect and regulate the type of fishing gear used. Five of those sixteen regional fishery bodies either deal with single species or have a very specific directive. Eleven regional fisheries organizations remain that have a significant level of competence over areas of the high seas: High Seas Task Force, "Closing the Net: Stopping Illegal Fishing on the High Seas" (Governments of Australia, Canada, Chile, Namibia, New Zealand, and the United Kingdom, WWF, IUCN, Earth Institute at Columbia University, 2006) 46. See also Chapter 10 in this volume on Fisheries Enforcement and the Concepts of Compliance and Monitoring, Control and Surveillance.

3 *United Nations Convention on the Law of the Sea*, opened for signature 10 December 1982, 1833 UNTS 3 (entered into force 16 November 1994) (LOSC).

4 Agreement for the Implementation of the Provisions of the United Nations Convention on the Law of the Sea of 10 December 1982 Relating to the Conservation and Management of Straddling Fish Stocks and Highly Migratory Fish Stocks, opened for signature 4 December 1995, 2167 UNTS 3 art 21(7) (entered into force 11 December 2001) (UNFSA).

5 *United Nations Convention on the Law of the Sea*, opened for signature 10 December 1982, 1833 UNTS 3 (entered into force 16 November 1994) (LOSC). LOSC has been ratified by 166 states: United Nations

6   Arts 61(5) and 119(2) LOSC.
7   Art 63(1)-(2) LOSC.
8   Arts 64(1) and 65 LOSC.
9   Art 66 LOSC.
10 Art 118 LOSC.
11 Art 63(1) LOSC.
12 Art 63(2) LOSC.
13 Art 64(1) LOSC. Notably, there is no obligation to cooperate through an existing RFMO. However, where there is none, there is a duty to cooperate to establish such an organization and participate in its work: B Applebaum and A Donohue, "The Role of Regional Fisheries Management Organizations" in E Hey (ed), *Developments in International Fisheries Law* (1999, Kluwer Law International, Netherlands) 228.
14 The International Whaling Commission (IWC) is the international organization concerned with the conservation and management of whales. It was established in 1946 pursuant to the International Convention for the Regulation of Whaling (opened for signature 2 December 1946, 161 UNTS 72 (entered into force 10 November 1948)). The IWC also conducts research into and provides advice on small cetaceans. The IWC currently has 88 member states: see generally, International Whaling Commission <https://iwc.int/home> at 18 March 2015.
15 *Agreement for the Implementation of the Provisions of the United Nations Convention on the Law of the Sea of 10 December 1982 Relating to the Conservation and Management of Straddling Fish Stocks and Highly Migratory Fish Stocks*, opened for signature 4 December 1995, 2167 UNTS 3 (entered into force 11 December 2001) (UNFSA). UNFSA has been ratified by 82 states: *United Nations Status of the United Nations Convention on the Law of the Sea, of the Agreement Relating to the Implementation of Part XI of the Convention and of the Agreement for the Implementation of the Provisions of the Convention Relating to the Conservation and Management of Straddling Fish Stocks and Highly Migratory Fish Stocks* (2014) United Nations <http://www.un.org/depts/los/reference_files/status2010.pdf> at 13 March 2015.
16 B Applebaum and A Donohue, "The Role of Regional Fisheries Management Organizations" in E Hey (ed), *Developments in International Fisheries Law* (1999, Kluwer Law International, Netherlands) 218.
17 Ibid.
18 Art 7(2) UNFSA.
19 Sub-articles 10(e), (f) and (g) relating to the role of RFMOs in the development of standards for the collection, reporting, verification and exchange of data on fisheries for the stocks; the compilation and dissemination of accurate and complete statistical data; and the promotion and conduct of scientific assessments of the stocks and relevant research and dissemination of the results are further developed under art 14 on the collection and provision of information and cooperation in scientific research and Annex I on Standard Requirements for the Collection and Sharing of Data.
20 Art 17(1) UNFSA.
21 Art 17(2) UNFSA.
22 Art 17(4) UNFSA.
23 Ibid. See also art 20(7) UNFSA.
24 Art 24(1) UNFSA.
25 Art 25(1)(a) UNFSA.
26 Art 25(1)(b)-(c) UNFSA.
27 Art 20(1) UNFSA.
28 Art 20(3) UNFSA.
29 Art 20(7) UNFSA.
30 Art 21(1) UNFSA.
31 Art 21(11)(i) UNFSA.
32 Art 21(15) UNFSA.
33 Art 30(2) UNFSA.
34 Art 30(5) UNFSA.
35 Art 192 LOSC.

36 Art 193 LOSC.
37 Art 194(1) LOSC.
38 Art 197 LOSC.
39 Art 198 LOSC.
40 Art 199 LOSC.
41 Art 200 LOSC.
42 Ibid.
43 Art 201 LOSC.
44 Art 202 LOSC.
45 Art 202(a)(i)-(v) LOSC.
46 Art 202(b)-(c) LOSC.
47 Art 203 LOSC.
48 Art 204 LOSC.
49 Art 205 LOSC.
50 Art 207(4) LOSC.
51 Art 207(3) LOSC.
52 Art 208(4)-(5) LOSC. For the role of global organizations in the regulation and enforcement of pollution from seabed activities beyond national jurisdiction, see art 209 LOSC and the role of the International Seabed Authority in Chapter 7 of this volume on The Role of Global Organizations.
53 Art 210 LOSC. Note there is no duty for states to harmonize their own policies at regional level regarding pollution by dumping.
54 Art 211 LOSC. Competent international organizations shall also promote the adoption, where appropriate, of routing systems designed to minimize the threat of accidents, which might cause pollution to the marine environment including the coastline and related interests of coastal states.
55 Art 212 LOSC. Note there is no duty for states to harmonize their own policies at regional level regarding pollution from or through the atmosphere.
56 Environmental issues covered by the Regional Seas Programmes include: coastal development, integrated coastal zone management, marine and coastal invasive species, coastal reefs, marine mammals, marine protected areas, large marine ecosystems, land-based sources of pollution, marine litter, vessel and sea-based pollution, and particular challenges facing small island developing states: see generally UNEP RSP <http://www.unep.org/regionalseas/issues/default.asp> at 3 March 2015.
57 See generally Black Sea Regional Seas Programme <http://www.unep.org/regionalseas/programmes/nonunep/blacksea/default.asp> at 3 March 2015.
58 See generally Wider Caribbean Regional Seas Programme <http://www.unep.org/regionalseas/programmes/unpro/caribbean/default.asp> at 3 March 2015.
59 See generally Eastern Africa Regional Seas Programme <http://www.unep.org/regionalseas/programmes/unpro/easternafrica/default.asp> at 3 March 2015.
60 See generally East Asian Seas Regional Seas Programme <http://www.unep.org/regionalseas/programmes/unpro/eastasian/default.asp> at 3 March 2015.
61 See generally South Asian Seas Regional Seas Programme <http://www.unep.org/regionalseas/programmes/nonunep/southasian/default.asp> at 3 March 2015.
62 See generally ROPME (Regional Organisation for the Protection of the Marine Environment) Sea Area Regional Seas Programme <http://www.unep.org/regionalseas/programmes/nonunep/ropme/default.asp> at 3 March 2015.
63 See generally Mediterranean Regional Seas Programme <http://www.unep.org/regionalseas/programmes/unpro/mediterranean/default.asp> at 3 March 2015.
64 See generally North-East Pacific Regional Seas Programme <http://www.unep.org/regionalseas/programmes/nonunep/nepacific/default.asp> at 3 March 2015.
65 See generally North-West Pacific Regional Seas Programme <http://www.unep.org/regionalseas/programmes/unpro/nwpacific/default.asp> at 3 March 2015.
66 See generally Red Sea and Gulf of Aden Regional Seas Programme <http://www.unep.org/regionalseas/programmes/nonunep/redsea/default.asp> at 3 March 2015.
67 See generally South-East Pacific Regional Seas Programme <http://www.unep.org/regionalseas/programmes/nonunep/sepacific/default.asp> at 3 March 2015.
68 See generally South Pacific Regional Seas Programme <http://www.unep.org/regionalseas/programmes/nonunep/pacific/default.asp> at 3 March 2015.

69 See generally West and Central Africa Regional Seas Programme <http://www.unep.org/regional seas/programmes/unpro/westernafrica/default.asp> at 3 March 2015.
70 UNEP RSP <http://www.unep.org/regionalseas/about/default.asp> and <http://www.unep.org/regionalseas/programmes/independent/default.asp> at 25 February 2015. See also sub-chapter on Independent Regional Seas Organisations.
71 For these Regional Seas Programmes, the UNEP RSP is responsible for the functions of the secretariat, the provision of financial and budgetary services as well as technical assistance and advice and is accountable for administering trust funds: UNEP RSP <http://www.unep.org/regionalseas/programmes/unpro/default.asp> at 15 February 2015.
72 UNEP RSP <http://www.unep.org/regionalseas/programmes/nonunep/default.asp> at 15 February 2015. By way of example, the Secretariat of the Pacific Regional Environment Programme (SPREP) fulfils this function in the South Pacific.
73 For more information on the roles of RCUs and RACs, see *Ecosystem Approach to the Regional Seas Conventions and Action Plans*, UNEP (DEPI) RS.15/WP.2.RS (2013). See also UNEP RSP <http://www.unep.org/regionalseas/programmes/default.asp> at 25 February 2015.
74 UNEP. *UNEP: Achievements and Planned Development of UNEP's Regional Seas Programme and Comparable Programmes Sponsored By Other Bodies*, UNEP Regional Seas Reports and Studies No.1 (UNEP, 1982) in *Ecosystem Approach to the Regional Seas Conventions and Action Plans*, UNEP (DEPI) RS.15/WP.2.RS (2013).
75 *Regional Seas Strategic Directions 2013–2016*, UNEP (DEPI) RS.15/WP.5.RS (2013).
76 The Commission for the Conservation of Antarctic Marine Living Resources (CCAMLR): see generally CCAMLR <https://www.ccamlr.org/> at 5 February 2015. By way of example, unlike other RFMOs, CCAMLR has a mandate to both conserve and manage fish stocks and also protect and preserve the marine environment through ecosystem based management. Article IX of the Convention for the Conservation of Antarctic Marine Living Resources states that the functions of CCAMLR are to give effect to the objectives and principles set out in art II. To this end, CCAMLR shall facilitate research into Antarctic marine living resources and the marine ecosystem, compile data on the status of and changes in marine living resources, ensure the acquisition of catch and effort statistics on harvest populations, analyze, disseminate and publish information regarding data and catch and effort statistics and reports of the Scientific Committee, identify conservation needs and analyze the effectiveness of conservation measures, formulate, adopt and revise conservation measures on the basis of best scientific evidence available, and implement the system of observation and inspection established under art XXIV of the Convention: CCAMLR <http://www.ccamlr.org/node/74528#II> at 3 March 2015. Under art V of the Convention for the Conservation of Antarctic Marine Living Resources, Contracting Parties, which are not Parties to the Antarctic Treaty, acknowledge the special obligations and responsibilities of the Antarctic Treaty Consultative Parties for the protection and preservation of the environment of the Antarctic Treaty area. Contracting Parties agree to observe Antarctic Treaty Consultative Meeting conservation measures for the protection of the Antarctic environment. Contracting Parties must abide by the 1998 Protocol on Environment Protection to the Antarctic Treaty relating to the protection of the Antarctic environment: CCAMLR <https://www.ccamlr.org/en/organisation/relationship-antarctic-treaty-system> at 3 March 2015.
77 The Arctic Council: see generally <http://www.arctic-council.org/index.php/en/> and <http://www.arctic-council.org/index.php/en/environment-and-people/oceans> at 3 March 2015.
78 The Baltic Marine Environment Protection Commission (Helsinki Commission or HELCOM): see generally <http://www.helcom.fi/about-us> at 3 March 2015.
79 The Caspian Environment Programme: see generally <http://www.tehranconvention.org/spip.php?article24> at 3 March 2015.
80 The OSPAR Commission: see generally: <http://www.ospar.org/html_documents/ospar/html/ospar_convention_e_updated_text_2007.pdf> at 3 March 2015.
81 "In order to conserve and manage straddling fish stocks and highly migratory fish stocks, coastal States and States fishing on the high seas shall, in giving effect to their duty to cooperate in accordance with the Convention: . . . (g) protect biodiversity in the marine environment": Art 5 UNFSA.
82 *Convention on the Conservation and Management of Highly Migratory Fish Stocks in the Western and Central Pacific Ocean*, opened for signature 5 September 2000, 2275 UNTS 43, art 5(f) (entered into force 19 June 2004).

83 R Warner, K Gjerde and D Freestone, "Regional Governance for Fisheries and Biodiversity" in S Garcia, T Charles and J Rice (eds), *Governance for Fisheries and Marine Conservation: Interactions and Co-evolution* (Wiley Blackwell Publishers, Chichester, United Kingdom, 2013).
84 A Boyle, "Further Development of the 1982 Convention on the Law of the Sea: Mechanisms for Change" in David Freestone, Richard Barnes and David Ong (eds), *The Law of the Sea: Progress and Prospects* (Oxford, Oxford University Press, 2006) 53 in D Rothwell and T Stephens, *The International Law of the Sea* (Oxford, Hart Publishing, 2010) 346. This is largely the result of a number of factors including the strong coordinating role and scientific, technical and administrative assistance provided by the UNEP RSP, regular global meetings for the exchange of information and advice, the regional implementation of the global UN Regional Seas Strategic Directions, and the fact that the UNEP directly administers six of the Regional Seas Programmes.
85 UNEP, *Regional Seas Strategic Directions 2013–2016*, UNEP (DEPI) RS.15/WP.5.RS (2013).
86 Ibid.
87 See also Chapter 23 in this volume on Developing New Regulatory Paradigms for the Conservation and Sustainable Use of Marine Biodiversity in Areas beyond National Jurisdiction.
88 The Pelagos Sanctuary was originally established in 1999 by France, Monaco and Italy. It has been suggested that the Pelagos Sanctuary might serve as an example of a "step-by-step approach" in which two or more states first establish a protective measure outside a competent organization and subsequently seek endorsement through a regional seas organization: J Rochette, S Unger and G Wright, "Governing the 'High Seas' – Linking Governance and Regional Implementation" (Issue Paper No 2, Potsdam Ocean Governance Workshop, 2014) 10. It should be noted that the situation in the Mediterranean is unique as ABNJ exist only due to the fact that states have chosen not to establish EEZs.
89 Ibid 9.
90 Ibid 10. Notably, CCAMLR is a regional organization combining elements of both an RFMO and RSO.
91 See generally: J Rochette, S Unger and G Wright, "Governing the 'High Seas' – Linking Governance and Regional Implementation" (Issue Paper No 2, Potsdam Ocean Governance Workshop, 2014).
92 Ibid 4.
93 OSPAR Commission, *Collective Arrangement Between Competent International Organisations on Cooperation and Coordination Regarding Selected Areas in Areas Beyond National Jurisdiction in the North-East Atlantic* (2014) <http://www.ospar.org/v_measures/browse.asp?menu=00750302120125_000002_000000> at 10 March 2015.
94 Ibid para 3. See also: J Rochette, S Unger and G Wright, "Governing the 'High Seas' – Linking Governance and Regional Implementation" (Issue Paper No 2, Potsdam Ocean Governance Workshop, 2014) 9.
95 J Rochette, S Unger and G Wright, "Governing the 'High Seas' – Linking Governance and Regional Implementation" (Issue Paper No 2, Potsdam Ocean Governance Workshop, 2014) 10.
96 The United Nations Conference on Sustainable Development committed to "address, on an urgent basis, the issue of the conservation and sustainable use of marine biological diversity of areas beyond national jurisdiction including by taking a decision on the development of an international instrument under UNCLOS": "The Future We Want" (United Nations Conference on Sustainable Development, Rio de Janeiro, Brazil, June 2012) para 162. The Ad Hoc Open-Ended Informal Working Group to Study Issues Relating to the Conservation and Sustainable Use of Marine Biodiversity Beyond National Jurisdiction has recommended that the UNGA develop a new legally binding instrument on biodiversity beyond national jurisdiction under LOSC. A decision will be taken at the 69th Session of the United Nations General Assembly: Ad Hoc Open-ended Informal Working Group to Study Issues Relating to the Conservation and Sustainable Use of Marine Biological Diversity Beyond Areas of National Jurisdiction, *Recommendations of the Ad Hoc Open-ended Informal Working Group to Study Issues Relating to the Conservation and Sustainable Use of Marine Biological Diversity Beyond Areas of National Jurisdiction to the Sixty-ninth Session of the General Assembly* (2015) 1 <http://www.un.org/Depts/los/biodiversityworkinggroup/documents/AHWG_9_recommendations.pdf> at 10 March 2015.
97 See also Chapter 23 in this volume on Developing New Regulatory Paradigms for the Conservation and Sustainable Use of Marine Biodiversity in Areas beyond National Jurisdiction.

9

The Role of Courts and Tribunals in Maritime Regulation and Enforcement

Dale Stephens

The 1982 Law of the Sea Convention ('LOSC')[1] seeks to attain a level of poised equilibrium between coastal State jurisdiction on the one hand and the navigational rights of maritime nations on the other. While it is the self-declared intent of the LOSC to create a single comprehensive legal order for the seas and oceans,[2] it is equally clear the LOSC affirms that matters not regulated by it continue to be governed by the rules and principles of general international law.[3] Hence broader principles of international law can, and do, apply to provide much needed context, which assists resolution of current potential dilemmas. The power of the LOSC though lies in its promise to authoritatively resolve peacefully the inevitable disputes that would arise under its framework. The key to such resolution is the compulsory dispute settlement provisions that underpin the structure of the governance regime.

The emphasis on mandatory dispute resolution is a critical element of the Convention. It represented a propitious moment in the imagination of the drafters who sought to corral older political impulses and to direct constructive engagement. The LOSC was heralded as a decisive expression of modernist will and method at the time of its framing.[4] There was a palpable sense of triumphalism and breakthrough, at the time of its completion. Writing in 1983, Philip Allott breathlessly wrote:

> The United Nations Convention on the Law of the Sea is a fact. It exists. Whether or not it becomes a fully operational treaty ... it is and will be the cause of significant effects. Its very existence modifies political, economic, and legal relationships in countless ways whose direction and intensity we can predict only in a most speculative way.[5]

The intellectual excitement that accompanied its introduction reflected a mood of the time that emphasized a model of law as 'cooperation' or at least 'coexistence' rather than law as 'competition' within the international legal firmament.[6] It not only promised a new framework for dispute resolution but also was indicative of a new international 'mood' about confronting and overcoming old challenges.

This chapter will assess the role of Courts and Tribunals in the context of maritime law. Key aspects of law relevant to use of force and law enforcement within the maritime judicial context will be particularly covered. It will comprise three sections. The first will examine the dispute resolution architecture envisaged for the settlement of the world's maritime disputes under the LOSC. The compulsory dispute settlement, so critical to the LOSC design, has proven to be a largely successful project that has generated considerable legal articulation on the management of the world's oceans. The second will focus on the themes of the maritime jurisprudence emanating from key bodies such as the International Court of Justice and the International Tribunal for the Law of the Sea. The final section will specifically examine the interaction between international and Australian domestic jurisprudence on law enforcement matters. It will highlight schisms that are emerging between these two jurisdictions and comment on attempts to reconcile the two.

The dispute resolution architecture of the LOSC

Unlike its predecessors, namely the 1958 Maritime Conventions that provided for the optional settlement of disputes, the LOSC adopted a comprehensive and compulsory system of dispute settlement. Under the LOSC, State Parties are obliged to settle disputes through either:

a. diplomatic means (negotiation and conciliation) or,
b. judicial procedures (compulsory procedures).

The comprehensive structure for settlement of disputes is found in Part XV of the LOSC. It is made up of three sections: Section 1 deals with general provisions, Section 2 deals with compulsory procedures 'entailing binding decisions'[7] and Section 3 deals with limitations and exceptions to the applicability of Section 2.

(a) Nature and content of Part XV

The basic premise underlying Part XV is that there is a positive obligation to settle disputes by peaceful means in accordance with the UN Charter;[8] that State Parties have the right to agree to settle disputes by any peaceful means chosen[9] and that when a dispute arises there is an obligation on the Parties to exchange views regarding its settlement.[10]

Where no settlement has been reached by diplomatic means such as through the exchange of views of the parties, conciliation[11] or other peaceful or amicable means, any party to a dispute may submit the dispute to the Court or Tribunal having jurisdiction under the Convention for a binding decision.[12] Article 287 outlines the choice of forum for such dispute settlement as including the International Tribunal of the Law of the Sea (ITLOS), the International Court of Justice (ICJ), an arbitral tribunal (constituted under Annex VII of the LOSC) or a special arbitral tribunal (constituted under Annex VIII of the LOSC).

The ICJ is established under the UN Charter and the Statute of the International Court of Justice itself.[13] It possesses general civil jurisdiction and the UN General Assembly elects members of the Court. While not specifically concerned with maritime issues, it has heard a number of cases relating to this subject matter over the years. ITLOS and the two Arbitral Tribunals, one general and one special, are specifically created under the LOSC.[14] These Tribunals specialize in the law of the sea. While ITLOS and the general arbitral tribunal have broad jurisdiction to settle disputes concerning the interpretation or application of the LOSC, the special arbitral tribunal has jurisdiction under Annex VIII to settle disputes on fisheries, protection and preservation of the marine environment, marine scientific research and navigation (including pollution and dumping).[15]

123

ITLOS is established by the LOSC in accordance with Annex VI 'Statute of the International Tribunal for the Law of the Sea.'[16] Both the ICJ and ITLOS have fixed membership, unlike the arbitration tribunal and special arbitration tribunal, which are constituted in accordance with Annexes VII and VIII of the LOSC and effectively have ad hoc appointment. ITLOS, being an independent judicial organ, elects its members by a meeting of the States Parties to the Convention.[17]

It has been noted that issues of coordination and conflict between various international Courts and Tribunals are particularly acute within the international field because there is no unified judiciary.[18] That is, within 'international law, every tribunal is a self-contained system.'[19] For this reason, conflict between the ICJ and ITLOS may arise especially in terms of jurisdiction and jurisprudence. Such an observation has also been identified in the highly influential ILC Fragmentation study that observes this phenomenon throughout the field of international law and that resolution between separate rule 'complexes' remain a challenge of both interpretative approach and policy preference.[20]

Possibly because of this, the agreement at UNCLOS III on compulsory dispute settlement was only made possible when the applicability of compulsory procedures contained optional exceptions. These dealt with a coastal State's exercise of sovereign right or jurisdiction with respect to disputes concerning sea boundary delimitations, military or enforcement activities, or where the UN Security Council is exercising its function.[21]

The cases, the forums, the themes

Given the elaborate adjudication machinery set up under the LOSC, it is not surprising that there has been a considerable amount of case law and other determinative outcomes reached over recent decades. Such determinations have necessarily provided considerable guidance to the planning of State maritime operations. In particular, issues relating to the use of force have emerged as well as law enforcement issues to specifically condition international standards of behaviour. Similarly, maritime navigational rights do figure prominently in the case law of the ICJ, which has been particularly affirming in its approach. Questions relating to the use of force in law enforcement activities within the maritime environment have been the subject of considerable ITLOS attention. These issues will be more fully explored in this section.

The International Court of Justice

Despite the general commitment to compulsory dispute settlement under the current LOSC regime, it is notable that military issues remain a possible exception to this mandatory process as envisioned under the LOSC.[22] Despite this concession under the LOSC, such matters may ostensibly fall within the general jurisdiction of the ICJ. Indeed, the first ever case of the ICJ, the *Corfu Channel Case*[23] dealt expressly with the question of passage rights of naval vessels and provided a basis for understanding how 'innocent passage' by warships was to be exercised.[24] More importantly, the Court was able to use the reality of the intersecting maritime jurisdictions of States to craft a more contemporary perspective on the nature of sovereignty and the purpose of international law in the post-war world. In particular, Judge Alvarez advanced a view that highlighted the social interdependence between States, stressing that sovereignty carried with it both rights and obligations. He noted specifically that 'we can no longer regard sovereignty as an absolute and individual right of every State as used to be done under the old law founded on the individualist regime.'[25] Such a sentiment acted as a riposte to the earlier decision of the Permanent Court of International Justice in the *Lotus* case,[26] another maritime based case, where an unadulterated version of sovereignty was originally developed. Judge Alvarez's view was also prescient in its anticipation of the balance of rights and obligations that infuse the LOSC that came some 30 years later.

The significance of the *Corfu Channel* case particularly lay in its positive assertion of maritime rights for warships during innocent passage. This constituted a resolution of a question of some uncertainty that had pervaded scholarly and Government debate on this issue for a number of decades. An older perspective had held that warships, because of their very nature, could not undertake innocent passage because of their inherently threating character.[27] The ICJ established that such a perspective was untenable, but did prescribe the manner in which such passage could be exercised by a warship with stipulations as to how weapons systems were to be configured. Moreover, and more controversially, the Court in that instance seemed to suggest that when navigational rights were denied in the maritime environment, then States had the capacity to affirm the exercise of such rights of passage with a necessary level of force.[28] This led to considerable academic criticism and reaction.[29]

The case did provide a very useful reference point during the UNCLOS III debates where a number of States still persisted in the view that warships required prior permission to undertake innocent passage. Indeed, others also pressed that warships intending to exercise rights of innocent passage within foreign territorial seas should be required to provide prior notification of such an exercise. Significantly neither position was accepted within the terms of the LOSC.[30]

Despite the significance of the *Corfu Channel* case, it was not until the 1980s that the ICJ again dealt with maritime issues in a reasonably substantive manner. In the 1986 *Nicaragua* case,[31] the ICJ addressed the question of naval mining and attacks on harbours in relation to the customary prohibition on the use of force as reflected Article 2(4) of the UN Charter. While maritime issues did not dominate the determination by the Court which focused on broader issues relating to the use of force, they nonetheless featured in the Court's assessment. As a reflection of the balance between coastal State sovereignty and the freedom of navigation, the Court provided a very useful assessment of the capacity of naval vessels to exercise navigational rights outside of territorial sea limits. In that instance, Nicaragua had alleged that programmed US naval manoeuvres outside the territorial sea limits of Nicaragua amounted to a threat of force contrary to Article 2(4) of the Charter and accompanying customary international law. Moreover, such manoeuvres were alleged to constitute a violation of the principle of non-intervention given their implicitly coercive character. Significantly, the Court did not accept such reasoning and consistently with their favourable disposition to promoting navigational rights in the *Corfu Channel* case, determined that such manoeuvres did not offend the principles prohibiting force otherwise stringently invoked by the Court in that case.[32] Indeed the Court was clear in deciding that freedom of navigation and rights of maritime communication were to be fully preserved.

The International Tribunal for the Law of the Sea

The establishment of ITLOS represented a key moment in the role of maritime jurisprudence. This Tribunal represents the apex of the hierarchy of dispute resolution mechanisms as entrenched within the LOSC. Whereas the ICJ would likely deal with 'strategic' maritime issues from time to time, ITLOS might be dealing with a greater range and frequency of 'tactical' or functional issues relating to maritime activities. Its work over the past decade has been extremely productive and it has not refrained from tackling key issues of maritime law with a sense of prescriptive purpose. The following analysis will focus on maritime law enforcement issues initially, but will then canvass more general, but no less important issues, arising particularly from the first ITLOS substantive litigation decided on its merits, namely the seminal *Saiga* case.

Use of force in maritime law enforcement at international law

The use of force for the purposes of law enforcement, particularly within the maritime context must be distinguished from the use of force in armed conflict and naval warfare.

While the regulation on the application of force within armed conflict has a long pedigree within international law, arising most notably from the mid-19th century, the regulation of law enforcement has been a more recent phenomenon. It had long been considered a matter of internal State policy as to what type or level of force was available to deal with law enforcement activity.[33]

In recent years, this phenomenon has reversed itself. The development of international standards regulating the use of force in the guise of the 1979 *Code of Conduct for Law Enforcement Officials*[34] represents a decisive statement of international consensus concerning the application of force in law enforcement contexts. Article 3 of the Code, states that 'law enforcement officials may use force only when strictly necessary and to the extent required for the performance of their duty.'[35] The general underlying principle of proportionality evident in the Code is reinforced by the *General Provisions of the Eighth United Nations Congress on the Preventions of Crime and the Treatment of Offenders*,[36] which mandates the exercise of calibrated judgment by law enforcement officials when applying proportionate force to a threat.

Not surprisingly perhaps, the need for an articulation on law enforcement thresholds and standards of application within the maritime environment has been the subject of considerable international attention over the years. In the 1933 '*I'm Alone*' case[37] an international commission determined what would be an international standard regarding the application of force. The matter concerned UK flagged and Canadian registered ship ('*I'm Alone*') in 1929 that had been smuggling alcohol along the Gulf of Mexico contrary to US domestic law. The US Coast Guard eventually sank it after a considerable chase. A subsequent International Commission determined that such an action was excessive and that 'the admittedly intentional sinking of the suspected vessel was not justified under the principles of international law.'[38] Hence, the US action assessed as unlawful and the US was obliged to pay compensation.

In the subsequent 1961 *Red Crusader* Case[39] a similar determination was made. The case involved Danish fishery protection vessels who had stopped and boarded a UK fishing trawler in a disputed fishing zone. The boarding party detained by crew of *Red Crusader* who fled the area. Danish vessels pursued, fired warning shots and then fired solid gunshot at the radar scanner and lights on the *Red Crusader*, thus threatening life. A subsequent International Commission of Enquiry determined that the Danish action exceeded the legitimate use of force in firing without warning and creating a danger to life on board the *Red Crusader*. Indeed, the Commission emphasized there were other means to resolve the situation.[40]

The *Saiga* case

Given the prominence of the question of maritime law enforcement and the level of force permitted under international law, it may not be surprising that the first substantive case heard by

ITLOS did involve tackling questions relating to the use of force in the maritime environment. In the 1999 case of the *M/V Saiga (No. 2)* Case,[41] ITLOS provided a very clear articulation on the limits on the use of force and in so doing created a decisive legal threshold of understanding as to what is acceptable or not within the realm of international maritime law enforcement.

The facts of the case involved the M/V *Saiga* (flagged to Saint Vincent and the Grenadines), an oil tanker that supplied gas oil and water to three fishing vessels that were licensed to fish in the Guinea exclusive economic zone (EEZ) (around 22 miles off Alcatraz Island).[42] The actions of the *Saiga* were not authorized by Government of Guinea, which alleged that the provision of gas oil was a violation of their customs laws. On October 28 1997, a Guinean patrol boat fired at, boarded and arrested crewmembers of the *Saiga* off the Sierra Leone Coast. Two people on board the *Saiga* suffered gunshot wounds. The ship and its crew were subsequently detained and the Master was prosecuted domestically for customs violations. Saint Vincent and the Grenadines brought an action in ITLOS.

The Tribunal determined that in relation to the application of force, international law mandates that force is to be avoided and where this is not possible, then only reasonable and necessary force is permitted in the exercise of law enforcement jurisdiction.[43] Conditions of 'humanity' are to condition the exercise of force. Moreover, an escalatory process of actions is required before force is ever contemplated and these include:

> a ship at sea is first to give an auditory or visual signal to stop, using internationally recognized signals. Where this does not succeed, a variety of actions may be taken, including the firing of shots across the bows of the ship. It is only after the appropriate actions fail that the pursuing vessel may, as a last resort, use force. Even then, appropriate warning must be issued to the ship and all efforts should be made to ensure that life is not endangered.[44]

In the circumstances at hand, the *Saiga* was low in the water, it had a top speed of only 10 knots and that it could have been boarded easily. The actions of the Guinea patrol boat in firing live ammunition from a fast patrol boat were determined to be excessive, indiscriminate and contrary to international legal standards.[45]

In the context of the use of force, the ITLOS in the *Saiga* case provided an emphatic statement on the limits on the use of force that drew considerably upon broader concepts of the use of force in both customary international law, as well as broader notions of restraint, namely conceptions of humanity. Instructively, in the subsequent 2007 Guyana/Suriname Permanent Court of Arbitration award case, the Tribunal drew upon this sentiment to further reinforce that only force that was 'unavoidable, reasonable and necessary' would pass muster.[46] Anything that was excessive to those conditions potentially activated broader concepts of 'military force' thus invoking heightened prohibitions contained within international law under Article 2(4) of the UN Charter.[47]

Broader issues of maritime law and ITLOS

The *Saiga* case represents a key foundational moment in the establishment of a technically proficient maritime jurisprudence. In addition to reaching conclusions as to the limits of the use of force in the maritime context, the case dealt with a number of other seminal topics relating to maritime law and practice. These included questions relating to the nationality of ships, customs enforcement jurisdiction, hot pursuit and the requirement for the exhaustion of local remedies

Nationality of ships

In the *Saiga* case Guinea sought to challenge the admissibility of claims by Saint Vincent and the Grenadines on grounds it did not have legal standing or competence to present claims on behalf of the ship, as it was alleged the *Saiga* was not validly registered under Saint Vincent and the Grenadines law at time of arrest. The argument was a technical one in that the registration was incomplete under existing Saint Vincent and the Grenadines domestic law and hence was provisional only. To this end, the contention made by Guinea was that the ship was without nationality.[48] Saint Vincent and the Grenadines responded by maintaining that a provisional registration was sufficient and that when a vessel was registered under its flag it remained so until deleted from registry. An analogy was made that a person does not lose nationality when a passport expires, similarly a vessel does not cease to be registered merely because of expiry of provisional certificate. Provisional certification, like a passport, is evidence about, and not source of, national status.[49]

The relevant LOSC provision is Article 91, which provides that each State has exclusive jurisdiction to determine the conditions that grant nationality and that there be a 'genuine link' between the State and the ship.

The Tribunal determined that the domestic law adopted regulates such conditions.[50] Hence, the determination of criteria and establishment for granting and withdrawing nationality to ships is within the exclusive jurisdiction of flag state.[51] Accordingly, the nationality of a ship is question of fact which was discharged by Saint Vincent and the Grenadines in this instance. In this instance provisional registration sufficed and the Tribunal also noted the indicia of nationality in various markings and documents on board the vessel.[52] Moreover, the Tribunal determined that Saint Vincent and the Grenadines' conduct reinforced this position as it had acted in the capacity of the flag state in invoking the jurisdiction of the Tribunal and Guinea had acted consistently with this position during the interlocutory proceedings of this matter.[53]

In relation to the question of 'genuine link' as stipulated in Article 91, the Tribunal determined this requirement was implemented to secure duties of the flag state to the ship rather than a mechanism for allowing other States to challenge validity of registration.[54] Hence, if challenging State determines no 'genuine link', it may report relevant facts to the flag state for them to investigate[55] under Article 94(6) of the LOSC, but there is no reference to allow challenging State to refuse to recognize nationality, or right to fly flag. Accordingly, the Tribunal determined that Guinea has no legal basis to refuse to recognize *Saiga*'s right to fly flag of Saint Vincent and the Grenadines' on ground of no genuine link.

Enforcement of customs laws

The facts of the incident involving the *Saiga* involved the purported exercise of customs law jurisdiction in the Guinea EEZ. The Tribunal needed to grapple with the question of whether the enforcement of custom laws of Guinea in the EEZ was compatible with the LOSC.

Under Articles 21 and 33 of the LOSC, a coastal State is entitled to apply custom laws and regulations in its territorial sea and contiguous zone. In the EEZ, Article 60(2) of the LOSC allows for jurisdiction to apply custom laws only to artificial islands, installations and structures.

Guinea sought to advance an argument that Articles 56 ('Rights, Jurisdiction and Duties of the coastal State in the EEZ') and 58 of LOSC ('Rights and Duties of other States in the Exclusive Economic Zone') allowed for the application of 'other rules of international law' to justify application and enforcement of general customs and contraband laws in the EEZ, so long as they are not incompatible with Part V LOSC. Guinea engaged principles of 'public interest' and 'necessity' to enable it to enforce local customs law. Public interest was argued to come from fiscal loss from illegal off-shore bunkering in its EEZ.[56]

The Tribunal determined recourse to 'public interest' not compatible with Articles 56 or 58, as this would entitle a coastal State enormous discretion to prohibit activities in its EEZ that it decides to charaterize as affecting its 'public interest', which would curtail the rights of other States in the EEZ[57] in a manner that directly undermines the integrity of Articles 56 and 58 of the LOSC.

The issue of 'necessity', which is a general ground for precluding wrongfulness under international law as reflected in the ILC *Articles on Responsibility of States for Internationally Wrongful Acts* at Article 25,[58] requires the act in question to be justified in safeguarding the State from a grave and imminent peril. The Tribunal determined that Guinea had provided no evidence its essential interests were in grave or imminent peril. Moreover, the application of customs laws was not the only way to safeguard its interest in maximizing tax revenue from sale of gas oil.[59]

Hence, the Tribunal determined where Guinea applied custom laws to EEZ, it acted contrary to LOSC. Therefore the arrest and detention of *Saiga*, the prosecution, conviction of master, the confiscation of cargo and seizure of ship were all contrary to the Convention.[60] Significantly, the Tribunal also determined that while the LOSC accords certain rights to coastal States and other States in the EEZ, the absence of express rights to coastal State do not belong to other State, and similarly the converse applies.[61] Such a determination provides a useful interpretative guide to resolving legal ambiguity under the LOSC that has general application.

Hot pursuit

The right of 'hot pursuit' is well established within international maritime jurisprudence. The *'I'm Alone'* case, discussed above, provided the first enunciation of the concept of hot pursuit and it is from this authority that the right gradually acquired customary status within international law. The LOSC subsequently codified this right in Article 111 and extended its reach to the EEZ, a new zone created through the LOSC.

Critically, when examining Article 111 in the *Saiga* case, ITLOS expressly stipulated that each of the criteria contained within Article 111 were cumulative.[62] Hence, when relying upon the right of hot pursuit to affect a lawful arrest the coastal State needed to ensure that all criteria were satisfied. Thus, the coastal State must have 'good reason to believe' that the vessel being pursued has violated the laws of the coastal state particular to the relevant maritime zone (Art. 111(1)). In addition, the pursuit must commence when the foreign ship (or one of its boats) is within the internal waters, archipelagic waters, territorial sea, contiguous zone, EEZ or on the continental shelf of the coastal State (Art. 111(1)(2)). In addition, the pursuit can only continue if it is not interrupted and the right ceases if the ship being pursued enters the territorial sea of any State other than the coastal State (Art. 111(3)). In addition, hot pursuit may only be commenced 'after a visual or auditory signal to stop has been given at a distance which enables it to be seen or heard by the foreign ship' (Art. 111(4)). Finally, in addition, only warships and military aircraft or other ships or aircraft that are clearly identifiable on government service of the coastal State may engage in a pursuit (Art. 111(5)).

As will be discussed in the third section, such criteria have been liberalized in Australian domestic legislation and have found tacit favour within Australian Courts. Moreover, attempts have been made to carve out a regional practice, supported by recently ratified agreements, that departs from the strictness of some of these elements and seeks to create a new normative international standard.

Exhaustion of local remedies

Article 295 of the LOSC mandates that recourse to international dispute resolution mechanisms are only allowed where local remedies have been exhausted, at least in circumstances where international law requires this. Guinea contended that Saint Vincent and the Grenadines claims were inadmissible because local remedies were not exhausted. Guinea claimed the Master could have gone to the Guinean Supreme Court and the owners of *Saiga* and the confiscated cargo could have initiated legal proceedings within the domestic legal system of Guinea. Further, all could have sought a compromise settlement under the domestic customs law.[63]

Saint Vincent and the Grenadines' argued, in response, that exhaustion of local remedies requirement did not apply, since Guinea violated their rights to have its vessels enjoy freedom of navigation and lawful use of the seas under the LOSC. In particular, the contention was that rule applies only where there is a jurisdictional connection between the State against which the claim is brought and the person in respect of which the claim is advanced. Such a connection was absent in this instance as the arrest of the ship took place outside the territorial jurisdiction of Guinea, and the ship was brought into jurisdiction by force. Further, the arrest occurred following an alleged hot pursuit that failed to satisfy requirements of LOSC.[64]

The requirement to exhaust local remedies is a feature of modern international law especially in the context of rights of diplomatic protection of its citizens. In respect of maritime law, the Tribunal drew a distinction between treatment of aliens and violation of rights against the State itself. It determined that Guinea violated rights of Saint Vincent and the Grenadines' under Articles 33, 56, 58, 111 and 292 LOSC. Accordingly, as the matter did not involve the treatment of aliens, the requirement to exhaust domestic remedies did not apply here. Moreover, the Tribunal determined that application of the rule required a jurisdictional connection between the person suffering the damage and State responsible for the wrongful act.[65]

In this instance no such jurisdictional connection could be established,[66] as Guinea's purported application of its customs laws to the EEZ was deficient.

ITLOS themes

The *Saiga* case decisively settled a number of issues relating to maritime law under the LOSC. The Tribunal in this inaugural case acted decisively and boldly in asserting its authority in this field. To date, there have been over twenty cases decided by the Tribunal. The 'tactical' focus of the Tribunal's jurisdiction has seen a predominance of procedural issues addressed. In fact, the case law reveals that the issues of 'prompt release' and 'reasonable bond' under Article 292 of the LOSC have featured in over half the cases coming before the Tribunal. In addition issues such as conservation measures, boundary delimitation, EEZ rights and warship immunity have also been the focus of litigation.

ITLOS is proving its relevance in this field and is providing a useful forum for meeting the ambitions of the drafters of the LOSC in fulfilling the compulsory dispute mechanism requirements. While it has been able to articulate a consistent and coherent vision of maritime legal rights and responsibilities under the LOSC, it nonetheless operates in a decentralized judicial environment. Such decentralization has significance for both competing bodies within the international legal sphere but also in relation to the question of domestic convergence and divergence. That issue will be addressed in the following section.

Australian courts and international law in the maritime context

In the domestic *Volga* cases that occurred in Australian State and Federal Courts in the early/mid-2000s, the intersection (and disconnection) between Australian law and international law was tested most fully. The issue of 'hot pursuit' was a particularly relevant point of contention in the facts of the *Volga* case and yet was not able to be squarely addressed. Unfortunately, the legislative scheme that applied under the then applicable *Fisheries Management Act* (FMA) to authorize automatic forfeiture of illegal fishing vessels effectively sidestepped domestic judicial consideration of the hot pursuit question.[67] Such an outcome has obvious international legal consequences, especially given the apparent inconsistency in regimes. However given Australia's dualist attitude to the incorporation of international law into domestic law, the Courts generally feel no compulsion to recognize international legal arguments and did not do so in this instance.

The facts of the incident are that in February 2002 a Russian-flagged long line fishing vessel, the *Volga*, was stopped and boarded on the high seas directly adjacent to the Australian AFZ/EEZ by members of the Royal Australian Navy and the Australian Fisheries Management Authority, on suspicion of unlawful fishing within the Australian AFZ/EEZ.[68] The navigation officers aboard the *HMAS Canberra* calculated that the *Volga* was 400 yards within the EEZ surrounding Heard and McDonald Islands (located in the southern ocean) when they ordered it to stop. Using more accurate mapping data, it was later determined that the *Volga* was, in fact, 0.5nm outside the EEZ when the order was given.

The *Volga* arrest resulted in a number of domestic legal proceedings in the Western Australian District Court,[69] the Western Australian Supreme Court[70] and the Federal Court of Australia.[71]

The domestic cases largely sidestepped the international law issues concerning hot pursuit and jurisdictional capacity by turning on a provision of the FMA, namely s 106A. This provision provided (remarkably), that foreign fishing vessels that were engaged in illegal fishing were immediately forfeited to the Commonwealth.

The owner of the *Volga*, Olbers, sought a declaration from the Federal Court that the seizure and detention of the *Volga* was unlawful and that the vessel and the equipment seized should be returned. Olbers submitted that the pursuit of the vessel and its subsequent seizure was not carried out in a way that was consistent with either the LOSC, namely the requirement of hot pursuit, nor its domestic equivalent in the FMA.

The submissions made by Olbers challenging the seizure were varied,[72] but largely centred on the operation of section 106A of the FMA and the forfeiture of ownership.[73] French J found that the provisions acted to transfer the title automatically from the owner of the vessel to the Commonwealth at the time that one or more of the qualifying fishing offences took place. Having found that the *Volga* breached sections of the FMA when it entered and unlawfully fished within the AFZ/EEZ,[74] French J found that title transferred from the *Volga* to the Commonwealth in

January 2002 despite the vessel not being apprehended until 7 February 2002.[75] Hence, given that this was an Australian vessel, issues of hot pursuit did not arise.

While French J did not make a determination on whether the *Volga* arrest was conducted in a manner consistent with the LOSC, he did comment on the provisions in the FMA giving rise to hot pursuit by way of *obiter dicta*. He noted that the hot pursuit provisions in s 87 of the FMA and those in Article 111 of the LOSC were apparently incompatible.[76] Specifically, French J noted that in the LOSC, the pursuit must not be interrupted (Art. 111(1)), but in the FMA, while a hot pursuit must likewise not be interrupted or terminated (s 87), interruption is qualified to not include interruptions such as when a pursuing officer loses sight of a vessel (s 87(2)) or loses output from a radar or other sensing device (s 87(3)). However, French J also noted in *obiter* that the interpretation of s 87 must 'have regard to the practical exigencies of the circumstances in which the pursuit might have to be undertaken.'[77]

The effect of French J's interpretation of s 106A of the FMA is that Olbers had no legal right to challenge the pursuit of the *Volga*.[78] The requirements of hot pursuit thereby become otiose because Olbers had already ceased to be the owner of the vessel by operation of the Australian law forfeiting the vessel.

Olbers appealed the decision of French J to the Full Court of the Federal Court on a number of constitutional law grounds. On the issue of the lawfulness of the pursuit, the Full Court did acknowledge Article 111 of the LOSC and s 87 of the FMA in relation to the facts, although the Full Court also stated that it was 'unnecessary for us to express a concluded view.'[79] Though there were a number of *obiter* comments that acknowledged the inconsistency between the LOSC requirements and the Australian legislation.[80]

The way in which the Court has interpreted the provisions in the FMA has given rise to substantial academic criticism for offending the principles underlying the various provisions of the LOSC that 'intended to safeguard rights of owners of foreign vessels.'[81] One commentator notes that the cases reveal that some Australian laws are inconsistent with the LOSC, but that in a domestic context 'implementation of international law in the domestic area is within the discretion of the executive and the legislature.'[82] Nonetheless, there is an obvious inconsistency in approach between the requirements of international law and the framework permitted under Australian national legislation.

As a remedial measure, Australia has undertaken negotiation of a number of bilateral agreements in the Southern Ocean to modify 'hot pursuit' requirements as a matter of international law.[83] This issue is more fully canvassed elsewhere in this volume, but it may be observed that this initiative does represent an attempt by Australian agencies to reconcile differences between domestic law and international law in a constructive manner. How an international Tribunal would reconcile a regional hot pursuit treaty regime in the face of the specific requirements of Article 111 of the LOSC (and the decision in *Saiga*) is uncertain. There would nonetheless be solid grounds to support such a derivation under the terms of the LOSC, which is itself expressed in numerous key areas to be 'subject to other rules of international law.'[84] More compellingly, such a derivation might be read as consistent with the terms of Article 111 in accordance with provisions of the *Vienna Convention on the Law of Treaties* that allows for 'any subsequent practice in the application of the treaty'[85] to be taken into account when discerning meaning. Finally, such a derivation may be reflective of a regional custom[86] that can co-exist with the LOSC as a matter of customary international law.

Moreover, having regard to French J's observation about contemporary law enforcement capacities, there exist strong policy arguments that a Tribunal such as ITLOS may have regard to when reconciling this modified regional articulation of hot pursuit. When in earlier decades the capacity of illegal maritime activity was restricted to near coastal zones, the traditional elements of hot pursuit were considered to strike the right balance. Even in the 1970's when the LOSC was being negotiated, capacities were still limited. Today, they are not and with the corresponding increase in criminal sophistication, Australia (and others) are asserting that there needs to be a correlative adjustment of the older principles pertaining to hot pursuit. As submitted above, there do seem to be a number of legal grounds open to press such claims within international judicial fora. It would appear to be only a matter of time before such a case will find its way to a body like ITLOS where value judgments about competing visions of maritime sanctity will need to be exercised. There is room for guarded optimism that a '21st century' conception of hot pursuit might be successfully advanced and accepted in such fora.

Conclusion

The Law of the Sea Convention creates a world order for Ocean governance. While ambitiously aimed, it necessarily requires reconciliation between numerous competing principles. Resource exploitation against resource preservation, coastal State security against navigational freedom, equitable principles against black letter rules and so on. In its goal to systematize and regulate the proliferation of claims to offshore maritime areas, the LOSC pits one principle against another in repeated instances of potential conflict throughout its text. While such balancing provides for the possibility of consensus agreement, it also presents obvious difficulties when interpreting and applying these competing provisions. As Kennedy observes:

> [r]eading the Convention is a puzzling experience. It is hard to identify either the source of its modernity or the mechanism by which it establishes itself as a substantive legal regime. The reader finds himself continually distracted, diverted and delayed. . . . No one is given the power to allocate and limit authorities in the world's aquatic regions. Instead the lengthy Convention submerges its voice, referring the reader through both its organization and content simultaneously forward to process and back to its own source or purposive origin in the Preamble.[87]

In addressing these conflicting goals, enormous faith is placed in a scheme of comprehensive dispute settlement. Indeed, the Convention anticipates a bewildering array of dispute settlement mechanisms. In this regard, both the ICJ and ITLOS in particular have contributed greatly towards the development of legal norms applicable in the maritime environment. Freedom of navigation is a theme that is frequently articulated and reinforced by the ICJ. At the same time when it comes to matters pertaining to the use of force, ITLOS has been both strident and decisive in its determination of exacting limits.

The enthusiasm that was expressed by commentators such as Philip Allott at the possibilities inherent in the LOSC, outlined at the beginning of this article, has been largely justified. The LOSC's goal of systematizing and regulating the proliferation of claims in the world oceans are being met and the dispute resolution mechanisms are fully operational. They are performing a creditable job in resolving disputes and ITLOS in particular has been both decisive and adroit in its approach to resolving disputes and articulating a sound jurisprudential foundation for effective maritime operational planning.

While the LOSC architecture may have been overly optimistic in the search for resolution of age-old maritime conundrums, it seems very unlikely that an UNCLOS IV Conference would achieve greater resolution of contentious issues. This is not to say that innovative solutions to contemporary problems should not be sought. Within the cascade of competing powers, rights and obligations of the LOSC, the resolution of matters pertaining to security and law enforcement issues will likely always be a dynamic practice. As Kennedy notes when reading the Convention, '[a]s the reader moves from the Preamble into the text he must move with faith, faith in the applicability of principles, the working out in practice, and the redemption of substance by process. If the Preamble is vague, the Convention will render it concrete. If the Convention is indeterminate, practice will clarify its terms.'[88] If the LOSC is a not just another dry legal document to be litigated in Court, but rather a living document, one that is also a state of mind, then let it act as a touchstone to guide ongoing, responsible dialogue as well as innovation to achieve the equilibrium necessary for international peace and security within the world's oceans.

Acknowledgments

The author would like to thank Ms Loise Wells, Ms Sarah Brown, Mr Mark Giddings and Ms Desislava Gancheva for their research assistance. Any errors in the chapter are solely the responsibility of the author.

Notes

1 *United Nations Convention on the Law of the Sea*, opened for signature 10 December 1982, 1833 UNTS 397 (entered into force 16 November 1994) (hereinafter 'LOSC').
2 LOSC Preamble, '*Recognizing* the desirability of establishing through this Convention, with due regard for the sovereignty of all States, a legal order for the seas and oceans which will facilitate international communication, and will promote the peaceful uses of the seas and oceans, the equitable and efficient utilization of their resources, the conservation of their living resources, and the study, protection and preservation of the marine environment' and '*Prompted*, by the desire to settle, in a spirit of mutual understanding and cooperation, *all* [emphasis mine] uses relating to the law of the sea'.
3 LOSC Preamble, '*Affirming* that matters not regulated by this Convention continue to be governed by the rules and principles of general international law'.
4 David Kennedy, *International Legal Structures* (Nomos Publishers, 1987), 202.
5 Philip Allott, *Power Sharing in the Law of the Sea*, 77 AJIL 1 (1983) 1.
6 See generally the discussion of these two approaches as manifested in the respective Columbia and Yale Law School orientations to International Law as discussed in David Kennedy, *When Renewal Repeats: Thinking Against the Box* (2000) 32 *NYU J. Int'l L. & Pol.* 335, 381.
7 *LOSC* Part XV.
8 *LOSC* Art. 279.
9 *LOSC* Art. 280.
10 *LOSC* Art. 283.
11 *LOSC* Art. 284.
12 *LOSC* Art. 286.
13 United Nations, *Statute of the International Court of Justice*, 18 April 1946; United Nations, *Charter of the United Nations*, 24 October 1945, 1 UNTS XVI, Chapter XIV: The International Court of Justice.
14 *LOSC* Annex VI, VII, and VIII.
15 *LOSC* Annex VIII, Art. 1
16 *LOSC* Annex VI.
17 *LOSC* Annex VI, Art. 4.
18 Tullio Treves, 'Conflicts between the International Tribunal for the Law of the Sea and the International Court of Justice' (1999) 31 *International Law and Politics* 809.
19 *Prosecutor v Tadic (Defence Motion for Interlocutory Appeal on Jurisdiction)* (International Criminal Tribunal for the Former Yugoslavia, Appeal Chamber, Case No IT-94-1-AR72, 2 October 1995), [11].

20 International Law Commission, *Fragmentation of International Law: Difficulties Arising from the Diversification and Expansion of International Law* – Report of the Study Group of the International Law Commission, UN Doc. A/CN.4/L.682 (Apr. 13, 2006), as corrected UN Doc. A/CN.4/L.682/Corr.1 (Aug. 11, 2006) (finalized by Martti Koskenniemi) (hereinafter 'ILC Fragmentation Study'), [8], 11.
21 See generally L.B. Sohn, 'Settlement of Law of the Sea Disputes' (1995) 10 *International Journal of Marine and Coastal Law*, 205–217.
22 *LOSC* Art. 298(1)(b).
23 *Corfu Channel (Merits) (U.K. v. Alb.)* (1949) ICJ Rep 4 ['Corfu Channel Case'].
24 See generally, Stephens, D.G., 'The Impact of the 1982 Law of the Sea Convention on the Conduct of Peacetime Naval/Military Operations' (1999) 29 *California Western International Law Journal*, 283.
25 *Corfu Channel Case* (1940) ICJ Rep 4, 39, Individual Opinion by Judge Alvarez.
26 *Case of the SS Lotus (France v Turkey)* [1927] PCIJ Rep5, 92.
27 This was an argument advanced by the US Counsel in the 1910 *North Atlantic Coast Fisheries Case* (Gr. Brit. v. U.S.) ICGJ 403 (PCA 1910).
28 *Corfu Channel*, 30; see also C.H.M. Waldock, 'The Regulation of the Use of Force by Individual States in International Law' (1952) 81 *Recuil Des Cours* 455, 501.
29 See for example, Ian Brownlie, *International Law and The Use of Force by States* (Clarendon Press, 1963).
30 Rob McLaughlin, *United Nations Naval Peace Operations in The Territorial Sea* (Martinus Nijhoff 2009) 100–102 for an outline of the resolution of this issue.
31 *Military and Paramilitary Activities in and Against Nicaragua (Nicaragua v United States Of America) (Merits)* [1986] ICJ Reps 14 [hereinafter *Nicaragua*].
32 *Ibid*, [227].
33 See generally, Rob McLaughlin, 'Legal-Policy Considerations and Conflict Characterisation at the Threshold between Law Enforcement and Non-International Armed Conflict', (2012) 13(1) *Melbourne J. Int'l Law* 94.
34 *Code of Conduct for Law Enforcement Officials*, GA Res 34/169, Thirty Fourth Session, UN Doc A/RES/34/169 (17 December 1979).
35 *Commentary* on *Code of Conduct for Law Enforcement Officials*, Art 3 emphasizes *(a)* that the use of force by law enforcement officials should be exceptional and should only be used when it is reasonably necessary; *(b)* national principles of proportionality should be respected in the interpretation of art 3; *(c)* the use of firearms is considered an extreme measure and generally should not be used except when a suspected offender offers armed resistance or otherwise jeopardizes the lives of others; in all cases where a firearm has been discharged a report should be made promptly to the competent authorities.
36 *Eighth United Nations Congress on the Prevention of Crime and the Treatment of Offenders*, UN Doc A/CONF 144/28/Rev 1.
37 *S.S. "I'm Alone"* (Canada, United States) (1935) Vol. III *Reports of International Arbitral Awards*, 1609–1618.
38 *Ibid*, 1615.
39 *Investigation of Certain Incidents Affecting the British Trawler Red Crusader* (United Kingdom and Denmark) (1962) Vol. XXIX *Reports of International Arbitral Awards* 521–539.
40 *Ibid*, 538.
41 *M/V "Saiga" (No 2) Case (Saint Vincent and the Grenadines v Guinea) (Merits)* (International Tribunal for the Law of the Sea Case No 2, 1 July 1999) [hereinafter *Saiga*].
42 Bernard Oxman, 'International Decisions' (2000) 94(1) *American Journal of International Law* 140.
43 *Saiga*, above n 40, [155].
44 *Ibid*. [156].
45 *Ibid*. [158].
46 Arbitral Tribunal Constituted Pursuant to Article 287, and in Accordance with Annex VII, of the United Nations Convention on the Law of the Sea in the Matter of an Arbitration between Guyana and Suriname [445], found at <http://www.pca-cpa.org/showpage.asp?pag_id=1147>.
47 *Ibid*.
48 *Saiga*, above n 40, [58]
49 *Ibid*, [60].
50 *Ibid*, [62–63].
51 *Ibid*, [65].
52 *Ibid*, [67].
53 *Ibid*, [68–69].
54 *Ibid*, [83].

55 *Ibid*, [82].
56 *Ibid*, [130].
57 *Ibid*, [131].
58 *Articles on Responsibility of States for Internationally Wrongful Acts* (2001) GA Res 56/836 of 12 December 2001, and corrected by document A/56/49 (Vol.I)/Corr.4.
59 *Saiga*, above n 40, [135].
60 *Ibid*, [172].
61 *Ibid*, [137].
62 *Ibid*, [146].
63 *Ibid*, [89–90].
64 *Ibid*, [91–92].
65 *Ibid*, [97–99].
66 *Ibid*, [99].
67 Section 106A of the Fisheries Management Act 2001; the section provides for the automatic forfeiture to the Commonwealth of vessels used in various fishing offences within the AFZ.
68 Such suspicion that was later found to be fact: *Olbers v Commonwealth (No 4)* [2004] FCA 229.
69 *R v Lijo* [2004] WADC 29 (criminal proceedings).
70 *Lijo v the Commonwealth Director of Public Prosecutions* [2003] WASCA 4 (an application to vary bail conditions).
71 *Olbers Co Ltd v Commonwealth* [2004] FCAFC 262, *Olbers v Commonwealth (No 4)* [2004] FCA 229, *Olbers v Commonwealth (No 3)* [2003] FCA 651, *Olbers Co Ltd v Commonwealth (No 2)* [2003] FCA 177, *Olbers Co Ltd v Commonwealth* [2002] FCA 1269.
72 That the vessel was not properly forfeited under the FMA, that the Act was unconstitutional (on several grounds) including that the provisions violated the separation of powers effected by Chapter III of the Constitution, that the provisions were beyond the scope of legislative power of the Commonwealth, and that the provisions effected acquisition of property other than on just terms.
73 Note that while s 106 of the FMA provides for forfeiture of a vessel following a court order, prior to 1999 when s 106A was introduced by the *Fisheries Legislation Amendment Act (No 1) 1999*, there was no provision for automatic forfeiture in the FMA.
74 *Olbers v Commonwealth of Australia* (No 4) [2004] FCA 229, [65].
75 *Ibid* [62], [63] and [80].
76 *Ibid*, [97].
77 *Ibid*, [96].
78 Warwick Gullet, 'Developments in Australian Fisheries Law: Setting the Law of the Sea Adrift?' (2004) 21 *EPLJ* 169, 173.
79 *Olbers Co Ltd v Commonwealth of Australia* (2004) 212 ALR 325 [19].
80 *Ibid*, [18]-[19].
81 Warrick Gullet, above n 78, 169.
82 Saiful Karim 'Conflicts over Protection of Marine Living Resources: The 'Volga Case' Revisted' (2011) 3 *Goettingen Journal of International Law* 1, 127.
83 *Agreement on Cooperation in the Maritime Areas Adjacent to the French Southern and Antarctic Territories, Heard Island and the McDonald Islands*, Australia-France, opened for signature 24 November 2003, [2005] ATS 6 (entered into force 1 February 2005); *Agreement on Cooperative Enforcement of Fisheries Laws in the Maritime Areas Adjacent to the French Southern and Antarctic Territories, Heard Island and the McDonald Islands*, opened for signature 8 July 2007, [2011] ATS 1 (entered into force 8 Jan 2011).
84 *LOSC*, above n 1, Preamble 'Affirming that matters not regulated by this Convention continue to be governed by the rules and principles of general international law'; Art. 2(3) LOSC 'The sovereignty over the territorial sea is exercised subject to this Convention and to other rules of international law'; see also Art. 19 (1), Art. 21(1), Art. 31, Art. 34, Art. 58, Art. 87, Art. 138 and Art. 303.
85 *Vienna Convention on the Law of Treaties*, opened for signature 23 May 1969, 1155 UNTS 331, (entered into force 27 January 1980), Art. 31(3).
86 *Asylum Case (Colombia v Peru) (Judgment)* [1950] ICJ 266.
87 David Kennedy, above n 4, 202.
88 Kennedy, above n 4, 206.

Part C
Regulation and Enforcement in Different Maritime Sectors

10

Fisheries Enforcement and the Concepts of Compliance and Monitoring, Control and Surveillance

Mary Ann Palma-Robles

Introduction

The trend in the production of global marine fisheries resources presents an alarming concern for sustainability. Fisheries resources which were initially regarded as inexhaustible are now either seriously depleted or overexploited.[1] According to the Food and Agriculture Organization (FAO), 28.8 per cent of global fish stocks are overfished and 61.3 per cent are fully fished.[2] Most of the ten most productive species in the world are fully fished and have no potential for increase in production.[3] Similarly one third of the commercially significant tuna species are already overfished.[4] Although catches in some regions such as the Western Central Pacific and the Eastern Indian Ocean are increasing and some stocks are showing signs of recovery in response to improved management, a number of fishing regions in the world are still subject to stress leading to a rapid decline in global fisheries.

The depletion of fisheries resources may be attributed to a number of factors, such as industrialisation, overfishing, environmental factors affecting stock productivity, the open access nature of many fisheries, and overcapacity in the world fishing fleet. Illegal, unreported and unregulated (IUU) fishing remains as "one of the greatest threats to fish stocks and marine ecosystems and continues to have serious and major implications for the conservation and management of ocean resources, as well as the food security and economies of many States, particularly developing States."[5] It is estimated that about one third of the total catch in some important fisheries is subject to IUU fishing representing an overall cost to developing countries of between USD2 to USD15 billion a year.[6] IUU fishing is associated with a gamut of issues, including ineffective flag State control and lack of capacity of States to adopt fisheries management plans that set sustainable limits based on scientific advice.[7]

Fish is the most internationally traded food commodity and plays a crucial role in food security. It is predicted that the demand for fish may reach 180 million tonnes in 2030 and neither aquaculture nor any terrestrial food production would be able to supplement the need for protein production provided by marine capture fisheries.[8] The World Bank also estimates the economic loss of USD51 billion from global fisheries between 1974 to 2007, with 2004 as the base year suggests the need for greater stakeholder awareness and comprehensive fisheries governance reform.[9]

There are a number of measures recommended to respond to the decline of fisheries, such as reduction of catch, restriction of fishing effort, designation of marine protected areas, and certification of sustainable fisheries.[10] Most of these measures have been developed within domestic laws and policies, regional conservation and management measures, and global binding and non-binding fisheries instruments. The FAO recommends that effective fisheries management should be conditioned by resource considerations, environmental constraints, ecological factors, technological development and socio-economic considerations.[11] Similarly, the governing legal framework should also address a broad range of issues relating to the conservation and management of fisheries.

The legal regime for fisheries has progressively developed since the 1990s and States have continuously adopted measures to control fishing activities. This has led to the gradual erosion of freedom of fishing supplanted by increased regulation of fishing activities and shared access under the 1982 United Nations Convention on the Law of the Sea (LOSC).[12] While the decades directly following the LOSC may be considered as an era of strengthening fisheries regulation, the succeeding period including the current one can be deemed as an important phase for fisheries enforcement. This is because key global fisheries agreements have now been established for a number of years providing sufficient time for individual States and regional organisations to amend relevant measures in line with international rights and obligations.

This chapter focuses on the enforcement of fisheries regulations, particularly the rights and obligations of States under international law and provides examples of State practice for analysis. It examines the fisheries enforcement framework under the LOSC and other global fisheries agreements in zones of sovereignty, zones under sovereign rights, and on the high seas. It also discusses port State enforcement as a supplement to flag State enforcement and an effective means to prevent the landing or transshipment of illegally caught fish. The chapter analyses the concept of monitoring, control and surveillance as an overarching concept of fisheries enforcement and contrasts it with the element of fisheries compliance. It concludes with a discussion of some of the emerging issues in fisheries that continuously challenge the fisheries enforcement capabilities of States.

International legal framework for fisheries enforcement

The international legal framework for fisheries enforcement comprises legally binding agreements, in particular the LOSC,[13] the 1993 FAO Compliance Agreement,[14] 1995 UN Fish Stocks Agreement,[15] and the 2009 FAO Port State Measures Agreement.[16] These agreements adopt the key principle of promoting equitable, efficient utilisation and conservation of living resources both in areas under national jurisdiction and on the high seas.[17] The LOSC provides the basic framework that outlines the general prescriptive rights and obligations of States in each maritime zone which in turn form the basis for exercising the enforcement powers of States. The limited provisions of the LOSC particularly with respect to fishing on the high seas and fishing for straddling and highly migratory stocks are strengthened by the FAO Compliance Agreement and the UN Fish Stocks Agreement.

The 1993 FAO Compliance Agreement was an effort to solve the problem of "reflagging of fishing vessels into flags of convenience to avoid compliance with agreed conservation and management measures".[18] It applies to all fishing vessels, including support vessels used or intended for fishing on the high seas, except for vessels of 24 metres or less in length[19] subject to certain conditions.[20] The application of this agreement is not restricted to specific species of fish. The FAO Compliance Agreement reiterates the provisions of the LOSC with respect to the effective control of fishing vessels and promotes the concept of compliance and enforcement. It focuses on the role of flag States to ensure the compliance of their vessels with international conservation and management measures on the high seas.

The UN Fish Stocks Agreement provides for the conservation and management of straddling and highly migratory fish stocks. Similar to the FAO Compliance Agreement, it emphasises the need for States to adopt effective mechanisms for compliance and enforcement of conservation measures on the high seas and due to the migratory nature of species subject to the agreement promotes the need to apply compatible measures in the exclusive economic zone (EEZ) and on the high seas.[21] In addition to flag State duties, the UN Fish Stocks Agreement emphasises the role of port States in promoting fisheries conservation measures.[22] The agreement also provides for international cooperation, through the creation of subregional and regional fisheries management organisations (RFMOs) and arrangements[23] and implementation of enforcement mechanisms such as high seas boarding and inspection.[24]

The FAO Port State Measures Agreement was negotiated and agreed by States more than ten years after key global fisheries instruments had been adopted post the LOSC. It outlines in greater detail the role of States in exercising their sovereignty over ports located in their territory as a means to ensure the long term conservation and sustainable use of living marine resources and ecosystems.[25] The FAO Port State Measures Agreement applies to foreign vessels seeking entry into port, with the exception of vessels of a neighbouring State that are engaged in artisanal fishing for subsistence and container vessels that are not carrying fish or, if carrying fish, only those with fish that have not been previously landed.[26] It elaborates on specific measures that may be applied by port States to combat IUU fishing, such as designation of ports, advance request of port entry, use of ports, inspections, and enforcement actions such as denial of port entry and prohibition of catch landing. Similar to the UN Fish Stocks Agreement, the FAO Port State Measures Agreement underscores the need for cooperation between flag and port States, as well as exchange of information with relevant States, RFMOs, the FAO and other international bodies.[27]

As examined in the succeeding sections, the LOSC has limited provisions on fisheries enforcement actions that may be undertaken by States. Apart from the enforcement powers of States under Article 73 of the LOSC in relation to the exercise of sovereign rights for the purpose of exploring, exploiting, conserving and managing living resources, much of the guidance on fisheries enforcement in other maritime zones may only be drawn from other global fisheries agreements. Non-binding fisheries instruments such as the FAO Code of Conduct for Responsible Fisheries[28] and the four International Plans of Action (IPOAs)[29] reiterate some of the enforcement related measures that may be implemented by States under the concept of monitoring, control and surveillance (MCS). The IPOA to Prevent, Deter and Eliminate Illegal, Unreported and Unregulated Fishing (IPOA-IUU) for example, provides that States should undertake comprehensive and effective MCS from the commencement of fishing, through the point of landing to the final destination.[30] The MCS measures provided under the IPOA-IUU encompass compliance and enforcement actions found in the LOSC, FAO Compliance Agreement and the UN Fish Stocks Agreement, such as authorisation to fish, record of fishing vessels, observer programme, vessel monitoring system, and boarding and inspection.

Fisheries enforcement in areas under sovereignty

The LOSC does not contain specific provisions that require States to conserve fisheries resources in areas under sovereignty. Consequently the Convention does not regulate fisheries enforcement in internal waters, territorial sea and archipelagic waters as these waters are subject to the full sovereignty of coastal States. In general the enforcement power of a State in areas under sovereignty under the LOSC largely encompasses the prevention of fishing by foreign vessels engaged in archipelagic sea lanes, innocent, and transit passages.[31]

Article 21 of the LOSC provides that a coastal State may adopt laws and regulations relating to innocent passage through the territorial sea in respect of a number of matters, including the conservation of living resources and prevention of infringement of fisheries laws and regulations of the coastal State.[32] Any fishing activity by a foreign fishing vessel in the territorial sea may be considered as a passage that is prejudicial to the peace, good order and security of a coastal State, and hence non-innocent.[33] This provision is clearly demonstrated in State practice as most coastal State legislation on the territorial sea categorises fishing activities by foreign vessels as passage that is not innocent.

In archipelagic waters the only reference to fisheries is with respect to traditional fishing. Article 51(1) of the LOSC provides that archipelagic States shall recognise traditional fishing rights of an immediately adjacent neighbouring State in areas falling within archipelagic waters. The terms and conditions associated with the exercise of traditional fishing rights are regulated by bilateral agreements between the archipelagic and neighbouring State and may not be transferred to or shared with a third State.[34] As an example Indonesia has concluded bilateral agreements with Malaysia and Papua New Guinea in recognition of traditional fishing rights.[35] Indonesia has imposed some requirements on neighbouring States exercising traditional fishing in Indonesian waters, such as the condition that the fishing practices must have been carried out for at least four generations, the use of fishing gears that are not prohibited under Indonesian law, and that the fishing activities may only be carried out by individuals rather than corporations.[36]

Fisheries enforcement in areas under sovereign rights

Similar to navigation, the LOSC considers competing interests relating to the exploitation and conservation of fisheries resources in an attempt to achieve a balance between the power of coastal States over resources in their areas under jurisdiction and freedom of fishing as part of the freedom of the high seas. Coastal State powers over resources in the EEZ include control over the activities of foreign fishing vessels accessing such resources, while the freedom of the high seas encompasses rights of foreign States and their nationals to conduct activities in the EEZ which may not be fisheries related, such as the exercise of the freedom of navigation. However the continuous decline of commercial fish stocks and stricter fisheries regulations have raised questions as to the balance of these rights tipping in favour of conservation, and increasingly limiting the rights of foreign fishing vessels in the EEZ and consequently on the high seas. In the South Pacific for example, small island States do not allow foreign vessels to fish on the high seas as a condition of access to adjacent EEZ fisheries.[37] These measures have subsequently led to fisheries closure in high seas pockets of the Western and Central Pacific ocean between 2010 and 2012, as well as an ongoing requirement for vessels transiting designated high seas areas to submit entry and exit information.[38]

Fisheries enforcement in the EEZ

As discussed in another chapter of this Handbook, the development of the legal regime of the EEZ marked a significant change in the law of the sea.[39] This is in particular reference to resource exploitation and management as the EEZ regime placed almost 90 per cent of fisheries resources under the sovereign rights of coastal States,[40] otherwise subject to the freedom of fishing prior to the LOSC. Consistent with the sovereign rights of coastal States in conserving and managing living resources in the EEZ,[41] the Convention confers on coastal States the discretion to develop measures that would carry out both its conservation and utilisation obligations under Articles 61 and 62, which includes adopting laws and regulations on foreign fishing access in the EEZ. These laws and regulations may relate to the licensing of fishers, fishing vessels and equipment; determining the type and amount of species to be caught and fixing quotas; regulating seasons and areas of fishing; fixing the age and size of fish and other species that may be caught; specifying information required of fishing vessels; placing of observers on board vessels; regulating conduct of research programmes; landing of catch; terms and conditions on joint ventures and other cooperative arrangements; training of personnel and transfer of fisheries technology; and enforcement procedures.[42]

Article 73 of the Law of the Sea Convention is the key provision on fisheries enforcement in the EEZ that ensures implementation of terms and conditions of foreign fishing access. It provides:

Article 73

Enforcement of laws and regulations of the coastal State

1. The coastal State may, in the exercise of its sovereign rights to explore, exploit, conserve and manage the living resources in the exclusive economic zone, take such measures, including boarding, inspection, arrest and judicial proceedings, as may be necessary *to* ensure compliance with its laws and regulations adopted by it in conformity with this Convention.
2. Arrested vessels and their crews shall be promptly released upon the posting of reasonable bond or other security.
3. Coastal State penalties for violations of fisheries laws and regulations in the exclusive economic zone may not include imprisonment, in the absence of agreements to the contrary by the States concerned, or any other form of corporal punishment.
4. In cases of arrest or detention of foreign vessels the coastal State shall promptly notify the flag State, through appropriate channels, of the action taken and of any penalties subsequently imposed.

There are a number of components and issues related to fisheries enforcement based on Article 73. One issue relates to the boarding and inspection of vessels. Article 73 provides for the enforcement power of coastal States to board and inspect vessels to ensure compliance with the laws and regulations of coastal States. The issue of boarding of vessels is threefold: 1) which vessels can be boarded; 2) what offences warrant the boarding of vessels; and 3) who can board vessels.

Which vessels can be boarded

It is clear that a vessel subject to enforcement powers under Article 73 is a fishing vessel, which is defined "as any vessel used or intended for use for the purposes of the commercial exploitation of living marine resources, including mother ships and any other vessels directly engaged in such fishing operations".[43] This definition however, does not unambiguously determine whether or not support ships such as bunkering vessels may be boarded for fisheries enforcement purposes. The response to this question relates to the type of offences that may warrant boarding of vessels which is further discussed below.

Where a vessel is licensed to fish in the EEZ of a coastal State, the flag State can be said to have conceded the right to inspect the vessel to that coastal State under the LOSC, as well as under any fisheries treaty between the two states. However Article 73 is not clear where the vessel is not licensed to fish but is exercising freedom of navigation through the EEZ of the coastal State. Article 73 does not state that only licensed or otherwise authorised vessels may be boarded and inspected. Rather, it grants the general right to enforce fisheries laws of the coastal State which may be interpreted by some as a blanket provision that all fishing vessels in the EEZ may be subjected to the exercise of this power simply because of their nature and usual purpose. On the other hand, it may be argued that transiting fishing vessels may exercise the freedom of navigation in the EEZ granted to all types of vessels; hence the right to navigate through the zone should be without any interference from the coastal State. Both are legitimate interpretations of the provision and an example of how opposing interests during the UNCLOS III negotiations attempted to balance jurisdiction of coastal States to protect their economic resources and freedom of navigation of foreign States in the EEZ. To address conflicting interpretations of this provision, some coastal States require the notification of entry and exit information by foreign fishing vessels transiting their EEZ, rather than providing for immediate boarding and inspection of these vessels for mere presence in the EEZ.

What offences are covered

Another issue that relates to the kind of fishing vessels subject to fisheries enforcement in the EEZ is the question of the type of fisheries offences that are covered by Article 73. This issue was addressed in the *M/V Saiga* case concerning an oil tanker flagged under the Saint Vincent and the Grenadines arrested by Guinean customs patrol vessels off the coast of Sierra Leone. One of the key issues raised in this case before the International Tribunal for the Law of the Sea (ITLOS) was whether bunkering or refuelling of a fishing vessel within the EEZ of a State is considered an activity which falls within the scope of a coastal State's exercise of its sovereign rights to explore, exploit, conserve and manage the living resources.[44] This view was supported by the Guinean *Code of Maritime Fishing* which provided that supplying of vessels or logistical support to fishing vessels are "operations connected to fishing" subject to licence.[45]

The view that refuelling is an activity ancillary to that of the refuelled ship is supported in State practice in the definition of driftnet fishing under the Convention for the Prohibition of Fishing with Long Driftnets in the South Pacific, where driftnet fishing activities, include "transporting, transhipping and processing any driftnet catch, and co-operation in the provision of food, fuel and other supplies for vessels equipped for or engaged in driftnet fishing."[46] On the other hand, it may be argued that bunkering at sea is an independent activity within the legal regime of freedom of navigation under Article 59 of the LOSC.[47] It may also be that States which have not adopted regulations concerning bunkering of fishing vessels do not regard refuelling as connected to fishing activities. In this debate the fundamental question becomes what constitutes fishing under domestic law.

Even though the LOSC does not provide a definition of "fishing", other international fisheries agreements have defined the same. Fishing, under the FAO Port State Measures Agreement means "searching for, attracting, locating, catching, taking or harvesting fish or any activity which can reasonably be expected to result in the attracting, locating, catching, taking or harvesting of fish."[48] This agreement further defines fishing-related activities as "any operation in support of, or in preparation for, fishing, including the landing, packaging, processing, transshipping or transporting of fish that have not been previously landed at a port, as well as the provisioning of personnel, fuel, gear and other supplies at sea."[49]

Who can board fishing vessels?

Article 73 does not provide any guidance on what agency or entity should be responsible for fisheries enforcement. Under Article 101 of the LOSC, "only warships or military aircraft, or other ships or aircraft on government service especially authorised to that effect" may conduct hot pursuit, which may include pursuit of foreign vessels breaching fisheries regulations of coastal States. Various States utilise different enforcement agencies for fisheries. Some States deploy military or naval vessels to address illegal fishing by foreign vessels to protect resources in the EEZ as if it were part of national security. Some States designate a civilian agency like the coast guard to deal with environmental and resource related infringement in areas under national jurisdiction. Between military and para-military vessels, the general practice has been to use civilian force for fisheries violations in the EEZ because naval intervention can be deemed as a hostile act by other nations and can create disputes if not managed carefully. The use of military vessels has also been faced with strong objections especially in fishing zones around disputed territories in East Asian waters and the South China Sea. Some countries have a multi-agency approach to combine assets in addressing various threats in the EEZ ranging from illegal fishing, marine pollution, illicit trafficking of narcotics, and people smuggling. For most developing countries, the response to illegal fishing depends on a number of considerations such as the availability of military or coastguard assets, the size of the EEZ, and other political priorities.

Prompt release of vessels

One of the most controversial aspects of Article 73 relates to the prompt release of vessels. Article 73(2) provides that arrested vessels and their crew shall be promptly released upon posting of a reasonable bond or other security. A number of cases involving fishing vessels have been heard before the ITLOS on the issue of prompt release. The two key issues in this provision relate to what a "reasonable bond" means and when a release is considered "prompt".

The LOSC does not define what is meant by a reasonable bond or other security. Although the ITLOS has not fixed the amount for a bond or financial security to be considered reasonable, it has identified a number of factors to be taken into account in determining the reasonableness of a bond. These factors include the amount, nature, and form of the bond or financial security,[50] gravity of the alleged offences, the penalties imposed or imposable under the laws of the detaining State, the value of the detained vessel and of the seized cargo, and the amount of the bond imposed by the detaining State and its form.[51] The ITLOS has not provided a complete list of criteria nor has it laid down rules as to the exact weight that should be attached to each factor.[52] The ITLOS has also ruled that non-financial conditions (e.g. good behaviour bond) cannot be considered components of a bond or financial security with respect to an alleged violation by a foreign fishing vessel in the EEZ of a coastal State.[53]

The issue of prompt release is related to the forfeiture of vessels imposed by many coastal States. The ITLOS noted in the *Tomimaru* case that Article 73 does not make reference to the confiscation of vessels; however many States provide for this enforcement action in their legislation with respect to the management and conservation of marine living resources.[54] An example which has arisen in state practice is whether or not the automatic forfeiture of vessels adopted in Australia is contrary to the prompt release requirement of the LOSC. In the case of the *Volga*, the Federal Court of Australia ruled that by operation of section 106A of the *Fisheries Management Act (Cth)* a transfer of title from the foreign fishing vessel owner to the Commonwealth occurred at the time when the fisheries offences were committed; hence when the pursuit, apprehension and forfeiture occurred, Australia was seizing its own vessel.[55] While the validity of section 106A of the *Fisheries Management Act* was upheld by the court, its legitimacy under international law still raises some issues.[56] For one the automatic forfeiture of a foreign vessel to the arresting country would cause the prompt release provision of the LOSC to be inoperable,[57] as it would simply render the application for the prompt release of a vessel without an object.[58]

Another issue in relation to enforcement action under Article 73 of the LOSC is the practice by States of destroying fishing vessels, including burning or sinking of vessels found to have violated domestic fisheries law in the EEZ. This is similarly not provided for under the LOSC but has been incorporated in the domestic legislation of some States. Similar to automatic forfeiture of foreign vessels, the basis for the destruction of fishing vessels for the purpose of combating IUU fishing may be questioned in light of the application of the prompt release provisions of the LOSC.

Imprisonment and considerations of humanity

Article 73(3) of the LOSC provides that penalties of coastal States in the EEZ may not include imprisonment or any other form of corporal punishment, in the absence of agreement to the contrary by the States concerned. This can be contrasted with the treatment of fishing violations by foreign nationals in the territorial sea subject to the full sovereignty of States. While most countries provide for the imprisonment of foreign vessel masters and crew as a form of punishment for violations in waters under their sovereignty, criminal penalties for illegal fishing in the EEZ are constrained by the LOSC. Other administrative penalties, such as the confiscation of catch and gears and prohibition of fish landing are applied by coastal States for fisheries violations in the EEZ. The ITLOS has ruled that Article 73(2) must be read in the context of Article 73 as a whole.[59] It has stated that "(t)he obligation of prompt release of vessels and crews includes elementary considerations of humanity and due process of law. The requirement that the bond or other financial security must be reasonable indicates that a concern for fairness is one of the purposes of this provision".[60]

Fisheries enforcement on the continental shelf

Part V of the LOSC on the EEZ provides that sedentary species do not belong to the EEZ but instead are subject to the continental shelf regime. Article 77(4) of the LOSC defines sedentary species as organisms which are at the harvestable stage, either immobile on or under the seabed or are unable to move except in constant physical contact with the seabed or the subsoil. Examples of species that are part of the living natural resources of the continental shelf are corals, sea anemones, sponges, sea urchins, sea cucumbers, gastropods, and bivalve molluscs such as oysters, pearl shell, mussels, clams, and cockles.[61]

Similar to the provisions on areas under sovereignty, the LOSC is silent on the need to conserve and utilise sedentary species.[62] But unlike the provisions on the EEZ, the sovereign rights given to the coastal State with respect to the continental shelf are exclusive.[63] Thus a coastal State is under no obligation to grant access to foreign nations to such species. Regulations on the use of sedentary species are generally covered under the domestic law of States. There is also no specific provision in the LOSC on enforcement relating to the conservation and management of sedentary species. Coastal States generally apply the fisheries enforcement regime in the EEZ to sedentary species on the continental shelf.

Difficulties arise for the enforcement of regulations on sedentary species in areas where the water column and seabed boundaries between adjacent States do not overlap due to the vagueness of the continental shelf regime in relation to sedentary species. Examples of these areas are shared boundaries between Australia and Indonesia in the Timor Sea and between Australia and Papua New Guinea in the Torres Strait. In the Timor Sea, the Australian continental shelf extends under the Indonesian water column; hence Australia cannot enforce its sovereign rights over the sedentary species on its continental shelf without access to the Indonesian water column. The different legal regimes also create confusion for Indonesian fishermen who may be fishing using an open access licence for pelagic fish in the water column of Indonesia and simultaneously catch sedentary species on the Australian continental shelf.

Fisheries enforcement for sedentary species in the extended continental shelf

The LOSC does not provide any guidelines on coastal State regulatory and enforcement powers on the extended continental shelf. Similar to challenges in enforcing fisheries regulations in shared maritime areas, there may be concerns in the future when sedentary species in the extended continental shelf are accessed by fishing vessels exercising the freedom of the high seas in the water column above. A clear international regulatory framework would need to be developed in order to address this issue, including the impact of fishing on vulnerable marine ecosystems on the seabed.[64]

Fisheries enforcement in the contiguous zone

The contiguous zone of a coastal State forms part of the EEZ for purposes of conservation and management of living resources. While the LOSC specifically provides that a coastal State can exercise control to prevent infringement of laws and regulations within its territory or territorial sea only in relation to customs, fiscal, immigration or sanitary laws,[65] the power of coastal States in the contiguous zone has been critical in terms of enforcing fisheries legislation. As an example, multi-agency cooperation between customs and fisheries officers has been crucial in apprehending illegal fishers. Immigration laws are used to issue deportation orders to foreign nationals onboard illegal fishing vessels. Similarly, customs regulations may apply in case of refuelling of fishing vessels.

Fisheries enforcement on the high seas

The LOSC provides for the exclusive jurisdiction of flag States over ships on the high seas,[66] except for certain illicit activities such as piracy and slave trading which require cooperation and are subject to universal jurisdiction. Part of exercising effective jurisdiction and control over vessels is the duty to take enforcement action against vessels that have not observed generally accepted international regulations and procedures. The development of the role of flag States in effective compliance and enforcement has led to the emergence of flag State duties or responsibilities that have specific application in fisheries. The need for cooperation to address IUU fishing has also led to the development of an enforcement mechanism that allows non-flag State authorities to conduct boarding and inspection on the high seas.

Flag state enforcement

Consistent with the principle of flag State responsibility under the LOSC, international fisheries specific instruments provide that a flag State whose vessels fish on the high seas shall take measures to ensure that its vessels comply with subregional and regional conservation and management measures.[67] In order to emphasise the responsibility of the flag State over the actions of its vessels, post LOSC fisheries agreements provide that a flag State shall authorise a vessel to fish on the high seas only where it is able to exercise its responsibilities with respect to such vessel.[68] A significant element in the exercise of this responsibility is flag State compliance and enforcement.

Article 19 of the UN Fish Stocks Agreement provides for the duty of a flag State to enforce subregional and regional conservation and management measures irrespective of where the violations occur. The flag State also has the duty to investigate immediately and fully any alleged violation and cooperate with other States including requiring its flagged vessel to give information to an investigating authority relating to fishing operations on the high seas. If sufficient evidence is available on the alleged violation by its vessel, the flag State is required to refer the case to its authorities with a view to instituting proceedings without delay in accordance with its laws, and to detain the vessel if appropriate.[69] It has the obligation to carry out investigations and judicial proceedings expeditiously and ensure that the vessel does not engage in fishing operations on the high seas until such time as all outstanding sanctions imposed by a flag State in respect of the violation have been complied with. Some of the sanctions for fisheries violations on the high seas that may be imposed by the flag State include the withdrawal, suspension or cancellation of the authorisation to fish,[70] or refusal to issue an authorisation to fish for a period of time.[71] The UN Fish Stocks Agreement and the FAO Compliance Agreement provide that sanctions should be adequate in severity to secure compliance, discourage violations, and deprive offenders of the benefits accruing from illegal activities.[72]

High seas boarding and inspection in fisheries

In general exclusive flag State jurisdiction means no interference from third States. The fisheries laws of coastal States over foreign vessels do not have application beyond the EEZ. Hence the powers of fisheries enforcement officers are limited to violations in the fisheries jurisdiction which include areas under sovereignty and sovereign rights. There are three exceptions to the limitation of this coastal State power on the high seas. One is in relation to the right of visit under Article 110 of the LOSC which does not apply to fisheries offences. The second relates to the right of hot pursuit under Article 111 of the LOSC. The third exception relates to high seas boarding and inspection under the UN Fish Stocks Agreement. Articles 21 and 22 of the UN Fish Stocks Agreement can be deemed as an exception to Article 92(1) of the LOSC which provides that ships are subject to the exclusive jurisdiction of the flag State on the high seas.

The framework for high seas boarding and inspection was developed under the UN Fish Stocks Agreement in Articles 21 and 22 to promote cooperation in fisheries enforcement. The high seas boarding and inspection regime outlines the procedure for boarding and inspection, and the rights and obligations of the inspecting State, authorised inspectors, flag States, and the vessel master. It also provides for actions that may be taken in the event that the master of a vessel refuses to be boarded and inspected on the high seas. The scope of application of this regime is the high seas areas covered by an appropriate RFMO[73] and includes vessels flying the flag of Parties to the UN Fish Stocks Agreement, vessels flying the flag of Parties to the UN Fish Stocks Agreement and members of relevant RFMOs, as well as vessels without nationality. Therefore a non-Party to the UN Fish Stocks Agreement that is also a non-member to a relevant RFMO and has otherwise not agreed to be bound by high seas boarding and inspection arguably cannot be subject to the regime in accordance with Article 36 of the Vienna Convention on Treaties.[74]

A Party to the UN Fish Stocks Agreement can be an inspecting State and should notify all States whose vessels fish on the high seas. It should ensure that vessels used for boarding and inspection are clearly marked and identifiable as being on government service, and should issue identification to duly authorised inspectors.[75]

The procedure for high seas boarding and inspection commences with an inspecting authority suspecting an alleged serious violation by a fishing vessel of a conservation and management measure established by a relevant RFMO or arrangement. A serious violation based on the UN Fish Stocks Agreement means:

- Fishing without a valid licence, authorisation or permit issued by the flag State;
- Failing to maintain accurate records of catch and catch-related data, as required by the relevant subregional or regional fisheries management organisation or arrangement, or serious misreporting of catch, contrary to the catch reporting requirements of such organisation or arrangement;
- Fishing in a closed area, fishing during a closed season or fishing without, or after attainment of, a quota established by the relevant subregional or regional fisheries management organisation or arrangement;
- Directed fishing for a stock which is subject to a moratorium or for which fishing is prohibited;
- Using prohibited fishing gear;
- Falsifying or concealing the markings, identity or registration of a fishing vessel;
- Concealing, tampering with or disposing of evidence relating to an investigation;
- Multiple violations which together constitute a serious disregard of conservation and management measures; or
- Such other violations as may be specified in procedures established by the relevant subregional or regional fisheries management organisation or arrangement.[76]

Boarding and inspection procedure on the high seas has been developed within the context of generally accepted international obligations, namely: taking into account the safety of the vessel and crew; conduct that would not constitute harassment of any fishing vessel; minimal interference with fishing operations; and avoiding action which would affect the quality of catch on board. Duly authorised inspectors of an inspecting State have the authority to inspect the vessel, its licence, gear, equipment, records, facilities, fish, fish products, and documents necessary to verify compliance with relevant conservation and management measures.[77] In the course of boarding and inspection, authorised inspectors have the duty to present credentials to the master of the vessel, produce a copy of the relevant conservation and management measure in question, initiate notice to the flag State at the time of boarding, and provide a copy of the report to the master and authorities of the flag State.[78] Inspectors also have the duty not to interfere with the master's ability to communicate with the authorities of the flag State and note any objection or statement which the master wishes to include in the report. Authorised inspectors have the obligation to avoid the use of force except when and to the degree necessary, only to ensure the safety of inspectors and where the inspectors are obstructed in the execution of their duties. If required, the degree of force to be used should not exceed that reasonably required under given circumstances.[79] Flag States on the other hand, have the obligation to ensure that vessel masters accept and facilitate prompt and safe boarding by inspectors, cooperate with the inspectors, and allow the inspectors to communicate with flag State authorities. Vessel masters should also provide reasonable facilities to the inspectors, not obstruct, intimidate, or interfere with the inspectors in the performance of their duties, and facilitate their safe disembarkation.[80]

Inspectors are required to promptly leave the vessel following completion of the inspection if they find no evidence of a serious violation.[81] However, where following a boarding and inspection there are clear grounds for believing that a vessel has engaged in an activity contrary to a relevant conservation and management measure, the inspecting State shall secure evidence and promptly notify the flag State of the alleged violation.[82] The flag State has the obligation to respond within three working days, and can do either of two options: one, investigate the matter and if evidence warrants, take enforcement action with respect to the vessel, in which case it needs to promptly inform the inspecting State of the results of the investigation and the enforcement action taken; or two, authorise the inspecting State to investigate.[83] If the flag State fails to respond or take action, the inspectors may remain on board and secure evidence and may require the master to assist in further investigation, including where appropriate, by bringing the vessel to the nearest port.[84] The inspecting State shall also immediately inform the flag State of the name of the port to which the vessel is to proceed. The inspecting State would need to inform the flag State and the relevant regional organisation or arrangement and its members or participants of the results of any investigation.[85] The flag State may, at any time during this course of investigation, request the inspecting State to release the vessel to the flag State along with full information on the progress and outcome of its investigation.[86]

In the event that the master of a vessel refuses to accept boarding and inspection in accordance with Articles 21 and 22 of the UN Fish Stocks Agreement or a similar regime established by the relevant RFMO, the flag State would need to direct the master of the vessel to submit immediately to boarding and inspection.[87] The exception to this would be if it is necessary to delay boarding and inspection due to issues relating to safety at sea. If the master does not comply with such direction, the flag State shall suspend the authorisation to fish of the vessel and order it to return immediately to port.[88]

The actions that may be taken by flag States against their vessels may vary and can include judicial proceedings and imposition of penalties. The UN Fish Stocks Agreement provides that actions that may be taken by States other than the flag State shall be proportionate to the seriousness of the violation.[89] It further provides that States shall be liable for damage or loss attributable to them arising from action taken which is unlawful or exceeds that reasonably required in the light of available information to implement the boarding and inspection procedure of the UN Fish Stocks Agreement.[90]

Port State enforcement

All fishing vessels have to land or tranship their catch, or refuel and reload provisions in port.[91] Port State measures are therefore considered to be an effective means of addressing illegal fishing as they augment the shortcomings of flag States in exercising control and jurisdiction over vessels. There are two major roles of port States in combating IUU fishing. First, a port State may adopt measures to supplement the prescriptive and enforcement measures taken by both flag and coastal States. Second, a port State can adopt measures that would ensure that IUU vessels which have escaped detection from flag and coastal States and have entered or are about to enter their ports are made liable for their actions and reported to the concerned States.

The LOSC provides for the full sovereignty of a State with respect to ports in its territory. Part of this right is to take necessary steps to prevent any breach of the conditions associated with a port call.[92] It may also undertake investigations or institute proceedings with respect to any vessel discharge in violation of applicable rules of international law when a vessel is voluntarily in its port or offshore terminal.[93] These provisions however, are not enforcement powers directly related to fisheries.[94]

It is in the UN Fish Stocks Agreement that the role of port States in fisheries enforcement and compliance has been clearly established. Article 23(1) of the UN Fish Stocks Agreement provides for both the right and duty of a port State to take measures to promote the effectiveness of subregional, regional, and global conservation and management measures. A port State has the right to inspect documents, fishing gear and catch on board fishing vessels when it is in port or offshore terminals.[95] The UN Fish Stocks Agreement also allows a port State to undertake enforcement actions such as the prohibition of landing and transshipment if it has been established that the catch has been taken in a manner which undermines the effectiveness of a conservation and management measure on the high seas.[96] As opposed to an exercise of full sovereignty over ports, which can mean the adoption of either no or very strict regulations at the discretion of port States, the emphasis on both the right and a duty has given port States an important role in promoting conservation and management measure for straddling and highly migratory stocks. The FAO Code of Conduct for Responsible Fisheries and the IPOA-IUU also emphasise the role of port States in promoting sustainable fisheries.[97]

The FAO Port State Measures Agreement elaborates on the various measures adopted under the IPOA-IUU and the Model Scheme on Port State Measures,[98] in order to ascertain whether the vessel requiring entry has actually engaged in IUU fishing. This is done through vessel inspection and the requirement to submit information that will assist port States in determining the compliance of a vessel with relevant regulations. The key enforcement action that may be taken by port States is provided for in Article 18(1) of the FAO Port State Measures Agreement. Similar to the provisions of the UN Fish Stocks Agreement and the IPOA-IUU, Article 18 provides that if there are clear grounds for believing that a vessel has engaged in IUU fishing or fishing activity in support of such fishing following an inspection, the port State shall:

> "...
>
> (a) promptly notify the flag State and, as appropriate, relevant coastal States, regional fisheries management organizations and other international organizations, and the State of which the vessel's master is a national of its findings; and
>
> (b) deny the vessel the use of its port for landing, transshipping, packaging and processing of fish that have not been previously landed and for other port services, including, *inter*

alia, refuelling and resupplying, maintenance and drydocking, if these actions have not already been taken in respect of the vessel, in a manner consistent with this Agreement, including Article 4."[99]

Reporting of findings to the flag State and other relevant States and RFMOs is consistent with the duty to cooperate between States provided not only under the FAO Port State Measures Agreement but also in other global fisheries agreements. The FAO Compliance Agreement for example provides that when a fishing vessel is voluntarily in its port and there are reasonable grounds for believing that the fishing vessel has been used for an activity that undermines the effectiveness of international conservation and management measures, the port State is required to promptly notify the flag State.[100] The flag and port States may enter into arrangements that would allow the port State to conduct investigations as may be considered necessary to establish the violation by the fishing vessel.[101]

Prohibition of landing and transshipment of fish is the most common enforcement action adopted by many port States against foreign vessels. The enforcement action on prohibition of fish landing has been subject to objections from States because it also takes the form of a market or trade restriction. In the dispute between Chile and the European Union on swordfish in the Southeastern Pacific Ocean, the EU claimed that Chile had prescribed and implemented a measure in a discriminatory manner when it prohibited the unloading of swordfish in its ports.[102] The dispute was settled amicably; however the burden to prove that the measure applied is non-discriminatory in nature rested on Chile as a port State. Therefore it is crucial that port States prescribe clear domestic regulations in taking enforcement actions against fishing vessels that have engaged in IUU fishing.

A distinctive port enforcement action against foreign fishing vessels only available under the FAO Port State Measures Agreement is the denial of port entry. Based on the information requested by a port State in advance from vessels intending to enter its port, a port State may deny the entry of a vessel if it believes that the vessel has engaged in IUU fishing or fishing activities in support of such fishing, especially if such vessel is included on an IUU list developed by a RFMO.[103] In the case of denial of entry, a Party to the FAO Port State Measures Agreement is required to communicate its decision to the flag State of the vessel, and where appropriate to the relevant coastal State, regional or international organisation.[104] The only exclusion from the application of the denial of port entry is *force majeure* or distress, consistent with international law.[105]

Even though the denial of port access is not expressly set out in the LOSC and other global fisheries agreements, a number of States had adopted this measure as an exercise of sovereignty over their ports prior to the development of FAO Port State Measures Agreement.[106] Another area of cooperation between the port State and other States is provided in the UN Fish Stocks Agreement in relation to high seas boarding and inspection. When an inspecting State deems it necessary to bring the vessel to the nearest port and the flag State has failed to respond or take actions against the vessel, the port State has the obligation to render its assistance to the inspecting State, including taking all necessary steps to ensure the well-being of the crew.[107] The exchange of port inspection information with the flag State is also a crucial component of cooperation as it enables the flag State to take punitive or corrective actions against its vessel. An example is the de-registration of the vessel *Paloma V* from the Namibian registry on the basis of the information obtained from the port inspection conducted by New Zealand authorities which proved that the vessel had been involved in IUU fishing.[108]

Monitoring, control and surveillance

Monitoring, control and surveillance (MCS) is a term developed by the FAO in 1981[109] which is now widely accepted as a key principle in sustainable fisheries management and identified as the "best hope in preventing, deterring and eliminating IUU fishing".[110] According to FAO, monitoring is the continuous requirement for the measurement of fishing effort characteristics and resource yields. This involves the collection, measurement, and analysis of fisheries data such as species composition, fishing effort, bycatch, discards, and areas of operation. Control is defined as the regulatory mechanism under which the exploitation of the resources may be conducted, such as the terms and conditions under which resources can be harvested which are normally embodied in national fisheries legislation and regional agreements. Lastly, surveillance is the degree and types of observations required to maintain compliance with the regulatory controls imposed on fishing activities.[111]

MCS has three spatial components: land, sea, and air.[112] The land component of MCS serves as the base of operations and involves the coordination of MCS activities and deployment of available resources. The sea component of MCS includes the surveillance of the maritime zones of a coastal State, and may include the use of radar, sonar, and vessel platforms. The air component includes air surveillance and also includes the use of satellite-based technology to identify possible fisheries violations.[113] The right combination of land, sea, and air assets based on the resources and capability of States determine success in responding to illegal fishing incidents in areas of national jurisdiction and on the high seas.

MCS has a wider scope than traditional fisheries enforcement in which patrol vessels mainly conduct surveillance operations and arrest of fishing vessels for alleged violations. MCS includes data collection and analysis, enactment of legislative instruments and implementation of management plans. There are a number of MCS tools provided in international instruments that may be used by States in support of fisheries enforcement, such as fishing licensing systems, record of fishing vessels, vessel monitoring systems (VMS), dockside monitoring, observer programmes, boarding and inspection regimes, catch certification, acquisition, storage and dissemination of MCS data, and port State measures.[114] These MCS tools may be applied to monitor compliance with fisheries regulations from the commencement of the fishing activity to the final destination of the fish.[115]

MCS tools such as VMS and observer programmes help enhance enforcement activities of States resulting from the limited coverage of fisheries patrols. For example, satellite-based VMS required for most vessels fishing on the high seas provides monitoring agencies with accurate locations, speed, and identity of fishing vessels at periodic time intervals. This information may be used to detect illegal fishing in closed or restricted areas or during closed seasons. It may also ascertain a potential fisheries violation based on the position and movement of a vessel, i.e. a considerable time being spent on the EEZ by a transiting vessel may be an indication that the vessel is fishing. In the South Pacific, the Pacific Island Forum Fisheries Agency describes the role of VMS as support to existing surveillance assets such as patrol vessels, surveillance flights and regional observers that currently operate in the Western and Central Pacific Ocean.[116]

Observer programmes are conducted for purposes of fishery science and compliance. Implementation of an observer programme for fishery science purposes involves the estimation of total catch and biological sampling.[117] However observers may also be given the task of validating logbooks, observing catch landing and inspecting relevant documents for purposes of compliance with fisheries regulations. Observer programmes allow for the verification of fisheries data which is an effective means of detecting unreported fishing. Observer reports may also be required as evidence in court for the prosecution of fisheries offenders.

Although there are limitations to the scope and application of VMS, observer programmes and other MCS tools, they assist authorities to identify potential violations which would otherwise be undetected by traditional fisheries enforcement. Second, these MCS tools are established within a domestic and regional legal framework which fishing vessels are required to adhere to as a condition for fishing. On the high seas, a breach of relevant regional conservation and management measures is considered a serious fisheries violation and provides a trigger to initiate other MCS tools such as boarding and inspection.

MCS, compliance, and enforcement

As described above, the broad concept of MCS suggests that various tools may be considered as fisheries enforcement measures. These MCS tools, although not referred to as such in global fisheries agreements such as the FAO Compliance Agreement also form part of the compliance and enforcement mechanisms developed under this agreement. The concept of compliance under the FAO Compliance Agreement centres on the role of the flag State to ensure that vessels abide by agreed conservation and management measures on the high seas. It calls for States to take effective action, consistent with international law, to deter reflagging of vessels to other nations as a means of avoiding compliance with conservation and management measures.[118] The agreement also calls upon States to join or enter into understanding with subregional or regional organisations with a view to achieving compliance with international conservation and management measures.[119] To this end the FAO Compliance Agreement provides a number of MCS-related measures that may be undertaken by flag States, such as record of fishing vessels, licensing system and imposition of sanctions of adequate severity.

The UN Fish Stocks Agreement contains similar provisions but specifically refers to its Part IV as 'Compliance and Enforcement'. It provides for compliance and enforcement mechanisms by flag States in the context of high seas enforcement, as well as international cooperation in high seas boarding and provision of assistance in terms of "monitoring, control, surveillance, compliance and enforcement".[120] In addition to these measures, the UN Fish Stocks Agreement provides for compliance and enforcement measures that may be taken by port States under Article 23. A number of regional fisheries management organisations such as the Western and Central Pacific Fisheries Commission (WCPFC) have developed a compliance mechanism where States are required to regularly report the measures they have adopted to implement agreed conservation and management measures;[121] however there is no sanction associated with the failure of States to adopt appropriate domestic measures. The WCPFC aims to adopt a graduated response to non-compliance by its members, cooperating non-members and participating territories by taking into account the type, severity, degree, and cause of the non-compliance in question.[122]

The relationship between MCS, compliance and enforcement is further outlined in the FAO Code of Conduct for Responsible Fisheries which provides that "States should ensure compliance with and enforcement of conservation and management measures and establish effective mechanisms, as appropriate, to monitor and control the activities of fishing vessels and fishing support vessels."[123] It also provides that these effective mechanisms are for "fisheries monitoring, surveillance, control and enforcement to ensure compliance with [their] conservation and management measures . . ."[124] These provisions suggest the close inter-relationship between the concepts of MCS, enforcement and compliance.

However while these agreements focus on the application of the three concepts to ensure that vessels comply with agreed conservation and management measures, State practice has also evolved to ensure that compliance is not limited to the imposition of sanctions but also incentives that will encourage obedience among fishing vessels. It further involves the inclusion or participation of the fishing industry in decision-making in order to enhance the level of compliance, resource stewardship, and legitimacy of management authorities. This type of self or voluntary compliance is an effective means to supplement traditional fisheries enforcement and improve the success of MCS measures.

Australia has adopted the Australian Fisheries Management Authority (AFMA) Domestic Compliance and Enforcement Policy based on risk management that aims to achieve an "optimum level of compliance", defined as "the level of non-compliance at an acceptable level, which can be maintained at a reasonable cost, while not compromising the integrity and sustainability of the resource".[125] This policy distinguishes between compliance, voluntary compliance, deterrence, and enforcement. The AFMA Domestic Compliance and Enforcement Policy provides for enforcement as one type of deterrence and compliance as a function of both voluntary compliance and deterrence. Although voluntary compliance is not the key focus of the policy, it is recognised as one of the many tools that can be used by fisheries officers to improve compliance.[126]

Emerging issues in IUU fishing

There are a number of issues in fisheries that are not sufficiently addressed by the limited prescriptive and enforcement powers of States under the LOSC and global and regional fisheries agreements. Hence they require the development of more innovative measures at the domestic level and strengthened and wider collaboration between States, including facilitation of exchange of information and cooperative enforcement mechanisms.

The lack of adequate fisheries management frameworks for specific fisheries and fishing activities give rise to the inability of States to address issues at the enforcement level. These fisheries management concerns include fishing for non-tuna resources on the high seas, illegal fishing for associated species such as sharks and other marine mammals, fishing for deep sea species and their impact on vulnerable marine ecosystems, and fishing activities as a hazard to navigation. As a response to these issues, tuna RFMOs have adopted measures making it illegal to catch or use certain gears that catch non-target species such as sharks, seabirds, dolphins, and sea turtles. Regional organisations have also been created to manage non-tuna and deep sea resources such as the South Pacific Regional Fisheries Management Organisation (SPRFMO). These organisations have further developed measures that prohibit members from trading with vessels or States whose vessels have engaged in or supported IUU fishing.

There are also issues that directly challenge traditional fisheries enforcement and MCS and are not addressed by specific global or regional agreements. Examples include illegal fishing perpetrated by transnational criminal groups or 'fisheries crime', such as trafficking of people for purpose of forced labour in the fishing industry and use of vessels for acts of terrorism and other criminal activities. As a response to fisheries crime, INTERPOL launched an initiative in 2013 called Project Scale whose objectives are to: (a) raise awareness regarding fisheries crime and its consequences; (b) establish National Environment Security Task Forces to ensure cooperation between national and international agencies; (c) assess the needs of vulnerable member countries to effectively combat fisheries crimes; (d) conduct operations to suppress crime, disrupt trafficking routes, and ensure the enforcement of national legislation. A Fisheries Crime Working Group was established under this initiative to develop the capacity and capability of member countries to effectively address fisheries crime.[127] A number of countries have cooperated and called upon INTERPOL to issue Purple Notices to illegal fishing vessels. INTERPOL's Purple Notices are used to seek or provide information on the modus operandi, objects, devices, and methods used by criminals associated with fishing. Where there are suspected illegal fishing activities involving elements of crime, a binding or a non-binding resolution may be adopted by members of RFMOs to refer the matter to the INTERPOL Fisheries Crime Working Group and encourage members to provide relevant information.

At a regional level, 25 West and Central African countries have adopted The Code of Conduct Concerning the Repression of Piracy, Armed Robbery Against Ships and Illicit Maritime Activity in West and Central Africa in 2013. The Code of Conduct recognises IUU fishing as a "transnational organised crime in the maritime domain" together with other well-established transnational criminal activities.[128] The Code of Conduct provides a framework for cooperation for sharing and reporting of information, interdiction, apprehension and prosecution of suspected vessels, as well as the facilitation of care, treatment, and repatriation of people subjected to transnational crime in the maritime domain.[129]

Conclusion

While the LOSC provides the basic framework for fisheries regulation and enforcement in the different maritime zones, the adoption of international agreements post LOSC has fortified the prescriptive and enforcement powers of States. The FAO Compliance Agreement, UN Fish Stocks Agreement and the FAO Port State Measures Agreement have introduced measures that address unique fisheries concerns. In sum, the strengthening of flag State responsibility through compliance mechanisms, high seas boarding and inspection, and port State jurisdiction in fisheries are three key aspects of relevant global agreements that have helped influence international fisheries enforcement. The emphasis on cooperation between States in modern international fisheries law has also led to bilateral, subregional, and regional agreements on MCS, compliance and enforcement that shape State practice to address IUU fishing.

The close relationship between the concepts of MCS, enforcement and compliance give States a range of tools and measures that may be adopted to address specific fisheries issues in the EEZ, on the continental shelf and on the high seas. However concerns in fisheries are continuously evolving and the lack of adequate management frameworks for certain species and fishing activities give rise to the inability of States to address such issues effectively. There are also issues that challenge traditional fisheries enforcement or revolve around broader political problems and require the development of more innovative measures beyond the scope of fisheries. These issues may be the subject of future fisheries enforcement mechanisms or arrangements between States.

Notes

1 Richard Ellis, *The Empty Ocean: Plundering the World's Marine Life* (Washington: Island Press, 2003), *cf* Thomax Huxley, 'The Fisheries Exhibition', 28 *Nature* (1883), pp. 176–177.
2 Food and Agriculture Organization (FAO), *The State of World Fisheries and Aquaculture: Opportunities and Challenges* (Rome: FAO, 2014), p. 37.
3 Ibid., p. 38.

4 Ibid.
5 United Nations General Assembly (UNGA), Sixty-ninth session, Agenda Item, 74(b), Sustainable fisheries, including through the 1995 Agreement for the Implementation of the Provisions of the United Nations Convention on the Law of the Sea of 10 December 1982 relating to the Conservation and Management of Straddling Fish Stocks and Highly Migratory Fish Stocks and related Instruments, *Resolution Adopted by the General Assembly on 9 December 2014, A/RES/69/109*, 06 February 2015, para. 56.
6 Marine Resources Assessment Group Ltd (MRAG), *Review of Impacts of Illegal, Unreported and Unregulated Fishing on Developing Countries: Final Report*, (London, 2005), p. 44.
7 See Mary Ann Palma, Martin Tsamenyi, and William Edeson, *Promoting Responsible Fisheries: The International Legal and Policy Framework to Combat Illegal, Unreported and Unregulated Fishing* (Netherlands: Brill, 2010).
8 FAO, *State of World Fisheries and Aquaculture 2004* (Rome: FAO, 2004), p. 86; See also The World Bank, *Fish to 2030: Prospects for Fisheries and Aquaculture* (Washington: World Bank, 2013).
9 The World Bank, *The Sunken Billions: the Economic Justification for Fisheries Reform* (Washington: World Bank, 2009), p. 43.
10 *World Ocean Review: Living with the Oceans 2010* (Hamburg: Maribus, 2010), pp. 130–139.
11 Food and Agriculture Organisation (FAO), Fisheries Management, *FAO Technical Guidelines for Responsible Fisheries No. 4* (Rome: FAO, 1997), at 14.
12 Francisco Orrego Vicuña, *The Changing International Law on High Seas Fisheries* (Cambridge: University Press, 1999), pp. 8–13; See also Shigeru Oda, *International Control of Sea Resources* (Dordrecht: Martinus Nijhoff Publishers, 1989).
13 United Nations Convention on the Law of the Sea, Montego Bay, Jamaica, concluded on 10 December 1982, in force 16 November 1994, 1833 UNTS 3; 21 ILM 1261 (1982).
14 *Agreement to Promote Compliance with International Conservation and Management Measures by Fishing Vessels on the High Seas*, signed 24 November 1993, 2221 UNTS 91 (entered into force 24 April 2003).
15 *United Nations Agreement for the Implementation of the Provision of the United Nations Convention on the Law of the Sea of 10 December 1982 Relating to the Conservation and Management of Straddling Fish Stocks and Highly Migratory Fish Stocks*, New York, concluded on 04 August 1995, in force 11 December 2001, 34 ILM 1542 (1995); 2167 UNTS 88.
16 FAO, *Agreement on Port State Measures to Prevent, deter and Eliminate Illegal, Unreported and Unregulated Fishing*, signed 22 November 2009 [2010] ATNIF 41.
17 *LOSC*, Preamble.
18 David Balton, 'The Compliance Agreement' in Ellen Hey, (ed.), *Developments in International Fisheries Law* (Hague: Kluwer Law International, 1999) p. 34.
19 *FAO Compliance Agreement*, Art. I(a) and II(2).
20 Article III of the FAO Compliance Agreement provides that in a fishing region where bordering coastal States have not yet declared EEZs, or equivalent zones of national jurisdiction over fisheries, such coastal State Parties to the agreement may agree to establish a minimum length of fishing vessels below which the agreement shall not apply.
21 UN Conference on Straddling and Highly Migratory Fish Stocks, Fourth Session, *Statement Made by the Chairman of the Conference at the Closing of the Fourth Session, on 26 August 1994*, A/CONF.164/24, para 5, in Jean-Pierre Lévy and Gunnar G Schram, *United Nations Conference on Straddling Fish Stocks and Highly Migratory Fish Stocks: Selected Documents* (Hague: Martinus Nijhoff Publishers, 1996).
22 *UN Fish Stocks Agreement*, Art. 23.
23 *UN Fish Stocks Agreement*, Art. 8.
24 *UN Fish Stocks Agreement*, Arts. 21 and 22
25 *FAO Port State Measures Agreement*, Art. 2.
26 *FAO Port State Measures Agreement*, Art. 3.
27 *FAO Port State Measures Agreement*, Art. 6.
28 Food and Agriculture Organization (FAO), *Code of Conduct for Responsible Fisheries*, FAO Conference, 28th sess (31 October 1995).
29 The four International Plans of Action developed under the FAO Code of Conduct are International Plan of Action for Reducing Incidental Catch of Seabirds in Longline Fisheries (IPOA-Seabirds) 1999, International Plan of Action for the Conservation and Management of Sharks (IPOA-Sharks) 1999, International Plan of Action for the Management of Fishing Capacity (IPOA-Capacity) 1999, and the

International Plan of Action to Prevent, Deter, and Eliminate Illegal, Unreported, and Unregulated Fishing (IPOA-IUU) 2001.
30 *International Plan of Action to Prevent, Deter and Eliminate Illegal, Unreported and Unregulated Fishing* (IPOA-IUU), Adopted on 23 June 2001 at the 120th Session of the FAO Council. IPOA-IUU, para. 24.
31 LOSC, Arts. 19(2)(i), 20(1)(d) and (e), 25, and 42(1)(c), and 54.
32 LOSC, Art. 21(c0 and (d).
33 LOSC, Art. 19(i).
34 LOSC, Art. 51(1).
35 Dysi Polite, 'Traditional Fishing Rights: Analysis of State Practice,' 5 *Australian Journal of Maritime and Ocean Affairs* (2013), 120, 126.
36 Ibid.
37 Parties to the Nauru Agreement, *A Third Arrangement Implementing the Nauru Agreement Setting Forth Additional Terms and Conditions of Access to the Fisheries Zones of the Parties*, Koror, 16 May 2008, amended 11 September 2010, Art. 3.
38 Western and Central Pacific Fisheries Commission, Conservation and Management Measure 2010–02, *Conservation and Management Measure for the Eastern High Seas Pocket Special Management Area*, Honolulu, 10 December 2010, para. 2.
39 See Chapter 1 of this volume.
40 Ellen Hey, 'The Fisheries Provisions of the LOS Convention' in Ellen Hey, (ed.), *Developments in International Fisheries Law* (Hague: Kluwer Law International, 1999), p. 27.
41 *LOSC*, Part V.
42 *LOSC*, Art. 62(4).
43 *FAO Compliance Agreement*, Art. 1(a).
44 International Tribunal for the Law of the Sea (ITLOS), The M/V "SAIGA" Case (Saint Vincent and the Grenadines v Guinea), Case No 1, Judgment of 04 December 1997, para. 56.
45 ITLOS, *The M/V "SAIGA"* Case No 1, para. 64.
46 *Convention for the Prohibition of Fishing with Long Driftnets in the South Pacific*, concluded on 24 November 1989, in force 17 May 1991, ATS 1992 No. 30, Art. 1.
47 ITLOS, *The M/V "SAIGA"* Case No 1, para. 56.
48 *FAO Port State Measures Agreement*, Art. 1(c).
49 *FAO Port State Measures Agreement*, Art. 1(d).
50 ITLOS, *The "M/V Saiga" Case (Saint Vincent and the Grenadines v. Guinea) (Prompt Release)*, Case No. 1, Judgment of 04 December 1997, para. 82.
51 ITLOS, *The "Camuoco" Case (Panama v. France) (Prompt Release)*, Case No. 5, Judgment of 07 February 2000, para. 67.
52 ITLOS, *The "Monte Confurco" Case (Seychelles v. France) (Prompt Release)*, Case No. 6, Judgment of 18 December 2000, para. 76.
53 ITLOS, *The "Volga" Case (Russian Federation v. Australia) (Prompt Release)*, Case No. 11, Judgement of 23 December 2002, para. 77.
54 ITLOS, *The "Tomimaru" Case* (Japan v. Russian Federation) *(Prompt Release)*, Case No. 15, Judgment of 06 August 2007, para. 72
55 *Olbers v Commonwealth of Australia* (No 4) [2004] FCA 229 at 80.
56 Warwick Gullett, 'Development of Australian Fisheries Law: Setting the Law of the Sea Convention Adrift?' 21 *Environmental and Planning Law Journal* (2004) 169, 174.
57 Ibid, 175.
58 *The "Tomimaru" Case*, Case No. 15, para. 73.
59 ITLOS, *The "Juno Trader" Case (Saint Vincent and the Grenadines v Guinea-Bissau) (Prompt Release)*, Case No. 13, Judgment of 18 December 2004, para. 77.
60 Ibid.
61 See for example Sedentary Organism Proclamation of the Governor-General of the Commonwealth of Australia in December 1995. Under section 12 of the Australian *Fisheries Management Act* 1991 (Cth), the Governor-General may declare an organism to be a sedentary organism to which the Act applies if he or she is satisfied that a marine organism of any kind, for the purpose of international law, is part of the living natural resources of the Australian continental shelf.
62 *LOSC*, Art. 77(4).

63 *LOSC*, Art. 77(2).
64 See FAO International Guidelines for the Management of Deep Sea Fisheries in the High Seas (Rome, 2009); See also a series of United Nations General Assembly Resolutions beginning with UNGA, Fifty-ninth session, Agenda Item 49(b), Resolution adopted by the General Assembly, Sustainable fisheries, including through the 1995 Agreement for the Implementation of the Provisions of the United Nations Convention on the Law of the Sea of 10 December 1982 relating to the Conservation and Management of Straddling Fish Stocks and Highly Migratory Fish Stocks, and related instruments, 17 January 2005, *A/RES/59/25*, para. 66.
65 *LOSC*, Art. 33.
66 LOSC, Art. 91(1).
67 *UN Fish Stocks Agreement*, Art. 19(1).
68 *UN Fish Stocks Agreement*, Art. 19(2).
69 *UN Fish Stocks Agreement*, Art 19(1)(d).
70 *UN Fish Stocks Agreement*, Art. 19(2); *FAO Compliance Agreement*, Art. III(8).
71 *FAO Compliance Agreement*, Art. III(5)(b).
72 *UN Fish Stocks Agreement*, Art. 19(2).
73 An appropriate RFMO in this context means an organisation with competence in managing tuna resources, such as the Indian Ocean Tuna Commission (IOTC), International Commission for the Conservation and Atlantic Tunas (ICCAT), Inter-American Tropical Tuna Commission (IATTC), and Western and Central Pacific Fisheries Commission (WCPFC). Currently, only WCPFC, IOTC and ICCAT have developed boarding and inspection schemes.
74 *Vienna Convention on the Law of Treaties*, Vienna, Austria, concluded 23 May 1969, in force 27 January 1980, UN Doc. A/Conf.39/27; 1155 UNTS 331; 8 ILM 679 (1969); 63 AJIL 875 (1969), Art. 36.
75 *UN Fish Stocks Agreement*, Art. 21(4).
76 *UN Fish Stocks Agreement*, Art. 21(11).
77 *UN Fish Stocks Agreement*, Art. 22(2).
78 *UN Fish Stocks Agreement*, Art. 22(1).
79 *UN Fish Stocks Agreement*, Art. 22(1)(f).
80 *UN Fish Stocks Agreement*, Art. 22(3).
81 *UN Fish Stocks Agreement*, Art. 22(1)(e).
82 *UN Fish Stocks Agreement*, Art. 21(5).
83 *UN Fish Stocks Agreement*, Art. 21(6).
84 *UN Fish Stocks Agreement*, Art. 21(8).
85 *UN Fish Stocks Agreement*, Art. 21(9).
86 *UN Fish Stocks Agreement*, Art. 21(12).
87 *UN Fish Stocks Agreement*, Art. 22(4).
88 *UN Fish Stocks Agreement*, Art. 22(4).
89 *UN Fish Stocks Agreement*, Art. 21(16).
90 *UN Fish Stocks Agreement*, Art. 21(18).
91 For the purpose of these discussions, ports include offshore terminals and other installations for landing, transhipping, refuelling, or re-supplying. *FAO Port State Measures Agreement*, Art. 1(g).
92 *LOSC*, Art. 25.2.
93 *LOSC*, Art. 218.
94 See also Chapter 6 of this volume.
95 *UN Fish Stocks Agreement*, Art. 23(2).
96 *UN Fish Stocks Agreement*, Art. 23(3).
97 FAO Code of Conduct, Art. 8.3; IPOA-IUU, paras. 52–64.
98 FAO, *Model Scheme on Port State Measures to Combat Illegal, Unreported and Unregulated Fishing* (Rome: FAO, 2007).
99 Article 4 of the FAO Port State Measures agreement provides for the relationship of the agreement with international law and other international instruments.
100 *FAO Compliance Agreement*, Art. V(2).
101 *FAO Compliance Agreement*, Art. V(2).
102 International Tribunal on the Law of the Sea (ITLOS), *Case Concerning the Conservation and Sustainable Exploitation of Swordfish Stocks in the South-eastern Pacific Ocean (Chile v. European Community)*, List of Cases No. 7, Constitution Chamber Order of 20 December 2000, para. 2.3(d).

103 *FAO Port State Measures Agreement*, Art. 9.
104 *FAO Port State Measures Agreement*, Art. 9(3).
105 *FAO Port State Measures Agreement*, Art. 10.
106 Terje Lobach, 'Measures to be Adopted by the Port State in Combating IUU Fishing,' *supra* note 69, at 69; Rachel Baird, 'CCAMLR Initiatives to Counter Flag State Non-enforcement in Southern Ocean Fisheries,' 36 *Victoria University of Wellington Law Review* (2005), at 745.
107 *UN Fish Stocks Agreement*, Art. 21(8).
108 High Court of New Zealand Wellington Registry, CIV 2008–485–1310 Under the Judicature Amendment Act 1972 in the matter of an application for judicial review between Omunkete Fishing (Pty) Limited and the Minister of Fisheries and the Minister of Foreign Affairs and Trade, Judgment, 01 July 2008.
109 FAO definition of MCS formulated in 1981 *as cited in* Peter Flewwelling, An Introduction to Monitoring, Control and Surveillance for Capture Fisheries. *FAO Fisheries Technical Paper No. 338, hereinafter referred to as* FAO Fisheries Technical Paper No. 338, (Rome: FAO, 1995), at 13.
110 FAO, Implementation of the International Plan of Action to Prevent, Deter and Eliminate Illegal, Unreported and Unregulated Fishing. *FAO Technical Guidelines for Responsible Fisheries No. 9* (Rome: FAO, 2002), para. 3.2.5.
111 *FAO Fisheries Technical Paper No. 338*, at 13.
112 Peter Flewwelling, Cormac Cullinan, David Balton, Raymond P. Sautter and J. Eric Reynolds, Guide to Monitoring, Control, and Surveillance Systems for Coastal and Offshore Capture Fisheries. *FAO Fisheries Technical Paper. No. 415* (Rome: Italy, 2003).
113 *FAO Fisheries Technical Paper No. 338*, at 13–14.
114 *LOSC*, Art. 62(4); *IPOA-IUU*, para. 24; UN Fish Stocks Agreement, Art. 18(3)(g).
115 *IPOA-IUU*, para. 24.
116 Pacific Islands Forum Fisheries Agency (FFA), "FFA Monitoring, Conrol and Surveillance Experts Meet About Illegal Fishing," www.ffa.int, Honiara, 3 April 2009. Accessed on 02 February 2015.
117 Davies, Sandy I. and Reynolds, J. Eric (eds.). Guidelines for Developing an At-Sea Fishery Observer Programme, *FAO Fisheries Technical Paper No. 414* (Rome: FAO, 2002), p. 5.
118 *FAO Compliance Agreement*, Preamble.
119 *FAO Compliance Agreement*, Preamble.
120 *UN Fish Stocks Agreement*, Art. 25(3)(c).
121 Western and Central Pacific Fisheries Commission, *Conservation and Management Measures for Compliance Monitoring Scheme*, CMM 2014–07, 5 December 2014.
122 WCPFC, CMM 2014–07, para. 23.
123 *FAO Code of Conduct*, Art. 6.10.
124 *FAO Code of Conduct*, Art. 7.17.
125 Australian Fisheries Management Authority, *AFMA Domestic Compliance and Enforcement Policy*, April 2010, p. 8.
126 *AFMA Domestic Compliance and Enforcement Policy*, p. 9.
127 INTERPOL, Environmental Compliance and Enforcement Committee, Project Scale, www.interpol.int. Accessed on 14 April 2014.
128 The Code of Conduct Concerning the Repression of Piracy, Armed Robbery Against Ships and Illicit Maritime Activity in West and Central Africa, Yaounde, 25 June 2013, Art. 1(5)(i).
129 Yaounde Code of Conduct, Art. 2(1).

11
Shipping: Safety of Life at Sea

Anthony Morrison

O hear us when we cry to Thee,
For those in peril on the Sea![1]

Introduction

Seafaring has always been one of the most dangerous occupations in the world.[2] From the earliest days of maritime navigation, innumerable seafarers have perished through sinkings, collisions, shipwrecks and other "perils of the sea" with little protection other than petitions such as those mentioned in the above quote.

It has long been an unwritten custom of the sea that seafarers will go to the aid of other seafarers in distress and this custom is recognised to such an extent that it now forms part of customary international law.[3] However, until recent times, this has rarely been codified in any practical sense. Mediaeval Maritime Codes and bilateral treaties between maritime nations sometimes made mention of requirements to go to the aid of vessels and seafarers in distress or to permit ships refuge in their ports,[4] but it was not until the sinking of the *Titanic* in 1912 that the maritime nations made a concerted effort to formulate enforceable international rules concerning the safety of life at sea.[5]

The ensuing *Safety of Life at Sea Convention (SOLAS)*, in its 1974 amended version,[6] continues to be the primary instrument governing the safety of life at sea. It is complemented by more recent conventions such as the *United Nations Convention on the Law of the Sea, 1982 (LOSC)*,[7] the *Search and Rescue Convention, 1979 (SAR Convention)*[8] and, to a lesser extent, the *Convention for the Unification of Certain Rules of Law Respecting Assistance and Salvage at Sea, 1910 (Brussels Convention)*,[9] the *International Convention on Salvage, 1989 (Salvage Convention)*,[10] the *Standards of Training, Certification and Watch-keeping Convention, 1995 (STCW)*[11] and the *Convention on the International Regulations for Preventing Collisions at Sea, 1972 (Colregs)*.[12]

Safety of life at sea has become a highly relevant issue in recent years because of the human tragedy of the loss of life of thousands of asylum seekers fleeing in overloaded, unseaworthy ships, particularly in the Mediterranean Sea.[13] In this regard, the catalyst for action to be taken by the International Maritime Organisation (IMO) was the *MV Tampa* incident in August and

September 2001, when the Australian government refused the vessel, with over 400 asylum seekers aboard, access to Christmas Island.[14] The ensuing stand-off, which resulted in the asylum seekers being removed from the vessel at sea onto an Australian naval vessel and transported to Nauru without ever landing on Australian territory, highlighted problems with the existing conventions in relation to both the overall treatment of asylum seekers as well as the position of the master of the vessel who rescued the persons in distress.[15] In addition to amending the existing conventions, the IMO has attempted to deal with the problem though non-binding guidelines, the most recent being the *IMO Guidelines on the Treatment of Persons Rescued at Sea, 2004 (Guidelines)*.[16]

This chapter will examine safety of life at sea in two main ways:

1. The obligations under customary international law and international conventions and non-binding instruments concerning safety of life at sea;
2. Specific problems relating to the enforcement of international obligations.

The first section of the chapter will critically examine the protection of life at sea under customary international law and the provisions of relevant conventions. This section will also examine relevant non-binding instruments such as the *Guidelines*. As well as giving a brief exposition of the main provisions, this study will highlight the gaps that exist in the international law and policy framework.

The second section of the chapter will look at some issues and factors which can affect the enforcement of obligations under the international legal regime. These issues and factors include:

1. The question of whether there exists in international law an obligation on coastal States to permit entry of ships in distress into their territory where there is a humanitarian risk involved. This in turn will require an examination of the concept of "distress", when a ship is "in distress" and the powers of the coastal States, flag States and search and rescue (SAR) States if such an obligation exists;
2. Regardless of the answer to (1), the question of whether there exists under customary international law or any of the conventions an obligation on the coastal State or SAR State to permit disembarkation of persons from the rescuing ship if the ship is in the territorial waters or SAR region of that State;
3. What rights, if any, exist for persons in distress to be rescued under refugee or humanitarian law.

In examining the factors and issues, specific reference will be made to the situation in waters surrounding Australia, particularly the effect of the *MV Tampa* incident and to the situation in the Mediterranean Sea and the attempts by coastal States in that region to address the same problem.

Safety of life at sea under international law

Safety of life at sea under customary international law

Until at least the early twentieth century, protection of life at sea was inextricably mixed with the safety of the ship so that the preservation of a ship either at sea or in places of refuge carried with it the preservation of the lives of the crew and passengers on that ship.

The practice of preserving both ships and lives grew up gradually through codes of maritime practice which evolved from the earliest times of maritime trade. The best known of the early maritime Codes, the Rhodian law, as incorporated into the *Code of Justinian*, attempted to codify existing maritime custom at the time.[17] The Rhodian Law does deal with dangers and difficulties of navigation but there is no mention of ships or seafarers in distress.[18] In fact, there was some evidence that where ships were wrecked on a foreign shore, the local inhabitants were permitted to seize the property from the ship and the crew and passengers could be either ransomed or enslaved.[19]

There is evidence of the growth of the custom of rescuing seafarers or granting refuge to ships in the later mediaeval Codes of the maritime European States. These Codes developed because of the need for consistency of treatment of merchants, ships and cargoes among all the trading ports. As trade was essentially an international concern it was necessary for there to be a common legal basis for trade and ships that carried trade.[20]

Lo Libre de Consolat de Mar which appeared in writing in Barcelona in 1435, but which had been in existence since before the First Crusade in 1096,[21] consolidated the customs then existing in Catalonia and made extensive reference to an obligation to aid ships in distress, which was a great advance on the uncontrolled anarchy of earlier centuries.[22] Codes of other maritime States had also alluded to the duty to protect and assist ships and sailors in distress. *The Maritime Ordinances of Trani (1063)*[23] alluded to ships being permitted to enter prohibited ports because of bad weather but did not oblige access to be given.[24] In France, the *Navigation Code of the Port of Arles (1150)* provided in clause 105 that fishermen living near the river must go to the assistance of any ship owned by another resident of Arles if it is in danger.[25] Later the *Rules of Oleron* (circa 1266) provided in Article XXIX that protection and assistance was to be given to sailors of ships wrecked on the shore.[26] A further refinement occurred in the *Ordinance of Louis XIV* in 1681 which codified the *Rules of Oleron* into French law.[27]

In the Baltic and other north European ports the maritime customs established by the Codes in Italy, Catalonia and France formed the basis for the practice in these ports. In Germany and the Baltic, the *Laws of Visby* were promulgated to deal with trade with and between the towns of the Hanseatic League in 1407. These were based on the *Rules of Oleron*.[28] Subsequently the *Laws of the Hanse Towns* were issued around 1597 and were based largely on the earlier Codes.[29]

In England maritime laws were codified into the Black Book of the Admiralty and were based largely on the *Rules of Oleron*.[30] Similarly, in Scotland the *Rules of Oleron* and the *Laws of Visby* formed the basis of maritime law.[31] By the 14th century the admiralty courts had been established and by the 16th century they were dealing with commercial disputes.[32] In the case of *Luke v Lyde*[33] in 1759, Lord Mansfield decided the case on the Rhodian Laws and justified this use of maritime Codes by stating that "... maritime law is not the law of any particular country, but the general law of nations...."[34] The judgment then surveys the origins of maritime law through the maritime codes commencing with the Rhodian Laws. This decision conveniently sets out the growth and development of the Codes from which it can be established that by the 18th century, there existed a common set of rules and practices among the major maritime States of Europe that could form the basis of customary law.[35]

So by at least the 18th century, and arguably much earlier, there were clearly accepted rules in the majority of the maritime trading nations and regions sufficient to establish that there existed in customary international law an obligation on all maritime nations to go to the assistance of ships and persons in distress at sea.

Safety of life at sea under international conventions

Until the 20th century, the duty to rescue persons in distress at sea rested on customary international law. The sinking of the *Titanic* in 1912 convinced major maritime nations of the need for codification not only of the duty to rescue but also the need to ensure that all ships were seaworthy enough to avoid the need for rescue. Therefore, in examining the safety of life at sea under international conventions, there are two separate categories of conventions:

(a) Conventions that deal with the preservation of life *per se*, including the obligation to go to the assistance of ships and persons in distress. This includes provisions in the *Brussels Convention*, the *Salvage Convention*, *SOLAS*, *LOSC* and the *SAR Convention*.

(b) Conventions that seek to eliminate, as far as possible, the circumstances in which there is a need for lives and ships at sea to be saved. These are designed to ensure that the ships themselves are capable of completing a voyage by being properly crewed, being seaworthy and cargo-worthy and being properly navigated. In this regard *SOLAS*, the *Colregs* and *STCW* are relevant.

Conventions that deal with the preservation of life *per se*

The first mention of the obligation on a ship to go to the aid of vessels or persons in danger in a multilateral convention is in Article 11 of the *Brussels Convention*. This states that:

> Every master is bound, so far as he can do so without serious danger to his vessel, her crew and her passengers, to render assistance to everybody, even though an enemy, found at sea in danger of being lost.
>
> The owner of the vessel incurs no liability by reason of contravention of the above provision.

A similar provision appears in the *Salvage Convention*. Article 10 states:

1. Every master is bound, so far as he can do so without serious danger to his vessel and persons thereon, to render assistance to any person in danger of being lost at sea.
2. The States Parties shall adopt the measures necessary to enforce the duty set out in paragraph 1.
3. The owner of the vessel shall incur no liability for a breach of the duty of the master under paragraph 1.

The main difference between the two is the requirement in paragraph 2 for States Parties to make the duty enforceable through domestic legislation. Thus, the *Salvage Convention* imposed on States rather than individual masters the obligation to put into effect the duty of saving of lives at sea.

While it may seem strange that the duty to save life is expounded in conventions dealing with salvage and salvage reward, particularly since reward is paid for saving of life only in very limited circumstances,[36] other conventions dealing with safety of navigation and life at sea more logically also contain this duty. In particular the *LOSC* prescribes in Article 98(1):

1. Every State shall require the master of a ship flying its flag, in so far as he can do so without serious danger to the ship, the crew or the passengers:
   (a) to render assistance to any person found at sea in danger of being lost;
   (b) to proceed with all possible speed to the rescue of persons in distress, if informed of their need of assistance, in so far as such action may reasonably be expected of him;

(c) after a collision, to render assistance to the other ship, its crew and its passengers and, where possible, to inform the other ship of the name of his own ship, its port of registry and the nearest port at which it will call.

This duty is wider and more explicit than the *Salvage Convention* in that the master must not only rescue persons actually found by the master to be in danger but must also respond to a reasonable request to proceed to rescue other persons not actually found by the master and also to render assistance after a collision. The seriousness of this provision and the duty it prescribes is emphasised by Article 18(2) of *LOSC* which provides, *inter alia*, that rendering assistance to persons in distress is an exception to innocent passage.[37] While all these duties could be seen as mere subsets of the overall duty they are more detailed and more onerous than the duty in the *Brussels Convention* and *Salvage Convention*.

More detailed and onerous still are the duties set out in Regulation 33 of Part V of *SOLAS*. While it does not repeat the duty to rescue, paragraph 5 of Regulation 33 provides that the regulation does not affect the operation of the *Brussels Convention*[38] "particularly the obligation to render assistance imposed by Article 11 of that Convention", thus preserving the duty. Most of Regulation 33 deals with the requirement for masters of ships to proceed, on receipt of information from any source, to the assistance of persons in distress where reasonably possible, regardless of the nationality and status of such persons or the circumstances which caused the distress.[39] Where the master does embark persons in distress they are to be treated "with humanity, within the capabilities and limitations of the ship".[40] If deemed unreasonable or unnecessary to answer the distress signal, the Master must insert in the ships log the reason for the decision.[41] Where the ship does answer the signal, the master of the ship in distress can requisition one or more of the ships replying, in which case the masters of the requisitioned ships must proceed with all speed to the assistance of the persons in distress.[42] The masters of ships not requisitioned are thereby released from the duty to assist.[43] The masters of ships that are requisitioned are released from the duty to assist if they are informed that another ship has reached the person in distress and assistance is no longer necessary.[44]

Another key element in the protection of life at sea is a coordinated search and rescue arrangement. Article 98(2) of *LOSC* sets the scene for such coordination by stating:

2. Every coastal State shall promote the establishment, operation and maintenance of an adequate and effective search and rescue service regarding safety on and over the sea and, where circumstances so require, by way of mutual regional arrangements cooperate with neighbouring States for this purpose.

Coincident with negotiations for *LOSC*, the *SAR Convention* was adopted in April 1979. This convention, which was substantially amended in 1998, provides for the establishment of a search and rescue arrangement for the saving of persons in distress at sea.

Article 2.1.3 of the Annex to the *SAR Convention* provides that search and rescue regions are to be set up under the responsibility of a coastal State, without prejudice to the territorial boundaries of coastal States within the region. This State is responsible for the establishment of and the equipping and operation of a search and rescue service which would ensure that any person in distress at sea within that region is provided with assistance irrespective of nationality or status of the person or the circumstances causing the distress.

Subsequently, the world's oceans were split into 13 areas each subdivided into SAR regions for each of which a coastal State is responsible.[45] Coordination centres and sub-centres are to be established within each SAR region and are to be coordinated as closely as possible with aeronautical search and rescue services. Of great importance is the close coordination of search and rescue services with neighbouring States including the grant of the right to neighbouring States to cross national maritime boundaries for the purposes of search and rescue.

The actual procedures for search and rescue are set out in detail in Chapter 4 of the *SAR Convention*. The search and rescue operation is split into three emergency phases – uncertainty phase (where the vessel or person is missing), alert phase (where the vessel or person fails to respond to requests by the search and rescue centre) and distress phase (where there is positive information that rescue is necessary). The procedures to be followed in each phase are set out in Article 4.5. Search and rescue operations are to continue until they have been successful or until "all reasonable hope of rescuing survivors has passed".

Once rescued, consideration must be given to the disembarkation of the rescued persons and the release of the master of the rescuing ship from further responsibility for them. The need to address both these issues arose from the *MV Tampa* incident. Amendments to both *SOLAS* and the *SAR Convention* were adopted in May 2004 where the issues were dealt with by the insertion of an identical provision into both conventions – Part V, Regulation 33, paragraph 1–1 of *SOLAS* and Article 3.1.9 of the Annex to the *SAR Convention*. Under these provisions, the parties to the conventions must first take steps to ensure that the master is released from all responsibility with the least deviation from the ships voyage as possible, provided that the safety of the persons rescued is not compromised. Secondly, the parties responsible for search and rescue operations must take steps to ensure that persons rescued are disembarked at a place of safety. Complying with the latter obligation is problematic and is more fully discussed later in this chapter.

The *MV Tampa* incident not only resulted in significant changes to both *SOLAS* and the *SAR Convention* but also resulted in the IMO promulgating the *Guidelines* in May 2004. The *Guidelines* are mostly a summary of the rights and obligations of Governments and shipmasters under international law as well as guidance on the proper implementation of rescue at sea and search and rescue operations generally. They are essentially practical and procedural in nature. It is important to understand that these *Guidelines* are not binding but only provide guidance to masters and coastal States providing Search and Rescue services.[46]

Conventions dealing with safety of shipping

While the conventions discussed above deal directly with the saving of life at sea, it is also important to examine other conventions which deal with the safety of shipping. The rationale is that if ships are properly built, maintained, navigated and crewed, distress situations will not be created thereby obviating the need for any rescue.

The most important convention dealing with the safety of ships is *SOLAS*. This convention is a long and detailed document which addresses, mainly in regulations, all aspects of the safety of ships including their construction, life-saving appliances, radio communication, requirements for carriage of various types of cargoes both general and hazardous, rules governing safety of navigation and other measures to enhance marine safety and security.

Since the catalyst for *SOLAS* was the sinking of the *Titanic* in 1912 with its great loss of life, there are extensive requirements in *SOLAS* concerning construction of ships, radio-communication and life-saving appliances. All these provisions are in place to prevent ships sinking on voyage, but if they do to ensure that there are proper means of communication to give distress signals and also sufficient life-saving equipment for the persons on board. All these features were notably absent on the *Titanic* when it sank. In addition *SOLAS* has extensive requirements for the handling and stowage of cargo to ensure that the ship is suitable for the cargo carried and that it is stowed in a manner that does not endanger the structural stability of the ship. This is particularly important in relation to the carriage of containers which must be distributed accurately according to weight to ensure stability.

However, even a properly constructed, maintained and stowed ship can sink with loss of life if it is not properly navigated. Chapter V of *SOLAS* goes into great detail about how a ship must be navigated and routed, what equipment needs to be on the ship, particularly navigation systems and equipment such as radar, long range tracking equipment, automatic identification systems and navigation charts and signals. These requirements all combine to ensure as far as possible the safety of the ship and with it the safety of life on the ship.

One vital element of safe navigation is how to avoid collisions at sea. With the huge expansion of shipping over the last century, rules had to be developed to ensure that ships did not collide, particularly in heavily used channels such as the Strait of Dover and the Malacca Strait. Rules had been in existence since 1840 when Trinity House established rules[47] that were subsequently enacted into the *Steam Navigation Act, 1846*.[48] Subsequent rules were developed and amended throughout the 19th century and were adopted by most of the major maritime nations. It was not until 1972 that the rules were put into a convention, the *Colregs*. These rules, known colloquially as the Rules of the Road, set out detailed rules which all ships must follow including conduct of vessels in particular situations, the use of lights and shapes and of sound and light signals. Again, they are designed to ensure that ships are navigated properly thus avoiding collisions and the creation of distress situations.

Finally, the human element plays a major role in any endeavour. In the maritime sphere, to eliminate human error, as far as possible, ships must be properly manned and the crew must be properly trained. Regulation 14 of Chapter V of *SOLAS* puts it succinctly – "... from the point of view of safety of life at sea, all ships shall be sufficiently and efficiently manned". To further this need, the IMO adopted the *STCW* in 1978, which was extensively amended in 1995. As its name suggests, the aim of the convention was to set out the requirements that contracting governments must adopt in relation to the training and certification of all officers and crew. Certification must be based on the attainment of qualifications approved by the IMO. This certification is essential for anyone seeking to work in the shipping industry. Again, with proper training of a ship's crew, the number of distress situations at sea should be reduced but, unfortunately, can never be eliminated.

Problems with implementing safety of life at sea

The combination of customary international law, international conventions and IMO Guidelines should create a system where there is little or no loss of life at sea. Unfortunately, the continuing loss of life in the Mediterranean Sea and elsewhere highlights that there are problems. These problems consist not only of gaps in the convention system but also the reluctance of some maritime States to undertake their responsibilities adequately.[49] The following issues highlight these problems and demonstrate a need for further action to be taken to overcome them.

Right of access to ports

One of the main problems that arose in the *MV Tampa* incident was the refusal of the Australian Government to permit the ship access to Christmas Island.[50] This raised the question of whether or not there exists under international law an obligation on a coastal State to grant access to a ship in distress, involving as it does the accepted right of a State to control its borders.[51]

At the international level, there is little support for the concept of a general right to access ports. A ship cannot access ports as of right and any request for entry can be permitted, conditioned or refused by the coastal State.[52] However, the situation may be different for ships in distress.[53]

Any right of access to a place of refuge to a ship when it is in distress raises the question of what "distress" means and what must be proven to establish that a ship is in distress. What constitutes "distress" has been examined in the national case law of various coastal States including the United Kingdom, the United States and Canada. What can be extracted from these decisions is that distress must primarily involve an element of danger to the ship, its cargo and crew, to the extent that a reasonable master is put in fear of losing the ship, cargo or crew.[54] This danger can come not only from physical elements such as severe weather and heavy seas,[55] but also from lack of fuel, stores and water.[56] Damage to the ship need not be such that destruction or sinking is inevitable, provided that it is deemed reasonably necessary to put into a place of refuge to repair or revictual to enable the voyage to continue.[57] It is also clear that the danger must be unavoidable and urgent and not self-induced by the failure to properly navigate the ship,[58] to victual the ship or load sufficient fuel.[59] Many of these dangers were peculiar to sailing ships and are no longer relevant to modern ships. However, the concept of distress, and the necessity for it when requesting a place of refuge, is still valid today.

As discussed earlier in this chapter, there exists under customary international law a duty to go to the assistance of a person or ship in distress. While there is no specific right under any multilateral treaty compelling a coastal State to grant access to ships in distress it has long been argued that there has existed and there continues to exist under customary international law an obligation on a coastal State to grant access to ships in distress, although the extent of the custom has changed over time.[60] At the time when preserving the ship included the preservation of life on it, it was argued that the duty to go to the assistance of persons in distress must *a fortiori* include the right to access a port if that is what is necessary to preserve life.[61] However, over the past century there has been a growing trend for coastal States to refuse access to ships in distress where there is a risk to the environment of the coastal State.[62] At the same time search and rescue capabilities have resulted in the ability of SAR States to preserve life of persons on board ships in distress in most cases by removing them from the ship by helicopter, boat or other means without the necessity of accessing a port or otherwise preserving the ship.

The situation was aptly summed up by Barr, J in the High Court of Ireland in *ACT Shipping (Pte) Ltd v The Minister for the Marine, Ireland and the Attorney General (The Toledo)*.[63] This decision was consistent with the growing trend that was appearing in State practice in a number of States[64] which was to refuse access to a place of refuge for ships in distress where the ship was in danger of damaging the coastline of the coastal State and there was no danger to human life on the ship. In such situations, there was no obligation owed to the ship under customary international law for it to be granted automatic right of access to a place of refuge.

Barr, J reviewed in detail the current position of ships in distress under customary international law and found:

> In summary, therefore, I am satisfied that the right of a foreign vessel in serious distress to the benefit of a safe haven in the waters of an adjacent state is primarily humanitarian rather than economic. It is not an absolute right. If safety of life is not a factor, then there is a widely recognised practice among maritime states to have proper regard to their own

interests and those of their citizens in deciding whether or not to accede to any such request.[65]

The distinction between permitting access where life is in danger[66] and where it is not has come about because of what Barr, J called a "fundamental metamorphosis" of modern shipping including the increase of risk of damage to the host State due to the increase in size of ships and the type of cargo carried. In recent years, the State practice of other coastal States, has also reflected this view.

Barr, J in *The Toledo* conveniently summarised this trend and the reasons for it:

> The right of refuge which traditionally has been available to foreign ships in serious distress is one which has evolved in customary international law in the course of several centuries. However, in modern times there has been a fundamental metamorphosis in the development of shipping and in the growth of maritime commerce. . . . In the modern era there appears to be a clearly discernable change in emphasis in the attitude of maritime states towards casualties seeking shelter in their waters, in that greater importance is given to the distinction between ships in distress where a humanitarian consideration of life is involved and those, such as the *MV Toledo*, where the risk to vessel and cargo is purely economic in nature. It is now commonplace for foreign ships in distress which are in the latter category to be refused entry to the territorial waters of states from which access is sought. . . .[67]

Today, it appears that the extent of any obligation under customary international law to grant access to ports of ships in distress has been greatly circumscribed to be one of humanitarian assistance only and that, outside the requirement to protect human life, a request by a ship in distress for access to a port or a place of refuge is now to be treated in the same way as any general request for access. Only if there is a risk to life and access to a port is the only way to remove that risk, should the ship be granted access to preserve that life.[68]

If, as in the case of the *MV Tampa*, an alternative, such as transferring the persons at risk to another vessel, is available then there would be no right to access a port nor would there be any right for the vessel to which the persons had been transferred to access a port unless it too was in distress. This then brings up the second, more practical, problem highlighted by the *MV Tampa* incident – whether or not there exists an obligation on the flag State or the SAR State to permit disembarkation in its territory.

Obligation to permit disembarkation

As mentioned earlier in this chapter, Part V, Regulation 33, paragraph 1–1 of *SOLAS* and Article 3.1.9 of the Annex to the *SAR Convention* provide that the parties responsible for search and rescue operations must take steps to ensure that persons rescued are disembarked at a place of safety. Also, under the definitions in Chapter 1 of the Annex to the *SAR Convention* "rescue" is defined as:

> an operation to retrieve persons in distress, provide for their initial medical or other needs, and deliver them to a place of safety.

No detail is provided as to how this is to be done and in particular what is meant by a place of safety or, more importantly, whether or not the flag State or the SAR State has any obligation to provide a place of safety in its territory.

The IMO attempted to overcome this lack of definition in the *Guidelines* which seek to clarify what is a place of safety for the purposes of search and rescue. The *Guidelines* define a place of safety as:

> a location where rescue operations are considered to terminate. It is also a place where the survivors' safety of life is no longer threatened and where their basic human needs ... can be met. Further it is a place from which transportation arrangements can be made for the survivors' next or final destination.[69]

The *Guidelines* continue by stating that an assisting ship should not be considered as a place of safety (as happened in the *MV Tampa* incident).[70] A place of safety could be a place on land or on another vessel or facility at sea but the *Guidelines* stress that identification of a place of safety depends on the peculiar factors of the case and that a variety of important factors need to be taken into account.[71] In particular the *Guidelines* state that screening and status assessment of rescued persons should not impede their disembarkation in a place of safety.[72] It is important to understand that these *Guidelines* are not binding but only provide guidance to masters and coastal States undertaking Search and Rescue services. While the IMO requests these parties to establish procedures based on the *Guidelines*, there is no compulsion to do so.[73]

To further bolster the *Guidelines*, in January 2009, the Facilitation Committee of the IMO (FAL) set out five principles for dealing with disembarkation of person rescued at sea.[74] These essentially reflect the *Guidelines* in most respects but go further in providing that, where rescued persons cannot be swiftly disembarked elsewhere, the government responsible for the SAR area should allow disembarkation into its territory. This is however quickly undermined by the requirement that such disembarkation must be in accordance with that State's immigration laws.[75] As with the *Guidelines*, these principles are not binding.

The lack of definition and process in the *SAR Convention* and *SOLAS* as to what, if any, obligation falls on the SAR State to provide for disembarkation of rescued persons and the fact that the *Guidelines* and the FAL five principles, which do address these issues, are only persuasive and not binding, mean that there is no obligation under international law for any State to allow disembarkation of rescued persons into its territory.[76]

In Europe, some moves have been made to coordinate procedures to disembark rescued persons. An initial meeting of 10 Mediterranean States, including Spain, Malta and Italy, which are the countries mainly affected by the influx of refugees from Africa, was held in October 2011 with a view to drawing up an MOU on procedures for disembarking persons rescued at sea.[77] This process was established pursuant to the *Guidelines* and is ongoing.[78] In the absence of any legal obligation to accept the disembarkation of rescued persons, this approach is the best option.

In a practical sense, a clear process for disembarking rescued persons is essential. When coastal States refuse permission to rescued persons to disembark in their territory, this can cause problems, particularly to ship masters. Shipping is a highly competitive business and any delay in completion of voyages through deviation to rescue persons in distress can be very expensive.[79] Any excessive delay could lead to the possibility that shipowners could instruct their masters to avoid rescuing persons at sea because of the uncertainty of disembarking them.[80] This is not hypothetical as there have been reported incidents of ships failing to rescue, particularly in the cruise industry in the Caribbean.[81] The reason has been aptly described:

> Dead men tell no tales. Nor do they sue. Only those castaways who survive, and who can identify a passing ship, would be able to sue the ship's captain for leaving them behind.

A decedent's family would have little means of discovering which ships may have passed by a loved one.[82]

While this statement was made in relation to United States law on the right to sue for failure to rescue,[83] it equally highlights the possibility that a failure to efficiently disembark rescued persons could lead to masters avoiding rescuing them.

The lack of any obligation to permit access to a port for ships in distress where there is no humanitarian risk or any obligation on a flag State or a SAR State to allow disembarkation into its territory, means that a solution to the problem of dealing with rescued persons cannot be found in international maritime law and a solution must be found elsewhere.[84] One possibility is under refugee and humanitarian law which will be considered next.

Refugee and humanitarian law

Improvement of the situation in dealing with rescued persons must inevitably be done in conjunction with refugee and humanitarian law.[85] Human rights apply to all persons regardless of geographical location including persons rescued at sea.[86]

The most important relevant convention is the *Convention Relating to the Status of Refugees* (*Refugee Convention*).[87] While the *Refugee Convention* fails to deal in any meaningful way with admission of asylum seekers, the UNHCR has made it clear that the central principle of non-refoulement contained in Article 33(1) of the *Refugee Convention* means that asylum seekers cannot be rejected at a frontier.[88] It was argued in the *MV Tampa* incident that this meant that Australia could not reject the rescued persons under the non-refoulement principle.[89] This argument was rejected by Australia[90] and has also been rejected by the United States Supreme Court in the case of *Sale v Haitian Centers Council*[91] where it was held that the non refoulement obligation applied only where the person is actually in the country and did not apply to persons outside a country and seeking entry to that country.[92] Other opinion is that the non refoulement principle applies to conduct of State officials wherever it occurs and is not limited to conduct within the territory of the State.[93]

In any event the *Refugee Convention* does not require the rescuing State to grant asylum to the rescued persons[94] but only that it cannot reject them at a frontier without arranging an alternate method of dealing with them that does not amount to refoulement.[95] This then implies some form of cooperation in the same way as the Mediterranean coastal States are attempting to arrange for disembarkation in line with the *Guidelines*. The UNHCR at a meeting in Djibouti in 2011 recommended that a model framework be developed to facilitate international cooperation on dealing with persons rescued at sea.[96] As with the Mediterranean MOU negotiations, this is ongoing.

It is this form of negotiation and cooperation which is necessary to find an answer to the problems surrounding the treatment of rescued persons and not the application of narrow legal interpretation.

Conclusion

The clear duty for vessels to proceed to the assistance of persons and vessels in distress at sea has been in existence since time immemorial and still applies as a norm of customary international law.

The development of conventions in the twentieth century has been towards establishing a comprehensive framework for the safety of life at sea and for the rescue of persons and ships in distress at sea. Changing circumstances in both shipping and the movement of people, especially the phenomenon of asylum seekers since the Vietnam "boat people" of the 1970s,[97] have created problems for the proper and efficient implementation of the responsibilities for preserving life at sea.

These problems concern largely how to deal with persons rescued. In looking for a solution for places of refuge and disembarkation of rescued persons international maritime law has proved to be largely ineffective. This emanates mainly from the concessive way obligations are expressed in the conventions and the lack of detail given to essential points. The problem is exacerbated by these essential points being elucidated in non-binding *Guidelines* and Principles. It is also caused by the fact that both places of refuge and disembarkation involve, to some extent, an infringement of the sovereignty of the flag States and coastal States who are being asked to admit persons prior to proper screening and evaluation of status. In these days of heightened security fears this is not likely to change.[98]

In the absence of satisfactory solutions being found in maritime law, the law relating to human rights and refugees could be invoked but here too there are problems of legal interpretation and application. At best, humanitarian law can be invoked in a negative sense to ensure that essential human rights are not infringed but this does not help in advancing a solution to the problems.

The best way to resolve the problems inherent in the saving of life at sea regime is by regional cooperation so that a number of countries agree to spread the load. This can lessen the fear that one, sometimes small, country will be left with the problem of dealing with a huge number of refugees, which is the fear often expressed by Malta.[99] It can also set up an efficient procedure for the speedy disembarkation of persons rescued and the processing of their status. It will still strike the problem of sovereignty but this too can be alleviated by the fact that a proper level of cooperation between countries in a region can ensure that proper procedures to ascertain the status of the persons seeking asylum are developed.

Urgent attention is required to find a workable solution to the problems inherent in the current safety of life at sea regime. Failure to do so will only increase the temptation for masters and shipowners to ignore the plight of persons in distress at sea.[100]

Notes

1 William Whiting, "Eternal Father, Strong to Save", in *Hymns Ancient and Modern* (J Alfred Novello, 1861), 222.
2 Killian S O'Brien, "Refugees on the High Seas: International Refugee Law Solutions to a Law of the Sea Problem" (2011) 3 *Goettingen Journal of International Law* 715, 716.
3 Richard Barnes, "Refugee Law at Sea" (2004) 53 *International and Comparative Law Quarterly* 47, 49; this custom has been recognised also in common law in the case of *Scaramanga v Stamp* (1880) C.P.D. 295, where it was stated at 304 that:
   To all who have trust themselves to the sea it is of utmost importance that the promptings of humanity in this respect should not be checked or interfered with by the prudential considerations which may result to a ship or cargo from the rendering of the needed aid.
4 Anthony Morrison, *Places of Refuge for Ships in Distress: Problems and Methods of Resolution* (Martinus Nijhoff, 2012), 77.
5 K X Li, "Maritime Legislation: New Areas for Safety of Life at Sea" (2001) 28/3 *Maritime Policy and Management* 225, 225; International Maritime Organisation, "History of SOLAS" <www.imo.org/KnowledgeCentre/ReferencesAndArchives/History of SOLAS>.
6 *International Convention for the Safety of Life at Sea*, opened for signature 1 November 1974, 1184 UNTS 2 (entered into force 25 May 1976) (*SOLAS*).

7 *United Nations Convention on the Law of the Sea*, opened for signature 10 December 1982, 1833 UNTS 3 (entered into force 16 November 1994) (*LOSC*).
8 *International Convention on Maritime Search and Rescue*, opened for signature April 27 1979, 1405 UNTS 97 (entered into force 22 June 1985) (*SAR Convention*).
9 *Convention for the Unification of Certain Rules of Law Respecting Assistance and Salvage at Sea*, opened for signature 23 September 1910, UKTS 4 (1913) Cd 6677 (entered into force 1 March 1913) (*Brussels Convention*).
10 *International Convention on Salvage*, opened for signature 28 April 1989, 93 UKTS 8; Cm 3458 (entered into force 14 July 1996) (*Salvage Convention*).
11 *International Convention on Standards of Training, Certification and Watchkeeping for Seafarers*, opened for signature 7 July 1978, 1361 UNTS 2 (entered into force 28 April 1984) (*STCW*).
12 *Convention on the International Regulations for Preventing Collisions at Sea*, opened for signature 20 October 1972, 1050 UNTS 16 (entered into force 15 July 1977) (*Colregs*).
13 Martin Scheinin, "Rescue at Sea – Human Rights Obligations of States and Private Actors, with a Focus on the EU's External Borders" (2012) *Robert Schuman Centre for Advanced Studies Policy Papers*, Paper 2012/05, 1.
14 Stuart Kaye, "Tampering with Border Protection: The Legal and Policy Implications of the Voyage of MV *Tampa*" in Martin Tsamenyi and Chris Rahman (eds), *Protecting Australia's Maritime Borders: MV Tampa and Beyond* (Centre for Maritime Policy, Wollongong, 2002) 59, 59.
15 Frederick J Kenny Jr. and Vasilios Tasikas, "The Tampa Incident: IMO Perspectives and Responses on the Treatment of Persons Rescued at Sea" (2003) 12/1 *Pacific Rim Law & Policy Journal* 143, 147, 177.
16 MSC, 78th Session, *Guidelines on the Treatment of Persons Rescued at Sea*, MSC 78/22/Add.2 dated 20 May 2004 (*Guidelines*).
17 Wolfgang Vitzhum, "From the Rhodian Sea Law to UNCLOS III" in Peter Ehlers, Elizabeth Mann-Borghese and Rudiger Wolfrum (eds), *Marine Issues from a Scientific, Political and Legal Perspective* (Kluwer, 2002) 2.
18 Walter Ashburner, *The Rhodian Sea – Law* (Clarendon, 1909) clxi.
19 Ibid vii.
20 Albert Musson, *Mediaeval Law in Context* (Manchester University Press, 2001) 11.
21 Martin Norris, "The Seaman as Ward of the Admiralty" (1954) 52 *Michigan Law Review* 479, 481.
22 This provision built on the earlier *Barcelona Maritime Code of 1258* which also provided for assistance to be given to ships in distress by storms <http://www.admiraltylawguide.com/documents/barcelona1258.html>.
23 Trani was a major trading port in southern Italy and flourished in the 10th century under the Kings of Sicily.
24 Article VIII <http://www.admiraltylawguide.com/documents/trani.html>.
25 <http://www.admiraltylawguide.com/documents/arles.html>.
26 <http://www.admiraltylawguide.com/documents/oleron.html>; Aldo Chircop, "The Customary Law of Refuge for Ships in Distress" in Aldo Chircop and Olof Linden (eds), *Places of Refuge for Ships – Emerging Environmental Concerns of a Maritime Custom* (Martinus Nijhoff, 2006) 163, 173–174.
27 Bridget Murphy, "Luke v Lyde – an Analysis" (2003) 9 *Auckland University Law Review* 1140, 1148.
28 Ibid., 147; Norris, above n. 21, 481.
29 <http://www.admiraltylawguide.com/documents/hanse.html>
30 Royal Connell and William Mack, *Naval Ceremonies, Customs and Traditions* (US Naval Institute Press, 6th ed., 2004) 25.
31 Norris, above n. 21, 481.
32 Aldo Forte, "'Kenning be Kenning and Course be Course': Maritime Jurimetrics in Scotland and Northern Europe 1400–1600" (1998) 2 *Edinburgh Law Review* 56, 57.
33 (1759) 2 Burr 882; 97 ER 614.
34 Ibid., 617.
35 Murphy, above n. 27, 1147–1148.
36 Mitchell McInnes, "Life Rescue in Maritime Law" (1994) 25/3 *Journal of Maritime Law and Commerce* 451, 466–467; Jason Parent, "No Duty to Save Lives, No Reward for Rescue. Is that Truly the Current State of International Salvage Law?" (2006) 12 *Annual Survey of International and Comparative Law* 87, 91.

37 "Passage shall be continuous and expeditious. However, passage includes stopping and anchoring, but only in so far as the same are incidental to ordinary navigation or are rendered necessary by *force majeure* or distress or for the purpose of rendering assistance to persons, ships or aircraft in danger or distress." Also see Stuart Kaye, above n. 14, 69.
38 Although the *Salvage Convention* is not mentioned in the 2009 Consolidated Text of *SOLAS*, curiously the citation of the *Brussels Convention* in the footnote is that of the *Salvage Convention*.
39 This rider was inserted after the *MV Tampa* incident in September 2001.
40 *SOLAS*, Part V, Regulation 33, paragraph 6.
41 Ibid., paragraph 1.
42 Ibid., paragraph 2.
43 Ibid., paragraph 3.
44 Ibid., paragraph 4.
45 Jasmine Coppens, "The Essential Role of Malta in Drafting the New Regional Agreement on Migrants at Sea in the Mediterranean Basin" (2013) 44/1 *Journal of Maritime Law and Commerce* 89, 93.
46 *Guidelines*, Annex, paragraph 1.2.
47 Simon Gault and Steven Hazlewood (eds), *Marsden on Collisions at Sea* (Sweet & Maxwell, 2003) 132.
48 9&10 Vict. 100.
49 Anja Klug, "Strengthening the Protection of Migrants and Refugees in Distress at Sea through International Cooperation and Burden-Sharing" (2014) 21/6 *International Journal of Refugee Law* 48, 50.
50 Frederick J Kenny Jr, above n. 15, 143, 144.
51 Ibid.
52 Morrison, above n. 4, 72.
53 Ibid., 75.
54 *The Eleanor* (1809) 165 ER 1058; *SS May v The King* (1931) 3 DLR 15; *The New York* 16 US 59 (1818).
55 *The Eleanor* (1809) 165 ER 1058.
56 *The Diana* 74 US 354 (1868).
57 *Kate A Hoff v the United Mexican States; The Rebecca* (1929) 23 *American Journal of International Law* 860, 863.
58 *SS May v The King* (1931) 3 DLR 15.
59 *Merk and Djakimah v the Queen* Supreme Court of St Helena Supreme Court Case No 12, 1991.
60 Morrison, above n. 4, 125–126.
61 Ibid., 12.
62 George Kasoulides, 'Vessels in Distress: Safe Havens for Crippled Tankers' (1987) 11 *Marine Policy* 184, 185–186.
63 [1995] 2 ILRM 30.
64 For example the Netherlands Courts in *Guangzhou Ocean Shipping Company v Minister of Transport, Public Works and Water Management (Long Lin)*, Council of State, Administrative Justice Division, 10 April 1995 AB (1995) No 498, S&S (1995) No 95.
65 *ACT Shipping*, above n. 63, 48–49.
66 Sophie Cacciaguidi-Fahy, 'The Law of the Sea and Human Rights' (2007) 19 *Sri Lanka Journal of International Law* 85, 97.
67 *ACT Shipping (Pte) Ltd* above n. 63, 45–46.
68 Morrison, above n. 4, 126.
69 *Guidelines*, Annex, paragraph 6.12.
70 Ibid., paragraph 6.2.
71 Ibid., paragraph 6.5. The current Australian approach of placing asylum seekers in large life boats and directing them to sail to Indonesia raises many of these factors. The life boats are seaworthy, air conditioned, adequately stocked with food and water for the journey and are not overloaded with people. They are crewed by the crew of the vessel which brought them from the country of embarkation, have adequate navigation equipment and are accompanied by a border protection vessel up to the territorial boundary of Indonesia. All these factors raise the supervening question of whether or not the life boat is in distress and therefore in need of rescue. Based on the definition of "distress" set out in the *Eleanor* (above n. 54), arguably they are not in distress, the rescue provisions under the *SAR Convention* need not be invoked and therefore the question of place of safety does not arise.
72 Ibid., paragraph 6.20.
73 Ibid., Article 2.

74 Coppens, "Towards New Rules on Disembarkation of Persons Rescued at Sea?" (2010) *The International Journal of Marine and Coastal Law* 337, 388–393.
75 FAL 32nd and 33rd Sessions, *Principles Relating to Administrative Procedures for Disembarking Persons Rescued at Sea* FAL.3/Circ.194 dated 22 January, 2009, paragraph 2.3.
76 Coppens, "Towards New Rules" above n. 74, 403.
77 Klug, above n. 49, 54–56.
78 Coppens, "The Essential Role of Malta" above n. 45, 93.
79 Martin Davies, "Obligations and Implications for Ships Encountering Persons in Need of Assistance at Sea" (2003) 12/1 *Pacific Rim Law & Policy Journal* 109, 133–139; Arthur Allan Severance, "The Duty to Render Assistance in the Satellite Age" (2005–2006) 36 *California Western International Law Journal* 377, 388–389.
80 Ernst Willheim, "MV *Tampa* : The Australian Response" (2003) 15/2 *International Journal of Refugee Law* 159, 170.
81 Robert D. Peltz, "Adrift at Sea – The Duty of Passing Ships to Rescue Stranded Seafarers" (2013–2014) 38 *Tulane Maritime Law Journal* 363, 364.
82 Patrick J. Long, "The Good Samaritan and Admiralty: A Parable of a Statute Lost at Sea" (2000) 48 *Buffalo Law Review* 591, 610.
83 Peltz, above n. 81, 366.
84 Richard Barnes, "Refugee Law at Sea" (2004) 53 *International and Comparative Law Quarterly* 47, 76.
85 Willheim, above n. 80, 170; Cacciaguidi-Fahy, above n. 66, 105–106.
86 Barnes, above n. 84, 61.
87 *Convention Relating to the Status of Refugees*, opened for signature 28 July 1951, 189 U.N.T.S. 150 (entered into force 22 April 1954).
88 Willheim, above n. 80, 175.
89 This argument is not as clear cut as this. Barnes, above n. 84, 64 argues that refusal of entry does not amount to refoulement but depends on the circumstances and whether or not the person(s) fall into one of the exceptions in Article 33(2) which include the right to refuse on security grounds or on the grounds that the applicant has committed a serious crime. Others go further and argue that the non-refoulement principle consequentially requires at least temporary right of disembarkation to assess status of the persons rescued – see O'Brien, above n. 2, 732.
90 Willheim, above n. 80, 173.
91 113 S. Ct. 2549, 509 US 155 (1993).
92 Ibid.
93 Barnes, above n. 84, 69; Willheim, above n. 80, 175; O'Brien, above n. 2, 727.
94 Barnes, above n. 84, 63; Willheim, above n. 80, 176.
95 Willheim, above n. 80, 173.
96 Klug, above n. 49, 54–60.
97 O'Brien, above n. 2, 718–719
98 Craig H. Allen, 'Australia's *Tampa* Incident: The Convergence of International and Domestic Refugee and Maritime Law in the Pacific Rim – Introduction to the Maritime Law Forum' (2003) 12 *Pacific Rim Law and Policy Journal* 97, 105.
99 Derek Lutterbeck, 'Small Frontier Islands: Malta and the Challenge of Irregular Immigration' (2009) 20/1 *Mediterranean Quarterly* 119, 143; Coppens, 'Malta and Migrants at Sea', above n. 45, 97.
100 Davies, above n. 79, 141.

12
Shipping: Vessel-source Pollution

Erik J. Molenaar

Introduction

This chapter focuses on the international law that has been developed at the global and regional levels for the purpose of the prevention, control and reduction of (further: combating) pollution of the marine environment by merchant ships (further: vessel-source pollution). The development of this body of law has to a large extent been brought about by shipping incidents. Whereas the sinking of the *RMS Titanic* south of Newfoundland, in 1912, triggered the international regulation of merchant shipping for the purpose of maritime safety – culminating in the adoption of the first SOLAS Convention[1] in 1914 – international regulation for the purpose of combating vessel-source pollution only seriously commenced following the *Torrey Canyon*'s shipwreck off Cornwall in 1967. OILPOL 54[2] had already been in force for almost a decade by then, but its regulations were widely acknowledged to be inadequate in light of the threats posed by the increasingly larger volumes of oil then transported by increasingly larger oil tankers.

The chapter consists of two main sections: 'International regulation of vessel-source pollution' and 'International enforcement of vessel-source pollution'. The former focuses largely on substantive international rules and standards (e.g. discharge standards) relating to vessel-source pollution, and the latter largely on international mechanisms (e.g. audits and harmonized inspection) aimed at ensuring compliance with these rules and standards. This chapter will not comprehensively cover the international law relating to jurisdiction by States in their capacities as flag, coastal or port States, as this is covered by Chapters 4–6. Finally, no attention will be paid here either to the substantive international rules and standards that have been developed primarily for the purpose of maritime safety or security, as this is covered by Chapter 11 'Shipping: Safety of Life at Sea'. It is nevertheless worth emphasizing that regulation that has maritime safety as its primary purpose may have combating vessel-source pollution as an explicit secondary purpose, or may implicitly contribute significantly to combating vessel-source pollution.

In addition to the two main sections described above, this chapter continues below with a discussion on the 'Scope of vessel-source pollution' and ends with 'Summary and concluding observations'.

Scope of vessel-source pollution

The scope of vessel-source pollution for the purpose of this chapter does not include 'dumping' as defined in Article 1(1)(5) of the LOS Convention.[3] The point of departure for further delimiting the scope of this chapter is the definition of 'pollution of the marine environment' (further: marine pollution) in Article 1(1)(4) of the LOS Convention, which reads as follows:

> "pollution of the marine environment" means the introduction by man, directly or indirectly, of substances or energy into the marine environment, including estuaries, which results or is likely to result in such deleterious effects as harm to living resources and marine life, hazards to human health, hindrance to marine activities, including fishing and other legitimate uses of the sea, impairment of quality for use of sea water and reduction of amenities;

Vessel-source pollution may therefore be caused intentionally or unintentionally and directly or indirectly (e.g. through emissions), may actually or possibly result in damage, and such damage can occur though "substances or energy". This latter phrase can be regarded as including heat, radiation, light, noise, electricity, vibrations and – arguably – physical impacts such as anchoring or grounding.[4]

Whether or not a human activity qualifies as marine pollution is important because it determines the applicability of the LOS Convention's jurisdictional framework relating to vessel-source pollution. If applicable, coastal State jurisdiction would in most scenarios be limited to imposing generally accepted international rules and standards (GAIRAS) on foreign ships passing through the coastal State's maritime zones. A coastal State could nevertheless seek IMO approval for imposing rules and standards that are more stringent than GAIRAS. These issues are discussed in more detail later.

The qualification as marine pollution has, among others, arisen in relation to anchoring and the introduction of organisms and pathogens through ballast water and sediments. The regulation of anchoring in areas with coral reefs located seaward of the territorial sea by the United States and the Netherlands indicates that they take the view that the LOS Convention's jurisdictional framework relating to vessel-source pollution is not applicable in these circumstances. Rather than seeking IMO approval, they justified their unilateral regulation of anchoring on the basis of their sovereign rights relating to the use and conservation of marine living resources of their exclusive economic zones (EEZs) or continental shelves.[5] This state practice does not appear to have led to formal objections by other States.

As regards aquatic organisms or pathogens, it is clear that they do not qualify as either substances or energy for the purpose of Article 1(1)(4) of the LOS Convention. However, Article 196(1) of the LOS Convention classifies significant and harmful changes to the marine environment caused by "intentional or accidental introduction of species, alien or new" as "resulting from" marine pollution. Subsequent practice by the international community no longer supports this classification in the shipping domain, however. Instead of including international regulation of ballast water and sediments in an Annex to the principal global treaty on vessel-source pollution, MARPOL 73/78[6], the Members of IMO preferred a stand-alone instrument, which ultimately became the BWM Convention.[7] While the Preamble to the BWM Convention opens with recalling Article 196(1) of the LOS Convention, it subsequently notes that the introduction of harmful aquatic organisms and pathogens via ship's ballast water and sediments threatens the conservation and sustainable use of marine biodiversity.[8] The non-applicability of the

LOS Convention's jurisdictional framework relating to vessel-source pollution is also apparent from the fact that the BWM Convention allows States – whether individually or collectively – to regulate ballast water exchange more stringently than prescribed by the BWM Convention, without IMO approval.[9] There are no indications that these views are affected by the circumstance that the BWM Convention had not yet entered into force at the time of writing, as the reasons for this do not seem related to the discussion above.[10]

In view of this practice on the regulation of anchoring and ballast water and sediments, it is decided that – for the purpose of this chapter – vessel-source pollution can be caused by the following actual and potential impacts on the marine environment and marine biodiversity:

1. Shipping practices and incidents leading to accidental discharges of polluting substances (cargo or fuel) or physical impact on components of the marine ecosystem (e.g., on the benthos and larger marine mammals);
2. Operational discharges (cargo residues, fuel residues (sludge), garbage and sewage) and emissions, as well as toxic and other impacts of anti-fouling systems;
3. Introduction of harmful organisms and pathogens through ballast-water exchanges or attachment to vessel hulls;
4. Other navigation impacts (noise pollution and other forms of impacts on, or interference with, marine species potentially causing, for instance, disruption of behavior, abandonment, or trampling of the young by fleeing animals or displacement from normal habitat); and
5. Anchoring impacts.[11]

International regulation of vessel-source pollution

Global regulation

LOS Convention

The LOS Convention and its implementation agreements[12] are to a large extent framework conventions and in many areas do not contain the substantive standards necessary for actual regulation (e.g. marine pollution standards or fisheries conservation and management measures) or, except for the International Seabed Authority (ISA), establish regulatory bodies with a mandate to do so. To ensure implementation at the appropriate level, the LOS Convention and its implementation agreements acknowledge the competence of pre-existing global or regional instruments and bodies, impose obligations on States to cooperate and agree on regulations through them, and encourage the adoption and establishment of new instruments and bodies.[13]

While pre-existing international bodies are occasionally mentioned by name,[14] it is more common for the LOS Convention to use non-specific references to "competent" or "relevant" international organizations or similar wording. This acknowledges not only that more than one pre-existing international body may have competence in certain scenarios, but also that the mandates of international bodies may develop over time, and that new international bodies may be established.[15]

Even though the IMO is only explicitly mentioned once in the LOS Convention,[16] it is generally accepted that the IMO is the primary competent international organization for the regulation of international merchant shipping.[17] At the same time, however, the IMO is not the only competent international organization for this sector.[18] Both the International Labour Organization (ILO) and the International Atomic Energy Agency (IAEA) have a long-lasting and widely recognized standard-setting role relating to shipping.[19] Moreover, several international organizations, such as the International Hydrographic Organization (IHO) and the World Meteorological Organization (WMO) are 'competent' as well, even though not for the purposes of standard-setting. Rather, the information and services provided by and through them, safeguard and facilitate safe shipping as well as provide the scientific basis for standard-setting by other organizations. Lastly, reference must be made to the important role in the merchant shipping sector of self-regulation by international non-governmental bodies, for instance the International Association of Classification Societies (IACS).

The pre-eminence of global bodies in the international regulation of merchant shipping is a direct consequence of the global nature of merchant shipping and the interest of the international community in globally uniform minimum regulation. The LOS Convention safeguards this interest and the pre-eminence of global bodies by linking flag and coastal State jurisdiction in most scenarios through so-called 'rules of reference' to the notion of GAIRAS, which was briefly introduced above. GAIRAS refer to the technical rules and standards laid down in instruments adopted by the competent global regulatory bodies discussed above. It is likely that the rules and standards laid down in legally binding instruments in force adopted by these bodies can at any rate be regarded as GAIRAS.[20]

The basic duty for flag States to exercise effective jurisdiction and control over ships flying their flag as laid down in Article 94 of the LOS Convention is further specified in Article 211(2), which stipulates that flag State prescriptive jurisdiction over vessel-source pollution is mandatory and must at least have the same level as GAIRAS. Flag States can of course choose to require their vessels to comply with more stringent rules and standards than GAIRAS, but this will then impact on their competitiveness.

While flag State jurisdiction is essentially a 'mandatory minimum', coastal State jurisdiction can be characterized as an 'optional maximum'. The LOS Convention does not require coastal States to impose laws and regulations on ships in lateral passage through their maritime zones, but if they do, they can in principle not impose rules and standards that are more stringent than GAIRAS.[21] The main exceptions to this general rule recognized by the LOS Convention are implied or provided by Articles 21(2) and 234. Moreover, as concluded above, IMO approval constitutes another exception,[22] as well as coastal State regulation of anchoring, and ballast water and sediments.

An important limitation on the LOS Convention's ability to safeguard globally uniform minimum regulation, is that it does not link port State jurisdiction by a rule of reference to GAIRAS. Articles 25(2), 211(3), and 255 of the LOS Convention implicitly confirm the absence of a right of access for foreign vessels to ports as well as the port State's wide discretion in exercising jurisdiction under customary international law. This so-called 'residual' jurisdiction is also recognized in several IMO instruments and has on some (crucial) occasions been exercised by the United States and the European Union (EU). Nevertheless, some exceptions apply – for instance in case of *force majeure* and distress – and uncertainties exist – for instance on the implications of international trade law.[23]

IMO

IMO – named International Maritime Consultative Organization (IMCO) until 1982 – was established in 1958 pursuant to the IMO Convention.[24] IMO's substantive mandate pursuant to Article 1(a) of the IMO Convention was initially limited to "maritime safety and efficiency of navigation". However, when OILPOL 54 entered into force only a few months after

IMO's establishment and charged it with certain tasks,[25] its mandate was in practice extended to vessel-source oil pollution. The 1975 amendments to the IMO Convention formally extended IMO's substantive mandate to "prevention and control of marine pollution from ships" and established the Marine Environment Protection Committee (MEPC) under a new Part IX of the IMO Convention.[26]

Since then, IMO's mandate on vessel-source pollution has continued to broaden, even though this has not been codified in the IMO Convention. IMO's current 'environmental' mandate is formulated in its 2013 Mission Statement as "environmentally sound [...] and sustainable shipping".[27] This broader mandate gradually emerged due to IMO's efforts on, *inter alia*, emissions, anchoring, ballast water and sediments, anti-fouling systems, ship recycling, ship strikes of cetaceans and noise. The treaties and non-legally binding instruments in which these efforts are laid down will be discussed below in a chronological order and/or grouped together. As noted above, no attention will be devoted to instruments that do not have vessel-source pollution – broadly understood – as their primary purpose. Information on the status of participation in treaties can be obtained from IMO's website.[28]

Intervention Convention

The 1969 Intervention Convention[29] confirms the right of coastal States to take the necessary measures on the high seas "to prevent, mitigate or eliminate grave and imminent danger to their coastline or related interests from pollution or threat of pollution of the sea by oil, following upon a maritime casualty",[30] and determines modalities for the right's exercise. Its adoption followed the 1967 *Torrey Canyon* disaster, which eventually made the British government decide to bomb the wreck to prevent further damage. The 1973 Protocol[31] extends the 1969 regime to substances other than oil. The Intervention Convention is an atypical IMO instrument because it deals primarily with jurisdiction, rather than setting technical rules and standards. A corresponding basis for jurisdiction "beyond the territorial sea" – thus also encompassing the EEZ – was included in Article 221 of the LOS Convention.

Instruments on liability, insurance and compensation

In addition to the Intervention Convention, the 1967 *Torrey Canyon* disaster also culminated in two treaties on liability, insurance and compensation for oil pollution damage: CLC 69[32] and FUND 71.[33] These treaties are currently known as CLC 92 and FUND 92 due to amendments contained in several protocols, and were complemented by the 2003 Supplementary Fund.[34] Other IMO treaties on liability and compensation for pollution are NUCLEAR 71,[35] HNS 96[36] and BUNKER 01.[37] The Nairobi Convention[38] on the removal of wrecks, which was adopted for the purpose of maritime safety as well as the protection of the marine environment, acknowledges that coastal States have the right to take measures relating to the removal of wrecks in their EEZs, and also includes provisions on liability and insurance.[39]

MARPOL 73/78

MARPOL 73/78[40] is IMO's principal treaty on vessel-source pollution and superseded OILPOL 54.[41] Its most important category of standards is discharge and emission standards. The only other IMO treaty that contains discharge standards is the BWM Convention. As regards other categories of standards, mention can be made of the well-known double-hull standard

– triggered by the 1989 *Exxon Valdez* disaster – laid down in Annex I to MARPOL 73/78. This construction standard belongs to the category of construction, design, equipment and manning (CDEM) standards. Due to the extra-territorial effects of CDEM standards and thereby their potential to undermine globally uniform minimum regulation,[42] coastal State prescriptive jurisdiction with regard to this category is more limited than with regard to the categories of discharge and emission standards, and navigation standards.

The Annexes to MARPOL 73/78 contain, *inter alia*, discharge standards for oil (Annex I), noxious liquid substances (Annex II), sewage (Annex IV) and garbage (Annex V) as well as emission standards for ozone depleting substances, nitrogen oxides (NOx), sulphur oxides (SOx), volatile organic compounds (VOCs) and shipboard incinerators (Annex VI). Annexes I, II, IV and V make use of so-called 'special areas' where more stringent discharge standards for the various substances apply, and Annex VI makes use of so-called 'Emission Control Areas' where more stringent emission standards for SOx, NOx and/or particulate matter apply.[43] The various amendments to Annex VI agreed in recent years seek to enhance the energy efficiency of ships – among other things through engine design (energy efficiency) requirements – and thereby reduce emissions of greenhouse gases (GHGs). The need and desirability for IMO to adopt market-based measures (MBMs) was debated for some time, but was eventually suspended indefinitely.[44] Dissatisfied with this outcome, the EU is currently considering unilateral action.[45]

OPRC 90 and the Salvage Convention

The adoption of OPRC 90[46] was one of the steps undertaken by IMO in the aftermath of the grounding of the *Exxon Valdez* in Prince William Sound, Alaska, in March 1989. The Convention requires parties "individually or jointly, to take all appropriate measures [. . .] to prepare for and respond to an oil pollution incident".[47] One of its most important substantive standards is the requirement for all ships and offshore units to have oil pollution emergency plans. OPRC 90 also establishes a framework for multilateral cooperation in oil pollution preparedness and response, which encourages regional implementation, including through regional legally-binding instruments.[48] In 2000, the HNS Protocol[49] to OPRC 90 was adopted. It expands the scope of OPRC 90 to incidents with hazardous and noxious substances and largely follows the structure and substance of the OPRC 90. One of the main differences with OPRC 90 is that – in addition to ships – it does not apply to offshore units but to sea ports and other facilities where hazardous and noxious substances are loaded into or unloaded from ships.[50]

The Salvage Convention[51] was adopted in April 1989, a month after the *Exxon Valdez* disaster. It addresses a shortcoming in the 1910 Brussels Salvage Convention,[52] which is based on the 'no cure, no pay' principle, implying that salvors failing to save a ship or its cargo do not get any compensation for their efforts, even though they prevented or minimized damage to the environment. Pursuant to Article 14 of the Salvage Convention, such 'environmental salvage' triggers entitlement to 'special compensation'.

AFS Convention

The AFS Convention[53] was developed in response to the harmful effects of organotin compounds in anti-fouling paints used to prevent the build-up of organisms such as algae and molluscs on the surface of ships, which decrease speed and increase fuel consumption. In addition to killing organisms attached to a ship's surface, however, organotin compounds have been found to also 'leach' into the marine environment, causing damage such as deformations in oysters, and possibly entering the food chain, thereby posing a potential threat to human health. Accordingly, the AFS Convention is aimed at reducing or eliminating "adverse effects on the marine environment and human health caused by anti-fouling systems".[54] Even though the term pollution only appears in the Preamble, the use of anti-fouling systems clearly qualifies as marine pollution as defined in Article 1(1)(4) of the LOS Convention. The AFS Convention prohibits parties from using harmful anti-fouling systems for ships flying their flag or operating under their authority, as well as within their ports, shipyards or offshore terminals.[55] It is finally important to note that the higher fuel efficiency that can be achieved by using anti-fouling systems is not only important for the global shipping industry, but also reduces emissions of GHGs and the spread of harmful aquatic organism and pathogens.

BWM Convention

The BWM Convention seeks "to prevent, minimize and ultimately eliminate the transfer of Harmful Aquatic Organisms and Pathogens through the control and management of ships' Ballast Water and Sediments".[56] As discussed above, the BWM Convention is aimed at combating vessel-source pollution, broadly understood. The standards and procedures for the management and control of ship's ballast water and sediments established by the BWM Convention include ballast water exchange standards and onboard ballast water treatment systems. The failure of the BWM Convention's entry into force for more than a decade since its adoption, is not only due to the high costs of implementation but also the concerns on the robustness of the type-approval review process and port State control actions. MEPC approved two sets of Guidelines in October 2014 to address these concerns.[57]

Hong Kong Convention

The Hong Kong Convention[58] on ship recycling was developed in response to concerns on the effects of ship recycling on the environment – not just the marine environment – and human health and safety.[59] Parties are required to ensure that ships flying their flag and ship recycling facilities under their jurisdiction comply with the requirements of the Convention.[60] At the same time, however, the Convention does not constrain the parties' right to regulate ship recycling more stringently.[61] The Convention's Annex contains detailed regulations aimed at avoiding health and environmental risks – for instance from hazardous materials such as asbestos, heavy metals and ozone-depleting substances – during the dismantling stage, as well as standards on the construction, design, operation and preparation of ships in view of future dismantling. The negotiation process of the Hong Kong Convention also had to address the relationship between the Hong Kong Convention on the one hand, and the Basel Convention[62] as well as ILO's regulatory efforts on the other hand.[63] No consensus exists among parties to the Basel Convention that the Hong Kong Convention provides an "equivalent level of control and enforcement" to that provided by the Basel Convention.[64]

Other IMO instruments

In addition to the IMO treaties discussed above, several other legally binding and non-legally binding IMO instruments are relevant to combating vessel-source pollution, broadly understood. These instruments, which can only be briefly touched upon, include:

1. Pursuant to the PSSA Guidelines,[65] an area can be designated as a particularly sensitive sea area (PSSA) "because of its significance for recognized ecological, socio-economic, or scientific attributes where such attributes may be vulnerable to damage by international shipping activities".[66] Such "damage" is compatible with the broad understanding of vessel-source pollution adhered to in this chapter. The actual protection against such damage is provided by so-called associated protective measures (APMs), which can include special discharge standards, ships' routeing systems (see below) and "other measures aimed at protecting specific sea areas against environmental damage from ships, provided that they have an identified legal basis".[67] Innovative standards are therefore not ruled out;
2. Regulation V/10 on 'Ships' routeing' of SOLAS 74[68] acknowledges that ships' routeing systems can be established exclusively for the purpose of the protection of the marine environment (e.g. 'no anchoring areas', or (recommendatory) speed restrictions to avoid ship strikes with cetaceans as part of a traffic separation scheme (TSS) or a deep-water route)[69] or partly for this purpose (e.g. 'precautionary areas' or 'areas to be avoided');[70]
3. Regulations V/11 on 'Ship reporting systems' and V/12 on 'Vessel traffic services' of SOLAS 74 acknowledge that these can be adopted exclusively or partly for the purpose of the protection of the marine environment (e.g. to avoid ship strikes with cetaceans);
4. Guidance on Minimizing Ship Strikes with Cetaceans;[71]
5. Guidelines on Underwater Noise;[72] and
6. The Polar Code, which will have a mandatory Part II-A entitled 'Pollution Prevention Measures' – containing discharge and CDEM standards relating to oil, noxious liquid substances, sewage and garbage along the lines of the Annexes to MARPOL 73/7nd a recommendatory Part II-B entitled 'Additional Guidance Regarding the Provisions of the Introduction and Part II-A' – relating among other things to ballast water exchange and anti-fouling systems.[73]

Regional regulation

As concluded above, while the LOS Convention emphasizes the pre-eminence of global bodies in the international regulation of vessel-source pollution and the interest of the international community in globally uniform minimum regulation, it nevertheless explicitly allows unilateral prescription by coastal States in some scenarios, and implicitly by port and flag States more generally. Nothing in the LOS Convention prevents coastal, port or flag States from exercising these rights collectively at the regional level. The legality of regional residual port State prescriptive jurisdiction is in fact acknowledged by Article 211(3) of the LOS Convention, which merely requires regional States to give due publicity to such action.

Moreover, IMO practices and several of its instruments explicitly acknowledge a State's residual prescriptive jurisdiction in its capacity as a port State,[74] as a coastal State (e.g. in relation to ballast water exchange and anchoring) or in all three capacities (provided such exercise is consistent with international law)[75]. It is nevertheless understandable that the official position by

IMO Members on regional regulation is that this should be avoided in view of the risk it poses to IMO's authority.[76] As such a risk is not posed by (anticipatory) regional implementation of IMO instruments, however, this is explicitly allowed or even encouraged. This has for instance led the Arctic Council to regional implementation of IMO's SAR Convention[77] by means of the Arctic SAR Agreement[78] and regional implementation of IMO's OPRC 90 and Intervention Convention by means of the Arctic MOPPR Agreement.[79] Another example is the anticipatory – but recommendatory – regional implementation of aspects of the BWM Convention pursued jointly by the members of the OSPAR Commission,[80] HELCOM[81] and the parties to the Barcelona Convention[82].[83]

These instances of (anticipatory) regional implementation do not affect other States: the first two because they only implement and operationalize coastal State obligations and the last because it is pursued exclusively on a flag State basis (even though within a specified geographical area).[84] Another example of a flag State approach is Annex IV on 'Prevention of Marine Pollution' of the Protocol on Environmental Protection to the Antarctic Treaty.[85]

There are in fact very few examples of regional exercises of residual coastal or port State prescriptive jurisdiction that affect non-Members. The main exception is the EU, which has exercised residual jurisdiction in a (*de facto*) port, coastal and flag State capacity.[86] In addition, various regulations in Annex IV to the Helsinki Convention[87] constitute residual prescriptive jurisdiction in all three capacities as well.[88] No residual prescriptive jurisdiction has been exercised within the framework of the regional seas programmes established under the auspices of the United Nations Environment Programme (UNEP)[89] – one of which includes the Barcelona Convention – or large marine ecosystem (LME) mechanisms – many of which are supported by the Global Environment Facility (GEF).[90] The regional port State control (PSC) Arrangements discussed below are not relevant for (residual) prescription as they are exclusively aimed at enforcement of internationally agreed standards.

Finally, regional bodies may not only pursue a regulatory role as discussed above or an enforcement/compliance role as discussed below, but could also strive to resolve jurisdictional issues by means of an agreement-to-disagree or a regional implementation of the duties of strait/coastal States and (financial) contributions by user-States towards covering the costs of strait/coastal States.[91]

International enforcement of vessel-source pollution

Introduction

As noted in the Introduction to this chapter, this section focuses largely on international mechanisms aimed at ensuring compliance with the substantive rules and standards discussed in the previous section. Two different types of mechanisms can be identified in this regard, namely mechanisms aimed at non-compliance by States, and mechanisms aimed at so-called 'non-compliance by ships'. The latter non-compliance can arise due to a ship's failure to meet 'static' (CDEM) standards or because the captain, crew, operator or owner have failed to comply with certain requirements (e.g. discharge standards or logbook requirements). The regional compliance mechanisms discussed below look predominantly at non-compliance by ships.

The principal international juridical mechanism to address a State's non-compliance with its international obligations is the international law relating to State responsibility, which encompasses, among other things, cessation, reparation and countermeasures.[92] State responsibility can also be invoked through available international dispute settlement mechanisms. Such mechanisms are for instance included in Part XV of the LOS Convention and Article 10 and Protocol II to MARPOL 73/78, but these have never been used in relation to vessel-source pollution.[93] Other types of mechanisms aimed at non-compliance by States that have so far been developed within IMO are covered below.

IMO compliance mechanisms

The most 'traditional' IMO compliance mechanisms are probably the reporting obligations laid down in IMO instruments.[94] Whereas many IMO instruments also contain provisions on in-port inspection,[95] and IMO has also encouraged the establishment of regional PSC Arrangements[96] as well as developed guidance on PSC,[97] it is submitted that this cannot be regarded as an IMO 'mechanism' as such. After all, in-port inspection is based on customary international law and IMO did not start to devote serious attention to PSC until the first regional PSC arrangement, the Paris MOU,[98] had been operating for almost a decade and proven successful.

The first genuine IMO compliance mechanism was incorporated in STCW 78[99] through amendments adopted in 1995[100] that built on its traditional reporting obligation in Article IV. The protection of the marine environment is one of the purposes of STCW 78.[101] Pursuant to Regulation I/7 of the Annex to STCW 78 and Section A-I/7 of the STCW Code, parties were required to provide detailed information to IMO on measures taken to ensure compliance with the Convention, education and training courses, certification procedures and other factors relevant to implementation. The information was to be reviewed by panels of competent persons, who would report on their findings to the IMO Secretary-General, who, in turn, would report to the IMO's Maritime Safety Committee (MSC) which Parties to STCW 78 were fully compliant. The MSC would then produce the 'list of confirmed STCW Parties' ('White List') in compliance with the STCW 78.[102] The 'Manila amendments' adopted in 2010 develop and strengthen this mechanism further.[103] Not being on the STCW List entitles port States to proceed immediately to more detailed or expanded inspection and thereby increases the likelihood of other port State enforcement measures, including a prohibition to leave port.[104]

Additional compliance mechanisms were developed by the MSC's Sub-Committee on Flag State Implementation (FSI), including the 'Self-Assessment of Flag State Performance' in 1999[105] and the 'Voluntary IMO Member State Audit Scheme' in 2005.[106] While both are voluntary, the latter mechanism covers not only obligations of IMO Member States in their capacities as flag States but also as coastal and port States. This broader focus is also reflected in the decision to replace FSI by the Sub-Committee on Implementation of IMO Instruments (III).

In 2009, IMO decided to work towards a mandatory or 'institutionalized' Audit Scheme, which will become effective once the required amendments to legally binding IMO instruments have entered into force; scheduled for early 2016.[107] Of the IMO instruments on vessel-source pollution, only MARPOL 73/78 will be subject to the mandatory Audit Scheme.[108] Audits eventually culminate in final audit reports containing feedback on the performance of the audited IMO Member State, which is to respond with a corrective action plan within 90 days.[109] The implementation of this corrective action plan will then be assessed by an audit follow-up.[110]

The Scheme can be characterized as a facilitative compliance mechanism because it lacks a response or enforcement component.[111] It is based above all on the principle of sovereignty, which is meant to imply that audits "should be positive and constructive in approach".[112] Both the audit process and report are intended to be confidential,[113] and the Scheme also lacks some sort of determination of overall compliance or non-compliance. As the audits are not limited to a State's performance as a flag State, but also extend to its performance as a port and coastal State, implicit response options are also not that apparent.

Regional compliance mechanisms

Regional PSC Arrangements

Regional PSC Arrangements for merchant shipping were established to enhance compliance with internationally agreed standards by means of commitments to carry out harmonized and coordinated inspections and to take predominantly corrective enforcement action (i.e. detention for the purpose of rectification). The instruments in which these internationally agreed standards are contained are commonly referred to as the 'relevant instruments'. These consist of the main IMO instruments, including IMO instruments relevant to vessel-source pollution.[114] A participating Maritime Authority must only apply standards that are not just in force generally but also for that Maritime Authority.[115] Some applicability gaps can therefore be expected.

The Arrangements are non-legally binding and – rather than States as such – Maritime Authorities are parties to them.[116] Saving-clauses have nevertheless been incorporated in the Arrangements to ensure that nothing in them affects residual port State jurisdiction, which includes the right to take more onerous enforcement measures.[117]

The expansion in participation in the Paris MOU and the creation and expansion of eight new arrangements since then (i.e. Asia and the Pacific (Tokyo MOU); Latin America (Acuerdo de Viña del Mar); Caribbean (Caribbean MOU); West and Central Africa (Abuja MOU); the Black Sea region (Black Sea MOU); the Mediterranean (Mediterranean MOU); the Indian Ocean (Indian Ocean MOU); and the Arab States of the Gulf (Riyadh MOU), means that almost complete global coverage has now been achieved.[118] While the Arctic Ocean/region and the Southern Ocean/Antarctic region constitute gaps in global coverage, this does not necessarily mean that these gaps require the establishment of new regional PSC Arrangements.[119] As regards the Paris MOU, it should be emphasized that the adoption of a 1995 Directive on PSC by the then European Community[120] and its 2009 revision (recast),[121] meant that the EU assumed an increasingly more prominent role in the evolution of the Paris MOU.[122]

Whereas regional PSC Arrangements are primarily aimed at addressing non-compliance by ships, account can also be taken of the performance of the flag States of these ships. The Paris MOU, for instance, not only requires its Maritime Authorities to detain a ship to ensure that deficiencies are rectified, but also to refuse a ship access to port following multiple detentions.[123] Refusal of access to port depends among other things on whether or not the flag State appears on the annual grey or black lists.[124]

Other regional compliance mechanisms

In addition to regional PSC Arrangements, the following other regional compliance mechanisms relevant to vessel-source pollution exist:

1. Regional arrangements on monitoring, control and surveillance in relation to pollution incidents, for instance the Bonn Agreement[125] or within the framework of HELCOM;[126]
2. The North Sea Network of Investigators and Prosecutors (NSN), which is a body established in 2002 by the OSPAR Commission in order to facilitate enforcement of international

regulation of vessel-source pollution in the North Sea, in close cooperation with the Bonn Agreement;[127]
3. The efforts of HELCOM towards harmonized and effective cooperation on enforcement of pollution violations;[128] and
4. The efforts of the EU, including on penalties for pollution offences[129] and the establishment of the European Maritime Safety Agency (EMSA), tasked among other things with operating various information systems, thereby reinforcing and supporting the enforcement capability of EU Member States in their capacities as port and coastal States.[130]

Summary and concluding observations

The LOS Convention provides the global legal framework for jurisdiction over vessel-source pollution. In support of its main objective in this regard – globally uniform minimum regulation – it emphasizes the pre-eminence of global bodies in the international regulation of vessel-source pollution and limits coastal State regulation – as a general rule – to implementing generally accepted international rules and standards (GAIRAS).

While IMO is the primary competent international organization for the substantive regulation of international merchant shipping at the global level, other global bodies are relevant as well, for instance ILO and IAEA. The efforts of the international community to combat vessel-source pollution commenced with a focus on oil pollution through OILPOL 54, but have since then expanded to a wide range of impacts of merchant shipping on the marine environment and its biodiversity, such as emissions, anchoring, ballast water and sediments, anti-fouling systems, ship recycling, ship strikes of cetaceans and noise. Some of these are not even necessarily covered by the definition of 'pollution of the marine environment' laid down in Article 1(1)(4) of the LOS Convention, for instance impacts of anchoring and ballast water and sediments.

Nothing in the LOS Convention prevents States from exercising residual jurisdiction over vessel-source pollution in their capacities as port, coastal or flag States. The same applies in principle to IMO instruments, some of which even have provisions that explicitly acknowledge residual jurisdiction in various capacities. So far, however, regional bodies have only sparingly exercised this right, and even more sparingly in relation to regulation that also affects non-Members.

The international law on State responsibility and the international dispute settlement mechanisms available under the LOS Convention and IMO instruments have not been resorted to in relation to vessel-source pollution so far. During the last two decades, IMO has gradually expanded its compliance mechanisms beyond the more 'traditional' reporting requirements towards the mandatory Audit Scheme that is scheduled to become operational in early 2016. The Scheme can be characterized as a facilitative compliance mechanism because it lacks a response or enforcement component. Whereas these IMO mechanisms are exclusively aimed at non-compliance by States, the various regional compliance mechanisms are largely aimed at non-compliance by 'ships'. The most well-known of these are regional PSC Arrangements.

Notes

1 *International Convention on Safety of Life at Sea*, signed 20 January 1914, His Majesty's Stationery Office by Harrison and Sons, 1914 (never entered into force).
2 *International Convention for the Prevention of Pollution of the Sea by Oil*, signed 12 May 1954, 327 UNTS 3 (entered into force 26 July 1958); as amended.

3 *United Nations Convention on the Law of the Sea*, signed 10 December 1982, 1833 UNTS 396 (entered into force 16 November 1994).
4 See Harm M. Dotinga and Alex G. Oude Elferink, 'Acoustic Pollution in the Oceans: The Search for Legal Standards' (2000) 31 *Ocean Development & International Law* 151–182, at p. 158; and Erik J. Molenaar, *Coastal State Jurisdiction over Vessel-Source Pollution* (Kluwer Law International, 1998), at pp. 16–17.
5 See Molenaar, note 4 supra, at pp. 416–418 and 'Regulation designating the Saba Bank as Nature Park' (*Regeling van de Staatssecretaris van Economische Zaken, Landbouw en Innovatie van 15 december 2010, nr. 169929, houdende aanwijzing van de Saba Bank als natuurpark*; Staatscourant Nr. 20424, 21 December 2010), at Art. 3.
6 *International Convention for the Prevention of Pollution from Ships*, signed 2 November 1973, as modified by the 1978 Protocol (London, 1 June 1978) and the 1997 Protocol (London, 26 September 1997) and as regularly amended. Entry into force varies for each Annex. At the time of writing Annexes I-VI were all in force.
7 *International Convention for the Control and Management of Ships' Ballast Water and Sediments*, signed 13 February 2004, IMO Doc. BWM/CONF/36, of 16 February 2004 (not yet in force).
8 The term 'biological diversity' is defined in Art. 2 of the CBD (*Convention on Biological Diversity*), signed 22 May 1992, 1760 UNTS 143 (entered into force 29 December 1993).
9 *Ibid.*, Arts 2(3) and 13(3), and Section C of the Annex. IMO Assembly Resolution, A.868(20), 27 November 1997, 'Guidelines for the Control and Management of Ships' Ballast Water to Minimize the Transfer of Harmful Aquatic Organisms and Pathogens', had already recognized in para. 11.2 that "Member States have the right to manage ballast water by national legislation".
10 See note 57 infra and accompanying text.
11 This list is consistent with the 'environmental hazards associated with shipping' listed in paras 2.1–2.2 of IMO Assembly Resolution A.982(24), of 1 December 2005, 'Revised Guidelines for the Identification and Designation of Particularly Sensitive Sea Areas'.
12 These are the Part XI Deep-Sea Mining Agreement (*Agreement relating to the Implementation of Part XI of the United Nations Convention on the Law of the Sea of 10 December 1982*), signed 28 July 1994, 1836 UNTS 42 (entered into force 28 July 1996) and the Fish Stocks Agreement (*Agreement for the Implementation of the Provisions of the United Nations Convention on the Law of the Sea of 10 December 1982 relating to the Conservation and Management of Straddling Fish Stocks and Highly Migratory Fish Stocks*), signed 4 August 1995, 2167 UNTS 3 (entered into force 11 December 2001).
13 See, for example, Arts 237 and 311 of the LOS Convention and Art. 8(5) of the Fish Stocks Agreement, note 12 supra.
14 E.g. the International Civil Aviation Organization (ICAO) in Art. 39(3)(a) of the LOS Convention.
15 See '"Competent or relevant international organizations" under the United Nations Convention on the Law of the Sea', (1996) *Law of the Sea Bulletin*, No. 31, pp. 79–96.
16 Art. 2(2) of Annex VIII to the LOS Convention.
17 Cf. 'Competent or Relevant International Organizations', note 15 supra. See also the IMO Secretariat Study 'Implications of the United Nations Convention on the Law of the Sea for the International Maritime Organization' (IMO doc. LEG/MISC.7, of 19 January 2012); Craig H. Allen, 'Revisiting the Thames Formula: The Evolving Role of the International Maritime Organization and its Member States in Implementing the 1982 Law of the Sea Convention' (2009) 10 *San Diego International Law Journal* 265–333 (2009).
18 Henrik Ringbom, 'Regulatory Layers in Shipping', in Davor Vidas and Peter J. Schei (eds.), *The World Ocean in Globalization. Climate Change, Sustainable Fisheries, Biodiversity, Shipping, Regional Issues* (Martinus Nijhoff, 2011) pp. 345–370, at p. 348. See also: Olav S. Stokke, 'Regime Interplay in Arctic Shipping Governance: Explaining Regional Niche Selection', (2013) 13 *International Environmental Agreements: Politics, Law and Economics* 65–85.
19 As regards ILO, reference can be made to the Maritime Labour Convention (Geneva, 23 February 2006. In force 20 August 2013; *United Nations Treaty Registration* No. I-51299; <www.ilo.org>), which consolidates and updates a large number of maritime conventions and recommendations adopted by ILO since 1920. As regards IAEA, reference can be made to the various IAEA Regulations for the Safe Transport of Radioactive Materials (available at <www.iaea.org>).
20 Molenaar, note 4 supra, pp. 140–167.
21 See, *inter alia*, Arts 21(2), 39(2) and 211(5) of the LOS Convention.
22 See, *inter alia*, Arts 41(4) and 211(6) of the LOS Convention.

23 Erik J. Molenaar 'Port State Jurisdiction' *Max Planck Encyclopedia of Public International Law* (October 2014). As regards international trade law, the key issue is whether its freedom of transit and prohibition of quantitative restrictions constrain residual port State jurisdiction in the domain of the law of the sea. This issue came up in the case on (Pacific) swordfish between Chile and the EU and in the case on Atlanto-Scandian herring between Denmark (in respect of the Faroe Islands) and the EU, both instituted under the World Trade Organization.
24 *Convention on the Intergovernmental Maritime Consultative Organization*, signed 6 March 1948, 289 UNTS 3 (entered into force 17 March 1958), as amended. A consolidated version is contained in *Basic Documents, Volume I* (IMO, 2010 ed.), pp. 8–32.
25 See Art. XXI of OILPOL 54.
26 These amendments were adopted pursuant to IMCO Assembly Resolution A.358(IX), of 14 November 1975. In force 22 May 1982 (1276 UNTS 468).
27 IMO Assembly Resolution A.1060(28), of 29 November 2013, 'Strategic Plan for the Organization (for the six-year period 2014–2019)', at para. 1.1 of the Annex. See also the phrase "the effect of shipping on the marine environment" included by means of amendments into Arts 1(d), 2(d), 15(j) and 59 of the IMO Convention.
28 Available at <www.imo.org>.
29 *International Convention relating to Intervention on the High Seas in Cases of Oil Pollution Casualties*, signed 29 November 1969, 970 UNTS 211 (entered into force 6 May 1975).
30 *Ibid.*, Art. I(1).
31 *Protocol Relating to Intervention on the High Seas in Cases of Marine Pollution by Substances Other than Oil*, signed 2 November 1973, 1313 UNTS 3 (entered into force 30 March 1983), as amended.
32 *International Convention on Civil Liability for Oil Pollution Damage*, signed 29 November 1969, 973 UNTS 3 (entered into force 19 June 1975).
33 *International Convention on the Establishment of an International Fund for Compensation for Oil Pollution Damage*, signed 18 December 1971, 1110 UNTS 57 (entered into force 16 October 1978), as amended.
34 See *Liability and Compensation for Oil Pollution Damage. Texts of the 1992 Civil Liability Convention, the 1992 Fund Convention and the Supplementary Fund Protocol* (IOPC, 2011 ed.; available at <www.iopcfunds.org>).
35 Convention Relating to Civil Liability in the Field of Maritime Carriage of Nuclear Material, signed 17 December 1971, 974 UNTS 255 (entered into force 15 July 1975).
36 *International Convention on Liability and Compensation for Damage in Connection with the Carriage of Hazardous and Noxious Substances by Sea*, signed 3 May 1996. Not in force; as superseded by the Protocol adopted on 30 April 2010; also not in force; consolidated text available at <www.hnsconvention.org>.
37 *International Convention on Civil Liability for Bunker Oil Pollution Damage*, signed 23 March 2001, IMO Doc. LEG/CONF.12/19, of 27 March 2001 (entered into force 21 November 2008).
38 *Nairobi International Convention on the Removal of Wrecks*, signed 18 May 2007, IMO Doc. LEG/CONF.16/19, of 23 May 2007 (will enter into force 14 April 2015).
39 See Arts 1(1), 2(1) and 10–12 of the Nairobi Convention.
40 See note 6 supra.
41 Art. 9(1) of MARPOL 73/78.
42 See in particular Art. 21(2) of the LOS Convention.
43 See the overview available at <www.imo.org/OurWork/Environment/PollutionPrevention/Special AreasUnderMARPOL>.
44 See IMO Doc. MEPC 65/22, of 24 May 2013, at para. 5.1
45 See COM(2013) 480 final, of 28 June 2013, 'on the monitoring, reporting and verification of carbon dioxide emissions from maritime transport and amending Regulation (EU) No 525/2013'. It is submitted that the proposed regulation's consistency with general international law depends above all on the type of enforcement action that will eventually be resorted to. Support for the view that more onerous enforcement action than denial of entry is consistent with international law, can be found in a 2011 Judgment of the European Court of Justice (ECJ; Case C-366/10, *Air Transport Association of America and Others v. Secretary of State for Energy and Climate Change*; Judgment of the Court (Grand Chamber) of 21 December 2011; *European Court Reports* 2011, p. I-13833, at paras 212–130). The ECJ's Judgment on this issue in this case may well have been built on the Advocate General Kokott's – arguably erroneous – conclusion (Opinion, of 6 October 2011, at para. 133) based on the earlier – arguably erroneous – conclusion of the ECJ in the *Poulsen* case (Case C-286/90, *Anklagemyndigheden*

(Public Prosecutor) v. P.M. Poulsen and Diva Navigation Corp, Judgment of 24 November 1992; *European Court Reports* (1992), p. I-6019, at paras 30–34). It is not evident, however, whether the ECJ's view would be upheld following a challenge before a global court or tribunal.

46 *International Convention on Oil Pollution Preparedness, Response and Cooperation*, signed 30 November 1990, 1891 UNTS 77 (entered into force 13 May 1995).
47 *Ibid.*, Art. 1(1).
48 *Ibid.*, Preamble and Arts 6 and 7.
49 *Protocol on Preparedness, Response and Co-operation to Pollution Incidents by Hazardous and Noxious Substances*, signed 15 March 2000, IMO Doc. HNS-OPRC/CONF/11/Rev.1, of 15 March 2000 (entered into force 14 June 2007).
50 *Ibid.*, Art. 3.
51 *International Convention on Salvage*, signed 28 April 1989, 1953 UNTS 194 (entered into force 14 July 1996).
52 *International Convention for the Unification of Certain Rules of Law related to Assistance and Salvage at Sea and Protocol of Signature*, signed 23 September 1910, *United Kingdom Treaty Series* 4 (1913), Cd. 6677 (entered into force 1 March 1913).
53 *International Convention on the Control of Harmful Anti-fouling Systems on Ships*, signed 5 October 2001, IMO Doc. AFS/CONF/26, of 18 October 2001 (entered into force 17 September 2008).
54 Art. 1(1) of the AFS Convention.
55 *Ibid.*, Arts 3(1) and 4(1).
56 Art. 2(1) of the BWM Convention.
57 See Resolutions MEPC.252(67), of 17 October 2014, 'Guidelines for port State control under the BWM Convention' and MEPC.253(67), of 17 October 2014, 'Measures to be taken to facilitate entry into force of the [BWM Convention]' (IMO Doc. MEPC 67/20, of 31 October 2014, Annexes 1 and 3).
58 *Hong Kong International Convention for the Safe and Environmentally Sound Recycling of Ships*, signed 15 May 2009, IMO Doc. SR/CONF/14, of 19 May 2009 (not yet in force).
59 *Ibid.*, Art. 1(1).
60 *Ibid.*, Art. 4.
61 *Ibid.*, Art. 1(2).
62 *Convention on the Control of Transboundary Movements of Hazardous Wastes and Their Disposal*, signed 22 March 1989, 1673 UNTS 126 (entered into force 5 May 1992), as amended.
63 See the Preamble and Regulation 3 of the Annex.
64 Conference of the Parties (COP) 10 Decision BC-10/17 (2011), para. 1.
65 Adopted by means of IMO Assembly Resolution A.720(17), of 6 November 1991, as amended. The version that is currently in effect is included in IMO Assembly Resolution A.982(24), note 11 supra.
66 *Ibid.*, para. 1.2.
67 *Ibid.*, para. 6.1.3.
68 *International Convention for the Safety of Life at Sea*, signed 1 November 1974, 1184 UNTS 277 (entered into force 25 May 1980), with protocols and regularly amended.
69 See IMO Doc. NAV 59/20, of 1 October 2013, at paras 3.2–3.4, 3.18 and 3.24 and Annex 2. See also IMO Doc. MEPC.1/Circ.833, of 7 April 2014, 'Guidelines for the reduction of underwater noise from commercial shipping to address adverse impacts on marine life', at para. 10.5.
70 See paras 2.1.12–2.1.14 of the 'General Provisions on Ships' Routeing' (IMO Resolution A.572(14), of 20 November 1985, as amended).
71 IMO Doc. MEPC.1/Circ.674, of 31 July 2009, 'Guidance Document for Minimizing the Risk of Ship Strikes with Cetaceans'.
72 IMO Doc. MEPC.1/Circ.833, note 69 supra.
73 A recent version is included in IMO Doc. MSC 94/21/Add.1, of 27 November 2014, at Annex 6.
74 E.g. Reg. 21(8)(2) of Annex I to MARPOL 73/78.
75 E.g. Art. 1(3) of the AFS Convention, Art. 2(3) of the BWM Convention, Reg. XI-2/2(4) of SOLAS 74 and para. B/4.34 of the International Ship and Port Facility Security Code (ISPS Code; IMO Doc. SOLAS/CONF.5/34, of 17 December 2002).
76 See e.g. IMO Assembly Resolution A.1060(28), note 27 *supra*, at para. 2.2 which reads – in part – that the challenge for IMO is to "provide an effective and efficient response to shipping trends, developments and incidents, and in so doing, stave off regional or unilateral tendencies which conflict with the Organization's regulatory framework".

77 International Convention on Maritime Search and Rescue, signed 27 April 1979, 1405 UNTS 118 (entered into force 22 June 1985), as amended.
78 *Agreement on Cooperation in Aeronautical and Maritime Search and Rescue in the Arctic*, signed 12 May 2011, 50 ILM 1119 (entered into force 19 January 2013).
79 *Agreement on Cooperation on Marine Oil Pollution Preparedness and Response in the Arctic*, signed 15 May 2013, available at <www.arctic-council.org> (not yet in force).
80 Established by the OSPAR Convention (*Convention for the Protection of the Marine Environment of the North-East Atlantic*, signed 22 September 1992, 2345 UNTS 67 (entered into force 25 March 1998), as amended. Annex V 'On the Protection and Conservation of the Ecosystems and Biological Diversity of the Maritime Area', signed 23 September 1998, consolidated text available at <www.ospar.org> (in force 30 August 2000), as amended.
81 Operating pursuant to the 1992 Helsinki Convention (*Convention on the Protection of the Marine Environment of the Baltic Sea Area*, signed 9 April 1992, 2099 UNTS 197 (entered into force 17 January 2000), as amended).
82 *Convention for the Protection of the Marine Environment and the Coastal Region of the Mediterranean*, signed 10 June 1995, <www.unepmap.org> (entered into force 9 July 2004).
83 Joint Notice to Shipping from the Contracting Parties of the Barcelona Convention, OSPAR and HELCOM on: 'General Guidance on the Voluntary Interim Application of the D1 Ballast Water Exchange Standard by Vessels Operating between the Mediterranean Sea and the North-East Atlantic and/or the Baltic Sea' (Annex 17 to 2012 OSPAR Summary Record).
84 See in this regard the acknowledgment of IMO's primacy in Art. 4(2) of Annex V to the OSPAR Convention, note 80 supra, as well as the more general requirement for consistency with international law included in Art. 6 of the Barcelona Convention, note 82 supra.
85 Annexes I-IV, Madrid, 4 October 1991. In force 14 January 1998; <www.ats.aq>.
86 See Ringbom note 18 supra,; Henrik Ringbom, *The EU Maritime Safety Policy and International Law* (Martinus Nijhoff Publishers, 2008); and Veronica Frank, *The European Community and Marine Environmental Protection in the International Law of the Sea. Implementing Global Obligations at the Regional Level* (Martinus Nijhoff Publishers, 2007), pp. 227–257.
87 See note 81 supra.
88 In particular Regs 4–6, some of which are based on EU enactments.
89 See <www.unep.org/regionalseas>.
90 See, *inter alia*, <www.lme.noaa.gov> and <www.iwlearn.net>.
91 See, e.g., Erik J. Molenaar, 'Options for Regional Regulation of Merchant Shipping Outside IMO, with Particular Reference to the Arctic Region' (2014) 45 *Ocean Development & International Law* 272–298, at pp. 289–290. The extensive cooperation between strait States and user-States with respect to the Straits of Malacca and Singapore could be used as a model.
92 James R. Crawford, 'State Responsibility', *Max Planck Encyclopedia of Public International Law* (September 2006).
93 See also Art. 94(6) of the LOS Convention.
94 E.g. Art. 11 of MARPOL 73/78 and Art. IV of STCW 78 (*International Convention on Standards of Training, Certification and Watchkeeping for Seafarers*, signed 1 December 1978, 1361 UNTS 190 (entered into force 28 April 1984); as amended). See also Yoshinobu Takei, 'Institutional Reactions to the Flag State that has Failed to Discharge Flag State Responsibilities' (2012) LIX *Netherlands International Law Review* 65–90.
95 E.g. Art. 5 of MARPOL 73/78.
96 IMO Assembly Resolution A.682(17), of 6 November 1991, 'Regional Co-operation in the Control of Ships and Discharges'.
97 IMO Assembly Resolution A.1052(27), of 30 November 2011, 'Procedures for Port State Control, 2011'.
98 Paris Memorandum of Understanding on Port State Control (adopted 26 January 1982, entered into force 1 July 1982; as amended; most recent version at <www.parismou.org>). This article uses the version that includes the 37th amendment and came into effect on 1 July 2014.
99 See note 94 *supra*.
100 See in particular IMO docs STCW/CONF/DC/1, of 5 July 1995 (containing the revised Annex) and STCW/CONF/DC/2, of 5 July 1995 (containing the STCW Code).
101 Art. I(2) of STCW 78.

102 See, e.g. IMO doc. MSC.1/Circ.1164/Rev.12, of 28 June 2013.
103 Consolidated versions of the Annex to the STCW 78 and the STCW Code are laid down in IMO docs STCW/CONF.2/33, of 1 July 2010, and STCW/CONF.2/34, of 3 August 2010.
104 Art. X(3) of STCW 78.
105 IMO Assembly Resolution A.912(22), of 29 November 2001, 'Self-Assessment of Flag State Performance' replaces an earlier IMO Assembly Resolution with the same title.
106 Whereas IMO Assembly Resolution A.946(23), of 27 November 2003, 'Voluntary IMO Member State Audit Scheme' endorsed the establishment and development of the Audit Scheme as such, the Scheme was essentially established by means of the adoption of the 'Framework and Procedures for the Voluntary IMO Member State Audit Scheme' (IMO Assembly Resolution A.974(24), of 1 December 2005) and the 'Code for the Implementation of Mandatory IMO Instruments' (III Code; IMO Assembly Resolution A.973(24), of 1 December 2005). The 'Framework and Procedures' and the III Code (currently entitled 'IMO Instruments Implementation Code') have been amended several times since (see note 107 below). See also IMO doc. A 28/9/2, of 10 September 2013.
107 See IMO Assembly Resolution A.1068(28), of 4 December 2013, 'Transition from the Voluntary IMO Member State Audit Scheme to the Mandatory IMO Member State Audit Scheme'. Separate IMO Assembly Resolutions adopted revised versions of the 'Framework and Procedures' and the III Code (Nos. A.1067(28), of 4 December 2013, and A.1070(28), of 4 December 2013, respectively). See also IMO Assembly Resolution A.1077(28), of 4 December 2013, '2013 Non-Exhaustive List of Obligations under Instruments Relevant to the IMO Instruments Implementation Code'.
108 See IMO Resolutions MEPC.246(66) and MEPC.247(66), both adopted on 4 April 2014.
109 Cf. Para. 8.4 of the Audit Procedures included in Part II of IMO Assembly Resolution A.1067(28), note 107 supra.
110 Ibid., para. 9.1.
111 Cf. James Harrison, 'Compliance Mechanisms and the IMO: How to Solve a Problem like Flag State Performance?', unpublished paper presented at the workshop held by the K.G. Jebsen Centre for the Law of the Sea (JCLOS), 23 September 2014, Tromsø (on file with author).
112 Para. 6.1.1 of the Audit Framework included in Part I of IMO Assembly Resolution A.1067(28), note 107 supra. See also the principle of 'continual improvement' in para. 6.5.1.
113 Ibid., para. 6.3.2. See also para. 6.2.5 of the Audit Procedures included in Part II of IMO Assembly Resolution A.1067(28), note 107 supra.
114 As regards the Paris MOU, these are MARPOL 73/78, CLC 69 and its 1992 Protocol, the AFS Convention, BUNKER 01 and the BWM Convention (despite its not being in force).
115 E.g. Sec. 2.3 of the Paris MOU.
116 Erik J. Molenaar, 'Port State Jurisdiction: Toward Comprehensive, Mandatory and Global Coverage' (2007) 38 *Ocean Development & International Law* 225–257, at p. 227.
117 E.g. Secs 1.7 and 9.1 of the Paris MOU.
118 See the information at <www.imo.org/OurWork/Safety/Implementation/Pages/PortStateControl>.
119 As regards the Arctic region see Molenaar, note 91 supra, at pp. 284–287.
120 Council Directive 95/21/EC, of 19 June 1995 (*OJ* 1995, L 157/1).
121 Directive 2009/16/EC, of 23 April 2009, 'on port State control' (*OJ* 2009, L 131/57), as amended.
122 See the reference to the need for prior agreement within the EU in the 13th preambular paragraph of the Directive.
123 Sections 3.4–3.13 of the Paris MOU.
124 Ibid., Sec. 4. See the 2013 Paris MOU Annual Report (available at <www.parismou.org>), at pp. 33 and 35.
125 Agreement for Cooperation in Dealing with Pollution of the North Sea by Oil and Other Harmful Substances, signed 13 September 1983, *OJ* 1984, L 188/9 (entered into force 1 September 1989), as amended.
126 Including the Informal Working Group on Aerial Surveillance (IWGAS).
127 See info at <www.ospar.org>.
128 E.g. HELCOM Recommendations 19/14, of 26 March 1998, and 19/16, of 24 March 1998 (available at <helcom.fi>).
129 Directive 2005/35/EC, of 7 September 2005, 'on ship-source pollution and on the introduction of penalties, including criminal penalties, for pollution offenses' (*OJ* 2005, L 255/11), as amended.
130 See information at <www.emsa.europa.eu>.

13
Regulation of Offshore Hydrocarbon Exploration and Exploitation under International Law

Youna Lyons

Introduction

Offshore exploration and exploitation of hydrocarbons began in the 1950s. It is estimated that there are now close to 7000 offshore oil and gas installations worldwide. Total offshore oil production in 2010 amounted to 33% of global production, a 10% increase from a decade before.[1] Oil companies use a variety of methods and processes that have evolved over time. Some operations rely on above-water fixed installations while others rely on floating installations, whether self-propelled or not. Operations also include the use of un-manned subsea installations of different sizes, pipelines and cables and sometimes offshore port terminals for offloading and loading operations. Exploration and exploitation of offshore hydrocarbon resources are handled by public or private entities according to the rights granted by the State having sovereign rights over the resources. This chapter focuses on the obligations of States under international law for offshore activities taking place in the territorial sea, archipelagic waters and the Exclusive Economic Zone (EEZ); it does not address the nature of the relationship of States with the offshore industry, nor does it discuss hydrocarbon activities beyond national jurisdiction on the deep seabed.

This chapter is divided into three sections. The first focuses on the overarching legal framework applicable to offshore exploration and exploitation for hydrocarbons. It reviews States' rights and obligations with respect to offshore exploration and exploitation of hydrocarbon resources as provided for in the United Nations Convention for the Law of the Sea (LOSC)[2] and in general rules of international law and discusses the failure of the international community to agree on global rules for offshore hydrocarbon activities and its consequences. The second section identifies and discusses international treaties that apply to specific issues which may arise out of or in the context of offshore exploration and exploitation for hydrocarbon resources. The third section discusses the remaining legal gaps with respect to the control of pollution of the marine environment from offshore hydrocarbon activities. Finally, although this chapter does not discuss and compare in depth regional agreements entered into for offshore hydrocarbon activities taking place in some regional seas, it mentions several examples of such agreements where they fill the gaps left by international law.

Framework provisions in LOSC and international law

States' responsibilities

Offshore structures deployed for hydrocarbon exploration and exploitation

LOSC regulates offshore exploration and exploitation for hydrocarbons through rules on the rights of States to seabed resources as well as rules on the jurisdiction of States over installations[3] placed in different maritime zones. Under LOSC, coastal States have sovereign rights over the non-living resources of the seabed up to the outer edge of their continental shelf.[4] As for the rules applicable to the placement of offshore structures at sea, they depend on the maritime zone in which the offshore structure is placed. Coastal States have sovereignty[5] over the territorial sea and have thus full jurisdiction over offshore structures placed in this zone, irrespective of their use. Coastal States must however signal the presence of offshore installations to allow for innocent passage of foreign vessels in their territorial sea.[6] Similarly, coastal States have sovereignty over their archipelagic waters and offshore structures located therein.[7] However, in addition to a right of innocent passage, other States also enjoy in this zone a right of archipelagic sea lanes passage. Archipelagic States must provide due notification of any offshore structure located in the proximity of these lanes as provided by generally accepted international regulations.[8]

Coastal States also have jurisdiction over offshore structures installed in the EEZ for the purpose of hydrocarbon exploration and exploitation.[9] They are also granted the exclusive right to authorise and regulate drilling on the continental shelf for all purposes.[10] However, this jurisdictional right is based on the fact that coastal States have sovereign rights over the living and non-living resources of the EEZ and not sovereignty over the zone. In the EEZ, coastal States also have an obligation to give due notice of the construction of offshore structures and maintain permanent warnings to all vessels in order to ensure safety of navigation in this zone as other States exercise their freedom of navigation.[11] The coastal State may also 'where necessary, establish reasonable safety zones around such (. . .) installations and structures in which it may take appropriate measures to ensure the safety both of navigation and of (. . .) installations and structures'.[12] However, safety zones shall not exceed a distance of 500 meters around such installations and structures except as authorised by generally accepted international standards or as recommended by the competent international organisation [the IMO].[13] However, navigation measures such as 'Areas To Be Avoided' may be applied for at the IMO in accordance to ships routeing rules.[14]

With respect to abandoned or disused offshore installations located in the EEZ, LOSC also provides that they must 'be removed to ensure safety of navigation, taking into account any generally accepted international standards established in this regard by the competent international organization'. However, the possibility to leave them in place is also envisaged, in which case appropriate publicity shall be given to the depth, position, dimensions of any installations or structures not entirely removed.'[15] The issues raised by these rules and by the decommissioning of disused offshore installations are further discussed below.

Cables and pipelines

The laying of pipelines and of submarine cables are dealt with together in LOSC, as a freedom of the high seas extending (albeit with some restrictions) to the EEZ and continental shelf.[16] While coastal States cannot impede the laying of pipelines on their continental shelf by other States, their consent must be obtained with regard to the route[17] and restrictions may be imposed with regard to the prevention, reduction and control of pollution from pipelines.[18] LOSC takes into consideration the potential environmental impact caused by pipelines in comparison to cables, where it is assumed that the latter is not a source of pollution.

Damage to submarine pipelines and cables located in the Area[19] are subject to specific obligations on the State of the flag of the vessel that caused the damage as well as the State having jurisdiction over the person who caused the damage.[20] By contrast, there are no specific provisions to address maintenance duties, or damage to or pollution from pipelines impacting on the marine environment of a coastal State's EEZ. The coastal State is recognised as having the right 'to take reasonable measures for (...) the prevention, reduction and control of pollution from pipelines' and the right to 'establish conditions for cables or pipelines entering its territory or territorial sea or its jurisdiction over cables and pipelines constructed or used in connection with its resources'. However, this State 'may not impede the laying or maintenance of such cables or pipelines'. Although LOSC adds that other submarine cable and pipeline laying States 'shall have due regard to cables or pipelines already in position' and that' possibilities of repairing existing cables or pipelines shall not be prejudiced', no provision grants enforcement jurisdiction to the coastal States against foreign entities responsible for damage to pipelines and cables under its jurisdiction located beyond the territorial sea.[21]

In relation to activities involving pipelines, cables and entities operating under their jurisdiction, coastal States are subject to obligations not to cause transboundary pollution, to take measures to prevent and control pollution, not to transform one type of pollution into another, to notify imminent or actual damage and to study and monitor the potential risks and effects of pollution from these activities.[22] Transboundary pollution from pipelines is subject to the same general provisions.

However, regionally adopted rules are applicable to offshore activities in regional seas such as the Baltic Sea where the Espoo Convention on Environmental Impact Assessment in a Transboundary Context[23] sets out the obligations of Parties to assess the transboundary environmental impact of certain activities[24] at an early stage of project planning.[25] It also obliges States to cooperate[26] by exchanging information, consulting[27] and notifying[28] one another of major projects that are likely to have a significant adverse impact across boundaries.[29] It provides that a 'party of origin'[30], i.e. parties to the Espoo Convention under whose jurisdiction the laying of such pipelines is envisaged to take place, has responsibilities towards affected parties, and is therefore obligated to process an EIA.[31]

Marine surveys

Offshore activities rely on seismic surveys (especially in the exploration phase) aimed at studying the depth profile of the study area, the geomorphology of the seabed as well as the thickness of sediment layers and identification of the seabed substrate. LOSC clearly provides that the consent of the coastal State is necessary for the conduct of Marine Scientific Research (MSR) by other States in its EEZ and on the continental shelf.[32] As for MSR conducted in the territorial sea or archipelagic waters by other States, LOSC contains no specific provision. However any MSR in these areas would fall under the sovereignty of coastal States and authorisation to conduct the research would be left to their discretion.

Although LOSC does not define MSR nor envisage any other kind of research, it provides clearly that if data collected or the results of MSR are of direct significance for the exploration and exploitation of natural resources or the MSR involves the use of explosives, consent from the coastal State can be withdrawn.[33] It is therefore clear that any marine surveys connected to exploration for hydrocarbons are subject to the discretionary consent of the coastal State, whether these take place in the territorial sea, archipelagic waters or the continental shelf of that State. The controversy about whether a hydrographic survey can be conducted on the continental shelf of a coastal State by another State without seeking the prior approval of the coastal State is thus theoretically irrelevant in the context of geological surveying for oil and gas. However, in practice similarities between seabed surveys conducted for different objectives, which are generally also carried out by the same research vessels, make it more difficult to distinguish between them. The purpose of the survey (and whether it is for offshore activities), rather than the content, seems to be critical.

Pollution of the marine environment and the incorporation by reference of global rules and standards

Under LOSC, States have a general obligation to protect and preserve the marine environment.[34] However, LOSC also includes specific obligations for different types of marine pollution. In the context of offshore hydrocarbon exploration and exploitation, relevant provisions include (i) the obligation to not cause transboundary pollution,[35] (ii) the obligation to take measures to prevent, reduce and control 'pollution from installations and devices used in exploration or exploitation of the natural resources of the seabed and subsoil, in particular for preventing accidents and dealing with emergencies, ensuring the safety of operations at sea';[36] they must include measures necessary to protect and preserve rare or fragile ecosystems as well as the habitat of depleted, threatened or endangered species and other forms of marine life,[37] (iii) the duty to not transform one type of pollution into another,[38] (iv) the obligation to prevent, reduce and control the intentional or accidental introduction of alien species,[39] (v) the obligation to notify imminent or actual damage,[40] (vi) the obligation to study and monitor the potential risks and effects of pollution from activities occurring under their control,[41] as well as to monitor the pollution risks and effects of actual activities under their control and the effect of actual pollution under their control[42] and the obligation to publish reports of the results of these analyses;[43] and, (vi) the obligation to adopt laws and regulations to prevent, reduce and control pollution arising from or in connection with seabed activities subject to their jurisdiction[44] and from dumping.[45]

These provisions on pollution from dumping and seabed activities require that States adopt laws, regulations and measures that are no less effective than the global rules and standards on dumping by pollution[46] and no less effective than international rules, standards and recommended practices and procedures[47] on pollution from seabed activities. The literal reading of these provisions[48] seems to imply that Parties to LOSC are deemed to have incorporated existing and future instruments by reference and that they might also be bound by the standard set in instruments which they may not have adopted provided that they qualify as 'global rules and standards'. This view might be considered as an unacceptable intrusion on the sovereignty of States by some.[49] However, any other interpretation would render these provisions superfluous and deprive them of their meaningfulness.[50] Although the wording of Articles 208, 210, 214 and 216 are slightly different, they all reiterate the obligation of coastal States to adopt and enforce laws and regulations and other measures taken to implement generally accepted international rules and standards established through competent international organisations. It follows from this that standards for pollution control and remediation contained in an international treaty should form the minimum standard to be implemented nationally, insofar as (i) they concern

Offshore Exploration and Exploitation

pollution from seabed activities; and, (ii) the treaty has been ratified by a sufficiently large number of States to make it a globally accepted treaty.[51]

In the absence of an international instrument regulating offshore hydrocarbon activities, this rule of incorporation by reference applies to relevant parts of international treaties that are applicable to some aspects of offshore hydrocarbon although their primary purpose is to regulate pollution from shipping rather than from offshore hydrocarbon activities. For example, the 1973 International Convention for the Prevention of Pollution from Ships as amended by the Protocol of 1978 (MARPOL)[52] and the 1990 International Convention on Oil Pollution Preparedness, Response and Cooperation (the OPRC Convention)[53] are shipping conventions that also apply to some offshore installations. This situation contributes to the fragmented nature of the legal regime of offshore hydrocarbon activities (see below for further discussion of the treaties applicable to offshore hydrocarbon activities).

Obligation to establish global rules against pollution from offshore activities

Lack of implementation of LOSC Articles 208 and 214

LOSC mandates coastal States to harmonise their policies at regional level and 'to establish global and regional rules, standards and recommended practices and procedures to prevent, reduce and control pollution of the marine environment' [from seabed activities].[54] The 1976 Convention on Civil Liability for Oil Pollution Damage Resulting from Exploration and Exploitation of Sea Bed Mineral Resources (CLEE Convention) was intended to play this role but it has never come into force.[55] One of the difficulties faced is the lack of a competent international organisation to host the convention and act as secretariat. The efforts deployed since 1977 by the International Maritime Organization (IMO) and the Comité Maritime International to negotiate a global instrument have failed[56] and although many regional agreements have been reached around the globe,[57] many rich hydrocarbon basins have no such agreement (for instance the South China Sea).[58]

Role played by the IMO

The only international treaties and guidelines applicable to offshore oil and gas activities have been adopted or negotiated through the IMO. Although the core mandate of this specialised agency is to promote shipping safety and to protect the marine environment from international shipping activities,[59] offshore oil and gas activities have fallen within the scope of its responsibility in so far as the activities involve ships (e.g. floating platforms) or interfere with shipping safety (as do installations, structures and platforms). While many shipping treaties and guidelines also apply to offshore installations (where the definition of 'ship' includes offshore platform or parts thereof such as Mobile Drilling Units (MODU), Floating, Storage and Offloading Unit or Vessel (FSO), Floating Production Storage and Offloading Unit or Vessel (FPSO) or Floating and Storage Unit (FSU)), this is not always the case.

Following the Montara blow-out which resulted in transboundary oil pollution from offshore activities from Australia's EEZ into Indonesia's EEZ, Indonesia proposed a new work programme to establish an international regime for liability and compensation for oil pollution damage from offshore drilling activities in connection with exploration and exploitation of oil.[60] However, after keeping this issue on the agenda for two sessions, the Legal Committee followed the recommendation of many delegations to remove the 'Liability and compensation issues connected with transboundary pollution damage from offshore oil exploration and exploitation activities' from the 2015 agenda on the basis that transboundary pollution damage from offshore oil activities does not constitute a planned output in the Strategic Plan and the High-level Action Plan.[61] Nevertheless, the IMO agreed to provide guidance for bilateral and multilateral agreements in the context of liability and compensation issues concerning transboundary pollution damage from offshore oil exploration and exploitation activities.[62]

This situation has resulted in a fragmented legal regime for offshore oil and gas activities based on a confusing set of rules derived from many different instruments. Furthermore, the scope of application of each set of rules is dependent on definitions such as whether the given installation or part thereof is a permanent installation or a disconnectable installation, whether it is self-propelled or non-propelled.[63] The IMO has acknowledged this difficulty and sought to clarify some issues in its 2010 Guidance for the application of safety, security and environmental protection provisions to FPSOs and FSUs where it insists on the importance of distinguishing non-disconnectable FPSOs and FSUs (designed to be permanently moored) as opposed to disconnectable ones, and self-propelled craft as opposed to non-propelled craft while operating in location.[64]

Circulars, resolutions, guidelines and standards adopted by the IMO and applicable to offshore installations can be loosely grouped into five topic areas: (i) safety of navigation through safety zones and routeing measures[65]; (ii) construction rules[66]; (iii) security[67]; (iv) training[68]; and (v) decommissioning[69]. While there is no guidance focusing on operational pollution alone, construction, navigation safety guidelines and decommissioning guidelines share a common goal of limiting pollution and environmental damage. Many of these IMO recommendations are designed to promote the implementation of applicable international treaties, most of which are discussed below.

Issue specific rules

Treaties applicable to offshore hydrocarbon activities

Preparedness and response planning for oil spill and other noxious substances

Under the OPRC Convention, which entered into force in 1995, operators of offshore units (either floating or fixed) located within the jurisdiction of States Parties must have an oil pollution emergency plan or similar arrangements which must be coordinated with national systems in order to respond promptly and effectively to oil pollution incidents. Similarly, platforms under the control of a State Party must carry a shipboard oil pollution emergency plan.[70] The OPRC Convention also requires that specific tools be developed and equipment be used, including oil spill combating equipment, programmes of exercises and training, detailed plans and communication capabilities as well as a mechanism or arrangement to coordinate the response to an oil pollution incident.[71] The 2000 Protocol on Preparedness, Response and Co-operation to Pollution Incidents by Hazardous and Noxious Substances (HNS 2000) to the 1990 OPRC Convention provides for similar rules to those applicable to prepare for oil spills.[72]

The OPRC Convention has been widely adopted globally (107 countries as of 28 July 2014, including many of the main offshore oil and gas producing States)[73] and has prompted the development of oil spill contingency and response plans at national level but also between two

Offshore Exploration and Exploitation

or more States where there is a risk of a transboundary spill. Regional contingency planning has also developed across the globe through regional binding agreements[74] and for regions where developments were slower despite high risks of pollution created by dense shipping traffic, the IMO and IPIECA (the global oil and gas industry association for environmental and social issues) have launched a joint Global Initiative Programme designed to enhance oil spill preparedness and response capacity for marine spills at priority locations around the world.[75]

Discharge of oil and other gaseous and hard waste

The 1973 MARPOL Convention is primarily aimed at the shipping industry but also applies to parts of offshore oil and gas operations. MARPOL operates through six technical annexes, each addressing a different kind of pollution: Annex I regulates pollution by oil[76]; Annex II pollution by noxious substances in bulk; Annex III pollution by harmful substances in packaged form; Annex IV pollution by sewage from ships; Annex V pollution by garbage from ships and Annex VI prevention of air pollution from ships. In MARPOL, the definition of 'ship' includes floating craft and fixed and floating platforms.[77] It should be noted that States that are parties to MARPOL are also bound by Annexes I and II but the other Annexes require specific and independent consent.

Although the main aim of MARPOL is to prevent the discharge of harmful substances in the marine environment, it excludes 'the release of harmful substances directly arising from the exploration, exploitation and associated off-shore processing of seabed minerals resources' from the definition of 'discharge' under the Convention. However, the revised Annex I contains special requirements for fixed or floating platforms including drilling rigs, FPSOs and FSUs. When they are engaged in the exploration, exploitation and associated offshore processing of seabed mineral resources and other platforms, they must comply with requirements applicable to ships of 400 gross tonnage and above other than oil tankers and other requirements including maintaining a record of all operations involving oil or oily mixture discharges, and complying with the prohibition on discharge into the sea of oil or oily mixtures except when the oil content of the discharge without dilution does not exceed 15 parts per million.[78] These provisions also apply to the oil concentration allowed in drill cuttings discharged.

In 2011, MARPOL Annex V Regulations for the prevention of pollution by garbage from ships was amended. Resolution MEPC 201(62) expands the requirements for placards and garbage management plans to fixed and floating platforms engaged in exploration and exploitation of the seabed.[79]

The disposal of pollutants resulting from offshore hydrocarbon activities

The disposal of pollutants generated by offshore hydrocarbon activities follow the same rules as pollutants produced by other activities. Two main international sets of rules apply; first the 1972 London Convention[80] and its 1996 Protocol[81] with respect to the dumping at sea of such pollutants; second the 1989 Basel Convention on the Control of Transboundary Movements of Hazardous Wastes and their Disposal (the 1989 Basel Convention)[82] applies to the transport of hazardous waste to another State Party (whether during exploration, production or post-production clean-up). The Convention obliges Parties to ensure that hazardous and other wastes are managed and disposed of in an environmentally sound manner and to adopt domestic measures for that purpose. It applies to used oils, Persistent Organic Pollutant wastes

(POPs wastes), chemicals that persist for many years in the environment and bio-accumulate (such as mercury), Polychlorinated Biphenyls (PCBs), and compounds used in industry such as heat exchange fluids as an example of substances relevant to offshore oil and gas activities.

With respect to disposal at sea, the 1972 London Convention and its 1996 Protocol prohibit the disposal at sea of mercury and radioactive matter as well as many other pollutants, unless they are only present in minute quantities (traces).[83] However, these rules only apply to the disposal of such pollutants. The creation (and spilling) of this type of pollution by normal oil and gas operations from a platform does not qualify as dumping under the London Convention or its Protocol.[84]

Invasive species (through ballast and fouling)

The 2001 International Convention on the Control of Harmful Anti-fouling Systems on Ships (the 2001 AFS Convention)[85] applies to ships and offshore platforms, both fixed and floating[86] and provides that after 1st January 2008, offshore installations will not be allowed to have organotin compounds on their external parts and surfaces, except under specific conditions to ensure that there is no contamination to the marine environment.[87]

However, despite the frequent use of anti-fouling treatments, most vessels and floating platforms still carry at least some fouling organisms, if not on the main hull, in some less treated and exposed areas of the vessels (e.g. around the external cooling pipes, the propeller, the bow thruster or the sea chest). Bio fouling (i.e. biological growth on man-made structures) is recognised as a major pathway for the transfer of species from a location to another. Additionally, marine ecosystems surrounding offshore platforms and installations are particularly exposed to the risk of introduction of foreign species through ballast movements due to the ship traffic they attract for loading or unloading people, material or other cargo. Ballast movements surrounding offshore installations can be similar to that of a busy port, depending on the size of the operations.

Although the 2004 International Convention for the Control and Management of Ships' Ballast Water and Sediments[88] is not relevant for offshore installations which do not have ballast tanks, it is applicable to floating devices such as FPSO and FSO as well as support vessels. While this convention is not yet in force, the oil and gas industry has prepared guidelines for the prevention and management of alien invasive species.[89] These guidelines emphasise pathways for travel of Alien Invasive Species within oil and gas activities and in particular through biofouling. The IMO has also adopted Guidelines for the Control and Management of Ships' Biofouling to Minimize the Transfer of Invasive Species.[90] They include recommendations for a biofouling Management Plan and Record Book, fouling control coating installation and maintenance, in-water inspection and cleaning, and considerations of design and construction, in order to reduce the risk of transfer of invasive species.

Protection against unlawful acts (including piracy)

In the event of piracy or other unlawful acts against offshore installations located in the territorial sea, Coastal States have indisputable jurisdiction to arrest potential perpetrators on the States' territory (including the territorial sea). However, in the EEZ, the enforcement powers of coastal States are generally limited to acts of piracy which under LOSC, excludes acts committed for political ends.[91] However, the 1988 Convention for the Suppression of Unlawful Acts against the Safety of Maritime Navigation[92] and its 1988 protocol[93] provides for protection against acts of violence against individuals on a ship or platform, regardless of whether the acts are committed for private or political ends.[94]

The post-development phase: decommissioning and site restoration

After years of oil and gas production, the seabed of offshore oil and gas fields usually hosts a variety of debris (including piles of drill cuttings) and subsea man-made structures and devices (including connectors, pipelines and subsea equipment), in addition to one or several fixed or floating platforms. However, the only specific international rules applicable to these phases of offshore activities are LOSC provisions on the removal of platforms and the dumping regime on placement at sea for disposal in the London Convention and London Protocol.

The obligation of removal and rules on dumping

Two distinct legal regimes apply and need to be read together when dealing with the post production phase of offshore installations and structures: (i) the provisions in LOSC and the 1989 IMO Guidelines[95] on removal of offshore installations; and (ii) the dumping rules as set forth in UNCLOS, the 1972 London Convention[96] and 1996 London Protocol.[97]

The partial removal of installations and structures provision in UNCLOS Article 60(3) was inserted as a result of concerns from industry majors on the potentially enormous costs entailed in earlier obligations of complete removal.[98] The IMO, being the competent authority referred to in this provision establishes standards which States need to take into account when removing such installations and structures. The 1989 IMO Guidelines impose a general requirement on coastal States to entirely remove all abandoned or disused installations and structures on the continental shelf or in the EEZ unless special circumstances can be shown to apply. Complete removal is recommended without exception only where disused installations and structures are located on officially designated or customary traffic lanes.[99] The Guidelines also provide for the possibility of converting abandoned or disused installations into other uses where this can enhance living resources by their placement on the seabed.[100]

Under LOSC the definition of dumping (the 'deliberate disposal at sea') as contained in the London Convention is reiterated.[101] Consistent with the London Convention, LOSC requires coastal States to ensure that dumping is not carried out without permission.[102] Both Conventions include the disposal of platforms or other man-made structures at sea in the definition of dumping.[103] Aligned with the principles of the precautionary approach and 'polluter pays', all dumping is prohibited under the 1996 London Protocol save for wastes specified on its 'reverse list' which include the disposal at sea of offshore installations.[104] Dumping conditions include a waste prevention audit, consideration of waste management options, description and characterisation of the waste, parameters on the dumping site selection as well as an assessment of effects and monitoring.[105] However, it is noted that cables and pipelines are excluded from the scope of the London Convention and Protocol.[106] Thus there is no clear provision to require the removal of a disused cable and pipeline nor to prevent its abandonment (or removal) on the seabed, to the extent that it does not breach the obligation of due diligence of States to protect the marine environment.

Decommissioning scenarios

Three scenarios can be envisaged. First the structure is fully removed and either disposed of (at sea or on land) or re-used. Second, the structure is partially removed; the part which is removed is either disposed of (at sea or on land) or re-used. Third, the structure is left *in situ* (either as a means of disposal or to be re-used).

The purpose of the new placement determines the applicable legal regime. If the platform is disposed of at sea, whether in whole or in part, whether on site or in another location, the dumping regime applies. The argument that the London Convention does not cover mere abandonment *in situ* but focuses instead on 'deliberate disposal at sea' has brought forward the view that abandonment of an offshore platform for no purpose other than disposal must be considered 'dumping'.[107] It also led to the expansion of the definition of dumping in the 1996 London Protocol to expressly include any abandonment of platforms or other man-made structures at sea, for the sole purpose of deliberate disposal.[108]

However, if the entire platform or a part of it is subject to a new legitimate use (whether in the same location or elsewhere), LOSC rules discussed above on the placement of offshore installations will apply (which includes the duty to respect the rights of other users in the zone, such as the freedom and safety of navigation in the EEZ), as well as special rules applicable to this type of use (be it another oil and gas use, fisheries management, aquaculture, marine tourism or biodiversity enhancement). To prevent cheap disposal of offshore installations disguised as re-use such as artificial reefs, the London Convention provides that the condition for its provisions not to apply is that the placement be not contrary to its aims.[109] The re-use of offshore installations as artificial reefs is the most debated of potential re-uses, especially where an installation is left *in situ* for this purpose.[110]

Obligation to restore the natural environment

No international rule mandates coastal States to remove drill cutting piles or generally restore the natural environment. However, the LOSC general duty to protect and preserve the marine environment (see above) and the rules of international law on transboundary pollution still apply. Regionally, OSPAR had effectively eliminated the discharge of cuttings contaminated with oil-based fluids[111] and proposed a management regime requiring all cutting piles to be assessed against set criteria to determine if they were of immediate environmental concern.[112]

At post-production phase, other questions arise with respect to the disposal or abandonment of accumulated pollutants such as mercury and NORMs (Normally Occurring Radioactive Material)[113] which may be found in pipelines or other connectors. However, for these also, the only specific international rules applicable are those relating to the transboundary disposal of these pollutants.[114]

International rules designed to protect endangered species or habitats can also prevent the rehabilitation of a site and the obligation of removal when disused installations and pipelines have served as attaching substrate for the development of endangered species or as habitat for endangered swimming species.[115]

International legal gaps with respect to the control of pollution of the marine environment

Noise pollution

Exploration activities, well developments and production of offshore oil and gas resources are known to produce underwater noise, vibrations and physical disturbances (e.g. seismic survey, underwater explosions, construction). However the extent of the impact is generally poorly understood and had until a decade ago not been the subject of much attention. Scientific research[116] has highlighted the potential impact and prompted its inclusion in the report of the United Nations' Secretary General on Oceans and the Law of the Sea.[117] The IMO has also included the impact of noise pollution from shipping on the marine environment in its programme of work. The first set of Guidelines for the reduction of underwater noise from commercial shipping to address adverse impacts on marine life were adopted in 2014 and more studies are in progress.[118] The MEPC is finding it difficult to adopt regulations which would fix a sound level target due to the lack of understanding of the type of sounds generated, their respective sources and their impact as well as the need to develop an acceptable measuring and reporting system.[119]

However, much of the attention is devoted to the impact from shipping rather than the oil and gas industries. Guidelines and rules adopted in this context may be binding on seismic vessels, offshore support vessels and other floating structures but they are unlikely to also apply to activities from fixed platforms and to address noise issues that are characteristic to stationary offshore oil and gas activities rather than shipping.

Nevertheless, international regulations on the protection of migratory species,[120] or on particularly sensitive sea areas, or stringent environmental regulations adopted in offshore oil and gas producing countries can include noise mitigation measures. New technology and methods have been developed to measure underwater sounds produced by offshore activities and limit them, for instance in areas of particular sensitivity[121] at specific times when such sounds would interfere with ecological processes such as the migration, breeding or reproduction of whales or other marine species.[122]

Operating discharges from oil and gas extraction

Apart from oily discharges which fall within the scope of MARPOL Annex I and may thus be subject to the discharge limitations of this convention, non-oily components of drilling fluids, produced water and offshore processing drainage and displacement water are not regulated under international law. Although MARPOL Annex II (which addresses pollution by noxious liquid substances) would be relevant, this Annex does not include specific provisions allowing for its application to offshore oil and gas operations. Nonetheless, the transport and handling of hazardous and noxious liquid substances in bulk on offshore support vessels fall within the scope of this Annex.[123]

With respect to sewage from offshore installations engaged in hydrocarbon exploration and exploitation activities, MARPOL Annex IV on pollution from sewage is not applicable. This Annex applies to ships engaged in international voyages and thus not to fixed or floating offshore platforms.[124] Pollution from pipelines or from faults in the seabed also fall between the cracks of the international legal framework.

Accidental pollution from offshore activities

Many scenarios involving offshore hydrocarbon activities can result in accidental oil leakage. While the largest and iconic examples are the 2009 Montara blow-out in the Timor Sea and the 2010 Deepwater Horizon oil spill in the Gulf of Mexico, many others are less well known and involve less spectacular incidents involving smaller spills, pipeline leaks and frequent seabed seepages from faults in the seabed whether from naturally occurring faults or faults engendered by offshore activities. As previously mentioned, by contrast with oil pollution accidents from shipping (for which international rules deal with liability,[125] clean-up and compensation mechanisms)[126] no such rules exist for a transboundary oil spill arising from offshore hydrocarbon activities.

Air pollution and carbon sequestration

There is currently no cap on carbon dioxide emissions from shipping nor from offshore activities. However, MARPOL Annex VI,[127] the first instrument dealing with pollution of the marine environment through the atmosphere from shipping is applicable to offshore petroleum activities. This new annex of MARPOL focused initially on the sulphur and nitrogen content of fuel oil, ozone-depleting substances such as halons and chlorofluorocarbons (CFCs), on-board incineration of certain products such as contaminated packaging materials and emissions of volatile organic compounds (VOCs) from tankers in ports or terminals. However, the landmark 2011 Amendment to Annex VI that added a chapter IV to the Annex aimed at decreasing GHG emissions[128] does not apply to offshore hydrocarbon activities.[129]

Sequestration of gas in sub-seabed formations in order to avoid air pollution is subject to a distinct regime. The Conference of the Parties to the 1996 London Protocol took on the task of regulating sequestration of carbon dioxide in sub-seabed formations, based on the text of the London Convention 1972. In 2006, Annex 1 of the 1996 London Protocol was amended to include the storage of carbon dioxide streams in the seabed and subsoil to the list of wastes or other matter that may be considered for dumping.[130] This amendment (in force since 2007)[131] regulates carbon dioxide sequestration in sub-seabed geological formations, aimed at permanent isolation of the carbon dioxide injected in order to avoid discharges of liquid carbon dioxide directly into the deep oceans.[132] Although the disposal of wastes arising out of offshore activities are excluded from the London Protocol, the disposal of CO_2 into the seabed falls within its scope and guidelines have been adopted to ensure cautious and best practice (by member States).

Conclusion

Although offshore activities occur across many ocean basins and although the spectacular accidental spills in the Gulf of Mexico and in the Timor Sea highlighted the lack of and need for an international regime for exploration and exploitation of offshore hydrocarbon activities as well as for responsibility and compensation for damage suffered from transboundary spills for offshore activities, there is still no such regime in place. Unfortunately, global inertia seems unfavourable to States entering into a global agreement to prevent and regulate pollution from offshore hydrocarbon activities, despite States' obligation to establish such rules. The international community of States has also failed to agree on international standards to guide exploration and exploitation of offshore oil and gas.

However, many international shipping treaties and environmental treaties apply to different aspects of offshore activities which results in a fragmented legal regime. This fragmentation is multi-faceted in that different international rules apply to different aspects of offshore activities but also to different States depending on their adoption of the relevant agreements (unless they qualify as globally accepted standards) and regions. Gaps remain with respect to pollution include noise pollution, operating discharges (other than oil, garbage and sewage), pipelines maintenance and air pollution, in addition to accidental oil and gas pollution. Nevertheless the development of international environmental law and of the duty of due diligence excepted from

States for the protection of the marine environment should convince States of their obligation to adopt industry best practices within their domestic legislation in order to respect and implement their international obligations.

Notes

1 Infield (2012) 'Offshore Outlook 2012'. Online. Available HTTP: <http://www.infield.com/Articles/offshore-outlook-2012.pdf> (accessed 2 July 2014).
2 United Nations Convention on the Law of the Sea, 1833 U.N.T.S. 397, 21 I.L.M. 1261 (entered into force 16 November 1994; adopted 10 December 1982). Online. Available HTTP: <http://www.un.org/Depts/los/convention_agreements/texts/unclos/unclos_e.pdf> (accessed 15 June 2014).
3 LOSC uses alternatively the terms 'man-made structures at sea' and 'installations and structures' without defining them. It seems that all offshore structures would qualify, whether above water or submerged. See Beckman, R., 'Global Legal Regime on the Decommissioning of Offshore Installations and Structures' in Nordquist M.H. et al. (eds.) (2013) *The Regulation of Continental Shelf Development: Rethinking International Standards*, Boston: Martinus Nijhoff, 259–280.
4 In the territorial sea, these rights are based on LOSC Article 2; in the EEZ, they are based on Articles 56, 60 and 77; beyond and to the outer edge of the continental shelf, they are based on LOSC Article 77. Note that the latter includes the extended continental shelf declared in accordance with article 76 of LOSC.
5 LOSC, Article 2.
6 1989 Guidelines and Standards for the Removal of Offshore Installations and Structures on the Continental Shelf and in the Exclusive Economic Zone (IMO Resolution A.672 (16)), adopted 19 October 1989, para 2(4). Online. Available HTTP: <http://www.imo.org/blast/mainframemenu.asp?topic_id=1514&doc_id=7608> (accessed 10 July 2014).
7 LOSC, Article 49.
8 LOSC, Article 53(8) and 1989 Guidelines *supra* note 6 para 3(8).
9 LOSC, Article 56 and 60.
10 LOSC, Article 81.
11 LOSC, Article 60(3).
12 LOSC, Article 60(4).
13 LOSC, Article 60(5), and IMO Resolution A.671(16) on Safety Zones of Navigation Around Offshore Installations and Structures (adopted 19 October 1989). Online. Available HTTP: <http://www.imo.org/blast/blastDataHelper.asp?data_id=22502&filename=A671.pdf>. Of note is that these Guidelines do not provide specific criteria or circumstances where the breadth of a safety zone may expand beyond 500m. The need for extended safety zones was advocated by some national delegations as a measure to mitigate the environmental and safety risk created by grouped offshore installations further apart than 500m but generating shipping traffic and high risk of incidents. Following an extensive discussion on the distinction between safety zones and navigation or ship routeing measures, the Sub-Committee on Safety of Navigation considered on 31 August 2010 that there was no need to establish safety zones larger than 500m around offshore installations nor develop guidelines to do so. This is further confirmed by the additional Guidelines for Safety Zones and Safety of Navigation Around Offshore Installations and Structures adopted by the IMO Maritime Safety Committee at its 88th session (24 Nov–3 Dec 2010) in SN.1/Circ.295. Online. Available HTTP: <http://www.imo.org/blast/blastDataHelper.asp?data_id=30258&filename=295.pdf>.
14 See for instance the successful application for an Area To be Avoided in waters off the Brazilian south-east coast, in the Campos Basin region, in order to reduce the risk of collisions in an area with a high concentration of oil rigs, production systems and FPSOs. Online. Available HTTP: < http://www.mpa.gov.sg/sites/pdf/nav56–20-final-report.pdf>
15 LOSC, Article 60(3).
16 LOSC, Articles 87 and 112 on the high seas, and Articles 58(1) and 79 on the EEZ and continental shelf.
17 LOSC, Article 79(3).
18 LOSC, Article 79(1).

19 The Area is the seabed and ocean floor and subsoil beyond the limits of national jurisdiction (LOSC, Article 1(1).
20 LOSC Articles 112 and 113: Right to lay submarine cables and pipelines; Article 113: Breaking or injury of a submarine cable or pipeline; Article 114: Breaking or injury by owners of a submarine cable or pipeline of another submarine cable or pipeline; Article 115: Indemnity for loss incurred in avoiding injury to a submarine cable or pipeline.
21 LOSC, Articles 79(2) and 79(4). For more details on this issue see, Kaye, S. (2007). 'International Measures to Protect Oil Platforms, Pipelines, and Submarine Cables from Attack', *Tulane Maritime Law Journal*, 31, pp. 377–423.
22 See below, Part I, A(4).
23 The Convention was adopted in 1991 and entered into force on 10 September 1997. Online. Available HTTP: <http://www.unece.org/fileadmin/DAM/env/eia/documents/legaltexts/Espoo_Convention_authentic_ENG.pdf> (accessed 3 July 2014).
24 Espoo, Appendix I. Where a proposed activity is not listed in Appendix I, concerned States party to the Convention, shall, at the initiative of any such State, enter into discussions on whether the proposed activity(s) is or are likely to cause a significant adverse transboundary impact and will as such be treated as if the activity(s) were so listed. Espoo Appendix III provides a general guidance for identifying criteria for determining the significant adverse transboundary impact.
25 Espoo, Article 2.
26 Espoo, Article 8 and Appendix VI.
27 Espoo, Article 5.
28 Espoo, Article 3(1).
29 See 'Introduction to Espoo Convention'. Online. Available HTTP: <http://www.unece.org/env/eia/eia.html> (accessed 3 July 2014).
30 Espoo, Article 1.
31 Koivurova, T. 'Could the Espoo Convention Become a Global Regime for Environmental Impact Assessment and Strategic Environmental Assessment', in Warner, R. and Marsden, S. (eds.) (2012) *Transboundary Environmental Governance – Inland, Coastal and Marine Perspectives*, England: Ashgate, 323–342.
32 LOSC, Article 246.
33 Some authors consider that LOSC provisions on MSR only apply to some but not all forms of data collection in the marine environment. For a discussion on the issue, see Yang, F. (2010) 'Exclusive Economic Zone (EEZ) Regime in East Asian Waters: Military and Intelligence-gathering Activities, Marine Scientific Research (MSR) and Hydrographic Surveys in EEZ', *RSIS Working Paper 198/10*. See also the views of J.A. Roach, 'Defining Scientific Research: Marine Data Collection', *30 Centre for Ocean Law and Policy*, 2007, 541–573 and S. Bateman, 'Hydrographic Surveying in the EEZ: Differences and Overlaps with Marine Scientific Research', *Marine Policy 29*, 2005, 163–174.
34 LOSC, Article 192.
35 LOSC, Article 194(2); The risk of transboundary pollution is more important for offshore exploration and exploitation occurring close to a maritime boundary or in an enclosed or semi-enclosed sea bordered by several States.
36 LOSC, Article 194(3)(c).
37 LOSC, Article 194(5).
38 LOSC, Article 195. This provision is for instance relevant in the context of the application of dispersant to an oil spill from an offshore well with the aim of enhancing the natural dissolution of the oil in the environment. The effectiveness of dispersant must be assessed in each case in order to determine whether the benefits outweigh the negative impacts which may be produced by the toxicity of the dispersant.
39 LOSC, Article 196. Marine organisms that have developed on a floating offshore installation can be transported to a new location when the installation is relocated and become invasive if the circumstances are appropriate unless the offshore installation is cleaned before it is moved.
40 LOSC, Article 199.
41 LOSC, Article 206.
42 LOSC, Article 204.
43 LOSC, Article 205.
44 LOSC, Articles 208 and 214.

45 LOSC, Articles 210 and 216. The term 'dumping' includes any deliberate disposal of waste or other matter from a vessel, platform or other man-made structure at sea, as well as disposal of a vessel, platform or other man-made structure at sea itself. However, disposals that are incidental to or derived from the normal operation of the vessel (or platform, or other man-made structure) or amount to an intentional placement rather than a disposal do not constitute 'dumping' (Article 1–1(1)(a) LOSC).

46 LOSC, Article 210(6).

47 LOSC, Article 208(3).

48 These are provisions relevant to this paper. However, many other provisions in the LOSC use the same mechanism with respect to, for instance, pollution from shipping (Article 211) and in the context of generally accepted standards applicable by coastal States towards States exercising their right of innocent passage (Article 21).

49 Boyle, A., (1985) 'Marine Pollution under the Law of the Sea Convention', 79 *American Journal of International Law*, pp. 347–372, at p. 356 and Timagenis, C.G. (1979) *The International Control of Marine Pollution*, University of Virginia: Oceana Publications.

50 The fundamental principle of *effet utile* is that a treaty interpreter is not free to adopt a meaning that would reduce parts of a treaty to redundancy or inutility. This principle is implied in the *Vienna Convention on the Law of Treaties*, opened for signature 23 May 1969, 1155 UNTS 331 (entered into force 27 January 1980), Articles 31 and 32. See, e.g., R. Jennings and A. Watts (1996) *Oppenheim's International Law*, 9th ed., New York: Longman, pp. 1280–1281, stating: 'an interpretation is inadmissible which would make a treaty provision meaningless or ineffective'.

51 On the notion of 'generally accepted standard' and 'global rule or standard', and references to the different views from the doctrine, see Lyons, Y. (2014) 'The New Offshore Oil and Gas Installation Abandonment Wave and the International Rules on Removal and Dumping', *International Journal of Coastal and Marine Law* 29, pp. 1–41. The London Convention, OPRC Convention and MARPOL Annexes I and II for instance would likely meet the test of global acceptance.

52 The 1997 Protocol To Amend The International Convention For The Prevention Of Pollution From Ships, 1973, As Modified By The Protocol Of 1978 Relating Thereto (Revised Version as of 2011) (entered into force 19 May 2005, adopted 26 September 1997). Online. Available HTTP: <http://cil.nus.edu.sg/1997/1997-protocol-to-amend-the-1973-international-convention-for-the-prevention-of-pollution-from-ships-as-modified-by-the-1978-protocol-including-annex-vi-revised-version-as-of-2011/> (accessed 2 July 2014).

53 1990 International Convention on Oil Pollution Preparedness, Response and Co-operation 1981 UNTS 51 / UKTS No. 84 (1999) Cm 4542 / 30 ILM 733 (1990), Article 3.1(c). Online. Available HTTP: <http://cil.nus.edu.sg/1990/1990-international-convention-on-oil-pollution-preparedness-response-and-co-operation/> (accessed on 16 July 2014).

54 LOSC, Article 208(4) and (5).

55 1977 Convention on Civil Liability for Oil Pollution Damage Resulting from Exploration for and Exploitation of Seabed Mineral Resources; signed 1 May 1977, London, United Kingdom. Online. Available HTTP: <http://cil.nus.edu.sg/1977/1977-convention-on-civil-liability-for-oil-pollution-damage-resulting-from-exploration-for-and-exploitation-of-seabed-mineral-resources/> (accessed 6 July 2014).

56 Several drafts have been prepared at the initiative of the IMO to create an international convention regulating offshore oil and gas activities. However, the general inertia encountered and reported change in some States' position led the IMO to remove this long-term plan from its work programme. The Draft Offshore Units Convention produced by the Canadian Maritime Law Association, which is pursuing the effort, has met strong opposition from the USA (Shaw, R. (2004) 'Report of the CMI Working Group on Offshore Mobile Craft', CMI Yearbook: 421 and Kashubsky, M. (2006) 'Marine pollution from the offshore oil and gas industry: review of major conventions and Russian law' (Part I) *Maritime Studies* 151, 1–11. For an update on the 2010 Russian initiative, see Rochette. J, Wemaëre, M., Chabason, L. and Callet, S. 'Seeing Beyond the Horizon for Deepwater Oil and Gas: Strengthening the International Regulation of Offshore Exploration and Exploitation', *Studies No. 01/14, IDDRI*, 2014 p. 10.

57 Examples include the 1992 Convention for the Protection of the Marine Environment of the North Atlantic (OSPAR Convention), the 1996 Convention for the Protection of the Mediterranean Sea against Pollution (1976 Barcelona Convention), the 1978 Regional Convention for Cooperation of the Protection of the Marine Environment from Pollution (1978 Kuwait Convention) and the

1989 Kuwait Protocol (1989 Protocol Concerning Marine Pollution Resulting From Exploration And Exploitation Of The Continental Shelf (entered into force 17 February 1990; adopted 29 March 1989)). For a recent list of regional agreements, see for example J. Rochette, 'International Regulation of Offshore Oil and Gas Activities: Time to Head Over the Parapet', *IDDRI-Policy Brief* 06/14, 2014 and Kashubsky (2006) *supra* note 56.

58 On the lack of implementation of Article 208 of LOSC and the call for the IMO to take on that role, see Roach, J.A., 'International Standards for Offshore Drilling' in Nordquist, M.H. et al. (eds.) (2013) *supra* note 3, pp. 105–150.

59 Convention on the International Maritime Organization adopted on 6 March 1948; and Article 57 of 1945 Charter of the United Nations (entered into force 24 October 1945; adopted 26 June 1945).

60 IMO Legal Committee, 10 September 2010, IMO LEG 97/14/1.

61 See Report of the Legal Committee on the Work of its 101st Session LEG101/12, 13 May 2014. Online. Available HTTP: < http://www.iadc.org/wp-content/uploads/2014/02/LEG-101-Report.pdf> p. 16 (accessed 9 July 2014).

62 IMO Legal Committee, 101st session, *ibid* note 60. Furthermore, as the focus of the IMO lies with shipping, national delegations generally comprise shipping regulators and rarely include representatives of national oil and gas regulatory bodies. This situation would need to be addressed if the IMO were to embrace a more comprehensive regulatory role with respect to seabed activities. See Spackman, A. (2003), 'Offshore Drilling Environmental Standards Evolving, Touch Oil and Gas', Online. Available HTTP: <http://www.drillingcontractor.org/dcpi/2003/dc-janfeb03/J3-Spackmanb.pdf> (accessed 10 July 2014).

63 1974 International Convention for the Safety of Life at Sea (SOLAS) (entered into force 25 May 1980; adopted 1 November 1974) provides a good application of this guidance as this critical shipping convention only applies to 'ships engaged in international voyages'. Regulation 3 specifies that the ship must be 'propelled by mechanical means' and if a cargo ship, it must be superior to 500 tons GT. (Annex, Chap I General Provisions, Part A – Regulations 1 and 3. Online. Available HTTP: <http://cil.nus.edu.sg/1974/1974-international-convention-for-the-safety-of-life-at-sea/)> (accessed 8 July 2014).

64 MSC-MEPC.2/Circ.9, dated 25 May 2010.

65 All ships must respect the safety zone designated around oil and gas installations and comply with generally international standards regarding navigation in their vicinity. Requests to extend safety zones beyond the maximum 500 m are being discussed at the IMO and have met conflicting views. Guidelines for consideration or requests for safety zones larger than 500m around artificial islands, installations and structures in the EEZ, Submitted by the United States, Sub-committee on safety of navigation, 56th session, NAV 56/4/1, 4 June 2010 and 2010 Draft SN Circular: Guidelines for safety zones and safety of navigation around offshore installations and structures, NAV 56/WP.3, 28 July 2010, Annex 14.

66 The Code for the Construction and Equipment of Mobile Offshore Drilling Units, 2009 (2009 MODU Code) was adopted by Assembly Resolution A.1023(26). It updates and revises the 1989 MODU Code adopted by Assembly Resolution A.649(16), which itself superseded the 1979 MODU Code adopted by Resolution A.414(XI). To be also noted, the 1981 Guidelines for the design and construction of offshore supply vessels adopted by Resolution A.464(XII). While it is still in force for existing ships, it is now replaced by MSC. 235(82) for new ships.

67 The International Ship and Port Facility Security Code (the ISPS Code), which defines a comprehensive set of measures to enhance the security of ships and port facilities, specifically applies to MODU.

68 Recommendations on training personnel on mobile offshore units (MOUs), IMO Resolution A.891(21), adopted on 25 November 1999. Of note also is Resolution A.863(20) 1997 adopting the Code of Safe Practice for the Carriage of Cargoes and Persons by Offshore Supply Vessels (OSV Code), as amended by MSC.237(82).

69 1989 IMO Guidelines *supra* note 6.

70 OPRC Convention, Article 3(1)(b).

71 OPRC Convention, Articles 6(1) and (2).

72 2000 Protocol on Preparedness, Response and Co-operation to Pollution Incidents by Hazardous and Noxious Substances entered into force 14 June 2007; adopted 14 March 2000, 2003 ATNIF 9.

73 See IMO, Status of multilateral Conventions and instruments in respect of which the International Maritime Organization or its Secretary-General performs depositary or other functions. Online. IMO

Available HTTP: <http://www.imo.org/About/Conventions/StatusOfConventions/Documents/Status%20-%202014.pdf> accessed 31 August 2014.
74 For example, in the Mediterranean Sea, the 2002 Prevention and Emergency Protocol concerning Co-operation in Preventing Pollution from Ships and, in Cases of Emergency, Combating Pollution of the Mediterranean Sea (entered into force 17 March 2004, adopted 25 January 2002) to the Barcelona Convention for the Protection of the Marine Environment and the Coastal Region of the Mediterranean (entered into force 12 February 1978, adopted 16 February 1976; 1102 UNTS 27) sets the main principles of contingency planning and cooperation in case of an oil spill.
75 IMO/IPIECA Global Initiative. Online. IPIECA <http://www.ipieca.org/focus-area/oil-spill-preparedness> accessed 20 June 2014; IMO's Integrated Technical Co-operation Programme. Online. International Maritime Organization <http://www.imo.org/OurWork/Environment/PollutionResponse/Pages/Default.aspx> (accessed 20 June 2014).
76 Revised Annex I adopted by resolution MEPC.117(52) on 15 October 2004.
77 MARPOL, Article 2(4).
78 Revised Annex I *supra* note 73 and Guidelines for the application of the revised MARPOL Annex I requirements to FPSOs and FSUs, Resolution MEPC.139(53). See also para 6(13) and 6(14) of MEPC 59/24 (July 2009) on the interpretation of the requirements of MARPOL Annex I Regulation 15 as regards Discharge of Oil and Oily Waste from Fixed and floating Platforms.
79 Online. Available HTTP: <http://www.imo.org/blast/blastDataHelper.asp?data_id=30760&filename=201(62).pdf> (accessed 10 July 2014).
80 1972 Convention on the Prevention of Marine Pollution by Dumping of Wastes and Other Matter, (entered into force 30 August 1975; adopted 29 December 1972).
81 1996 Protocol to the 1972 Convention on the Prevention of Marine Pollution by Dumping of Wastes and Other Matter, (entered into force 24 March 2006; adopted 7 November 1996).
82 Online. Available HTTP: <http://cil.nus.edu.sg/1989/1989-basel-convention-on-the-control-of-transboundary-movements-of-hazardous-wastes-and-their-disposal/> (accessed 5 August 2011).
83 London Convention, Annex I and 1996 London Protocol Annex 2.
84 LOSC, Article 1(5)(b)(i) and London Convention, Article 3(1)(c).
85 Online. Available HTTP: <http://www.austlii.edu.au/au/other/dfat/treaties/2008/15.html> (accessed 16 July 2014).
86 AFS Convention, Article 2.9.
87 AFS Convention, Annex 2.
88 Adopted 13 February 2004; not yet in force. Online. Available HTTP: <http://cil.nus.edu.sg/2004/2004-international-convention-for-the-control-and-management-of-ships-ballast-water-and-sediments/> (accessed 2 July 2014).
89 IPIECE/OGP (2010) 'Alien invasive species and the oil and gas industry, Guidance for prevention and management, OGP Report Number 436'. Online. Available HTTP: <http://www.ogp.org.uk/pubs/436.pdf> (accessed 10 July 2014). Note the inclusion of a list of species identified as potentially particularly invasive.
90 Resolution MEPC. 207(62), adopted 15 July 2011. Online. Available HTTP: <http://www.imo.org/blast/blastDataHelper.asp?data_id=30766> (accessed 10 July 2014).
91 LOSC, Articles 58 and 101.
92 Adopted 10 March 1988, 1678 UNTS 201.
93 Protocol for the Suppression of Unlawful Acts Against the Safety of Fixed Platforms Located on the Continental Shelf, 10 March 1988, 1678 UNTS 304. Online. Available HTTP: <http://cil.nus.edu.sg/1988/1988-protocol-for-the-suppression-of-unlawful-acts-against-the-safety-of-fixed-platforms-located-on-the-continental-shelf/> (accessed 9 July 2014).
94 For a full discussion of the SUA Convention and Protocol to offshore activities, see Kaye S. (2007) *supra* note 21, pp. 389–394.
95 The 1989 Guidelines *supra* note 6. For a discussion on the history of the 1989 IMO Guidelines, see Kasoulides, G.C. (1989) 'Removal of Offshore Platforms and the Development of International Standards', *Marine Policy 13*, 249–265; as updated in Marine Policy 14 (1990) 84–86.
96 *Supra* note 97.
97 *Supra* note 98.
98 Nordquist, M.H., ed., (1993) *United Nations Convention on the Law of The Sea 1982 A Commentary*, Vol. II, Nandan. S, and Rosenne, S. eds., Center for Oceans Law and Policy: Martinus Nijhoff, p. 582.

99 1989 IMO Guidelines, *supra* note 6, para 3(7).
100 *Ibid* para 3(12).
101 LOSC, Article 1(5); 1972 London Convention, Article 3(1). It is noted that pollution arising out of the normal operations of a platform do not qualify as dumping (UNCLOS, Article 1(5)(b)(i)).
102 LOSC, Articles 210(5), and 216(1)(b).
103 London Convention, Articles 3(1)(a), 4(1)(b) and Annex II (B).
104 1996 London Protocol, Annex 1.
105 1996 London Protocol, Annex 2. See also 2000 Specific Guidelines for Assessment of Platforms or Other Man-Made Structures at Sea, adopted 22 September 2000. Online. Available HTTP: <http://cil.nus.edu.sg/2000/2000-specific-guidelines-for-assessment-of-platforms-or-other-man-made-structures-at-sea/> (accessed 15 July 2014).
106 Although this was unclear under the London Convention. The abandonment of cables, pipelines and marine research devices initially placed for a purpose other than mere disposal is not covered by the Protocol (Article 1(2)(3)).
107 13th Consultative Meeting of the Contracting Parties to the Convention on the Prevention of Marine Pollution by Dumping of Wastes and Other Matter, 29 October – 2 November 1990. Online. Available HTTP: <http://www.imo.org/KnowledgeCentre/ReferencesAndArchives/IMO_Conferences_and_Meetings/London_Convention/LCandLDCReports/Documents/Report%20of%20LDC%2013%20October%201990.pdf> (accessed 15 July 2014). See also de La Fayette, L. (1998) 'The London Convention 1972: Preparing for the Future' 13(4) *International Journal of Marine and Coastal Law*, p. 525) and Lyons, Y. (2014), *supra* note 50.
108 1996 London Protocol, Article 1(4).
109 London Convention, Article 1(b)(ii).
110 This debate is the origin of the *London Convention and Protocol/UNEP Guidelines for the Placement of Artificial Reefs* (2009) London: International Maritime Organization.
111 OSPAR Decision 2000/3 on the Use of Organic-phase Drilling Fluids (OPF) and the Discharge of OPF-Contaminated Cuttings.
112 OSPAR Recommendation 2006/5 on a Management Regime for Offshore Cutting Piles. The assessment confirmed that OSPAR Decision 2000/3 has resulted in significant reduction in pollution and recovery of the seabed. The OSPAR Commission states that Contracting Parties should reassess the situation and possible impacts in the meeting cycle 2013/2014 in the light of results of further post-decommissioning environmental surveys – see OSPAR Commission – Assessment of the possible effects of releases of oil and chemicals from any disturbance of cuttings piles (2009 update). Online. Available HTTP: <http://qsr2010.ospar.org/media/assessments/p00337_OA_2_update2009.pdf> (accessed 15 July 2014).
113 For a description of this issue, see 'Naturally Occurring Radioactive Materials (NORM) in Produced Water and Oil-Field Equipment – An Issue for the Energy Industry'. Online. Available HTTP: <http://pubs.usgs.gov/fs/fs-0142-99/fs-0142-99.pdf> (accessed 15 July 2014).
114 See above, Part II A(3).
115 For instance green sea turtles foraging on organisms growing on platforms' legs. See references and discussion in Lyons, Y. (2014) *supra* note 51, p. 3.
116 International Council for the Exploration of the Sea (ICES) (2005) 'Report of the Ad-Hoc Group on the Impacts of Sonar on Cetaceans and Fish (AGISC)', Copenhagen: ICES. Online. Available HTTP: <http://ec.europa.eu/environment/nature/conservation/species/whales_dolphins/docs/ices_second_report.pdf> (accessed 2 July 2014). See also List of Peer-reviewed scientific studies on the impacts of ocean noise on marine living resources, submitted pursuant to paragraph 107 of General Assembly Resolution 61/222, maintained by the UN Secretary-General. Online. Available HTTP: <http://www.un.org/depts/los/general_assembly/noise/noise_belgium.pdf> (accessed 9 July 2014).
117 Since 2004, UN doc. A/59/62/Add.1, para 220. For a comprehensive discussion on this topic, see Papanicolopulu, I. (2008) 'Current legal developments – Underwater Noise' 23 *International Journal of Marine and Coastal Law*, pp. 365–376.
118 MEPC 1/Circ. 833.
119 MEPC Report on its 66th Session, MEPC 66/21 Agenda 21 p. 58.
120 See for instance species protected under the 1979 Convention on the Conservation of Migratory Species of Wild Animals (entered into force 1 November 1983; adopted 23 June 1979), or the critical

habitats of endangered species under CITES (1973 Convention on International Trade in Endangered Species of Wild Fauna and Flora (entered into force 1 July 1975 ; adopted 3 March 1973)).

121 Such as Ecologically and Biologically Significant Areas under the 1992 Convention on Biological Diversity (entered into force 29 December 1993; adopted 5 June 1992) and Particularly Sensitive Sea Area (PSSA) designated by the IMO (Online. Available HTTP: <http://www.imo.org/blast/main frame.asp?topic_id=1357> (accessed 9 July 2014)).

122 See for instance, André, M. et al., (2011) 'Live Monitoring of Ocean Noise and Cetacean Acoustic Signals' 63 *Marine Pollution Bulletin*, pp. 18–26 at p. 25.

123 IMO Assembly Resolution A.673(16) adopted on 19 October 1989, as amended by the Resolutions of the Maritime Safety Committee MSC 184(79) and MSC.236.

124 Regulation 2.1 of the 2004 Revised Annex IV of MARPOL 73/78, Resolution MEPC.115(51) Amendments to the annex of the Protocol of 1978 relating to the international Convention for the Prevention of Pollution from Ships, entered into force on 1 August 2005. The provisions on sewage fall outside scope of the exclusion of discharge from exploration, exploitation and associated offshore processing of seabed minerals resources as sewage does not result from such activities. However, the application of the regulations on sewage discharge to offshore installations is limited by the requirement that the discharge occurs from a vessel involved in an international voyage.

125 International Convention on Civil Liability for Oil Pollution Damage, adopted 29 November 1969, 973 UNTS 3 (entered into force 19 June 1975; being replaced by 1992 Protocol).

126 International Convention on the Establishment of an International Fund for Compensation for Oil Pollution Damage, adopted 18 December 1971, 11 ILM 284 (entered into force 16 October 1978; superseded by 1992 Protocol to Amend the 1969 International Convention on Civil Liability for Oil Pollution Damage (entered into force 30 May 1996; adopted 27 November 1992)) and IPIECA-ITOPF (2007) 'Oil Spill Compensation: A Guide to the International Conventions on Liability and Compensation for Oil Pollution Damage'. Online. Available HTTP: <http://www.ipieca.org/publication/oil-spill-compensation> (accessed 21 June 2014).

127 Annex VI entered into force on 19 May 2005 and a revised Annex VI was adopted in October 2008 which entered into force on 1 July 2010. Online. Available HTTP: <http://www.imo.org/OurWork/Environment/PollutionPrevention/AirPollution/Pages/Default.aspx> (accessed 2 July 2014).

128 Amendments to the Annex of the Protocol of 1997 to amend the International Convention for the Prevention of Pollution from Ship, 1973, as Modified by the Protocol of 1978 Relating Thereto, Resolution MEPC 203(62) adopted on 15 July 2011. Online. Available HTTP: <http://www.imo.org/blast/blastDataHelper.asp?data_id=30762&filename=203(62).pdf>

129 Combustion and flaring result in emissions of carbon dioxide (CO_2), carbon monoxide (CO), methane (CH_4) and oxides of nitrogen (NOx) and sulphur (SOx). Venting releases Volatile Organic Compounds (VOCs) and methane, whilst firefighting and refrigeration releases Halon and chlorofluorocarbons (CFCs). Online. Available HTTP: <http://www.oilandgasuk.co.uk/knowledgecentre/atmospheric_emissions.cfm> (accessed 17 July 2014).

130 Annex 1, 1(8)

131 The entry into force is governed by Article 22 of the 1996 London Protocol pursuant to which amendments to the Annexes automatically enter into force for all contracting parties that have not objected within 100 days of the day of adoption.

132 Amendment to Annex 1 to the London Protocol; Resolution LP.1(1) On The Amendment To Include Co2 Sequestration In Sub-Seabed Geological Formations In Annex 1 To The London Protocol. Online. Available HTTP: <http://www.imo.org/OurWork/Environment/PollutionPrevention/AirPollution/Documents/COP 16 Submissions/IMO note on LC-LP matters.pdf> (accessed 16 July 2014).

14

The Regulation of Marine Scientific Research:

Addressing Challenges, Advancing Knowledge

Harriet Harden Davies

Introduction

Marine scientific research is critical to enhance human understanding of the marine environment and respond to challenges facing ocean governance. Scientific advances and technological developments drive transformative changes in how, where and by whom, marine scientific research can be conducted. These advances present opportunities to enhance knowledge and deliver benefits. However, they also bring new challenges for governance, particularly where the legal classification of research activities is unclear or there is the potential for adverse environmental impacts. This chapter will examine the nature and importance of marine scientific research, the international framework for the regulation of marine scientific research and some of the emerging challenges for regulation.

Advancing knowledge through marine scientific research

Defining marine scientific research

Marine scientific research is undertaken to explore and investigate the oceans in order to expand scientific knowledge. It is not defined by the United Nations Convention on the Law of the Sea (LOSC).[1] Various definitions were proposed during the LOSC negotiations but difficulty in distinguishing between pure research (i.e. to advance knowledge) and applied research (i.e. for industrial purposes or economic gain) became a core and unresolved issue in the negotiations.[2] Despite the inclusion in the 1976 Informal Single Negotiating Text of a definition of marine scientific research as 'any study or related experimental work designed to increase mankind's knowledge of the marine environment', the definition was not retained in the final text of the LOSC.[3]

The legal definition of marine scientific research and the distinction between pure and applied research activities is still debated today. Some argue that the LOSC regime for marine scientific research is applicable to both pure and applied activities. Others propose an emphasis on knowledge furtherance only as the fundamental purpose for marine scientific research. One working definition of marine scientific research proposed by the Subsidiary Body on Scientific, Technical and Technological Advice (SBSTTA) emphasises the importance of openness, dissemination of data, exchange of samples and the publication of research results, in enhancing knowledge of the marine environment.[4]

Marine scientific research is used as a general term to encompass the many forms of scientific investigation concerned with the 'essence of phenomena and processes occurring in the marine environment and interrelations between them'.[5] It can take many forms, including observations, surveying or sampling to investigate physical, chemical, biological, geological and other characteristics of the ocean. Research might be exploratory, targeted or aim to support a specific industry sector. Some data collection activities conducted at sea are not generally considered to fall within the scope of the LOSC regime for marine scientific research, including resources exploration, *ex situ* observation technologies and hydrographic and military surveying.[6]

Perhaps in recognition of the challenges that could arise from the lack of definition of marine scientific research, the LOSC requires States to promote the establishment of general criteria and guidelines to assist in ascertaining the nature and implications of marine scientific research.[7] In practice, the validation of a marine scientific research project by a coastal State can be a useful indicator in defining the nature of marine scientific research.[8] Nevertheless, the lack of a definition of marine scientific research leads to ambiguity and challenges for regulation, as this chapter will discuss.

Investigating the oceans

Humans have long been fascinated by the marine environment. Since ancient times, the lure of the depths has tempted explorers and scientists alike to venture into the ocean. In the past century, giant leaps have been made in the human endeavour to explore and study the ocean. From trailblazers such as William Beebe and Otis Barton, who became the first humans to dive deeper than 3000 feet in the early 1930s, and Sylvia Earle who has pioneered the use of underwater technology to study the ocean since the 1960s, submersibles and other underwater vehicles are increasingly used to learn about the marine environment.[9] With the advent of the self-contained underwater breathing apparatus (SCUBA) in the 1940s humans have been increasingly able to access the underwater world, and scientific diving has become a useful and cost-effective means of investigating shallow-water marine environments such as coral reefs.[10]

Long before humans were venturing beneath the waves, marine scientific research was being conducted from vessels, often using trawls, nets and other instruments to sample marine life and investigate oceanographic processes. Among the more famous examples are the voyages of Charles Darwin aboard the *Beagle* 1831–36, Wyville Thompson and William Carpenter aboard the *Challenger* 1872–76,[11] and Fridtjof Nansen aboard the *Fram* in the 1890s. These early pioneers confronted long-held views about the nature and extent of life in the ocean, illuminating the diversity of marine life and paving the way for subsequent advances in understanding the marine environment. Today, there are more than 800 marine scientific research vessels in operation worldwide.[12]

Advances in science and technology are transforming how marine scientific research can be conducted, blurring traditional disciplinary boundaries. The knowledge enhancing outcomes of marine scientific research are reflected in the rising levels of scientific publications.[13] Also, serendipitous scientific discoveries can be applied for commercial purposes, reflecting the often overlapping nature of 'pure' and 'applied' research.

Marine scientific research is conducted all over the world. Although some States have published reviews of their marine scientific research capability (e.g. Canada[14] and the USA)[15], a comprehensive worldwide picture of marine scientific research is still lacking. This represents a significant gap in the understanding of where and how marine scientific research is conducted and hinders the identification of opportunities for scientific collaboration and capacity building. In recognition, the establishment of a Global Ocean Science Report under the auspices of the Intergovernmental Oceanographic Commission of the United Nations Educational, Scientific and Cultural Organisation (IOC) has been proposed to address this gap.[16]

Public funding remains a major enabler of marine research, however the private sector and citizens also play a role. For example, privately-owned research equipment can be used for marine scientific research as part of collaborations between research and industry (e.g. SERPENT project)[17] or through the use of vessels as 'ships of opportunity'.[18] Private citizens might also be involved in the conduct of marine science, for example through volunteer citizen science projects.

Marine scientific research has long been an inherently global endeavour and international collaborations have been a prominent feature throughout its history – from the establishment in 1903 of the International Council for the Exploration of the Sea, the International Geophysical Year in 1957–58, the early 1960s International Indian Ocean Expedition and more recently the 2000–10 Census of Marine Life. International collaboration continues to be a key element of marine scientific research, particularly as large volumes of data are increasingly available from marine research.

The importance of marine scientific research

Advancing our knowledge of the marine environment brings many environmental, social and economic benefits. The importance of marine science for eradicating poverty; contributing to food security; conserving and managing the marine environment and resources; helping to understand, predict and respond to natural events (including marine hazards such as tsunamis, storm surges and harmful algal blooms)[19] and promoting sustainable development has been recognised by the United Nations General Assembly (UNGA).[20] There is increasing recognition of the significant role of the 'blue economy', for which marine scientific research is a prominent driver,[21] in supporting sustainable development,[22] capacity building and technology transfer.

Scientific evidence is crucial in underpinning ocean governance. The importance of advancing knowledge through marine scientific research is frequently recognised in the LOSC. It is highlighted in the LOSC Preamble, with a reference to 'promoting the study of the marine environment', and in relation to the conservation and management of marine resources and the protection and preservation of the marine environment. For example, scientific methods are needed to measure and evaluate the risks of pollution.[23]

Marine scientific research offers opportunities to advance discovery and understanding of the oceans. The ocean remains largely unexplored, particularly the deep ocean where the discovery of hydrothermal vents in the 1970s opened new opportunities to understand the origins of life. The potential for new marine biodiversity discoveries was demonstrated by the Census of Marine Life (2000–10) and the marine microbial realm still remains little understood,[24] sparking interest in marine genetic resources.[25] The use of ocean observing systems can provide natural hazard warnings and other useful information. Given the multiple benefits associated with understanding the marine environment, it is crucial to advance marine scientific research.

Addressing the complex array of challenges for ocean governance increasingly requires international and interdisciplinary approaches, highlighting the continuing need to identify opportunities and means for collaboration. The marine scientific community can play an important role in this regard, as well in the broader development and implementation of the international law of the sea. This is illustrated by the continuity and prominence of scientific and technical committees linked to the international law of the sea,[26] with roles ranging from identifying research priorities to translating scientific evidence into policy relevant advice.

The regulatory framework for marine scientific research

The LOSC provides the legal framework for the regulation of marine scientific research. It is complemented in this regard by other international, regional and national legal instruments that also contain provisions for the regulation of marine scientific research, for example the Antarctic Treaty System, the Convention on Biological Diversity,[27] the London Convention[28] and the London Protocol,[29] as well as soft law measures such as voluntary codes of conduct.

The United Nations Convention on the Law of the Sea

Throughout the LOSC there are provisions relating to the regulation of marine scientific research, particularly in Part XIII which is dedicated to the issue. These provisions include four mandatory principles for the conduct of marine scientific research:[30]

1. Marine scientific research shall be conducted exclusively for peaceful purposes;
2. Marine scientific research shall be conducted with appropriate scientific methods and means;
3. Marine scientific research shall not unjustifiably interfere with other legitimate uses of the sea, and shall be duly respected in the course of such uses; and
4. Marine scientific research shall be conducted in compliance with all relevant regulations, including those for the protection and preservation of the marine environment.

The right to conduct marine scientific research is conferred upon all States and competent international organisations.[31] They must all ensure that marine scientific research is undertaken in accordance with the LOSC and provide compensation for damage, such as pollution, resulting from measures taken in contravention of the LOSC.[32] The provisions of the LOSC regarding marine scientific research are generally considered to reflect existing and emerging customary international law. Marine scientific research is subject to different regimes in areas within, and beyond, national jurisdiction.

Marine scientific research in areas within national jurisdiction

The development of the LOSC considerably expanded the geographical extent, scope and content of coastal State jurisdiction over marine scientific research activities.[33] The LOSC establishes rights and responsibilities for both coastal States and researching States or international organisations in relation to the conduct of marine scientific research in areas under national jurisdiction, including consent regimes and a duty to provide information to the coastal State.

Consent regimes

Coastal States have the right to regulate, authorise and conduct marine scientific research in their territorial seas, exclusive economic zones and continental shelves.[34] Marine scientific research can only be conducted in these zones with the express consent of, and under any conditions set by, the coastal State.[35]

The LOSC provides that in normal circumstances States shall grant their consent for marine scientific research in their exclusive economic zones or on their continental shelves provided that it is exclusively for peaceful purposes, to increase scientific knowledge of the marine environment and for the benefit of all mankind.[36] There is a regime of implied consent under the LOSC to allow States or international organisations to proceed with a marine scientific research project provided that the coastal State has not responded to the application for consent within six months.[37] Article 247 provides for a simplified consent regime for the conduct of marine scientific research by international organisations.[38] In practice, express consent is the pathway generally used by researching States, although implied consent is used in some instances.[39]

States are obliged to establish procedures to ensure that such consent will not be delayed or unreasonably denied. There is a high approval rate for marine scientific research applications.[40] However, Article 246(5) provides that consent may be withheld by the coastal State on four accounts, namely, if the project:

1. Is of direct significance for exploration and exploitation of natural resources;
2. Involves drilling into the continental shelf, use of explosives or the introduction of harmful substances into the marine environment;
3. Involves the construction, operation or use of artificial islands, installations and structures; or
4. The consent application contains inaccurate information or if there are outstanding obligations from a prior research project.

Furthermore, the coastal State may demand the suspension or cessation of marine scientific research activities, such as in cases of non-compliance with certain conditions.[41] However, in practice, orders of suspension or cessation are rare.[42]

Official channels should be used for communications relating to consent for the conduct of marine scientific research.[43] The IOC provides template draft standard forms for applications for, and confirmation of, consent to conduct marine scientific research and preliminary cruise reports.[44] States are obliged to enact measures to facilitate marine scientific research and assist research vessels, including access to harbours.[45]

Duty to provide the coastal State with information and comply with certain conditions

Researching States and international organisations have a duty to provide the coastal State with information relating to the marine scientific research project, at least six months prior to the project commencement. This should include details of the nature, objectives, methods, geographical scope, timeframe, institutions and principal investigator involved in the project.[46]

States and international organisations undertaking marine scientific research have a duty to comply with certain conditions, including ensuring the right of the coastal State to participate or be represented in the marine scientific research project.[47] The cost of coastal State participation in a marine scientific research project is carried by the researching State or international organisation, which are advised to maximise the coastal State's involvement at all stages in order to facilitate the planning, operation and cost-effectiveness of the activity.[48] In addition to making research results internationally available, researching States are required to provide preliminary reports, results and conclusions as well as access to data and samples derived from the research to the coastal State, and to assist in the assessment and interpretation of the data.[49]

Marine scientific research in areas beyond national jurisdiction

The LOSC provisions on marine scientific research in areas beyond national jurisdiction (ABNJ) are far more liberal than in areas within national jurisdiction. The freedom to conduct marine scientific research is one of the six freedoms of the high seas.[50] Further, the right for all States and competent international organisations to conduct marine scientific research in ABNJ, i.e. in both the Area and high seas, is reiterated in Articles 256 and 257 of the LOSC. State practice indicates that data obtained through marine scientific research, particularly from ABNJ, is shared via international data repositories such as the ocean biogeographic information system (OBIS) as well as via publication in international journals.[51]

The provisions for the conduct of marine scientific research in the Area are more detailed than those for the high seas. Part XI of the LOSC provides that marine scientific research in the Area shall be conducted for the benefit of mankind as a whole.[52] The International Seabed Authority has a duty to promote and encourage the conduct of marine scientific research in the Area, the dissemination of results and the transfer of related technology and scientific knowledge to developing States. States are obliged to promote international cooperation in marine scientific research in the Area.[53]

International cooperation, capacity building and the development and transfer of marine technology

The importance of international cooperation in the development and conduct of marine scientific research and the transfer of related information and technology is highlighted in Parts XIII and XIV of the LOSC.[54] For example, technical cooperation, joint events and the exchange of experts are highlighted as means to promote the development and transfer of marine technology.[55] The establishment of national and regional marine scientific and technological research centres is identified as a means to deliver training programmes and facilitate the acquisition, processing and dissemination of marine data.[56] The importance of coordinating scientific research policies and undertaking joint programmes of research is emphasised for States bordering enclosed or semi-enclosed seas.[57]

In particular, the need to promote the development of marine science and technological capacity in developing States, for example by facilitating access to knowledge, information and technology and the development of human resources, is highlighted.[58] This is emphasised in relation to the Area[59] and in relation to the participation of land-locked and geographically disadvantaged States in marine scientific research projects.[60] The LOSC also highlights the provision of scientific and technical assistance to developing States as a priority for the protection and preservation of the marine environment.[61] The publication and dissemination of information and knowledge arising from marine scientific research is also stipulated.[62]

The importance of promoting international scientific and technical cooperation is echoed in other international treaties: for example the Convention on Biological Diversity (CBD), which also highlights the establishment of research and training programmes for the conservation and sustainable use of biodiversity,[63] and the London Convention[64] (LC) and London Protocol[65]

(LP), which emphasise the importance of cooperation in research and training for the prevention, reduction and elimination of marine pollution.[66]

Marine scientific research installations or equipment

The deployment and use of marine scientific research installations and equipment is regulated by the LOSC.[67] Researching States are generally required to remove scientific research installations or equipment on completion of the research.[68] Safety zones, not exceeding 500 metres, may be created around scientific research installations but must not obstruct established shipping routes or compromise safety at sea or navigation.[69] The challenge of protecting marine scientific research instruments and equipment deployed at sea from damage and loss remains a key issue for both researching and coastal States.[70]

Implementation

Some States have national legislation relating to marine scientific research, including 39 of the 72 member States of IOC.[71] States are encouraged to harmonise national legislation with the provisions of the LOSC.[72] The IOC and the United Nations Division for Ocean Affairs and the Law of the Sea (UNDOALOS) support States in the implementation of the LOSC provisions for marine scientific research, particularly those in Parts XIII and XIV.

The IOC has a role in promoting international cooperation in marine scientific research, capacity building, technology transfer and data-sharing. The IOC Advisory Body of Experts on the Law of the Sea (ABE-LOS) provides advice on the role of the IOC in relation to the LOSC.

The IOC collects, analyses and publishes information from States on practices in marine scientific research and technology transfer.[73] It has published guidelines for States on the transfer of marine technology,[74] and has established a capacity-building development programme to strengthen marine science institutes and a mechanism to help States to identify relevant experts and partnership opportunities. It plays a role in international cooperation projects such as the Joint Meteorological Organisation/IOC Commission for Oceanography and Marine Meteorology *in situ* observing platform support centre (JCOMMOPS) and International Oceanographic Data and Information Exchange (IODE) which facilitates international cooperation on data format standards to facilitate use of data between States. It has also developed guidelines relating to legal and practical issues associated with the deployment of profiling floats in the high seas.[75]

The UNDOALOS guide to the implementation of the provisions of the LOSC relevant to marine scientific research[76] provides a detailed description of the legal provisions of the LOSC related to marine scientific research, a discussion of the experience of States in implementing those provisions (drawing upon data collected by the IOC) and practical guidance on the implementation of the LOSC provisions.

The Antarctic Treaty System

The importance of scientific research and international cooperation in the governance of global commons is illustrated by the prominent focus given to scientific cooperation in the Antarctic Treaty System (ATS). With the establishment of the Antarctic Treaty[77] (AT) in 1959, Antarctica was proclaimed as 'a continent for peace and science'. Pre-dating the LOSC by more than two decades, the AT foreshadowed at least three of the key principles for marine scientific research that emerged in the LOSC: peaceful purposes, freedom of scientific investigation and international scientific cooperation.[78] Furthermore, the AT introduced in its Preamble the concept of scientific investigation in Antarctica being for the interests of all mankind. This concept is reflected in LOSC Part XI, namely that, the conduct of scientific investigation in the Area is to be for the benefit of all mankind. The protection of the environment, including from the adverse impacts of marine scientific research, is also a key focus of the ATS, as strengthened by the Madrid Protocol.[79]

To facilitate international cooperation in scientific investigation in Antarctica, parties are required to exchange information relating to planned scientific programmes, scientific personnel and scientific observations and results.[80] Parties have a duty to inform other parties of planned expeditions and stations in Antarctica, and other parties have a right of inspection.[81]

The Convention on the Conservation of Antarctic Marine Living Resources (CCAMLR)[82] highlights the need for international cooperation and the establishment of suitable mechanisms to promote and coordinate scientific research. Two institutions under CCAMLR are charged with facilitating and promoting scientific research, cooperation, information exchange and publication of data,[83] the Commission for the Conservation of Antarctic Marine Living Resources and the Scientific Committee on Antarctic Research (SCAR).

Self-regulation and voluntary measures

The scientific community and relevant industries have voluntarily established codes of conduct to address potential environmental impacts arising from marine scientific research. For example, the International Marine Minerals Society developed a voluntary 'Code for Environmental Management of Marine Mining', including a statement of six environmental principles for marine mining and a set of ten operating guidelines for application as appropriate at specific mining sites, applicable to scientists and industry.[84] InterRidge, an international non-profit organisation concerned with the promotion of mid-ocean ridge research, published a 'statement of commitment to responsible research practices at deep-sea hydrothermal vents' that encourages scientists to abide by a set of six guidelines with the aim to minimise disturbances to the marine environment during the course of research and ensure scientifically and environmentally sustainable use of hydrothermal vents by scientists.[85] Furthermore, the Convention for the Protection of the Marine Environment of the North-East Atlantic (OSPAR) has published a Code of Conduct for Responsible Marine Research in the Deep Seas and High Seas of the OSPAR Maritime Area.[86]

Codes of conduct illustrate an awareness in the scientific community of the potential for adverse environmental impacts arising from marine scientific research and actions taken towards minimising such impacts. However, most codes lack measures to assess effectiveness or impact, this combined their voluntary nature makes it difficult to assess their effectiveness and impact.[87]

Emerging challenges for the regulation of marine scientific research

Many of the challenges for the regulation of marine scientific research stem from technological advances since the establishment of the LOSC or from definitional gaps or ambiguity in the LOSC provisions. Scientific and technological advances can enable significant developments in marine scientific research to enhance understanding of the marine environment. However, there are also questions surrounding the legal classification of some research activities, sharing the benefits of research and environmental protection.

The absence of an internationally agreed definition of marine scientific research causes uncertainty on whether certain activities fall within the scope of the LOSC regime for marine scientific research, particularly where research involves new technologies, novel actors, marine resources or measures that entail lethal harm to marine life or manipulation of the marine environment. The application of the precautionary approach has particular relevance to marine scientific research that has the potential to conflict with the duty to protect and preserve the marine environment, codified in Article 192 of the LOSC.

Survey activities provide an example of a regulatory challenge stemming both from technological advances and a lack of legal definitions. A lack of definitions in the LOSC causes difficulty in drawing legal distinctions between hydrographic surveying and marine scientific research. Technological advances, including global positioning systems (GPS) and remotely operated vehicles, have caused controversy over the potential for a vessel to remain outside an exclusive economic zone (EEZ) whilst conducting hydrographic surveys within it. It has been suggested that the distinction between different categories of surveying and marine scientific research hinges on more than the intent and purpose for collecting data, and that the potential economic value and utility of data to coastal States must also be considered.[88]

Collaborative efforts are increasingly necessary to interpret the large volumes of marine data acquired from sophisticated ocean observation systems and disseminated through national, regional and global oceanographic data centres. The continued emergence of internationally collaborative programmes requires the coordinated involvement of many States and could provide opportunities for capacity building and technology transfer.[89]

The challenge of achieving a regulatory balance between the promotion of marine scientific research and sometimes competing factors of marine environmental protection and jurisdictional control will be illustrated through the following examples: minimising environmental impacts of marine scientific research, ocean fertilisation, ocean observation systems and marine genetic resources.

Minimising environmental impacts of marine scientific research

Marine scientific research is subject to the LOSC regime for marine environmental protection.[90] As technological advances extend the possible reach of marine scientific research to deeper and more remote parts of the ocean and the types of possible research activities expand, concerns are raised about the environmental impact of marine scientific research. A key challenge for regulation is to balance the promotion of marine scientific research, to benefit and advance our understanding of the marine environment, with the protection of the marine environment from potential adverse impacts arising from such research.

Adverse environmental impacts of marine scientific research could include physical, chemical, acoustic or accidental impacts such as the introduction of alien species, as well as general environmental impacts associated with vessels (e.g. exhaust emissions, waste, noise).[91] For example, adverse impacts of deep-sea research could be caused by: dredging; scientific drilling; the removal, displacement or disturbance of fauna; oversampling; the deployment, recovery or abandonment of research equipment; physical damage to the marine environment or high-intensity illumination from remotely operated and human occupied vehicles.[92] There are particular concerns about the environmental impacts of marine scientific research activities that intentionally perturb or manipulate the marine environment, such as conducting experiments *in situ* and ocean fertilisation.[93]

Repeat visits to some marine environments raise concerns of compounding adverse impacts of scientific research activities on fragile marine ecosystems; for example scientific research is one of the main sources of anthropogenic disturbance at hydrothermal vents.[94] There are particular concerns about the environmental impact of marine scientific research in deep-sea areas beyond national jurisdiction due to gaps in the legal regime for those areas.[95] The known environmental impacts of such scientific exploration activities are considered to be minor or negligible and short-term. However, the rate of natural recovery from anthropogenic disturbances to hydrothermal vents remains largely unknown.[96] The scientific community continues to play an active role in recognising, understanding and minimising the environmental impacts of marine scientific research, including through the development and adoption of voluntary codes of conduct[97] and the establishment of protected areas.[98]

Where marine scientific research activities involve the deliberate perturbation of the marine environment, it is prudent for research projects to seek to maximise the advancement of knowledge that can be used to support the protection of the marine environment, whilst minimising the adverse impacts of the research.[99] The LOSC duty to cooperate is an important driver of measures to achieve a balance between the duty to promote marine scientific research and the duty to protect the marine environment, for example, by reducing unnecessary repeat visits to sites.

Ocean fertilisation

Geoengineering is a deliberate intervention in the Earth's climate system, it has been proposed as an option to moderate climate change and has raised significant governance questions.[100] There are also implications for the regulation of marine scientific research involving marine geoengineering methods, such as ocean fertilisation, ocean alkalinity enhancement or carbon sequestration.[101] Ocean fertilisation has been hotly debated in the context of the international regime for the prevention of marine pollution and the control of dumping waste at sea.[102]

Ocean fertilisation activities seek to increase the production of plankton in the ocean, for example, by the direct addition of nutrients such as iron, or by increasing nutrient supply from deep water.[103] Such activities could be conducted for scientific research purposes, for example to understand the role of micro-nutrients in biological processes, or for commercial purposes. Due to an interest in ocean fertilisation as a potential geoengineering method to remove carbon dioxide from the atmosphere, and the knowledge gaps relating to the long-term environmental impacts of this activity, questions have been raised as to whether or not such activities are in breach of the LC and LP.

In 2007, the Scientific Groups of the LC and LP issued a statement of concern regarding iron fertilisation of the oceans to sequester carbon dioxide and raised questions surrounding the regulation of large-scale ocean iron fertilisation operations. The resulting resolution[104] agreed that, given the limited knowledge on the effectiveness and potential environmental impacts of ocean fertilisation, these activities should not be allowed other than for legitimate scientific research.[105] This resolution confirmed that research activities for ocean fertilisation do not constitute dumping under the LC or LP, but it also raised a subsequent question of how to assess research proposals to determine if they qualified as 'legitimate scientific research'.

Therefore, a subsequent resolution[106] adopted an Assessment Framework for Scientific Research Involving Ocean Fertilisation to be used to assess scientific research proposals on a case by case basis to determine whether a proposal constitutes legitimate scientific research.

This resolution affirmed a role for the LC-LP to work towards a global, transparent and effective control and regulatory mechanism for ocean fertilisation activities. The LC-LP Assessment Framework creates an approval process for proposed ocean fertilisation scientific research projects, consistent with the provisions of the LOSC, that requires that proposed projects satisfactorily demonstrate that the project displays 'proper scientific attributes' and that environmental impact assessment criteria have been met. The framework provides a tool to create transparency and promote international coordination in knowledge creation relating to ocean fertilisation research.[107]

The strong involvement of scientific experts within the LC-LP Scientific Groups has played an influential role in the development of the Assessment Framework and in making prompt and well-grounded decisions on ocean fertilisation possible.[108] Given the potential of geoengineering to cause conflict, engaging the scientific community in dialogue on the environmental and social implications of ocean fertilisation and other marine geoengineering activities will continue to be important to promote transparency and research into the long-term effects of such activities. The measures adopted by the LC-LP provide an example of how environmental protection provisions of the LOSC can be implemented consistently with the promotion of legitimate marine scientific research. This illustrates the importance of upholding freedom of marine scientific research while environmental protection measures are strengthened.[109]

Ocean observation systems: profiling floats and drifting buoys

Profiling floats and drifting buoys are widely used to conduct operational oceanographic observations. The use of these technologies has grown significantly since the establishment of the LOSC, particularly through initiatives such as the Array for Real-time Geostrophic Oceanography (Argo) programme, which collects and distributes temperature and salinity observations. The Global Ocean Observing System (GOOS) currently includes 3000 Argo floats and more than 1250 drifting buoys, which record surface currents, temperature and atmospheric pressure.[110] These programmes generate large amounts of data, some of which is made freely available in real-time to a wide audience, and international collaboration is increasingly necessary to analyse and interpret this data.

The use of free-floating instruments such as profiling floats and drifting buoys has raised three interlinked questions for regulation. Firstly, because the scale and nature of these programmes arguably surpasses earlier concepts of marine scientific research reflected in the LOSC, the legal status of the instruments is unclear. This raises questions on whether their use falls within the LOSC regime for marine scientific research and the extent of jurisdictional control that can be exerted by the coastal and researching State – whether it is considered as a high seas freedom or subject to coastal State jurisdictional control. Secondly, there are issues surrounding how the instruments can be protected from interference, measures for the safety of other users of the sea and the removal and recovery of instruments. Thirdly, there is a need to promote international collaboration to analyse and interpret the data obtained. Crucially, given the scale of these programmes, the regime of prior consent is impractical and challenging for compliance purposes. Therefore, it has been suggested that the current international legal framework is not able to address the issues raised by floating and drifting ocean observing instruments.[111]

These challenges are not new, they have been under consideration by relevant international organisations for some decades. Issues arising in the conduct of ocean data acquisition systems and devices (ODAS) were considered by the IOC and the Intergovernmental Maritime

Consultative Organisation (IMCO now IMO) as early as the 1960s. A draft agreement to comprehensively regulate ODAS was developed in numerous forms over the ensuing three decades,[112] however the process was inconclusive.

The potential issues of deploying profiling floats that could drift into areas under the jurisdiction of another coastal State has been recognised by IOC, including the importance of informing coastal States in advance of deployments of profiling floats that could drift into waters under their jurisdiction.[113] Draft Practical Guidelines for the collection of oceanographic data have been developed by IOC's ABE-LOS with the aim of clarifying some of the gaps left in the legal framework;[114] the provision of information to the coastal State regarding the activities is a key feature of the guidelines. IOC has also developed guidelines relating to legal and practical issues associated with the deployment of profiling floats in the Argo Program in the high seas.[115]

Floats and gliders can arguably be considered as marine scientific equipment within the LOSC regime for marine scientific research, provided that activities using this equipment are conducted consistently with the LOSC principles for the conduct of marine scientific research – for example that the data collected is used for peaceful purposes and is not intended for use in exploiting the resources of an EEZ or compilation of hydrographic or military surveys. It has been observed that a new legal regime to regulate the use of the ever increasing numbers of buoys, floats and gliders may be desirable, but not probable.[116]

Marine genetic resources

Humans still have much to discover about the nature and extent of marine life. The rich biological diversity of the oceans could offer potential opportunities for the development of new biotechnologies. The term 'bioprospecting' is often used to refer to the dynamic processes involved in research and development of marine genetic resources.[117] There are many possible applications for products derived from marine genetic resources, in industries including pharmaceuticals, cosmetics and food, and in scientific and industrial processes. However, gaps in the governance framework for marine genetic resources, particularly in ABNJ, raise regulatory considerations relating to access and benefit-sharing that have implications for marine scientific research.[118]

The potential environmental impact considerations for research activities relating to accessing marine genetic resources *in situ* include disturbance or harm to fragile marine environments and the removal or harvest of organisms.[119] Furthermore, scientific and technological developments continue to open new avenues to access genetic resources, including via online data platforms or techniques such as synthetic biology.[120]

One of the challenges for the regulation of marine genetic resources is that they are not defined in the LOSC. Given that marine scientific research is also not defined in the LOSC, it is difficult to differentiate between marine scientific research and commercially oriented 'bioprospecting' activities – particularly given that commercial outcomes could arise from serendipitous scientific discovery. This highlights the difficulty of separating pure from applied research in practice.

Research findings and benefits derived from collection activities undertaken within areas under the national jurisdiction of a coastal State, fall within the LOSC regimes for marine scientific research and technology transfer. They are also subject to the provisions of the CBD and the Nagoya Protocol on Access to Genetic Resources and the Fair and Equitable Sharing of Benefits Arising from Their Utilisation (the Nagoya Protocol),[121] in addition to any contract terms imposed upon researchers by the coastal State.[122] However, there are still uncertainties surrounding the legal status of marine genetic resources on the continental shelf beyond 200 nautical miles, particularly given challenges of applying the 'sedentary species' test.[123]

The LOSC stipulates that marine scientific research activities must not constitute the legal basis for any claim to any part of the marine environment or its resources.[124] Bio-piracy is a concern which raises questions for the legitimacy of scientific research by non-traditional actors. For example, the global ocean sampling expedition of *Sorcerer II*, which commenced in 2003, raised questions surrounding access and benefit-sharing of the genetic material obtained during the course of the voyages, which crossed areas both within and beyond national jurisdiction.[125]

Although, the CBD and the Nagoya Protocol provide some guidance for addressing concerns of access and benefit-sharing for marine genetic resources derived from areas within national jurisdiction, their applicability is limited in ABNJ.[126] Reflecting this gap in the international legal framework, marine genetic resources including questions of access and benefit-sharing are one of four key issues under consideration by the UN Ad-hoc Open-Ended Working Group to study issues relating to the conservation and sustainable use of biodiversity beyond national jurisdiction (BBNJ), which has recommended that the General Assembly decide to establish a preparatory committee to develop a new legally binding instrument under the LOSC.[127] The development of such an instrument could have implications for the regulation of marine scientific research relating to marine genetic resources in ABNJ.

Conclusion – harnessing opportunities for knowledge enhancement

Marine scientific research is crucial to enhance understanding of the marine environment, inform ocean governance and provide societal benefits. The LOSC provides a regime for the conduct of marine scientific research that emphasises international cooperation, capacity building and technology transfer, and balancing freedom of marine scientific research with coastal State jurisdictional control.

However, the lack of an internationally agreed definition for marine scientific research raises legal questions on the extent to which some activities are covered by the LOSC regime – particularly as technological developments transform where, how and by whom marine scientific research can be conducted. Examples of research activities that could cause contention include: the manipulation of the marine environment (e.g. geoengineering), the sharing of benefits (e.g. marine genetic resources) or the protection of jurisdictional rights (e.g. ocean observing systems). This creates a challenge for regulation to balance the promotion of scientific research with the protection of both the marine environment and jurisdictional rights.

The protection of the marine environment is a critical priority, particularly in ABNJ where the legal regime is far less stringent than in areas within national jurisdiction. However, there is also an urgent need to promote and facilitate marine scientific research in order to further understanding of the marine environment and inform approaches to protect it. Environmental protection considerations must be weighed against the benefits of marine scientific research, which continue to play a critical role in innovation. The scientific community is a vital stakeholder in achieving the required balance.

Strong and sustained scientific input has already been a key ingredient for success in operationalising the precautionary principle and aiding the development of legal regimes to ensure that research activities that could harm the marine environment are conducted to maximise knowledge advancement and minimise environmental impact (e.g. the assessment framework for ocean fertilisation under the LC-LP). Voluntary codes of conduct have already been developed with the aim of minimising adverse environmental impacts from scientific research; it could be interesting to explore whether there is potential for the broader application or augmentation of such measures.

There is still much to learn about the marine environment and the challenges facing ocean governance add increasing urgency to the fostering of technological advances in marine scientific research in order to enhance knowledge. It will be increasingly important to enable technologies to be promoted in national and international research programmes, whilst addressing any regulatory questions raised regarding the legal status of such technologies – a challenge that could intensify in the future as an increasing need to finance marine research from novel sources, such as the private sector, could further blur the boundary between 'pure' and 'applied' research. The promotion of marine scientific research must remain a key priority.

The promotion of marine scientific research could be supported by measures to promote international cooperation and streamline consent systems for the conduct of marine scientific research. Capacity building and the development and transfer of marine technology, inextricably linked to the progress of marine scientific research, can be facilitated by enhanced participation of young scientists and improved access to human and financial resources. Crucially, an understanding of the process of scientific endeavour is necessary in order to ensure desired outcomes and regulation that is not overly burdensome. The involvement of the marine scientific community in such a process is important, and stronger connectivity between marine science and policy is an important step in this direction.

Notes

1 *United Nations Convention on the Law of the Sea*, Opened for Signature 10 December 1982, 1833 UNTS 3 (Entered into Force 16 November 1994).
2 United Nations Division for Ocean Affairs and the Law of the Sea Office of Legal Affairs, *Marine Scientific Research: A Revised Guide to the Implementation of the Relevant Provisions of the United Nations Convention on the Law of the Sea* (United Nations, 2010) 4–6.
3 *Official Records of the Third United Nations Conference on the Law of the Sea, Revised Single Negotiating Text (part III)*, Vol 5, UN Doc. A/CONF.62/WP.8/Rev.1/Part III (6 May 1976) art 48, art 49.
4 Subsidiary Body on Scientific, Technical and Technological Advice, *Study of the Relationship between the Convention on Biological Diversity and the United Nations Convention on the Law of the Sea with Regard to the Conservation and Sustainable Use of Genetic Resources on the Deep Seabed (decision II/10 of the Conference of the Parties to the Convention on Biological Diversity)*. UN Doc. UNEP/CBD/SBSTTA/8/INF/3/Rev.1 (22 February 2003) para 47.
5 LOSC art 243.
6 See for example: Donald R Rothwell and Tim Stephens, *The International Law of the Sea* (Hart, 2010) 322; Sam Bateman, 'Hydrographic Surveying in the EEZ: Differences and Overlaps with Marine Scientific Research' (2005) 29(2) *Marine Policy* 163.
7 LOSC art 251.
8 United Nations Division for Ocean Affairs and the Law of the Sea Office of Legal Affairs, *Marine Scientific Research: A Revised Guide to the Implementation of the Relevant Provisions of the United Nations Convention on the Law of the Sea* (United Nations, 2010) 29.
9 See for example Robert D Ballard, *The Eternal Darkness: A Personal History of Deep-Sea Exploration* (Princeton University Press, 2000); Trevor Norton, *Stars beneath the Sea: The Extraordinary Lives of the Pioneers of Diving* (Arrow, 1999).
10 M A Lang, 'Coral Reef Research: Advances through the Use of Scuba' (2012) 31(1) *Underwater Technology* 21.
11 Anthony J Koslow, *Silent Deep: The Discovery, Ecology and Conservation of the Deep Sea* (University of New South Wales Press, 2007).

12 International Research Vessel Schedules and Information, http://www.researchvessels.org/about_ships.html accessed 05/02/2015.
13 See for example Laurent Godet, Kevin A Zelnio and Cindy L Van Dover, 'Scientists as Stakeholders in Conservation of Hydrothermal Vents' (2011) 25(2) *Conservation Biology* 214; Paul Oldham et al, 'Valuing the Deep: Marine Genetic Resources in Areas Beyond National Jurisdiction' (One World Analytics, 2014) 73–89.
14 Council of Canadian Academies, *Ocean Science in Canada: Meeting the Challenge, Seizing the Opportunity* (Council of Canadian Academies, 2013).
15 National Academy of Sciences, *Sea Change: 2015–2025 Decadal Survey of Ocean Sciences* (National Academies Press, 2015).
16 *Rationale for a Global Ocean Science Report*, UNESCO-IOC Assembly, 27th sess, (26 June – 5 July 2013) IOC-XXVII/Dec.5.5.2; *Proposal of a Global Ocean Science Report (GOSR)*, UNESCO-IOC Executive Council, 47th sess, IOC/EC-XLVII/3 (1–4 July 2014) EC-XLVII/Dec.6.2.
17 Scientific and Environmental ROV Partnership Using Existing Industrial Technology (SERPENT) project http://www.serpentproject.com/ accessed 26/02/2015.
18 See for example: JCOMMOPS Ship Of Opportunity Program http://www.jcommops.org/sot/soop/ accessed 26/02/2015.
19 See for example: Pacific Tsunami Warning System http://www.unesco.org/new/en/natural-sciences/ioc-oceans/sections-and-programmes/tsunami/ accessed 26/02/2015.
20 *Oceans and the Law of the Sea, Report of the Secretary-General*, UN GAOR, 64th sess, Agenda Item 76, UN Doc. A/64/66/Add.2 (19 October 2009) para 15.
21 Oceans Policy Science Advisory Group, Australian Government, *Marine Nation 2025: Marine Science to Support Australia's Blue Economy* (2013).
22 *The Future We Want*, GA Res 66/288, UN GAOR, 66th sess, 123rd plen mtg, Agenda Item 19, UN Doc. A/RES/66/288 (11 September 2012, adopted 27 July 2012); *The Road to dignity by 2030: ending poverty, transforming all lives and protecting the planet. Synthethis report of the Secretary-General on the post-2015 sustainable development agenda*, UN GAOR, 69th sess, Agenda Items 13(a) and 115, UN Doc. A/69/700 (4 December 2014).
23 See for example LOSC art 204.
24 H Abida et al, 'Bioprospecting Marine Plankton' (2013) 11(11) *Marine Drugs* 4594.
25 Genetic resources are defined as genetic material of actual or potential value under the Convention on Biological Diversity (CBD art 2).
26 For example, the Scientific Committee on Antarctic Research (SCAR) and the Scientific Groups of the London Convention and London Protocol.
27 *Convention on Biological Diversity*, Opened for Signature 5 June 1992, 1760 UNTS 79 (Entered into Force 29 December 1993).
28 *Convention on the Prevention of Marine Pollution by Dumping of Wastes and Other Matter*, Opened for Signature 29 December 1972, 1046 UNTS138 (Entered into Force 30 August 1975).
29 *Protocol to the Convention on the Prevention of Marine Pollution by Dumping of Wastes and Other Matter, 1972*, Opened for Signature 7 November 1996 (Entered into Force 24 March 2006).
30 LOSC art 240.
31 LOSC art 238.
32 LOSC art 263.
33 Donald R Rothwell and Tim Stephens, *The International Law of the Sea* (Hart, 2010) 324.
34 LOSC arts 56 (1)(b)(ii), 245, 246.
35 LOSC arts 245, 246.
36 LOSC art 246.
37 LOSC art 252.
38 See for example: '*Procedure for the application of art. 247 of the Convention by the Intergovernmental Oceanographic Commission*' IOC Res XXIII-8, UN Doc IOC-XXIII/3 (30 July 2005).
39 United Nations Division for Ocean Affairs and the Law of the Sea Office of Legal Affairs, *Marine Scientific Research: A Revised Guide to the Implementation of the Relevant Provisions of the United Nations Convention on the Law of the Sea* (United Nations, 2010) para 100.
40 Ibid para 101.
41 LOSC art 253.

42 United Nations Division for Ocean Affairs and the Law of the Sea Office of Legal Affairs, *Marine Scientific Research: A Revised Guide to the Implementation of the Relevant Provisions of the United Nations Convention on the Law of the Sea* (United Nations, 2010) para 112.
43 LOSC art 250. Examples of official channels include: Sea Law, Environment Law and Antarctic Law Section, Department of Foreign Affairs and Trade (Australia) http://www.dfat.gov.au/international-relations/themes/environment-sea-law/marine-scientific-research/Pages/marine-scientific-research-msr-requests.aspx and Maritime Policy Unit, Legal Directorate, Foreign & Commonwealth Office (UK) https://www.gov.uk/government/publications/marine-scientific-research-application-form-for-the-uk-and-overseas-territories accessed 18/01/15.
44 IOC draft standard consent forms for the conduct of marine scientific research: http://ioc-unesco.org/images/stories/LawoftheSea/Documents/MarineScientificResearch/MSR_FormA.pdf accessed 18/01/15.
45 LOSC art 255.
46 LOSC art 248.
47 LOSC art 249.
48 United Nations Division for Ocean Affairs and the Law of the Sea Office of Legal Affairs, *Marine Scientific Research: A Revised Guide to the Implementation of the Relevant Provisions of the United Nations Convention on the Law of the Sea* (United Nations, 2010) para 158.
49 LOSC art 249.
50 LOSC art 87 (1)(f).
51 United Nations Division for Ocean Affairs and the Law of the Sea Office of Legal Affairs, *Marine Scientific Research: A Revised Guide to the Implementation of the Relevant Provisions of the United Nations Convention on the Law of the Sea* (United Nations, 2010) para 116.
52 LOSC art 143.
53 LOSC arts 143, 144.
54 LOSC arts 239, 242, 243, 266, 269.
55 LOSC art 269.
56 LOSC arts 275, 276.
57 LOSC art 123.
58 LOSC arts 266, 268.
59 LOSC art 143.
60 LOSC art 254.
61 LOSC art 202.
62 LOSC art 244.
63 CBD arts 7, 12, 18.
64 LC art VIII.
65 LP art 13.
66 See also the section 'Antarctic Treaty System' of this chapter.
67 LOSC art 258.
68 LOSC art 249.
69 LOSC arts 260, 261, 261.
70 United Nations Division for Ocean Affairs and the Law of the Sea Office of Legal Affairs, *Marine Scientific Research: A Revised Guide to the Implementation of the Relevant Provisions of the United Nations Convention on the Law of the Sea* (United Nations, 2010) para 124.
71 Elizabeth J Tirpak, *Practices of States in the Fields of Marine Scientific Research and Transfer of Marine Technology: An Update of the 2005 Analysis of Member State Responses to Questionnaire No. 3*, UN Doc. IOC/ABE-LOS VIII/8 (19 March 2008).
72 *Oceans and the Law of the Sea*, GA Res 63/111, UN GAOR, 63rd sess, Agenda Item 70 (a), UN Doc A/RES/63/111 (12 February 2009, adopted 5 December 2008) para 5.
73 Elizabeth J Tirpak, *Practices of States in the Fields of Marine Scientific Research and Transfer of Marine Technology: An Update of the 2005 Analysis of Member State Responses to Questionnaire No. 3*, UN Doc. IOC/ABE-LOS VIII/8 (19 March 2008).
74 Intergovernmental Oceanographic Commission, *IOC Criteria and Guidelines on the Transfer of Marine Technology*, IOC Information Document, 1203 (UNESCO, 2005).
75 See the section 'Ocean observation systems: profiling floats and drifting buoys' of this chapter.

76 United Nations Division for Ocean Affairs and the Law of the Sea Office of Legal Affairs, *Marine Scientific Research: A Revised Guide to the Implementation of the Relevant Provisions of the United Nations Convention on the Law of the Sea* (United Nations, 2010).
77 *Antarctic Treaty*, Opened for Signature 01 December 1959, 402 UNTS (Entered into Force 23 June 1961).
78 AT arts I, II, III.
79 *Protocol on Environmental Protection to the Antarctic Treaty*, Opened for Signature 04 October 1991 (Entered into Force 14 January 1998).
80 AT arts III, VIII.
81 AT art VII.
82 *Convention on the Conservation of Antarctic Marine Living Resources*, Opened for Signature 20 May 1980, 1329 UNTS (Entered into Force 7 April 1982).
83 CCAMLR Art XI and XV.
84 *IMMS Code for Environmental Management of Marine Mining*, International Marine Minerals Society, 2001, revised 2011. http://www.immsoc.org/IMMS_code.htm accessed 7/2/15.
85 *InterRidge statement of commitment to responsible research practices at deep-sea hydrothermal vents*, (17, February 2006, Kiel) http://www.interridge.org/irstatement accessed 7/2/15; Colin Devey, Charles Fisher and Steven Scott, 'Responsible Science at Hydrothermal Vents' (2007) 20(1) *Oceanography* 162.
86 *OSPAR Code of Conduct for Responsible Marine Research in the Deep Seas and High Seas of the OSPAR Maritime Area*, OSPAR Convention for the Protection of the Marine Environment of the North-East Atlantic, 2008–1 (24 January 2008).
87 For a discussion of the implementation of the InterRidge code of conduct see: Laurent Godet, Kevin A Zelnio and Cindy L Van Dover, 'Scientists as Stakeholders in Conservation of Hydrothermal Vents' (2011) 25(2) *Conservation Biology* 214.
88 Sam Bateman, 'Hydrographic Surveying in the EEZ: Differences and Overlaps with Marine Scientific Research' (2005) 29(2) *Marine Policy* 163.
89 United Nations Division for Ocean Affairs and the Law of the Sea Office of Legal Affairs, *Marine Scientific Research: A Revised Guide to the Implementation of the Relevant Provisions of the United Nations Convention on the Law of the Sea* (United Nations, 2010).
90 LOSC art 196 and 240(d).
91 Anna-Maria Hubert, 'The New Paradox in Marine Scientific Research: Regulating the Potential Environmental Impacts of Conducting Ocean Science' (2011) 42(4) *Ocean Development and International Law* 329.
92 Cindy Lee Van Dover, 'Impacts of Anthropogenic Disturbances at Deep-Sea Hydrothermal Vent Ecosystems: A Review' in press *Marine Environmental Research*.
93 Philomène Verlaan, 'Experimental Activities That Intentionally Perturb the Marine Environment: Implications for the Marine Environmental Protection and Marine Scientific Research Provisions of the 1982 United Nations Convention on the Law of the Sea' (2007) 31(2) *Marine Policy* 210.
94 Lyle Glowka, 'Putting Marine Scientific Research on a Sustainable Footing at Hydrothermal Vents' (2003) 27(4) ibid. 303.
95 Robin Warner, 'Protecting the Diversity of the Depths: Environmenal Regulation of Bioprospecting and Marine Scientific Research Beyond National Jurisdiction' (2008) 22 *Ocean Yearbook* 411.
96 Cindy Lee Van Dover, 'Impacts of Anthropogenic Disturbances at Deep-Sea Hydrothermal Vent Ecosystems: A Review' in press *Marine Environmental Research*.
97 See the section 'Self-regulation and voluntary measures' of this chapter.
98 Lyle Glowka, 'Putting Marine Scientific Research on a Sustainable Footing at Hydrothermal Vents' (2003) 27(4) *Marine Policy* 303.
99 Philomène Verlaan, 'Experimental Activities That Intentionally Perturb the Marine Environment: Implications for the Marine Environmental Protection and Marine Scientific Research Provisions of the 1982 United Nations Convention on the Law of the Sea' (2007) 31(2) ibid. 210.
100 Royal Society, *Geoengineering the Climate: Science, Governance and Uncertainty* (Royal Society, 2009); Catherine Redgwell, 'Geoengineering the Climate: Technological Solutions to Mitigation – Failure or Continuing Carbon Addiction?' (2011) 5(2) *Carbon & Climate Law Review* 178.
101 Karen N Scott, 'The Day after Tomorrow: Ocean CO2 Sequestration and the Future of Climate Change' (2005) 18(1) *Georgetown International Environmental Law Review* 57.

102 Rosemary Rayfuse and Robin Warner, 'Climate Change Mitigation Activities in the Ocean: Turning up the Regulatory Heat' in Robin Warner and Clive Schofield (eds), *Climate Change and the Oceans: Gauging the Legal and Policy Currents in the Asia Pacific and Beyond* (Edward Elgar, 2012) 234.
103 Doug W R Wallace et al, *Ocean Fertilisation: A Scientific Summary for Policymakers* (UNESCO-IOC, 2010).
104 *Resolution LC-LP.1 (2008) on the Regulation of Ocean Fertilisation*, 30th mtg of the Contracting Parties to the London Convention and 3rd mtg of the Contracting Parties to the London Protocol (31 October 2008).
105 Legitimate scientific research is regarded as placement of matter for a purpose other than the mere disposal thereof Resolution LC-LP.1 para 3.
106 *Resolution LC-LP.2 (2010) on the Assessment Framework for Scientific Research Involving Ocean Fertilisation*, 32nd Consultative Mtg of the Contracting Parties to the London Convention and 5th mtg of the Contracting Parties to the London Protocol (14 October 2010).
107 Till Markus and Harald Ginzky, 'Regulating Climate Engineering: Paradigmatic Aspects of the Regulation of Ocean Fertilization' (2011) 5(4) *Carbon & Climate Law Review* 477.
108 Ibid.
109 Anna-Maria Hubert, 'The New Paradox in Marine Scientific Research: Regulating the Potential Environmental Impacts of Conducting Ocean Science' (2011) 42(4) *Ocean Development and International Law* 329.
110 GOOS http://ioc-goos.org/ accessed 26/02/2015.
111 Katharina Bork et al, 'The Legal Regulation of Floats and Gliders – in Quest of a New Regime?' (2008) 39(3) *Ocean Development & International Law* 298.
112 See for example *Draft Convention on the Legal Status of Ocean Data Acquisition Systems, Aids and Devices (ODAS)* Intergovernmental Oceanographic Commission of UNESCO (IOC), IOC Assembly, 17th sess, Agenda Item 9.1.2, UN doc IOC-XVII/Inf.1 (21 January 1993).
113 *The Argo Project*, IOC Res XX-6, Intergovernmental Oceanographic Commission of UNESCO (IOC) Assembly, 20th sess, Agenda Item 3.1.2, UN Doc IOC-XX/3 Annex II (20 August 1999).
114 *Draft [Practical] Guidelines of IOC, Within the Context of UNCLOS, for the Collection of Oceanographic Data By Specific Means*, Intergovernmental Oceanographic Commission of UNESCO, 7th mtg of the Advisory Body of Experts on the Law of the Sea, IOC, Agenda Item 3.2, UN Doc IOC/ABE-LOS VII/7 (19 February 2007).
115 *Guidelines for the Implementation of Resolution XX-6 of the IOC Assembly Regarding the Deployment of Profiling Floats in the high seas within the framework of the Argo programme*, IOC Executive Council Res EC-XLI.4, Executive Council of the Intergovernmental Oceanographic Commission of UNESCO (IOC), 41st sess, Agenda Item 4.2.2, UN Doc IOC/EC-XLI/3 Annex II (29 July 2008).
116 Katharina Bork et al, 'The Legal Regulation of Floats and Gliders – in Quest of a New Regime?' (2008) 39(3) *Ocean Development & International Law* 298.
117 See Chapter 19.
118 See for example: David K Leary, *Publications on Ocean Development, Volume 56: International Law and the Genetic Resources of the Deep Sea* (Brill Academic Publishers, 2006); Lyle Glowka, 'Evolving Perspectives on the International Seabed Area's Genetic Resources: Fifteen Years after the Deepest of Ironies' in David Vidas (ed), *Law, Technology and Science for Oceans in Globalisation: Iuu Fishing, Oil Pollution, Bioprospecting, Outer Continental Shelf* (Martinus Nijhoff, 2010) 397; Arianna Broggiato et al, 'Fair and Equitable Sharing of Benefits from the Utilization of Marine Genetic Resources in Areas Beyond National Jurisdiction: Bridging the Gaps between Science and Policy' (2014) 49(0) *Marine Policy* 176.
119 Cindy Lee Van Dover, 'Impacts of Anthropogenic Disturbances at Deep-Sea Hydrothermal Vent Ecosystems: A Review' in press *Marine Environmental Research*.
120 David Leary and S Kim Juniper, 'Addressing the Marine Genetic Resources Issue: Is the Debate Heading in the Wrong Direction?' in Clive H Schofield, Seokwoo Lee and Moon-Sang Kwon (eds), *The Limits of Maritime Jurisdiction* (Brill Academic Publishers, 2013) 769.
121 *Nagoya Protocol on Access to Genetic Resources and the Fair and Equitable Sharing of Benefits Arising from Their Utilization to the Convention on Biological Diversity*, Opened for Signature 29 October 2010 (Entered into Force 12 October 2014).
122 See for example Craig H Allen, 'Protecting the Oceanic Gardens of Eden: International Law Issues in Deep-Sea Vent Resource Conservation and Management' (2001) 13(3) *Georgetown International Environmental Law Review* 563.

123 Joanna Mossop, 'Regulating Uses of Marine Biodiversity on the Outer Continental Shelf' in David Vidas (ed), *Law, Technology and Science for Oceans in Globalisation: IUU Fishing, Oil Pollution, Bioprospecting, Outer Continental Shelf* (2010) 319.
124 LOSC art 241.
125 http://www.jcvi.org/cms/research/projects/gos/overview accessed 31/01/15; Henry Nicholls, 'Sorcerer II: The Search for Microbial Diversity Roils the Waters' (2007) 5(3) *PLoS Biology* e74.
126 Robin Warner, 'Protecting the Diversity of the Depths: Environmenal Regulation of Bioprospecting and Marine Scientific Research Beyond National Jurisdiction' (2008) 22 *Ocean Yearbook* 411.
127 Recommendations of the Ad Hoc Open-Ended Informal Working Group to study issues relating to the conservation and sustainable use of marine biological diversity beyond areas of national jurisdiction to the sixty-ninth session of the General Assembly, 23 January 2015 https://www.un.org/depts/los/biodiversityworkinggroup/documents/AHWG_9_recommendations.pdf.

15

Deep Seabed Mining: Key Obligations in the Emerging Regulation of Exploration and Development in the Pacific

Robert Makgill and Ana P. Linhares*

Introduction

New technological developments and increasing commodity prices mean that mining of the deep seabed is increasingly seen as commercially feasible.[1] The Pacific Ocean's vast seabed mineral deposits are viewed as a potential treasure trove for those able to fund deep seabed exploration and development. However, deep sea mineral deposits are often found at depths of between 4,500 to 5,500 metres and are located in unique environments.[2] The process of mining deep seabed resources is immensely difficult.[3] Technically it "has been compared to standing atop a New York City skyscraper on a windy day, trying to suck up marbles off the street below with a vacuum cleaner attached to a long hose".[4] In environmental terms little scientific information on the effects of seabed mining on deep sea ecosystems currently exists,[5] but it is thought that they are likely to be sensitive to changes in light, noise and vibration caused by mining activities.[6]

The capital-intensive character of deep seabed mining makes it an investment that relies on funding from developed States or the private sector. To date, despite the potential rewards,[7] there has only been a modest level of investment in deep seabed mining throughout the Pacific. Nevertheless, a number of fledgling proposals within the Region may represent an emerging deep seabed minerals industry. One such proposal led the Republic of Nauru, in 2008, to seek an advisory opinion from the Seabed Disputes Chamber of the International Tribunal for the Law of the Sea (the Chamber) on questions regarding States Parties' obligations and liability/responsibility for deep seabed mining in the Area. The Chamber agreed to exercise its advisory opinion jurisdiction and proceedings took place in the later part of 2010.

The Chamber delivered its Advisory Opinion on 1 February 2011[8] finding that State Parties have a general obligation of due diligence to adopt "laws and regulations" and to take "administrative measures which are, within the framework of its legal system, reasonably appropriate for securing compliance by persons under its jurisdiction".[9] Putting meat on the bones of due diligence the Chamber went on to identify the direct obligations of sponsoring States under the 1982 United Nations Convention on the Law of the Sea (LOSC) and general international law. Key amongst these direct obligations is the precautionary approach, best environmental practices, and environmental impact assessment (EIA).[10] The Chamber afforded particular attention to the meaning and application of these obligations international law. Importantly, the Chamber found that States would be liable for damage to the environment arising from any failure to satisfy these obligations.[11] Equally, satisfying these obligations would exempt State Parties from "liability for damage".[12]

The Advisory Opinion, therefore, provided strong incentive for Pacific States, entertaining seabed mining activities within their jurisdiction, to enact appropriate laws and regulation. Consequently the precautionary approach, best environmental practices, and EIA have all found expression in a number of subsequent legislative initiatives across the Region. These include the: (a) European Union and Secretariat of the Pacific Community Regional Legislative and Regulatory Framework for Deep Sea Minerals Exploration and Exploitation (Regional Framework);[13] (b) Cook Islands National Seabed Minerals Policy 2014; (c) Tongan Seabed Mining Act 2014; and (d) New Zealand's Exclusive Economic Zone and Continental Shelf (Environmental Effects) Act 2012 (EEZ Act). It is noteworthy that despite the fact the Chamber's opinion concerned the Area, these initiatives generally seek to apply the key obligations to deep sea mining within the exclusive economic zone (EEZ) and continental shelf of various States. This is because Pacific States have sovereign rights over extensive marine areas that are rich in seabed minerals,[14] and there is a general acceptance that the Chamber's opinion applies more broadly than the Area.

Despite the potential riches locked within deep sea minerals, significant hurdles stand in the way of development. Even when the technical obstacles to recovering deep sea minerals have been arguably overcome, the practical steps required to satisfy the key obligations have remained a significant obstacle. This was indeed the case of the first two seabed mining proposals to be considered under New Zealand's EEZ Act. As with other Pacific States, New Zealand's EEZ and continental shelf covers a vast area and information concerning the marine environment and existing users (e.g. fisheries) is sparse. The proponents of seabed mining have found it difficult to fill the gaps (and more often void) in the baseline information necessary to support their applications. This has meant that the EIAs supporting their applications have been unable to even satisfy the reduced information requirements enabled under a precautionary approach, or demonstrate that they satisfy best environmental practices. This has resulted in criticism from certain members of the mining industry that the obligations are too stringent. However, neither of the New Zealand applications was led by a major international company with a proven track record in mining activities (e.g. BHP Billiton or De Beers). It may be that such companies have decided the lack of information concerning New Zealand's EEZ makes seabed mining too commercially risky at this juncture in time. Whatever the case, the decisions made in New Zealand have signalled that baseline data is required to proceed where imperfect information requires a precautionary approach. It might be said in these circumstances, that the key obligations identified by the Chamber are serving the regulatory function for which they were intended.

This chapter does not attempt to provide an exhaustive commentary on all the arguments surrounding the exploration and development of deep sea minerals. Rather, it examines how the key obligations identified in the Advisory Opinion have been adopted in the Pacific Region as regulatory prerequisites to deep sea mining exploration and development. The lead author was legal counsel in the Advisory Opinion proceedings, advised Pacific governmental and inter-governmental agencies in the wake of the Advisory Opinion, represented the New Zealand Law Society during the enactment of the EEZ Act, and went on to represent commercial fishing interests in the first public hearing of an application to undertake seabed mining in

New Zealand's EEZ. This chapter draws on that background, primary documents, and recent literature to provide a picture of how the obligations identified by the Chamber have been approached by regulators across the Pacific and interpreted by decision-makers in respect of recent seabed mining proposals under New Zealand's EEZ Act.

The Chamber's Advisory Opinion on Deep Sea Mining

The Law of the Sea Convention and the Area

The LOSC governs the exploration and development of marine natural resources both within and beyond areas of national jurisdiction. It delimits marine areas into different zones and regulates States Parties' jurisdiction. Rights to develop natural resources are attended by corresponding obligations to protect and preserve the marine environment. Seabed mining in marine areas beyond national jurisdiction is provided for under Part XI of the LOSC. These marine spaces are collectively described as the Area. The Area is defined as "the seabed and ocean floor and subsoil thereof, beyond the limits of national jurisdiction".[15] "Activities in the Area" is defined as meaning "all activities of exploration for, and exploitation of, the resources of the Area".[16] The resources[17] of the Area are described as the *common heritage of mankind*.[18] Simply, put, resources of the Area are vested in mankind as a whole, and are not subject to alienation, except in accordance with Part XI of the LOSC and the rules, regulations and procedures of the International Seabed Authority (ISA).[19]

Activities in the Area may be undertaken by "States Parties, or state enterprises or natural or juridical persons which possess the nationality of States Parties or are effectively controlled by them or their nationals".[20] While States Parties are entitled to apply to the ISA to undertake activities in the Area under the LOSC, in practice (particularly in the case of developing States) such activities will usually be carried out by private companies or state owned entities.[21] Mining companies or state-owned entities need to be sponsored by a State Party to the LOSC prior to seeking approval for mining activities. All mining activities must be carried out in accordance with a plan of work approved by the ISA.[22] The Chamber is a judicial body within ITLOS with the exclusive function of interpreting the LOSC's provisions on the Area (Part XI).[23] The Chamber has jurisdiction to provide advisory opinions at the request of the ISA on legal questions arising within the scope of their functions.[24] The purpose of the advisory jurisdiction of the Chamber is to provide the ISA with independent judicial assistance in interpretation of the LOSC.[25]

Nauru's request for an advisory opinion

On 10 April 2008, the ISA received the first two applications to explore for polymetallic nodules in the Area. The applications concerned the Clarion-Clipperton Zone, which is located in the eastern central Pacific to the south and south-east of the Hawaiian Islands. The Clarion-Clipperton Zone is considered to hold the most promise in terms of commercially viable manganese nodule recovery within the Area.[26] The applications were sponsored by the Republic of Nauru and the Kingdom of Tonga and applied to that part of the Clarion-Clipperton Zone reserved for developing nations. In each case, the companies submitting the application had been recently incorporated in the sponsoring State and were subsidiaries of Nautilus Minerals Inc.,[27] a Canadian ocean mining company already involved in the development of polymetallic sulphides in the EEZ of Papua New Guinea. However, Nauru became concerned about its potential liability for environmental damage to the Area and requested the ISA seek an advisory opinion from the Chamber on the obligations and liability of sponsoring States.[28]

Nauru's chief concern was whether it would be held liable for a seabed mining incident in the Area caused by a third party (i.e. the sponsored entity). In its request for an advisory opinion, Nauru argued that it could not afford exposure to the legal risks potentially associated with deep seabed mining. Further, its sponsorship of the company was premised on the assumption that Nauru could effectively mitigate (with a high degree of certainty) the potential liabilities or costs arising from its sponsorship.[29] Nauru maintained that, without clarity on issues of State responsibility and liability it would be difficult for developing States to sponsor activities in the Area, as it would not be possible for them to adequately assess the potential risks and liabilities that may arise, or to be in a position to take steps to mitigate such risks. Nauru concluded by submitting that all this meant that developing States might be precluded from effectively participating in activities in the Area.[30] The ISA granted Nauru's request for an advisory opinion and put three questions to the Chamber, which can be summarised as : (a) obligations with respect to the sponsorship of activities in the Area; (b) liability for any failure to comply with those obligations; and (c) necessary measures that must be taken in order to fulfil those obligations.[31] The Chamber's answers to those questions are discussed below.

Obligations of state parties

The Chamber identified three critical provisions of the LOSC setting out the obligations of sponsoring States. These provisions are: (a) article 139(1) that "States Parties shall have *the responsibility to ensure* that activities in the Area ... shall be carried out in conformity with" Part XI (the Area) of the LOSC; (b) article 153(1) that "States Parties shall assist the Authority by *taking all measures necessary to ensure such compliance* in accordance with article 139"; and (c) Annex III, article 4(4) that a "State Party has *adopted laws and regulations and taken administrative measures* which are, within the framework of its legal system, reasonably appropriate for securing compliance by persons under its jurisdiction." The Chamber chose to focus on the meaning of the phrase "responsibility to ensure" under article 139 determining that it establishes an obligation on States to apply the rules of the LOSC to entities of their nationality and under their control.[32] To ensure that sponsored contractors meet the standards required under the LOSC, sponsoring States are under an obligation to appropriately control entities within their jurisdiction through implementation and enforcement of domestic legislation. A breach of this obligation may attract liability to the sponsoring State.[33]

Importantly, the sponsoring State's obligation "to ensure" is not an obligation to achieve the sponsored contractor's compliance with domestic law in each and every case. Instead, it is an obligation for the sponsoring State to "deploy adequate means, to exercise best possible efforts, to do the utmost to achieve this result". The Chamber found that this obligation can be characterised as an obligation "of conduct" and not "of result", and as an obligation of "due diligence".[34] Due diligence requires States to ensure that activities within their jurisdiction or control do not cause damage to the environment of other States or to areas beyond the limits of national jurisdiction.[35] The Chamber drew on authority from the International Court of Justice (ICJ) in *Pulp Mills on the River Uruguay*[36] to illustrate the connection between the obligation to ensure and due diligence. Particular emphasis was placed on the ICJ's description of due diligence as "an obligation which entails not only the adoption of appropriate rules and measures, but also a certain level of *vigilance* in their enforcement and the exercise of administrative control applicable to public and private operators."[37] In short, due diligence requires rules, enforcement and effective public administration. This requires States to enact laws, make regulations, and take administrative measures which are "reasonably appropriate for securing compliance by persons under [their] jurisdiction".[38]

The Advisory Opinion states that the obligations of States are not limited to the due diligence "obligation to ensure". The LOSC and related instruments make provision for a number of "direct obligations".[39] Compliance with these obligations can be relevant factors in satisfying the due diligence obligation.[40] The Advisory Opinion lists a number of these direct obligations including: (a) the obligation to assist the ISA in the exercise of control over activities in the Area; (b) the obligation to apply a precautionary approach; (c) the obligation to apply best environmental practices; (d) the obligation to take measures to ensure the provision of guarantees in the event of an emergency order by the ISA for protection of the marine environment; (e) the obligation to ensure the availability of recourse for compensation in respect of damage caused by pollution; and (f) the obligation to conduct EIAs.[41] This chapter focuses on three key obligations including the precautionary approach, best environmental practice and EIA (key obligations). These obligations are distinct from the other obligations identified by the Chamber for four principal reasons.

First, they are norms of international environmental law with broad application. Despite their soft law foundations, these key obligations are increasingly included in a wide range of international agreements. This has led the ICJ and the Chamber to identify the precautionary approach and EIA as emergent norms of customary international law. The ICJ found in *Pulp Mills* that undertaking an EIA "may now be considered a requirement under general international law ... where there is a risk that the proposed industrial activity may have a significant adverse impact in a transboundary context, in particular, on a shared resource".[42] The Chamber more cautiously observed in the advisory opinion "that the precautionary approach has been incorporated into a growing number of international treaties and other instruments, many of which reflect the formulation of Principle 15 of the Rio Declaration ... this has initiated a trend towards making this approach part of customary international law."[43] David Freestone appears to consider that such caution is unnecessary contending that "[t]hese highly important environmental obligations may now be argued to be requirements of general application."[44] Although the principle of best environmental practice has not been similarly endorsed by the international judiciary at this point in time, it is notable that the term does appear in a number of important international treaties governing marine areas.[45]

Second, these obligations put the meat on the bones of the due diligence obligation.[46] They seek to prevent damage to the environment, or at least minimise the risk of such damage, by directly addressing the potential adverse impacts a proposed activity might have on the environment. As such, they fall into a category of obligations that can be satisfied prior to undertaking seabed mining activities.

Third, preventative measures are an important part of the Advisory Opinion because, as the Chamber points out, their purpose is to exempt States from "liability for damage".[47] Furthermore, however, from a practical point of view, the adoption of preventive measures minimises the risk of damage from which liability might arise. Where there is no damage, there is no liability. Irrespective of whether preventative measures apply as customary law, their implementation must be considered prudent because it reduces the risk of liability even being brought into question. In simple terms, it makes sense to take preventative measures if it reduces the risk of a dispute about liability with another state. Thus, even if these obligations did not apply outside the Area as a matter of customary law, it would be prudent for States to include them in their domestic legislation in order to minimise the risk of liability in the case of environmental damage to areas over which they do not have exclusive jurisdiction.

Fourth, the precautionary approach, best environmental practices and EIA are more widely applicable under the LOSC ocean governance framework than the other direct obligations enunciated in the Advisory Opinion. This means that they can be utilised by States Parties in the exercise of their rights and obligations, or jurisdiction, within other LOSC zones. As will be discussed, the Advisory Opinion has indeed encouraged States Parties within the Pacific Region to apply these obligations in domestic legislation intended to govern natural resource activities in both the Area and the EEZ.

Liability for failure to comply with obligations

Nauru sought the Advisory Opinion to establish whether it had liability for environmental damage caused by a sponsored contractor in the Area. The principal concern put forward by Nauru was that "if a developing State can be held liable for activities in the Area, the State may potentially face losing more than it actually has".[48] Nauru's concern highlights a dilemma faced by all States considering deep sea resource development. The Deep Water Horizon disaster provides a vivid reminder to States of the risks associated with deep sea drilling, with the final cost to British Petroleum estimated to be somewhere in the vicinity of $US 41 billion.[49] Seabed development presents a multitude of hazards connected with the volatile nature of the marine environment and biological hazards directly connected with development.[50] It is too early to determine whether nodule exploitation will cause serious environmental effects.[51] Developed States could find it difficult to compensate an injured State, *erga omnes* based claim,[52] in the event of significant environmental damage. Developing States, as evidenced through Nauru's concerns, could quite simply find compensation beyond their financial means.[53] It was against this background that the ISA sought the Chamber's opinion on "the extent of liability of a State Party for any failure to comply with the provisions of the Convention".

Liability arises from the failure of a State to carry out its obligations, rather than the failure of a contractor to meet its obligations.[54] Therefore, damage arises from a State's failure to ensure activities are carried out in accordance with the LOSC.[55] To establish liability, a causal link must exist between the damage caused by the contractor and the failure of the State to meet its obligations.[56] Such a link cannot be presumed.[57] To prove the causal link it must be shown there is damage resulting from a State's failure to meet its obligations under the LOSC.[58] States are exempt from liability if they have taken "all necessary and appropriate measures to secure effective compliance" under the LOSC.[59]

The Chamber noted that neither the LOSC, nor the Regulations, specify what constitutes compensable damage, or who is entitled to claim damage. Nevertheless, the Chamber found that damage includes "damage to the Area and its resources constituting the common heritage of mankind, and damage to the marine environment".[60] Likely claimants in respect of damages include the ISA, entities engaged in seabed mining, users of the sea, and coastal States.[61] Importantly, "[e]ach State Party may also be entitled to claim compensation in light of the *erga omnes* character of obligations relating to preservation of the environment of the high seas in the Area".[62] As to the quantum of damage, the Chamber referred to Annex III, article 22 which states that liability is for the actual amount of damage.[63] The Chamber further observed that the obligation for a State to provide full compensation (*restituto in integrum*) is part of international law.[64] Consequently, liability of a sponsoring State is said to be for actual damage.[65] The form of compensation would depend on both the nature of the damage and the technical feasibility of restoring the situation to the *status quo ante*.[66]

It would be prudent for States Parties to heed the Chamber's findings on liability with regard to their rights and obligations outside the Area. For example, a more general provision on state responsibility and liability for protection of the marine environment is found under article 235 of the LOSC. Anton adds that "[d]espite any limits that exist under" Part XI of the LOSC "states have comprehensive and detailed obligations established by a large number of treaties and customary international law to protect and preserve the marine environment . . .", and "[a] breach of these wide ranging obligations . . . that is attributable to a state is a wrongful act for which a state is responsible under international law and for which the state must make reparations".[67] This is a salient reminder that there are a broader set of obligations under international law for States to ensure that activities within their jurisdiction do not cause damage to another State, or States exercising the right of *erga omnes*. States may be held liable for failure to satisfy obligations applying to other jurisdictions within the LOSC framework. States wishing to reduce the risk of liability would be sensible to look to the Chamber's findings.

Necessary and appropriate measures to fulfil obligations

The question on measures was the most difficult one for the Chamber to answer in detail. The LOSC stipulates that States must adopt laws and regulations, and take administrative measures, including the establishment of enforcement mechanisms.[68] However, it does not provide any express guidance on the laws and regulations that should be adopted in order to fulfil a State's obligations. The Chamber was clearly cognisant of the need to exercise care in respect of sovereign decision-making. The Advisory Opinion, therefore, states the scope and extent of the laws and regulations, and administrative measures required, will depend upon the legal system of each State.[69] It is for States to determine appropriate policy measures.[70] The Chamber limited itself to statements of sound regulatory and administrative principles such as: (a) necessary laws, regulations and administrative measures should be in force at all times;[71] and (b) national measures must be reviewed on an on-going basis to ensure that they continue to meet current standards, and that contractors are meeting their obligations.[72]

In keeping with sound regulation, the Chamber found Nauru's proposal that it could satisfy its obligations through contract with a sponsored entity to be unsatisfactory.[73] It observed that "[m]ere contractual obligations between the sponsoring State and the sponsored contractor may not serve as an effective substitute for the laws and regulations and administrative measures" as they would not "establish legal obligations that could be invoked against the sponsoring State by entities other than the sponsored contractor."[74] Moreover, a contractual approach would lack transparency making it "difficult to verify, through publicly available measures, that the sponsoring State had met its obligations".[75] Rather, "the role of the sponsoring State is to contribute to the common interest of all States in the proper implementation of the principle of the common heritage of mankind . . . with a view to ensuring that entities under its jurisdiction conform to the rules on deep seabed mining. Contractual arrangements alone cannot satisfy the obligation . . .".[76]

Although the Chamber took pains to distance itself from making findings on the regulatory and administrative measures States should take, the reality is, it did not need to identify specific measures. This had already been achieved through the identification of State obligations. The logic contained in the Chamber's answers to the first two questions provides sufficient guidance as to the types of measures States should seek to implement if they wish to avoid liability. States are required under the LOSC and general international law to satisfy a number of direct obligations. Failure to satisfy those obligations causing damage to the marine environment will result in State liability for that damage. Liability may be avoided through the adoption of regulatory and administrative measures that give effect to the direct obligations (e.g. precautionary approach, best environmental practices and EIA). Regulatory and administrative implementation of these obligations will also serve to reduce the risks associated with development. They therefore provide a practical form of insurance against the potential for damage and liability.

The advisory opinion's key obligations

Precautionary approach

An integral part of a States Party's due diligence obligation (and arguably the most critical direct obligation set out in the Advisory Opinion) is the requirement to take a precautionary approach "in situations where scientific evidence concerning the scope and potential negative impact of the activity in question is insufficient but where there are plausible indications of potential risks".[77] The absence of full scientific information is one of the most fundamental problems faced by regulatory bodies tasked with complex environmental decisions concerning the development of natural resources. One of the chief roles of science in the preparation of an EIA is the prediction of potential impacts. This is a virtually insurmountable responsibility when prediction is hampered by a lack of knowledge concerning the biophysical environment.[78] The precautionary approach provides a mechanism for managing the risk of damage in the absence of complete scientific information. It moves away from the primacy of scientific proof. Instead, it emphasises the limitations of scientific prediction, and "the need for decision-making that errs on the side of allowing for worst case scenarios".[79]

International recognition of the importance of taking a precautionary approach in the absence of full scientific information was achieved during the Rio Summit in 1992. Principle 15 of the Rio Declaration urges States not to postpone environmental action due to lack of full scientific certainty:[80]

> In order to protect the environment, the precautionary approach shall be widely applied.... Where there are threats of serious or irreversible damage, lack of full scientific certainty shall not be used as a reason for postponing cost-effective measures to prevent environmental degradation.

The precautionary approach reverses the idea that it is better to obtain scientific information before action is taken.[81] It represents an important departure from "scientific absolutism" which extols "that decisions should be taken on the basis of scientific findings or in light of knowledge available at the time, an approach whose consequence was that lack of full certainty meant no action."[82] The precautionary approach is, therefore, important because it enables activities with uncertain risks to be undertaken if appropriate steps are taken to identify and prevent serious or irreversible damage before it occurs.

The application of the precautionary approach is by no means free from debate. The diversity of formulations means that there is a degree of pluralism in terms of its meaning and implementation, especially at a domestic level.[83] Argument exists as to whether the precautionary approach only requires consideration of precautionary action as opposed to taking precautionary action.[84] Questions have been raised as to whether the "serious or irreversible damage" threshold for the triggering the approach is too high. The degree to which the precautionary approach should be driven by science as opposed to public perception has also been a source of contention.[85] These concerns invariably boil down to simple arguments of whether the application of precaution is too onerous, or not onerous enough. These are valid considerations for States wishing to encourage economic development and prosperity while ensuring that proponents of development adopt sufficient steps to avoid the possibility of environmental catastrophe. Nevertheless, as discussed, the precautionary approach provides a mechanism not only for managing the risk of damage, but also the risk of liability for damage. States relying on the precautionary approach to limit potential liability for transboundary pollution are going to be put under close scrutiny by States on the receiving end of any failure to prevent environmental degradation (including those exercising *erga omnes* rights).

The LOSC does not make express provision for the precautionary approach. Nevertheless, the Chamber observed in its Advisory Opinion that the precautionary approach has been incorporated into a growing number of international treaties and other instruments, many of which reflect the formulation of Principle 15 of the Rio Declaration. This has, as discussed, initiated a trend towards making the precautionary approach part of customary international law.[86] The Chamber noted, in respect of the obligation to apply a precautionary approach, that the ISA's Nodules Regulations[87] and the Sulphides Regulations[88] contain provisions requiring sponsoring States to "apply a precautionary approach, as reflected in Principle 15 of the Rio Declaration".[89] This principle has therefore been elevated from a non-binding statement into a legal obligation binding on States Parties to the LOSC.[90]

Importantly, the Chamber found that a precautionary approach is an integral part of the general obligation of due diligence of sponsoring States, and is therefore applicable outside the scope of the Regulations.[91] The Chamber's finding on the precautionary principles trend towards customary law together with its application beyond the Regulations, strongly suggest that the precautionary obligation applies more broadly than just the Area. These findings also support the view that the Rio Declaration's version of the precautionary approach is the one that is generally applicable under international law. This is consistent with observations that there is no substantive distinction between the precautionary principle and the precautionary approach under international law. Rather, the content of the obligation and the way it is enforced is defined by the context within which it is implemented.[92] It is also consistent with observations that Principle 15 reflects the content of the precautionary approach under customary international law.[93]

The ISA and Secretariat of the Pacific Community held a joint workshop in Fiji in late 2011 entitled *Environmental Management Needs for Exploration and Exploitation of Deep Sea Minerals* (Fiji Workshop). The outcomes of workshops conducted on EIA, legal issues and capacity building are reported in ISA Technical Study No. 10.[94] The Study indicates that the precautionary approach might be incorporated into decision-making through:[95]

- Regular reporting of data on environmental impacts and pre-emptive action to avert serious harm to the marine environment.
- Adopting an incremental test bed approach to a mining activity where impacts are uncertain, e.g. authorise test mining rather than immediately authorising commercial-scale activity.

These are examples of an adaptive management approach. Adaptive management promotes learning based decision-making in circumstances where there is imperfect scientific information concerning the likely effects of a proposed activity. It enables regulators to obtain further information throughout the life of a project and allows for on-going assessment of the impacts of activities.[96] Adaptive management is in line with the precautionary approach because it acknowledges scientific uncertainty, but enables action to be undertaken while remaining flexible enough to respond to new information.[97] Initial regulatory approval for an activity is followed by a period of monitoring and reporting. If monitoring reveals adverse effects, or new information becomes available which indicates that current practices are no longer appropriate (for example, if it becomes apparent certain unacceptable environmental effects are occurring), the programme of work should be amended to reflect any changes that are necessary to avoid or mitigate those effects.[98] If those effects cannot be avoided or mitigated, and there is a risk of serious or irreversible damage, the operation of the activity may need to cease until such time as the risk is brought under control.

Best environmental practices

The Chamber states in the Advisory Opinion that, "in light of the advancement in scientific knowledge", States Parties have become convinced of the need "to apply 'best environmental practices' in general terms so that they may be seen to have become enshrined in the ... obligation of due diligence."[99] This statement illustrates how the Chamber views due diligence as a variable obligation that can change over time in response to new information.[100] It is also significant because its use of the word "enshrined" supports interpretations of the advisory opinion which suggest that due diligence has elevated best environmental practices to an obligation of customary status. If best environmental practice does have customary status by virtue of due diligence, it would follow that States have an obligation to apply best environmental practices where activities under their jurisdictional control create a risk of transboundary damage to other States.

The Sulphides Regulations and standard clauses oblige States to apply best environmental practices.[101] There is no reference to best environmental practices in the earlier Nodules Regulations, which employs instead the term best technology available. The Chamber appears to be of the view that the requirement for best environmental practices under the regulations and standard clauses heralds a rise in standard from the use of best technology available.[102] Best environmental practice certainly appears to be a much broader concept than best technology available. A survey of the former in a variety of international instruments shows that it means "the application of the most appropriate combination of environmental control measures and strategies",[103] whereas the latter appears to be limited by what is technologically achievable at the time.

Best environmental practices are defined in the ISA Technical Study as "widely accepted norms or customs of environmental risk management".[104] This definition acknowledges the soft law roots of best environmental practice and the fact that certain practices are evolving into harder forms of international law (e.g. EIA and the precautionary approach). The term best environmental practice derives from the more general term "best practices". Best practices refer to exemplary models of action for addressing social, economic and environmental challenges. They are approaches that have been shown, over time, to be the most effective. Traditionally used by corporations to establish industry standards, best practices are now also used by governments and regulatory agencies to identify minimum standards of conduct.[105] This includes the use of best practices in international non-binding agreements and to co-ordinate domestic regulatory action between different States.[106]

The Rio Declaration's 27 non-binding principles for sustainable development can be fairly described as the foundation stones of international best environmental practice.[107] Those principles include: the application of the precautionary approach to prevent environmental degradation

Deep Seabed Mining: Key Obligations

(Principle 15); and undertaking EIA where an activity is likely to have a significant adverse impact on the environment (Principle 17). The precautionary approach and EIA can therefore be described as examples of international best environmental practices for achieving sustainable development. These principles are often employed in conjunction with one another. The ISA Technical Study recommends, for example, that "where there is incomplete information and no established best practices, best environmental practice requires that the precautionary approach be applied".[108]

It was probably not lost on the Chamber that the key direct obligations are provided for together under a number of other international agreements designed to protect the marine environment. The Helsinki Convention and the OSPAR Convention both make provision for best environmental practices and the precautionary approach as corresponding obligations.[109] The Helsinki Convention also uses the precautionary approach to inform the application of best environmental practice stating that, in determining what combination of measures constitutes best environmental practice, particular consideration should be given to (*inter alia*) the precautionary principle.[110] Notwithstanding the different ways in which these conventions juxtapose best environmental practice with the other key obligations, they all define best environmental practice as meaning the most appropriate mix of controls and strategies

Environmental impact assessment

The requirement for EIA in respect of the marine environment is provided for under article 206 of the LOSC. More specifically, an application for approval for a plan of work under Part XI must be accompanied by "an assessment of potential environmental impacts of the proposed activities".[111] A contractor who intends to carry out activities in the Area is, therefore, under an obligation to conduct an EIA in respect of its proposal. The State has a corresponding due diligence obligation to ensure that the contractor meets its obligations in this regard.[112] The Advisory Opinion stresses that the obligation to conduct an EIA is both a direct obligation under the LOSC, and a general obligation under customary international law.[113] The Chamber referred to the Judgment in *Pulp Mills on the River Uruguay* in which the ICJ found that undertaking an EIA "may now be considered a requirement under general international law ... where there is a risk that the proposed industrial activity may have a significant adverse impact in a transboundary context, in particular, on a shared resource".[114] It determined that these principles could equally extend to activities in the Area beyond the scope of the Regulations.[115] The Chamber went on to suggest that the ICJ's reasoning in a transboundary context may also extend to activities beyond the limits of national jurisdiction, and references to "shared resources" may apply to resources that are the common heritage of mankind.[116] In light of these findings, the Chamber concluded that the obligations of contractors and sponsoring States concerning EIAs extend beyond the scope of application of specific provisions of the Regulations.[117]

Emerging regulation for the key obligations in the Pacific

Seabed minerals located within areas of national jurisdiction

The Pacific holds considerable potential for mineral development within areas of state jurisdiction. Research has established the existence of a range of seabed minerals within the EEZs of many Pacific Island Countries including polymetallic massive sulphides, cobalt-rich manganese crusts and manganese nodules. Resource evaluation has confirmed that the potential for seabed mining in the Region is significant.[118] Pacific Island States consider that being involved in mining activities, whether directly or indirectly, can potentially improve their GDP and the standard of living for their nationals. Many of these States view the exploitation of the mineral resources of their surrounding seas as a means to economic prosperity.[119] It is thought that the benefits of mining developments in the waters surrounding Pacific States will flow into the local economy through such factors as location of headquarters of mining companies in the jurisdiction, job creation, improvement of public services and the use by mining companies (and their employees) of local goods and services.[120] Although Pacific Island States remain interested in minerals located within the Area, the minerals within their own areas of jurisdiction often have the advantage of being located at shallower depths and proximate to land-based services and infrastructure. Furthermore the sovereign rights exercised over these areas mean that States do not need to seek permission for exploration and development from the ISA.

The law of the sea convention, the EEZ and the continental shelf

The EEZ extends from the outer limit of the territorial sea (12 nautical miles (nm)) to 200 nm from the territorial sea baseline.[121] The continental shelf comprises the seabed and subsoil which is "the natural prolongation" of a coastal State's land territory and may extend beyond the EEZ.[122] Neither the EEZ nor the continental shelf is part of a country's sovereign territory under the LOSC. Rather, States exercise exclusive sovereign rights over these marine areas. Sovereign rights over the EEZ entitle States to engage in "exploring and exploiting, conserving and managing" the living and non-living natural resources of the waters, seabed and subsoil.[123] Sovereign rights in respect of the continental shelf, where it extends beyond the EEZ, are narrower. They are limited to exploring and exploiting natural resources on or under the continental shelf,[124] as there are no special rights in respect of the water column.[125]

Sovereign rights are subject to a number of obligations set out under the LOSC, various international agreements and customary international law. Sovereign rights do not, for example, affect the freedoms enjoyed by other States in the EEZ and above the continental shelf.[126] More importantly, in the context of this chapter, sovereign rights to undertake seabed mining in either the EEZ or continental shelf are subject to the general obligations to protect and preserve the marine environment under Part XII,[127] and, prevent, reduce and control pollution of the marine environment under article 194 of the LOSC. Coastal States, therefore, have jurisdiction over the protection and preservation of the marine environment.[128] This is accompanied by a corresponding obligation to adopt laws and regulations under article 208(1), and take necessary measures, to prevent, reduce and control pollution of the marine environment arising from seabed activities subject to their jurisdiction under article 208(2).[129] Article 208(3) requires that the "laws, regulations and measures shall be no less effective than international rules, standards and recommended practices and procedures".[130] The LOSC also requires coastal States to enforce laws and regulations adopted to prevent, reduce and control pollution of the marine environment.[131]

There are clear similarities between the aforementioned obligations applying to seabed mining within EEZ and continental shelf and those applying to the Area as set out under the Advisory Opinion. Article 194(2), for example, requires that "States shall *take all measures necessary to ensure* that activities under their jurisdiction or control are so conducted as not to cause damage to other States and their environment". As discussed, the Chamber determined that the requirement under article 139(1) that "States Parties have *the responsibility to ensure* that activities in the Area" are carried out in conformity with international law was an obligation of due diligence.

It is not of any real significance that article 194(2) is concerned with ensuring activities do not cause damage, whereas article 139(1) is concerned with ensuring activities comply with international law.

Firstly, the due diligence obligation drawn upon under the Advisory Opinion seeks to ensure that activities under a State's jurisdiction do not cause damage to other States. Colloquially, one might say that the obligations expressed in articles 194(2) and 139(1) are two sides of the same coin insofar as both are premised on the prevention of damage. Second, the obligation under article 194(2) is accompanied by the requirement under article 208 to adopt laws, regulations and measures "no less effective than international rules, standards and recommended practices and procedures". The key obligations identified in this chapter must come within the remit of that requirement. The precautionary approach and EIA have become norms of customary international law and must qualify on that basis alone, while best environmental practice could be formed of either standards or recommended practices and procedures. Third, as in the case of the Area, coastal States are liable for any failure to fulfill their international obligations concerning protection and preservation of the marine environment. These similarities mean that the Advisory Opinion can offer strong guidance to States seeking to satisfy regulatory and administrative obligations for seabed mining activities within areas of national jurisdiction.

Regional measures taken to implement the key obligations

As early as 1999, a workshop was convened in Papua New Guinea to produce seabed mining guidelines for Pacific Island Countries.[132] The workshop produced the Madang Guidelines, born out of the concern that nations should begin the process of "developing appropriate regimes and legislation to manage present and future mineral exploration, development and exploitation within their EEZs".[133] The Guidelines recognise that marine deposits are part of a complex and interdependent ecosystem, the "pioneering nature" of exploration and the importance of ensuring that the development of the resources is responsible and sustainable.[134] Governments are encouraged to take a proactive stance[135] and to issue specific legislation for offshore mining.[136] Legislative regimes should address risk,[137] and the collection of baseline data is identified as a prerequisite to development of the resources.[138] The Guidelines also specify that any risks associated with the exploration and exploitation of offshore mineral resources should be assessed and given consideration. However, there was little real progress made in the immediate wake of the Madang Guidelines as development in the Pacific was constrained by the lack of cost effective seabed mining technology.[139]

In 2010, the European Union agreed to fund a deep sea minerals project in collaboration with the Secretariat of the Pacific Community. It is intended to provide support and advice to those Pacific Island States[140] interested in becoming involved in deep seabed mining activities. The objective of the project is to expand the economic resource base of the participating States by developing a viable and sustainable marine minerals industry. This is be achieved through the development and implementation of sound and regionally integrated legal, fiscal and environmental frameworks, improved human capacity and effective monitoring systems. The project has four specific deliverables including: (a) formulation of the Regional Framework for marine mineral exploration and mining; (b) development of national policy, legislation and regulations for the governance of offshore mineral resources within national jurisdictions; (c) strengthening national capacity to support Pacific nationals in the offshore mining industry; and (d) ensure effective environmental management and monitoring regimes are in place.[141]

The Secretariat of the Pacific Community released the Regional Framework in July 2012.[142] The Framework proposes that a regionally-agreed set of standards should be developed to support Pacific States in the preparation of regulatory regimes that are "comprehensive, efficient, workable, and consistent with international obligations, rules and standards".[143] The Framework aims to assist States "ensure that activities with national jurisdiction or control are consistent with the precautionary approach; are conducted with a view to minimising and mitigating the risk of environmental harm; and appropriately take into account other sea users".[144] It asserts that States need to act proactively, and develop and implement national legislative frameworks for seabed mining. The document adds that the LOSC creates a general obligation for all States to protect and preserve the entire marine environment, and that this obligation "extends to activities both within and outside areas of national jurisdiction"[145] Quoting from the Advisory Opinion, the Framework recognises that States undertaking seabed mining activities must satisfy the general due diligence obligation and direct obligations including: (a) applying the precautionary principle; (b) employing the best environmental practice; and (c) conducting EIA.[146]

The Framework recommends that one way for regulation to incorporate international law obligations is to include "high-level statements reflecting these obligations as a preliminary "purpose and principles" part of the legislation, against which decision-making under the legislation would be considered".[147] It goes on to suggest that incorporation of the LOSC into domestic legislation can be achieved through inclusion of a preliminary purpose provision, such as: "[t]his Act must be interpreted, and all persons performing functions and duties of exercising powers under it must act, consistently with the State's international obligations under the LOSC".[148] It needs to be questioned, however, whether the suggested provision is in fact a purpose-based provision, and not simply an acknowledgement that jurisdiction over non-sovereign waters derives from the LOSC.[149] Purpose provisions should provide a clear statement of the policy intent of the legislative regime, which must be achieved by decision-makers when exercising functions or powers under that regime. For example, sustainability is the purpose of a number of domestic statutes in New Zealand.[150] Sustainable development could serve as an appropriate purpose for deep sea mining legislation within the Pacific. However, it appears that concerns have been raised by some Pacific States that social and economic considerations implicit within the concept of sustainable development are inappropriate when considering applications to develop finite resources, the impacts of which are generally located well beyond most land based stakeholders. Similar concerns arose during the passage of New Zealand's EEZ Act. Parliament's response to these concerns was to maintain a sustainable purpose, but limit considerations to biophysical impacts.

The Regional Framework points to the limited extent of the information currently known about the deep sea environment and the potential effects of new deep sea mining technologies on that environment. It then directs States to apply a precautionary approach, as reflected in principle 15 of the Rio Declaration.[151] The document states that the precautionary approach does not necessarily prevent activities with unknown effects from proceeding. Rather "it requires that if they proceed, they only do so with caution; and cognisant of unknown potential impacts, with appropriate checks and risk-minimising controls in place."[152] Precaution is described as requiring the evaluation of alternatives and on-going monitoring "with a view eventually to moving into more scientifically-certain risk management mechanisms".[153] Significantly, the Regional Framework states that precaution shifts the burden of proof as to the effects of a proposed activity to the proponents of that activity. Accordingly it is recommended that, where there is a possibility of an adverse effect, the provision of evidence as to whether the nature or scale of the effect is acceptable should rest with the proponent of the activity.[154] An effects-based regime is proposed for the approval of permits or licences, where activities are classified as permitted, discretionary or prohibited depending on the nature and scale of their potential effects.[155]

The Regional Framework recommends that, in order to satisfy due diligence, a State should complete sufficient checks at the outset of any proposal to ensure that a proponent will be able to perform its activities in a timely, safe, environmentally responsible, and efficient manner.[156] It states that consideration of an EIA prepared by the proponent is a critical step in this initial checking process. It is, therefore, necessary that any legislative regime makes provision for preparation and consideration of EIAs. The Framework suggests that legislation should require the applicant to complete an EIA "as soon as the DSM project is sufficiently defined to permit meaningful analysis, and before any mining activity takes place".[157] It should cover, not only environmental effects, but also social, cultural and health impacts.[158] The recommendation to require an assessment of social and cultural impacts will probably face a certain amount of resistance given the concerns of some States that these values are unlikely to be affected beyond territorial limits. One response to such concerns is that if these values are not affected, proponents should not find it too difficult to evidentially establish this within their EIA.

The Regional Framework recommends that seabed mining licences should include conditions requiring operators to implement the precautionary approach, employ best environmental practices, and collect environmental baseline data.[159] This would include such things as amending operational activities in circumstances where the adverse effects (or the risk of effects) need to be avoided or mitigated. It is suggested that a state regulatory body is in turn provided with the power to review or change the conditions of a licence, and, in extreme circumstances, to cancel the licence.[160] It is further recommended that penalties in cases of non-compliance with licence conditions should be severe enough not to be simply dismissed as a business cost.[161]

Seabed mining regulation in Pacific Island countries

As of February 2015, the Cook Islands, Fiji, Tonga and Tuvalu had enacted specific legislation for deep sea mineral activities. Kiribati is drafting specific legislation with the assistance of the DSM project. The Cook Islands pioneered legislation for seabed mining with the enactment of the Seabed Minerals Act 2009 (SBM Act). Initial drafts were prepared with the assistance of the Commonwealth Secretariat, based in London, and went through various consultations and re-drafting to meet the needs of the Cook Islands.[162] The SBM Act provides a snapshot of international legal thinking at the time it was enacted. Unsurprisingly it does not place as much emphasis on the key obligations as legislation enacted in the Advisory Opinion's wake. The objectives of the Act include the requirement "to ensure that seabed minerals activity is carried out in a manner that is consistent with internationally accepted rules, standards, principles and practices".[163] However, this objective is worded more like a statement of legislative intent than a direction to those making decisions under the Act. Accordingly, the objective is likely circumscribed by the extent to which the Act makes provision for internationally accepted rules, standards, principles and practices.

The SBM Act is principally concerned with the ownership of seabed minerals within national jurisdiction,[164] and the allocation of licences to mine those minerals.[165] Environmental regulation is chiefly provided for under the Environment Act 2003.[166] This means that a licence to mine seabed minerals will not be granted until a permit has been granted under the Environment Act.[167] The completion of an EIA is a prerequisite to the grant of a permit.[168] However, the EIA requirements under the Environment Act are bare and there is no requirement to take a precautionary approach or apply best environmental practices. The present Seabed Minerals

Commissioner has described provision for environmental permitting under the Environment Act as a temporary "quick fix", and stated that the Act needs to be updated to make its own provision for the management of environmental impacts.[169]

The Seabed Minerals Authority oddly appears to have more environmental power over existing mining licences than applications for new mining licences under the SBM Act. Accordingly, the Authority may direct a mining licence holder "to mitigate to the extent that is practicable to do so in accordance with best international practice, any damage to the environment in the title area or the buffer area caused by those operations".[170] The SBM Act also enables regulations to be prepared for the protection of the environment, clean-up or other remediation of the effects of DSM activities and the prevention of damages.[171] Since the SBM Act came into force, the Cook Islands has taken part in the European Union funded deep sea minerals project. The subsequent Seabed Minerals Policy 2014 requires adherence "to international standards of environmental protection". The Policy pledges that the Cook Islands "will comply with applicable principles of international law targeting protection of the environment, including adoption of best environmental practice and application of the precautionary approach".[172] At the time of writing this chapter the Cook Island's government had signalled that new regulations are due to be promulgated which will flesh out the EIA requirements for permits under the Environment Act.

The International Seabed Mineral Management Decree 2013 of the Government of Fiji (Fiji Seabed Mineral Decree) enables Fiji to act as a sponsoring State for the purposes of engaging in seabed mineral activities in the Area.[173] The Fiji Seabed Mineral Decree requires any person engaged in seabed mineral actives under the Decree to apply the precautionary approach and employ best environmental practices in order to avoid, mitigate, or remedy adverse effects of Seabed Mineral Activities on the marine environment[174]. The Decree is a relatively comprehensive document insofar as it provides for mining activities in the Area. Seabed mining activities conducted within Fiji's EEZ or continental shelf are regulated by the Mining Act (Amendment) Decree 2010. This adds a new section to the Mining Act 1966 which defines land as including water and land covered by water, for the purposes of prospective licences. EIA for mining applications is provided for under the Environment Management Act 2005.[175] Unlike the Decree, the Environment Act does not make provision for protection of the marine environment, the precautionary approach or best environmental practice. It is worth noting, in respect of the EEZ and continental shelf, the out-dated and conflicting nature of different legislation involved has been given as one reason for the poorly integrated management of Fiji's coastal areas.[176]

The Tonga Seabed Minerals Act 2014 and Tuvalu Seabed Minerals Act 2014 both incorporate the key obligations, identified in this chapter, as set out in the Advisory Opinion. The similarity in the wording of the Acts indicates that they have both benefited from the European Union and Secretariat of the Pacific Community deep sea minerals project. Both Acts exercise jurisdiction over the EEZ, continental shelf and Area.[177] Section 2(2) of each Act employs the same language requiring that the Acts "shall where possible be interpreted, and all persons performing functions and duties or exercising powers under it shall act, subject to any Act . . . the contrary, consistently with . . . international obligations under the UN Convention on the Law of the Sea, and other relevant international instruments". Specific duties under this section include *inter alia*: (a) protection and preservation of the marine environment; (b) application of the precautionary approach; (c) employment of best environmental practice; and (d) prior EIA of activities likely to cause serious harm to the marine environment.[178] It is worth noting that the threshold of serious harm for EIA may not be consistent with best environmental practice as impacts that fall short of serious, but are more than minor, may still need to be mitigated in order to protect and preserve the marine environment. Notwithstanding, both Acts have attempted to comprehensively address the Advisory Opinion's obligations under a single legislative framework and in that respect can be considered an advance on the Cook Islands SBM Act and Fiji Mining Act.

Enactment of key obligations in New Zealand's EEZ

The legislative regime prior to the EEZ Act

New Zealand's EEZ is the fifth largest in the world, with an area of about 15 times that of its land mass (or 5.7 per cent of the world's EEZ).[179] When the legal continental shelf extensions are included, New Zealand's current ocean area jurisdiction spans more than 20 times the area of its land – 1.2 per cent of the earth's surface area. Its vast size is conversely matched by the limited amount of scientific information available concerning its ecosystem values and natural resource potential.[180] This lack of information was, until recently, compounded, by legislative silence as to the environmental management of New Zealand's EEZ and continental shelf. Prior to the enactment of the EEZ Act a legislative *lacuna* existed in New Zealand with regard to managing the effects of exploration and development within the EEZ.[181] This *lacuna* was demonstrated in the decision of the High Court in *Greenpeace v Minister of Energy and Resources*,[182] where Greenpeace brought judicial review proceedings against the government for failing to undertake an EIA prior to granting oil exploration rights over an area of the EEZ.

The Court observed that Greenpeace's principal proposition was that the government was required to take into account international obligations concerning EIA. In failing to do so, Greenpeace contended the government had erred in law.[183] The High Court found on this point that the Resource Management Act 1991(RMA), New Zealand's principal overarching statute for managing natural and physical resources,[184] "did not apply to activities outside the territorial waters. If questions arise as to the extent to which New Zealand – as a State – met its international obligations that must be a matter upon which Parliament might choose to legislate. It is not a matter upon which the Court can direct Parliament."[185] The High Court's decision highlighted the inadequacy of the legislative framework for seabed mining activities within the EEZ at that time. The RMA, with its guiding purpose of sustainable management,[186] provided a comprehensive framework for environmental assessment of land-based activities and those within the territorial sea. By contrast, the EEZ's legislation was less developed and conferred a broad discretion on the government to approve (or not approve) exploration or mining activity.[187] The government moved to close the gap with the enactment of the EEZ Act. This new regime would have a sustainable management purpose to be achieved through decision-making that gave effect to the Advisory Opinion's key obligations identified under the preceding headings in this chapter.

Environmental impact assessment, caution and adaptive management

The EEZ Bill was introduced to Parliament on 24 August 2011 in order to give effect to New Zealand's obligations under the LOSC to manage and protect the natural resources of its EEZ and continental shelf. Initially scheduled to come into effect on 1 July 2012, the Bill was eventually enacted on 3 September 2012. The s 10 sustainable management purpose of the EEZ Act closely resembles the s 5 purpose of the RMA. While sustainable development seeks to redress imbalances in resource allocation, sustainable management does not seek to regulate social equity. It does not seek to redistribute wealth, and it does not seek to equitably allocate rights to development. It is effectively a form of environmental control and regulation.[188] Although sustainable management includes social and cultural wellbeing under the RMA, consideration is limited to the effects of development activities on those values. In a significant departure from s 5 under the RMA, s 10 of the EEZ Act does not provide for social or cultural wellbeing. Likewise, the definition of environment under s 4 does not include people and communities, or social, aesthetic and cultural conditions. This is because New Zealand policy makers, as is the case with some Pacific Island Countries, did not consider social and cultural values to be relevant beyond territorial waters. The application of the Act is, therefore, limited to natural values within the EEZ and continental shelf.[189] Notwithstanding, economic wellbeing remains a relevant consideration under s 10. This requires consideration of the economic benefits of seabed mining proposals, and the economic impacts of such proposals on existing interests (e.g. commercial fishing).

The Environmental Protection Authority (EPA) is charged with deciding applications for marine consents, monitoring compliance and enforcement.[190] All seabed mining activities within the EEZ and continental shelf must either be permitted under regulations or authorised by marine consent under the EEZ Act.[191] Consistent with the Advisory Opinion's EIA obligation, all marine consent applications must be supported by an impact assessment.[192] An impact assessment must: (a) describe the proposed activity; (b) describe the state of the existing environment; (c) identify the effects of the activity on the environment and existing interests; (d) describe any consultation undertaken with existing interests; and (e) measures proposed to avoid, remedy, or mitigate the adverse effects.[193] The information in the impact assessment should include such detail as corresponds to the scale and significance of effects that the proposed activity may have on the environment or existing interests, and sufficient detail to enable the EPA and potentially affected persons to understand the nature of the activity and its effects on the environment.[194]

Public participation is encouraged under the Act, and notice must be given in respect of activities that do not have a low probability of a significant adverse effect.[195] Any person may make a submission to the EPA on an application for marine consent to undertake seabed mining.[196] The EPA may conduct a hearing if it considers one desirable, and must conduct a hearing if one is requested by the applicant or a submitter.[197] The EPA must establish a procedure that is fair and reasonable (e.g. accords with the principles of natural justice). The hearing must avoid unnecessary formality, and to these ends cross-examination is not allowed unless the EPA gives permission.[198] Despite the requirement to avoid formality, the scale and evidential complexity of proposals have seen legal counsel and cross-examination play a large role in hearings to date.

In assessing an application the EPA must consider a comprehensive list of matters principally concerned with effects on the environment (i.e. natural and physical values).[199] However, as discussed above, the proposal's effects on existing interests and its economic benefit to New Zealand must also be taken into account. As with decisions on applications for consent made under the RMA, the EPA must not have regard to trade competition or the effects of trade competition.[200] Matters that must be regarded when considering the extent of adverse effects on existing interests include: (a) the area in common; (b) the degree to which both activities must be carried out to the exclusion of others; and (c) whether the existing interest can only be exercised in the area to which the application relates.[201]

The precautionary approach is provided for under the EEZ Act's information principles.[202] These principles require the EPA to: (a) make full use of its powers to request information and obtain advice; (b) base decisions on the best available information; and (c) take into account any uncertainty or inadequacy in the information available.[203] Best available information means the best information available without unreasonable cost, effort or time.[204] Reasonableness in this context is likely to be assessed in relation to the nature of the risk and scale of potential adverse effect. The information principles require the EPA to "favour caution and environmental protection" where the information available is uncertain or inadequate.[205] If favouring caution and environmental protection means that an application for an activity is likely to be prohibited, the decision-maker must first consider whether an adaptive management approach would allow the activity to be undertaken.[206] The EPA may, for example, impose adaptive management requirements as conditions of a marine consent. An adaptive management approach may include: (a) commencing on a small scale, or for a short period so that effects can be monitored; or (b) any other approach that allows an activity to be undertaken so that its effects can be assessed and the activity discontinued, or continued with or without amendment, on the basis of those effects.[207]

Although not legislatively provided for, adaptive management is a common tool for managing risk and change under the RMA. Adaptive management approaches under the RMA regularly include such things as environmental management plans, staging, monitoring and contingency plans, environmental audits, best practicable option analysis and the review mechanisms under conditions of consent. The Environment Court held in *Crest Energy Kaipara Ltd v Northland Regional Council*[208] that key features of an adaptive management approach include: (a) setting out the stages of development; (b) establishing the existing environment through robust baseline monitoring; (c) clear and strong monitoring, reporting and checking mechanisms so that steps can be taken before significant adverse effects eventuate; (d) that these mechanisms are supported by enforceable conditions which must be satisfied before subsequent stages can proceed; and (e) a real ability to remove all (or some of the development that has occurred) if monitoring warrants it.[209]

The Supreme Court's decision in *Sustain Our Sounds Inc. v NZ King Salmon Company Ltd*[210] is the most authoritative finding on adaptive management in New Zealand. The Court commenced this part of the decision by questioning "whether any adaptive management regime can be considered consistent with a precautionary approach".[211] It identified "the vital part of the test" as being "the extent to which an adaptive management approach will sufficiently diminish the risk and the uncertainty".[212] The Court went on to identify the appropriate factors for assessing the degree to which adaptive management will diminish risk and uncertainty. Resembling the findings of the Environment Court in the *Crest Energy Kaipara Ltd* the Supreme Court held these are: (a) there will be good baseline information about the receiving environment; (b) the proposed conditions provide for effective monitoring of adverse effects using appropriate indicators; (c) thresholds are set to trigger remedial action before the effects become overly damaging; and (d) effects that might arise can be remedied before they become irreversible.[213] As in the case of the Environment Court, the Supreme Court was considering the application of adaptive management under the RMA. It has been pointed out that the different wording under the EEZ Act means "that an adaptive management approach is not inherently inconsistent with favouring caution and environmental protection, and therefore the particular threshold question addressed by the Court in *King Salmon* may be unnecessary".[214] In the authors' view that approach is too literal, and the threshold identified by the Supreme Court serves to encapsulate the purpose of the factors identified as appropriate for the application of adaptive management. Whatever the case, it is agreed that the Court's findings on the broader question of adaptive management effectively identify "what constitutes good practice".[215]

Decisions on seabed mining proposals under the EEZ Act

There have been two publicly notified applications for seabed mining activities since the enactment of the EEZ Act. The importance of the precautionary approach and adaptive management to obtaining marine consent for seabed mining is evident in the EPA's decision on both applications. The applications were made by companies specifically incorporated to undertake the respective proposals. They did not, therefore, have corporate track records in seabed mining activities. This was a likely factor in the level of operational detail each applicant could provide on the proposed activity. The first application by Trans-Tasman Resources Ltd sought to mine 50 million tonnes of iron ore per annum within the South Taranaki Bight EEZ. The iron sand was to be processed at sea into iron ore concentrate for export. The residual material (approximately 45 million tonnes per annum) was to be returned to the seabed as de-ored sediment. The disposition of the residual sediment and the area of its plume were to attract significant opposition from Māori interests (indigenous interests), commercial fishing interests and the general public. The second application concerned Chatham Rock Phosphate Limited's proposal to mine phosphorite over 10,192 km^2 of the Chatham Rise, a 1,000km stretch of the EEZ containing significant seabed mineral deposits. This proposal attracted similar opposition in respect of the extraction and deposition of sediment on the seabed. Both applications involved large public hearings and were ultimately declined on the basis that the information supplied through EIA was uncertain, and the adaptive management measures proposed did not meet the factors (or good practice) identified as prerequisites to satisfying a precautionary approach.

The EPA found in the *Trans-Tasman Resources decision* that there was considerable uncertainty as to the information provided in support of the application, and as a consequence uncertainty as to the effects of the proposal.[216] In particular, the EPA found that: (a) the information on the existing environment and the way the mining operation might affect it was considerably uncertain; (b) the information on existing Māori interests was inadequate and incomplete; and (c) the impacts on commercial fishing interests in the area were uncertain. The EPA also recorded that there was a lack of clarity as to the mining operation itself, and that it would have had greater confidence had the applicant been able to provide greater operational detail.[217] The EPA favoured caution and environmental protection in light of the level of uncertainty accompanying the proposal as required under s 62(1) of the EEZ Act. In considering this requirement the EPA found that: "[t]his provision is an explicit statement that, within the context of the EEZ Act, the promotion of sustainable management requires a cautious approach. The taking of risks in this environment is not encouraged, and we note that this direction is not to be traded off against the attainment of economic well-being. In other words, the requirement to favour caution and environmental protection in the face of uncertain or inadequate information is an absolute one, and we remind ourselves of section 10(3), which makes it clear that applying the information principles in section 61 is one of the ways the purpose of the EEZ Act is achieved."[218]

The EPA then turned to consideration of the applicant's proposal to employ adaptive management to address the uncertainties in the application as required under the Act.[219] The applicant stated that a staged approach to the activity was not possible in this case, and instead proposed a risk-based tiered approach to adaptive management.[220] It suggested that operational changes could be made before adverse effects became irreversible. The EPA conceptually agreed that this approach could be an appropriate adaptive management framework, but that its applicability would be fact specific. It noted, in this respect, that the applicant had created an expectation at the commencement of the hearing that there would be considerably more quantitative detail in support of its adaptive management approach.[221] The EPA then considered the applicant's proposal against the Supreme Court's test for determining whether an adaptive management approach is appropriate.[222] In relation to the extent of environmental risk, the EPA found that there was considerable uncertainty due to the lack of baseline monitoring and real data, as opposed to the modelled information that the applicant had provided in support of its approach.[223]

The EPA then cited the Supreme Court's finding that "there must be an adequate evidential foundation to have reasonable assurance that the adaptive management approach will achieve its goals of sufficiently reducing uncertainty and adequately managing any remaining risk."[224] Returning to its point that the adaptive management approach had started as one that had quantitative triggers, the EPA stated the gaps in information exposed during the hearing had led to an approach where a process was prescribed to enable the establishment of those triggers.[225] The EPA went on to find that it was not convinced by the applicant's contention that the proposed activity would only have minor potential effects. This was because there was not a good baseline understanding of the receiving environment.[226] The EPA considered that while it was not necessary to have all the information, it was not satisfied there was a sufficient baseline understanding of the existing environment. On the evidence presented the EPA decided that the environment would not be safeguarded or that the adverse effects of the proposal could be avoided, remedied or mitigated.[227] Overall the EPA found that the application was premature and more time should have been taken to understand the proposed operation, its effects on the receiving environment and existing interests. For those reasons the application did not meet the sustainable management purpose of the EEZ Act.[228]

The *Trans-Tasman Resources decision* sent shock waves through the New Zealand mining sector, not least because of the much publicized $NZ 65 million that the company had spent on the project since its incorporation in September 2007.[229] This sent a clear signal that, despite significant capital expenditure, applicants might not be able to meet the information thresholds concerning the existing environment prerequisite to having an application favorably determined. Nevertheless, Chatham Rock Phosphates was confident that, despite the uncertainties involved in seabed mining, it had completed sufficient work to show that the proposal would satisfy the sustainable management purpose of the Act.[230] The EPA found in the *Chatham Rock Phosphate decision* that considerable efforts had been made to provide the necessary baseline information on the marine environment, and to commission expert modelling and analysis in support of the application. However, it was "incontestably the case that there remained significant gaps in the data and information provided about the consent area's marine environment as well as uncertainty about the impact of the proposal on existing interests and the environment."[231] Again the EPA observed that a good level of baseline information is necessary in determining the standards, limits, thresholds and triggers for any proposed adaptive management framework.[232]

The EPA noted that it was mindful that the proposed activity was intended in the open ocean, at a depth and in an environment about which there exists significant uncertainty of knowledge and consequences.[233] However, it accepted that the crucial issue is not about uncertainty *per se*, but what is an acceptable and appropriate level of risk in the gap between certainty and uncertainty. It observed "[t]hat gap is never likely to close entirely for a proposal of this scale in the environment in which it is proposed. Closing the gap to an acceptable risk-tolerance point is, however, critical to the granting of consent under the EEZ Act."[234] The EPA considered that the adaptive management approach offered by the applicant did not address fundamental concerns such as the need to validate habitat predictions concerning the existing environment in advance of mining. Distinct from the *Trans-Tasman Resources decision* the EPA appears to have considered that there was sufficient baseline information to offer a condition requiring validation of modelled impacts during a trial mining period. However, the applicant contended that such an approach would render the project financially unviable.[235]

Another difference when compared to the *Trans-Tasman Resources decision* was the EPA's finding that there was sufficient evidence that there would be significant and permanent adverse effects on other parts of the existing environment.[236] Deciding to decline the proposal the EPA found it was convinced that the proposal would create significant and permanent adverse effects on the environment, which were incapable of being avoided, remedied or mitigated. The EPA concluded that it was appropriate to be guided by this concern, particularly when taking into account that the requirement to favour caution and environmental protection had been invoked.[237] The applicant responded to the decision in the media with claims that the decision sent a seriously bad signal to business: "[i]f we can't succeed having invested $33 million over seven years, then obviously the government is not serious about economic development."[238] Unsurprisingly, there have also been claims from the mining sector that New Zealand's resource development framework has serious problems and needs urgent reform.[239]

The New Zealand government should be careful, however, about bowing to pressure from the mining industry. The present legislative framework was formulated with a view to complying with New Zealand's obligations under the LOSC and more generally under international law. Watering down the EEZ Act to enable proposals to proceed without strong baseline information on the environment would be a breach of those obligations. Although the effects of the proposals under discussion might be considered to be localised, it needs to borne in mind that poor regulation resulting in damage to the environment could expose New Zealand to liability. This is important in light of the fact that the EEZ Act does not just govern seabed mining, but also oil and gas exploration and development.[240] It might be contended in light of the existing paucity of strong baseline environmental information concerning New Zealand's EEZ that the Act is effectively fulfilling the function for which it was intended to serve.

Conclusion

New technology and increasing commodity prices mean that seabed mining has the potential to generate economic wealth. Despite the capital-intensive nature of development, a number of proposals to undertake different forms of seabed mining have been advanced across the Pacific. These range from Nauru seeking the Chamber's opinion on the obligations and liability of developing States for mining within the Area, through to the public hearing of large volumes of evidence both for and against seabed mining within New Zealand's EEZ. It may be drawing a long bow to suggest there is a direct line between the Chamber's opinion and the subsequent seabed mining decisions in New Zealand. Such an assertion would ignore the fact that the EEZ Act does not expressly require decision-makers to comply with the LOSC or international law. It must not be overlooked, however, that this is because the EEZ Act purports to enable the implementation of New Zealand's obligations under the LOSC and other conventions.[241] Herein lays the importance of the Advisory Opinion across the Pacific Region. The Chamber's clarification of States' obligations under the LOSC provided both legal and practical incentive to implement domestic regulation for seabed mining outside sovereign territory in order to reduce exposure to liability.

It would be a disservice to States to suggest that the avoidance of liability is the only reason that regulation is being promulgated throughout the Region. After all, the 1999 Madang Guidelines were born out of general concern that legislation was needed to manage seabed mineral exploration and development within the Regions' EEZs. It is true that the Advisory Opinion encouraged a flurry of regulatory activity within some Pacific Island States. It should be recognised, however, that the opinion's effect in other jurisdictions was rather one of influence on regulation already in various stages of gestation. The Cook Islands and New Zealand, for example, had both taken steps towards enactment prior to the Advisory Opinion. Both States were cognisant of the need to more effectively regulate their EEZs. It is fair to say that the Advisory Opinion significantly advanced international jurisprudence through its finding that States have a due diligence obligation to enact laws, make regulations and take administrative measures to secure compliance with the LOSC by persons under their jurisdiction. The direct obligations identified by the Chamber in turn provided goals and objectives that States could seek to implement through regulation in order to secure compliance with the LOSC outside sovereign territory.

The key obligations identified by the Chamber are the precautionary approach, best environmental practice and EIA. These obligations received particular attention because they are norms of international law with broad application. EIA clearly forms part of customary law, while the precautionary approach, if not there, must be on the very cusp of such status. Although best environmental practices *per se* has yet to be elevated to similar customary status, the broad application of this obligation across a variety of international agreements signals a general concurrence as to its application in environmental regulation. Furthermore, these obligations are central to regulating the use of new technologies in the exploration and development of marine areas over which little scientific information exists. They do not require regulators to prevent exploration and development in the face of uncertain information. Rather, they require regulators to ensure that any potential impacts which might arise due to uncertain information do not result in serious or irreversible damage. This requires the collection of adequate baseline data on existing environments prior to commencing exploration or development to ensure that any potential environmental changes arising out of uncertainty are able to be monitored and controlled before they result in a significant adverse effect.

Regulatory initiatives for seabed mining following the Advisory Opinion commenced with the preparation of the Regional Framework. Citing the Advisory Opinion, the Regional Framework recognises that States undertaking seabed mining must satisfy the due diligence obligation, the precautionary principle, best environmental practice and EIA. Emphasis is placed on the limited extent of knowledge available in respect of the deep sea environment and the potential effects of seabed mining. It recommends that this uncertainty should be addressed through a precautionary approach and the collection of environmental baseline data. The Regional Framework has significantly influenced legislation and regulation since it was promulgated in 2012. Despite the enactment of pre-existing legislation the Cook Islands has developed policy that pledges compliance with international law, including the precautionary approach and best environmental practice. Presumably this will be reflected in regulations under consideration at the time of writing. Fiji's Seabed Mineral Degree makes similar provision. However, the Decree only applies to the Area, and more general legislation applying to Fiji's EEZ is neither comprehensive nor integrated. Tonga Seabed Minerals Act 2014 and Tuvalu Seabed Minerals Act 2014 are the more comprehensive beneficiaries of the Regional Framework. These enactments: (a) exercise jurisdiction over the EEZ, continental shelf and Area; (b) require decisions-makers to act consistently with the LOSC; and (c) include provision for all three key obligations (i.e. precautionary approach, best environmental practice and EIA).

Despite progress made by Pacific Island States in developing seabed mining regulation, it is in New Zealand where the most significant seabed mining proposals have been advanced since the release of the Advisory Opinion.[242] This is likely due to the fact that New Zealand is a developed State, with stable government and strong regulatory and technical infrastructure. The Regional Framework signals in this respect that, even with the promulgation of appropriate regulation, administrative and technical capacity will remain significant impediments to the exploration and development of seabed minerals within the Pacific Islands.[243] New Zealand, in contrast to Pacific Island States, has steered away from a sectoral focus on one industry and instead seeks to regulate the effects of all forms of exploration and development within its EEZ. The EEZ Act's purpose is sustainable management and considerable emphasis is placed on robust EIA and public participation. The precautionary approach is given effect through the Act's information principles, which require decision-makers to favour caution and environmental protection where the information is uncertain or inadequate. If favouring caution and environmental protection means that an exploration or development proposal is likely to be declined the decision-maker must first consider whether an adaptive management approach would allow the activity to be undertaken. The Supreme Court found in the *King Salmon decision* that the degree to which adaptive management can diminish risk and uncertainty is governed by: (a) good baseline information about the receiving environment; (b) effective monitoring of adverse effect indicators; (c) clear thresholds that trigger remedial action; and (d) the ability to remedy any adverse effects that do occur before they become irreversible.

The EEZ Act's precautionary approach and application of adaptive management have been key factors in decisions to decline the first two seabed mining proposals to fall to be considered under the Act. The *Trans-Tasman Resources* and *Chatham Rock Phosphate decisions* involved lengthy public hearings and many volumes of expert evidence. Notwithstanding the significant numbers of experts that were brought to bear in both sets of proceedings, the applicants were found to have failed to provide good baseline information about the receiving environment. The adaptive management approaches proposed in both cases were over-reliant on modeling of the receiving environment. They were not supported by a level of baseline information necessary to enable the monitoring of effects against clear thresholds, let alone ensure that any potential effects were not irreversible. It is a salutary lesson that, despite considerable investment in both seabed mining applications, neither applicant was able to establish a sufficiently robust baseline environment. It is perhaps not that surprising, however, given the fact that academic literature, the Chamber, the Regional Framework and State regulators have all stressed the lack of scientific information which presently exists concerning these marine environments. While some within the seabed mining industry might chastise the precautionary approach as too restrictive, the only other option in the face of incomplete information is to take a "suck it and see" approach. It would be a brave government who exposed itself (or those within its jurisdiction) to liability for damage to the marine environment or existing interests resulting from a failure to heed the Chamber's opinion.

Notes

* The authors would like to acknowledge contributions made to this chapter by Kellie Dawson and Timothy Orr, Barristers and Solicitors of the High Court of New Zealand.
1 International Seabed Authority, *Workshop on Polymetallic Nodule Mining Technology – Current Status and Challenges Ahead* (National Institute of Ocean Technology, Chennai India, Background Document, February 2008) at 5.
2 *Ibid*; and Halfar, J. and Fujita, R., "Precautionary management of deep-sea mining" (2002) 26 *Marine Policy* 103 at 104.
3 Nelson, J., "The Contemporary Seabed Mining Regime: A Critical Analysis of Mining Regulations Promulgated by the International Seabed Authority" (2005) 16:1 *Colorado Journal of International Environmental Law and Policy* 27 at 40.
4 United Nations Division for Ocean Affairs and Laws of the Sea "The United Nations Convention on the Law of the Sea (A Historical Perspective)" (1998) http://www.un.org/depts/los/convention_agreements/convention_historical_perspective

5 International Seabed Authority, *Biodiversity, species ranges, and gene flow in the abyssal Pacific nodule province: predicting and managing the impacts of deep seabed mining* (ISA Technical Study No. 3), at 4 to 6; Bonney, Stephanie, "Bioprospecting, Scientific Research and Deep Sea Resources in Areas Beyond National Jurisdiction: A Critical Legal Analysis" (2006) 10 *New Zealand Journal of Environmental Law* 41 at 52; and Halfar and Fujita, above n 2, at 105.
6 McGinnis, M., *Ocean Governance: The New Zealand dimension (Summary Report)*, Emerging Issues Programme, School of Government, Victoria University of Wellington (2012) at 33; and National Institute of Water and Atmospheric Research Limited, *Expert Risk Assessment of Activities in the New Zealand Exclusive Economic Zone and Continental Shelf (Prepared for the Ministry for the Environment* (National Institute of Water and Atmospheric Research Limited, August 2012) at 67 to 71, 77 to 81, 87 to 90 and 95 to 97.
7 Macalister, T., "David Cameron says seabed mining could be worth £40bn to Britain", *The Guardian*, 14 March 2013. "David Cameron has pledged to put Britain at the forefront of a new international seabed mining industry, which he claimed could be worth £40bn to the UK economy over the next 30 years."
8 Seabed Disputes Chamber of the International Tribunal for the Law of the Sea *Responsibilities and Obligations of States Sponsoring Persons and Entities with Respect to Activities in the Area (Advisory Opinion)* (1 February 2011) ("Advisory Opinion").
9 Advisory Opinion, at para 110.
10 Anton, D., Makgill, R. and Payne, C., 'Advisory Opinion on Responsibility and Liability for International Seabed Mining (ITLOS Case No. 17): International Environmental Law in the Seabed Disputes Chamber', (2011) 41/2 *Environmental Policy and Law* 60 to 65, at 63.
11 Advisory Opinion, at para [109].
12 Advisory Opinion, at para [119].
13 Secretariat of the Pacific Community (SOPAC Division), *Pacific-ACP States Regional Legislative and Regulatory Framework for Deep Sea Minerals Exploration and Exploitation prepared under the SPC-EU EDF10 Deep Sea Minerals Project*, (1st ed. July 2012).
14 Neate, R., "Seabed Mining Could Earn Cook Islands Tens of Billions of Dollars", *The Guardian*, 5 August 2013. "A new geological survey by Imperial College marine geochemist David Cronan estimates that the Cook Islands' 2 million square kilometre exclusive economic zone contains 10bn tonnes of manganese nodules. The nodules, which vary from the size of a potato to that of a dining table, contain manganese, nickel, copper, cobalt and rare earth minerals used in electronics."
15 LOSC, art 1(1)(1).
16 LOSC, art 1(1)(3).
17 Resources are defined in art 133(a) of the LOSC as "all solid, liquid or gaseous mineral resources in situ in the Area at or beneath the seabed, including polymetallic nodules".
18 LOSC, art 136.
19 LOSC, art 137. The International Seabed Authority is the organ through which State Parties "organise and control activities in the Area, particularly with a view to administering the resources of the Area" (LOSC, art 157(1)). For a discussion of the powers and functions of the Assembly, the Council, and the Legal and Technical Commission see: Rothwell, D. and Stephens, T., *The International Law of the Sea*, (Hart Publishing, Oxford, 2010) at 136 to 143.
20 LOSC, art 153(2)(b).
21 French, D., "From the Depths: Rich Pickings of Principles of Sustainable Development and General International Law on the Ocean Floor – the Seabed Disputes Chamber's 2011 Advisory Opinion", (2011) 26 *The International Journal of Marine and Coastal Law* 525 at 529.
22 LOSC, art 153(2) and (3).
23 Advisory Opinion, at para [25].
24 LOSC, art 191.
25 Advisory Opinion, at para [26].
26 Agarwal, B., "Feasibility Study on Manganese Nodules Recovery in the Clarion-Clipperton Zone", in Ajit Shenoi et al. (eds.), *The Lloyd's Register Educational Trust Collegium 2012 Series*, (University of Southampton, Highfield 2012) at 21. Polymetallic manganese nodules, for example, contain varying amounts of valuable metals including manganese, cobalt, copper and nickel. Agarwal et al. state that the market demand for these minerals has risen dramatically over the last 10 years. The price of copper, for example, has tripled while those of cobalt, nickel and manganese have doubled since 2002. Despite a

decline in demand following the 2008 economic crisis, the global market is recovering together with metal prices. This trend has made the mineral markets an attractive investment for both private and government enterprises.

27 Nauru sponsored Nauru Ocean Resources Inc., and Tonga sponsored Tonga Offshore Mining Ltd.
28 Advisory Opinion, at para [4].
29 International Seabed Authority, *Proposal to seek an advisory opinion from the Seabed Disputes Chamber of the International Tribunal for the Law of the Sea on matters regarding sponsoring State Responsibility Submitted by the delegation of Nauru* Sixteenth Session, Kingston, Jamaica 26 April to 7 May 2010, ASBA/16/C/6 (2010) at 1.
30 *Ibid* at 2.
31 Council of the International Seabed Authority *Decision of the Council of the International Seabed Authority requesting an advisory opinion pursuant to Article 191 of the United Nations Convention on the Law of the Sea* (6 May 2010).
32 Advisory Opinion, at para [108].
33 Advisory Opinion, at para [109].
34 Advisory Opinion, at para [110].
35 *Corfu Channel (United Kingdom v. Albania)* (Merits) [1949] ICJ Rep 22: It is "every State's obligation not to allow knowingly its territory to be used for acts contrary to the rights of other States". *Advisory Opinion on the Legality of the Threat or Use of Nuclear Weapons* [1949] ICJ Rep 226: "The existence of the general obligation of states to ensure that activities within their jurisdiction and control respect the environment of other states and of areas beyond national control is now part of the corpus of international law relating to the environment."
36 *Pulp Mills on the River Uruguay (Argentina v Uruguay) (Merits)* [2010] ICJ Rep 54 ("*Pulp Mills*").
37 Advisory Opinion, at [115]; and Pulp Mills, at para [197].
38 Advisory Opinion, at [119].
39 Advisory Opinion, at para [121].
40 Advisory Opinion, at para [123].
41 Advisory Opinion, at para [122].
42 Advisory Opinion, at para [147]; and Pulp Mills, at para [204].
43 Advisory Opinion, at [135].
44 Freestone, D., "Responsibilities and obligations of States Sponsoring Persons and entities with Respect to Activities in the Area", Vol. 105 (2011) *The American Journal of International Law* 1 at 6.
45 See the LOSC Regulations on Prospecting and Exploration for Polymetallic Sulphides in the Area (adopted 7 May 2010); the Convention on the Protection of the Marine Environment of the Baltic Sea Area 1992 (Helsinki Convention); and Convention for the Protection of the Marine Environment of the North-East Atlantic (OSPAR Convention).
46 Anton, Makgill and Payne, above n 10, at 63.
47 Advisory Opinion, at [119].
48 Advisory Opinion, at [4]; and ISBA/16/C/6, paragraph 1.
49 "BP and the Deepwater Horizon disaster: Cleaning up the legal spill", 15 November 2012 *The Economist*, http://www.economist.com/blogs/schumpeter/2012/11/bp-and-deepwater-horizon-disaster
50 Agarwal, above n 26, at 57.
51 Agarwal, above n 26, at 60.
52 Anton, Makgill and Payne, above n 10, at 64: "In connection with Question 2, the Chamber indicated, citing the ILC Articles on State Responsibility, Article 48, that obligations to preserve the environment of the high seas and in the Area may be *erga omnes*, that is, owed to the international community as a whole, or *erga omnes partes*, "to a group of States" [if the obligation] is established for the protection of a collective interest of the group."; and *Barcelona Traction, Light and Power Company, Ltd.* (*Belgium v. Spain*) [1970] I.C.J. Rep. 3 at para. 33: "The Court explained that '[b]y their very nature [such obligations] are the concern of all States. In view of the importance of the rights involved, all States can be held to have a legal interest in their protection; they are obligations *erga omnes*'." For a thorough discussion of *erga omnes* and seabed mining see Payne, C., *Collective Responsibility for Sound Resource Management: Erga Omnes Obligations and Deep Sea Mining*, Inter-American Congress on the Environmental Rule of Law, Montego Bay, Jamaica, 30 to 31 March 2015.
53 Gibson. J., "Deep Seabed Mining and Marine Environmental Protection: Advisory Opinion of the International Tribunal for the Law of the Sea on the Responsibilities and Obligations of States Sponsoring

Activities in the Area", (2011) 21 *Water Law* 189 at 192 to 193. Gibson observes that collaborative arrangements with the private sector may be the only practical way that developing states can participate in seabed mining. He notes, however, it may be questioned whether developed countries should be allowed to take advantage of flexible international corporate structures in order to gain access to mineral resources in reserved areas. He cautions that LOSC has long suffered from poor environmental compliance under "flags of convenience", and that it would be unfortunate if companies sponsored by "states of convenience" created a similar problem in the context of offshore mineral development.

54 LOSC, art 139(2); and Advisory Opinion, at [172].
55 Advisory Opinion, at para [178].
56 Advisory Opinion, at para [181].
57 Advisory Opinion, at para [184].
58 Advisory Opinion, at para [182].
59 LOSC, art 139(2); and Advisory Opinion, para at [186].
60 Advisory Opinion, at para [179].
61 Advisory Opinion, at para [179].
62 Advisory Opinion, at para [180].
63 Advisory Opinion, at para [193].
64 Advisory Opinion, at para [194].
65 Advisory Opinion, at para [195].
66 Advisory Opinion, at para [197].
67 Anton, D., "The Principle of Residual Liability in the Seabed Disputes Chamber of the International Tribunal for the Law of the Sea: The Advisory Opinion on Responsibility and Liability for International Seabed Mining (ITLOS case No. 17)", (2012) 7 *McGill International Journal of Sustainable Development Law and Policy* 241 at 250. Anton's observation is made in light of his discussion on the question of whether there is (or should be) residual liability for states in the case that there is a liability gap.
68 LOSC, art 4(4) of Annex III.
69 Advisory Opinion, at para [218].
70 Advisory Opinion, at para [227].
71 Advisory Opinion, at para [219].
72 Advisory Opinion, at para [222].
73 Advisory Opinion, at para [223].
74 Advisory Opinion, at para [224].
75 Advisory Opinion, at para [225].
76 Advisory Opinion, at para [226].
77 Anton, Makgill and Payne, above n 33, at 63.
78 Jones, J., "Regulatory design for scientific uncertainty: Acknowledging the diversity of approaches in environmental regulation and public administration", (2007) 19:3 *Journal of Environmental Law* 347 at 349.
79 Foster, C., *Science and the Precautionary Principle in International Courts and Tribunals: Expert Evidence, Burden of Proof and Finality* (Cambridge University Press, New York, 2011) at 18.
80 Declaration of the UN Conference on Environment and Development, adopted by the UN Conference on Environment and Development at Rio de Janeiro, 14 June 1992, UN Doc.A/CONF.48/14. 11 ILM 1416, Principle 15.
81 Foster, C., above n 79, at 18. Foster argues that the precautionary approach recognises "that it may be better to act first and then set about ascertaining the facts more closely. While preventive action involves intervention prior to the occurrence of damage in relation to known risks, precaution involves preparedness by public authorities to intervene in advance in relation to potential, uncertain or hypothetical threats. If the risk is sufficiently serious in character, precaution may posit intervention even where risk is simply suspected, conjectured or feared."
82 Weiss, C., "Scientific Uncertainty and Science-Based Precaution", (2003) 3 *International Environmental Agreements: Politics, Law and Economics* 137 at 139.
83 Jones, above n 78, at 363.
84 Weiss, above n 82, at 140.
85 VanderZwaag, D., Fuller, S. and Myers, R., "Canada and the Precautionary Principle/Approach in Ocean and Coastal Management" in David Rothwell and David VanderZwaag (eds.), *Towards Principled Ocean Governance* (Routledge, London and New York 2006) 145 at 145.

86 Advisory Opinion, at [135].
87 International Seabed Authority, Regulations on Prospecting and Exploration for Polymetallic Nodules in the Area of 2000.
88 International Seabed Authority, Regulations on Prospecting and Exploration for Polymetallic Sulphides in the Area of 2010.
89 Advisory Opinion, at para [125].
90 Advisory Opinion, at para [127].
91 Advisory Opinion, at para [131].
92 Trouwborst, A., *Precautionary Rights and Duties of States* (Martinus Nijhoff Publishers, Leiden, 2006) at 11; and Marr, Simon, *The Precautionary Principle in the Law of the Sea: Modern Decision Making in International Law* (Martinus Nijhoff Publishers, Leiden, 2003) at 17 to 21.
93 Trouwborst, A., at 286 to 287.
94 International Seabed Authority, *Environmental management needs for exploration and exploitation of deep sea minerals: report of a workshop held by the International Seabed Authority in collaboration with the Government of Fiji and the SOPAC Division of the Secretariat of the Pacific Community in Nadi, Fiji, from 29 November to 2 December, 2011* (International Seabed Authority, ISA Technical Study No. 10, 2012).
95 *Ibid* at 29 to 33. The legal issues chapter is adopted from the Legal Working Group Report. See http://www.isa.org.jm/files/documents/EN/Workshops/2011/WG2-LegalIssues.pdf
96 McGinnis, above n 6, at 41.
97 Allen, R., "The United States' Application of Precaution in Managing Living Marine Resources", (2011) 26 *International Journal of Marine and Coastal Law* 643 at 646, and Jones, J., above n 78, at 363.
98 ISA Technical Study No. 10, above n 95, at 33; and Jones, J., above n 78, at 361.
99 Advisory Opinion, at para [136].
100 Advisory Opinion, at para [117].
101 Advisory Opinion, at para [136].
102 Anton, Makgill and Payne, above n 10, at 63.
103 Use of the terms best available techniques, best environmental practice and related concepts in international environmental instrument, Expert Group on best available techniques, best environmental practice, UNEP/POPS/EGB.1/INF/3 (29 January 2003).
104 ISA Technical Study No. 10, above n 94, at 33.
105 Dickerson, H., "Best Practices" in *Max Planck Encyclopedia of Public International Law* (Oxford University Press, 2013) at [1] and [2].
106 Dickerson, H., at [7].
107 Dickerson, H., at [18].
108 ISA Technical Study No. 10, above n 94, at 33.
109 Convention on the Protection of the Marine Environment of the Baltic Sea Area (1992), article 3; and Convention for the Protection of the Marine Environment of the North-East Atlantic (1992), article 2(3).
110 Helsinki Convention, Annex II, regulation 2(3).
111 LOSC, art 206.
112 Advisory Opinion, at paras [141] to [142].
113 Advisory Opinion, at paras [145].
114 Advisory Opinion, at para [147]; and Pulp Mills, at para [204].
115 Advisory Opinion, at para [148].
116 Advisory Opinion, at para [148].
117 Advisory Opinion, at para [150].
118 Secretariat of the Pacific Community (SOPAC Division), *Information Brochure 6: Deep Sea Minerals Potential of the Pacific Islands Region*, SPC-EU EDF10 Deep Sea Minerals (DSM) Project; and Pratt, C. and Howorth, R., *Oceans Issues in the Pacific Region in 2000: Initiatives and Priorities* SOPAC Miscellaneous Report 415 (April 2001) at 13.
119 Matos, C. and Kotobalavu, J., *Ocean Minerals – Prospects for Pacific Island Nations* (Prepared for the Workshop on New Marine Technology and Social Change in the Pacific, Canberra, March 1986).
120 Henley, P., "Minerals and Mechanisms: The Legal Significance of the Notice of the "Common Heritage of Mankind" in the Advisory Opinion of the Seabed Disputes Chamber", (2011) 12 *Melbourne Journal of International Law* 1 at 20 to 21; and Regional Framework, above n 2, at 6 and 45 to 46.
121 LOSC, arts 55 and 57.
122 LOSC, art 76(1).

123 LOSC, art 56(1)(a).
124 LOSC, art 77(4). Natural resources under art 77 mean "mineral and other non-living resources of the seabed and subsoil together with living organisms belonging to sedentary species."
125 LOSC, art 78.
126 EEZ rights are subject to navigation, over-flight and the laying of submarine cables and pipelines under art 58; continental shelf rights are subject to the laying submarine cables and pipelines under art 79(1); and coastal States are required to pay royalties to the ISA for resources exploited within the continental shelf under art 82.
127 LOSC, arts 192 and 193.
128 LOSC, art 56(b)(iii), and through the obligation to adopt laws under art 208.
129 LOSC, arts 208(1) and (2).
130 LOSC, arts 208(3).
131 LOSC, art 214.
132 The Workshop was convened by the government of Papua New Guinea, the Metal Association of Japan, the Pacific Islands Forum, and the Secretariat of the Pacific Community.
133 Secretariat of the Pacific Community (SOPAC Division), *The Madang Guidelines: Principles for the Development of National Offshore Mineral Policies*, Report of the Offshore Mineral Policy Workshop Madang, Papua New Guinea (22 to 26 February 1999), at 5.
134 Pratt and Howorth, above n 118, page 4.
135 Madang Guidelines, recommendation 12.
136 Madang Guidelines, recommendation 6.
137 Madang Guidelines, recommendation 7,
138 Madang Guidelines, recommendation 13.
139 Pratt and Howorth, above n 118, at 14.
140 The Cook Islands, Federated States of Micronesia, Fiji, Kiribati, Marshall Islands, Nauru, Niue, Palau, Papua New Guinea, Samoa, Solomon Islands, Timor Leste, Tonga, Tuvalu and Vanuatu.
141 SP-EU EDF10 Deep Sea Minerals (DSM) Project Four Year Work Plan, at http://www.sopac.org/dsm/public/files/meetings/DSM_Project_Four_year_Detailed_Work_Plan_July2011_AT.pdf
142 For the full citation for the Regional Framework see above n 13.
143 Regional Framework, at 1.4.
144 Regional Framework, at 1.4.
145 Regional Framework, at 6.2.
146 Regional Framework, at 6.4.
147 Regional Framework, at 7.1.
148 Regional Framework, at 7.2.
149 The provision suggested in the Regional Framework was drawn from clause 11 of the first draft of New Zealand's EEZ Bill. Clause 11 of that Bill was intended to confirm the exercise of decision-making under the Bill was to be consistent with the LOSC and other relevant international conventions. It is more a tool of statutory interpretation than a statement of policy intent. Reflecting its interpretative function, the enacted s 11 was ultimately reduced to a statement, along the lines, that the EEZ Act 2012 enables implementation of the LOSC and international law.
150 Resource Management Act 1991, Fisheries Act 1996 and EEZ Act 2012.
151 Regional Framework, at 18.5.
152 Regional Framework, at 18.18.
153 Regional Framework, at 18.18.
154 Regional Framework, at 18.21.
155 Regional Framework, at 2.1.
156 Regional Framework, at 5.5.
157 Regional Framework, at 5.5.
158 Regional Framework, at 5.5.
159 Regional Framework, at 6.4.
160 Regional Framework, at 14.34.
161 Regional Framework, at 14.48.
162 Lynch, P., *Towards the Development of a National Regulatory Framework for Deep Sea Mining in the Cook Islands*, Research Paper (October 2011) at 15.
163 Cook Islands Seabed Minerals Act 2009 (CKSMB Act), s 3(1)(c). http://www.seabedmineralsauthority.gov.ck/PicsHotel/SeabedMinerals/Brochure/Seabed%20Minerals%20Bill%202009.pdf

164 CKSMB Act, s 5.
165 CKSMB Act, s 3(2)(a).
166 CKSMB Act, s 3(2)(e).
167 CKSBM Act, s 302(2).
168 Cook Islands Environment Act 2009, s 36. http://www.seabedmineralsauthority.gov.ck/PicsHotel/SeabedMinerals/Brochure/Environment%20Act%202003.pdf
169 Lynch, above n 162, at 27.
170 CKSBM Act, s 304(2)(c).
171 CKSBM Act, 332(2)(8), (9) and (10).
172 Cook Islands Seabed Minerals Authority, *Cook Islands National Seabed Minerals Policy*, March 2014, at 7.
173 Fiji Seabed Mineral Decree, s 3(1).
174 Fiji Seabed Mineral Decree, s 32(e).
175 Fiji Environment Management Act 2005, s 27.
176 Alley, D., Makgill, R., and Stalenberg, N., *Full Report: Integrated Coastal Management in Fiji and Recommendations for Improved Decision Making*, IUCN (February 2009) at 8.
177 Tonga Sea Bed Minerals Act 2014 at http://www.sopac.org/sopac/dsm/dsm_laws/Tonga_SeabedMineralsAct2014_1.pdf; Tuvalu Sea Bed Minerals Act 2014 at www.faolex.fao.org/docs/pdf/tuv140149.pdf.
178 Tonga SBM Act and Tuvalu SBM Act, s 2(2)(a), (e), (f) and (g).
179 Ministry for the Environment, *Improving Regulation of Environmental Effects in New Zealand's Exclusive Economic Zone*, (Wellington: MfE August 2007) at 1.
180 Ministry for the Environment Regulatory Impact Statement: Exclusive Economic Zone and Extended Continental Shelf Environmental Effects Legislation April 2011 at 1.
181 Makgill, R., "Sounding Out Riches and Risk: Approaching Environmental Regulation of Oil and Gas within New Zealand" in *Exploration and Development within the EEZ – Offshore Oil and Gas* (New Zealand Law Society, Wellington 2011) 1 to 34, at 7.
182 [2012] NZHC 1422 (HC).
183 [2012] NZHC 1422 (HC), at [64].
184 Makgill, R., "New Zealand", in R. Martella and B. Grosko (eds.) *International Environmental Law: The Practitioner's Guide to the Laws of the Planet* (American Bar Association, Chicago 2014) 909 to 932, at 910.
185 [2012] NZHC 1422 (HC), at [105].
186 Section 5 of the RMA provides that all decision-making under the RMA is subsidiary to and must achieve the purpose of sustainable management.
187 Palmer, K., "Environmental Management of Oil and Gas Activities in New Zealand" [2013] Vol 31 No 2 *Journal of Energy & Natural Resources Law* 123, at 131.
188 Makgill, above n 184, at 910 to 911.
189 EEZ Act, s 4.
190 EEZ Act, s 13.
191 EEZ Act, s 20(1).
192 EEZ Act, s 38.
193 EEZ Act, s 39(1).
194 EEZ Act, s 39(2)(a) and (b).
195 EEZ Act, s 45.
196 EEZ Act, s 46.
197 EEZ Act, s 50.
198 EEZ Act, s 53.
199 EEZ Act, s 59(2).
200 EEZ Act, s 59.
201 EEZ Act, s 60.
202 EEZ Act, s 61.
203 EEZ Act, s 61(1)(a), (b) and (c).
204 EEZ Act, s 61(5).
205 EEZ Act, s 61(2).
206 EEZ Act, s 61(3).
207 EEZ Act, s 64(2).

208 A132/2009 (EC).
209 A132/2009 at [101] (EC). For a detailed discussion of adaptive management and approaches to risk under the RMA see: Somerville Q.C.R., "Policy Adjudication, Adaptive Management and the Environment Court", (2013) Vol 9 *Resource Management Theory and Practice*, 1 to 28.
210 *Sustain Our Sounds Inc. v NZ King Salmon Company Ltd*, [2014] NZSC 40 (SC).
211 [2014] NZSC 40 at para [129] (SC).
212 [2014] NZSC 40 at para [133] (SC).
213 [2014] NZSC 40 at para [133] (SC).
214 *Decision on Marine Consent Application by Chatham Rock Phosphate Limited*, Application Ref: EEZ000006, Environmental Protection Authority, 10 February 205, at para [835].
215 *Chatham Rock Phosphate decision*, at para [836].
216 *Trans-Tasman Resources Ltd Marine Consent Decision*, Environmental Protection Authority, dated 17 June 2014, at para [762].
217 *Trans-Tasman Resources decision*, at para [772].
218 *Trans-Tasman Resources decision*, at para [139]
219 EEZ Act, s 61(2) and (3).
220 *Trans-Tasman Resources decision*, at para [794].
221 *Trans-Tasman Resources decision*, at para [797].
222 *Trans-Tasman Resources decision*, at paras [798] and [799].
223 *Trans-Tasman Resources decision*, at para [800].
224 *Trans-Tasman Resources decision*, at para [805]; and [2014] NZSC 40 at para [125] (SC).
225 *Trans-Tasman Resources decision*, at para [816].
226 *Trans-Tasman Resources decision*, at para [834].
227 *Trans-Tasman Resources decision*, at para [852].
228 *Trans-Tasman Resources decision*, at para [853].
229 Smellie, P., "'We're not going away,' says Trans-Tasman Resources, as EPA appeal dropped", *National Business Review* 13 Dec 2014.
230 Hartely, S., "Chatham Rock Criticises EPA for Report Release", *Otago Daily Times*, 20 Aug 2014. Chatham managing director Chris Castle stated that "while there were uncertainties to seafloor mining, that was what the marine consent process was designed to identify and clarify. We remain confident we have done the work to show we can undertake our mining operations in a sustainable way, and we believe the marine consent process will demonstrate this."
231 *Chatham Rock Phosphate decision*, at para [823].
232 *Chatham Rock Phosphate decision*, at para [824].
233 *Chatham Rock Phosphate decision*, at para [843].
234 *Chatham Rock Phosphate decision*, at para [845].
235 *Chatham Rock Phosphate decision*, at para [927].
236 *Chatham Rock Phosphate decision*, at para [923].
237 *Chatham Rock Phosphate decision*, at para [929].
238 Morton, J., "EPA Rejects Second Seabed Mining Bid", *The New Zealand Herald*, 11 Feb 2015.
239 Hartely, S., "Pro, Anti-mining Groups at Odds over EEZ Act change", *Otago Daily Times*, 14 Feb 2014.
240 Makgill, R., "Sounding Out Riches and Risk", above n 181, at 27 to 31.
241 EEZ Act, s 11.
242 Nautilus Minerals Inc. lodged submitted its seabed mining application to the Government of Papua New Guinea on 3 October 2008. Approval was granted on 17 January 2011, which was 2 weeks before the release of the Advisory Opinion.
243 Regional Framework, above n 13, at 20.

16
Transnational Crime

Douglas Guilfoyle

Introduction

The concept of transnational crime is potentially nebulous.[1] The 2000 United Nations Convention against Transnational Organized Crime (UNTOC) defines "transnational crime" to include any crime:

- committed in more than one state;
- committed in one state but a substantial part of its preparation, planning, direction, or control takes place in another state;
- committed in one state but involving an organized criminal group that engages in criminal activities in more than one state; or if
- committed in one state and having substantial effects in another state.[2]

The list of activities which might fall within such a definition is self-evidently not closed. Piracy, at least as practised off the coast of Somalia in the early twenty-first century, would qualify. Some governments have taken the position that illegal, unregulated and unreported fishing constitutes, in many cases, a form of highly organised transnational crime.[3] The focus of this chapter, however, will be upon maritime trade or smuggling of goods or people in a manner contrary to international conventions or relevant Security Council resolutions, as well as crimes of violence or "terrorism" other than piracy.

This chapter will consider first several general questions of the law of the sea relevant to maritime action aimed at countering transnational crime before considering the questions of maritime terrorism and weapons proliferation and the smuggling of migrants and prohibited drugs by sea in more detail. The chapter will conclude with an assessment of current challenges in addressing these various illicit activities.

Jurisdiction over maritime crime under public international law

Jurisdiction under LOSC: coastal states

The extent of a coastal state's law prescriptive and enforcement jurisdiction in different areas of ocean space is covered in other chapters, in particular those in Part A. As a general observation, coastal states have in fact a relatively limited competence to intercept traffic in goods or people in adjacent waters if one considers the regimes of the contiguous zone and the territorial sea. (Such activities will not fall within the jurisdiction allocated to a coastal state within its Exclusive Economic Zone (EEZ).) To begin, while the contiguous zone has its origins in the suppression of maritime smuggling (with the so-called hovering acts),[4] the powers it confers at international law are more limited than is commonly appreciated. Within the contiguous zone a coastal state has authority to either prevent or punish infringements of its customs, fiscal, immigration and sanitary laws in its territorial sea or land territory (Article 33, LOSC). As Ivan Shearer has noted, the connotations of the word "punish" require an offence to already have occurred within territorial jurisdiction; while the connotations of "prevent" might extend to inspections and warnings, they could not justify further measures such as arrest, seizure or detention.[5] Nonetheless, there are states that take in their law or practice more expansive views, extending to the exercise of enforcement jurisdiction under the "preventative" limb. The Australian practice of permitting the seizure of drugs in the contiguous zone perhaps colourably falls within the concept of prevention (though deprivation of property rights before an offence has been committed would seem to stretch the concept).[6] The *US Naval Commander's Handbook on the Law of Naval Operations* goes rather further, asserting that a coastal state enjoys full law-enforcement authority over customs, fiscal, immigration and sanitary matters out to 24 nm.[7] Such an approach collapses the distinction between prevention and punishment entirely. Finally, unless a vessel in the territorial sea is bound to or from port, it will obviously enjoy the right of innocent passage.[8] While the list of non-innocent activities contained within LOSC is not exhaustive, the assertion of enforcement jurisdiction by the coastal state against a vessel merely passing through its territorial sea normally requires that the any illicit activity by a vessel be such as to prejudice the peace, good order or security of the coastal state or its territorial sea.[9] (That is, the offence must have some impact going *beyond* the ship itself.) The result then, is that for present purposes coastal states will not generally be able to take action against vessels engaged in transnational crime unless they are in port, bound to or from port and located within the territorial sea or have committed some crime having an effect in the coastal state's territorial sea or land territory. Intervention must otherwise rely on the law applicable to vessels on the high seas (including the ability of a flag state to waive its exclusive jurisdiction over a vessel by consent).

Jurisdiction under LOSC: the high seas

On the high seas, of course, a vessel is subject to the exclusive jurisdiction of its flag state.[10] The main object of this rule is to confer an immunity on vessels exercising freedom of navigation on the high seas from interference by the public vessels of foreign states.[11] The presumption finds expression in the chapeau to Article 110 of LOSC:

> Except where acts of interference derive from powers conferred by treaty, a warship which encounters on the high seas a foreign ship . . . is not justified in boarding it [unless an exception applies].

The general exceptions to the rule concern cases where there are reasonable grounds for suspecting that the vessel is engaged in one of a limited number of activities (i.e. the slave trade, piracy, unauthorised broadcasting) or where there is reasonable suspicion that a vessel is either without nationality (the position of such "stateless" vessels is discussed further below) or despite "flying a foreign flag or refusing to show its flag, . . . is, in reality, of the same nationality as the [interdicting] warship".[12] Otherwise, the vessel's state of nationality (flag state) must have consented to the exercise of jurisdiction either under a treaty or an *ad hoc* arrangement. The difficulty with the general exceptions is that not every activity attracts the same powers of enforcement. In the case of either slave trading or suspicion of being a vessel without nationality, LOSC only provides expressly for a right of visit and inspection. By contrast, universal enforcement jurisdiction (encompassing powers of arrest and prosecution) is only expressly provided for in the case of piracy[13] and to a certain extent in the case of high seas broadcasting.[14]

The position of stateless vessels deserves further brief consideration. A vessel need not be registered to enjoy nationality. The national laws of many states provide that small craft below a certain weight or length may enjoy a right to fly a flag (without registration) based on the nationality of the owner alone.[15] A vessel with such a *right* to fly its flag enjoys the nationality its flag state under LOSC, irrespective of whether it actually flies a flag or displays national markings.[16] In practice, this may make it difficult to determine the nationality of small craft. Nonetheless, if the master of such a small craft claims nationality in a particular state and that presumptive flag state upon inquiry rejects that claim of nationality, the vessel is rendered constructively stateless.[17] This follows from the fact that a vessel may not claim two nationalities and use them at its convenience; indeed, a vessel doing so may be "assimilated" to a stateless vessel.[18] Views differ on the further question of whether under customary international law a stateless vessel as such may be subjected to the jurisdiction of the interdicting state. There is some case law for the proposition that such a vessel may be subjected to the jurisdiction of any state because it enjoys the protection of none,[19] however much of the academic commentary suggests a further jurisdictional nexus to the interdicting state is required before law enforcement action can be taken.[20]

As regards consent by the flag state to interdiction under a treaty or *ad hoc* arrangement, there are numerous relevant examples[21] some of which are discussed below. At present it is enough to observe that such treaties tend to have a narrow subject matter and a specific focus, such as the maritime interdiction provision of the Vienna Convention on Narcotic Drugs 1988 (providing a mechanism whereby a flag state may consent to foreign states boarding its vessels on the high seas).[22] This may lead to the problem of boarding a vessel on suspicion that it is engaged in one activity only to find it is engaged in a different illegal activity not covered by the treaty arrangement. Alternatively, a flag state may validly consent (often by *note verbale*) to one of its vessels being visited and inspected on the high seas and even to the exercise of law enforcement jurisdiction by the interdicting state over the vessel and those aboard. It is worth noting, however, that it will be difficult to prosecute any offences discovered in such cases absent an applicable national law with extraterritorial effect and that such *ad hoc* arrangements may also raise human rights questions (e.g. whether even a well-advised defendant would have had notice they could be subjected to the foreign criminal jurisdiction in question).[23]

A further exception worth brief consideration is the doctrine of hot pursuit.[24] Thus, where a vessel has infringed the laws of the coastal state in a maritime zone where it has relevant enforcement jurisdiction, the authorities of the coastal state may pursue the vessel onto the high seas and arrest it there (provided a number of conditions are met).[25] While the doctrine has generated a number of high profile cases and considerable academic commentary, it is difficult to obtain reliable data on how frequently it is used in practice. In general, its use appears more the exception than the rule.

The very narrowness of these general exceptions (and specific treaty regimes) serves to reinforce the evident importance placed by states on the principle of exclusive flag jurisdiction as the principal means of upholding freedom of navigation on the high seas. Given the number of "threats from the commons" we now face in the field of maritime security,[26] one may well ask whether we have struck the right balance between collective security and freedom of navigation.²⁷ Quite apart from the legal restrictions, the hazard and expense of maritime interdiction operations already tends to ensure that they are an exceptional measure. It will typically be easier to take measures against vessels and their masters and crew when they arrive in port.²⁸

Jurisdiction under general principles of public international law

The alternative, of course, is to rely on general principles of prescriptive jurisdiction under public international law and use them to criminalise acts occurring at sea. Conventions taking such an approach (sometimes known as crime suppression treaties) may also provide for mutual legal assistance and/or "extradite or prosecute" obligations to assist in investigations and prosecutions. The alternative source of general international obligations (or powers) in this field arises through the use of Security Council resolutions, typically targeting the proliferation of weapons of mass destruction. These too may oblige UN member states to modify their national law. Such cases are discussed in more detail below.

Terrorism and crimes of violence at sea

The SUA convention

The Convention for the Suppression of Unlawful Acts against the Safety of Maritime Navigation (the SUA Convention)²⁹ was notoriously inspired by the *Achille Lauro* hijacking which made two things painfully apparent. The first was that the maritime transport industry was not covered by any equivalent to the numerous conventions dealing with aircraft hijacking and other offences against the safety of air transportation. The second was the arbitrary limitations present within the definition of piracy, most notably that piracy is defined under treaty law to involve an attack by a private vessel against another vessel (the two ship requirement) and the further requirement that piracy be "for private ends"³⁰ (which is commonly, if mistakenly, taken to exclude politically motivated violence).³¹ Given that the *Achille Lauro* was internally hijacked it was not a case of piracy and neither the exception to flag state jurisdiction on the high seas nor universal jurisdiction to prosecute applied.

Rather than analogise such acts of maritime violence to piracy (thus creating universal prescriptive jurisdiction and universal enforcement jurisdiction on the high seas), the SUA Convention followed the so-called "Hague model" of terrorism suppression conventions.³² Under the SUA Convention parties undertake to criminalise in national law a variety of offences including seizing or exercising control over a ship by force or intimidation, performing acts of violence likely to endanger the safe navigation of a ship, or causing damage to a ship which is likely to endanger its safe navigation, or, indeed, simply destroying a ship.³³ States parties must extend their criminal law to cover such acts when committed aboard their flag vessel or by their nationals.³⁴

States parties must be able to assert jurisdiction over offences covered by the convention where a suspect is simply found within their territory. The offences created are thus subject to a classic extradite or prosecute obligation.³⁵ Such provisions "stipulate[] that in every case where an alleged offender is found within the state's territory that state must either extradite him to face trial in another state that seeks him for the purposes of prosecution. . . or if it does not extradite him, it must submit the case to its competent authorities for the purpose of prosecution."³⁶ The result "is in essence a form of universal jurisdiction as between the parties" though it is important to note that this jurisdiction is "only applicable between the parties".[37] Further, the duty to investigate a suspect is triggered by the suspect's territorial presence rather than an extradition request.[38] Thus, a state party has a free choice whether to extradite or prosecute a suspect; and an obligation to prosecute where no other states are willing to do so. The SUA convention also contains a provision allowing the master of a ship which has a suspect aboard to put that suspect off into port at a contracting party.[39] While the port state may refuse to take delivery of the suspect, it is clearly expected that this will be done only exceptionally and there is a requirement for such a refusing state to give reasons.[40]

Finally, the SUA convention contains no express reference to any requirement that an offender must act with a political motive. Given the events that inspired it, and references to the problem of international terrorism contained in its preamble, some authors apparently assume that such a terrorist or political motive is required for an offence under the Convention.[41] The better view is that the SUA convention, like most of the "terrorism" suppression conventions, simply prohibits certain conduct without specifying that such acts must be committed with any particular motive. The very limited national case law on point supports this proposition.[42] This absence of any motive requirement means that some of the offences outlined in the SUA convention could in fact be committed by pirates. Somali hostage-taking piracy would clearly fall foul of the prohibition on seizing control of a vessel by force or intimidation. The two bodies of law, however, while they may overlap are clearly not co-extensive. The most obvious gap between the two regimes is that LOSC provides for visit and search *at sea* of a vessel suspected of piracy and allows enforcement jurisdiction to be exercised by a state other than the flag state in such cases. The SUA Convention, however, creates neither such unilateral law-enforcement rights over foreign vessels nor does it contain provisions facilitating obtaining flag state consent to such a boarding.

SUA 2005

Following the events of 11 September 2001, policy-makers began to fear the possibility of a maritime "September 11" in which a vessel might be hijacked and used as a floating bomb against a major port. This concern was likely always overstated. Maritime targets are less visible to the general public and therefore less attractive to terrorist and groups, which tend to be methodologically conservative.[43] In addition, even flammable cargoes are rather harder to ignite at sea than is commonly understood. The more likely model of maritime terrorism remains the use of small boats in suicide attacks against military targets, such as occurred in the USS *Cole* incident in 2000. A further post-2001 concern was the proliferation of precursor technologies that could be used to make biological, chemical or nuclear weapons (BCN weapons) and the proliferation of associated delivery systems. Following the *So San* incident, the US-led Proliferation Security Initiative (PSI) sought, as one of its declared objectives, to strengthen relevant international laws on such proliferation, including where it occurred by sea. One consequence of this was a push by the US to conclude bilateral agreements with major shipping registries to permit the boarding and search of vessels suspected of involvement in maritime proliferation of BCN weapons, precursors or delivery systems to state or non-state actors of proliferation concern.[44] Beyond such bilateral initiatives, the US and UK also spearheaded moves to negotiate a 2005 Protocol to the SUA Convention.[45]

In essence, the resulting SUA Protocol 2005 grafts a series of offences on to the original convention dealing with the use of ships as weapons in themselves or their involvement in the proliferation of BCN weapons or precursor technologies.[46] The exercise was not without controversy for a number of reasons. First, the convention potentially covers transfers of such technology to a government unless it is a party to the nuclear non-proliferation treaty (NPT).[47] Thus, its provisions were seen as discriminatory by some non-NPT states.[48] Second, and even more controversially, it included a provision on high seas boarding. The default position under the convention is that a vessel suspected of being involved in a SUA Protocol 2005 offence may only be boarded and inspected on the high seas with the consent of the flag state.[49] The convention does, however, allow states parties to opt into provisions which allow other parties to board their vessels either without seeking authorisation (effectively granting comprehensive permission in advance) or where a request to board is made and acknowledged but no further responses forthcoming within four hours (deemed consent).[50] The United States was a strong advocate of including such provisions which are commonly found in its bilateral drug interdiction treaties, especially those concluded with neighbouring Latin American and Caribbean states.[51] The idea of high seas boarding even predicated upon case-by-case flag state authorisation proved sufficiently controversial, as evidenced by the extensive list of safeguard provisions governing the conduct of such boardings included in the 2005 Protocol.[52]

Effectiveness of the SUA convention and 2005 protocol

The effectiveness of both the SUA Convention and its 2005 Protocol are open to question. While the convention contains an obligation to report to the International Maritime Organization (IMO) any prosecutions that occur under it, a major study of the terrorism suppression conventions was unable to identify any case in which this had actually happened.[53] Despite the Security Council having repeatedly implied in its resolutions on Somali piracy that the convention could be used to prosecute such acts, it does not appear to have formed the basis of many such prosecutions or, indeed, extraditions.

For the 2005 SUA Protocol to be regarded as a success, two requirements must be met. First, it must be sufficiently widely ratified.[54] On this basis, as I have noted elsewhere, the SUA Protocol is, at best, a qualified success.[55] Despite the diplomatic effort made by the US, UK and like-minded states to secure its conclusion, as at 17 October 2014 it has gained only 32 ratifications.[56] None of these are from the US, UK or other G8 states. Certainly two of the world's three largest flag states by registered tonnage, Panama and the Marshall Islands, have ratified the Protocol and have relevant laws prohibiting WMD transfers.[57] While this might allow suspect cargoes aboard such vessels to be interdicted at sea by a third state under the Protocol, this could only occur if a significant naval power ratified it.[58] None has. Second, the SUA Protocol is ultimately reliant upon national legislation for its enforcement: the crimes it creates can only be prosecuted under national law.[59] Even following Security Council resolution 1540, which expressly required states to take action in national law to prevent transfers of BCN weapons and precursor technologies to non-state actors, it is unclear whether many states have fully implemented that obligation. While the United States is not a party to the SUA Protocol 2005, it does have laws which cover, more or less, the activities it prescribes (at least where there is a nexus to the US).[60] The Australian government has taken the position that certain SUA Protocol 2005 offences are covered by existing laws,[61] specific implementing legislation has been expected for some years though there is none at present.[62] The legislative position of other Proliferation Security Initiative participants is unclear. Such laws, to be effective, would also have to be capable of application to foreign vessels intercepted with flag state consent. This is likely to require specific legislative reform rather than a reliance on existing offences which will usually require a direct nexus to the prosecuting state.

Smuggling: migrants and narcotics

Introduction

A classical literature on transnational organised crime tended to portray the phenomenon in terms of rigid, hierarchical and mafia-like organisations. More recently "the emphasis has been on models of a more fluid kind, networks of traffickers that challenge the state's definition of what a legal market is and which respond to constantly shifting markets and changing conditions by being highly adaptable and operating globally."[63] Where once it was assumed different criminal organisations specialised in the movement of different goods, now specialisation is "the network itself, and its ability to procure, transport, and deliver illegal merchandise across countries. What the merchandise was became almost irrelevant."[64] There is good reason to believe that the same networks which are involved in the smuggling of narcotics may also be involved in the smuggling of other commodities, including people.

The history of international cooperation in the suppression of maritime smuggling and trafficking has its origins in efforts to counter drug smuggling. Indeed, the earliest examples of such cooperation were probably between the United States and the United Kingdom to suppress the liquor traffic during prohibition[65] and the US now has some "45 maritime counterdrug bilateral agreements or operational procedures in place . . . [with] partner nations."[66] As already noted in relation to the SUA Protocol 2005, many of the treaty provisions developed to deal with other concerns, such as the proliferation of BCN weapons or smuggling of migrants draw heavily on drug interdiction models.[67]

Efforts to deal with the smuggling of both narcotics and migrants have generally been addressed in specialised bilateral, regional or multilateral treaties.[68] This follows from the fact that the relevant provisions of LOSC are either unhelpful or wholly inadequate to dealing with these problems. Migrant smuggling *per se* is not addressed in LOSC at all, although some have argued its provisions on suppression of the slave trade are potentially relevant to the issue.[69] Smuggled migrants may fall into a number of categories: refugees and asylum seekers fleeing conflict or persecution; economic migrants seeking a better life; and those being trafficked into exploitative conditions. In practice these categories may overlap considerably. However, it is whether human trafficking may be considered a contemporary form of slavery that concerns us at present. I have noted elsewhere that historically international law held slavery and "practices similar to slavery" to be distinct categories; indeed, I have argued that most modern forms of human trafficking do not involve the exercise of ownership over people, but rather forms of debt-bondage which constitute not slavery *per se* but a "similar practice".[70] A good argument may be made, however, that migrant trafficking may involve slavery. The argument runs that the coercive movement of people in order to exploit their labour, under conditions where they have little personal autonomy and are treated as units capable of being bought and sold, does effectively involve the exercise of *de facto* control over a person tantamount to slavery and it should thus be considered slavery.[71] This, however, does not assist much when it comes to providing a legal basis for interdicting migrant smugglers or human traffickers on the high seas.

Articles 99 and 110 of LOSC do make provision for the suppression of the slave trade at sea, but lamentably represent only a relic of 19th century law. These articles provide for visit and inspection of ships suspected of the slave trade but leave the question of enforcing that prohibition, implicitly at least, to the flag state.[72] (Although a curious provision of the law of the sea automatically emancipates slaves who 'take refuge' aboard another ship; opening, perhaps, the door to inviting such slaves aboard an interdicting vessel.)[73] In any event, the vast majority of migrants moved by sea are *not* being delivered into exploitation. Trafficked persons are far more likely to arrive in the destination country legally and on tourist or other visas. There are, however, exceptions. There have been occasional reports of child slaves being moved by sea in West Africa,[74] as well as the existence of slavery-like practices within the most poorly regulated parts of the fishing industry.[75] Reports of the latter include cases of people held indefinitely at sea through their being transhipped between fishing vessels thus preventing them from ever arriving in a port at which they could flee.[76]

The LOSC provisions on drug smuggling at sea are equally limited. They provide only for a generalised duty of cooperation to suppress narcotics trafficking at sea, and provide that a flag state which suspects one of its vessels is being used for narcotics smuggling may request the assistance of other states to suppress that activity.[77] As Gilmore has noted, this omits the more usual situation where an interdicting state wishes to take action against a foreign-flagged vessel which it suspects of involvement in drug smuggling.[78] In this context, as in others such as the regulation of fishing or countering piracy off Somalia, LOSC is best regarded as a framework convention under which other, more detailed agreements may be concluded. Indeed as noted above, when it comes to high seas law enforcement, Article 110 of the Convention expressly contemplates that boarding and search of foreign vessels may occur under other international treaties and agreements. It is to examples of such agreements this chapter now turns.

Narcotic smuggling

The most widely ratified provision on maritime interception of narcotic drugs is found in Article 17(3) of the Vienna Narcotics Convention. This allows an interdicting state which has identified a suspect vessel to contact that vessel's flag state and request confirmation of registry. If registration is confirmed by the flag state, it may seek permission to board, inspect and possibly take "other appropriate" law enforcement action against the vessel. This exercise of enforcement jurisdiction is supported by a grant of *legislative* jurisdiction in the Narcotics Convention. This convention expressly contemplates that the state which intercepts a drug smuggling vessel on the basis of flag states consent (provided either under the convention or under another arrangement), may enact national laws permitting the exercise of law-enforcement jurisdiction over offences discovered on board.[79] This seemingly simple system conceals a number of complexities.[80] First, it may be difficult to identify the state in which the vessel is registered. Second, the Narcotics Convention does not provide for boarding and inspection of the suspect vessel unless registration is *confirmed*. As noted above, not all small craft (such as yachts) which may be used in drug smuggling necessarily need to be registered under national law. They may enjoy nationality – and therefore a right of navigation on the high seas – by virtue of ownership alone. Third, it may be difficult to find the national agency responsible for confirming registration and giving permission for foreign states to board a vessel on the high seas – if they are even the same agency. Fourth, the list of powers given in Article 17 is disjunctive and sequential. Visit and search is a distinct exercise of enforcement jurisdiction from arrest and prosecution. Consent to the former is not necessarily consent to the latter. This may lead to delays if a crime is discovered as the interdicting state will need to seek "disposition instructions" from the flag state. (In effect, a decision about which state will conduct any prosecution arising.) Fifth, there is no provision on what is sometimes called "reverse hot pursuit". That is, a suspect vessel may attempt to evade interception by entering the territorial sea of a third state.[81]

As noted above, the United States is the world-leader in concluding bilateral and regional agreements regarding interdiction of vessels suspected of narcotic smuggling. Its web of treaties shows a certain variation in drafting and flexibility of approach. This is largely based on what partner states are willing – or constitutionally able – to agree to. Broadly, however, these treaties use (selectively or in combination) a number of the following techniques to try and resolve a number of the problems outlined above. Such US bilateral treaties:

1) may refer to vessels claiming the *nationality* of a state party, rather than being registered in a state party. This allows the presumptive flag state to authorise boarding and inspection, if only for the purposes of confirming nationality. (Of course, if the vessel was carrying two sets of papers and using them at its convenience, it would be rendered constructively stateless and boarding would be permissible under Article 110, UNCLOS);[82]
2) increasingly require that parties stipulate a single point of contact capable of authorising interdiction (a "competent authority"). Details of the relevant competent authorities are usually updated between the parties by diplomatic note;[83]
3) may give permission in advance to conduct boarding and inspection of a state party's flag vessel (though not to the exercise of further law-enforcement powers of arrest or prosecution) through one of two mechanisms. First, each party may simply grant a unilateral right of visit and inspection over its flag vessels to the other party to the treaty, obviating any need for case-by-case authorisation. Alternatively, a treaty may require a request for permission to board and inspect being made and acknowledged by the competent authority of the flag state, but then grant a right to board and inspect if no reply is made within a fixed time period, usually two to four hours (a "deemed consent" provision);[84]
4) may provide for ship-riders, a particular US innovation. The essential concept of a ship-rider is that, for example, a Jamaican law-enforcement official might be embarked upon a US Coast Guard cutter. In the event that the US cutter encounters a suspect vessel of Jamaican nationality, the ship-rider will be able to authorise a boarding and inspection (in which the US Coast Guard crew may assist as requested);[85]
5) may authorise interdiction operations in a partner state's territorial sea (thus allowing "reverse hot pursuit" or even patrolling). This may occur under a number of models. Comprehensive permission in advance to conduct territorial sea operations is uncommon, but not unheard-of. Where a ship-rider is present, he or she may be able to authorise entry into the territorial sea of the state he or she represents. Finally, such treaties may set out an obligation to seek permission to intervene against a vessel present in the territorial sea but may nonetheless allow intervention in cases where time does not permit such a request to be made. (In the latter case, contact must usually be made with coastal state authorities as soon as possible.)[86]

A number of these mechanisms are also found in regional treaties dealing with narcotics interdiction.[87]

Migrant smuggling

The Migrant Smuggling Protocol to UNTOC provides for the criminalisation of movement of persons across international borders into a state of which they are not a national contrary to local migration law for profit ("migrant smuggling"), and includes as aggravating circumstances either endangering the lives or safety of migrants or their "inhuman or degrading treatment, including . . . exploitation".[88] The word "exploitation" acknowledges possible overlap with human trafficking. The relevant provisions of the Protocol on maritime interdiction are cast in similar turns to the Vienna Narcotics Convention. In particular, the Protocol's interdiction provisions closely follow Article 17 of the UN Narcotics Convention. Article 8 of the Migrant Smuggling Protocol provides that a party may request other parties' assistance where it reasonably suspects that one of its flag vessels is engaged in migrant smuggling. Where a party reasonably suspects that another party's flag vessel is smuggling migrants, it may request confirmation of registry and subsequent permission to take action against the vessel, including boarding, search and, upon finding evidence of migrant smuggling, "appropriate measures . . . as authorized by the flag State". The exclusive jurisdiction of the flag state will thus prevail unless it permits the interdicting state to prosecute (and providing the latter has an appropriate law). This drafting also replicates the problems that flow from requiring "confirmation of registry" as discussed above. Boarding states may not take measures beyond those authorised, unless authorised under relevant treaties or necessary to "relieve imminent danger" to human life.[89] Consent to boarding may also be granted on conditions, including as to matters of state responsibility "and the extent of effective measures to be taken".[90]

Parties are not expressly required to create offences in national law covering offences committed aboard interdicted foreign vessels. Article 15(2)(c) of UNTOC itself may, however, indirectly require states to provide for domestic jurisdiction over offences committed on other parties' flag vessels under the Migrant Smuggling Protocol. It requires each state party to establish jurisdiction over conspiracies or activities undertaken outside its territory "with a view to the commission of a serious crime [punishable by four years' imprisonment] within its territory". This will often cover acts undertaken aboard foreign-flag vessels with a view to illegally disembarking migrants in the territory of the interdicting or boarding state. Further, under UNTOC Article 14(4) a state party may "establish its jurisdiction over the offences covered by this Convention [or its Protocols] when the alleged offender is present in its territory and it does not extradite him or her".

Despite this, the Protocol's provisions on jurisdiction and boarding and inspection remain quite general. Unsurprisingly, there does not appear to be any state practice in which the convention has formed the basis for interdicting migrants. One might thus expect that states would enter more detailed bilateral agreements as has occurred in fields such as drug interdiction. To some extent this is the case. However, rather than bilateral or regional treaties, counter migrant-smuggling measures are more typically pursued on the basis of unilateral measures or bilateral arrangements concluded as technical agreements *below the level of treaties* between states of departure and destination (or arrival, where migrants intend to move on to other states as a final destination, as has been the experience in Europe). This has particularly been the case in European practice where a range of agreements between individual EU member states with countries of departure such as Senegal have formed the basis for operations facilitated by the EU border agency Frontex and directed in part at interceptions in the territorial sea of the state of departure.[91]

A further development has been the emergence of consultative forums for information sharing and the discussion of common concerns among states involved in particular irregular migration routes, whether as states of origin, transit or destination. Such forums usually also involve concerned international organisations. Two particular examples are the Budapest Process (focused on questions of migration affecting Europe and its eastern neighbours)[92] and the

Bali Process (which while focused on South East Asia includes states of origin and destination as far-flung as Afghanistan and the US).[93] These processes have certain similarities with other relatively flexible, informal, horizontal networks drawing together experts and decision makers. While lacking decision-making powers, at their best such networks can raise levels of trust, share best practices (including through training events), and promote pragmatic working relationships which are consistent with the parties (often varied) legal commitments. The relevant literature on these developments remains, however, relatively thin and their impact on state practice hard to quantify.[94]

Conclusion

If one is looking for a general pattern of international cooperation in respect of maritime transnational organised crime revealed by this brief discussion, then it is probably that there are often layers of international agreement involved. UNCLOS usually provides the broad backdrop for powers of law enforcement at sea. Multilateral treaties such as the SUA Convention, the Vienna Narcotics Convention or the Migrant Smuggling Protocol may then establish frameworks for sectoral cooperation, but these are often not directly relied upon by states. More often these multilateral conventions serve to inspire further arrangements commonly in the form of regional or bilateral treaties and increasingly, at least in the field of irregular migration by sea, even agreements concluded below the level of treaties. This may have the advantage of creating solutions tailored to particular bilateral (or regional) relationships. This approach may work well where, for example, there is a high volume of goods or people being smuggled by sea between particular states of departure and destination. It also, however, has distinct weaknesses. The limited membership of bilateral or regional arrangements will obviously limit their reach; tailored bilateralism can result in "hub and spoke" situations where a powerful player can extract bilateral concessions that would not be available in a multilateral forum; and interdictions concluded on the basis of agreements below the level of treaties may have difficulty founding a prosecution given human rights or rule of law considerations.

The response to maritime organised crime at the level of international law is notably sectoral and fragmented. While there has been significant "copy-pasting" between legal regimes, the focus has generally been on creating maritime interdiction rights regarding only the particular subject matter at hand and based – as the invariable starting point – on obtaining case-by-case flag state consent to interdiction operations. The operational difficulties this may give rise to were discussed, in particular, in relation to narcotics smuggling. The discussion of the attempt under the SUA Protocol 2005 to contain the proliferation of BCN weapons by sea further noted the problems that arise when such a regime is less than universally subscribed to or remains unimplemented at the level of national law. Most pressing is the potential problem of having legal authority to board a vessel suspected of one offence but then discovering another over which one has no jurisdiction once aboard. The point is not moot: vessels boarded in waters off Somalia on suspicion of piracy may in fact prove to be engaged in migrant-smuggling into Yemen.

As I have noted elsewhere, "[a]t-sea interdictions are logistically complex, potentially dangerous and often very expensive."[95] It is, therefore, unsurprising that they remain an exceptional measure. What the formal treaty law on interdiction of maritime transnational organised crime may tend to conceal, however, is the steady growth of less formal mechanisms aimed at dealing with these problems. The potential trend is most apparent in the field of irregular migration, and the response to Somali piracy. While memoranda of understanding and horizontal networks of experts are perfectly legitimate means of responding to complex challenges they risk being (or being perceived as) "non-transparent and technocratic".[96]

Notes

1 N. Boister, *An Introduction to Transnational Criminal Law* (Oxford: OUP, 2012), pp. 3–4.
2 Art. 3(2), United Nations Convention Against Transnational Organized Crime, 15 November 2000, 2225 UNTS 209, in force 29 September 2003.
3 E.g. comments of Australia in: *Report of the Twenty-First Meeting of the Commission for the Conservation of Antarctic Marine Living Resources* (2002) (CCAMLR-XXI), 162 at para. 5.3.
4 A.V. Lowe, 'The development of the concept of the contiguous zone' (1981) 52 *The British Yearbook of International Law* 109–69.
5 I. Shearer, 'Problems of jurisdiction and law enforcement against delinquent vessels' (1986) 35 ICLQ 320, 330.
6 s. 67(1)(b)(ii), Maritime Powers Act 2013 (No. 15, 2013), and compare s. 41(1)(c) (distinguishing prevention and punishment).
7 US Navy, *Commander's Handbook on the Law of Naval Operations* (2007), paragraphs 1.5 and 3.11.4.1.5; and compare *American Law Institute, Restatement of the Law Third: The Foreign Relations Law of the United States* (St. Paul, Minn.: American Law Institute, 1987), vol. II, pp. 30, 49.
8 Technically, a vessel bound to port enjoys rights of innocent passage but access to port may be subjected to conditions which may be enforced prior to entry: compare Arts. 18(1)(b) and 25(2), LOSC.
9 Art. 19(1), LOSC.
10 Art. 92(1), LOSC.
11 D. Guilfoyle, *Shipping Interdiction and the Law of the Sea* (Cambridge: CUP, 2007), p. 276.
12 Art. 110(1), LOSC.
13 Art. 105, LOSC.
14 Art. 109(4), LOSC. See further Guilfoyle, *Shipping Interdiction*, pp. 176–7.
15 D.P. O'Connell, *The International Law of the Sea*, I. Shearer, ed. (Oxford: Clarendon Press, 1984) p. 753; H. Meyers, *The Nationality of Ships* (The Hague: Martinus Nijhoff, 1967), pp. 149–50.
16 Art. 91(1), LOSC.
17 For practical examples of larger fishing vessels being rendered constructively stateless when a flag state refuted their claimed registry see: D. Guilfoyle, *Shipping Interdiction*, p. 121.
18 Art. 92(2), LOSC.
19 *Molvan v. Attorney General for Palestine* [1948] AC 351 at 369; 15 ILR 115 at 124.
20 R.R. Churchill and A.V. Lowe, *The Law of the Sea* (Manchester: Manchester University Press, 1988), p. 214; compare E. Papastavridis, *The Interception of Vessels on the High Seas* (Oxford: Hart, 2013), p. 266.
21 See generally: Papastavridis, *The Interception of Vessels*; Guilfoyle, *Shipping Interdiction*.
22 Art. 17, United Nations Convention against Illicit Traffic in Narcotic Drugs and Psychotropic Substances, Vienna, 20 December 1988, 1582 UNTS 95. Entered force 11 November 1990 (Vienna Narcotics Convention).
23 D. Guilfoyle, '*Medvedyev and Others v. France*, European Court of Human Rights' (2010) 25(3) *International Journal of Marine and Coastal Law*, 437–42.
24 The classic study is: N.M. Poulantzas, *The Right of Hot Pursuit in International Law*, 2nd edn (The Hague: Martinus Nijhoff, 2002).
25 Art. 111, LOSC.
26 S. Kaye, 'Threats from the global commons: Problems of jurisdiction and enforcement' (2007) 8 *Melbourne Journal of International Law* 185.
27 N. Klein, *Maritime Security and the Law of the Sea* (Oxford: Oxford University Press, 2011), pp. 324–7.
28 This conclusion is reinforced by cases such as Australia, a party to the Vienna Narcotics Convention, which has entered no subsequent bilateral narcotics interdiction arrangements and does not appear ever to have relied upon Art. 17 *ad hoc* boarding authorisation.
29 Rome, 10 March 1988, (1992) 1678 UNTS 201 ('SUA Convention').
30 Art. 101, LOSC.

31 See: Guilfoyle, *Shipping Interdiction*, 32–42; and 'Piracy and Terrorism' in P. Koutrakos and A. Skordas (eds), *The Law and Practice of Piracy at Sea* (Oxford: Hart, 2014), 33–52; R. Geiss and A. Petrig, *Piracy and Armed Robbery at Sea: The Legal Framework for Counter-Piracy Operations in Somalia and the Gulf of Aden* (Oxford: OUP, 2014), 61; M. Halberstam, 'Terrorism on the high seas: the Achille Lauro, piracy and the IMO convention on maritime safety' (1988) 82 *AJIL* 269, 290; and *Institute of Cetacean Research v. Sea Shepherd Conservation Society* (US Court of Appeals, 9th Circuit, No. 12–35266, 25 February 2013), pp. 4–5.
32 Geiss and Petrig, *Piracy and Armed Robbery at Sea*, 163.
33 Arts. 3(1) and 5, SUA Convention.
34 Art. 6, SUA Convention.
35 Arts. 7 and 10, SUA Convention.
36 V. Lowe and C. Staker, 'Jurisdiction' in M. Evans (ed), *International Law* 3rd ed (Oxford: Oxford University Press, 2010), p. 328.
37 Ibid.
38 Art. 7(1), (2) and (5) and Art. 10(1), SUA Convention.
39 Art. 8, SUA Convention.
40 Art. 8(3), SUA Convention.
41 E.g. T. Garmon, 'International law of the sea: Reconciling the law of piracy and terrorism in the wake of September 11th' (2002) 27 *Tulane Maritime Law Journal* 257, 270; compare B. Saul, *Defining Terrorism in International Law* (Oxford: Oxford University Press, 2006), 39 (arguing a political motive is an essential element of any definition of terrorism).
42 *United States v. Shi*, 525 F.3d 709 (2008), and case note by E. Kontorovich in (2009) 103 AJIL 734.
43 See generally: P. Chalk, *The Maritime Dimension of International Security: Terrorism, Piracy, and Challenges for the United States* (Santa Monica, CA: Rand, 2008), Chapter 3.
44 There is an extensive literature on the PSI bilateral boarding agreements including: Guilfoyle, *Shipping Interdiction*, Chapter 9; Papastavridis, *Interception of Vessels*, Chapter, 5; Klein, *Maritime Security*, Chapter 4. Such agreements were concluded with: Antigua and Barbuda, Bahamas, Belize, Croatia, Cyprus, Liberia, Malta, Marshall Islands, Mongolia, Panama, and St. Vincent and the Grenadines. See: http://www.state.gov/t/isn/c27733.htm.
45 Not to be confused with the original 1988 Protocol to the SUA Convention: Protocol for the Suppression of Unlawful Acts against the Safety of Fixed Platforms Located on the Continental Shelf, Rome, 10 March 1988, 1678 UNTS 304.
46 A consolidated text of the SUA Convention as amended by the SUA Protocol 2005 is available in A.V. Lowe and S.A.G. Talmon (eds), *The Legal Order of the Oceans: Basic Documents on the Law of the Sea* (Oxford: Hart, 2009) as Document 79 ("SUA Protocol 2005").
47 *Ibid*, Article 3*bis*(2).
48 E.g.: IMO Doc. LEG 90/15, Annex 2 (statement of India).
49 Art 8*bis*, SUA Protocol 2005.
50 Art 8*bis*(5)(d) and (e), SUA Protocol 2005.
51 See generally: Guilfoyle, *Shipping Interdiction*, pp. 89–94; Papastavridis, *Interception of Vessels*, pp. 229–36; Klein, *Maritime Security*, pp. 132–4.
52 Art 8*bis*(10), SUA Protocol 2005.
53 Art. 15, SUA Convention; K.N. Trapp, *State Responsibility for International Terrorism* (Oxford: Oxford University Press, 2011). See n. 42 for a rare national prosecution.
54 See further: Scott D. MacDonald, 'The SUA 2005 Protocol: A Critical Reflection' (2013) 28 *International Journal of Marine and Coastal Law* 485, 511–15.
55 D. Guilfoyle, 'Counter Proliferation Activities and Freedom of Navigation', in Myron H. Nordquist et al (eds), *Freedom of Navigation and Globalization* (Leiden: Brill, 2014) 71, 75–9 and 81.
56 Algeria, Austria, Bulgaria, Cook Islands, Côte d'Ivoire, Cuba, Dominican Republic, Djibouti, Estonia, Fiji, Greece, Jamaica, Latvia, Liechtenstein, Marshall Islands, Mauritania, Netherlands, Nauru, Norway, Palau, Panama, Qatar, Saint Kitts and Nevis, Saint Lucia, Saint Vincent and the Grenadines, Saudi Arabia, Serbia, Spain, Sweden, Switzerland, Turkey and Vanuatu. See: <http://www.imo.org/About/Conventions/StatusOfConventions/Documents/Status%20-%202014.pdf> (as at 17 October 2014).
57 See relevant 1540 Committee Reports: UN Doc S/AC.44/2004/(02)/82 (Marshall Islands, 10 December 2004); S/AC.44/2004/(02)/120/Add.1 (Panama, 8 March 2006).

58 The US could seek to interdict suspect WMD shipments aboard Panamanian or the Marshall Islands flag vessels under its bilateral agreements with them. See the treaties listed at: <http://www.state.gov/t/isn/c27733.htm>.
59 Compare: M.D. Fink, 'The Right of Visit for Warships: Some Challenges in Applying the Law of Maritime Interdiction on the High Seas', 49 *Military Law and Law of War Review*, 2010, 19.
60 See e.g. 18 USC §2332a and b and compare 18 USC §2283. As regards the latter, the offence must also constitute an offence under 18 USC §2332b(g)(5)(B) all of which require a nexus to the US.
61 See e.g. the 2006 response of the Attorney General's Department to the Senate Legal and Constitutional Legislation Committee (citing terrorist offences in ss 101.4, 101.6, 102.7 and 102.8 of the Criminal Code Act 1995): <http://www.aph.gov.au/~/media/Estimates/Live/legcon_ctte/estimates/add_0506/ag/qon_28.ashx> (last visited 12 November 2014).
62 See the table of Australian legislation implementing terrorism treaties at: <http://www.aph.gov.au/About_Parliament/Parliamentary_Departments/Parliamentary_Library/Browse_by_Topic/TerrorismLaw/terrorismtreaties> (last visited 12 November 2014).
63 Boister, *An Introduction*, p. 76.
64 Ibid, p. 76 quoting M. Naim, *Illicit: How Smugglers, Traffickers, and Copycats are Hijacking the Global Economy* (New York: Anchor, 2006), p. 32.
65 Convention between the United Kingdom and the USA respecting the Regulation of the Liquor Traffic 1924, (1924) Treaty Series No. 22.
66 US Department of State, *International Narcotics Control Strategy Report* (March 2013), Vol. I, 42, <http://www.state.gov/documents/organization/204265.pdf> (last visited 12 November 2014).
67 See e.g.: F. Spadi, 'Bolstering the Proliferation Security Initiative at sea: a comparative analysis of ship-boarding as a bilateral and multilateral implementing mechanism' (2006) 75 *Nordic Journal of International Law* 249.
68 On US bilateral treaty practice see n. 51, above. The most influential regional treaty on point (drawing heavily on US experience in negotiating/drafting such treaties) is the Agreement Concerning Co-operation in Suppressing Illicit Maritime and Air Trafficking in Narcotic Drugs and Psychotropic Substances in the Caribbean Area 2003 (Caribbean Area Agreement), <http://www.state.gov/s/l/2005/87198.htm> (last visited 12 November 2014); and the most commonly replicated multinational treaty provision is: Art. 17, Vienna Narcotics Convention.
69 Papastavridis, *Interception of Vessels*, p. 267 ff.
70 Guilfoyle, *Shipping Interdiction*, pp. 228–31.
71 Papastavridis, *Interception of Vessels*, pp. 274–5.
72 Guilfoyle, *Shipping Interdiction*, p. 76; Klein, *Maritime Security*, p. 122; *contra* R. Reuland, 'Interference with non-national ships on the high seas: peacetime exceptions to the exclusivity rule of flag state jurisdiction' (1989) 22 *Vanderbilt Journal of Transnational Law* 1161, 1195–6.
73 Art. 99, LOSC.
74 Guilfoyle, *Shipping Interdiction*, pp. 76–7.
75 Eve de Coning et al, *Caught at Sea: Forced Labour and Trafficking in Fisheries* (International Labour Organization, 2013), <http://www.ilo.org/wcmsp5/groups/public/—-ed_norm/—-declaration/documents/publication/wcms_214472.pdf> (last visited 12 November 2014).
76 Environmental Justice Foundation, *Slavery at Sea: The Continued Plight of Trafficked Migrants in Thailand's Fishing Industry* (2014), 28, <http://ejfoundation.org/sites/default/files/public/EJF_Slavery-at-Sea_report_2014_web-ok.pdf> (last visited 12 November 2014).
77 Art. 108, LOSC.
78 W. Gilmore, 'Drug trafficking by sea: the 1988 United Nations Convention against Illicit Traffic in Narcotic Drugs and Psychotropic Substances' (1991) 15 Marine Policy 183, 185.
79 Art. 4(1)(b)(ii), Vienna Narcotics Convention.
80 See generally: Guilfoyle, *Shipping Interdiction*, pp. 83–5, 95–6.
81 There is some treaty practice on allowing hot pursuit to continue through another State's maritime zones: e.g. Treaty between the Government of Australia and the Government of the French Republic on Cooperation in the Maritime Areas adjacent to the French Southern and Antarctic Territories (TAAF), Heard Island and the McDonald Islands, 24 November 2003, [2005] ATS 6 (entered into force 1 February 2005); Agreement on Cooperative Enforcement of Fisheries Laws between the Government of Australia and the Government of the French Republic in the Maritime Areas Adjacent to the

French Southern and Antarctic Territories, Heard Island and the McDonald Islands, 8 January 2007, [2011] ATS 1 (entered into force 7 January 2011).
82 See further: Guilfoyle, *Shipping Interdiction*, p. 96.
83 Ibid, p. 95.
84 Ibid, pp. 89–90.
85 Ibid, p. 91; and compare Klein, *Maritime Security*, pp. 83, 121, 134, 136 and 185.
86 Ibid, pp. 93–94.
87 E.g. Art. 16, Caribbean Area Agreement.
88 Arts. 3(a) and 6(3)(b), Protocol against the Smuggling of Migrants by Land, Sea and Air, Supplementing the United Nations Convention against Transnational Organized Crime, 15 November 2000, 2241 UNTS 507, (entry into force 28 January 2004).
89 Ibid, Art. 8(5).
90 Ibid.
91 These operations have proved highly controversial: Papastavridis, *Interception of Vessels*, pp. 283–91; V. Moreno-Lax, 'Seeking Asylum in the Mediterranean: Against a Fragmentary Reading of EU Member States' Obligations Accruing at Sea', (2011) 23 *International Journal of Refugee Law* 174–220.
92 See: <https://www.budapestprocess.org/> (last visited 12 November 2014).
93 See: <http://www.baliprocess.net/> (last visited 12 November 2014).
94 See e.g. Susan Kneebone, 'The Governance of Labor Migration in Southeast Asia' (2010) 16 *Global Governance* 383, 391–5. For an analysis of the strengths/weaknesses of such networks in a different context see: D. Guilfoyle, 'Prosecuting Pirates: The Contact Group on Piracy off the Coast of Somalia, Governance and International Law' (2013) 4 *Global Policy* 73–9.
95 Guilfoyle, *Shipping Interdiction*, p. 95.
96 Guilfoyle, 'Prosecuting Pirates', p. 77.

17

Combating Piracy and Armed Robbery at Sea:

from Somalia to the Gulf of Guinea

Clive Schofield and Kamal-Deen Ali

Introduction

Piracy and armed attacks against shipping represent a longstanding and enduring threat to maritime trade and safety at sea. Recognised as a hazard to navigation from times of antiquity, the "golden age" of piracy took in the latter part of the seventeenth and early part of the eighteenth centuries – a period celebrated and embedded in the popular imagination thanks to novels such as Robert Louis Stevenson's *Treasure Island*,[1] the swashbuckling films of Errol Flynn and company,[2] and more recently Johnny Depp *et al*. in *Pirates of the Caribbean*.[3] While piracy subsequently declined significantly, in large part thanks to the concerted efforts of the navies of colonial powers keen to secure vital trade routes to possessions overseas, nonetheless piracy and armed robbery at sea was never entirely eradicated. Indeed, there has been a contemporary resurgence in piracy and armed robbery against ships. This has especially been the case in the north-western quadrant of the Indian Ocean and particularly off the Horn of Africa which witnessed a significant and sustained increase in attacks against shipping from 2007. The statistics of attacks in the Gulf of Guinea have also been high since 2008, while the dynamics and trends of the incidents are increasingly complex.

The objective of this chapter is to examine ways to combat the threat of piracy and armed robbery at sea through the lens of case studies of piracy off the Horn of Africa, where incidents of piracy are now in decline, and in the Gulf of Guinea, which has witnessed a surge in such illegal activities in recent years. The aim of this exercise is to try to identify what lessons may be gleaned from the experience of combating piracy and armed robbery against ships off the Somali coastline and how they may be applied to address the increasing threat of analogous activities in the Gulf of Guinea and elsewhere. Prior to tackling these case studies the chapter addresses the status and adequacy of the international law framework for combating piracy and armed robbery at sea with particular emphasis on the relevant LOSC provisions and the application of the *Convention for the Suppression of Unlawful Acts against the Safety of Maritime Navigation 1988* (SUA Convention) to such incidents.

Pirates versus sea robbers: the concept of piracy and armed robbery in international law

The above-mentioned campaign on the part of European colonial powers in particular against the "pirate scourge" led to piracy becoming the first of the limited number of crimes to be subject to universal jurisdiction.[4] However, even if the capturing State has enacted relevant legislation against piracy and armed robbery against ships – something that is by no means certain – they are not *obliged* to do so. Indeed, as highlighted below, the significant practical challenges that exist in relation to transferring, prosecuting and imprisoning pirates means that capturing States are often dissuaded from pursuing such prosecutions.

The contemporary definition of piracy is included in the United Nations Convention on the Law of the Sea (LOSC) of 1982,[5] which provides the generally accepted legal framework governing the law of the sea as a whole. LOSC has achieved broad international recognition and has, at the time of writing, 166 parties.[6] Under LOSC, which is generally taken to be reflective of customary international law on the issue, States Parties are committed to cooperate in the suppression of piracy on the high seas (LOSC, Article 100). Key elements of piracy, as defined under Article 101 of LOSC, include criminal intent, the use of force, the taking over of a vessel against the wishes of its master, and the robbery of cargo, the possessions of those on board, or even the vessel itself.[7] Piracy also extends to the operation of a pirate ship which is a ship used to commit piratical acts (LOSC, Article 103), a provision that encompasses the use of, for example, "mother ships" (see below). A particular feature of the LOSC definition is that piracy is undertaken for private ends (*lucri causa*) and the term does not cover politically motivated acts.[8] This requirement is problematic since it is practically difficult to prove the private motive for a crime.[9]

A further point of distinction in the international law definition of piracy is that, in accordance with Article 101 of LOSC, piracy only refers to acts taking place outside the territorial sea. A key achievement of the LOSC framework was that it established clear spatial limits to national claims to maritime jurisdiction. Under the terms of Article 3 of LOSC, the breadth of the territorial sea may be "up to a limit not exceeding 12 nautical miles" measured from baselines along the coast. Unsurprisingly, the vast majority of coastal States have taken advantage of this provision and claimed 12 nautical mile breadth territorial seas.[10] As many piracy-style acts in fact take place in relatively close proximity to the coast, the term "piracy" is often misapplied. In international law terms such piracy-like act taking place within the territorial sea are instead referred to as "armed robbery against ships".[11] Here, however, the term "piracy" is used inclusively to cover both attacks against shipping within the territorial sea and acts of piracy taking place seaward of territorial sea limits.

The international legal framework for combating piracy, however, goes beyond the LOSC. The Convention for the Suppression of Unlawful Acts against the Safety of Maritime Navigation (SUA Convention), 1988, equally addresses the threat of piracy-like acts under a broader rubric of criminal activities referred to in the Convention as "unlawful acts".[12] The relevance of the SUA Convention is that it addresses and aims to "cure" some of the gaps in the LOSC definition of piracy which excludes other violent attacks which nonetheless endanger the safety and security of ships.[13] Under the SUA Convention, an actual attack or threat of violence constitutes a crime, irrespective of whether it comes from within or outside the ship and regardless of the motive of the actors.[14]

The rise and decline of piracy off the Horn of Africa

If there was a popular perception of piracy as a thing of the past, events off the Somali coast in recent years served to shatter this comfortable view. In fact, piracy had never entirely disappeared, with the waters off the Horn of Africa being one of several areas of focus for acts of piracy and armed robbery against ships. For example, over 700 attacks against ships were recorded in the period 1993–2005.[15] However, the precipitous rise in the incidence of piracy and armed attacks against ships, predominantly off the Somali coast, that occurred from 2007 catapulted piracy to global prominence as a significant threat to navigation.

During 2007 pirate attacks off Somalia more than doubled to 51 from 22 in 2006.[16] The following year, 2008, witnessed a further surge in piratical activity with an increase in attacks of nearly 200% over the previous year to 111 reported or nearly 40% of the 293 attacks reported globally.[17] In spite of counter-piracy efforts on the part of the international community, including the despatch of multiple naval vessels to patrol the waters off Somalia, attacks increased substantially in 2009, nearly doubling once again with the total number of incidents attributed to the Somali pirates reaching 217 (of 406 globally).[18] The number of reported incidents increased further in 2010 (219 of 445 globally)[19] and 2011 (237 of 439 globally).[20] In the period 2009–2011 therefore Somali pirates accounted for in excess of half of the number of reported piracy attacks worldwide.

A significant shift has, however, occurred since 2011 with a precipitous decline in the number of reported attacks to 75 reported for 2012.[21] Further, this downward trend has been sustained with 15 incidents being reported off Somalia in 2013,[22] and 11 for 2014 all of which were thwarted.[23] A further notable aspect of these figures is that the rising trend in successful attacks on ships resulting in hijackings and hostage-taking has also been reversed as illustrated by the fact that over 40 ships per year were hijacked in the northwestern Indian Ocean in 2009 and 2010 with hijackings being progressively reduced to 28 incidents in 2011, 14 in 2012, two in 2013 (with both vessels being released within 24 hours as a result of naval interventions) and no successful hijackings in the region in 2014.

The significant decline in piracy and armed attacks against shipping that has been achieved in the north-western Indian Ocean is attributable to a number of factors.

Multilateral efforts to counter piracy

As noted above, the international community moved swiftly to respond to the surge in piracy attacks off Somalia in the latter part of 2008 by deploying naval forces on counter-piracy missions in the north-western Indian Ocean. Numerous interested States rushed warships to the Horn of Africa region. This has led to the establishment of a series of inter-related naval operations, notably NATO's operation *Allied Provider* (later operation *Allied Protector* and, from August 2009, operation *Ocean Shield*),[24] the European Union's *Operation Atalanta* and the US-led Combined Task Force (CTF) 151.[25] Additionally, naval vessels have been deployed from a number of "independent deployers" including Australia, Canada, the People's Republic of China, Japan, the Republic of Korea, Malaysia and Russia, as well as more local or regional States such as India, Iran and Pakistan. Cooperation amongst the international naval presence off the Horn of Africa has been achieved largely under the auspices of a regional code of conduct designed to address piracy and armed robbery against ships in the Western Indian Ocean, generally termed the "Djibouti Code",[26] as well as through the Contact Group on Piracy off the coast of Somalia which facilitates regular meetings allowing for tactical coordination among representatives of the deployed navies and the shipping community.[27] These operations have been authorised by a series of increasingly robust United Nations Security Council Resolutions.[28]

The significant difficulties presented by the Somali piracy threat, including the expanded reach of the pirates (see below), and thus the vast area to patrol, coupled with the speed of attacks led to a number of strategies being developed. These have included the organisation of convoys and provision of escorts, and the embarkation of vessel protection teams on merchant vessels, often though not exclusively of their own flag, to provide ship borne security.[29] A related means to ensure better protection for shipping has been the establishment of a safe route, the Internationally Recommended Transit Corridor (IRTC) through the especially piracy-prone Gulf of Aden, protected by ships from CTF 151, NATO and EU NAVFOR.[30] However, even this approach did not necessarily guarantee against attacks on shipping.[31]

Additionally, more robust and proactive counter-piracy efforts have increasingly been undertaken. These have included initiatives to deal with the pirate "mother ships" which are crucial to extending the range of pirate operations and to disrupt "Pirate Action Groups" before they were in a position to initiate attacks on shipping.[32] Similarly, the willingness of international forces to take action on land, including mounting a combined naval forces raid on a pirate base on shore in May 2012, has been credited with discouraging pirates from putting to sea.[33]

Efforts towards overcoming legal and capacity challenges

A key drawback to the international cooperative naval effort has been uncertainty as to what to do with pirates, or alleged pirates, once apprehended. As noted above, despite the fact that piracy is acknowledged as a crime subject to universal jurisdiction, punishable by any State regardless of the nationality of the victim or perpetrators, a number of practical and legal challenges have arisen which have tended to complicate or forestall efforts to prosecute and incarcerate pirates. For example, and despite repeated calls for States to criminalise piracy in their national laws in UN Security Council Resolutions, by no means do all States have adequate and up to date domestic laws criminalising piracy.[34] Further, the costs of prosecuting and incarcerating pirates have proved strong disincentives to action. Concerns have also been raised that once convicted pirates have served their time it may be difficult to return them to Somalia because of human rights concerns.[35] Consequently, many navies operating off the Horn of Africa have been operating on a "catch and release" basis where captured pirates are disarmed but otherwise face no real consequences for their actions such as prosecution and imprisonment. This led the UN Secretary-General's Special Adviser on Legal Issues related to Piracy off the Coast of Somalia, Jack Lang to suggested that "more than 90 per cent of the pirates apprehended by States patrolling the seas will be released without being prosecuted."[36]

The absence, at least until recently, of a functioning government and judicial system in Somalia itself and capacity issues within the wider region have been recognised as fundamental problems by the international community, resulting in strenuous efforts to address these concerns.[37] In this context criminal justice capacity building efforts have been made to assist those States whose judicial systems have been facing considerable challenges in dealing with a significant influx of piracy-related cases and prisoners.[38] These initiatives have been coordinated by the UN Office on Drugs and Crime (UNODC) counter-piracy programme (CPP) in Kenya, Somalia, the Seychelles, Mauritius, Tanzania and the Maldives. Additionally, efforts have been made to cooperatively deal with pirates on a regional basis. In particular, apprehending States such as those of the EU and US, have negotiated bilateral transfer agreements allowing for the prosecution of alleged pirates in regional third States such as Kenya, the Seychelles and Tanzania for trial in their jurisdictions.[39] This practice has, however, placed great strain on the criminal justice systems of the States receiving the alleged pirates as well as raising concerns over handing suspects over to such jurisdictions on human rights grounds.[40] Further, there exist multiple practical difficulties for the transferring State as personnel involved in the capture of alleged pirates may be required to give evidence at their trial.[41]

Combating Piracy and Armed Robbery at Sea

Shipping industry responses

The shipping industry has also developed a range of responses to the rise in piracy attacks off the Somali coast. Whilst the proximity of key sea lanes such as that linking the Northwest Indian Ocean to the Mediterranean and Europe via the Suez Canal, Red Sea, Bab al Mandeb Straits and Gulf of Aden, to the Somali coast, coupled with the substantial range of pirate operations has meant that simply avoiding pirate prone areas is extremely challenging, some re-routeing options designed to minimise the risk of attack do exist.

In particular, many vessels have opted to divert their routes as far as possible away from the Somali coast such that they hug the western coast of India, therefore skirting the eastern side of the piracy risk zone.[42] This is economically attractive as this adds only around one day to a transit through the High Risk Area (HRA) for piracy in the north-western Indian Ocean.[43] Concerns have, however, been raised that adherence to the recommended practice of divergence around the fringes of the HRA rather than directly across it is gradually eroding as the threat of piracy attacks declines and as shippers seek to cut corners.[44]

The shipping industry has also developed a range of precautionary measures to minimise their risk of being attacked and hijacked. These are encapsulated by industry Best Management Practice (BMP) guidelines for protection against Somali-based Piracy.[45] Among these guidelines is the recommendation for vessels traversing pirate-threatened waters to maintain a strict 24-hour radar and anti-piracy watch. Early detection of a potential attack allows the threatened vessel to increase speed and engage in evasive manoeuvres.[46] Indeed, speed is a key factor with vessels travelling at 18 knots and above generally considered to be immune to boarding from small boats, largely because of the bow wave and wake that they generate.[47] Early detection also provides the opportunity to mobilise anti-piracy responses such as the use of high-pressure water hoses and foam.

Other options to deter attacks include the use of obstacles to boarding such as barbed or razor wire. Efforts have also been made to make accessing key parts of the ship such as the bridge, engine room and crew accommodation area more challenging for boarders. A related option is for the crew of an attacked vessel to lock themselves in a safe room or "citadel" should the pirates manage to board their vessel. The objective of these measures is essentially to delay boarders from gaining full control over the vessel and taking hostages and thus potentially providing time for intervention by international forces. The use of citadels does not necessarily guarantee safety from hijacking and the ship's crew being taken hostage, however. This is illustrated by the experience of the freighter, the *Beluga Nomination*, in early 2011. Having been attacked and boarded, the crew of the vessel withdrew to their citadel below-decks. Unfortunately international naval assistance was unavailable and after two days the pirates managed to cut their way into the safe room using welding gear and took the crew hostage.[48]

Additionally, innovative technologies such as long-range acoustic devices (LRAD), designed to generate noises at painful, but non-lethal decibel levels with the aim of disorienting and deterring potential pirates have been deployed in the region though with mixed success. For example, an LRAD was used by the crew of the cruise liner *Seabourn Spirit*, as one of a number of counter-piracy measures deployed when it was attacked on 5 November 2005. This counter-piracy effort can be deemed to be successful in that the *Seabourn Spirit* escaped without being boarded. However, one rocket-propelled grenade round did penetrate the hull, while another reportedly bounced off the ship's stern.[49]

Increasingly, and despite traditional reluctance on the part of both mariners and ship owners to the arming of merchant vessels, the shipping industry is countering the piracy threat by employing armed guards – privately contracted armed security personnel (PCASP). Despite the reservations within the shipping industry regarding their employment, utilising PCASP has proved to be effective and increasingly popular. While having such a security team on board does not necessarily forestall attacks, at the time of writing, no ship carrying armed security personnel had been successfully hijacked. Significant concerns have, however, been raised over the regulation of this growing maritime security sector.[50] While acknowledging the "deterrent effect" of PCASP as playing a part in the reduced number of successful hijackings in 2011, the International Maritime Bureau (IMB) noted that the "regulation and vetting" of such personnel "still needs to be adequately addressed."[51]

In concluding on Somalia and by extension the Indian Ocean and Gulf of Aden, it can be said that despite the challenges and limitations of each of the responses discussed above, they have collectively contributed to decreasing the threat of piracy in the region. The international community has equally learnt crucial lessons that may be applicable to combating the threat of piracy beyond that region. The following section addresses the rising threat of piracy in the Gulf of Guinea in particular before a concluding assessment is made concerning whether the approaches that worked in Somalia may be suitable and effective to apply to piracy threats elsewhere.

The evolving dynamics of Gulf of Guinea piracy

As the global response to piracy off the coast of Somalia was building up, alarm bells were ringing concerning growing maritime insecurity on the 'other side' of Africa, specifically in the Gulf of Guinea region. Indeed, following the recent rapid decline in piracy off Somalia, the Gulf of Guinea stands as the most dangerous maritime area in the world in terms of successful rate of attacks and increasing violence. This prompted two resolutions of the UN Security Council in 2011 and 2012 expressing concerns about the rising insecurity in the region, its impact on regional and global security and calling on regional States and the global community to take remedial action.[52]

A rising threat

While the threat of piracy in the Gulf of Guinea is presently on a different scale to that of Somali piracy at its peak, it can be regarded as an increasingly pressing concern. This is not only because of the rapidly increasing rate of incidents but due to the complex dynamics of the attacks.

In clear contrast to the waters off Somalia, the Gulf of Guinea is witnessing rising incidents as well as a broadening scope of operations on the part of the pirates. Reported incidents rose from 23 in 2005 to 60 in 2007, which is more than 100% rise in two years.[53] The records took a slight dip in 2008 and 2009 but have since swelled from 2010 to 2013, with 2012 recording the highest at 64 incidents.[54] It is also noteworthy that at the close of 2013, the Gulf of Guinea recorded more incidents of attacks in the high seas compared to the previous years.[55] Moreover, in 2014 41 incidents were reported off West Africa with five vessels being hijacked.[56] Additionally, the situation is also arguably worse than the statistics depict because it is believed that unlike other regions, approximately half of the incidents of piracy in the Gulf of Guinea are actually reported by ships' captains and operators due to fears of reprisal attacks upon their next visit.[57] Notwithstanding the limited reports, the Gulf of Guinea region has since 2009 been noted as the new piracy "territory", displacing Somalia especially with regards to violence employed in the attacks.[58]

From parasitic to full-scale piracy

Global attention on piracy has generally been limited to examinations of the statistics of attacks with occasional, more nuanced attempts to understand the root causes of piracy. Between these two extremes is a significant gap – analyses of the evolutionary tracks of piracy. This is an essential requirement for matching the trends of piracy with effective counter-piracy measures. To appreciate that evolutionary process in the Gulf of Guinea it is important to first understand the fundamental landscape, or better still seascape, of piracy in the region. Here, we distinguish between the occurrence of a piracy incident, which can happen anywhere, and the development of what can be characterised as a "piracy enclave" which is the possible location of pirates and focus for their operations.[59] Nigeria stands out as the epicentre of Gulf of Guinea piracy and is therefore classified as the primary piracy enclave. Nigeria alone accounts for 80% of reported incidents of piracy in the Gulf of Guinea.[60] Indeed, the Nigerian primary-piracy enclave has progressed from its parasitic character in and about 2005 to what can be termed full-scale piracy in 2012. Embedded in this criminal cycle is the fact that a large part of Nigerian piracy is born out of the Niger Delta insurgency.[61]

The parasitic or opportunistic phase of Gulf of Guinea piracy fits piracy incidents up to 2005 but also extends to 2007. Two-thirds of attacks during this period took place in ports and anchorages, interspersed with limited robberies in the territorial sea. It needs to be emphasised that the taxonomy of this phase as "opportunistic" is not based on the capability of the actors but relates to sea robbery as a subsidiary activity. The attention of insurgents during this period was on attacking offshore platforms, however, ships were also hijacked and crew kidnapped for ransom. Piracy reports during this period gave indications of what would become core in the profile of threats to sea lanes of communication (SLOC) security, that is, gangs of hijackers using speedboats armed with heavy weapons.

For example, in 2006 four crew members of the *Northern Comrade* were kidnapped for ransom; then over 40 people armed with guns in six speedboats attacked the *Dlb Cheyen* in May 2007. They were engaged by the Nigerian military in a shootout but succeeded in kidnapping the crew. Moreover, in the same month *Oloibiri* was attacked using explosives and its crew was again kidnapped for ransom.[62] Thus the tactic of kidnapping for ransom of expatriate oil workers was being employed in the hijacking of ships but largely as an occasional activity. From this parasitic phase, the pirates widened the enclave to cover the neighbouring coasts of Cameroon and Equatorial Guinea but still in the context of opportunistic piracy. Most of the accounts of illegal boarding of ships on the coasts of the two States in 2008 described the pirates and robbers as "Nigerian rebels", "Nigerian militants" and "protectors of the Bonny River".[63] The point to note is that the spread of the pirate threat to neighbouring coasts signalled the ability of the insurgents to extend the intensity and scope of their activities with wider security consequences.

As piracy proved to be a lucrative crime, the insurgents moved into a new phase in the cycle where vessels where specifically targeted; thus the *pursuits* began. This type of activity, typically featured the identification of a high value target which would then be shadowed further out to sea and violently attacked at the most vulnerable location possible. In February 2009 grenades were thrown at an oil tanker (*Front Chief*) killing a crew member. The crew of *Emirates Swam*, *Sevastopolskaya Buhta* and other vessels also suffered serious injuries during attacks in the same year.[64] These high levels of violence paralleled the Gulf of Guinea with historical instances where pirates employed violence and killing to subjugate their theatre of operations.[65] What it also implied is that by 2009 Gulf of Guinea piracy had incubated all the elements of a regional and global threat. This would become manifest in 2011 when pirates widened the enclave westwards and the coasts of Benin and Togo effectively came under siege. In both cases pirates were able to come deep into port areas and anchorages to hijack vessels. In the case of the hijacking of *Aristofanis* which took place in the port of Benin, the vessel was sailed to open seas where its cargo was discharged.[66]

The hijacking of the *Duzgit Venture* in 2011 also demonstrated the growth of transnational criminal networking in the Gulf of Guinea.[67] The *Duzgit Venture* was hijacked off the coast of Benin and the Captain was forced to sail the vessel all the way to the coast of Gabon, where the pirates planned to transfer the oil onto a barge.[68] Having failed to meet with the barge, the Captain was forced to sail to a location off Warri, Nigeria in order to try to offload the cargo. After a series of unsuccessful attempts, the pirates disembarked into fast boats, kidnapping the Captain and another crew member. This reflects the growth in piracy networks that facilitate the sale of stolen cargo. The pirates were in cahoots with other actors about 4,000km away from the point of hijack, and successfully commandeered the ship to sail across the coastal spaces of five States.[69] The incident also raises serious questions about the capability of Gulf of Guinea States to monitor their maritime domain.

By the close of 2011, therefore, piracy in the primary piracy enclave had consolidated and the coasts of Togo and Benin had become piracy hotspots in addition to the epicentre – Nigeria. From this consolidation came the westerly extensions of piracy activities to the coast of Cote d'Ivoire marked by the hijacking of the *Orfeas* in October 2012. After gaining control of the vessel, the pirates sailed over 2,000km to the coast of the Niger Delta, stole the ship's oil cargo, and released the vessel two days later.[70] Further, in July 2013 the Maltese flagged vessel, the *Cotton*, was hijacked off the coast of Gabon, the first of its kind off that coast, portending a widening of the piracy threat southwards.[71] This deepening threat has continued into 2014 with Angola and Ghana registering their first significant cases of hijackings, thus reinforcing the urgency of implementing effective counter-piracy measures in the region.

Further down south the *Kerala* was hijacked off Angola in January 2014.[72] The tanker was subsequently sighted under the control of the hijackers off the coast of Nigeria where part of its oil cargo worth an estimated US$8 million was stolen.[73] Then in the months of June and July the coast of Ghana registered three cases of hijacking, two of which were on oil tankers, signifying a further entrenchment of the piracy threat.[74]

Of particular note, the attacks off Angola and Ghana shattered the record of the two States as among the safest coastal waters in the region. These incidents also underscore the oil-related focus of attacks, suggesting that oil facilities and particularly tankers and supply vessels are highly likely to continue to be targeted by pirates because the financial rewards involved for the pirates, their accomplices, as well as the buyers of the stolen oil, are extremely high.[75] However, while the Niger Delta pirates hunt for these high value targets, all other vessels become potential prey and susceptible to attack.

Legal and jurisdictional challenges

The problem of Gulf of Guinea piracy lies not only in the complexity of its evolutionary tracks but in current and emerging legal challenges. First is the legislative deficit with respect to the crime of piracy in the Gulf of Guinea. A review of the national legislation database of the United Nations Division on the Law of the Sea (UNDOALOS) shows that Liberia and Togo are the only States in the region that have enacted piracy legislation.[76] It is only since January 2013 that Nigeria is reported to have initiated a process for the enactment of a law to combat piracy and other maritime crimes.[77] The UN Assessment Mission to the Gulf of Guinea also observed that the definition of the crime of piracy in the national laws of Benin was outdated and not consistent with the provisions of the LOSC.[78] Thus, even if Gulf of Guinea States are able to conduct patrols off their coasts, the efficacy of such patrols would be seriously undermined by the absence of domestic legislation to prosecute and punish for the crime of piracy. This will practically lead to a case of "catch and release" in the Gulf of Guinea as happened in Somalia or the pirates may be prosecuted for crimes other than piracy.

The second legal challenge in the Gulf of Guinea is with respect to the slow progress evident in the delimitation of maritime boundaries in the region leading to an incomplete regional maritime jurisdictional picture. Although some parts of the Gulf of Guinea have been delimited, or at least there exist arrangements of Joint Development Zones (JDZs), the coast stretching from Nigeria through to Guinea, featuring multiple potential maritime boundaries, remains undelimited.[79] This renders the legal distinction between piracy and sea robbery tenuous and equally leads to maritime security jurisdictional uncertainties.[80] Incidentally this is also the area featuring endemic piracy especially from Nigeria to Cote d'Ivoire.

Conclusion and lessons for combating piracy

Despite past successes in combating piracy, most recently off the Horn of Africa, it is abundantly clear that the "pirate scourge" has not been eradicated. Among the current "hotspots" for piracy the Gulf of Guinea looms large. That said, it should be noted that even in areas where progress has been made in the past, the threat of incidents of piracy and armed attacks against shipping recurring remains, as recently demonstrated by a fresh spate of incidents in the South China Sea.[81] The objective of this concluding section is to draw out some of the responses to piracy derived from the foregoing discussion. What becomes clear is that the complex nature of piracy today dictates a multi-faceted approach and this must take into consideration the different piracy environments and the crime profile. The experience of the global community in Somalia, which represents the most remarkable case of modern piracy, has reinforced the need for a combination of different tools; from the pen to the sword,[82] and the responses must be simultaneously flexible and robust. Six responses of particular importance are highlighted here: *governance, effective legal regime, patrols and enforcement, regional cooperation and global support.*

Governance

The mention of governance in any discourse tends to provoke many questions, but few easy answers. The common questions will include: how can we empirically connect governance and maritime (in)security, in this case piracy? What is the measurement of the governance gap and how can that be corrected? Which interventions are necessary to ensure good governance? Further, how will success be measured and with what indicators?

Answers to these questions must be on a case by case basis but the governance-maritime security connection can certainly not be discounted. Poor or weak governance is partly responsible for the perpetuation of piracy in Somalia, and this can be viewed in two ways. First, there is always the likelihood for crime to be prevalent in communities where people live in disadvantaged or impoverished conditions.[83] Weak governance also makes it impossible for law and order to be maintained and edges the particular state and the whole international community towards anarchy.[84] The lack of a credible and effective government meant that without external intervention criminality and transnational crimes including piracy could persist in Somalia.[85]

While the Gulf of Guinea may not be described as a region of "failed States," available statistics show that many States in the region suffer systemic weaknesses and are confronted with enormous socio-economic challenges. Nigeria has systematically slipped from a relatively strong position of number 54 in the "failed State" rankings of 2005 to number 14 in 2011, thus joining the top 20 fragile countries in the global "failed State" rankings.[86] During the same period piratical attacks off the coast of Nigeria have risen to high levels. Global counter-piracy measures must therefore prioritise improving governance in the counter-piracy response tool-kit.

Patrols and enforcement

Presence is crucial in all situations of fighting crime. Prior to multilateral naval deployments in the Indian Ocean, Somali pirates essentially had free reign at sea and the safety and security of commercial shipping was in the hands of the marauders. The impunity with which ship hijackings are conducted in the Gulf of Guinea, at times deep into the port areas of States, is similarly symptomatic of weakness in terms of maritime policing, surveillance and response capabilities across the Gulf of Guinea.[87]

Although security sector funding is generally inadequate, the situation with respect to navies and coastguards is more problematic. Angola's allocation of resources with respect to the protection of its maritime estate is typical of Gulf of Guinea States. Angola has an estimated coastline of 1,600km – the longest in the Gulf of Guinea. Its GDP is the second highest in the region, and much of that is derived from offshore resources. Yet the personnel strength of the Angolan Navy is only 1,000 (compared to 100,000 for its Army and 6,000 for its Air Force) and the equipment state of the Angolan Navy is palpably inadequate when contrasted with that of the Army.[88] The Nigerian Navy is similarly underfunded and has limited capability.[89] Its personnel strength is 8,000 – the largest in the Gulf of Guinea, but that is in sharp contrast to its 62,000-strong Army.[90] Thus there is a clear gap in naval capability in the Gulf of Guinea. However, unlike Somalia, where foreign navies filled the gap, this seems unlikely to occur in the Gulf of Guinea, not least because of the sovereignty concerns of the coastal States involved. The solution may lie in bilateral initiatives where third States would use existing political and security cooperation to facilitate counter-piracy deployments.

Effective legal regime

Piracy normally thrives in the environment of a weak legal regime with Somalia providing the classic case of this occurring. Indeed, it was only when the naval deployment in Somalia was backed with effective investigation and prosecution of pirates that the tide begun to turn. To effectively combat piracy in the Gulf of Guinea, the existing legislative deficit must be addressed. This observation is underscored by a review of the national legislation database of the UNDOALOS which shows that Liberia and Togo are the only States in the region to have enacted piracy legislation.[91] Indeed, it is only since January 2013 that Nigeria is reported to have initiated a process for the enactment of a law to combat piracy and other maritime crimes.[92]

Thus, even if Gulf of Guinea States are able to conduct patrols off their coasts, the efficacy of such patrols would be seriously undermined by the absence of domestic legislation to prosecute and punish for the crime of piracy. This will practically lead to a case of "catch and release" in the Gulf of Guinea as happened in Somalia or the pirates may be prosecuted for crimes other than piracy. The second legal challenge in the Gulf of Guinea is with respect to inconclusive maritime boundary delimitation. Although other parts of the Gulf of Guinea have been delimited, or at least there exist arrangements of Joint Development Zones (JDZs), the region from Nigeria through to Guinea remain un-delimited.[93] This renders the legal distinction between piracy and sea robbery tenuous and equally leads to maritime security jurisdictional uncertainties.[94]

Regional cooperation

Article 100 of the LOSC encapsulates the obligation of cooperation in the repression of piracy.[95] Here the importance of the Djibouti Code can be highlighted. Similarly, there is a positive trend of regional cooperation in the Gulf of Guinea. This started with the adoption of a Maritime Security Protocol in 2009 by member States of the Economic Community of Central African States (ECCAS) based on a structure that divides the ECCAS region into zones to enhance joint patrols, monitoring and enforcement.[96] The ECCAS initiative provided the impetus for a region-wide framework – the Yaoundé Code of Conduct for the repression of illicit activities at sea.[97] This is an important achievement in the context of a regional approach to maritime security, although it is by no means sufficient. On the one hand the Yaoundé Code will promote information sharing and cooperative responses in general, on the other hand, its effectiveness is likely to be undermined by the absence of legal framework and lack of enforcement capability, as outlined above.

Multilateral engagement

Finally, international support or multilateral engagement is critical in combating piracy and has proved to be an especially important facet of countering piracy off Somalia. Indeed, the obligation to cooperate in the LOSC is not limited to regional initiatives. The corollary to piracy being a crime of universal jurisdiction is the expectation that the global community will contribute to counter-piracy efforts in every region and so in a viable way. Resolutions 2018 and 2036 of the UN Security Council have laid the foundation for multilateral support to maritime security in the Gulf of Guinea. Already, the United States through its Africa Partnership and some other agencies is delivering maritime security support to the Gulf of Guinea.[98] The European Union also launched the Critical Maritime Routes in the Gulf of Guinea (CRIMGO) project in January 2013.[99] The project is designed to improve safety and security off the coasts of seven States in the Gulf of Guinea.[100] Although international cooperation holds prospects for enhancing maritime security in the Gulf of Guinea, a number of challenges would have to be addressed. Particularly deserving of attention is the need for coordination of international partnerships, something in large part achieved through multiple deployments of naval forces off Somalia. Multiple cooperative initiatives are currently being unpacked in the Gulf of Guinea region to which national administrators and regional institutions are required to respond and implement. This overcrowds national and regional policy, adversely affecting maritime security decision-making and coordination. The lesson from this experience is that external actors, donor agencies and relevant international organisations all need to engage with maritime security challenges through a harmonised platform.

Notes

1 Robert Louis Stevenson, *Treasure Island* (1883).
2 For example, 1935's *Captain Blood*. See for example, http://www.imdb.com/title/tt0026174/?ref_=nm_knf_i2.

3 Notably 2003's *Pirates of the Caribbean: The Curse of the Black Pearl*. See, for example, http://www.imdb.com/title/tt0325980/?ref_=nv_sr_2.
4 Daniel Patrick O'Connell, *The International Law of the Sea* (1984, Vol. II), 966.
5 United Nations, *United Nations Convention on the Law of the Sea*, Publication no.E97.V10 (1983). See 1833 United Nations Treaty Series (UNTS) 3, opened for signature December 10, 1982, Montego Bay, Jamaica (entered into force 16 November 1994).
6 Comprising 165 States plus the European Union. See, United Nations, Division for Ocean Affairs and the Law of the Sea, Office of Legal Affairs, '*Chronological List of Ratifications of, Accessions and Successions to the Convention and the Related Agreements as at 10 October 2014*' (2013), online: http://www.un.org/Depts/los/reference_files/status2010.pdf.
7 O'Connell, *The International Law of the Sea*, 968–970.
8 Robin R. Churchill, and A.V. Lowe, *The Law of the Sea*, 3rd edition, (1999), 210.
9 Douglas Guilfoyle, *Shipping Interdiction and the Law of the Sea*, (2009), 254–259. Maximo Q. Mejia Jr, 'Modern Piracy at Sea: Selected Legal Aspects', *International Proceedings of Economics Development an Research* 48, 21, 2012: 96–100.
10 See, for example, Division for Ocean Affairs and the Law of the Sea, Office of Legal Affairs, United Nations, *Table of Claims to Maritime Jurisdiction*, as at 15 July 2011, available at http://www.un.org/Depts/los/LEGISLATIONANDTREATIES/PDFFILES/table_summary_of_claims.pdf. A small number of States do, however, claim territorial seas that are either less than 12 nautical miles in breadth, such as Jordan on account of its restricted coastal front and the proximity of neighbouring States at the head of the Gulf of Aqaba, and Greece and Turkey with respect to the Aegean Sea, or are broader than 12 nautical miles in breadth, for instance the anachronistic 200 nautical mile territorial sea claims of Benin, Congo (Brazzaville), Ecuador and Peru. See, J. Ashley Roach and Robert W. Smith, *Excessive Maritime Claims*, 3rd edition, (2012), 137 and 144–148.
11 On the definition of armed robbery against ships see, International Maritime Organization (IMO), Assembly Resolution A.1025 (26), adopted on 2 December 2009 at the 26th Assembly Session of the IMO, available at, http://www.imo.org/About/Pages/DocumentsResources.aspx.
12 1988 Convention for the Suppression of Unlawful Acts against the Safety of Maritime Navigation, 10 March 1988, Rome, Italy, Entry into Force: 01 March 1992, 156 Parties as of 2 December 2010, 1678 UNTS 201 / [1993] ATS 10 / 27 ILM 672 (1988); hereinafter referred to as 1988 SUA Convention.
13 Malvina Halberstam, 'Terrorism on the High Seas: The *Achille Lauro*, Piracy and the IMO Convention on Maritime Safety', *American Journal of International Law* 88, 1988: 269–292.
14 See, in particular, Articles 3 to 6. For a detailed explanation of the scope of these articles, see Douglas Guilfoyle, *Shipping Interdiction and the Law of the Sea*, 2009, pp. 254–259.
15 K. von Hoesslin, *Making sense of Somalia's anarchic waters*, Philippine Star Online, 25 March 2006.
16 United Nations Office on Drugs and Crime (UNODC), *The Globalization of Crime: A Transnational Organized Crime Threat Assessment*, Vienna, UNODC, 2010, at 193, available at http://www.unodc.org/documents/data-and-analysis/tocta/TOCTA_Report_2010_low_res.pdf.
17 IMB, *Piracy and Armed Robbery Against Ships – Annual Report 1 January–31 December 2008*, (2009), at 26.
18 IMB, *Worldwide piracy figures surpass 400*, 14 January 2010, available at http://www.icc-ccs.org/news/385-2009-worldwide-piracy-figures-surpass-400.
19 IMB, *Hostage-taking at sea rises to record levels, says IMB*, 17 January 2011, available at http://www.icc-ccs.org/news/429-hostage-taking-at-sea-rises-to-record-levels-says-imb.
20 IMB, *Piracy and Armed Robbery against Ships – Annual Report 1 January–31 December 2011*, (2012), at 5–6 and 20.
21 IMB, *Piracy falls in 2012, but seas off East and West Africa remain dangerous, says IMB*, 16 January 2013, available at http://www.icc-ccs.org/news/836-piracy-falls-in-2012-but-seas-off-east-and-west-africa-remain-dangerous-says-imb.
22 IMB, *Somali pirate clampdown caused drop in global piracy IMB reveals*, 15 January 2014, available at, http://www.icc-ccs.org/news/904-somali-pirate-clampdown-caused-drop-in-global-piracy-imb-reveals.
23 IMB, *SE Asia tanker hijacks rose in 2014 despite global drop in sea piracy, IMB report reveals*, 12 January 2015, available at https://icc-ccs.org/news/1040-se-asia-tanker-hijacks-rose-in-2014-despite-global-drop-in-sea-piracy-imb-report-reveals.
24 Operation *Allied Provider* (October–December 2008) evolved into Operation *Allied Protector* in early 2009 and subsequently, in August 2009, became Operation *Ocean Shield* which at the time of writing was ongoing. See, North Atlantic Treaty Organization (NATO), Maritime Command (MARCOM),

'Counter-piracy operations', available at http://www.mc.nato.int/about/Pages/NATO%20and%20 Maritime%20Piracy.aspx; see also, NATO MARCOM, 'Operation Ocean Shield', MARCOM Factsheet, available at http://www.mc.nato.int/about/Pages/Operation%20Ocean%20Shield.aspx.

25 NATO Parliamentary Assembly, 'The Growing Threat of Piracy to Regional and Global Security', Committee Report 169 CDS 09 E, 2009 Annual Session, paragraphs 64–73, www.nato-pa.int/Default.asp/SHORTCUT=1770.
26 *Code of Conduct concerning the Repression of Piracy and Armed Robbery Against Ships in the western Indian Ocean*, concluded in Djibouti, 29 January 2009, available at http://www.imo.org/OurWork/Security/PIU/Pages/DCoC.aspx.
27 Notably through monthly Shared Awareness and Deconfliction (SHADE) group meetings. See, NATO Parliamentary Assembly, 'The Growing Threat of Piracy to Regional and Global Security', Committee Report 169 CDS 09 E, 2009 Annual Session, paragraphs 7–73, www.nato-pa.int/Default.asp/SHORTCUT=1770.
28 For example, unlike earlier resolutions such as UNSC Resolutions 1816, 1838 and 1848, UNSC Resolution 1851 of 16 December 2008 authorised the international community to operate not only within Somali waters but also within the land territory of Somalia which is used to plan, facilitate or undertake acts of piracy and armed robbery. Subsequent UNSC Resolutions include Resolutions 1918 and 1950 of 2010, Resolutions 1976, 2015 and 2020 of 2011, and Resolutions 2124 and 2125 of 2013. UN Security Council Resolutions available at, http://www.un.org/Docs/sc/.
29 C.H. Schofield and R. Warner, 'Scuppering Somali Piracy: Global Responses and Paths to Justice', in A. Forbes (Ed.), *Australia's Response to Piracy: A Legal Perspective*, Papers in Australian Maritime Affairs, No.31, 45–74 (2011), 57.
30 NATO, 'The Growing Threat of Piracy to Regional and Global Security', para.73
31 For example, the *Malaspina Castle* was attacked and hijacked whilst transiting the forerunner to the IRTC, the Maritime Security Patrol Area (MSPA) in 2009. See Mark Tran, 'Somali pirates seize British owned ship', *The Guardian*, 6 April 2009, www.guardian.co.uk/world/2009/apr/06/somali-pirates-hijack.
32 IMB, 'Annual Report 2011', 24.
33 BBC, 'Somali piracy: A broken business model?', 29 December 2012, *BBC News Online*, available at http://www.bbc.co.uk/news/world-africa-20549056.
34 See, for example, United Nations Security Council Resolution 1918 (2010), S/RES/1918, 27 April 2010. http://www.un.org/Docs/sc/unsc_resolutions10.htm.
35 Schofield and Warner, 'Scuppering Somali Piracy', 60.
36 See, Jack Lang, 'Report of the Special Adviser to the Secretary-General on Legal
Issues Related to Piracy off the Coast of Somalia', 13, Annex to the letter dated 24 January 2011 from the Secretary-General to the President of the Security Council, S/2011/30, available at http://www.securitycouncilreport.org/atf/cf/%7B65BFCF9B-6D27-4E9C-8CD3-CF6E4FF96FF9%7D/Somalia%20S%202011%2030.pdf.
37 In particular see, United Nations Security Council Resolution 1976 (2011), S/RES/2020, 11 April 2011. http://www.un.org/Docs/sc/unsc_resolutions11.htm.
38 United Nations Security Council Resolution 2015 (2011), S/RES/2020, 24 October 2011. http://www.un.org/Docs/sc/unsc_resolutions11.htm.
39 See, for example, 'Exchange of Letters for the conditions and modalities for the transfer of persons having committed acts of piracy and detained by the European Union-led Naval Force (EU NAVFOR), and seized property in the possession of EU NAVFOR, from EU NAVFOR to Kenya', in Official Journal (2009) L79/49, annex to EU Council decision 2009/293CFSP of 26 February 2009.
40 House of Lords, 'Combating Somali Piracy: the EU's Naval Operation Atalanta', April, 23, 2010, http://www.publications.parliament.uk/pa/ld200910/ldselect/ldeucom/103/10304.htm. See also, Katherine Hourfield, 'Ships fill up with pirates after Kenya balks', *Navy Times*, 15 April 2010, http://www.navytimes.com/news/2010/04/ap_pirates_kenya_041510/; and, Kathryn Westcott, 'Pirates in the Dock', *BBC News*, March 21, 2009, http://news.bbc.co.uk/2/hi/africa/8059345.stm.
41 Warner and Schofield, 'Scuppering Somali Piracy', 62–63.
42 Bowden and Basnet, 'The Economic Cost of Maritime Piracy 2011', 19.
43 *Ibid*. See also, IMO Maritime Safety Committee (MSC) circular, MSC.1/Circ.1339, Best Management Practices for Protection against Somalia Based Piracy, version 4, (BMP 4), August 2011, available at http://www.imo.org/MediaCentre/HotTopics/piracy/Documents/1339.pdf, at 86–87.

44 See, Huggins and Kane-Hartnett, 'Somali Piracy – Are we at the End Game?'
45 BMP 4.
46 *Ibid.*
47 Schofield and Warner, 'Scuppering Somali Piracy', 57.
48 Clemens Höges, Holger Stark and Andreas Ulrich 'German Shipowners Turn to Mercenaries to Protect Against Pirates', *Der Spiegel*, February 1, 2011, available at http://www.spiegel.de/international/world/0,1518,742685,00.html.
49 Schofield 2007, 47; and, Peter Lehr and Hendrick Lehmann, 'Somalia – Pirates' New Paradise', 1–22 in Peter Lehr (ed.), *Violence at Sea*, (2007), 2–5.
50 See, James Kraska, *International Regulation of Private Maritime Security Companies*, Information Paper Series, International Law Department, U.S. Naval War College, 13–14, 5 June 2013. Katrina Manson and Robert Wright, 'Somali pirates spawn lucrative security trade', *Financial Times*, 8 February 2012, available at http://www.ft.com/intl/cms/s/0/410d1b40–45b0–11e1-acc9–00144feabdc0.html#axzz1nu0aP2rS.
51 IMB, 'Annual Report 2011', 24.
52 United Nations Security Council (UNSC), *Resolution 2018-Piracy and Security in Africa*, (31 October 2011). UNSC, *Resolution 2039 — Peace Consolidation in West Africa*, (29 February 2012).
53 IMO, *Reports on Acts of Piracy and Armed Robbery Against Ships – Annual Report 2005*, MSC.4/Circ.81. 22 March 2006. IMO, Reports on Acts of Piracy and Armed Robbery Against Ships – Annual Report 2007, MSC.4/Circ.115, 10 April 2008.
54 IMO, *Reports on Acts of Piracy and Armed Robbery Against Ships – Annual Report 2012*, MSC.4/Circ.193, 2 April 2013.
55 IMO, *Reports on Acts of Piracy and Armed Robbery Against Ships: Annual report 2013*, MSC.4/Cir.208, 1 March 2013. It is noted that there is an error in the date of adoption of the Annual Report 2013. The correct date should be 1 March 2014.
56 IMB, *SE Asia tanker hijacks rose in 2014 despite global drop in sea piracy, IMB report reveals*, 12 January 2015.
57 IMB, Piracy and Armed Robbery against Ships: Annual Report 2009, 41.
58 Peter J. Pham, 'Africa's Other Dangerous Waters: Piracy in the Gulf of Guinea', *World Defence Review* 3, December 2009. Scott Baldauf, 'Pirates take new territory: West African Gulf of Guinea', *The Christian Science Monitor*, 15 January 2010.
59 Kamal-Deen Ali, 'The Anatomy of Gulf of Guinea Piracy', *Naval War College Review*, 68, 2, 2015: 93–118, at 95.
60 IMB, *Piracy and Armed Robbery against Ships: Annual Report 2008*, 26. UNOCD, *Transnational Organized Crime in West Africa: A Threat Assessment*, February 2013.
61 Ali Kamal-Deen, The Anatomy of Gulf of Guinea Piracy, *Naval War College Review*, 68, 2, 2015, pp. 93–118.
62 IMO, *Reports on Acts of Piracy and Armed Robbery against Ships: Acts Reported during August 2006* (MSC.4/Circ.91, 11 September 2006. IMO, *Reports on Acts of Piracy and Armed Robbery against Ships: Acts Reported during May 2007*, MSC.4/Circ.103, 9 July 2007.
63 IMB, Piracy and Armed Robbery against Ships – Annual Report 2008, pp. 62–69.
64 IMB, Piracy and Armed Robbery Against Ships – Annual Report 2009.
65 See generally Alexander O. Exquemelin, *The Buccaneers of America* (1993).
66 IMO Piracy Reports June and July 2011, MSC.4/Circ.173 (11 July 2011).
67 Ali Kamal-Deen, The Anatomy of Gulf of Guinea Piracy, *Naval War College Review*, 68, 2, 2015: 93–118.
68 IMB, *Piracy and Armed Robbery against Ships – Annual Report 2011*.
69 *Ibid.*
70 IMO, *Reports of Piracy and Armed Robbery Against Ships: Acts Reported During October 2012*, MSC.4/Circ.190, 21 January 2013.
71 IMO, *Reports on Acts of Piracy and Armed Robbery Against Ships: Acts reported during July 2013*, MSC.4/Cir.200, 15 August 2013.
72 IMO, *Reports of Piracy and Armed Robbery against Ships January 2014*, MSC.4Cir/206, 7 March 2014.
73 'MT Kerala Returned to Angolan Authorities After Hijacking', *Reuters*, February 2014.
74 The hijacked vessels in June are *MT Fair Artemis*, a Greek-owned oil tanker flying Liberian Flag, a Ghanaian registered fishing vessel, *MV Mariner 771*, while *Hai Soon 6*, a Kiribati flagged oil tanker was hijacked in July.

75 Christina Katsouris and Aaron Sayne, 'Nigeria's Criminal Crude: International Options to Combat Export of Stolen Oil', *Chatham House*, September 2013, 2–12.
76 See Penal Code of Liberia, 2008, and Code de la Marine Marchande, Togo, 1971, UNDOALOS, Legislation and Treaties Data Base, http://www.un.org/Depts/los/LEGISLATIONANDTREATIES/index.htm, 1 January 2013.
77 See 'NIMASA Seeks Legal Backing to Fight Piracy', *This Day*, 14 February 2013.
78 See page 5, United Nations, *Report of the United Nations Assessment Mission on Piracy in the Gulf of Guinea*, Security Council S/2012/45, 19 January 2012.
79 Victor Prescott and Clive Schofield, *The Maritime Political Boundaries of the World*, 2nd edition, 338–342.
80 Kamal-deen Ali and Martin Tsamenyi, 'Fault Lines in Maritime Security: Analysis of maritime boundaries uncertainties in the Gulf of Guinea', *Africa Security Review*, Vol.22, no.3 (August 2013): 95–110.
81 IMB, *SE Asia tanker hijacks rose in 2014 despite global drop in sea piracy, IMB report reveals*, 12 January 2015.
82 James Kraska, Brian Wilson, 'Fighting Piracy: The Pen and the Sword', *World Policy Journal*, 2008: 41–52.
83 Abdi Ismail Samatar, Mark Lindberg and Basil Mayani, 'The Dialectics of Piracy in Somalia: the Rich Versus the Poor', *Third World Quarterly* 31, 8, 2011: 1377–94. See also, Eric Frecon, 'Piracy in the Malacca Straits: notes from the field', *International Institute for Asian Studies* Newsletter 36, 2005.
84 Robert Kaplan, 'The Coming Anarchy', *Atlantic Monthly*, February 1994, 44–76; Robert I. Rotberg, (ed.), *When States Fail: Causes and Consequences* (2004).
85 Kerstin Petretto, 'Weak States, Offshore Piracy in Modern Times', *East African Human Security Forum Discussion Paper*, March 2008; Stig J. Hansen and Atle Mesoy, 'The Pirates of the Horn: State Collapse and the Maritime Threat', *Strategic Insights* 3, 1, 2006; and, Ger Teitler, 'Piracy in Southeast Asia: A Historical Comparison', *Maritime Studies* 1, 1, 2001.
86 The details are as follows: 54(2005), 22 (2006), 17 (2007), 11(2008), 15(2009), 14(2010), 14(2011). See, 'Failed State Index: 2005–2011', Peace for Fund, http://global.fundforpeace.org/, 15 September 2013.
87 Generally on the implications of weak naval and policing capability for maritime security, see, Martin Murphy, *Small Boats, Weak States, Dirty Money: Piracy and Maritime Terrorism in the Modern World*, (Hurst, 2010).
88 'Chapter Nine: Sub-Saharan Africa', The Military Balance, 2012, 421–422.
89 See, 'Nigerian Navy is underfunded, former Naval Capt. tells senate committee', 4 June 2013, http://wwww.gejites.com/news/item/24792-nigerian-navy-is-underfunded---ex-naval-capt-tells-senate-committee, 30 November 2013. See also 'Senate Seeks Better Funding for Navy', *NBF News*, 18 June 2009, http://www.nigerianbestforum.com/blog/senate-seeks-better-funding-for-navy/, 30 November 2009.
90 The International Institute for Strategic Studies (IISS) 'Chapter Nine: Sub-Saharan Africa', *The Military Balance, 2012* (Routledge, 2012): 447–448.
91 See Penal Code of Liberia, 2008, and Code de la Marine Marchande, Togo, 1971, UNDOALOS, Legislation and Treaties Data Base, http://www.un.org/Depts/los/LEGISLATIONANDTREATIES/index.htm, 1 January 2013.
92 See 'NIMASA Seeks Legal Backing to Fight Piracy', *This Day*, 14 February 2013.
93 Prescott and Schofield, *The Maritime Political Boundaries of the World*, 338–342.
94 Kamal-Deen Ali and Tsamenyi, 'Fault Lines in Maritime Security'.
95 Article 100 of UNCLOS provides: "All States shall cooperate to the fullest possible extent in the repression of piracy on the high seas or in any other place outside the jurisdiction of any State."
96 See ECCAS, Protocole Relatif a la Strategie de Securitisation des Interest Vitaux en Mer des Etats de la CEEAC du Golfe de Guinea (Yaoundé, Cameroon. 24 October 2009). Zone A: Angola, DR Congo; Zone B: Angola, Congo (Brazzaville), Gabon; Zone D: Cameroon, Equatorial Guinea, Gabon, São Tomé and Príncipe.
97 Summit of Heads of State and Governments of ECOWAS and ECCAS, Yaoundé, Cameroon on 24–25 June 2013.
98 On APS see Commander US Naval Forces Africa, 'About Africa Partnership Station', http://www.c6f.navy.mil/about%20us.html, 12 December 2013. See also, David E. Brown, 'AFRICOM AT 5 Years: The Maturation of a New U.S. Combatant Command', The Letort Papers, Strategic Studies Institute,

U.S. Army War College, 2013; and, Sean McFate, 'U.S. Africa Command: A New Strategic Paradigm?', *Military Review* 88, 1 (January-February 2008): 1–28.
99 European Commission, New EU initiative to combat piracy in the Gulf of Guinea, Press Release, Ref IP/13/14, Brussels, 10 January 2013.
100 Benin, Cameroon, Equatorial Guinea, Gabon, Nigeria, Sâo Tomé and Principe and Togo.

Part D
Current Issues and Future Challenges

18
Regulation of Marine Renewable Energy

Anne Marie O'Hagan

Introduction to marine renewable energy

Drivers

The legal drivers for Marine Renewable Energy (MRE) generation are numerous and reflect both environmental and energy priorities. From an environmental perspective increasing energy from marine renewable sources has the potential to help mitigate and adapt to the effects of climate change and reduce emissions of harmful greenhouse gases, including carbon dioxide. Renewable energy resources are, by definition, sustainable, unlimited and not subject to depletion hence they have a major role to play in contributing to energy security. At a regional scale, deployment can create wealth through job creation not only through device deployment, but also growth of a supply chain sector. Marine renewables are often the only indigenous energy source in many countries, which can also promote energy independence and national economic development. As a result, and to maximise the benefits from development of the MRE sector, several national governments have published dedicated strategies and targets for different types of MRE to encourage its development and growth. This in turn complements the legal requirements to reduce carbon dioxide emissions through a move away from fossil fuels.

In the European Union, Member States are obliged to comply with over-arching legislation to achieve three key objectives by 2020.[1] These are: a 20% reduction in greenhouse gas emissions from 1990 levels, a raise in the share of EU energy consumption produced from renewables to 20% and a 20% improvement in the EU's energy efficiency. As a result of the EU's Renewable Energy Directive (2009/28/EC), Member States have accepted binding national targets for increasing the share of renewable energy in their energy consumption. A detailed plan of how these targets are to be achieved is provided in National Renewable Energy Action Plans (NREAPs). These set out sectoral targets, the technology mix expected, the trajectory to be followed and any reforms necessary to overcome the barriers to developing renewable energy. Of the 28 EU Member States, 23 are coastal States. Fifteen of the coastal EU Member States have specified national targets for offshore wind in their NREAPs by 2020. In contrast, only seven have identified targets for wave and tidal energy. This is indicative of the development status of the various MRE technologies. Internationally, China has an ambitious national target of 5 GW of offshore wind by 2015 and 30 GW by 2020. The Global Wind Energy Council[2] state that in Japan an estimated 5–6 GW of offshore capacity could be reached by 2030 and South Korea has a target of 2 GW by 2030. Australia remains heavily dependent on oil (38% in 2012–13) and coal (33% in 2012–13) with renewables accounting for only 6% of the country's energy mix in 2012–13.[3] The Renewable Energy Target (RET) scheme was designed to transform the energy sector and ensure that 20% of Australia's electricity comes from renewable sources by 2020. The RET was reviewed by an Expert Panel in 2014 who put forward options to the Australian Government for both the Large-scale Renewable Energy Target and the Small-scale Renewable Energy Scheme.[4] The Government and Opposition parties have been in a stalemate over the target since August 2014. A deal agreed in May 2015 broke this impasse and, in June, the Senate passed a Bill to reduce the renewable energy target for 2020 from 41,000 gigawatt hours (GWh) to 33,000 GWh.[5]

A note on terminology

Marine renewable energy, in this chapter, refers to three key energy sources: offshore wind, tidal and wave. In different parts of the world alternative terms are used: 'offshore renewable energy' is usually synonymous with MRE. The term 'Ocean Energy' (OE) tends to be reserved for sources of energy that are derived directly from the ocean itself, namely waves, tides, [ocean] currents, salinity gradients and thermal gradients.

Sources and status of marine renewable energy

Offshore wind

Offshore wind is the most commercially advanced form of MRE. Essentially wind turbines capture the energy of moving air and convert it to electricity. The turbines start to generate energy at wind speeds of 4–5 metres per second (m/s) up to a maximum speed of 25 m/s, when the turbine will shut down. In recent years there has been a tendency to deploy larger turbines as these can avail of the higher wind speeds further from the ground, utilise longer blades to maximise the energy capture from the wind and have a slower rotation speed, which can be important with respect to noise and visual considerations. Turbine diameters range from 80–126m, depending on the manufacturer and the rated power (usually 2–5 MW), with hub heights above sea level of 90–108m.[6] Recent technology developments have focussed on design and deployment of floating wind turbines. These consist of the same turbines but have a floating base structure which can be stabilised using ballast, buoyant area[7] or tethering. One possibility with floating wind turbines is that they can be deployed in deeper waters, typically designed for depths of 50–500m. In 2013 there was 7,046 MW of offshore wind power installed globally, with 6,562 MW coming solely from European waters.[8] More than 90% of this figure is installed in the waters of northern Europe, namely the North, Baltic and Irish Seas and the English Channel. Whilst the majority of offshore wind farms are located in Territorial Seas there are also a number in the Exclusive Economic Zone, for example in Belgium and Germany, though deployments further offshore have significant impacts on cost (cabling costs rise with increased distance to shore).

Tidal energy

Tidal energy includes both tidal range and tidal stream (marine current). The Intergovernmental Panel on Climate Change (IPCC) has stated that tidal range technology is the most advanced and only form of ocean energy technology that can currently be considered as mature.[9] It includes tidal barrages, lagoons, fences and reefs. Tidal barrages are perhaps the most well understood. A barrage spans the estuary, bay or river, in a similar way to a hydroelectric dam, and comprises sluices and turbines that control the flood and ebb of the tides to drive the turbines and generate electricity.[10] The best known example is the La Rance barrage near St. Malo in France, which opened in 1966, and has a peak output of 240 MW with an annual output of approximately 540 GWh. Functioning tidal barrages can also be found in Canada, China and South Korea. Tidal lagoons can be either free-standing structures built offshore or a semi-circular type arrangement connected to the shoreline at each end. These differ from barrages in that they do not fully cross a river or estuary. No operational tidal lagoons exist at this time though plans have been submitted and are undergoing review for a 240 MW nominal rated capacity lagoon in Swansea Bay, Wales in the UK.[11] Tidal barrages may have significant environmental impacts through, for example, disruption to marine mammal and fish migration patterns and alteration of hydrology and sediment transport.

Tidal stream technologies are designed to extract energy from fast-flowing water in tidal streams, which can be accelerated by coastal topography. Devices in this category are at pre-commercial stage and are limited to areas with a high tidal energy resource. The majority of tidal stream devices under development are based on rotating rotors with either horizontal or vertical axis turbines. They are broadly similar to wind turbines and can benefit from the lessons learned in that industry as they progress to commercial scale. Two of the most established tidal stream companies are Marine Current Turbines (MCT) (SeaGen device) and OpenHydro (Open Centre turbine). MCT deployed its SeaGen device in Strangford Lough, Northern Ireland in 2008 and this generates 1.2 MW for between 18 and 20 hours per day[12] with no significant environmental impacts having completed a comprehensive environmental monitoring programme.[13] The Siemens-operated company also has projects planned for Scotland, Wales and the Bay of Fundy in Canada. OpenHydro is an Irish technology company, with French company DCNS Group the major shareholder since 2013. Its Open Centre turbine is designed to be deployed directly onto the seafloor. Its slow rotation speed and lubricant-free operation can potentially minimise risks to surrounding marine life. OpenHydro has a broad portfolio of projects underway in multiple jurisdictions including the UK, France, Canada and the United States.

Wave energy

Unlike large wind turbines, there is a wide variety of wave energy technologies, resulting from the different ways in which energy can be absorbed from the waves and also depending on the water depth and proximity to the shore. Six main working principles for wave energy converters have been identified. These are explained in detail elsewhere[14] and include:

1. Oscillating water column[15]
2. Attenuator[16]
3. Point absorber[17]
4. Submerged pressure differential[18]
5. Oscillating surge convertor[19] and
6. Overtopping.[20]

It is important to understand these operating principles as different technologies occupy different depths and spatial areas of the sea (water column, seabed etc.) and accordingly there will be different planning, regulatory and management considerations. To date there has been no technology convergence, with a variety of devices still at the R&D stage, and testing on-going in laboratories and varying sea states. Most devices are currently deployed in dedicated Test Centres that allow device developers to test or demonstrate the performance of their devices in an open sea environment.[21] These centres can be subject to different consenting processes given deployments are often on a time-limited basis and involve single-units of small scale devices. Operational test centres for wave energy devices are all located within internal waters and territorial seas. Carnegie Wave Energy began constructing the Perth Wave Energy project in 2012, using its CETO device. In February 2015 the project was connected to the electricity grid, becoming the first demonstration of a complete grid-connected CETO system in the world. It is also the only wave energy project to comprise of more than one device and the only one that produces both power and freshwater, through a wave-powered desalination plant.[22]

Other forms of MRE

Ocean currents

Ocean current energy is defined as the kinetic energy available in large-scale, open-ocean currents derived from latitudinal distributions of winds and thermohaline ocean circulation. These currents flow continuously in the same direction and have low variability. The potential for power generation and technologies to harness the energy from such currents has received attention in different parts of the world, including Florida[23] and Taiwan,[24] though it remains at the early stage of development. The Bureau of Ocean Energy Management (BOEM) in the USA has stated that of all the forms of marine renewable energy, ocean currents are the least understood and its technology the least mature.[25] To date the technology has focused on submerged turbines, similar to wind turbines with either horizontal or vertical axes.[26] No commercial devices of this type are currently operational. BOEM issued a lease to Florida Atlantic University (FAU) in 2014 for testing and evaluating the use of turbines powered by ocean currents.[27]

Ocean thermal energy conversion (OTEC)

OTEC converts the difference in temperature between the surface and deep layers of the ocean into electrical power. To be economically viable, the temperature difference must be 20°C (36°F) and the cold deep water must be no more than 100m below the surface.[28] This means that sites suitable for OTEC exist between latitudes 20° and 24° North and South of the equator (e.g. tropical zones of the Caribbean and the Pacific). Where this temperature difference exists it is possible to drive a heat engine. OTEC plants can be ship-based, land-based or nearshore, attached to the shelf, moored or floating facilities in deep ocean waters.[29] There have been a number of successful pilot scale OTEC plants in Japan and Hawaii but all attempts to move OTEC from the pilot scale to commercial scale have so far failed.[30]

Salinity gradient power

Salinity gradient power or "the energy represented by the salinity concentration gradient between fresh water and seawater"[31] has the highest energy concentration (i.e. energy density) of all forms of MRE.[32] Three forms are currently being researched: Pressure Retarded Osmosis (PRO) and Reverse Electrodialysis (RED), both of which use a membrane, and Hydrocratic energy, which is membrane free. None of these technologies are at commercial scale. A small-scale pilot PRO project (4 kW) exists in Norway and concentrates primarily on testing and development and a smaller capacity (1 kW) RED pilot project has been installed in the Netherlands.[33]

Regulatory aspects

Development of any MRE project necessitates the consideration and application of legislation and agreements from local, national, regional and sometimes international scales. Different development stages, reflecting the planning, construction and installation, operation and decommissioning of a project, may also require adherence to different regulatory requirements. The regulatory system applicable can also vary according to the proposed location, specifically the maritime jurisdictional zone in which it is to be sited. An over-arching duty to protect and preserve the marine environment often results in comprehensive environmental assessment requirements.

International law

UN Law of the Sea Convention (LOSC)

The UN LOSC prescribes different maritime jurisdictional zones and the legal regime applicable to these ocean spaces. Currently, in 2014, the majority of MRE developments are located wholly within the limits of the Territorial Sea (12M, 12 miles) meaning that States have full sovereignty, subject to the right of innocent passage, over the water, airspace, bed and subsoil. The law surrounding innocent passage and offshore structures has largely been resolved as a result of the construction of offshore oil and gas rigs.[34] A coastal State may require "foreign ships exercising the right of innocent passage through its Territorial Sea to use such sea lanes and traffic separation schemes as it may designate or prescribe for the regulation of the passage of ships".[35] Beyond 12M, in the Exclusive Economic Zone (EEZ), there have been some offshore wind energy developments, for example in Belgium, Denmark and Germany. The LOSC provides that a coastal State "has sovereign rights for the purposes of exploring and exploiting, conserving and managing the natural resources, whether living or non-living, of the waters superjacent to the seabed and of the seabed and its subsoil, and with regard to other activities for the economic exploitation and exploration of the zone, such as *the production of energy from the water, currents and winds*" [emphasis added].[36] The coastal State also has jurisdiction with respect to the "establishment and use of artificial islands, installations and structures" and "the protection and preservation of the marine environment".[37] A coastal State has exclusive jurisdiction over any such artificial islands, installations and structures.[38]

In terms of the Continental Shelf, a coastal State exercises sovereign rights for the purpose of exploring and exploiting its natural resources. Natural resources, in this context, consist of the mineral and other non-living resources of the seabed and subsoil together with living organisms belonging to sedentary species.[39] All States are entitled to lay submarine cables and pipelines on the continental shelf.[40] Likewise, Article 60 on artificial islands, installations and structures in the EEZ applies "*mutatis mutandis*" to the Continental Shelf.[41] Beyond the EEZ, are the High Seas which cover all parts of the sea not included in the EEZ, the Territorial Sea or the internal waters of a State, or in the archipelagic waters of an archipelagic State. In the High Seas freedoms of navigation, overflight, and the freedom to lay submarine cables and pipelines, subject to Part VI of LOSC, exist. There is also the freedom to construct artificial islands and other installations permitted under international law, freedom of fishing and scientific research, subject to legal requirements specified elsewhere. Where an EEZ has not been claimed by a State, the High Seas regime is applicable, which could have implications for future development of MRE therein. On occasion the High Seas are also referred to as Areas Beyond National Jurisdiction (ABNJ). Though theoretically possible[42] presently it is not economically viable to develop MRE on the extended Continental Shelf or in the High Seas, hence they are not considered further in this chapter.

The LOSC contains a specific obligation to protect and preserve the marine environment.[43] Part XII of the Convention refers to pollution and its prevention but there is also a duty to protect and preserve rare or fragile ecosystems and the habitat of depleted, threatened or endangered species and other forms of marine life[44] as well as the prevention of intentional or accidental introduction of species, alien or new, to a particular part of the marine environment which may cause significant and harmful changes thereto.[45] Following a Report of the Secretary-General on Oceans and Law of the Sea on marine renewables in April 2012,[46] the UN Open-ended Informal Consultative Process on Oceans and the Law of the Sea focused on MRE during its thirteenth meeting, in New York from 29 May to 1 June 2012.[47] The latter reiterated that the LOSC was the appropriate legal framework for all activities in the oceans and seas, including MRE. Several delegations emphasised the need to pay particular attention to the potential adverse environmental, social and cultural impacts of MRE.[48] A structured process for allocation of ocean space for future development of MRE was also deemed necessary.[49]

Other relevant international law

MRE development is not neatly covered by a single legal instrument but rather its regulation is dispersed across multiple legal instruments. Table 18.1 presents a non-exhaustive list of other relevant international legal instruments that may, implicitly or explicitly, impact upon the planning, development and management of MRE installations. As MRE development touches upon a number of discrete elements (see later), the majority of regulation derives from national legislation, which enshrines broader international and regional legal commitments.

Table 18.1 International legal instruments with potential implications for MRE development

Instrument	Topic(s) with implication(s) for MRE	Example references
UN Convention on Biological Diversity	Environmental Impact Assessment	Article 14, CBD and Decision XI/18
	Protected Areas	Article 7, CBD and Decision VII/5 on Marine and Coastal Biodiversity
	Underwater noise and its impacts	UNEP/CBD/SBSTTA/14/L.14 19 May 2010 (emerging issues in CBD)
	Invasive species	Article 8(h), CBD
	Marine Spatial Planning (MSP)	Marine spatial planning in the context of the CBD: a study carried out in response to CBD COP 10 decision X/29. (2012). CBD Technical Series No. 68
UN Framework Convention on Climate Change	Reduction of greenhouse gases	Article 4, UNFCCC & Kyoto Protocol
	Clean Development Mechanism	Article 12, Kyoto Protocol
	Technology Mechanism	Cancun Agreement (2010) Decision 1/CP.16, paras.113–127

Instrument	Topic(s) with implication(s) for MRE	Example references
Convention on International Civil Aviation	Offshore wind turbine heights, location and lighting	International Civil Aviation Organisation (ICAO) Annex 14 standards, chapter 6
	Implications for radar and aerial navigation	ICAO. (2009). European Guidance Material on Managing Building Restricted Areas, Technical Report, ICAO Eur. Doc. 015
IMO Protocols and Resolutions	Ships routeing	General Provisions on Ships' Routeing, IMO Resolution A.572(14), 20 November 1985
	Safety of navigation around offshore installations and structures	Safety Zones and Safety of Navigation Around Offshore Installations and Structures, IMO Resolution A.671(16), 19 October 1989
	Decommissioning of offshore structures	Guidelines and Standards for the Removal of Offshore Installations and Structures on the Continental Shelf and in the Exclusive Economic Zone, IMO Resolution A.672(16), 19 October 1989
International Convention for the Prevention of Pollution from Ships, 1973 (MARPOL), as amended	Prevention of pollution	Article 1. Generally applicable to 'ships' servicing energy installations.
Safety of Life at Sea Convention (SOLAS) 1974	Ships routeing Exclusion zones	Chapter V, Safety of Navigation
Espoo Convention on Transboundary EIA 1991	Obligation on States to notify and consult each other on all major projects under consideration that are likely to have a significant adverse environmental impact across boundaries.	All Articles

Regional Seas Conventions

The UN launched the Regional Seas Programme in 1974, subsequent to its Conference on the Human Environment held in Stockholm, Sweden in 1972. The Programme had the initial aim of addressing the increasing degradation of the world's marine and coastal environments through improved and more sustainable management. This required neighbouring countries to engage on a range of actions specific to their region in order to better protect their shared marine environment. A number of Regional Seas programmes became active, often underpinned by a strong legal basis and implemented by countries sharing a common body of water. The issues to be addressed through joint activities and Action Plans are tailored to the particular region. Not all Regional Seas Conventions (RSCs) may consider MRE explicitly. The Pacific Regional Environment Programme (SPREP) acts as the Secretariat for the three associated Conventions.[50] The SPREP Strategic Plan for 2011–2015, for example, promotes the development of cost-effective renewable energy as a way of reducing greenhouse gases though it does not explicitly mention MRE.[51]

OSPAR Convention on the protection of the marine environment of the North-East Atlantic

The OSPAR Convention entered into force on 25 March 1998. The Convention has been signed and ratified by Belgium, Denmark, the European Union, Finland, France, Germany, Iceland, Ireland, the Netherlands, Norway, Portugal, Spain, Sweden, the UK, Luxembourg and Switzerland. As the EU is a party to the Convention, many OSPAR commitments are taken forward through EU law. The original focus of the Convention was the prevention and reduction of all sources of pollution. The OSPAR Commission has also traditionally worked on oil and gas installations but legal drivers to reduce greenhouse gases and increase renewable energy have resulted in the OSPAR Commission adopting a new focus on offshore wind as this activity is increasing in the North Sea and Celtic Seas, both part of the OSPAR area. In 2004, the OSPAR Commission published a background document on potential advantages and disadvantages associated with the development of offshore wind farms.[52] Subsequently the Commission produced a review of the state of knowledge on the environmental impacts associated with offshore wind farms[53] which culminated in the publication of a dedicated guidance document on environmental considerations for offshore wind farm development.[54]

Elements of consenting for marine renewable energy

Introduction

Consenting commonly involves occupation of sea space (leasing), environmental impacts, connection to the electricity grid, terrestrial planning and decommissioning. Consenting varies according to country and sometimes also maritime jurisdictional zone as well as technology type. Applicable processes may also vary within countries.

Occupation of sea space

To occupy and utilise an area of sea space a developer will generally require a lease of that area. This is usually available from the national government or one of its agencies, as it normally proclaims ownership of the seabed subject to certain public rights, such as navigation and fishing. A distinction between exclusive and non-exclusive use of sea space and whether the 'development' is temporary or permanent is often made in leasing procedures. If a development is temporary or for a defined period of time, a licence may be issued. Conversely where the use is expected to be for a longer time-frame, a lease may be granted. Different countries will use different terms depending on the nomenclature used in their governing legislation. In the UK, the Crown Estate manages lands held by the Crown as sovereign including the foreshore and seabed, usually to 12M, around the UK. As such, the Crown Estate can alienate property meaning the Crown can grant a right in the seabed or foreshore to a third party for specific purposes such as mineral extraction, fish farming or MRE generation. These uses are normally regulated by specific statutes. The Crown Estate has a responsibility to enhance the value of Crown property and for MRE this occurs primarily through its leasing rounds (see UK section) which generate an income to revert to the Crown.

Elsewhere the maritime jurisdictional zone may have a pronounced effect on consenting processes. In Germany the central Government's Federal Maritime and Hydrographic Agency (BSH) has responsibility for offshore wind energy developments in the EEZ. From the shore to the 12M limit, it is the coastal States[55] that are responsible for processing offshore wind energy permits. If an underground electrical cable from a wind farm in the EEZ crosses State waters to an onshore grid access point then the State must grant permission for this.[56] In other countries with a federal system of government, such as Australia and Canada, State and federal laws also apply to offshore development. This type of governance system has the potential to create difficulties where a development straddles a number of planning competencies within different levels of government resulting in the need for multiple consents, usually from different authorities.

Terrestrial planning

All MRE must come ashore, either through a cable, a processing plant or electrical sub-station. These ancillary features require planning permission under the terrestrial planning system, or equivalent, in operation in that country. There is usually a separate application process which operates independently from consenting for sea-based activities. In Ireland local planning authority jurisdiction ends at the Mean High Water Mark. In contrast, local authorities in the UK have jurisdiction to the Low Water Mark. In Germany State planning jurisdiction extends to 12M. In the USA, processes vary from State to State covering construction of associated works as well as the impacts related to cabling, such as avoidance of pollution, and potential impacts to recreational or commercial fisheries.[57] Under planning law, there may also be a requirement to consult with other regulatory authorities e.g. nature conservation bodies, health and safety authorities, other industry representatives and the public on relevant planning applications. The scale of development may also determine the application of terrestrial planning law and the role of local authorities.

Environmental impacts

Under international law, there is a duty to protect and preserve the marine environment. A major component of this obligation is the requirement for a developer to carry out an Environmental Impact Assessment (EIA) so as to ensure that the environmental implications of a development are taken into account before a decision to proceed is made by the competent authority.[58] In the case of MRE projects, the requirement to submit an EIA is generally dependent on the nature, size and location of the proposed development. In the EU, the EIA Directive[59] distinguishes between projects requiring a mandatory EIA (Annex I) and those where Member State authorities must determine if projects are likely to have significant effects (Annex II), taking into account criteria listed in Annex III of the Directive. Wind energy projects are included in Annex II and as such EIA is at the discretion of Member State authorities. Wave and tidal energy are not explicitly mentioned in the Directive so EIA is at the discretion of the Member State. Smaller scale developments seem to have less rigorous EIA requirements in many countries, for example, in Mexico, Spain and Portugal.[60] In Spain, a reduced number of topics in comparison to larger, full scale projects are considered and the competent authority will then examine these with a view to deciding whether a full EIA is necessary. In Scotland, if a development is over

1 MW and within 12M or under 50 MW and beyond 12M it will require an EIA, depending on its nature and location.[61]

Many of the expected effects from MRE devices are similar to other forms of marine development. To date EIA of wave and tidal energy projects has been modelled on EIA for offshore wind. Removal of energy directly from the water column distinguishes wave and tidal energy generation from the offshore wind experience and presents a host of new potential issues which have not been confronted in offshore wind. One obvious example is the introduction of moving components to the underwater environment.[62] Consenting processes, and EIA in particular, must consider the potential interactions between marine species and devices, possible alterations of marine habitats from operational activities and long term ecosystem effects of deploying and operating arrays of MRE devices in coastal and estuarine waters.[63] Effects may be specific to the type of energy being harnessed, the individual device type or the reduction in energy in marine systems. Smaller scale wave and tidal devices have been tested and deployed in real sea conditions but the short duration of such deployments means there is limited data available to assess their potential environmental effects. Uncertainty, therefore, remains a major challenge for regulators and developers and ranges from uncertainty of the effects of a single device to those associated with multiple devices and cumulatively with other marine activities. Consequently some countries are looking towards new and innovative ways of enabling MRE development whilst complying with over-arching legal requirements (see later).

One outcome of the EIA process is informing the design of an environmental monitoring programme to accompany the associated consent(s). An analysis of 14 wave and one tidal test sites across the EU classified the monitoring activities going on at those sites into nine categories: benthos, seabirds, fish and fish habitats, marine mammals, other marine megavertebrates (sharks and turtles), physical oceanographic environment, acoustics, terrestrial habitats and socio-economic considerations, plus an additional category for other activities which did not fall within the aforementioned classes.[64] Unsurprisingly, given the intended purpose of development, physical oceanography parameters were the most common parameter investigated. An interesting finding from this study is that there was widespread variation in the methods utilised, such that even when several sites were essentially addressing the same ecological question, they were often using strikingly different methods to do so. This emphasises the need for a more unified approach to the EIA process, particularly in countries that are working from a common legal basis. A second finding, with implications for acceptance of the sector, was the lack of consideration of the socio-economic effects of MRE development. These typically include elements like demography, employment and regional income; sea and land use; aesthetics; infrastructure; socio-cultural systems and implications for other maritime activities such as fisheries, tourism and recreation.[65] There is a paucity of guidance on how to address such elements which might also explain their relative invisibility in EIAs to date.

Electrical connection

MRE is exploited at source meaning it requires suitable grid infrastructure interconnected to the transmission network. In a number of EU countries the offshore energy resource is situated in remote coastal locations where there is only a weak distribution network available, if any, and this can result in costly grid reinforcements raising project costs to a prohibitive level. There are also weak interconnections between EU Member States,[66] the power market is generally inflexible, liable to change and fragmented and there is a lack of offshore electricity grids.[67] Thus there is a need to consider long-term strategic level grid infrastructure along with site level connections during project planning and consenting. There are differences between countries in terms of the support schemes for offshore wind, wave and tidal as well as in the regulatory frameworks and grid codes. Grid access and grid connection are also governed separately. In many countries there is no common power market.

For projects, grid connections tend to be governed by distinct legal and administrative processes and obtained from the national energy ministry or agency under an Electricity Act, or equivalent. In practice before consent to construct or generate electricity can be acquired, a range of other conditions must be complied with including planning permission or exemption, EIA, a connection offer from the relevant operator and a Power Purchase Agreement (PPA). Grid connection offers can be made by either the Transmission System Operator (TSO), who operates the high voltage system, or the Distribution System Operator (DSO) who operates the medium and low voltage systems depending on the type of connection needed by the project. A PPA is a contractual agreement between an electricity generator and a licensed supplier obliging the latter to purchase the output from a new renewable energy powered electricity generation plant.

The variety of permits, licences and permissions involved in consenting solely the electrical elements of a project are complex, time-consuming and often difficult to integrate into a single project licence. Only Denmark, Italy and the Netherlands have a single permit system for all renewable energy projects.[68] This issue has been repeatedly raised in the EU: the Directive on Renewable Energy (2009/28/EC) provides that "administrative procedures are streamlined and expedited at the appropriate administrative level" and that such procedures are "clearly coordinated and defined, with transparent timetables for determining planning and building applications".[69] This provision extends to provide that, if possible under the applicable regulatory framework, "simplified and less burdensome authorisation procedures" are established for smaller projects and for decentralised devices.[70] The European Commission has recognised that progress in removing administrative barriers remains limited and slow, can raise the costs of renewable energy generally and will require further efforts if the 2020 targets are to be achieved.[71]

At site level, there may be a requirement to obtain permission to lay cables e.g. in Belgium, Germany, the Netherlands and Sweden. This can also result in the need for an [additional] EIA given the likelihood for seabed disturbance. Customary practice has led to cables generally being buried at a depth of 2m so as to avoid interference with, and damage from, other sea uses. Recent best practice from developers in the UK has highlighted the need for flexibility in consenting procedures for grid connections and cable laying. Experience there has shown that specifying fixed burial depths as a condition of consent is problematic because ground conditions are likely to vary substantially along the route and this may not be known when applying for consent due to the limitations of geophysical and geotechnical surveying techniques.[72] Beyond site level considerations, there is a need to examine the concept of a dedicated offshore grid and how this could be realised. This would require the integration of several power networks and consequently a substantial number of entities might be responsible for granting consents but, in the longer-term, it could reduce costs as the cables could work as interconnectors as well as for power transmission from offshore generation sites to onshore and offshore consuming centres.[73]

Decommissioning and abandonment

Any installations or structures which are abandoned or disused in the EEZ must be removed to ensure safety of navigation in accordance with any accepted international standards.[74] These

IMO standards date from 1989 and provide that all installations are to be removed except where "non-removal or partial removal is consistent with these Guidelines and Standards."[75] Decisions should be made on the basis of a case-by-case evaluation taking into account the following matters:

1. potential effect on safety of navigation or other uses,
2. deterioration of material and future effects,
3. potential effect on the marine environment including living resources,
4. risk of shift from position,
5. costs, technical feasibility and risk of injury to personnel, and
6. determination of new use or other reasonable justification.[76]

The Guidelines outline the factors that should be considered in determining each of the above matters. In relation to a determination of any potential effect on the marine environment, the guidelines state this should be based upon scientific evidence taking into account the effect on water quality; geological and hydrographic characteristics; the presence of endangered or threatened species; existing habitat types; local fishery resources; and the potential for pollution or contamination of the site.[77]

The Resolution recommends that the following standards are taken into account when a decision is made regarding removal:

- entire removal of abandoned or disused installations or structures in <75m of water and weighing <4000 tonnes in air (excluding deck and superstructure);
- entire removal of abandoned or disused installations or structures if placed after 1 January 1998 if standing in <100m of water and weighing <4000 tonnes in air (excluding deck and superstructure).[78]

Removal should cause no adverse effects on navigation or the marine environment including living resources. A coastal State may decide that the installation or structure does not need to be removed. If this is the case, the coastal State must ensure that the remaining parts are stable, indicated on nautical charts and marked by aids to navigation, where necessary. The coastal State must also identify the party responsible for maintaining those aids and for conducting monitoring of the material left behind so as to ensure these guidelines are observed. Legal title to the installations and structures that have not been entirely removed from the seabed must be unambiguous so that there are no financial issues relating to liability in the future.

The IMO Guidelines recognise that a coastal State can decide to allow an installation or structure to remain, in whole or in part, on the seabed if it would serve a new use such as an enhancement of a living resource.[79] MRE devices may alleviate fishing pressure and potentially allow fish to breed and grow[80]; introduce new hard substrate that may have artificial reef effects[81] and also act as fish aggregating devices.[82] Abandonment of man-made structures at sea comes within the definition of 'dumping' in the 1996 Protocol to the London Convention on the Prevention of Marine Pollution by Dumping of Wastes and Other Matter (1972) but it must be for the "sole purpose of deliberate disposal".[83] This stipulates that dumping does not include "abandonment in the sea of matter (e.g. cables, pipelines and marine research devices) placed for a purpose other than the mere disposal thereof".[84] The potential to have an artificial reef effect could, in some cases, be used to legitimise dumping at sea and for this reason the

IMO, as the entity responsible for the London Convention and Protocol along with the United Nations Environment Programme (UNEP), developed guidelines for the Placement of Artificial Reefs in 2009.[85] The definition of artificial reef used in the guidelines, however, unequivocally excludes "submerged structures deliberately placed to perform functions not related to those of a natural reef [. . .] even if they incidentally imitate some functions of a natural reef".[86]

Selected national approaches to consenting of MRE developments

Australia

Australia has a federal system of government so both Commonwealth and State legislation applies to MRE projects. EIA legislation as well as planning legislation also applies. Currently there are no operational offshore wind or tidal energy projects in Australian waters The Carnegie Wave Energy project in Perth was grid connected in February 2015.[87] For offshore wind this has been attributed to a number of factors including the higher development costs associated with offshore wind farms in comparison with their onshore counterparts and also the fact that existing offshore turbines are not wholly suited to the deep waters (>30 metres) around Australia.[88] A number of sites have been identified as suitable for offshore wind farms[89] and there are also some planned wave energy projects such as the 3 MW grid connected wave energy array located at Garden Island, Perth, Western Australia which will be fully operational in 2016.[90] The Australian company Oceanlinx Ltd. successfully deployed the world's first 1/3 scale, grid-connected, wave energy device in Port Kembla in February 2010 for three months with the aim of proving the generating power of the technology. In 2012, CSIRO identified 16 Australian companies that are either actively developing ocean energy projects, have received substantial government and/or private funding or have announced project development plans.[91]

Currently there is no legislation dealing specifically with MRE at any level of Australian government.[92] Projects within 3M of the coastline are regulated through State legislation and the over-arching Environment Protection and Biodiversity Conservation Act 1999 along with federal legislation on the electricity market, maritime safety and renewable energy generally. The State of Victoria has been cited as one where an integrated framework for MRE licensing and environmental impact has been discussed though this seems to have stalled recently.[93] Separately the suite of legislation applicable to renewable energy projects has been described as a "maze" to a Victorian Government Committee.[94] In Victoria projects require planning approval, environmental assessment and approval; works approval; infrastructure approval; heritage and Aboriginal impact approvals and electricity and gas approvals.[95] This multitude of approvals coupled with the novelty of the technology and the lack of available information on the physical resource has resulted in MRE developers having to 'forge a process' for approval of their projects.[96]

Beyond 3M, in Commonwealth waters, federal legislation applies. Carnegie's Garden Island wave energy project is located on a Commonwealth-owned and active defence base, HMAS Stirling, hence it has been subject to federal legislation. In addition, approvals are also required under State (Western Australia) law including the Environmental Protection Act 1986, the Navigable Waters Regulations 1958 and the Wildlife Conservation Act 1950. The terrestrial elements of the project were managed by the Department of Defence that issued an Environmental Clearance Certificate for the project in November 2012. Under the auspices of the Standing Council on Energy and Resources, a Clean Energy Working Group has been created that has been tasked with working on the development of a national framework for MRE, supported by an appropriate legal framework to apply in Commonwealth waters.[97] With respect to grid connection, the majority of Australia's MRE resource is situated far from the transmission network or load centres. The National Electricity Market is governed by the rules of four core governing bodies: the Standing Committee on Energy and Resources, the Australian Energy Market Commission, the Australian Energy Regulator and the Australian Energy Market Operator who are responsible for market policy, rules, enforcement and physical operation, respectively.[98] The response by the Australian Government to the recommendations contained in the aforementioned review of the Renewable Energy Target will be instrumental in determining the future of marine renewable energy in the country.[99]

Germany

Germany has a federal system of government with 16 states or *Länder*, three of which are coastal and therefore exercise jurisdiction to the 12M limit. Beyond 12M, the federal government has jurisdiction for planning and licensing activities. The majority of operational and planned offshore wind farms are located in the EEZ. In 2002, the German Government published its strategy for offshore wind which indicated that up to 20–25 GW could be achieved by 2030.[100] The Federal Maritime and Hydrographic Agency (BSH) coordinates consenting, grid connection and public consultation for offshore wind farms in the EEZ under Article 2 of the Marine Facilities Ordinance (*SeeAnlV*). This Ordinance stipulates that a wind farm project can only be approved where:

a) it does not impair the safety and efficiency of navigation, and
b) it is not detrimental to the marine environment.

Germany does not require its MRE developers to pay leasing fees or rent as this was viewed as undermining existing subsidies such as feed-in tariffs.[101] Under Article 3 of the Marine Facilities Ordinance, an approval is a non-discretionary administrative act. This means that there is a presumption in favour of development unless the project falls into one of the categories listed above, and only if the expected impact cannot be mitigated effectively. The permit lasts for 25 years from the start of operation and also covers design, safety and decommissioning. On receipt of an application for consent, the BSH informs other competent authorities such as the regional Waterways and Shipping Directorates, the mining authority, the Federal Environmental Agency and the Federal Agency for Nature Conservation of the application and invites them to provide comments. Following this, wider participation begins, involving industry associations, special interest groups and the general public, who have the ability to inspect the documents associated with the proposed development. The adjoining *Länder* are also involved at this stage as their permission is required for any cables that have to cross the Territorial Sea to get ashore.

The next stage of consenting is the preparation of an EIA. The EIA Act (*UVPG*) provides that a development with more than 20 turbines requires an EIA. To assist developers, the BSH issued regulations specifying the required scope of the investigations to be carried out by developers on each of the features to be protected. This is contained in the Standard for Investigation of the Impacts of Offshore Wind Turbines on the Marine Environment (*StUK*).[102] A two year baseline study to determine the present circumstances is required as a basis for subsequent monitoring and compilation of the EIA.[103] Monitoring must take place during the entire period of construction whilst operational phase monitoring has to be performed for a period of three to five years, depending on the specific conditions at the site and any features of conservation interest. This guidance is very detailed and stipulates the exact spatial areas to be covered in fish, bird, marine mammal surveys as well as their associated reference sites.[104] The BSH has also published guidance on underwater sound monitoring for baseline characterisation and for construction, operation and decommissioning phases of the project.[105]

Contemporaneously a navigational impact assessment, to establish the probability of vessels colliding with wind farm installations, must be conducted. This along with all other EIA documentation is made available to the public and other agencies for comment before a final decision is made. Following this, BSH reviews whether the requirements for granting approval have been met. In accordance with Article 6 of the Marine Facilities Ordinance, BSH can grant approval if the regional Waterways and Shipping Directorate has also granted consent and confirmed that the project does not impair the safety and efficiency of navigation. Once both authorities have agreed, a notification of approval is issued. This is subject to a range of standard supplementary conditions which cover, for example, a requirement to begin installation of the turbines within 2.5 years of receiving approval; to fit the turbines with lights; and a bank guarantee covering the cost of decommissioning. The Federal Mining Act (*BbergG*) covers approvals for the laying and operation of cables, however, it is the Infrastructure Planning Acceleration Act 2006 that obliges the TSO to install the grid connection of offshore wind farms in its area and cover the associated costs. The Federal Network Agency Regulator (*BundesNetzAgentur*) is the entity responsible for approving applications for offshore grid on economic grounds. As a result of the scale of offshore wind farm installation in the German EEZ, offshore grid development has become a key focus area. In 2013, the German TSOs published the first version of an Offshore Grid Development Plan.[106]

Another unique feature of the German consenting system is the implementation of Marine Spatial Planning (MSP) in the EEZ. The German Spatial Planning Act (ROG) became applicable to the EEZ in 2004 and specific legislation was enacted for spatial planning in the EEZs of both the North Sea and the Baltic Sea in September and December 2009, respectively. This was instigated by the economic interest in increasing offshore wind farms viewed as essential to achieving the Government's emission targets.[107] In order to secure the levels of investment needed for such large scale projects, a stable and predictable planning framework was required with MSP identified as the preferred approach.[108] Subsequently as the marine spatial plans were designed, dedicated areas for offshore wind farms were zoned in the North Sea and the Baltic.[109] Germany has no ocean energy (wave and tidal) projects as yet.[110]

Scotland (United Kingdom)

The UK is comprised of England and Wales, Scotland and Northern Ireland. Only Scotland is considered here due to the level of development planned in that jurisdiction and also the significant effort that has gone into tailoring consenting processes for MRE in Scottish waters. The devolved government for Scotland has a range of responsibilities but some powers have been retained by the UK Government in Westminster, including energy policy. The Crown Estate can lease areas of the seabed for development purposes. There have been six commercial offshore wind leasing rounds since 2000. More recently two commercial leasing rounds for wave and tidal in the Pentland Firth and Orkney waters of Scotland and Rathlin and Torr Head in Northern Ireland have been held. Previously seabed leases for wave and tidal energy pertained to test and demonstration sites only, namely the European Marine Energy Centre (EMEC) in Orkney, Scotland and the Wave Hub in Cornwall, England.

The Crown Estate leasing process for MRE projects involves at least two stages. An Exclusivity Agreement may be awarded where it is necessary for a strategic assessment to be conducted prior to the development of a series of projects.[111] This is essentially a contractual commitment from The Crown Estate that it will not allow any other developer of the same technology to use that same area of seabed for the duration of the agreement. The principal agreements involve an Agreement for Lease ('AfL') which conveys a conditional right for the developer to request a lease for a seabed site and/or seabed rights. Under the AfL a developer may undertake technical and environmental survey work and deploy equipment necessary for further project planning, subject to securing the necessary statutory consents. At this stage the developer does not have any right to start construction or operation of the project. Once the developer has received the necessary statutory consents and fulfilled the conditions associated with the AfL, the developer can then obtain a lease of the seabed. The Crown Estate lease enables construction and operation of the project for a period of 50 years (Round 3 wind projects) in return for a negotiated annual rent.

The statutory consents required will vary according to the location (jurisdiction) of the planned project. It is in this context that Scotland has invested substantial time and effort into streamlining the applicable procedures. The UK's Marine and Coastal Access Act 2009 sought to modernise and reform marine planning and licensing arrangements. This has been augmented in Scotland with the Marine (Scotland) Act 2010.[112] The Scottish Act provides for the creation of a national or regional marine plan(s) (Part 3), a rationalised marine licensing process (Part 4), as well as provisions on enforcement (Part 7). The licensing provisions introduce a single marine licence which replaces the previously required licences for deposits under the Food and Environment Protection Act 1985 (FEPA) and navigation under the Coast Protection Act 1949. In addition, the consent required for constructing electricity generating stations, under section 36 of the Electricity Act 1989, can now be considered at the same time as the marine licence for an MRE project. The new Act also introduced a pre-application consultation process where prospective applicants are required to submit a pre-application notice and report before submitting their application.

The marine licensing functions are carried out by a dedicated team, the Marine Licensing Operations Team (MS-LOT), within the marine management authority, Marine Scotland, that operates as a one-stop-shop, meaning there is a single point of contact that coordinates the processing of development applications. It aims to provide a decision on all applications within nine months provided the requisite environmental information is available and no local public inquiry is warranted. To assist developers in navigating the consenting process, a licensing manual[113] was produced for anyone intending to develop in Scottish waters. This also reflects responsibilities under EU law such as EIA and Appropriate Assessment under the Habitats Directive, known as Habitats Regulation Appraisal (HRA) in Scotland. Licence fees are payable and these are determined by the scale and complexity of the project in conjunction with MS-LOT. More recently the guidance has been refined and targeted to particular marine activities with specific guidance for offshore wind, wave and tidal.[114]

Marine Scotland is progressing the implementation of sectoral marine planning encompassing the development of a Sectoral Marine Plan for Offshore Wind Energy in Scottish Territorial Waters.[115] This was preceded by a Strategic Environmental Assessment (SEA) in 2007 which resulted in separate Regional Locational Guidance for offshore wind,[116] wave[117] and tidal[118] respectively in 2012. A key part of this was research on the environmental effects of MRE devices with complementary management approaches to enable development whilst ensuring environmental protection. The latter takes the form of a 'Survey Deploy and Monitor' policy that is risk-based on the basis of environmental sensitivity of the receiving environment, scale of development and device (or technology) classification.[119] Sensitivity relates to designated conservation sites and protected species. Pre-prepared sensitivity maps enable Marine Scotland to distinguish between areas of higher and lower sensitivity. Scale of development is based on the proposed installed generating capacity, from low (up to 10 MW), to medium (10–50 MW) and up to high (above 50 MW). Device classification is an expression of the risk associated with device or technology installation (e.g. moorings), movement (e.g. parts that move above or below the water surface), behaviour and interaction. The developer may be asked to submit a report on the risks associated with their device which is then coupled with the risk assessment based on the aforementioned three factors in order for MS-LOT to make a final determination.

United States of America

The US Department of Energy (DOE) has been supporting research and development of Marine and Hydrokinetic (MHK) Technologies, that convert the energy of waves, tides, and river and ocean currents into electricity, since 2005 following changes to the Energy Policy Act 2005 (EPAct). Since 2009, the Bureau of Ocean Energy Management's (BOEM) Office of Renewable Energy Programs (OREP) has issued five commercial wind energy leases offshore including the controversial Cape Wind project off Massachusetts and others off Delaware, New Jersey, Rhode Island and Virginia.[120] None of these projects are currently operational. The US DOE has been instrumental in funding work on OE technology development; market acceleration and deployment; resource assessment and characterisation. The DOE's MHK portfolio for 2013 consisted of 87 projects representing investments of $33.8 million.[121] This investment concentrated primarily on technology advancement and demonstration as well as the associated testing infrastructure. The Northwest National Marine Renewable Energy Center (NNMREC) is in the process of developing a Pacific Marine Energy Center South Energy Test Site (PMEC-SETS) that will be grid connected and is expected to have four berths at which individual or small arrays (3–5) of devices can be tested. It is anticipated that up to 10 wave energy devices at any one time will be permitted which is likely to produce 10 MW of electricity to the grid.[122]

Under the Federal Power Act, the Federal Energy Regulatory Commission (FERC) asserts regulatory jurisdiction over MHK projects on navigable waters (within 3M of the shore) and on any projects with an onshore grid connection. FERC does not have regulatory authority for OTEC projects, as these are under the remit of the NOAA pursuant to the OTEC Act 1980. The Outer Continental Shelf (OCS) under US legislation comprises all submerged lands, subsoil, and seabed lying between the seaward extent of the States' jurisdiction, usually 3M to the limit of federal jurisdiction, i.e. 200M. On the OCS, a lease from BOEM will be required if the project produces, transports or transmits energy, is located on the OCS and involves the temporary or permanent attachment of a structure or device to the seabed. FERC, however, retain responsibility for issuing licences for the construction and operation of an MHK project on the OCS. In an attempt to clarify the complex jurisdictional issues, both agencies issued detailed Guidelines on Regulation of Marine and Hydrokinetic Energy Projects on the OCS in 2012.[123] These guidelines state that restricted testing is permissible under a BOEM lease without a FERC licence if certain conditions are complied with:

1. the technology is experimental,
2. the proposed installation is temporary in preparation for a further licence or for educational purposes, and
3. power generated would not be transmitted to the grid.

The BOEM consenting process involves four phases: planning, leasing, site assessment and construction and operations.

BOEM has the authority to grant three types of leases for MHK projects.[124] A commercial lease is necessary for a commercial scale project. Research leases are issued only to a federal agency or a State for renewable energy research activities that support the future production, transportation or transmission of renewable energy. In contrast, a limited lease is granted for projects of limited scope, usually in cases where the duration of activities associated with the proposed project is limited to five years, and any power generated by the project would also be limited (e.g. 5 MW) through the terms and conditions of the lease.[125] BOEM work collaboratively with many individual States on developing their MRE resources. Generally they coordinate Federal-State task forces to facilitate project development. In addition they are also involved in regional proposals, for example, the Atlantic Wind Connection proposal which would see the construction of a high-voltage direct-current system that would connect offshore wind turbines in the wind energy areas off New York, New Jersey, Maryland, Delaware and Virginia to the onshore grid.[126] In principle, all leases are considered on a case-by-case by BOEM in collaboration with other regulatory agencies such as FERC or State agencies. In certain instances FERC may grant licence waivers or exemptions. The Guidelines stipulate that to come within the scope of an exemption, a pilot project must be small, short term, located outside sensitive areas (based on FERC's own review), removable and able to be shut down at short notice, removed, with the site restored before the end of the licence term and initiated by a draft application with sufficient information to support environmental analysis.[127] If a licence has been granted for a pilot project, FERC will generally allow an applicant to transition to a standard licence.[128]

Leasing rounds operate in a similar way to elsewhere: a competitive leasing round is announced by BOEM and applicants are invited to respond. Applicants may also submit an unsolicited application indicating an interest in obtaining a BOEM lease for a certain OCS location. Applications must detail the area of interest, a description of the project proponent's objectives and proposed facilities, an outline of planned activities and any environmental or resource data available as well as proof of qualification to hold a lease as specified in the Code of Federal Regulations (CFR). Where there are no other applicants, a developer will then be requested to submit a Site Assessment Plan, which must detail the physical characterisation surveys and baseline environmental surveys to support the planned activities.[129] The FERC licensing process is arguably more complex and can take one of three forms as detailed in the published guidelines.[130] Where a BOEM lease and FERC licence are required, the two processes can be aligned in the interests of efficiency and expediency.[131] The timeframes for receipt of a BOEM lease will also vary according to whether the application is competitive or non-competitive, ranging from 1 year in the case of a non-competitive situation to 2.5 years in a competitive round.[132] This includes stakeholder consultation and environmental surveys. For a FERC licence the time taken is anticipated to be one year provided that the application is complete and includes the requisite environmental information.[133] Pilot projects can take half that time provided the application is complete. Both BOEM and FERC require payment for their respective permits.

Together with the above permits, authorisation from the U.S. Army Corps of Engineers is almost always required where a structure is to be placed in navigable waters, under the Rivers and Harbors Act §10. Table 18.2 lists a number of other permits and consultations that may be required before final permission is granted. Any device or structure that might obstruct navigation must be marked by the appropriate navigational aid granted under a Private Aid to Navigation (PATON) Permit regulated by the U.S. Coast Guard under Title 33 of the Code of

Table 18.2 Additional Federal Statutes and their relevant implications for MHK applications.

Statute	Requirement
National Historic Preservation Act (NHPA)	Assess potential effects on historic resources
Endangered Species Act (ESA)	Evaluate impacts on endangered species and critical habitats
Marine Mammal Protection Act	Assess potential impacts on marine mammals
Migratory Bird Treaty Act	Assess potential impacts on migratory birds
Magnuson-Stevens Fishery Conservation Act	Evaluate actions that may adversely affect essential fish habitat
Clean Water Act	Assess to comply with water quality standards
Clean Air Act	Assess to comply with air quality standards
Coastal Zone Management Act (CZMA)	Review proposal to ensure consistency with State coastal management policies

Federal Regulations, Part 66. MHK projects are also subject to the requirements of the National Environmental Policy Act (NEPA) which provides a framework for identifying and assessing the environmental effects and reasonable alternatives to the proposed project. Firstly the federal agency will decide whether the proposed project can be excluded from a comprehensive environmental review (categorical exclusion). Where this is not the case, then an Environmental Assessment (EA) will be prepared by the federal agency. This provides sufficient evidence and analysis for determining whether to prepare an Environmental Impact Statement (EIS). If no significant issues are identified during EA, federal agency staff will prepare an assessment indicating that the project is unlikely to have significant effects coupled with a Finding of No Significant Impact (FONSI). Where significant environmental impacts are anticipated an EIS will be produced with the assistance of other regulatory agencies and stakeholders.

The Guidelines produced by BOEM and FERC consider hybrid projects.[134] These are defined as including technologies that generate electricity from more than one form of renewable energy, one of which is an MHK technology (e.g., wind and wave-generation) under the same lease. This could accommodate new, combined structures which are currently at the R&D phase in the EU such as the Poseidon Floating Power Plant.[135] Where projects straddle State waters and the OCS, the guidelines stipulate that a federal lease from BOEM will be required for the OCS part of the project whilst a FERC licence will be necessary for both the OCS and State waters parts of the project.[136] In relation to decommissioning of renewable energy projects, the regulations covering this are found in 30 CFR, Part 285. This provides that all facilities, including pipelines, cables and other structures and obstructions must be removed when they are no longer used for operations. Removal must occur no later than two years after the termination of the related lease, easement or right of way.[137] The latter has been identified as potentially problematic for larger scale offshore wind farms which would be required to complete decommissioning in the same timeframe as a much smaller development.[138] This in turn could have negative implications for project costs. Developers must provide a decommissioning bond or other acceptable form of financial assurance under the terms of the BOEM lease and/or FERC licence.[139]

Enforcement

Responsibility

As a relatively new sector, responsibilities for MRE projects are still evolving. Regulation and enforcement involves actors from the public, private and non-governmental sectors. Public institutional responsibility is primarily determined by the location of the project, namely the maritime jurisdictional zone within which it is located. As most projects are situated in internal waters or the Territorial Sea, national bodies are ultimately responsible for ensuring their operation complies with all relevant legislation. Such requirements are usually specified in the actual terms and conditions of the lease or licence granted. Non-compliance becomes an issue of contract law between the relevant authority and the developer. In certain situations non-compliance may lead to the consent being revoked and the project suspended. Coastal State enforcement of the duties under the relevant lease or licence can follow through the courts in addition to the enforcement methods prescribed in law. There can also be private enforcement of responsibilities by way of civil action. Beyond the Territorial Sea, the situation becomes more complex; arguably attributable to the current state of the industry. The limited number of MRE projects in EEZs means that responsibilities may not be formally allocated to a particular government authority as yet. Generally the coastal State will have jurisdiction in the EEZ and accordingly its competent authorities will have enforcement jurisdiction. In the case of Germany, for example, the Federal Ministry of Transport, Building and Urban Development (BMVBS) oversees planning, authorisation and also safety aspects of offshore wind farms in the EEZ. Consequently it defines the obligations that offshore operators must conform to and determine whether or not they are compliant.

Health and safety

The offshore environment presents a range of potential risks to those tasked with working in these areas. A range of international legal instruments contain specific provisions on various aspects of Health & Safety. These include:

- International Convention for the Safety of Life at Sea (SOLAS),
- Convention on the International Regulations for Preventing Collisions at Sea (COLREGS),
- International Load Line Convention,
- International Convention on Standards of Training, Certification and Watchkeeping for Seafarers (STCW), and
- International Convention for the Prevention of Pollution from Ships (MARPOL).

The provisions of the above Conventions are transposed into national legislation and this will specify the responsible authority. Coastal States may have supplementary health and safety (H&S) legislation which seeks to address common activities and hazards, however, in many cases this has not been designed with the offshore environment or MRE structures in mind. There is no specific legislation covering H&S concerns associated with MRE activities in the UK and consequently the regulatory approach has been to extend the provisions of the Health & Safety at Work Etc. Act 1974, (HSWA) and secondary regulations, to cover offshore activities.[140] Following the enactment of the HSWA (Application outside Great Britain) Order 2013, the provisions of the original Act now apply to the limit of the Territorial Sea and in the Renewable Energy Zone, which encompasses the entire area in which the Crown Estate may issue leases. The Order covers the full life-cycle of a MRE device, including construction, operation and maintenance (O&M), decommissioning, personnel transfers from vessels or aircraft (including helicopters), diving and cable works. Due to the multitude of issues included within H&S legislation, there can be several enforcement authorities. In Germany a Health & Safety Plan must be submitted with the permit application and is assessed by the BSH even though it does not have a health and safety remit. Operational and occupational health and safety is overseen by regional level authorities (*Gewerbeaufsichtsamt*) and at the federal level, by the accident prevention and insurance association (*Berufsgenossenschaft*). Dedicated H&S legislation applicable only to MRE developments is uncommon, although in some countries voluntary codes of conduct are being adopted in an effort to ensure that MRE is subject to the same or similar practices as land-based workplaces.[141]

Navigational safety

Responsibility for navigational safety in the marine environment rests with the IMO and national governments. Offshore wind farms present a collision risk to other marine users. As a way of preventing collisions, navigation channels and shipping lanes tend to be mapped as 'constraint' areas when planning MRE projects. A Navigational Impact Assessment is usually conducted as part of project planning or for EIA purposes. This identifies where problems may arise as well as determining appropriate mitigation measures. Passive mitigation measures include marking the site with appropriate navigation aids and lights in accordance with national and/or international guidelines. The International Association of Lighthouse Authorities (IALA) previously issued recommendations on the marking of a single turbine,[142] offshore wind farms[143] and wave and tidal devices.[144] These have since been consolidated and superseded by IALA Recommendation O-139 on the Marking of Man-Made Offshore Structures.[145] With respect to wave and tidal devices, the Recommendation stipulates that "consultation between the stakeholders such as developers, national administrations, Aids to Navigation authorities, competent authorities and wave and tidal contractors should take place at an early stage".[146]

Under the LOSC any installations or structures which are abandoned or disused must be removed to ensure safety of navigation taking into account any relevant international standards and with due regard to fishing activities, protection of the marine environment and the rights and duties of other States.[147] Coastal States have the discretion to establish reasonable safety zones around artificial islands, structures and installations and appropriate measures therein in the interests of safety, both of navigation and of the structures themselves.[148] In the Territorial Sea, Articles 20 and 21 of LOSC provide that coastal States have a right to adopt laws and regulations for the safety of navigation and, in particular, may adopt sea-lanes, routeing systems and traffic separation schemes in order to ensure the safety of vessels and avoid collision.[149] In the English Channel, the UK regulatory agencies in association with the IMO amended the recognised Traffic Separation Scheme (TSS) off Land's End, between the UK mainland and the Isles of Scilly on the south west coast of England due to safety considerations resulting from the development of the Wave Hub offshore testing facility in Cornwall. The TSS was moved 12M to the north of the current boundaries, also amending the Inshore Traffic Zone to the east.[150]

Safety zones can be defined as an area of water around or adjacent to an MRE device or installation from which certain or all classes of vessels are excluded and within which activities can be regulated. The terms 'safety zone' and 'exclusion zone' are often used interchangeably though, in a strict sense, exclusion zones imply that no activities or vessels are permitted and hence these could impact much more significantly on shipping, fishing and other sea uses. Safety zones are common practice around large offshore wind farms, given their scale. The breadth of safety zones is at the discretion of the coastal State but should not exceed 500m except where authorised by accepted international standards or as recommended by the competent international organisation.[151] The IMO has not yet adopted standards on this topic though, in 2008, both Brazil and the United States of America proposed the drafting of such standards.[152] The UK's Maritime & Coastguard Agency have estimated that a maximum exclusion zone of 500m around a large wind farm of 300 plus turbines would put in excess of 200km^2 of sea off limits.[153] The IMO Resolution A.671(16) recommends that Governments consider the establishment of safety zones around offshore installations or structures as well as the establishment and charting of fairways or routeing systems through exploration areas.[154] Wave and tidal devices are generally less visible than offshore wind turbines and it is anticipated that in future, safety zones around these will have a smaller spatial footprint. These will have mooring cables and anchor points which will need to be reflected in the dimensions of any operational safety zone.

Safety zones operate during specific phases of a project namely, construction, maintenance operations and decommissioning only and not during the operational phase. At site level, it is up to the national regulatory authority together with the project developer to decide the appropriate size of the safety zone and from where the distance should be measured. The UK Guidance on Safety Zones recommends that during construction, major maintenance and decommissioning phases, safety zones should be established on a 'rolling' basis, so that the safety zone applies only to those areas where activities are actually taking place in order to limit disruption to other maritime users.[155] After an activity in one location has finished, the safety zone can then 'roll on' to the next location. This approach is supported by the European Boating Association (EBA) that has expressed the view that the total exclusion of small craft is likely to be "unnecessary, impracticable and disproportionate".[156] It highlights that excluding small craft from offshore wind farms could force them into busy commercial shipping lanes hence increasing the risk of collision. The German Government has also recognised the negative implications of imposing safety zones on small craft (under 24m) and has exempted them from such zones in certain situations.[157]

Gaps and opportunities

The legal framework for MRE is firmly rooted in the LOSC,[158] though not regulated in detail, and is complemented by a range of relevant instruments and measures at international, regional and national levels. There are few limitations from international law that will inhibit deployment of MRE devices; however, from the experience of selected countries it is clear that there is limited application of existing regulatory systems beyond the Territorial Sea. Projects in the EEZ are limited to offshore wind located predominantly in northern Europe. Currently there is no real desire to deploy devices beyond the 12M limit where deployments are more financially and technically challenging. Detailed legislation covering these areas is crucial to ensure that in future such developments can occur further offshore. Some countries, such as the UK, have dealt with this issue through designation of a Renewable Energy Zone extending to the limit of the EEZ. R&D activities in offshore wind are focused on floating device concepts as well as larger turbines for deeper offshore waters which may instigate regulatory change over time. Beyond the EEZ (High Seas) it remains unclear whether a State individually or through sponsored companies has the right to extract wind and waves from these areas and what additional regulatory systems would need to be in place to make this possible, particularly given well established High

Seas freedoms. The LOSC is silent on freedom to collect renewable resources from the High Seas yet it does recognise the right to lay submarine cables and pipelines and construct artificial islands and other installations with only nominal restrictions.[159]

Regulatory systems for MRE are evolving. Offshore wind has triggered the formation of a more appropriate consenting system in many jurisdictions. Elsewhere the regulatory system could be described as reactive, being amended in response to project demand. To harness the available MRE resource, investors and project developers look towards countries with a stable, transparent and predictable regulatory system. This suggests that governments and their agencies need to be more proactive in how they deal with MRE proposals. The example of Scotland is instructive in this regard: with strategic level marine planning down to site level guidance on applicable procedures. Germany has also published comprehensive guidance and standards for offshore wind. For developing technologies such as wave and tidal energy devices, the regulatory system needs to facilitate adaptive management and those tasked with decision-making need to be pragmatic in their approach until such time as more devices are deployed and greater scientific evidence exists as to their efficacy and environmental impacts. Regulators can only operate on the basis of experience gained or they leave themselves, and hence the developer, open to the risk of legal challenge. The decisions made by regulators must be based on scientific evidence which underpins their advice and consequently enables them to defend the decision made. Certainty is difficult when activities (devices) are new and there is limited 'evidence' available. The Survey, Deploy and Monitor policy utilised in Scotland represents an attempt to address this issue.[160]

From a procedural perspective, MRE developments require various permits and consents depending on the jurisdiction in question. There have been efforts to streamline the consenting process in a number of locations with a centralised approach or one-stop-shop approach becoming more evident. Electrical and grid connections remain problematic and often operate separately to other administrative processes. Scale of development remains a dominant influencing factor. In some locations small scale demonstration and prototype devices are treated in the same way as multi-megawatt developments despite potentially having lesser social and environmental impacts. Test centres designed for device demonstration are successful at the early R&D stages but there must be a development and regulatory path for pre-commercial devices to progress. Environmental monitoring at test centres has increased data and information on environmental effects of devices. This, coupled with international efforts to disseminate information on environmental effects,[161] is continuously adding evidence and generating knowledge, however, fundamental environmental research questions for wave and tidal energy remain. These are difficult to address at site level by developers and will require more concerted national action.

Acknowledgment

This material is based upon works supported by Science Foundation Ireland (SFI) under the Charles Parsons Award (Grant number 06/CP/E003) in collaboration with Marine Renewable Energy Ireland (MaREI), the SFI Centre for Marine Renewable Energy Research (12/RC/2305).

Notes

1 European Commission. 2008. Communication from the Commission: Energy efficiency: delivering the 20% target (COM(2008) 772 final). Commission of the European Communities, Brussels, Belgium.
2 Global Wind Energy Council. 2014. Global Wind Report: Annual Market Update 2013. Global Wind Energy Council, Brussels, Belgium.

3 Australian Government: Bureau of Resources and Energy Economics. 2014. 2014 Australian Energy Update. http://www.bree.gov.au/sites/bree.gov.au/files/files//publications/aes/2014-australian-energy-statistics.pdf
4 Commonwealth of Australia. 2014. Renewable Energy Target Scheme – Report of the Expert Panel. http://retreview.dpmc.gov.au/sites/default/files/files/RET_Review_Report.pdf
5 See http://www.theguardian.com/environment/2015/jun/24/renewable-energy-target-senate-sits-late-to-pass-bill-without-amendment and http://www.skynews.com.au/news/top-stories/2015/06/24/renewable-energy-target-cut-as-bill-passes.html
6 Lynch, K. and Murphy, J. 2012. Overview of offshore wind and ocean energy technologies (D3.6). Report published as part of the EU FP7 MARINA Platform project. http://www.marina-platform.info/dissemination.aspx
7 Whereby a device is buoyancy stabilised, similar to a barge, with catenary mooring lines. See NREL. 2007. Engineering Challenges for Floating Offshore Wind Turbines. Presented at Offshore Wind Conference, Copenhagen, Denmark, October 26–28, 2005. http://wind.nrel.gov/public/SeaCon/Proceedings/Copenhagen.Offshore.Wind.2005/documents/papers/Future_innovative_solutions/S.Butterfield_Engineering_Challenges_for_Floating.pdf
8 *Op. cit.* fn 2.
9 Lewis, A., Estefen, S., Huckerby, J., Musial, W., Pontes, T., and Torres-Martinez, J. 2011. Ocean Energy. In IPCC Special Report on Renewable Energy Sources and Climate Change Mitigation [O. Edenhofer, R. Pichs-Madruga, Y. Sokona, K. Seyboth, P. Matschoss, S. Kadner, T. Zwickel, P. Eickemeier, G. Hansen, S. Schlömer, C. von Stechow (eds.)], Cambridge University Press, Cambridge, UK and New York, NY, USA.
10 Shanahan, G. 2008. Tidal Range Technologies. In IEA-OES Annual Report 2008. OES Executive Committee, Lisbon, Portugal.
11 Tidal Lagoon Swansea Bay. 2013. Preliminary Environmental Information Report: Non-Technical Summary. July 2013. Tidal Lagoon (Swansea Bay) plc. Swansea, Wales. http://tidallagoon.opendebate.co.uk/files/TidalLagoon/PEIR/Non_Technical_Summary_ENG_TLSB_PEIR.pdf
12 See http://www.marineturbines.com/3/news/article/7/seagen__the_world_s_first_commercial_scale_tidal_energy_turbine_deployed_in_northern_ireland
13 Marine Current Turbines (MCT). 2010. SeaGen Environmental Monitoring Programme: SeaGen Biannual Environmental monitoring March 2010 – Oct 2010. Report produced by Royal Haskoning, Edinburgh, Scotland.
14 See http://wavec.org/client/files/April_2010_Report_State_of_Art_Ocean_Energy_efm_reduced.pdf
15 See, e.g., the Ocean Energy buoy http://www.oceanenergy.ie/
16 See, e.g., Pelamis http://www.pelamiswave.com/
17 See, e.g., OPT's PowerBuoy http://www.oceanpowertechnologies.com/
18 See, e.g., Carnegie's CETO http://www.carnegiewave.com/
19 See, e.g., Aquamarine Power's Oyster http://www.aquamarinepower.com/
20 See, e.g. Wave Dragon http://www.wavedragon.net/
21 Huertas Olivares, C., Holmes, B., O'Hagan, A.M. 2011. Catalogue of Wave Energy Test Centres and Review of National Targets (D2.1). Project report from the EU IEE funded SOWFIA project. http://www.sowfia.eu/index.php?id=22
22 Carnegie Wave Energy. 2015. Perth Project Newsletter, Issue 6, April 2015. http://www.carnegiewave.com/projects/perth-project.html [link at bottom of page].
23 See Von Arx, W.S., H.B. Stewart and Apel, J.R. 1974. The Florida Current as a Potential Source of Useable Energy. Proceedings of the MacArthur Workshop on the Feasibility of Extracting Usable energy from the Florida Current, Palm Beach Shores, Florida and Duerr, A.E.S., Dhanak, M.R. and Van Zwieten, J. 2012. Utilizing the Hybrid Coordinate Ocean Model Data for the Assessment of the Florida Current's Hydrokinetic Renewable Energy Resource. Marine Technology Society Journal, vol. 12, pp. 24–33.
24 Chen, F. 2010. Kuroshio Power Plant Development Plan. Journal of Renewable and Sustainable Energy Reviews, 14(9), 2655–2668.
25 See http://www.boem.gov/Renewable-Energy-Program/Renewable-Energy-Guide/Ocean-Current-Energy.aspx accessed 22/09/14.
26 Minerals Management Service. 2006. Technology White Paper on Ocean Current Energy Potential on the U.S. Outer Continental Shelf. http://www.boem.gov/uploadedFiles/BOEM/

Renewable_Energy_Program/Renewable_Energy_Guide/Technology%20White%20Paper%20on%20Wind%20Energy%20Potential%20on%20the%20OCS.pdf

27 See http://www.boem.gov/press06032014/
28 Department of Energy. 2009. Ocean Energy Technology Overview. Prepared by NREL for the U.S. DOE Office of Energy Efficiency and Renewable Energy, Federal Energy Management Program. DOE/GO-102009–2823. NREL, Golden, Colorado, U.S.A.
29 Solar Energy Research Institute. 1989. Ocean Thermal Energy Conversion: An Overview. Produced for the Wind Ocean Technologies Division, US DOE. SERI, Golden, Colorado, U.S.A.
30 Fujita, R., Markman, A.C., Diaz, J.E.D., Garcia, J.R.M., Scarborough, C., Greenfield, P., Black, P., Aguilera, S.E. 2012. Revisiting ocean thermal energy conversion. Marine Policy 36(2), 463–465.
31 Wick, G.L. and Isaacs, J. 1976. Utilization of the energy from Salinity Gradients. Wave and Salinity Gradient Energy Conversion Workshop, University of Delaware, 1976 cited in Jones and Finley, 2003.
32 Jones, A.T. and Finley, W. 2003. Recent Developments in Salinity Gradient Power. OCEANS 2003 Conference, San Diego, California, 22–26 September 2003. OCEANS 2003 Proceedings, Volume 4, pp. 2284–2287. DOI 10.1109/OCEANS.2003.178265.
33 Ocean Energy Systems (OES). 2009. IEA Implementing Agreement on Ocean Energy Systems Annual Report 2009. OES-IA document A09.
34 Esmaeli, H. 2001. The Legal Regime of Offshore Oil Rigs in International Law. Ashgate Publishers, Dartmouth, UK. ISBN 9780754621935.
35 Article 22, LOSC.
36 Article 56(1)(a), LOSC.
37 Article 56(1)(b)(i) and (iii), LOSC.
38 Article 60(2), LOSC.
39 Article 77(4), LOSC.
40 Article 79, LOSC.
41 Article 80, LOSC.
42 Discussed in UN GA, 2012, A 67/120, para.44.
43 Article 192, LOSC.
44 Article 194(5), LOSC.
45 Article 196(1), LOSC.
46 UN GA, 2012, A/67/79.
47 UN GA, 2012, A/67/120.
48 *Op. cit.* para. 58.
49 *Op. cit.* para. 56.
50 Namely the Convention on the Protection of the Natural Resources and Environment in the South Pacific Region (and Protocols), 1986 [Noumea Convention]; the Convention to Ban the Importation into Forum Island Countries of Hazardous and Radioactive Wastes and to Control the Transboundary Movement and Management of Hazardous Wastes within the South Pacific Region, 1995 [Waigani Convention] and the Convention on Conservation of Nature in the South Pacific, 1976 [Apia Convention, suspended in 2006].
51 Secretariat of the Pacific Regional Environment Programme (SPREP). 2011. SPREP Strategic Plan 2011–2015. Apia, Samoa. http://www.sprep.org/attachments/000921_SPREPStrategicPlan2011_2015.pdf
52 OSPAR. 2004. Background Document on Problems and Benefits Associated with the Development of Offshore Wind Farms. Publication number: 214–2004. OSPAR Commission, London, UK.
53 OSPAR. 2006. Review of the Current State of Knowledge on the Environmental Impacts of the Location, Operation and Removal/Disposal of Offshore Wind-Farms. Publication number: 278–2006. OSPAR Commission, London, UK.
54 OSPAR. 2008. OSPAR Guidance on Environmental Considerations for Offshore Wind Farm Development. Publication number: 2008–3. OSPAR Commission, London, UK.
55 Lower Saxony, Schleswig-Holstein and Mecklenburg-Vorpommern.
56 Thomsen, K.E. 2012. Offshore Wind: A Comprehensive Guide to Successful Offshore Wind Farm Installation. Academic Press, Waltham, MA, USA. ISBN 9780123859365.
57 *Op. cit.*
58 Article 206, LOSC.

59 Directive 2011/92/EU of 13 December 2011 on the assessment of the effects of certain public and private projects on the environment (EIA Directive), codified version.
60 O'Hagan, A.M. 2012. Maritime Spatial Planning (MSP) in the European Union and its Application to Marine Renewable Energy. Annual Report of the IEA-OES; 101–109.
61 Scottish Government. 2013. Marine Planning Circular MSF 106/2013, p. 2. www.scotland.gov.uk/Resource/0042/00426388.doc
62 Leeney, R.H., Greaves, D., Conley, D. and O'Hagan, A.M. 2014. Environmental Impact Assessments for wave energy developments – Learning from existing activities and informing future research priorities, Ocean & Coastal Management, http://dx.doi.org/10.1016/j.ocecoaman.2014.05.025
63 Copping, A., Battey, H., Brown-Saracino, J., Massaua, M., and Smith, C. 2014. An international assessment of the environmental effects of marine energy development, Ocean & Coastal Management, http://dx.doi.org/10.1016/j.ocecoaman.2014.04.002
64 Op. cit. fn 62.
65 See, Bailey, I., West, J., Whitehead, I. 2011. Out of sight but not out of mind? Public perceptions of wave energy. J. Environ. Pol. Plann. 13(2), 139–157; Haggett, C. 2008. Over the sea and far away? A consideration of the planning, politics and public perception of offshore wind farms. J. Environ. Policy Plan. 10(3), 289–306. http://dx.doi.org/10.1080/15239080802242787; Lilley, M.B., Firestone, J., Kempton, W. 2010. The effect of wind power installations on coastal tourism. Energies 3(1), 1–22. http://dx.doi.org/10.3390/en3010001; and WAVEPLAM, 2010. Wave Energy: A Guide for Investors and Policy Makers. Report from the EU WAVEPLAM project. http://www.waveplam.eu/files/downloads/D.3.2.Guidelienes_FINAL.pdf
66 Van Hulle, F. 2009. Integrating Wind: Developing Europe's Power Market for the Large Scale Integration of Wind Power. Tradewind project Deliverable. http://www.uwig.org/TradeWind.pdf
67 Chozas, J.F., Soerensen, H.C. and Korpås, M. 2010. Integration of Wave and Offshore Wind Energy in a European Offshore Grid. Proceedings of the Twentieth International Offshore and Polar Engineering Conference, Beijing, China, 20–25 June 2010, pp. 926–933.
68 European Commission. 2013. Report from the Commission to the European Parliament, the Council, the European Economic and Social Committee and the Committee of the Regions. Renewable energy progress report (COM(2013) 175 final) {SWD(2013) 102 final}. Commission of the European Communities, Brussels, Belgium.
69 Article 13(1)(a) and (c), Directive 2009/28/EC.
70 Op. cit. Article 13(1)(f).
71 Op. cit. fn 68, p. 7.
72 DNV GL. 2014. Sharing Lessons Learned and Good Practice in Offshore Transmission. A report for The Crown Estate by DNV GL. Report No.: 112843-UKBR-R-01-F. DNV GL – Energy Renewables Advisory, Bristol, UK.
73 Op. cit. fn 67.
74 Article 60, LOSC.
75 IMO. 2008. Guidelines and Standards for the Removal of Offshore Installations and Structures on the Continental Shelf and in the EEZ. IMO Resolution A.672(16). IMO, London.
76 Op. cit. Section 2, paras. 2.1.1–2.1.6.
77 Op. cit. Section 2.3.
78 Op. cit. section 3, paras. 3.1–3.2.
79 Op. cit. section 3, para. 3.4.1.
80 Witt, M.J., Sheehan, E.V., Bearhop, S., Broderick, A.C., Conley, D.C., Cotterell, S.P., Crow, E., Grecian, W.J., Halsband, C., Hodgson, D.J., Hosegood, P., Inger, R., Miller, P.I., Sims, D.W., Thompson, R.C., Vanstaen, K., Votier, S.C., Attrill, M.J. and Godley, B.J. 2012. Assessing wave energy effects on biodiversity: the Wave Hub experience. Philos. Transact. A Math. Phys. Eng. Sci. 370(1959), 502–529.
81 Linley, E.A.S., Wilding, T.A., Black, K., Hawkins, A.J.S., Mangi, S. 2007. Review of the reef effects of offshore wind farm structures and their potential for enhancement and mitigation. Report to Department for Business, Enterprise and Regulatory Reform (BERR), No. RFCA/005/0029P. BERR, London, UK.
82 Wilhelmsson, D., Malm, T., Öhman, M.C. 2006. The influence of offshore wind power on demersal fish. ICES Journal of Marine Science, 63, 775–784.
83 Article 1.4.1.4, 1996 Protocol.
84 Article 1.4.2.3, 1996 Protocol.

85 London Convention and Protocol/UNEP. 2009. London Convention and Protocol/UNEP Guidelines for the Placement of Artificial Reefs. IMO, London, UK.
86 *Op. cit.* p. 2.
87 See fn 22.
88 Diesendorf, M. 2011. Europe has offshore wind farms . . . why can't Australia? Online article http://theconversation.com/europe-has-offshore-wind-farms-why-cant-australia-3574 [published 5 October 2011, accessed 29 June 2014].
89 Messali, E. and Diesendorf, M. 2009. Potential sites for off-shore wind power in Australia, Wind Engineering, 33(4), 335–348.
90 Carnegie Wave Energy Limited. 2012. Perth Wave Energy Project, Garden Island, Western Australia – Summary of Environmental Impact Assessment and Approvals.
91 CSIRO. 2012. Ocean renewable energy: 2015–2050 — An analysis of ocean energy in Australia. CSIRO, Victoria, Australia. http://www.csiro.au/Organisation-Structure/Flagships/Energy-Flagship/Ocean-renewable-energy.aspx
92 Ocean Energy Systems (OES). 2014. Annual Report: Implementing Agreement on Ocean Energy Systems (IEA-OES). OES Executive Committee, Lisbon, Portugal.
93 Wright, G. 2012. Wanted: regulatory reform in Australian marine energy. EcoGeneration [online]. July/August 2012. http://ecogeneration.com.au/news/wanted_regulatory_reform_in_australian_marine_energy/076883/
94 Environment and Natural Resources Committee. 2010. Final Report for the Inquiry into the Approvals Process for Renewable Energy Projects in Victoria. Parliament of Victoria, Melbourne, Australia. http://www.parliament.vic.gov.au/enrc/inquiries/article/870
95 Department of Primary Industries, briefing with the Environment and Natural Resources Committee – Melbourne, 22 June 2009 quoted in Environment and Natural Resources Committee (2010) [see fn 94].
96 *Op. cit.* fn 94.
97 *Op. cit.* fn 92.
98 Wright, G. 2012. Facilitating efficient augmentation of transmission networks to connect renewable energy generation: the Australian experience. Energy Policy, 44, 79–91.
99 See fn 4 and 5.
100 Government of Germany. 2002. Strategy of the German Government on the use of off-shore wind energy in the context of its national sustainability strategy (English version). German Government, Berlin, Germany http://www.offshorewindenergy.org/reports/report_033.pdf
101 Portman, M., Duff, J.A., Köppel, J., Reisert, J., Higgins, M.E. 2009. Offshore wind energy development in the Exclusive Economic Zone: legal and policy supports and impediments in Germany and the US. Energy Policy, 37, 3596–3607.
102 BSH. 2013. Standard for Investigation of the Impacts of Offshore Wind Turbines on the Marine Environment. BSH-Nr. 7003. BSH, Hamburg, Germany. http://www.bsh.de/en/Products/Books/Standard/7003eng.pdf
103 *Op. cit.* p. 10.
104 *Op. cit.* p. 11–13.
105 BSH. 2011. Offshore wind farms – Measuring instruction for underwater sound monitoring: current approach with annotations Application instructions. Prepared by Müller-BBM GmbH, Hamburg. BSH, Hamburg, Germany. http://www.bsh.de/de/Produkte/Buecher/Standard/Measuring_instruction.pdf
106 See http://www.netzentwicklungsplan.de/content/offshore-netzentwicklungsplan-2013-zweiter-entwurf
107 MRAG/European Commission. 2008. Legal Aspects of Maritime Spatial Planning; Framework Service Contract No. FISH/2006/09 – LOT2 for DG Maritime Affairs and Fisheries, European Commission, Brussels, Belgium.
108 *Op. cit.* fn 60.
109 BMVBS. 2009. Spatial Plan for the German EEZ in the North Sea – Text and Map sections and Spatial Plan for the German EEZ in the Baltic Sea – Text and Map sections. BMVBS, Hamburg. 2009. http://www.bsh.de/en/Marine_uses/Industry/Wind_farms/EEZ.jsp
110 *Op. cit.* fn 92.

111 The Crown Estate. 2014. The Crown Estate Role in Offshore Renewable Energy Developments: Briefing (Jan. 2014 version). The Crown Estate, London, England. http://www.thecrownestate.co.uk/media/5411/ei-the-crown-estate-role-in-offshore-renewable-energy.pdf
112 See http://www.legislation.gov.uk/asp/2010/5/contents
113 Scottish Government. 2012. A Guide to Marine Licensing: Marine Licensing In Scotland's Seas Under The Marine (Scotland) Act 2010 and The Marine And Coastal Access Act 2009 (May 2012 version) http://www.scotland.gov.uk/Resource/0039/00394406.pdf
114 Scottish Government. 2012. Marine Scotland Licensing and Consents Manual Covering Marine Renewables and Offshore Wind Energy Development. Report R.1957, October 2012. http://www.scotland.gov.uk/Resource/0040/00405806.pdf
115 Scottish Government. 2011. Blue Seas – Green Energy: A Sectoral Marine Plan for Offshore Wind Energy in Scottish Territorial Waters. Part A: The Plan. http://www.scotland.gov.uk/Publications/2011/03/18141232/0
116 Offshore Wind Energy in Scottish Waters – Draft Regional Locational Guidance. Parts 1–11. August 2012. http://www.scotland.gov.uk/Topics/marine/marineenergy/Planning/windrlg
117 Offshore Wave Energy in Scottish Waters – Draft Regional Locational Guidance. Parts 1–6. August 2012. http://www.scotland.gov.uk/Topics/marine/marineenergy/Planning/waverlg
118 Offshore Tidal Energy in Scottish Waters – Draft Regional Locational Guidance. Parts 1–7. August 2012. http://www.scotland.gov.uk/Topics/marine/marineenergy/Planning/tidalrlg
119 Scottish Government. 2012. Survey, Deploy and Monitor Licensing Policy Guidance. August 2012. http://www.scotland.gov.uk/Topics/marine/Licensing/marine/Applications/SDM
120 BOEM. 2014. Renewable Energy on the Outer Continental Shelf Factsheet. BOEM, Washington, D.C., USA. http://www.boem.gov/BOEM-Overview-Renewable-Energy/
121 *Op. cit.* fn 92.
122 Batten, B. and Polagye, B.L. 2013. NNMREC Accomplishments and Impacts 2009–2013. NNMREC Report #5. NNMREC, Corvallis, USA. 55 pp. http://ir.library.oregonstate.edu/xmlui/handle/1957/39929
123 Bureau of Ocean Energy Management and Federal Energy Regulatory Commission (BOEM/FERC). 2012. BOEM / FERC Guidelines on Regulation of Marine and Hydrokinetic Energy Projects on the OCS. Version 2, 19 July 2012. http://www.ferc.gov/industries//hydropower/gen-info/licensing/hydrokinetics/pdf/mms080309.pdf
124 *Ibid* section 2.8.
125 *Ibid* section 2.10.
126 Atlantic Wind Connection. 2013. Right-of-Way Application Supplement for the Bureau of Ocean Energy Management on the Atlantic Wind Connection Project. Docket No. BOEM–2011–0023. http://www.boem.gov/uploadedFiles/BOEM/Renewable_Energy_Program/State_Activities/Supplement%20to%20the%20ROW%20application.pdf
127 *Op. cit.* fn 123, section 2.12.
128 *Ibid* fn 123, section 2.14.
129 *Ibid* fn 123, section 3.2.
130 *Ibid* fn 123, section 3.3.
131 *Ibid* fn 123, section 3.5.
132 *Ibid* fn 123, section 3.11.
133 *Ibid*.
134 *Ibid* fn 123, sections 8.1–8.4.
135 See, e.g. FP7 ORECCA (http://www.orecca.eu/) and MARINA Platform (http://www.marina-platform.info/) project outputs.
136 *Op. cit.* fn 123, section 9.2.
137 30 CFR §285.902.
138 Kaiser, M.J. and Snyder, B. 2010. Offshore Wind Energy Installation and Decommissioning Cost Estimation in the U.S. Outer Continental Shelf. U.S. Dept. of the Interior, Bureau of Ocean Energy Management, Regulation and Enforcement, Herndon, VA. TA&R study 648. 340 pp. http://www.bsee.gov/uploadedfiles/bsee/research_and_training/technology_assessment_and_research/648aa.pdf
139 *Op. cit.* fn 123, section 6.2.

140 RenewableUK. 2014. Offshore Wind and Marine Energy Health and Safety Guidelines: Issue 2. Prepared for RenewableUK by SgurrEnergy Ltd. Renewable UK, London, UK. http://www.renewableuk.com/en/publications/index.cfm/2013-03-13-hs-guidelines-offshore-wind-marine-energy
141 GL Garrad Hassan Canada. 2012. International overview of marine renewable energy regulatory frameworks. GL Garrad Hassan, Ottawa, Canada.
142 Recommendation O-114 in 1998.
143 Recommendation O-117 in 2004.
144 Recommendation O-131 in 2005.
145 IALA. 2008. IALA Recommendation O-139 on the Marking of Man-Made Offshore Structures. Edition 1, December 2008. IALA, Saint Germain en Laye, France.
146 *Ibid.*, section 2.1.1.
147 Article 60(3), LOSC.
148 Article 60(4), LOSC.
149 These are taken forward in the IMO's General Provisions on Ships' Routeing. Resolution A.572 (14), adopted on 20 November 1985.
150 IMO. 2008. Routeing of Ships, Ship Reporting and Related Matters. Amendments to the Traffic Separation Scheme "Off Land's End, Between Longships and Seven Stones", Submitted by the UK. Sub-Committee on Safety of Navigation, 54th session. IMO Doc. NAV 54/3/5, 28 March 2008.
151 Article 60(5), LOSC.
152 IMO. 2008. Development of Guidelines for Consideration of Requests for Safety Zones Larger than 500 Metres Around Artificial Islands, Installations and Structures in the EEZ: submitted by the USA and Brazil. IMO Doc. MSC 84/22/4, 4 February 2008.
153 Department for Business, Enterprise and Regulatory Reform (BERR). 2007. Explanatory Memorandum to the Electricity (Offshore Generating Stations) (Safety Zones) (Application Procedures and Control of Access) Regulations 2007, No.48. Final Regulatory Impact Assessment. BERR, London, England.
154 *Op. cit.* fn 75.
155 DECC. 2011. Applying for safety zones around offshore renewable energy installations: Guidance notes. DECC, London, England. https://www.og.decc.gov.uk/EIP/pages/files/file40651.pdf [accessed 16 July 2014]
156 EBA. 2013. EBA Position Statement Offshore Wind Farms. EBA Secretariat, c/o RYA, Southampton, England. http://www.eba.eu.com/site-documents/eba-position-statements/eba-position-wind-farms.pdf
157 Currently this is limited to one operational wind farm in the Baltic Sea, no others are yet legally classified as operational. https://www.elwis.de/BfS/bfs_start.php?target=3&source=1&aboexport=abo&db_id=87456
158 Article 56(1)(a), LOSC.
159 Article 88, LOSC.
160 *Op. cit.* fn 119.
161 IEA-OES Annex IV work and Tethys database http://tethys.pnnl.gov/

19
The Potential to Regulate Bioprospecting for Marine Genetic Resources: Two Case Studies

Julia Jabour

Introduction

The aim of this chapter is to search for the *perfect* regime for the protection of marine genetic resources in areas beyond national jurisdiction (ABNJ),[1] if indeed such a thing exists. The chapter is framed within the wider theme of this Handbook and presents studies on the difficulties of accessing marine genetic resources in ABNJ and sharing the benefits of their development, while also protecting biodiversity generally through, for example, implementing suitable environmental safeguards in areas which are outside the control of a state. Two case studies explore what the advantages and disadvantages of a dedicated regime might be and what barriers to adoption and implementation it might face. The first example is that of Antarctic bioprospecting, which is not regulated specifically under the Antarctic Treaty regime.[2] The Antarctic is a legally and politically *sui generis* region, although analogous to areas beyond national jurisdiction, and with marine genetic resources which are characteristically novel, but with a poorly developed legal regime relating to them. The first study explains why the Antarctic Treaty Consultative Parties have not adopted a dedicated legal regime for access and benefit sharing, and what they have accepted in its place.

The second study is of the Commission for the Conservation of Antarctic Marine Living Resources (CCAMLR) and its rejection of a number of proposals for marine protected areas (MPAs) in the Southern Ocean. The Convention,[3] which the Commission implements, contains an ecosystem-based set of provisions for conservation and rational use of Antarctic marine living resources. It is a mature regime applying to marine living resources (including marine genetic resources, seabirds, seals and whales but not sealing or whaling, both of which are covered under separate international instruments) in areas both within and beyond national jurisdiction.[4] CCAMLR has adopted the task of creating a representative 10% of the Convention's area of application as MPAs by 2020 but so far it has been unable to reach consensus on the practical and normative aspects of MPAs, particularly no-take fishing zones.

The case studies were chosen because of their value as examples of the complexities and difficulties of regulating access to and benefits derived from the development of marine genetic resources sourced from ABNJ. They are themselves linked; the Antarctic Treaty Consultative

Parties adopted CCAMLR under their mandate to make decisions about matters affecting the Antarctic. They anticipated a need to regulate access to marine resources (especially krill) in areas outside the jurisdiction of any one state, well in advance of those resources becoming compromised by over exploitation.[5]

Before proceeding, it is important to explain the nomenclature used in this chapter, to avoid misinterpretations of key terms:

- *biological diversity* – usually and hereafter shortened to *biodiversity*: 'the variability among living organisms from all sources including, *inter alia*, terrestrial, marine and other aquatic ecosystems and the ecological complexes of which they are part: this includes diversity within species, between species and of ecosystems'.[6]
- *biological prospecting* – usually and hereafter shortened to *bioprospecting*, is taken to be exploratory scientific research that is or will be 'of direct significance for the exploration and exploitation of natural resources'.[7] In other words, it is applied scientific research with commercial intent.
- *marine genetic resources* – 'genetic material of actual or potential value' found in the marine environment.[8] The diversity of this genetic material is covered broadly under *biological diversity*.
- *national jurisdiction* and *beyond national jurisdiction* (as per LOSC Articles on maritime zones).

Why there is no marine genetic resources convention now

The global community has not given high priority to regulating access to marine genetic resources in areas beyond national jurisdiction in the past as a separate activity from – say – fishing or scientific research.[9] There are a couple of main reasons why this is so. First, 'marine genetic resources' can be sourced from species as far apart on the taxonomic scale as vertebrates and microbes; anything living in the marine environment is potentially a marine genetic resource. Managing human activities that relate to megafauna (e.g. fish) is difficult enough; managing those same activities when they relate to microfauna (e.g. something smaller than 0.3 of a millimetre) is orders of magnitude more complicated.

Secondly, there is relatively poor scientific knowledge about what the marine environment contains, even though (or perhaps *because*) it makes up over 70% of planet earth's surface. Contributing to this paucity of information is the fact that distant water marine scientific research is expensive and becoming more so with the increasing costs of running ships (including the prices of fuel and compliance with marine regulations). Even once the mining industry became aware of the potential storehouse of mineral riches on the ocean floor as many as four or five decades ago, the technological sophistication to access them was not necessarily available or cost-effective. Not only was technology an inhibiting factor, but while land-sourced minerals were viable, there was no need to source marine minerals.

Finally, the list of marine species potentially of interest to the biological prospecting industry is not only *unknown*, but most likely *unknowable* as well. Trying to erect policy frames around a suppositional ecosystem where a resource might be located, then regulating access to it and sharing the benefits derived from its use, is unrealistic without detailed knowledge of the functioning of that ecosystem.

Nevertheless there is a greater chance of finding genetic resources that might have commercial utility in the pharmaceutical (medicine) or nutraceutical (functional food) industries in the marine environment as opposed to the terrestrial environment, primarily because the marine environment is particularly biodiverse. Species that make adaptations to help them survive and thrive in unusual marine environments take on elements of novelty themselves. It is the search for novelty – for example on the deep abyssal plains where there is little or no light or oxygen; around hydrothermal vents with very hot, sulphur-rich water; or in very cold polar water – that characterizes the activity of biological prospecting. When novel marine genetic resources are found in areas outside national boundaries, the effective regulation of human activity associated with access to them becomes complex and challenging. However, it is important to note that many of the topographic features of these novel ocean spaces are, in fact, also found in areas *within* national jurisdiction, which greatly simplifies regulation and management for a number of reasons. First, because the areas are relatively closer to the coast, there is a higher probability of commercial interest in potential novelty on the basis that the resources are relatively easier to access, making scientific research relatively cheaper, and consequently there is probably a higher level of scientific understanding about them. Secondly, regulation of access to and benefits derived from resources sourced domestically does not involve another state, unless those resources actually straddle an adjacent state's EEZ.[10]

Previously, factors such as isolation; prospecting, exploration and extraction regulations and costs; and uncertain ongoing access arrangements have meant that potentially high value resources in ABNJ have attracted little commercial attention. Yet it is a natural scientific progression from taxonomic identification and classification of newly discovered species to investigation of what these marine genetic resources can 'do' for humans. And thus in recent years the global community of environmental policy- and law-makers, spearheaded by the United Nations General Assembly and the UN Ad Hoc Open Ended Informal Working Group on Biodiversity Beyond National Jurisdiction (BBNJ 2013), has elevated regulating and managing access to and the distribution of benefits from marine genetic resources in ABNJ from one of speculative interest to one of very real concern (Arrieta et al 2010). Aware that technology and interest are developing in tandem, the idea seems to be that any regulation is better than none, and dedicated regulation is thought to be the ideal. This is what the United Nations has charged the global community of stakeholders with investigating. The specific proposal is that a new agreement of some kind (an implementing agreement appended to the LOSC for example)[11] is required.

There was an opportunity for the 1982 LOSC itself to regulate (through law) and manage (through the establishment of an administrative structure) access to marine genetic resources outside national maritime boundaries, since their novelty and utility were already known (or at least speculated) and since it was within this Convention that maritime boundaries were codified and the mineral resources of the deep seabed beyond national jurisdiction characterized as representing the 'common heritage of mankind'.[12] Nevertheless, marine genetic resources were not expressly regulated under LOSC provisions, with its more aspirational conservation goals applying only broadly to all marine resources, including those both living in the water column and found on the sea floor.

The adoption of the Convention on Biological Diversity (CBD)[13] 10 years after LOSC also provided an opportunity to regulate and manage access to marine genetic resources. The CBD provided a useful definition of biodiversity but, although the potential was there, the CBD (and its later Nagoya Protocol)[14] did not declare itself the principal regulatory regime for biological prospecting or access to marine resources *beyond national jurisdiction*. Its provisions certainly create obligations on states over such resources within their jurisdiction, and the processes and activities carried out by their nationals in relation to such resources, but the CBD contains no broader international or multinational accountability for regulating such resources in ABNJ.[15]

Even though CBD article 5 requires Parties to cooperate in the sustainable use of biological diversity in ABNJ, that requirement is too weak to be of assistance in the development of mandatory regulations.

In fact, a divergence of opinion about whether or not a dedicated legal instrument is necessary is now reflected in the reports of meetings of the BBNJ – established to take up this challenge.[16] Since there is no scientific body attached to the BBNJ working group, it remains to be seen how a suitable governance structure can possibly be developed sans scientific advice. While the CBD currently fulfils this role for BBNJ on an interim basis, any new convention should include a suitable scientific body able to conduct directed scientific research and participate in the policy-making process. Furthermore, any such convention would benefit from acknowledging that scientific body as integral to its decision-making, rather than diminishing its status to advisory-only.

It can be concluded that existing obligations to protect and preserve marine genetic diversity that are as broad in scope as those found in LOSC and CBD do not provide a regime commensurate with the substantive legal requirements demanded by modern technological advances, modern conservation norms and increased commercial attention, and that would also satisfy access to what many see as 'common property' resources. But does this necessarily mean that a new regulatory instrument is necessary?

A new international law instrument would need to fill the gaps and uncertainties surrounding the regulation of access to marine genetic resources and the sharing of any benefits accruing from their commercialization. To accomplish this the BBNJ group would need to determine whether there is sufficient scientific information to make objective assessments about the impacts of bioprospecting or extraction on the resources and their dependent and associated ecosystems. Such assessments would provide evidence of the *need* for a dedicated legal instrument to regulate and manage activities. The need is by no means obvious and must be comprehensively demonstrated. Take the example of an activity that obtains samples of marine genetic material once only from the marine environment: the sample is processed in a laboratory somewhere under national regulations; a novel gene or process is identified, synthesized, developed; and a compound or product is put into the marketplace as a commercial product. What are the issues raised by this activity? First, let's assume that the sample is small, say 10 litres of seawater. There is no obvious environmental impact. Let's assume then that the biodiversity in that seawater is robust and not under threat: it would be relatively unaffected by the removal of such a small amount of material in any case. The most important issue that arises is one of *ownership*: is the seawater and any biological material it contains a common property resource that the rest of the world deserves to benefit from? This latter topic will be followed up in a later section of the chapter.

Knowledge about marine biodiversity

There are a number of questions concerning our level of knowledge about biodiversity, the answers to which will help provide evidence of the need for a dedicated legal regime: why is marine biodiversity desirable? How is biodiversity measured? What makes it vulnerable?

Why is marine biodiversity desirable?

The leading preambular paragraph of the CBD partly answers this question about why biodiversity is important, stating: '[Conscious of] the intrinsic value of biological diversity and of the ecological, genetic, social, economic, scientific, educational, cultural, recreational and aesthetic values of biological diversity and its components'. Since the early work of Costanza et al (1997, 1998), the answer to the question has increasingly been as much about utilitarian as intrinsic value. The economic value of services provided by a healthy ecosystem to support human well-being is quantifiable and therefore a fundamental defence for conserving and sustainably using biodiversity.[17] In short, biodiversity is insurance against the future possibility of deficient ecosystems leading to diminished ecosystem services flowing to humans.

How is marine biodiversity measured?

Marine biodiversity is measured through the investigations of scientific research programmes, from small-scale local studies to multinational, multi-year activities conducted throughout the world's oceans by government-funded research agencies and privately funded commercial researchers (Arrieta et al 2010; Barber and Boyce 2006; Moritz and Cicero 2004). In the 1990s it was reported that there were possibly 300,000 known marine species, but that there could in fact be 10 million (Gray 1997). The increasing sophistication of scientific research methods (e.g. DNA barcoding), although sometimes contentious, has led to more confidence in marine biodiversity assessment research and a more appropriate structure for its reporting. But more confidence does not necessarily mean universal acceptance of techniques and results, speculations and extrapolations.

The most notable large-scale project in recent years has been the Census of Marine Life, which was a coordinated international research project spanning 10 years (Costello et al 2010). In the last century our knowledge of marine taxonomy in particular maritime regions of the globe has grown from the virtually unknown (for example, deep water was considered to be azoic or without life) to well known for some taxa in some regions, such as in national exclusive economic zones (Costello et al 2010). The Census of Marine Life established national and regional implementation committees to assist with its global research efforts and early results from some of the published Census research have proved to be a useful source of knowledge about marine genetic resources (e.g. Costello et al 2010). WoRMS – a database of marine species compiled by taxonomic experts – also collects data, with over 200,000 marine species on record (WoRMS 2014). In summary though, we simply do not know the level of marine biodiversity either within or beyond national jurisdiction and a regional approach to quantifying marine biodiversity is probably the best way that our knowledge can be advanced.

The Antarctic was one of the regions studied during the Census of Marine Life decade (CoML 2014; CAML 2014). It had the largest seabed area and largest sea volume of all the research sites, but the lowest diversity at only 0.4 species per area, compared with, say, 32.3 in the South Korean exclusive economic zone (Costello et al 2010). Notwithstanding, the Census of Antarctic Marine Life and its companion project, SCAR-MarBIN (SCAR Marine Biodiversity Information Network) was tasked with 'assessing the nature, distribution and abundance of the Southern Ocean biodiversity' and keeping a database of research records, available to future generations of researchers (SCAR MarBIN 2014). The results of the Antarctic research, though largely disregarded in many quantitative research papers on the basis that the region is an outlier (Costello et al 2010: 3), is of particular interest for this chapter because of the nature of access to these seemingly common pool marine genetic resources.

What makes marine biodiversity vulnerable?

One of the key messages from recent ecosystems research has been that 'The most important direct drivers of biodiversity loss and ecosystem service changes are habitat change (such as land use changes, physical modification of rivers or water withdrawal from rivers, loss of coral reefs, and damage to sea floors due to trawling), climate change, invasive alien species, overexploitation, and pollution' (Millennium Ecosystem Assessment 2005: vi). This statement gives direction to the efforts at both national and international scales to proactively manage the effects of human impact on marine genetic resources.

Some of these drivers of biodiversity loss are already managed in one way or another *in situ* in the marine environment beyond national jurisdiction. Bottom trawl fisheries and the impact of heavy trawl gear on the sea floor have been likened to 'ploughing the deep sea floor' (Puig et al 2012). A proposal put forward to the European Parliament in 2013 to ban bottom trawling and gill netting failed, although extra restrictions were placed on these environmentally unpopular fishing activities (European Parliament 2013). The transfer of harmful aquatic organisms and pathogens in ships' ballast water is the topic of the new convention on ballast water management.[18] Ten years after its adoption, this International Maritime Organization (IMO) Convention is still not in force,[19] highlighting the complex and expensive technical issues associated with new rules about the storage, discharge and re-ballast of water to stabilize ships. Similarly, maintaining the integrity of the marine environment is handled through the suite of IMO conventions including those dealing with ship safety, marine pollution, crew preparedness and training, rules for avoiding collisions, safe loading and emissions (IMO 2014). Accident prevention is the cornerstone to the success of these maritime conventions, with heavy responsibilities on flag states, ship insurers and classification societies to ensure the regulations are, or can be, complied with, legally, politically and technically.

Preventing overexploitation is the province of many regional fisheries management organizations and similar types of multilateral fisheries regulators. The maintenance of marine biodiversity has the caveat that conservation includes use, and this two-fold approach to management is very often uneven in its application. Whaling is one case in point; tuna fisheries are another (Birnie 1985; Clapham et al 2007; Heazle 2006; Polacheck 2002; Kolody et al 2008). The unequal distribution of conservation as opposed to harvesting effort is, unfortunately, very often cause for dysfunction, mismanagement, vitriol, abandonment of the rule of law, criticism, stock collapse and international court cases – none of which will be dealt with in detail here. Suffice to say, managing human uses of megafauna (fish, whales and seals for example) at both national and international levels is fraught with difficulty – and these are species you can see, track through DNA barcoding, visually identify in marketplaces, in nets, or onboard vessels in locations they are licensed or not licensed to fish. If access to marine genetic resources is perceived as being through 'fishing' for them, then existing models of regulation might prove sufficient. These models might not always be efficient, but they do provide a starting point.

Other impacts on marine biodiversity are the result of *ex situ* activities. Run off from agricultural activities into the marine environment, for example, are linked to all kinds of near-shore degradations, including the promotion of harmful algal blooms (Hallegraeff 2010). Emissions of large amounts of CO_2 into the atmosphere are directly linked to, among other things, increased uptake of CO_2 in the global (particularly polar) oceans and lowering the pH (thus increasing acidity) (e.g. Hoegh-Guldberg et al 2007). Many of the indirect effects of human activities on marine biodiversity have solutions elsewhere, outside the brief of this chapter, and are no less complex.

An evaluation of our knowledge about marine genetic resources

In conclusion, do we have sufficient information about biodiversity in areas beyond national jurisdiction to objectively assess the impact of marine genetic resource bioprospecting and therefore the need for specific regulation? It seems fairly clear that: i) we do not know the scale of marine genetic resource diversity; ii) we have existing regulatory mechanisms for protecting marine biodiversity broadly but not specifically, and iii) under these circumstances, the logical approach is to invoke the precautionary approach and aim for the adoption of regulation irrespective of the state of knowledge. Two case studies will help to illustrate the difficulties with this approach.

Case study: Antarctic bioprospecting

By their nature, case studies are only a snapshot in time and place and circumstance. Nevertheless their value in this chapter lies in scoping the range of concerns attached to the activity of bioprospecting, commercialization or spatial management in the conservation of marine genetic resources in an area outside national jurisdiction. This place, Antarctica, has a symbolic significance and hence one could be lead into thinking that the custodians would have a far more sophisticated approach to the conservation of marine genetic resources than they do in reality.

This section introduces the case study area – Antarctica – to illustrate how the Antarctic Treaty Consultative Parties, many of which have mature and sophisticated domestic legislation on biodiversity (though perhaps not marine genetic resources specifically), treat Antarctica as *sui generis* but in an inconsistent and under-developed way. It could be argued that the stakes in the Antarctic are so low that it is relatively easier to make groundbreaking environmental law since there is no constituency to please or offend with environmental decisions that go well beyond the public's ideological limits (also known as 'social licence to operate'). While this might be true of such moves as the total prohibition on mineral resource activities, it has not been the case in relation to Antarctic bioprospecting.

International Antarctica

Antarctica's credentials as a place *beyond national jurisdiction* stem from the Antarctic Treaty of 1959.[20] The contentious issue of claims, overlapping claims and reservations to make claims to Antarctic territory some time in the future led the 12 states most interested in an outcome to put aside their differences and adopt the Antarctic Treaty. In its Article IV, the issue of claims was put to one side in favour of the dual objectives of peace and science. Article IV does not resolve claims in favour of one position over another. Rather, it resolves disputes about them while the Treaty is in force. This releases the Parties to get on with keeping the peace and conducting scientific research.

Because there is no single sovereign over Antarctica, the area south of 60° South is in one sense *beyond national jurisdiction*. And in fact Article VI declares that nothing in the Treaty derogates from the existing rights that states' parties have in relation to the high seas (a concept not to be codified until the LOSC negotiations approximately 20 years later). However, this is only one interpretation. To those seven states that have made claims to Antarctic territory (Argentina, Australia, Chile, France, New Zealand, Norway and the United Kingdom) their claimed areas are indisputably subject to their national jurisdiction (Dodds & Hemmings 2009). Further, Australia, for example, has proclaimed a 200NM maritime zone off the Australian Antarctic Territory and thus asserts sovereign rights and jurisdiction over this area as well – at least in relation to its nationals (Jabour 2006, 2008). Overt assertions of sovereignty, sovereign rights and jurisdiction arise, either in reality or simply in the minds of others, but they are not permitted to spoil the otherwise good working relationship among the Consultative Parties (Dodds and

Hemmings 2009; Haward and Bergin 2010). Nationalism ultimately takes a back seat to the harmony of the meetings and the good of the majority. The definition of consensus in the Antarctic Treaty and related instruments typifies this point: it is either agreement, or the lack of formal objection.[21] Failing to formally object, which is achieved by speaking against a proposal, deems states to be part of the consensus. There is no show of hands, no secret ballot; consensus is negotiated, silence is acquiescence.

The Antarctic treaty and its Environmental Protocol[22]

The Antarctic legal regime comprises a complementary set of free standing conventions, a protocol and a range of outcomes from meetings that have some degree of legal obligation attached to them. In relation to bioprospecting, there are a number of important provisions in the Treaty and its Protocol on Environmental Protection (Madrid Protocol):

- Antarctic Treaty Article II – freedom of scientific investigation and cooperation. This permits any Antarctic Treaty party to conduct scientific research in any part of the area south of 60° South latitude. Antarctic territorial claims place no overt barriers on where scientists can conduct their research or collect samples.
- Antarctic Treaty Article III – scientific observations and results from Antarctica must be exchanged and made freely available 'to the greatest extent feasible and practicable' (Jabour-Green and Nicol 2003).
- Madrid Protocol Article 8, Annex I[23] – all activities must be evaluated for environmental impact prior to their conduct in Antarctica. This includes scientific research.

Scientific activity

Scientific activity is preeminent in the Antarctic. It is enshrined as the essence of the Treaty, alongside peace. In fact, those parties to the Treaty that display high levels of scientific interest earn the right to become Consultative Parties – decision-makers. It is no surprise that all the original signatories to the Treaty are also Consultative Parties and that subsequently 17 others have earned their place at the table through the conduct of scientific research expeditions, the establishment of bases and the like. It is also no surprise that most of the world's capacity to study and perhaps exploit marine genetic resources is to be found among the Consultative Parties.

The Parties consult with non-governmental organizations such as the Scientific Committee on Antarctic Research (SCAR) to provide advice on activities such as bioprospecting and the state of the environment. SCAR has an Antarctic biodiversity database which captures 'all recorded species observations and their locations from the Antarctic and sub-Antarctic. It also holds a reference set of all terrestrial and freshwater taxa for all regions below 45° south latitude'.[24] SCAR and the Antarctic Treaty Consultative Parties work together to identify scientific needs and provide scientific advice; bioprospecting is classified as an 'emerging issue' (SCAR 2014:31).

The United Nations University, with support from UNEP and the Belgian Federal Ministry of Environment, maintains a database called the Bioprospector, which catalogues research activity and commercialized products sourced from Antarctic material.[25] It is possible to browse all 185 records in this database for the title, research sector, organization, state sponsors and taxonomy. Not all records are complete, nor are there any indications of when the database and its accompanying references were last updated. However it can be used as an indication of the types, if not the scale of activity undertaken. Another source of information is the tracing of patents for Antarctic-sourced bioprospecting activities (Nicol and Foster 2003; Foster et al 2011), which can give a good indication of how far the industry has advanced in the commercialization process but once again, does not give an account of the scale of activities.

One of the key planks of democracy within the Antarctic Treaty System is the free exchange of information about Antarctic activities, submitted as annual reports to the Antarctic Treaty Secretariat.[26] This exchange also means that the public can access the annual reports of each Antarctic operator. Reports often include a summary of their scientific research activities, and accessing these helps to fill in gaps in the information available from other sources.

Despite all indications that bioprospecting activities are increasing, the Antarctic Treaty Consultative Parties have not taken the next step of regulating bioprospecting to protect marine genetic resources, provide benefits to the rest of the world from 'common pool' Antarctic resources or mitigate against any environmental risk. Their rationale is simple: bioprospecting is a scientific activity, well covered under the Antarctic Treaty and the Protocol on Environmental Protection. If bioprospecting involves the harvesting of a resource, say krill, then the activity is 'fishing', which is covered under CCAMLR.

Policy position of Antarctic treaty consultative parties

The policy position outlined above has been in place for 10 years (Jabour-Green and Nicol 2003). Bioprospecting is a standing agenda item at the annual Antarctic Treaty Consultative Meetings (ATCM) and is introduced every year, usually by Belgium.[27] Each year the discussion produces rhetoric but no decisive action, with the possible exception of the portfolio of non-binding Resolutions that are accruing under this topic. For example, at ATCM XXXVI in 2013 the Parties adopted Resolution 6(2013) on Biological Prospecting in Antarctica that concluded with the comments that the Representatives:

> *Reaffirm that the Antarctic Treaty System is the appropriate framework for managing the collection of biological material in the Antarctic Treaty area and for considering its use;*
>
> *Recommend that their governments report, as appropriate, on biological prospecting carried out under their respective legal regimes, with a view to facilitating a better understanding and assessment of these types of activities; and Encourage their governments to examine ways to improve information exchange in this regard and to consider whether to adapt the Electronic Information Exchange System for this purpose.*[28]

Then at ATCM XXXVII in 2014, Belgium proposed that the Parties, among other things, consider and adopt a working definition of 'bioprospecting' for the purposes of implementing Resolution 6(2013). Noting that other international fora were also working on defining this term and that their definitions would not be Antarctic-specific, Belgium proposed the following for consideration:

> *Any activity of search, identification, description, collection, survey, monitoring, cultivation, replication, or any other scientific investigation processes, performed on indigenous biological species, carried on within the area defined in Article VI of the Antarctic Treaty, with the initial intention to consider potential industrial or commercial derived products or applications, notably through the development of patentable material or process.*

The final report of the meeting reflects the semantic difficulties the Parties had with this approach: some thought the definition too broad and others, too narrow.[29] Rejecting this proposal (i.e. without reaching consensus on it), the Parties discussed how to progress the topic and decided, as they typically do, that further discussion was warranted and that bioprospecting should remain a standing agenda item.

A second plank to Belgium's 2014 proposition was that when environmental evaluations are conducted on scientific activities (as per Article 8 and Annex 1 of the Madrid Protocol), Parties should include in their permitting requirements, the duty to disclose when bioprospecting is the purpose of the scientific activity. The report of the meeting did not record the fate of this duty of disclosure proposal and it can be assumed that there was no substantive discussion on the matter. The 2015 ATCM is expected to be business as usual in relation to the regulation of bioprospecting.

Strengths and weaknesses

It is quite apparent that there is no desire on the part of Antarctic Treaty Consultative Parties to adopt another layer of regulation on bioprospecting as a separate activity from scientific research. The strength of this approach is that the system is not burdened with extra, onerous regulation. Rather it relies on and gives legitimacy to the universal requirement to conduct environmental evaluations of all activities – including scientific research – prior to them being carried out in Antarctica. Whether or not states parties choose to take up the proposal for a duty of disclosure – which is actually a good idea because it clarifies the intent of their scientific research – will be a national policy decision since the requirements would fall within national legal frameworks. At the very least, all Antarctic scientific endeavours (including bioprospecting) will continue to be captured by the Antarctic Treaty's free exchange provisions and the Madrid Protocol's environmental provisions.

The weakness of this approach is that it does not deal with benefit sharing. There is an inherent risk in placing benefit sharing alongside sovereign neutrality of the kind practiced in Antarctica (Jabour-Green and Nicol 2003). As with fishing, sharing the benefits from the commercialization of products or processes derived from Antarctic material is simply not on the radar in the Antarctic Treaty arena (Jabour 2010). How this continues to play out might well be influenced by what happens in other international fora, particularly the BBNJ working group. Its investigations and possible eventual adoption of a legal instrument that will no doubt include provisions on sharing the proceeds from commercialization of marine genetic resources sourced from beyond national jurisdiction. This is complicated because any new instrument that has an area of application overlapping with any instruments in the Antarctic Treaty System will need to take account of those existing legal regimes. This is analogous to the situation in which CCAMLR finds itself, discussed in the next section: one of accepting international responsibilities for marine protected areas but then being unable to reconcile the practical and normative elements of the idea within the Antarctic context.

Case study: CCAMLR and marine protected areas

During the 1960s and 1970s fishers turned to harvesting the resources of the Southern Ocean, with fishing effort directed primarily at fish, although krill was also taken (Everson 2000). Given the consequences of the appalling history of unregulated harvesting for whales, seals and penguins, the Antarctic Treaty Consultative Parties became concerned that unregulated harvesting of krill – a keystone species in the Southern Ocean ecosystem – could have serious impacts (Agnew 1997). The Parties adopted a convention that was, in 1980, and still is today, a visionary legal instrument.

Southern ocean resources under CCAMLR

In the Convention, marine living resources are defined as 'populations of fin-fish, molluscs, crustaceans and all other species of living organisms, including birds, found south of the Antarctic Convergence'.[30] Technically this means that all marine genetic resources derived from living organisms are under the dual custody of the Antarctic Treaty Consultative Parties (since their area of interest is south of 60° South) and the CCAMLR Commission members, whose area of interest overlaps. If the Antarctic Treaty Consultative Parties are unwilling to adopt substantive regulation over these resources, perhaps CCAMLR will? One way of achieving this would be by designating marine protected areas and regulating what can and cannot occur there.

Scientific activity

CCAMLR uses an ecosystem and precautionary approach to conservation of Antarctic marine living resources (Constable et al 2000)[31] and facilitates the work of the Commission by establishing a number of subsidiary bodies, including a Scientific Committee and a Standing Committee on Implementation and Compliance. All Commission Members are also Scientific Committee members. Because decisions of the Commission are to be based on the 'best scientific evidence available',[32] it is obligated to take full account of the recommendations and advice of its scientific experts. These experts are informed by the research of national programmes and the Commission's own research into fisheries monitoring, onboard observing, ecosystem monitoring and marine debris. A number of working groups assist the Scientific Committee including ecosystem monitoring and management, fish stock assessment, statistics, assessments and modelling and incidental mortality associated with fishing. All things considered, decisions in CCAMLR involve a high degree of scientific input.

As a result of this advice the Commission has the power to designate regions and sub-regions based on species population distribution; set catch limits for specific regions and sub-regions; determine species requiring special protection; designate age, size and sex of harvested species; open and close seasons; open and close areas, regions and sub-regions for study or conservation; and regulate effort, gear and methods of harvesting (Jabour 2012, 2013).

CCAMLR also has a programme for the identification of vulnerable marine ecosystems (VMEs) – areas such as the tops of seamounts, hydrothermal vents, cold water corals and sponge beds – which can be damaged during bottom fishing activities.[33] Once identified, there is a prohibition on bottom trawling and deep-sea gillnetting in these vulnerable areas, with notification requirements and move-on rules. Notifications about the location of VMEs from fishers are submitted to scientific working groups for discussion, review, assessment and updating of information on fishing impact. Exclusion zones may be put in place around VMEs to protect them from the direct impacts of fishing. Decisions on legally binding Conservation Measures are then made in the Commission meetings. Based on the powers within the Convention to effect substantial ecosystem protection, and hence maintain the integrity of marine genetic resources, the Commission not only took up the challenge of marine protected areas but was in fact, the first to designate a high seas marine protected area.

The Potential to Regulate Bioprospecting

Policy position of CCAMLR members

The South Orkney Islands MPA was the world's first high seas marine protected area, encompassing 94,000 km² of the southern shelf zone below the island chain. Acting on the advice of its Scientific Committee, the Commission adopted the MPA in 2009.[34] There was no current fishing activity in the area of the proposed MPA. Although adopted by consensus, discussion on this proposal reflected a lack of agreement on the scope and form of Southern Ocean MPAs more broadly.[35] However, after a further two years of discussion, the Commission adopted a general framework for the establishment of MPAs, based on recommendations from the Scientific Committee.[36]

A total of four proposals have subsequently been submitted for consideration under the general framework's six key objectives: maintaining the viability and integrity of representative examples of marine ecosystems; protecting key ecosystem processes, habitats and species; establishing scientific reference areas; protecting vulnerable areas; protecting features critical to local ecosystems; and protecting the resilience of areas to climate change. All subsequent proposals have been rejected, first in 2012, then at a special meeting in mid-2013 and thirdly at the CCAMLR Commission meetings at the end of 2013 (Jabour 2013) and 2014. Objections seemed to be based partly on their size (several million square kilometres in total), partly on their duration (up to 50 years, with decadal review cycles), and partly on the legal standing of CCAMLR to take such actions (Hislop and Jabour 2014). For the proponents of those MPAs, it is back to the drawing board yet again, in the hope that sometime soon a breakthrough will occur.

Strengths and weaknesses

CCAMLR applies to a marine biogeographic region that includes sub-Antarctic islands that are the sovereign territory of member states. This Southern Ocean legal regime is, therefore, both *within* and *beyond* national jurisdiction. Commission Members whose sub-Antarctic islands are not in dispute can choose to apply CCAMLR rules or create their own (Turner et al 2008). Members treat other areas as beyond national jurisdiction and accept the preeminence of CCAMLR in regulating the conservation and rational use of marine living resources.

The Commission has an arsenal of tools that it can use to help conserve marine genetic resources. In addition to setting catch limits for target species, it uses these tools to make legally binding rules on such matters as compliance, notifications, gear regulations, data reporting, research and experiments, minimization of incidental mortality, environmental protection, fishing seasons, closed areas and prohibition of fishing, by-catch limits and protected areas.[37] The rules apply to all marine living resources, but marine genetic resources are not singled out for special treatment. The strength of withholding consensus on MPAs highlights the uncertainty surrounding this approach to high seas conservation and underscores the Convention's historical credentials as the principal legal regime applying to the conservation of Antarctic marine living resources.

The weakness of the Commission's failure to adopt an oceanic corral of marine protected areas is that some Member States will continue to advocate for such MPAs and valuable time, effort and resources will be diverted away from other important matters, such as illegal, unreported and unregulated fishing and the impacts of a warming climate. Clearly more work is needed to convince Commission members of the utility of massive MPAs in an area which is already a marine protected area under a different name. There is no doubt that progress being made in other fora (especially the CBD and its ecologically and biologically significant areas) will filter into and influence CCAMLR members who feel that some of the particularly vulnerable marine ecosystems in its area of application would benefit from greater protection. The story is not over yet: the proposals for MPAs will most likely continue to be presented to Commission meetings until a broader agreement can be reached, and ultimately, consensus.

Conclusions

This chapter examined the need for a new instrument to regulate access to and share the benefits of marine genetic resources in ABNJ by presenting lessons from two analogous case studies – Antarctic bioprospecting and Southern Ocean MPAs. It highlighted how little we know about the marine environment and the interactions between an ecosystem's components and those of dependent and associated ecosystems. Our knowledge about marine biodiversity and ecosystem linkages in a changing world is so limited – NOAA estimate that only 5% of ocean spaces have been explored[38] – it was concluded that a precautionary approach should be taken to protecting marine genetic resources (marine biodiversity generally). In marine areas under sovereign jurisdiction, this is hardly problematic since coastal states parties have an array of powers derived from the LOSC and the CBD to assist them. In marine areas beyond national jurisdiction, however, it is a different story. Conceding that the Southern Ocean south of the Antarctic Convergence and 60° South is high seas and evaluating how the Parties to Antarctic Treaty instruments treat marine genetic resources is illustrative of how a regime might work in other high seas areas.

In Antarctica, access to marine genetic resources is gained through the activity being classified as either scientific research (regulated under the Antarctic Treaty and the Madrid Protocol) or fishing (regulated under CCAMLR). There is no provision in the Antarctic legal regime for sharing the benefits of commercializing Antarctic-derived marine genetic material. Furthermore, Antarctic marine genetic resources are not considered common property resources, even though they quite clearly lie outside national jurisdiction. The Antarctic Treaty Consultative Parties have taken a narrow approach to bioprospecting, treating it only as scientific research and regulating it only insofar as all scientific research is subject to environmental evaluation. A clever call for bioprospecting to appear in mandatory exchange of information documents as the intention of the scientific research is interesting, but unlikely to be adopted by the Parties because it would set a precedent for identifying the intentions of all scientific research and open up a Pandora's box of debate. Furthermore, the uses of marine resources such as krill are regulated as fishing – the activity used to harvest them – irrespective of the purposes for which the krill is intended beyond the harvest.

Since the 1990s the development of MPAs has been on the global environmental agenda. There are, of course, quite reasonable concerns about the maintenance of biodiversity, particularly in information-poor regions such as the high seas (IUCN 2003). An implementing agreement nested into the LOSC is one way to approach protection of vulnerable marine ecosystems and their genetic resources. But the notion of the global representative system of MPAs covering 10% of the marine environment has collided with the practicalities of governing areas beyond national jurisdiction. Aside from the merits of the argument for the protection of marine genetic resources, the mere drawing of boundaries around an area will not protect it. Without the ability to monitor and enforce high seas MPAs boundaries to prevent activities identified as being harmful and therefore excluded from the area, the MPA serves no practical purpose.

In Antarctica, it seems there are bigger issues of concern than the explicit protection and rational use of marine genetic resources, e.g. understanding and measuring biodiversity, gaining a greater knowledge about ecosystem interactions, and projecting how the climate will change and what effect these changes will have on biodiversity. Prioritizing scientific research effort will become more important as climatic changes increase in speed and intensity. Protecting something without really understanding it is not an idea easily sold to states with an interest in using resources and a considerable amount of further work is needed to convince them of the merits of protecting diversity they cannot even necessarily see in areas beyond their direct sphere of influence and interest.

Bibliography

Agnew, D. (1997) 'Review: The CCAMLR Ecosystem Monitoring Programme,' *Antarctic Science* 9, 3: 235–242.

Arrieta, J.M., Arnaud-Haond, S. and Duarte, C.M. (2010) 'What lies underneath: Conserving the oceans' genetic resources', *PNAS* 107,43: 18318–18324.

Barber, P. and S. L. Boyce (2006) 'Estimating diversity of Indo-Pacific coral reef stomatopods through DNA barcoding of stomatopod larvae', *Proceedings of the Royal Society B: Biological Sciences* doi: 10.1098/rspb.2006.3540.

BBNJ, 2013. Ad Hoc Open-ended Informal Working Group to study issues relating to the conservation and sustainable use of marine biological diversity beyond areas of national jurisdiction, *Intersessional workshops aimed at improving understanding of the issues and clarifying key questions as an input to the work of the Working Group in accordance with the terms of reference annexed to General Assembly resolution 67/78*.

Birnie, P. (1985) *International Regulation of Whaling; From conservation of whaling to conservation of whales and regulation of whale-watching* (Vols. 1 and 2). New York: Oceana Publications.

Census of Antarctic Marine Life, http://www.caml.aq/ (accessed 1 June 2014).

Census of Marine Life, http://www.coml.org/ (accessed 1 June 2014).

Clapham, P.J., Childerhouse, S., Gales, N.J., Rojas-Bracho, L., Tillman, M.F. and Brownell, R. (2007). "The Whaling Issue: Conservation, confusion, and casuistry". *Marine Policy*, 31:314–319.

Constable, A., de la Mare, W., Agnew, D., Everson, I. and D. Miller (2000) 'Managing fisheries to conserve the Antarctic marine ecosystem: Practical implementation of the Convention on the Conservation of Antarctic Marine Living Resources (CCAMLR),' *ICES Journal of Marine Science* 57:778–791.

Costanza, R., d'Arge, R., de Groot, R., Farberk, S., Grasso, M., Hannon, B., Limburg, K., Naeem, S., O'Neill, R.V., Paruelo, J., Raskin, R.G., Sutton, P. and van den Belt, M. (1997) 'The value of the world's ecosystem services and natural capital', *Nature*, 387 (15 May 1997):253–260.

Costanza, R., d'Arge, R., de Groot, R., Farberk, S., Grasso, M., Hannon, B., Limburg, K., Naeem, S., O'Neill, R.V., Paruelo, J., Raskin, R.G., Sutton, P. and van den Belt, M. (1998) 'The value of ecosystem services: putting the issues in perspective', *Ecological Economics*, 25: 67–72.

Costello, M.J., Coll, M., Danovaro, R., Halpin, P., Ojaveer, H., et al. (2010) 'A Census of Marine Biodiversity, Knowledge, Resources, and Future Challenges', *PLoS ONE* 5(8): e12110. doi:10.1371/journal.pone.0012110.

DiMento, Joseph F.C. and Hickman, Alexis J. *Environmental Governance of the Great Seas: Law and Effect* (Cheltenham: Edward Elgar, 2012).

Document A/AC.276/6, August 2013, available online at http://www.un.org/depts/los/bio diversityworkinggroup/biodiversityworkinggroup.htm (accessed 5 May 2014).

Dodds, K. and Hemmings, A. (2009) 'Frontier Vigilantism? Australia and Contemporary Representations of Australian Antarctic Territory', *Australian Journal of Politics and History*, 55:4, 513–529.

European Parliament, Press Release, 'Deep-sea fisheries: Parliament calls for bottom trawling ban in vulnerable areas', 10 December 2013, available online at http://www.europarl.europa.eu/

news/en/news-room/content/20131206IPR30022/html/Deep-sea-fisheries-Parliament-calls-for-bottom-trawling-ban-in-vulnerable-areas (accessed 23 May 2014).

Everson, I. (2000) *Krill: Biology, Ecology and Fisheries* (Oxford: Blackwell Science).

Foster, J., Nicol, S. and Kawaguchi, S. (2011) 'The use of patent databases to detect trends in the krill fishery'. *CCAMLR Science* 18, 135–144.

Gray, J.S (1997) 'Marine biodiversity: patterns, threats and conservation needs' *Biodiversity and Conservation* 6: 153–175, at 155.

Hallegraeff, G.M., (2010) 'Ocean climate change, phytoplankton community responses, and harmful algal blooms: a formidable predictive challenge', *Journal of Phycology* 46 (2):220-235.

Haward, M. and Bergin, A. (2010) 'Vision not vigilantism: Reply to Dodds and Hemmings', *Australian Journal of Politics and History*, 56:4, 612–616.

Heazle, M. (2006). *Scientific Uncertainty and the Politics of Whaling.* Washington: University of Washington Press.

Hislop, C. and Jabour, J. (2014) 'Quality Matters: High Seas MPAs in the Southern Ocean', *Ocean Yearbook* 29, 2014 (*in press*).

Hoegh-Guldberg, O., Mumby, P.J., Hooten, A.J., Steneck, R.S. Greenfield, P., Gomez, E., Harvell, C.D., Sale, P.F., Edwards, A.J., Caldeira, K., Knowlton, N., Eakin, C.M., Inglesias-Prieto, R., Muthiga, N., Bradbury, R.H., Dubi, A. and Harziolos, M.E. (2007) 'Coral reefs under rapid climate change and ocean acidification', *Science* 318 (5857) (2007) 1737–1742.

Hoshino, E., Hillary, R.M. and Pearce, J. (2010) 'Economically Optimal Management Strategies for the South Georgia Patagonian Toothfish Fishery', *Marine Resource Economics*, 25: 265–280.

International Maritime Organization, *List of IMO Conventions*, available online at http://www.imo.org/About/Conventions/ListOfConventions/Pages/Default.aspx (accessed 23 May 2014).

IUCN (2003) 'Towards a Strategy for High Seas Marine Protected Areas' (K. Gjerde and C. Briede eds.) *Proceedings of the IUCN, WCPA and WWF Expert Workshop on High Seas Marine Protected Areas* 15–17 January 2003, Malaga Spain.

Jabour-Green, J. and Nicol, D. (2003) 'Bioprospecting in areas outside national jurisdiction: Antarctica and the Southern Ocean', *Melbourne Journal of International Law* 4:1, 76.

Jabour, J. (2006) 'High Latitude Diplomacy: Australia's Antarctic extended continental shelf', *Marine Policy* 30:2, 197.

Jabour, J. (2008) 'The Australian Continental Shelf: Has Australia's high latitude diplomacy paid off?' *Marine Policy* 33, 429.

Jabour, J. (2010) 'Biological prospecting: the ethics of exclusive reward from Antarctic activity', *Ethics in Science and Environment* 10:19–29.

Jabour, J. (30 November 2012) Trend Lines: Antarctic marine protection is working, World Politics Review, http://www.worldpoliticsreview.com/trend-lines/12492/antarctic-marine-protection-is-working.

Jabour, J. (22 July 2013) Trend Lines: Global Insider: Antarctic Marine Protection Process Still Healthy Despite Talks' Failure, World Politics Review, http://www.worldpoliticsreview.com/trend-lines/13109/global-insider-antarctic-marine-protection-process-still-healthy-despite-talks-failure.

Kolody, D., Polacheck, T., Basson, M. and Davies, C. (2008) 'Salvaged pearls: lessons learned from a floundering attempt to develop a management procedure for Southern Bluefin Tuna', *Fisheries Research* 94:339–350.

Liu, S., Costanza, R., Farber, S. and Troy, A. (2010) 'Valuing ecosystem services: Theory, practice, and the need for a transdisciplinary synthesis', Annals of the New York Academy of Sciences, 1185:54–78.

Mäler, K-G., Aniyar, S. and Jansson, Å. (2008) 'Accounting for ecosystem services as a way to understand the requirements for sustainable development', *PNAS* 105:28:9501-9506.

Midgley, G.F. (2012) 'Biodiversity and Ecosystem Function', *Science* 335, 13 January 2012: 174–175.

Millennium Ecosystem Assessment, *Ecosystems and Human Well-being: Biodiversity Synthesis* (Washington, DC: World Resources Institute, 2005) available through http://www.maweb.org/documents/document.354.aspx.pdf (accessed 5 May 2014).

Molenaar, Erik J. and Alex G. Oude Elferink (eds) *The International Legal Regime of Areas Beyond National Jurisdiction: Current and Future Developments* (Leiden: Martinus Nijhoff, 2012).

Moritz, C. and Cicero, C. (2004) 'DNA barcoding: promise and pitfalls', *PLoS Biol*, 2004 Oct; 2(10):e354.

Nicol, S. and Foster, J. (2003) Recent trends in the fishery for Antarctic krill. *Aquatic Living Resources* 16 (1): 42–45.

Palmer, M.A. and Febria, C.M. (2012) 'The Heartbeat of Ecosystems', *Science* 336, 15 June 2012: 1393–1394.

Polacheck, T. (2002) 'Experimental catches and the precautionary approach: The Southern Bluefin Tuna dispute', *Marine Policy* 26:283–294.

Puig, P., Canals, M., Company, J. B., Martin, J., Amblas, D., Lastras, G., Palanques, A., and Calafat, A. M., 'Ploughing the deep sea floor', *Nature* 489:7415, 2012: 286–289.

Scientific Committee on Antarctic Research, *Antarctic Science and Policy Advice in a Changing World, Strategic Plan 2011 – 2016*, available online at http://www.scar.org/strategicplan2011/SCAR_Strat_Plan_2011-16.pdf (accessed 2 June 2014).

Scientific Committee on Antarctic Research, SCAR-MarBIN, *Linking, Integrating and Disseminating Antarctic Marine Biodiversity Information*, available online at http://www.scarmarbin.be/ (accessed 23 May 2014).

Turner, J., Jabour, J. and Miller, D. (2008) 'Consensus or Not Consensus: That Is the CCAMLR Question', *Ocean Yearbook* 22: 117–157.

Vidas, Davor and Schei, Peter J. (2011) *The World Ocean in Globalisation* (Leiden: Martinus Nijhoff).

Worm, B., Barbier, E.B., Beaumont, N., Duffy, J.E., Folke, C., Halpern, B.S., Jackson, J.B.C., Lotze, H.K., Micheli, F., Palumbi, S.R., Sala, E., Selkoe, K.A., Stachowicz, J.J. and Watson, R. (2006) 'Impacts of Biodiversity Loss on Ocean Ecosystem Services', *Science*, 314, 3 November 2006: 787–790.

WoRMS Editorial Board (2014) *World Register of Marine Species*, available online from http://www.marinespecies.org (accessed 8 May 2014).

Notes

1 See *United Nations Convention on the Law of the Sea* (LOSC, adopted 10 December 1982, in force 16 November 1994, 1833 U.N.T.S. 3). The terms 'national jurisdiction' and 'beyond national jurisdiction' are not defined in LOSC but are to be viewed in the context of those parts of the LOSC that define maritime zones, e.g. Article 1(1) definition of 'Area' and Part II Territorial Sea and Contiguous Zone, Part V Exclusive Economic Zone, Part VI Continental Shelf and Part VII High Seas. The term 'area/s beyond national jurisdiction' – or ABNJ – is framed within these LOSC definitions. ABNJ does not, in this instance, refer to the seabed below the high seas, as covered under Part XI The Area.

2 *Antarctic Treaty* (adopted 1 December 1959, in force 23 June 1961, 402 U.N.T.S. 71).

3 *Convention on the Conservation of Antarctic Marine Living Resources* (Convention, adopted 20 May 1980, in force 07 April 1982) 19 I.L.M. 837.

4 The area of application of the Convention is outlined in Article 1.2 as south of 60° South latitude and north to the Antarctic convergence, the coordinates of which are outlined in Article 1.4. An illustrative map can be found at http://www.ccamlr.org/en/organisation/convention-area that shows the northern boundary of the area, and the sub-Antarctic islands that are included.
5 Their caution acknowledged that whales, seals and penguins had been over-exploited during the 19th and into the mid-20th century and that they did not want a repeat for fish stocks. The precautionary approach is, in fact, a key element of the Convention.
6 *Convention on Biological Diversity* (CBD, adopted on 22 May 1992, entered into force 29 December 1993, 31 I.L.M. 822), Article 2. Marine genetic diversity is a subset of marine biological diversity and the two are used interchangeably in this chapter.
7 LOSC Article 246 (5). Note that many international fora are also working on definitions. A definition proposed at the Antarctic Treaty Consultative Meeting in Brasilia in 2014 was not adopted, although it was noted that a definition was the first step along the road towards regulation. See Antarctic case study for further details. *Draft Final Report of the Thirty-seventh Antarctic Treaty Consultative Meeting*, not publicly available, paragraphs 343–349.
8 CBD Article 2. The syntax of the article suggests that 'value' relates to commercial rather than intrinsic value, given that the words 'actual or potential' are hardly likely to be appended to the value of something in and of itself.
9 One example is the harvesting of Antarctic krill, *Euphausia superba*, as a regulated fishing activity, but with the intention of using the resource for its Omega-3 oil and other pharmaceutical uses.
10 For example, see the map produced by GRID-Arendal showing the exclusive economic zones overlaid on seafloor topography in the western Pacific. Map 'Depth region of potential nodule development' available online at http://www.grida.no/graphicslib/detail/depth-region-of-potential-nodule-development_0b4b (accessed 23 May 2014)
11 United Nations General Assembly Resolution 68/70. 'Oceans and the law of the sea.' UN doc. A/RES/68/70, 9 December 2013.
12 LOSC Article 136.
13 CBD note 5.
14 Nagoya Protocol on Access to Genetic Resources and the Fair and Equitable Sharing of Benefits Arising From Their Utilization to the Convention on Biological Diversity, (adopted 29 October 2010, opened for signature 02 February 2011) U.N.T.S. NEW-30619, available online at http://www.cbd.int/abs/doc/protocol/nagoya-protocol-en.pdf (accessed 23 May 2014).
15 CDB Article 4(b).
16 For a thorough treatment of the establishment, mandate and progress of this Group, see Warner, Chapter 23 in this volume. See also International Institute for Sustainable Development (IISD) briefing notes on the BBNJ Working Group, available online from http://www.iisd.ca/oceans/marinebiodiv7/ (accessed 27 May 2014).
17 A useful summary is found in the Millennium Ecosystem Assessment report 'Ecosystems and Human Well-Being: Biodiversity Synthesis' published in 2005, available online from http://www.maweb.org/documents/document.354.aspx.pdf (accessed 5 May 2014). See particularly Figure A 'Conceptual Framework of Interactions between Biodiversity, Ecosystem Services, Human Well-being, and Drivers of Change'. See also Costanza et al 1997; Costanza et al 1998; Hoshino et al 2010; Mäler et al 2008; Liu et al 2010; Midgley 2012; Palmer and Febria 2012; and Worm et al 2006.
18 International Convention for the Control and Management of Ships' Ballast Water and Sediments (adopted in London, 13 February 2004, not yet in force).
19 Although there were 39 signatories as at 16 May 2014, the total tonnage represented was only 30.25% – still 4.75% short of the requisite representation to bring the Convention into force.
20 Antarctic Treaty (adopted in Washington, 01 December 1959, in force 23 June 1961) 402 U.N.T.S. 71.
21 For a description of the provenance, function and use of consensus in CCAMLR see Turner et al 2008.
22 Protocol on Environmental Protection to the Antarctic Treaty (adopted in Madrid, 4 October 1991, in force 14 January 1998) 30 I.L.M. 1416 (Madrid Protocol).
23 Article 8 and Annex I of the Madrid Protocol provide a comprehensive description of the rationale and what evaluations are to cover. Article 8 is specific:

1   Proposed activities referred to in paragraph 2 below shall be subject to the procedures set out in Annex I for prior assessment of the impacts of those activities on the Antarctic environment or on dependent or associated ecosystems according to whether those activities are identified as having:
    (a) less than a minor or transitory impact;
    (b) a minor or transitory impact; or
    (c) more than a minor or transitory impact.
2   Each Party shall ensure that the assessment procedures set out in Annex I are applied in the planning processes leading to decisions about any activities undertaken in the Antarctic Treaty area pursuant to scientific research programmes, tourism and all other governmental and non-governmental activities in the Antarctic Treaty area for which advance notice is required under Article VII (5) of the Antarctic Treaty, including associated logistic support activities.
3   The assessment procedures set out in Annex I shall apply to any change in an activity whether the change arises from an increase or decrease in the intensity of an existing activity, from the addition of an activity, the decommissioning of a facility, or otherwise.
4   Where activities are planned jointly by more than one Party, the Parties involved shall nominate one of their number to coordinate the implementation of the environmental impact assessment procedures set out in Annex I.

24 SCAR Antarctic Biodiversity Database, information online at http://www.scar.org/researchgroups/productsandservices/#biodiversity (accessed 1 June 2014). Database online at https://data.aad.gov.au/aadc/biodiversity/ (accessed 1 June 2014).
25 United Nations University – Institute of Advanced Studies, *Bioprospecting Information Resource*, available online at http://www.bioprospector.org/ (accessed 1 June 014).
26 Antarctic Treaty Secretariat, Information Exchange, *Annual Report*, available online at http://www.ats.aq/devAS/ie_annual.aspx?lang=e (accessed 2 June 2014).
27 For example, at the Antarctic Treaty Consultative Meeting XXXVII in Brasilia in 2014, Belgium introduced Working Paper 12, *Assessing Bioprospecting in Antarctica*. Available online at Antarctic Treaty Secretariat, http://www.ats.aq/devAS/ats_meetings_doc_database.aspx?lang=e&menu=2 (accessed 1 June 2014).
28 ATCM Resolution 6 (2013) available online from Antarctic Treaty Secretariat, http://www.ats.aq/devAS/ats_meetings_meeting_measure.aspx?lang=e (accessed 1 June 2014).
29 ATCM XXXVII, Final Report, Item 17 Biological Prospecting in Antarctica, available at http://www.ats.aq/devAS/info_finalrep.aspx?lang=e&menu=2 (accessed 1 June 2014).
30 Article I.2. Whales and seals are factored into ecosystem models, as dependent and associated species of target fish, but neither activity of whaling or sealing are regulated under CCAMLR.
31 CCAMLR Article I and Article II.
32 CCAMLR Article IX.1(f).
33 CCAMLR, Conservation Measure 22–06 (2012) *Bottom fishing in the Convention Area*, and CCAMLR, Conservation Measure 22–07 (2013) *Interim measure for bottom fishing activities subject to Conservation Measure 22–06 encountering potential vulnerable marine ecosystems in the Conservation Area*, both available online at http://www.ccamlr.org/en/measure-22–07–2013 (accessed 3 June 2014).
34 CCAMLR Conservation Measure 91–03 (2009) *Protection of the South Orkney Islands southern shelf*, available online at http://www.ccamlr.org/en/conservation-and-management/browse-conservation-measures (accessed 16 May 2014).
35 CCAMLR, *Report of the Twenty-Eighth Meeting of the Commission, CCAMLR-XXVIII 2009*, available online at http://www.ccamlr.org/en/system/files/e-cc-xxviii.pdf (accessed 1 June 2014) paras 7.1 to 7.19.
36 CCAMLR Conservation Measure 91–04 (2011) *General framework for the establishment of CCAMLR Marine Protected Areas*, available online at http://www.ccamlr.org/en/conservation-and-management/browse-conservation-measures (accessed 16 May 2014).
37 All CCAMLR Conservation Measures and their history are available online at http://www.ccamlr.org/en/conservation-and-management/browse-conservation-measures (accessed 1 June 2014).
38 National Oceanic and Atmospheric Administration (NOAA), *Ocean Facts*, available online at http://oceanservice.noaa.gov/facts/exploration.html (accessed 3 June 2014).

20

Ocean Acidification: Scientific Surges, Lagging Law and Policy Responses[*]

Katja Fennel and David L. VanderZwaag[**]

Introduction

The increasing acidity of the world's oceans, linked to elevated carbon dioxide levels in the atmosphere from anthropogenic CO_2 emissions, is capturing more and more scientific and political attention. The scientific literature has exploded with a fifteen-fold increase in the number of ocean acidification publications from 2004 to 2012[1] and the number of multi-national and national ocean acidification research projects are ever expanding.[2] The need to mitigate and adapt to ocean acidification has been highlighted in recent UN General Assembly resolutions,[3] and new Sustainable Development Goals drafted in 2014 include a specific political target to minimize and address the impacts of ocean acidification including through enhanced scientific cooperation.[4]

Getting a regulatory grip on ocean acidification has not been easy. No international agreement has been negotiated to specifically address ocean acidification.[5] A fragmented array of international agreements, documents and initiatives has emerged having relevance to climate change and ocean acidification.[6] International negotiation efforts for a new agreement by 2015 to control global greenhouse gas emissions have focused on the need to address climate change and rising atmospheric temperatures rather than ocean acidification.[7]

This chapter reviews both the scientific and international law and policy dimensions of ocean acidification. Part 1 highlights the surging scientific reality. After reviewing the basic chemistry of ocean acidification, it summarizes the extensive scientific information regarding biological effects and ecosystem-level responses and the numerous scientific uncertainties and information gaps still remaining. Part 2 surveys the international law and policy seascape relevant to ocean acidification and the lagging nature of the regulatory framework to date. Five global dimensions are described and assessed: the UN Convention on the Law of the Sea (LOSC);[8] the UN climate change regime; marine pollution control instruments; the Convention on Biological Diversity;[9] and relevant UN General Assembly resolutions and processes. The chapter concludes with thoughts on future directions for international law and policy responses to ocean acidification and a summary of key questions looming on the horizon. A review of regional,[10] national[11] and local responses[12] to ocean acidification is beyond the scope of this chapter.

Surging ocean acidification science

Ocean chemistry and "man's greatest geophysical experiment"

Ocean acidification most commonly refers to the long-term increase in ocean acidity caused by the ocean's uptake of anthropogenic carbon dioxide (CO_2) from the atmosphere, although the ocean's acidity can increase due to other processes as well, e.g. acid rain and decomposition of organic material. Since the industrial revolution human activities have led to the emission of roughly 590 Gt of carbon, primarily due to fossil fuel combustion and land use changes.[13] As a result atmospheric CO_2 has increased dramatically from a pre-industrial value of 280 parts per million by volume (ppmv) to 400 ppmv in 2014 with an accelerating rate.[14] By the year 2100 atmospheric CO_2 may reach levels of 900 ppmv unless CO_2 emissions are reduced dramatically.[15]

The ocean is taking up about 2 Gt of anthropogenic carbon per year.[16] Cumulatively the ocean has taken up a quarter to a third of anthropogenic CO_2[17] and is thus mitigating human-induced global warming; however, this massive uptake of CO_2 affects the ocean's chemistry. When CO_2 is taken up by the ocean it does not merely dissolve in seawater; instead most of the dissolving CO_2 reacts with water to form carbonic acid (H_2CO_3) which then dissociates to form bicarbonate ions (HCO_3^-), carbonate ions (CO_3^{2-}) and hydrogen ions (H^+).[18] The fraction of inorganic carbon that remains in the form of CO_2 molecules is referred to as aqueous CO_2. The combination of all inorganic carbon forms, i.e. aqueous CO_2, carbonic acid, carbonate ions and bicarbonate ions, is referred to as Dissolved Inorganic Carbon (DIC). Only the small fraction of aqueous CO_2 can be used directly by photosynthetic organisms.[19] The addition of anthropogenic CO_2 to the ocean shifts the equilibrium between aqueous CO_2, carbonate and bicarbonate such that the concentrations of CO_2, hydrogen and bicarbonate ions increase compared to preindustrial concentrations (the increase in hydrogen ions is synonymous with increasing acidity) while the concentration of carbonate ions decreases. These chemical reactions are well understood and quantified.

It is important to note that the uptake of anthropogenic CO_2 by the ocean (i.e. a net flux into the ocean) is the relatively small residual of much larger, spatially and temporally varying CO_2 fluxes into and out of the ocean (IPCC 2001 estimated that roughly 90 Gt C/yr are exchanged between ocean and atmosphere).[20] Some ocean regions are continuous sources of CO_2 to the atmosphere, e.g., the upwelling region in the eastern tropical Pacific Ocean where a combination of wind patterns and the Coriolis force exerted by earth's rotation leads to perpetual upwelling of deep ocean water that is supersaturated in DIC. Other regions are continuous sinks of atmospheric CO_2 or switch seasonally between acting as a sink and source. Switches between uptake and outgassing of CO_2 can be driven by local processes such as surface water cooling and warming (since the solubility of CO_2 is temperature-dependent) and photosynthetic production and respiration of organic matter (since CO_2 is consumed and produced by these processes, respectively) and by remotely driven changes in surface ocean pCO_2 such as variations in the horizontal import of high or low DIC waters by ocean currents. Ocean DIC concentrations increase in the vertical direction with increasing water depth, primarily because a portion of the organic matter that is produced by photosynthesis in the surface ocean sinks and is respired at depth by microbes that consume oxygen and produce CO_2. This process, referred to as the biological pump, contributes to the storage of inorganic carbon in the deep ocean.

The acidity of seawater refers to its concentration of hydrogen ions and is expressed in pH, defined as the negative logarithm of hydrogen ion concentration. Because of this convention a decrease in pH refers to an increase in acidity, and a change by one pH unit corresponds to a change in hydrogen ion concentration by a factor of 10. Solutions with pH values less than 7.0 are said to be acidic; solutions with pH values larger than 7.0 are alkaline. Surface ocean water is weakly alkaline with an average pre-industrial pH of 8.2. Surface water pH has already fallen to 8.1[21] which corresponds to an increase in surface ocean acidity by 26 per cent. By the year 2100, pH values are projected to drop to 7.8 or 7.9,[22] which would represent a doubling in acidity. While most of the surface ocean is still far from becoming truly acidic (pH < 7.0), the term acidification refers to the ongoing shift toward acidic conditions.

As mentioned above, an increase in acidity coincides with a decrease in carbonate ion concentration. Lowering of the carbonate ion concentration makes seawater more corrosive to calcium carbonate minerals, which are major building blocks of the shells and skeletons of many marine organisms. From the pre-industrial time to 2007 the solubility of calcium carbonate has increased by about 20 per cent and is projected to increase by another 40 per cent by the year 2100.[23]

The chemistry of ocean acidification as outlined above is well understood. Already more than 50 years ago the chemist Roger Revelle referred to the accelerating human CO_2 emissions as an unprecedented "large scale geophysical experiment" anticipating its fundamental effects on ocean chemistry.[24] There is observational evidence documenting ongoing trends in acidification from time-series stations in the open ocean.[25] These trends are consistent with the rate of increase in atmospheric CO_2. Hydrographic and biogeochemical properties have been measured at the Bermuda Atlantic Time-series Study (BATS) station, a site in the subtropical North Atlantic Ocean near Bermuda, since 1983 with more regular, monthly measurements beginning in 1988[26] and at the Hawaii Ocean Time-series (HOT) station in the subtropical Pacific Ocean near Hawaii since October 1988.[27] Surface ocean pCO_2 at these two stations is shown in comparison with atmospheric CO_2 in Figure 20.1. Acidity derived from these measurements is shown in Figure 20.2.

The time-series show recurring seasonal variations in atmospheric CO_2 (due to the seasonal greening of forests in the northern hemisphere) and in surface ocean pH and pCO_2 superimposed on a clear long-term trend.[28] The seasonal cycle in seawater pCO_2 and pH is largely driven by seasonal warming (cooling) of seawater, which decreases (increases) the solubility of CO_2 leading to outgassing (uptake) of CO_2 to (from) the atmosphere. The recurring seasonal pattern of planktonic photosynthesis and respiration of organic matter contributes also to the seasonal cycle in pH and pCO_2. Inter-annual differences occur at both the Hawaii and the Bermuda station due to various episodic events.[29] However, the trends of pCO_2 increase (1.91 and 1.89 ppm/yr at HOT and BATS, respectively) are consistent with the trend in atmospheric pCO_2 (1.87 ppm/yr after 1990).

The seasonal fluctuations and long-term trends in pH that are observed in open ocean waters are much smaller than those in coastal waters. For example, an 11-year record of high-resolution pH measurements obtained annually from late spring or early summer to late summer is available from Tatoosh Island at the coast of Washington State (USA) in the northeast Pacific Ocean.[30] At Tatoosh Island, pH exhibits a pronounced daily oscillation, substantial fluctuations over a range of longer timescales (days to seasons) and a clear long-term trend.[31] The daily cycle has a typical amplitude of 0.24 pH units; in other words, pH changes within 24 hours by more than twice the change that has occurred from preindustrial times to the present in the surface open ocean. The daily oscillation is due to the day-night cycle of photosynthesis (which consumes CO_2 thus increasing pH) in combination with continuous respiration (which produces CO_2 thus lowering pH). The seasonal pH fluctuations are more extreme, for example, in 2007 pH changed by more

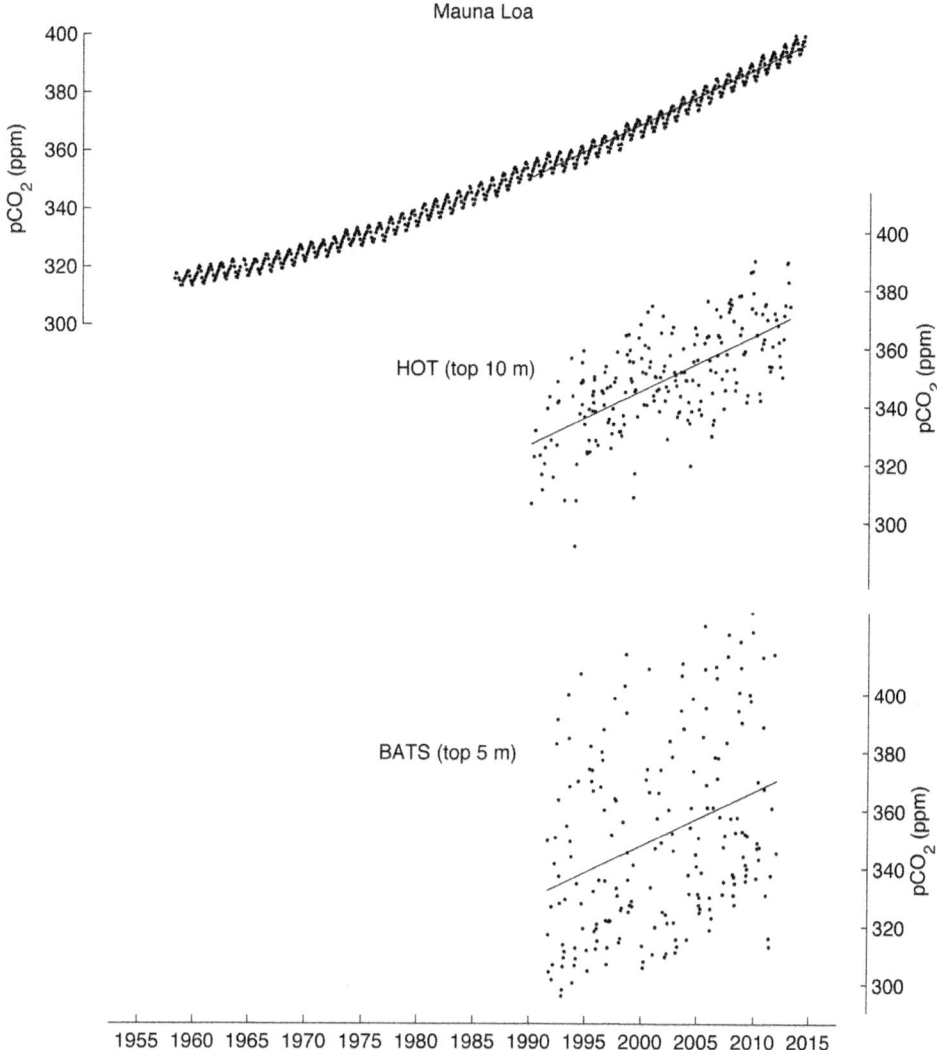

Figure 20.1 Atmospheric CO_2 concentrations measured at the Mauna Loa observatory in Hawaii from 1958 onward, and surface ocean concentrations of dissolved CO_2 (gas phase only in partial pressure) from the HOT station near Hawaii and the BATS station near Bermuda. Observations are shown as black dots; black lines indicate linear trends after 1990. Atmospheric pCO_2 increased by 1.87 ppm per year; surface ocean pCO_2 increased by 1.91 and 1.89 ppm per year at the HOT and BATS stations, respectively.

than 1 pH unit; this is more than twice the estimated pH change between preindustrial and year 2100 conditions in the surface open ocean. Superimposed on these signals is a long-term decline of 0.065 pH units per year[32].

The likely reason for the faster rate of acidification observed at the coast of Washington State is that it is an upwelling region where prevalent wind patterns lead to transport of carbon-rich, low-pH water from the deep ocean to the surface. The upwelling phenomenon combined with

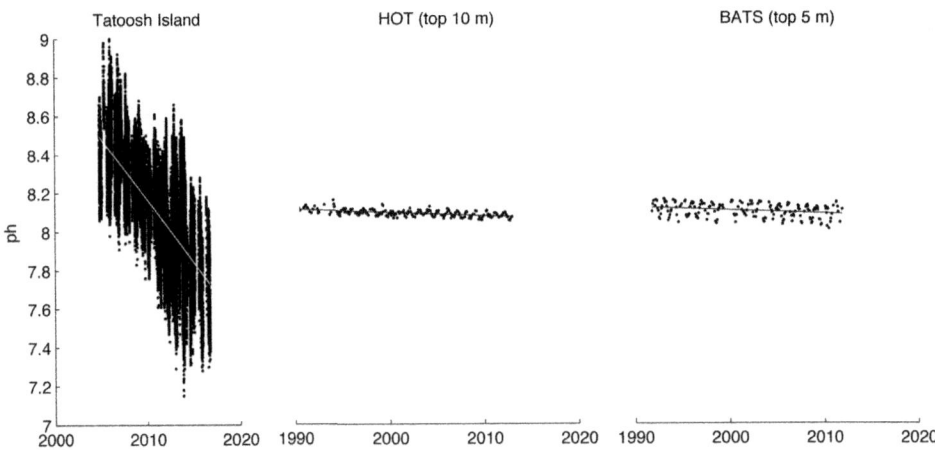

Figure 20.2 Ocean pH in surface waters at Tatoosh Island (left), at the HOT station near Hawaii (middle), and at the BATS station near Bermuda (right). pH measurements are shown as black dots; solid white and black lines indicate linear trends. At the two open ocean sites (HOT and BATS) pH is declining at a rate of 0.002 pH units per year. At Tatoosh Island (Washington State) pH is declining at a much faster rate of 0.065 pH units per year, and pH is exhibiting extreme fluctuations.[12]

the anthropogenic carbon addition to the ocean is making the coasts of Washington State, Oregon (USA) and British Columbia (Canada) more susceptible to acidification than subtropical and temperate open ocean regions. Other susceptible regions include coastal waters that are impacted by heavy nutrient loads from land (for example, the coastal northern Gulf of Mexico, which receives massive nutrient inputs from the Mississippi River)[33], subsurface oxygen minimum zones in the open ocean and the polar oceans.[34] Oxygen minimum zones and polar oceans have naturally elevated DIC and low pH because of accumulation of microbially respired carbon in the former and because cold water holds more CO_2 in the latter.

Biological effects of ocean acidification

Ocean acidification will affect marine organisms in a number of ways. Direct effects include changes in solubility of calcium carbonate (the material of shells and hard skeletons in many marine organisms), stimulation of photosynthesis due to increases in the concentration of aqueous CO_2 and bicarbonate ions, and disturbance of the acid-base balance of animals because many physiological processes require the pH in body fluids and within cells to be regulated within narrow limits. The direct effects may have repercussions far beyond changes in abundance of individual species, potentially leading to reorganizations of whole ecosystems and affecting the ocean's ability to export carbon through biological mechanisms.

Direct effects

Ocean acidification is expected to directly affect the process of calcification (the biologically mediated precipitation of calcium carbonate); hence, early studies have primarily focused on the responses of calcifying phytoplankton and invertebrate species (calcifying or calcareous organisms are those with calcium carbonate shells or skeletons). Examples include benthic invertebrates such as corals, clams, mussels, oysters, crabs, lobsters and sea urchins, and planktonic organisms such as coccolithophores and foraminifera. There are two common forms of calcium carbonate: aragonite, which is built by corals and many molluscs and is relatively soluble, and calcite, which is less soluble and built by coccolithophores, foraminifera and some molluscs. Acidification increases the solubility of these bio-minerals because fewer carbonate ions are available in solution.

Studies on corals have consistently shown decreasing rates of calcification when aragonite solubility increases following acidification.[35] In a study on two coral species Fine and Tchernov[36] have shown that corals can lose their skeletons completely in highly acidified water, but that the coral polyps remain healthy in a controlled environment and able to regrow their skeletons when exposed again to normal pH conditions. In natural coral reefs the naked polyps would be subject to predation and likely not viable for long. There are many other benthic invertebrates with calcareous parts, but responses to acidification have been studied only in a few. Examples include the study by Gazeau et al.,[37] which showed decreasing calcification rates in a mussel and an oyster species, and by Shirayama and Thornton,[38] which documented reduced shell growth in a gastropod and two sea urchin species following acidification. In addition to decreasing calcification rates, the early development of benthic invertebrates can be affected by acidification with reduced rates of fertilization success and development, and smaller larval sizes.[39] Although few calcareous organisms can tolerate pH that is significantly below present levels, there are exceptions. Tunnicliffe et al.[40] observed dense clusters of mussels near a deep ocean hydrothermal vent in the Mariana arc (western equatorial Pacific) where liquid CO_2 and hydrogen sulphide emerge from the vent. The vent fluids reduce pH in surrounding waters to between 5.4 and 7.3. Despite these acidic conditions the vent mussels are able to precipitate shells, albeit at reduced rates and with thinner shell walls indicating that calcification under these low pH conditions comes at a metabolic cost. Many studies have also found decreased calcification rates and thinner shells in the major calcareous plankton groups coccolithophores and foraminifera,[41] although there are exceptions as well. For example, Iglesias-Rodriguez et al.[42] found a significant increase in shell thickness of a coccolithophore under high CO_2, while its growth rate decreased.

The above examples illustrate that, for a variety of calcareous organisms, calcification rates are reduced following acidification, but the sensitivity to decreasing pH varies among species and some show the counterintuitive response of increased calcification. These complications arise because calcification is a biologically mediated process regulated by the organism to varying degrees. Organismal compensation and acclimation mechanisms affecting the calcification process are not sufficiently understood as of yet to explain the observed species-to-species differences.

Acidification is expected to increase rates of photosynthesis because the process uses aqueous CO_2 rather than the more abundant bicarbonate ions.[43] Aqueous CO_2 makes up only a small fraction of DIC, but this fraction increases with falling pH. Marine photosynthetic organisms (the most important of which are phytoplankton) have to expend energy on internally concentrating CO_2 at their sites of photosynthesis. With falling pH, photosynthesizers will have to spend less energy on concentrating CO_2 and photosynthetic rates should increase. Indeed this stimulating effect on photosynthesis has been shown to occur in a variety of phytoplankton species, but not all, and for natural plankton assemblages, although the effect is relatively small.[44] The stimulation of photosynthesis does not necessarily lead to increased rates of cell division; instead it appears to be limited to producing larger cells with more intracellular carbon relative to other elements.[45] In contrast to planktonic photosynthesizers, seagrasses consistently show dramatic increases in their photosynthetic rate when the concentration of aqueous CO_2 increases.[46]

Decreasing ocean pH may not only affect calcifying organisms but may also have detrimental effects on the survival, growth and reproduction of marine animals in general. For example, fishes require their blood pH to remain within tight limits. Disturbances of blood pH are known to impair oxygen transport by the circulatory system and thus the overall fitness of the animal. Information to date suggests that most marine fishes can effectively maintain their blood pH even at extreme ambient pH levels (regulation involves the excretion of acid primarily through gills but also kidneys and gut as compensatory mechanism)[47]. However, the energetic costs associated with pH regulation may impair other energy-demanding bodily functions such as swimming, immune defense, digestion, reproduction and growth, and thus overall fitness.[48] Responses of fishes to acidification will be species-specific. Most temperate fish species, including Atlantic cod,[49] appear to be well adapted to handle pH variations in ambient water.[50] A notable exception are two species of cardinal fish from a tropical coral reef which suffered a significant decrease in their capacity to swim and carry out other vital functions in response to decreasing pH levels.[51] Only a few species have been studied systematically in terms of their response to decreasing pH and detailed understanding of physiological compensation mechanisms is too limited at present to explain species-to-species differences and make projections about how fish will respond to acidification.

Ecosystem-level responses

As discussed above, ocean acidification will directly affect the physiology and growth of marine organisms in various ways. Acidification is also likely to alter biogeochemical processes with potential feedbacks on climate. The direct organismal responses to acidification will likely alter ecological relationships and trophic dynamics, which determine the flow of energy and nutrients through the marine food web. Changes in acidity affect different species differently, which will result in perturbations of individual ecosystem components that can have cascading effects across the food web. Major reorganizations of pelagic and benthic ecosystems may lie ahead, but projecting such ecosystem-level responses is extremely difficult because single-species laboratory experiments and multi-species mesocosm manipulations are not easily extrapolated to natural systems or the whole ecosystem, and because cascading effects are notoriously difficult to predict.

A slowdown of calcification may reduce the ability of calcifying organisms to compete with those that do not. Reductions in the abundance of those calcifying organisms that act as important trophic links (e.g. pteropods can be an important food source for Pacific salmon)[52] may interrupt feeding relationships and result in broad ecosystem responses. Loss of calcium carbonate structures in coral reefs, although not immediately fatal to corals in controlled environments, would remove their protective structures, making them susceptible to predation, and would remove the habitat of the whole, diverse reef community. Increased dissolution of calcium carbonate in the water column of the open ocean may decrease the ballasting of sinking organic matter, resulting in shallower re-mineralization and less efficient biological carbon export with potential feedbacks on climate.

Photosynthesis in planktonic ecosystems will likely be stimulated, but responses will almost certainly be species-specific with organisms thereby altering competitive relationships.[53] The elemental composition of photosynthetically produced organic matter will likely shift toward more carbon per atom of nitrogen, potentially lowering the food quality for consumers but possibly increasing the efficiency of biological carbon export. To date there is no solid observational evidence for acidification-induced species shifts in planktonic open-ocean ecosystems, which may in part be due to the fact that these systems are chronically under-sampled and, in part, because the changes may be subtle and hard to detect. Tatoosh Island is a rare example where community level shifts have been observed in an intertidal community and attributed to pH changes. More specifically, Wootton et al.[54] have shown that calcareous species performed poorly compared to non-calcareous species when pH was low.

The difficulty in projecting how ecosystems may reorganize is further complicated by the fact that marine species will adapt to changing environments to some degree. Ocean pH has varied over various timescales in the geological past, the massive carbon release during the Paleocene-Eocene Thermal Maximum (PETM) about 55 million years ago probably being the closest known analog to the present anthropogenic acidification.[55] Despite many similarities between the anthropogenic carbon release and the PETM, the latter is an imperfect analog to current changes because climatic and carbon cycle background conditions were different then (for example, the continental plate configuration was different and ice sheets on land were absent) and because carbon release was slower than the rate of the present anthropogenic release.[56] While the PETM can provide valuable information about the response of ocean carbon chemistry to a massive and sudden input of carbon,[57] responses of marine species and ecosystems are again difficult to infer given the limits of paleontological records. The potential for marine organisms to adapt to higher levels of CO_2 is presently not known.

In summary, the details and significance of ecosystem-level effects remain largely speculative. It is also important to note that ocean acidification is not the only stressor affecting marine ecosystems. Ocean warming and de-oxygenation will act synergistically with acidification.

Lagging law and policy responses

UN Convention on the Law of the Sea

Although LOSC was concluded in 1982 and thus predates global concerns over climate change and ocean acidification, the Convention contains general provisions that may be applicable to the threats of ocean acidification.[58] Pursuant to Article 192, States have the general obligation to protect and preserve the marine environment. States must also take all measures necessary to ensure that activities under their jurisdiction or control do not cause damage by pollution to other States and their environment (Art. 194(2)). States must further take necessary measures to protect and preserve rare or fragile ecosystems as well as the habitat of depleted, threatened or endangered species and other forms of marine life (Art. 194(5)). States must also adopt laws and regulations to prevent, reduce and control pollution from or through the atmosphere (Art. 212(1)).

The Convention's definition of pollution found in Article 1(4) appears broad enough to cover CO_2 emissions that are eventually absorbed into the oceans contributing to acidification.[59] Pollution is defined as the introduction by man, directly or indirectly of substances or energy into the marine environment which results in or is likely to result in deleterious effects, such as harm to living resources and hindrances to fishing and other legitimate uses of the sea.

The Convention also imposes a general environmental impact assessment responsibility that may be interpreted to cover proposed projects and activities at the national level that may contribute substantial CO_2 emissions and thus lead indirectly to ocean acidification. Article 206 requires States to undertake environmental impact assessments for planned activities under their jurisdiction or control that may cause substantial pollution or significant and harmful changes to the marine environment.

LOSC also contains aspirational provisions encouraging States to further develop global and regional standards to control pollution of the marine environment from various sources. Such standards are urged for land-based pollution (Art. 207), seabed activities (Art. 208) and atmospheric pollution (Art. 212). Article 211 requires the further development of international rules and standards to prevent and control vessel-source pollution. While the aspirational provisions do not specifically mention the control of pollutants contributing to ocean acidification, they offer a reminder of the need to address the multiple sources of marine pollution, for example, not just CO_2 emissions from ships but also from offshore petroleum operations and land-based burning of fossil fuels.

LOSC also contains dispute resolution procedures that might be used to place the legal spotlight on the failure of States to adequately address climate change and ocean acidification threats to the oceans.[60] Part XV of LOSC, establishing a rather complicated set of dispute settlement rules,[61] includes Article 297 which allows a case to be brought against a coastal State for contravening international rules and standards for the protection and preservation of the marine environment. The Convention also established the International Tribunal for the Law of the Sea (ITLOS) and ITLOS through its Rules of Procedure has opened the door for advisory opinions to be sought.[62] An advisory opinion has already been given on state responsibilities relating to deep-seabed mineral activities[63] and one could foresee a similar type of case being brought to seek advice as to state responsibilities to protect the marine environment from ocean acidification.

Whether future cases will be brought relating to climate change or ocean acidification remains highly doubtful. Adversarial litigation would depend on finding a plaintiff State willing to devote the time and money to contest the excessive CO_2 emissions of another State and major doctrinal hurdles would be faced including the need to establish a breach of an international legal obligation and to prove causation.[64] The breadth of ITLOS advisory opinion jurisdiction remains in question and the LOSC itself only explicitly bestowed a limited advisory role for ITLOS to address legal questions surrounding deep seabed activities (Art. 191).[65]

Climate change regime

The two global climate change agreements, the UN Framework Convention on Climate Change and the Kyoto Protocol, are obviously relevant to ocean acidification but in limited ways. Neither agreement mentions ocean acidification and their overall focus is on addressing the atmospheric aspects of climate change.[66]

The UNFCCC calls for the stabilization of greenhouse gas concentrations in the atmosphere at a level that would prevent dangerous anthropogenic interference with the climate system. Since climate system is defined broadly to cover "the totality of the atmosphere, hydrosphere, biosphere and geosphere and their interactions",[67] the need to consider ocean impacts of greenhouse gas emissions seems called for.[68] What constitutes dangerous interference is left open to interpretation.[69] The stabilization level for concentrations should allow ecosystems to adapt naturally, ensure food production is not threatened and allow economic development to proceed in a sustainable manner.[70]

The UNFCCC actually promotes the idea of enhancing the use of the oceans as sinks and reservoirs of greenhouse gases, including CO_2, which is the main contributor to ocean acidification.[71] Article 4(1)(d) requires Parties to promote and cooperate in the conservation and enhancement of sinks and reservoirs of all greenhouse gases not controlled by the Montreal Protocol, including forests, oceans and other coastal and marine ecosystems.

The Kyoto Protocol also displays substantial limitations as an avenue to address ocean acidification. The Protocol does not actually require reduction of CO_2 emissions. Industrialized countries listed in Annex I do have overall reduction targets for greenhouse emissions based on CO_2 equivalence,[72] but countries may choose not to give priority to reducing CO_2 emissions in favour of reducing emissions of one or more of the other five listed greenhouse gases: methane, nitrous oxide, hydrofluorocarbons, perfluorocarbons, and sulphur hexafluoride.[73] The Protocol does not require emission reductions for developing countries and key developed countries, including Japan, New Zealand and the Russian Federation, have not agreed to emission reductions for a second commitment period.[74] Canada and the United States are not Parties.[75]

The fifth assessment reports of the Intergovernmental Panel on Climate Change (IPCC), published in 2013–2014, have given increased attention to ocean acidification but policy-related advice remains quite weak. Working Group I, examining the physical science of climate change, highlighted the increase in carbon dioxide concentrations by 40 per cent since pre-industrial times with the ocean absorbing about 30 per cent of emitted anthropogenic CO_2, causing ocean acidification.[76] The decrease in pH of ocean surface water by 0.1 since the beginning of the industrial era was also noted corresponding to a 26 per cent increase in ocean acidity.[77] Working Group II, addressing impacts and adaptations to climate change, emphasized that for medium and high-emission scenarios, ocean acidification poses substantial risks to marine ecosystems, especially polar ecosystems and coral reefs.[78] The Working Group listed key adaptation options to reduce other stresses in an acidifying ocean environment, such as improving wastewater treatment and controlling overfishing.[79]

The IPCC's Working Group III, addressing mitigation of climate change, did not address ocean acidification specifically but emphasized the overall needs to reduce greenhouse gas emissions. To keep temperature change below 2°C relative to pre-industrial levels, the Working Group suggested the need for substantial GHG emission reductions, 40 to 70 per cent lower in 2050 than in 2010 and emission levels near zero or below by 2100.[80]

Negotiations for a post-Kyoto regime have not paid much attention to ocean acidification threats.[81] Political attention has been focused on obtaining enhanced commitments by countries to reduce GHG emissions but with a focus on controlling global temperature increases.[82] At the UN Climate Change Conference in Cancun in 2010, Parties agreed to a long-term goal of limiting global temperature increase to no more than 2°C above pre-industrial levels with a further review on the need for a strengthened goal (1.5°C) to be concluded by 2015.[83]

At the 2011 Climate Change Conference in Durban, countries agreed to launch a process to develop a protocol, another legal instrument or an agreed outcome with legal force applicable to all Parties. Negotiations are expected to be concluded in 2015 with entry into force and implementation in 2020.[84] Consideration of oceans and ocean acidification in the flurry of negotiations in the wake of the Durban decision has continued to lag.[85]

Marine pollution control instruments

Three marine pollution control instruments are especially relevant to ocean acidification. Two key international agreements are the 1996 Protocol to the London Convention,[86] which addresses ocean fertilization and its possible contribution to acidity increases, and the International Convention for the Prevention of Pollution from Ships (MARPOL)[87] which has partly addressed CO_2 emissions from ships. The Global Programme of Action for the Protection of the Marine Environment from Land-based Activities (GPA),[88] a legally non-binding document, is relevant for its supportive role in reducing the stresses from land-based marine pollution.

1996 Protocol to the London Convention

The 1996 Protocol, adopting a precautionary approach to ocean dumping where only wastes listed on a global "safe list" may be disposed of at sea,[89] is relevant to ocean acidification in two main ways. First, it addresses the potential sequestration of CO_2 into the ocean, for example, from offshore hydrocarbon operations. Sequestration of CO_2 into the seabed is one of the accepted disposal options under the Protocol.[90] Such sequestration would be subject to permit and waste assessment requirements.[91] Specific Guidelines for the Assessment of Carbon Dioxide for Disposal into Sub-Seabed Geological Formations, adopted in November 2012, flesh out various considerations that decision makers should evaluate when deciding whether to authorize seabed sequestration, for example, the availability of other disposal options, potential migration and leakage pathways and potential environmental effects of escaped carbon dioxide in the overlying water, including changes in pH.[92] The Protocol prohibits the sequestration of CO_2 into the water column.[93]

A second relevance of the Protocol is the placing of strict limitations on proposed ocean fertilization activities, another potential contributor to ocean acidification.[94] Through amendments to the Protocol, adopted in October 2013,[95] an ocean fertilization activity may only be considered for a permit if it is assessed as constituting legitimate scientific research, taking into account any specific placement assessment framework.[96] A new Annex 5 to the Protocol sets out details on how proposed ocean fertilization projects should be assessed and clarifies what constitutes legitimate scientific research.[97] Permits are only to be issued if an assessment determines that pollution of the marine environment is as far as practicable prevented or reduced to a minimum.[98] Additional geoengineering activities could also be subject to control under the Protocol if they are added to Annex 4.

MARPOL

Addressing CO_2 emissions from ships is another important component of the global fight against ocean acidification. The latest IMO study on GHG emissions from ships estimates that for the period 2007–2012, on average, shipping accounted for 3.1 per cent of annual global CO_2 emissions.[99] Maritime CO_2 emissions are projected to increase significantly in the coming decades with increases of 50 to 250 per cent predicted by 2050.[100]

The MARPOL Convention has only partly addressed the emission of carbon dioxide from ships. In July 2011 initial steps were taken to address GHG emissions from ships through amendments to Annex VI of MARPOL. A new Chapter 4 was added establishing energy efficiency requirements.[101] New ships will be obligated to meet Energy Efficiency Design Index (EEDI) requirements.[102] Each ship, including existing ships, will be required to develop a Ship Energy Efficiency Management Plan (SEEMP).[103]

Possible additional measures on GHG emissions have been controversial.[104] Tensions have arisen over whether a common but differentiated principle should apply in the shipping context. Debates have also occurred over whether market-based measures (MBM), for example, applying a levy on fossil fuel use and setting emission reduction targets should be adopted. The

IMOs Marine Environment Protection Committee at its May 2013 meeting agreed to suspend discussion of MBM issues to a future session.[105]

Global Programme of Action for the Protection of the Marine Environment from Land-based Activities (GPA)

The GPA is relevant to ocean acidification since it calls for the development and strengthening of national and regional programmes of action to prevent and control land-based sources of marine pollution.[106] Reducing land-based marine pollution is one of the key adaptation measures for responding to ocean acidification. Controlling the discharges of sewage and nutrients into the marine environment are two of the nine source categories targeted by the GPA and both sewage and nutrient discharges may enhance ocean acidification. The GPA's programme of work for 2012–2016 is focused on wastewater and nutrient management as two priorities in addition to marine litter.[107] Global partnerships have been formed to further address wastewater and nutrient pollution.[108]

However, the GPA has not effectively countered ocean acidification. CO_2 emissions are not listed as one of the nine source categories of land-based marine pollution to be addressed. The GPA might be described as "limping along" with substantial limitations. The GPA is a soft law document and has struggled with limited funding support.[109] There appears to be waning political support for GPA implementation.[110]

Convention on Biological Diversity

The CBD has been relevant to ocean acidification in four main ways.[111] First, the CBD has played a central role in tracking and summarizing the state of scientific knowledge on ocean acidification and its impacts on biodiversity. Two synthesis reports on the impacts of ocean acidification on marine biodiversity have been prepared, the first in 2009[112] and the second in 2014.[113]

A second CBD role has been to highlight the need for taking adaptation measures to counter ocean acidification. The CBD's Strategic Action Plan for Biodiversity 2011–2020, adopted through decision X/2 at the 10th Conference of the Parties in 2010,[114] sets out 20 "Aichi targets" with three particularly pushing for adaptation actions. Target 10 expressly mentions ocean acidification: "By 2015, the multiple anthropogenic pressures on coral reefs and other vulnerable ecosystems impacted by climate change or ocean acidification are minimized, so as to maintain their integrity and functioning."[115]

The other two targets important for adapting to ocean acidification are Target 6 and Target 11. Target 6 urges that by 2020 all fish and invertebrate stocks are managed sustainably and applying ecosystem approaches, so that overfishing is avoided and recovery plans and measures are in place for all depleted species.[116] Target 11 calls for at least 10 per cent of coastal and marine areas to be conserved through ecologically representative and well connected systems of protected areas and other effective area-based conservation measures by 2020.[117]

A third relevance of the CBD has been to emphasize the need for mitigation measures to counter climate change. For example, decision X/33, adopted at the 10th COP, calls for ecosystem approaches to mitigation, through such means as protection of natural forests, sustainable wetland management, and conservation of salt marshes and seagrass beds.[118]

A fourth role of the CBD has been to collect information on climate-related geo-engineering prospects and to encourage a precautionary approach to future geo-engineering projects. A technical and regulatory report on geo-engineering and potential impacts on biodiversity was published in 2012[119] and a further interim update was issued in 2014.[120] Through decision IX/16C in 2008, the Conference of the Parties called for a precautionary approach to ocean fertilization activities whereby such activities should not be allowed, except for small scale scientific research studies within coastal waters, until there is an adequate scientific basis for justification, and a global and effective regulatory mechanism to cover those activities.[121] Through decision XI/20 in 2012, the COP noted the lack of science-based, global, transparent and effective control and regulatory mechanisms for climate-related geo-engineering and the need for a precautionary approach to address future geo-engineering activities.[122] The COP also emphasized that climate change should be primarily addressed by reducing anthropogenic emissions of greenhouse gases and by increasing their removal by sinks.[123]

General Assembly resolutions and processes

UN General Assembly resolutions have also begun to address ocean acidification. For example, Resolution 68/70 on Oceans and Law of the Sea of December 2013 encourages States, international organizations and other relevant institutions to urgently pursue further research on ocean acidification and to increase national, regional and global efforts to address levels of ocean acidity and the negative impact of acidity on vulnerable marine ecosystems, particularly coral reefs.[124] The resolution expressed a General Assembly commitment to continue paying attention to ocean acidification and to take into account the first global integrated marine assessment and the ongoing work of the recently established Ocean Acidification International Coordination Centre of the International Atomic Energy Agency.[125]

The General Assembly's sustainable fisheries resolution of December 2013 also gave attention to ocean acidification.[126] The resolution urges States to intensify efforts to assess and address the impacts of global climate change and ocean acidification on the sustainability of fish stocks and their habitats.[127] The resolution emphasizes the importance of developing adaptive marine resource management strategies and enhancing capacity-building to implement such strategies so as to enhance the resilience of marine ecosystems to the impacts of ocean acidification.[128]

Processes occurring under the auspices of the UN General Assembly have also addressed ocean acidification. The UN Open-ended Informal Consultative Process on Oceans and Law of the Sea devoted its 14th meeting in June 2013 to the topic of ocean acidification, and the meeting emphasized the need to address the issue through both mitigation and adaptation.[129] Regarding mitigation, delegations stressed the principal mitigation measure must be reduction of CO_2 emissions but also noted the potential for other mitigation methods, such as carbon capture and storage.[130] The importance of reducing energy demands and developing renewable energy sources was also emphasized.[131] Regarding adaptation, the report of the meeting highlighted the need to reduce the multiple stressors on the marine environment including pollution, coastal erosion, destructive fishing practices and overfishing.[132] The importance of key management tools to assist with adaptation was noted, including environmental impact assessment, marine protected areas and marine spatial planning.[133]

Two other General Assembly related processes have also addressed ocean acidification. The UN Conference on Sustainable Development (2012) and its outcome document, 'The future we want', reiterated the need to work collectively to prevent further ocean acidification and called for enhanced international cooperation in marine scientific research, monitoring and observation of ocean acidification.[134] The Open Working Group on Sustainable Development Goals, established to develop a set of sustainable development goals for consideration and appropriate action by the General Assembly at its 68th session, in its 2014 outcome document includes a goal on conserving and sustainably using the oceans and marine resources for sustainable development.[135] One of the targets under the goal is to minimize and address the impacts of ocean acidification, including through enhanced scientific cooperation at all levels.[136]

Conclusion: future directions and key questions

Negotiating a new international agreement to specifically address ocean acidification has been suggested by various authors as a possible future course,[137] but prospects do not look good due to various factors. They include the lack of a political champion and most importantly the presence of existing international fora, described above, that have or are beginning to address ocean acidification.[138]

The main global response route for curbing ocean acidification is obviously pursuant to the UNFCCC regime.[139] While the extent to which CO_2 emissions will be further mitigated under the UNFCCC regime remains uncertain as negotiations for a new post-Kyoto agreement are still ongoing, future ways forward stand out that could be realized through a new agreement and/or a COP decision. First might be the adoption of a pH level target for the oceans.[140] The setting of a global average temperature target of not going above 2°C from pre-industrial levels establishes a type of precedent. However, getting international agreement on the appropriate pH level or range might be difficult in light of the highly variable nature of ocean acidity locally and regionally.[141] Setting a reasonable minimum pH level is further complicated by inertia in the global carbon system (even if CO_2 emissions were halted completely, ocean pH would continue to fall for at least decades). A second future course might be the establishment of a fund or giving funding priority under the climate change framework to support States in conserving critical coastal sinks for carbon, including mangroves, saltmarshes and seagrass beds.[142] UNEPs Blue Carbon report has already called for the protection of at least 80 per cent of such areas.[143] Perhaps the most straightforward and effective measure would be to set a CO_2 atmospheric level benchmark that would address both climate change and ocean acidification concerns.[144]

Future steps to address ocean acidification will have to extend on many fronts beyond the UNFCCC regime. The CBD will certainly continue to be an important international venue for further synthesizing scientific knowledge on the impacts of ocean acidity on marine biodiversity and for further raising, through CBD decisions relating to marine and coastal diversity, the need for mitigative and adaptive actions.[145] Reducing the multiple stressors on marine ecosystems, such as overfishing, deoxygenation and pollutants, are key adaptation strategies needing implementation at both regional and national levels.[146]

Numerous law and policy questions loom on the horizon. Key questions at the global level include:

- Should the GPA be strengthened to better address climate change and ocean acidification?
- Should the world community move from a 'soft law' approach towards land-based marine pollution to a legally binding treaty?[147]
- Should the CBD target of protecting 10 per cent of marine areas by 2020 be substantially raised in light of the need to adapt to ocean acidification?

- Will there be further need to regulate marine geo-engineering proposals beyond ocean fertilization projects?[148]
- What role should UN General Assembly resolutions play in further addressing ocean fertilization acidification?

At the regional level, key questions include:

- Are regional fisheries management organizations (RFMOs) and regional sea programmes adequately responding to the threats of ocean acidification and will they do so in the future?[149]
- To what extent might ocean acidification be mitigated at the regional level?
- Will governance arrangements in polar regions be up to the task of addressing the serious threats of ocean acidification in polar waters?[150]

Questions also abound at the national level. For example:

- Is there sufficient political, financial and human resource support for scientific research relating to ocean acidification?
- Are national CO_2 mitigation commitments and implementation efforts adequate in light of climate change and ocean acidification threats?
- What are the national adaptation implications of ocean acidification for fisheries management, aquaculture development and regulation, pollution standards, marine species at risk protection and marine protected area establishment?[151]

One thing is clear about the future regulation of human activities that contribute to ocean acidification and the degradation of marine ecosystems. It will remain a work in progress for decades to come. Mitigation not adaptation must be the global mantra. The work has hardly begun.

Notes

* This chapter attempts to be accurate as of 15 September 2014.
** The authors would like to acknowledge the research assistance of Emily Adams, JD candidate (2015), Schulich School of Law, and the research support of the Marine Environmental Observation Prediction and Response Network (MEOPAR), based at Dalhousie University and funded by the Government of Canada's Networks of Centres of Excellence Program. The support of the Social Sciences and Humanities Research Council of Canada is also gratefully acknowledged.
1 The number of peer-reviewed papers grew from 18 in 2004 to 356 in 2012. Secretariat of the Convention on Biological Diversity, *An Updated Synthesis of the Impacts of Ocean Acidification on Marine Biodiversity*, UNEP/CBD/SBSTTA/18/INF/6 (19 June 2014), p. 16.
2 For a detailed review, see ibid., pp. 16–18.
3 See section 'General Assembly resolutions and processes' below.
4 Target 14.3 as agreed to by the Open Working Group on Sustainable Development Goals in its *Outcome Document* (2014), submitted for consideration by the 68th session of the UN General Assembly. Available <http://www.sustainabledevelopment.un.org> (accessed 7 September 2014).
5 M. Simons and T. Stephens, 'Ocean acidification: addressing the other CO_2 problem', *Asia Pacific Journal of Environmental Law* 12, 2009, 1-19.
6 A. Proelss and M. Krivickaite, 'Marine biodiversity and climate change', *Carbon & Climate Law Review* 4, 2009, 437–445; Y. Downing, 'Ocean acidification and protection under international law from negative effects: a burning issue amongst a sea of regimes?', *Cambridge Journal of International and Comparative Law* 2, 2013, 242–273.

7 G. Galland, E. Harrould-Kolieb and D. Herr, 'The ocean and climate change policy', *Climate Policy* 12, 2012, 764–771.
8 United Nations Convention on the Law of the Sea, 10 December 1982, 1933 U.N.T.S. 3.
9 June 5, 1992, 1760 U.N.T.S. 79.
10 For a review of regional efforts to study and address ocean acidification, including for polar regions with the Arctic Council's 2013 *Arctic Ocean Acidification Assessment* being central, see T. Stephens, 'Ocean acidification', in R. Rayfuse (ed.), *Research Handbook on International Marine Environmental Law*, Cheltenham, UK; Edward Elgar, forthcoming 2015, chapter 20 and D. Herr, K. Isensee and C. Turley, 'Ocean acidification: Overview of the international policy landscape and activities on ocean acidification', *White Paper*, Gland Switzerland: IUCN, 2013.
11 For reviews of how climate change and ocean acidification might be addressed at the national and sub-national levels in the United States, see R.P. Kelly and M.R. Caldwell, 'Ten ways states can combat ocean acidification (and why they should)', *Harvard Environmental Law Review* 37 (2013), 57–103 and J. Thaler and P. Lyons, 'The seas are changing: it's time to use ocean-based renewable energy, the public trust doctrine, and a green thumb to protect seas from our changing climate', *Ocean and Coastal Law Journal* 19, 2014, 241–296.
12 J. Gupta, K. Van Der Leeuw and H. De Moel, 'Climate change: a 'global' problem requiring 'glocal' action', *Environmental Science* 4(3), 2007, 139–148; C. Turley and J.P. Gattuso, 'Future biological and ecosystem impacts of ocean acidification and their socioeconomic-policy implications', *Current Opinion in Environmental Sustainability* 4, 2012, 278–286; and R.P. Kelly et al., 'Mitigating local causes of acidification within existing laws', *Science* 332, 2011, 1036–1037.
13 C. Le Quéré et al., 'Global carbon budget 2013', *Earth Systems Science Data* 6, 2014, 235–263. The authors estimate that between 1750 and 2012 385±20 Gt C were emitted due to fossil fuel burning and cement production and 205±70 Gt C due to land use changes.
14 Figure 20.1.
15 D.P. van Vuuren et al., 'The representative concentration pathways: an overview', *Climatic Change* 109, 2011, 5–31. See representative concentration pathways 8.5.
16 Le Quéré et al., 'Global carbon budget 2013', 235–263.
17 C.L. Sabine and T. Tanhua, 'Estimation of anthropogenic CO_2 inventories in the ocean', *Annual Review of Marine Science*, 2, 2010, 175–198.
18 R.E. Zeebe and Wolf-Gladrow, CO_2 *in Seawater: Equilibrium, Kinetics, Isotopes*, Amsterdam: Elsevier Oceanography Series, Vol. 65, 2001, pp. 346.
19 J.R. Reinfelder, 'Carbon concentrating mechanisms in eukaryotic marine phytoplankton', *Annual Review of Marine Science* 3, 2011, 291–315.
20 IPCC Third Assessment Report 'The scientific basis', 2001. Chapter 3, p. 188.
21 J.-P. Gattuso and H. Lavigne, 'Technical note: approaches and software tools to investigate the impact of ocean acidification', *Biogeoscience* 6, 2009, 2121–2133.
22 J.C. Orr et al., 'Anthropogenic ocean acidification over the twenty-first century and its impact on calcifying organisms', *Nature* 437(7059), 2005, 681–686.; L. Bopp et al., 'Multiple stressors of ocean ecosystems in the 21st century: projections with CMIP5 models', *Biogeosciences* 10, doi:10.5194/bg-10-6225-2013, 2013, 6225–6245.
23 Gattuso and Lavigne, 'Technical Note', 2121–2133.
24 R. Revelle and H.E. Suess, 'Carbon dioxide exchange between atmosphere and ocean and the question of an increase of atmospheric CO_2 during the past decades', *Tellus* 9, 1957, 18–27.
25 Figure 1.
26 N.R. Bates, 'Interannual variability of the oceanic CO_2 sink in the subtropical gyre of the North Atlantic Ocean over the last 2 decades', *Journal of Geophysical Research* 112, C09013, doi:10.1029/2006JC003759, 2007.
27 J.E. Dore et al., 'Physical and biogeochemical modulation of ocean acidification in the central North Pacific', *Proceedings of the National Academy of Sciences* 106(30), 2009, 12235–12240.
28 Figures 20.1 and 20.2.
29 Dore et al., 'Physical and biogeochemical modulation of ocean acidification in the central North Pacific' 12235–12240; Bates, 'Interannual variability of the oceanic CO_2 sink in the subtropical gyre of the North Atlantic Ocean over the last 2 decades'.
30 J.T. Wooton, C.A. Pfister and J.D. Forester, 'Dynamical patterns and ecological impacts of changing ocean pH in a high-resolution multiyear dataset', *Proceedings of the National Academy of Sciences* 105,

2008, 18848–18853; J.T. Wooton and C.A. Pfister, 'Carbon system measurements and potential climatic drivers at a site of rapidly declining ocean pH', *PLoS ONE* 7(12), e53396, doi:10.1371/journal.pone.0053396, 2012.
31 Figure 20.2.
32 Figure 20.2.
33 W.-J. Cai et al., 'Acidification of subsurface coastal waters enhanced by eutrophication', *Nature Geoscience* 4, 2011, 766–770.
34 Orr et al., 'Anthropogenic ocean acidification over the twenty-first century and its impact on calcifying organisms', 681–686; M. Steinacher et al., 'Imminent ocean acidification in the Arctic projected with the NCAR global coupled carbon cycle-climate model', *Biogeosciences* 6, 2009, 515–533.
35 S.C. Doney et al., 'Ocean Acidification: The Other CO_2 Problem', *Annual Review of Marine Science* 1, 2009, 169–192.
36 M. Fine and D. Tchernov, 'Scleractinian coral species survive and recover from decalcification', *Science* 315, 2007, 1811.
37 F. Gazeau et al., 'Impact of elevated CO_2 on shellfish calcification', *Geophysical Research Letters* 34, L07603, doi: 10.1029/2006GL028554, 2007.
38 Y. Shirayama and H. Thornton, 'Effect of increased atmospheric CO2 on shallow water marine benthos', *Journal of Geophysical Research* 110, C09S08, doi:10.1029/2004JC002618, 2005.
39 H. Kurihara and Y. Shirayama, 'Effects of increased atmospheric CO_2 on sea urchin early development', *Marine Ecology Progress Series* 274, 2004, 161–169.
40 V. Tunnicliffe et al., 'Survival of mussels in extremely acidic waters on a submarine volcano', *Nature Geoscience* 2, 2009, 344–348.
41 U. Riebesell et al., 'Reduced calcification of marine plankton in response to increased atmospheric CO_2,', *Nature* 407, 2000, 364–367; J. Bijma, H.J. Spero, and D.W. Lea, 'Reassessing foraminiferal stable isotope geochemistry: impact of the oceanic carbonate system (experimental results)', in G. Fischer and G. Wefer (ed.) *Use of Proxies in Paleoceanography: Examples from the South Atlantic*, Springer-Verlag, 1999, pp. 489–512; J. Bijma, B. Hönisch and R.E. Zeebe, 'Impact of the ocean carbonate chemistry on living foraminiferal shell weight: comment on "Carbonate ion concentration in glacial-age deep waters of the Caribbean Sea" by W.S. Broecker and E. Clark', *Geochemistry, Geophysics, Geosystems* 3(11), 2002, 1064.
42 M.D. Iglesias-Rodriguez et al., 'Phytoplankton calcification in a high CO_2 world', *Science* 320, 2008, 336–340.
43 U. Riebesell and P.D. Tortell, 'Effects of ocean acidification on pelagic organisms and ecosystems', in J.-P. Gattuso and L. Hansson (eds.) *Ocean Acidification*, Oxford: Oxford University Press, 2011, pp. 99–121.
44 Ibid.
45 I. Zondervan, B. Rost and U. Riebesell, 'Effect of CO_2 concentration on the PIC/POC ratio in the coccolithophore *Emiliania huxleyi* grown under light-limiting conditions and different daylengths', *Journal of Experimental Marine Biology and Ecology* 272, 2002, 55–70.
46 S. Palacios and R.C. Zimmerman, 'Response of eelgrass *Zostera marina* to CO_2 enrichment: possible impacts of climate change and potential for remediation of coastal habitats', *Marine Ecology Progress Series* 344, 2007, 1–13.
47 S.F. Perry and K.M. Gilmour, 'Acid-base balance and CO_2 excretion in fish: unanswered questions and emerging models', *Respiratory Physiology & Neurology* 154, 2006, 199–215.
48 F. Melzner et al., 'Physiological basis for high CO_2 tolerance in marine ectothermic animals: pre-adaptation through lifestyle and ontogeny?', *Biogeoscience* 6, 2009, 2313–2331.
49 F. Melzner et al., 'Swimming performance in Atlantic Cod (*Gadus morhua*) following long-term (4–12 months) acclimation to elevated sea water pCO_2', *Aquatic Toxicology* 92, 2009, 30–37.
50 H.-O. Pörtner et al., 'Effects of ocean acidification on nektonic organisms', in J.-P. Gattuso and L. Hansson (eds.) *Ocean Acidification*, Oxford: Oxford University Press, 2011, pp. 154–175.
51 P.L. Munday, N.E. Crawley and G.E. Nilsson, 'Interacting effects of elevated temperature and ocean acidification on the aerobic performance of coral reef fishes', *Marine Ecology Progress Series* 388, 2009, 235–242.
52 J.L. Armstrong et al., 'Distribution, size, and interannual, seasonal and diel? food habits of northern Gulf of Alaska juvenile pink salmon, *Oncorhynchus gorbuscha*', *Deep-Sea Research Part II: Topical Studies in Oceanography* 52, 2005, 247–265.

53 Riebesell and Tortell, 'Effects of ocean acidification on pelagic organisms and ecosystems', pp. 99–121.
54 J.T. Wooton, C.A. Pfister and J.D. Forester, 'Dynamical patterns and ecological impacts of changing ocean pH in a high-resolution multiyear dataset', *Proceedings of the National Academy of Sciences* 105, 2008, 18848–18853.
55 J.P. Kennett and L.D. Stott, 'Abrupt deep-sea warming, palaeoceanographic changes and benthic extinctions at the end of the Palaeocene', *Nature* 353, 1991, 225–229.
56 R.E. Zeebe, 'History of Seawater Carbonate Chemistry, Atmospheric CO_2, and Ocean Acidification', *Annual Review of Earth and Planetary Sciences* 40, 2012, 141–165.
57 Ibid.
58 Herr, Isensee and Turley, 'Ocean acidification: Overview', p. 8.
59 V. Gonzalez, 'An Alternative Approach for Addressing CO_2-Driven Ocean Acidification' *Sustainable Development Law & Policy* 12, 2011, 45, 69.
60 D. Bialek and J. Ariel, 'Ocean acidification: international legal avenues under the UN Convention on the Law of the Sea' in M.B. Gerrard and G.E. Vannier (eds.) *Threatened Island Nations: Legal Implications of Rising Seas and a Changing Climate*, Cambridge: Cambridge University Press, 2013, pp. 473–529.
61 D.R. Rothwell and T. Stephens, *The International Law of the Sea*, Oxford and Portland, Oregon: Hart Publishing, 2010, pp. 439–460.
62 ITLOS, Rules of the Tribunal, Art. 138. The provision states that the Tribunal may give an advisory opinion on a legal question if an international agreement related to the purpose of the Convention specifically provides for the submission to the Tribunal of a request for such an opinion.
63 *Responsibilities and obligations of States sponsoring persons and entities with respect to activities in the Area*, Advisory Opinion, 1 February 2011, ITLOS Reports 2011, p. 10. Case No. 17, available <http://www/itlos.org> (accessed 4 September 2014).
64 Bialek and Ariel, 'Ocean Acidification', pp. 510–516; M. Burkett, 'Legal rights and remedies', in M.B. Gerrard and K. Fisher Kuh (eds.) *The Law of Adaptation to Climate Change: U.S. and International Aspects*, Chicago: American Bar Association, 2012, pp. 815–846.
65 Bialek and Ariel, 'Ocean acidification', pp. 524–527.
66 Simons and Stephens, 'Addressing the other CO_2 problem', pp. 1–19.
67 UNFCCC, Art. 1(3).
68 Simons and Stephens, 'Addressing the other CO_2 problem', p. 7.
69 On the difficulty of interpretation with both scientific and normative considerations, see Intergovernmental Panel on Climate Change (IPCC) Working Group III, *Climate Change 2014: Mitigation of Climate Change* (2014), chapter 1, p. 124, available <http://www.ipcc.ch> (accessed 12 September 2014).
70 UNFCCC, Art. 2.
71 R. Baird, M. Simons and T. Stephens, 'Ocean Acidification: A Litmus Test for International Law', *Carbon and Climate Law Review* 3 (2009) 459–471.
72 Article 3(1) of the Protocol establishes an overall commitment to reduce GHG emissions by at least 5 per cent below 1990 levels in the commitment period 2008–2012, while Annex B of the Protocol sets out quantified emission limitation or reduction commitments for individual countries.
73 T. Stephens, 'Warming waters and souring seas: climate change and ocean acidification', in D.R. Rothwell, K.N. Scott, A.G. Oude-Elferink and T. Stephens (eds.) *The Oxford Handbook of the Law of the Sea*, Oxford: Oxford University Press, forthcoming 2015, chapter 34.
74 IPCC Working Group III *Mitigation of Climate Change*, chapter 13, p. 1043.
75 UNFCCC, 'Status of ratification of the Kyoto Protocol', available <http://unfccc.int> (accessed 5 September 2014).
76 IPCC Working Group I, 'Summary for policymakers', in T.F. Stoker et al. (eds.) *Climate Change 2013: The Physical Science Basis*, Cambridge: Cambridge University Press, 2013, p. 11.
77 *Ibid.* p. 12.
78 IPCC Working Group II, 'Summary for policymakers', in C.B. Field et al. (eds.) *Climate Change 2014: Impacts, Adaptation, and Vulnerability*, Cambridge: Cambridge University Press, 2014, p. 17.
79 *Ibid.*, p. 27.
80 IPCC Working Group III, *Mitigation of Climate Change*, 'Summary for Policymakers', pp. 10–11.
81 E.R. Harrould-Kolieb and D. Herr, 'Ocean acidification and climate change: synergies and challenges of addressing both under the UNFCCC', *Climate Policy* 12, 2012, 378–389.
82 Galland, Harrould-Kolieb and Herr, 'The ocean and climate change policy', pp. 764–771.

83 The Cancun Agreements: Outcome of the Work of the Ad Hoc Working Group on Long-term Cooperative Action under the Convention, Decision 1/CP.16 (2010).
84 Decision 1/CP.17, Establishment of an Ad Hoc Working Group on the Durban Platform for Enhanced Action (2011).
85 Galland, Harrould-Kolieb and Herr, 'Ocean and climate change policy', p. 766.
86 1996 Protocol to the Convention on the Prevention of Marine Pollution by Dumping of Wastes and other Matter, 7 November 1996, 36 I.L.M. 1 (1997).
87 IMO, *MARPOL Consolidated Edition 2011*, London: IMO, 2011.
88 UNEP (OCA)/LBA/IG.2/7 (5 December 1995).
89 D.L. VanderZwaag and A. Daniel, 'International Law and Ocean Dumping: Steering a Precautionary Course Aboard the 1996 Protocol, but Still an Unfinished Voyage', in A. Chircop, T.L. McDorman and S.J. Rolston (eds.) *The Future of Ocean Regime Building: Essays in Tribute to Douglas M. Johnston*, Leiden: Martinus Nijhoff, 2009, 515–550; A. Sielen, 'The new international rules on ocean dumping: promise and performance', *Georgetown International Environmental Law Review* 21, 2009, 295–336.
90 Amendments, adopted in November 2006, include sub-seabed sequestration of CO_2 as one of the permitted disposals allowed under Annex 1 to the Protocol. IMO, 'New international rules allow storage of CO_2 under the seabed' (2007), <http://www.imo.org> accessed 4 September 2014.
91 Annex 2 of the Protocol sets out detailed waste assessment requirements that must be weighed before ocean dumping permits may be granted and this includes consideration of waste management options and assessment of potential environmental effects.
92 2012 Specific Guidelines for the Assessment of Carbon Dioxide for Disposal into Sub-Seabed Geological Formations, LC 34/15, annex 8, 2 November 2012.
93 Under Annex 1 of the Protocol only seabed sequestration is allowed.
94 For example, fertilizing the ocean with iron facilitates the uptake of CO_2 which may increase ocean acidity. D.L. VanderZwaag, 'Ocean dumping and fertilization in the antarctic: tangled legal currents, sea of challenges', in P.A. Berkman, M.A. Lang, D.W.H. Walton and O.R. Young (eds.) *Science-Diplomacy: Antarctica, Science, and the Governance of International Spaces*, Washington DC: Smithsonian Institution Scholarly Press, 2011, pp. 245–252.
95 IMO, *Report of the Thirty-fifth Consultative Meeting and the Eighth Meeting of Contracting Parties*, LC 35/15 Annex 4, 21 October 2013. For a review of the amendments *see* P. Verlaan, 'New regulation of marine geo-engineering and ocean fertilization', *The International Journal of Marine and Coastal Law* 28, 2013, 729–736.
96 Paragraph 1.3 of a new Annex 4 to the Protocol. *Ibid.*
97 For example, key considerations include whether the proposed activity is subject to scientific peer review and whether there is any financial and/or economic gain arising directly from the experiment or its outcomes. Ibid., Annex 5, para. 8.
98 Ibid., Article 6*bis*.
99 IMO, *Third IMO GHG Study 2014*, MEPC 67/INF. 3 (25 July 2014), p. 13.
100 *Ibid.*, pp. 17–18.
101 Marine Environment Protection Committee (MEPC), *Report of the Marine Environment Protection Committee on Its Sixty-Second Session*, MEPC 62/24/ Add. 1, (26 July 2011) Annex 19.
102 *Ibid.*, Regulation 21.
103 *Ibid.*, Regulation 22.
104 D.L. VanderZwaag, 'The IMO and arctic marine environmental protection: tangled currents, sea of challenges' in O.R. Young, J.D. Kim and Y.H. Kim (eds.) *The Arctic in World Affairs: A North Pacific Dialogue on Arctic Marine Issues, 2012 North Pacific Arctic Conference Proceedings*, Seoul, Korea: Korea Maritime Institute and Honolulu, Hawaii at East West Center, 2012, pp. 99–128, pp. 113–114.
105 MEPC, *Report of the Marine Environment Protection Committee on Its Sixty-Fifth Session*, MEPC 65/22 (24 May 2013), para. 5.1.
106 GPA, para. 19 and 31.
107 UNEP, *Report of the third session of the Intergovernmental Review Meeting on the Implementation of the Global Programme of Action for the Protection of the Marine Environment from land-based Activities*, UNEP/GPA/I6R.3/6 (26 January 2012), Annex, Manila Declaration, para. 5.
108 GPA, 'Global Wastewater Initiative', available <http://www.gpa.unep.org/index.php/global-wastewater-initiative> (accessed 11 September 2014 and GPA, 'Global Partnership on Nutrient Management',

available <http://www.gpa.unep.org/index.php/global-partnership-on-nutrient-management> (accessed 11 September 2014).
109 D.L. VanderZwaag and A. Powers, 'The protection of the marine environment from land-based pollution and activities: gauging the tides of global and regional governance', *The International Journal of Marine and Coastal Law* 23, 2008, 423–452, 439–440.
110 *Ibid.*, 438.
111 For a further review of the Convention's roles, see Herr, Isensee and Turley, 'Ocean acidification: overview', pp. 9–10.
112 Secretariat of the CBD, *Scientific Synthesis of the Impacts of Ocean Acidification on Marine Biodiversity*, CBD Technical Services No. 46, Montreal, 2009.
113 Secretariat of the CBD, *An Undated Synthesis of the Impacts of Ocean Acidification on Marine Biodiversity*, CBD Technical Series No. 75, Montreal 2014.
114 COP 10 decision X/2, 'Strategic Plan for Biodiversity 2011–2020' (2010).
115 *Ibid.*, Annex, para. 13.
116 *Ibid.*
117 *Ibid.*
118 COP 10 decision X/33, 'Biodiversity and Climate Change' (2010), para. 8(A).
119 Secretariat of the CBD, *Geoengineering in Relation to the Convention on Biological Diversity: Technical and Regulatory Matters*, CBD Technical Series No. 66, Montreal, 2010.
120 CBD Secretariat, *Interim Update of Information on the Potential Impacts of Climate Geoengineering on Biodiversity and the Regulatory Framework Relevant to the Convention on Biological Diversity*, UNEP/CBD/SBSTTA/18/INF5 (22 May 2014).
121 COP decision IX/16 'Biodiversity and Climate Change', (2008) part C, para. 4.
122 COP 11 decision XI/20 'Climate – related geoengineering', (2012) para. 8.
123 *Ibid.*, para. 4.
124 A/RES/68/70, 'Oceans and the law of the sea' (adopted on 9 December 2013), para. 153.
125 *Ibid.*, para. 156.
126 A/RES/68/71, 'Sustainable fisheries including through the 1995 Agreement for the Implementation of the Provisions of the United Nations Convention on the Law of the Sea of 10 December 1982 relating to the Conservation and Management of Straddling Fish Stocks and Highly Migratory Fish Stocks, and related Instruments' (adopted on 9 December 2013).
127 *Ibid.*, para. 5.
128 *Ibid.*, para. 157.
129 UNGA, *Report on the Work of the United Nations Open-ended Informal Consultative Process on Oceans and the Law of the Sea at its fourteenth meeting*, A/68/159 (17 July 2013).
130 *Ibid.*, para. 15.
131 *Ibid.*
132 *Ibid.*, para. 16.
133 *Ibid.*
134 A/RES/66/288, 'The future we want' (adopted on 27 July 2012), para. 166.
135 Open Working Group on Sustainable Development Goals, *Outcome Document* (2014), goal # 14, available <http://www.sustianabledevelopment.un.org> (accessed 7 September 2014).
136 *Ibid.*, target 14.3.
137 *See* González, 'An alternative approach for addressing CO_2-driven ocean acidification' (suggesting an ocean acidification instrument under the UN Convention on the Law of the Sea) and R.E. Kim, "Is a new multilateral agreement on ocean acidification necessary?', *Review of European Community & International Environmental Law* 21, 2012, 243–258.
138 Simons and Stephens, 'Addressing the other CO_2 problem', p. 19.
139 Stephens, 'Ocean Acidification.'
140 Harould-Kolieb and Kerr, 'Ocean acidification and climate change', p. 383; Stephens, 'Warming waters and souring seas.'
141 For a suggestion to establish an ocean acidification target based on the global mean saturation state of aragonite, a form of calcium carbonate that becomes more soluble as the acidity of seawater rises, see J. Rockström et al. 'A safe operating space for humanity', *Nature* 46, 24 September 2009, 472–475. A saturation state of 2.75 is proposed compared to a current status of 2.90 and a pre-industrial value of 3.44. *Ibid.*, p. 473.

142 D.E.J. Currie and K. Wowk, 'Climate change and CO_2 in the oceans and global oceans governance', *Carbon & Climate Law Review* 4, 2009, 387–404, 403.
143 C. Nellemann et al. (eds.), *Blue Carbon: A Rapid Response Assessment*, UNEP, GRID-Arendal, 2009, p. 8.
144 Stephens, 'Warming waters and souring seas.'
145 COP 10 decision X/29 (2010) on marine and coastal diversity already raised serious concerns over increasing ocean acidification (para. 64) and called on Parties to incorporate emerging knowledge into national biodiversity strategies and action plans and into national and local marine / coastal management plans (para. 67).
146 R. Kundis Craig, 'Marine Biodiversity, Climate Change, and Governance of the Oceans', *Diversity* 4, 2012, 224–238 and IGBP, IOC, SCOR, *Ocean Acidification Summary for Policymakers – Third Symposium on the Oceans in a High-CO_2 World*, Stockholm, Sweden: International Geosphere-Biosphere Programme, 2013.
147 For arguments in favour of a new global agreement, see D. Hassan, *Protecting the Marine Environment from Land-Based Sources of Pollution: Towards Effective International Cooperation*, Burlington, VT, Ashgate Publishing Company, 2006.
148 For example, buffering the global ocean with limestone looms as a possibility, although the huge amounts required represent a major constraint. See, *20 Facts about Ocean Acidification* (November 2013), available <http://www.whoi.edu/filesaver.do?id=165564&pt=2tp=150429> (accessed 11 September 2014).
149 On the difficulties RFMOs have faced in managing fisheries in a sustainable manner even without the complications of climate change and ocean acidification, see D.A. Russell and D.L. VanderZwaag, *Recasting Transboundary Fisheries Management Arrangements in Light of Sustainability Principles: Canadian and International Perspectives*, Leiden, Martinus Nijhoff, 2010.
150 T. Stephens and D.L. VanderZwaag, 'Polar oceans governance: shifting seascapes, hazy horizons', in T. Stephens and D.L. VanderZwaag (eds.), *Polar Oceans Governance in an Era of Environmental Change*, Cheltenham, UK; Edward Elgar, 2014, pp. 1–17.
151 For a review of the numerous adaptation implications of climate change and ocean acidification in the United States, see P. Parenteau, 'Species and ecosystem impacts', in Gerrard and Fisher Kuh, *The Law of Adaptation*, pp. 307–349.

21
Use of Technology in Maritime Regulation and Enforcement

Chris Rahman

The *United Nations Convention on the Law of the Sea* (*LOSC*) codified maritime regulatory and enforcement powers and the limits to those powers.[1] Enforcement power is dependent in any particular instance upon jurisdiction. Jurisdiction is inherently technology neutral, yet the *LOSC* was agreed in 1982 only after decades of international negotiations. The most intense negotiating period occurred during the 1970s. However, that period represents an entirely different technological context to that of today. Rapid developments in areas such as miniaturization, digitization, communications technologies and advanced materials over the past four decades have considerably altered the realm of what is technologically possible, including in the domain of the oceans. The application of technology for maritime regulation and enforcement consequently has burgeoned. The *LOSC* fundamentals regarding maritime jurisdiction, on the other hand, have remained static, even though the law of the sea, more broadly viewed, has slowly evolved. This has led to a situation in which a growing gap has appeared between what is technologically possible and that which is permissible under the constraints of extant international law.

This chapter demonstrates how a growing number of technology applications have emerged for both maritime regulation and enforcement. To illustrate the trend it particularly focuses on technologies used for vessel tracking and emissions reductions. Before beginning that discussion, a distinction needs to be made, in the context of technology applications, between maritime regulation, on the one hand, and enforcement, on the other. It is also important to reiterate the problem that whilst enforcement-enabling technologies have multiplied in their availability and potential application, the enforcement powers enjoyed by States remain bounded by the international law framework on jurisdiction which applies within each maritime zone.[2]

Regulation versus enforcement

The distinction employed here treats regulation as those rules involving the prescription of technology applications which apply to activities conducted within the maritime domain, inclusive of the land-sea interface, especially ports. For the purpose of this chapter enforcement involves the use of technological means to enable or undertake an enforcement action at sea. Compliance activities, such as inspections carried out by port State control officers to ensure that

Chris Rahman

prescribed equipment is being carried and is in good working order, thus fall outside of the enforcement scope of this chapter. Although it could be argued that detaining a ship under port State control powers is a form of enforcement rather than a compliance activity, the approach used here is to limit the treatment of enforcement to technologies which contribute to at-sea enforcement operations.

Much of the regulatory framework that applies in the maritime domain is based on treaties negotiated between States, and the legislation consequently enacted by States Parties to those agreements which give effect to treaty provisions. Such treaty arrangements may be bilateral, regional or global in character. In addition, different layers of government and other domestic regulatory authorities, such as port authorities in some countries, may develop their own regulations pertaining to matters over which they have jurisdiction. Many maritime regulations, whether domestic or international in origin, have a technological component. The prescription of technology applications is particularly common in the International Maritime Organization (IMO) conventions that regulate international shipping, and in monitoring, control and surveillance (MCS) systems for the management of fisheries, whether at sub-national, national or regional levels. However, technological aspects of maritime regulation are becoming widespread, more generally, as the technical options available to regulatory authorities proliferate and costs of their application decline. As will be demonstrated below, such applications often involve specific prescribed technologies, but can also follow a more general prescription for the development of sometimes unspecified technological solutions to fulfil a regulatory requirement.

Technology can also play a significant role in maritime enforcement. This may be a consequence of regulatory requirements for the use of a particular technology application, or simply due to the utility of certain technologies for enforcement operations. In the former case, good examples are regulations requiring devices to be carried by vessels to enable their identification and tracking, such as vessel monitoring systems (VMS) prescribed by fisheries management authorities or devices mandated for regulated classes of vessel under Chapter V of the *International Convention for the Safety of Life at Sea* (*SOLAS*).[3] In the latter case, any relevant technological means could be used in the process of maritime enforcement, whether or not those technologies are prescribed by regulation.

The next section elaborates on these distinctions by examining a number of examples of each type of technology application. The structure employed to do this will address, first, examples of regulations that prescribe the application of specific technologies; second, regulations that promote the application of non-specified technologies to achieve regulatory goals; and third, the use of technology in maritime enforcement. Lastly, it will conclude by commenting on some *LOSC* implications of technology developments in the enforcement realm.

Regulation of specific technologies

Regulation that requires the application of specific technologies has become increasingly common. The sections below focus on examples of technology applications for the common general purpose of vessel tracking in the fisheries management sector and the *SOLAS* realm of merchant ship safety, security and marine environmental protection. All sources of vessel tracking have come to be viewed as an increasingly important aspect of national maritime security and regional and international 'good order at sea,'[4] particularly in the post-9/11 international security environment. Vessel tracking is an essential element of the different information sources which contribute to maritime situational awareness, itself an essential component of maritime domain awareness (MDA); a term now in common use to describe comprehensive knowledge of all things at, or related to, the sea.[5]

VMS

VMS are an important MCS tool for fisheries management authorities. The relevant authorities could be national or sub-national depending on the jurisdictional context of a particular fishery.[6] In the case of a regional fisheries management organization (RFMO), States may cooperate to establish a coordinated regional VMS system for high seas areas (i.e., areas beyond coastal State jurisdiction) related particularly to highly-migratory species such as tuna;[7] an example of which is the scheme operated in the western and central Pacific by the Western and Central Pacific Fisheries Commission (WCPFC).[8] The need for such a system was driven by the decline of fish stocks due to a growing demand for fish, in a context of the relative ineffectiveness of traditional enforcement measures against illegal, unreported and unregulated (IUU) fishing activity. Development of fisheries VMS was thus viewed as a cost-efficient way to improve the effectiveness of limited enforcement assets.[9] The first VMS scheme was implemented by Portugal in 1988,[10] and VMS use has burgeoned globally since that time.

Each VMS system may differ in detail, but the fundamental elements are functionally equivalent. Fisheries VMS schemes commonly work as satellite-enabled monitoring systems, although, in principle, other technical means could be employed.[11] Each licensed fishing boat or support vessel regulated by a fisheries management authority is required to carry a communications device variously called either an automatic location communicator (ALC) or mobile transceiver unit (MTU).[12] The ALC/MTU is required, at a minimum, to provide a vessel's identity, position, and time and date of position automatically via a satellite at intervals established by the relevant authority. The reporting interval is commonly set as one hour but could be less or more frequent. A typical VMS arrangement would allow for a variable rate of polling by the management authority, including an option for on-demand polling of regulated, VMS-equipped boats. There are a number of mobile communications service satellite providers that can be used, and typically each regulator sets ALC/MTU type approval standards and may publish a list of approved devices.[13] Due to the commercially sensitive nature of the information, as the location of fishing activity connotes the location of valuable fish, it is communicated in a strictly secure and confidential manner to the receiving station of the management authority.

Fisheries management authorities stipulate which vessels must carry such a device. For example, New Zealand requires that, in waters under its jurisdiction, *inter alia*, foreign licensed fishing vessels, foreign-owned New Zealand fishing vessels, registered fish carriers, New Zealand fishing vessels over 28 metres in length and New Zealand fishing vessels under 28 metres in length used to fish in certain specified fisheries, are required to carry an ALC.[14] A compliant ALC for a New Zealand-regulated boat must transmit the following information:[15]

- ALC identification (which cannot be altered by the user)
- Date and time of position
- Latitude and longitude of position
- Speed of position
- Heading at time of position
- Type/event of position.

The use by some fisheries management authorities of enhanced MTUs (E-MTUs) to transmit catch and effort (for example, number of days fishing) data via VMS is also growing. An E-MTU device is an MTU capable of two-way communication, messaging and the transmission of electronic forms, which requires both a message display and a keyboard or other device with which to input data.[16] Such increased functionality creates an opportunity to potentially incorporate and transmit other data sets via VMS, although, as with catch or effort data, such information would need to be manually inputted by the vessel operator. This leaves open the possibility of fraud and manipulation by operators unless data can be matched with other MCS tools to ensure full compliance.

Beyond VMS: other electronic technologies for fisheries MCS

Increasingly, fisheries management authorities are promulgating regulations that require ever greater reporting and monitoring requirements. For example, in the United States the National Marine Fisheries Service (NMFS) increasingly requires near real-time reporting of species-specific catch data for both target stock and bycatch species.[17] The use of electronic means to accomplish required monitoring can potentially be far more efficient and cost effective than, for example, on-board observers, paper-based data filings and dockside monitoring. Such technologies also may facilitate greatly enhanced fish stock assessments.[18] Authorities in the United States and elsewhere therefore view the adoption of new electronic technologies as a means by which improved data collection for better fisheries monitoring and compliance can affordably be achieved, and effected in a more timely and accurate manner than at present. The NMFS issued a policy directive to this end in 2013. In addition to VMS, it notes other technology solutions as comprising electronic logbooks, video cameras and other technologies for electronic monitoring (EM) and electronic reporting.[19]

In Australia, the Australian Fisheries Management Authority (AFMA) has conducted EM trials for a decade. In 2009–2010 a pilot project was carried out with a leading commercial developer of fisheries EM systems, the Canadian company Archipelago Marine Research (AMR), in the tuna and billfish fishery off the east coast of Australia.[20] This involved equipping ten fishing vessels with an AMR system. The system comprised four closed circuit television cameras, a Global Positioning System receiver to provide vessel location, location times and vessel track information, a control centre housed in the wheelhouse to monitor sensors, record data and provide a system display, and two different types of sensors to detect and record fishing activity. When these sensors detected the activation of fishing equipment, video recording was automatically triggered. A satellite transceiver modem was also included to send via satellite an hourly status message when EM systems were powered, involving vessel location, activity and the system's health status. Both sensor and image data were recorded directly onto hard drives.[21] Each hard drive could last for approximately three months and then would require swapping, with the used drive sent to AFMA for data analysis.[22] The project concluded that, although some compliance costs, such as the need for in-port inspections were unchanged, others, such as the need for sea patrols in a fishery employing EM-equipped fishing boats may be reduced. Stock data assessment and other scientific information was improved through the use of EM systems. Most significantly, it was found that observer costs were cut by 80 per cent.[23] Observers are also inherently limited in number, but EM systems could be carried by all boats licensed to fish in any particular fishery. The trial has led to AMR being awarded a substantial contract to provide EM services in particular Australian fisheries.

There are limitations to such systems, though, including the fact that communications bandwidth constraints mean that near real-time monitoring of video streams is not currently viable. Nor are EM systems currently linked directly to VMS, although greater integration of MCS technologies may be a sphere ripe for future development.

AIS

The ship automatic identification system (AIS) was adopted in 2000 as part of regulation 19 of Chapter V of *SOLAS*; the chapter which deals with safety of navigation.[24] AIS was originally intended to be fitted to *SOLAS*-regulated merchant ships to function as a collision avoidance device, a mechanism via which a coastal State can collate data on ships and their respective cargoes, and as a traffic management tool for shore-based vessel traffic services (VTS).[25] However, following the terrorist attacks of 9/11 the utility of vessel tracking technologies for maritime security became obvious and, as a result, a 2002 *SOLAS* Conference shortened the original AIS implementation deadline to 31 December 2004. The AIS regulation requires all ships of 300 gross tonnes or above engaged on international voyages, ships of 500 gross tonnes and above not engaged on international voyages, and all passenger ships irrespective of tonnage to carry a compliant AIS device.[26]

Warships and other vessels owned or operated by governments are not required to carry AIS, although many individual governments do require such ships to be equipped with the system. Furthermore, the *SOLAS* regulation also doesn't apply to other types of vessel that fall outside of the application of the convention, such as fishing boats, small leisure craft and other small vessels. Some coastal States, however, do require the wider application of AIS for vessels or waters over which they have jurisdiction. For example, the United States amended its AIS carriage rules in January 2015, increasing the scope of their application. Under the revised regulations the list of vessels required to carry AIS in most navigable US waters was expanded to include, *inter alia*, all self-propelled vessels of 65 feet (c.20 metres) or more in length engaged in commercial service, not just those engaged on international voyages as previously had been the case. Most notably the regulation now encompasses fishing boats, which previously had been excluded. It also applies to self-propelled dredging vessels when engaged in dredging in circumstances where navigation of other vessels could be affected, and vessels carrying certain dangerous cargoes and bulk flammable or combustible liquids. However, the new regulations do allow certain classes of vessel, including regulated fishing boats, to carry a US Coast Guard-certified AIS Class B device rather than the standard *SOLAS*-mandated Class A unit.[27] Class B AIS units are a cheaper version of AIS, with lesser capability and functionality.[28]

The wider adoption of AIS is likely to continue beyond *SOLAS*-regulated vessels. For example, in the southwest Pacific, the Pacific Islands Forum Fisheries Agency (FFA), a multinational cooperative body which assists its 17 member States to manage and control their respective tuna fisheries, has issued a circular advising that all foreign fishing vessels applying for Good Standing on the FFA Vessel Register – a prerequisite for being allowed to fish in member States' waters – must from 1 July 2015 be outfitted with AIS.[29]

AIS equipment must be able to automatically provide information on the ship, including its identity, type, position, course, speed and navigational status, to other ships, aircraft and shore stations so equipped to receive the data, and to be able to receive AIS information from other AIS-equipped ships. A ship's AIS equipment must be able to track other ships and monitor their navigational status, and exchange data with onshore facilities.[30] The IMO does not require ships to be equipped with manufacturer-specific units, but has promulgated AIS performance standards which, although implemented on a voluntary basis, should nevertheless be followed to ensure compliance with the regulation and system effectiveness. Guidelines on the operational use of AIS also have been established. The performance standards require that the installed system be capable of automatically and continuously providing information, as well as being able to function in an 'assigned' mode in which a competent authority such as a VTS operator can set the transmission interval, and a 'polling' mode in which information is transferred on interrogation from a competent authority or another ship.[31] A compliant system should provide four categories of information: static, dynamic, voyage-related, and short safety-related messages.[32] The categorized information sent by ships under the regulation is reproduced below:

1. *Static*
   - Maritime Mobile Service Identity (MMSI)
   - Call sign and name
   - IMO Number
   - Length and beam
   - Type of ship
   - Location of position-fixing antenna
2. *Dynamic*
   - Ship's position with accuracy indication and integrity status
   - Position Time stamp in coordinated universal time
   - Course over ground
   - Speed over ground
   - Heading
   - Navigational status (e.g., 'underway by engines,' 'at anchor' etc.)
   - Rate of turn
   - Angle of heel (optional)
   - Pitch and roll (optional)
3. *Voyage-related*
   - Ship's draught
   - Hazardous cargo (type: e.g., dangerous goods, harmful substances, marine pollutants; as required by the competent authority)
   - Destination and estimated time of arrival
   - Route plan (waypoints: optional at the master's discretion)
4. *Short safety-related messages*

Static information is set on installation. Dynamic information is mostly updated automatically via connections to the ship's position sensor, heading sensor and gyro, except for navigational status information, which is entered and updated manually. Voyage-related data is entered manually at the outset of a voyage and updated as required. And short safety-related messages are entered manually when required.[33] The system transmits the information by very high frequency (VHF) radio broadcasts. A Class A AIS device generally comprises VHF transmitters and receivers, antennas, a central processing unit, a position-fixing system, display and keyboard, and interfaces with shipborne sensors, radar and other electronic navigation systems.[34]

Ships' automatic identification systems are expected to be operational at all times other than in circumstances in which navigational information needs to be protected.[35] This can occur, for example, if a ship's master perceives that the ship may be endangered by a particular threat, such as pirates in possession of their own AIS device or with access to near real-time

Use of Technology

AIS information. Access to such information can be useful to pirates or to potential maritime terrorists, as it enables specific targets to be chosen, located, tracked and attacked. The security risks of freely available AIS data was raised at the IMO,[36] but the nature of the technology as an open broadcast system makes this issue difficult to overcome. Moreover, in the case of ships navigating through areas targeted by Somali pirates, the advice by multinational security forces and industry groups has been for ships to leave AIS turned on throughout the designated High Risk Area.[37]

Thus, despite its utility, AIS nonetheless has a number of shortcomings, including lack of confidentiality due to its open broadcast design, and the range limitations of VHF, which under usual circumstances equate to the range to the horizon, or approximately 20 nautical miles; at least until the advent of satellite AIS services. But in the immediate aftermath of the 9/11 attacks there was a considerable push by certain States to expand the ability to identify and track ships over much longer distances. The result was the adoption in 2006 of a new *SOLAS* regulation,[38] regulation 19–1 on long-range identification and tracking (LRIT), which was to be fully implemented in 2009. Although the regulation itself simply establishes a legal framework for the secure and confidential accessing and sharing of vessel identity, position and time of position data rather than specifying a particular technology solution, the technology currently employed uses a satellite system for communications between ships and their flag State's LRIT Data Centre, plus a complex system of information sharing between Data Centres via the International LRIT Data Exchange.[39]

An alternative to LRIT which is unconstrained by *SOLAS* regulation 19–1's complicated and restrictive data sharing protocols, is to use space-based AIS receivers on Low Earth Orbit satellites.[40] This technology is now in widespread use and, although satellite AIS services are relatively expensive, it can provide more or less global coverage without the data access encumbrances of LRIT.

Regulation and non-specific technologies

In this next category of regulation, unspecified technology solutions may be available as a means of compliance. In the following examples, technologies typically must achieve a particular regulatory objective, but particular technological solutions are not prescribed. Rather, the technological solution to a regulated objective or standard can be a matter of choice, albeit in most cases requiring approval by the regulatory authority.

Californian vessel emissions controls

In 2006 a major plan to improve air quality throughout California's South Coast Air Basin was initiated. The region represents the second largest urban area in the United States, with some of that nation's worst air quality indicators. The activities of the leading ports were found to be major contributors to the air pollution problem. Therefore, the Port of Long Beach and the Port of Los Angeles, in collaboration with the South Coast Air Quality Management District, the California Air Resources Board (CARB) and the U.S. Environmental Protection Agency (EPA), developed the San Pedro Bay Ports Clean Air Action Plan (CAAP) to drastically reduce harmful emissions from port-related activities. The primary motivation is to lessen public health risks generated by air pollutants from port-related activities; most notably nitrogen oxides (NO_x), sulphur oxides (SO_x), and diesel particulate matter (PM). The reduction of greenhouse gas emissions is a secondary rationale for the initiative, but not the determinative factor.[41]

Based on 2001/2002 baseline emissions inventories it was determined that port-related activities were responsible for 12 per cent of PM, 9 per cent of NO_x and 45 per cent of SO_x emissions in the South Coast Air Basin area.[42] Of those port-related emissions percentages, ocean-going vessels were responsible for 59 per cent of PM, 36 per cent of NO_x and 90 per cent of SO_x emissions; while harbour craft were responsible for 11 per cent of PM, 13 per cent of NO_x and 6 per cent of SO_x emissions.[43] The remainder of the ports' emissions inventory is generated by land-based equipment such as rail locomotives, trucks and other heavy vehicles, and cargo handling equipment, none of which are strictly 'maritime' in the context of this Handbook and thus will not be discussed further.

The CAAP involves a suite of measures, including CARB regulations, new emissions standards, improved fuel standards and voluntary measures such as the Vessel Speed Reduction Program, which relies on financial incentives and port facility lease conditions when shipping company leases come up for renegotiation, to encourage ship operators to reduce vessel transit speeds when approaching or departing port, rather than regulation.[44] The focus of this section, though, is on two CARB regulatory controls which invoke the adoption of technological solutions as one method of regulatory compliance.

The first of these involves the reduction of ocean-going vessel 'hotelling'-derived emissions, that is, those emissions generated due to a ship's electricity needs when it is at berth. The 2007 CARB regulation seeks to slash PM and NO_x emissions produced by the auxiliary diesel engines of container ships, passenger vessels (i.e., cruise ships), and refrigerated cargo vessels whilst docked at berth in Californian ports.[45] The primary means to achieve this reduction involves switching the power source from on-board generation to shore-based power from the terrestrial electricity grid. However, not all ships are suited to using shore power and, in some cases, the shore-based infrastructure is not available. In such cases the regulation allows for the use of 'alternative control technologies' as a means of at-berth emissions reduction, defined as 'technologies, techniques, or measures that reduce the emissions of NO_x and PM from an auxiliary diesel engine other than shutting down the engine.'[46] The regulation doesn't specify which alternative technology should be used, only the standards of emissions reduction that should be achieved: set at a 10 per cent reduction from baseline emissions by 31 December 2011, 25 per cent by the end of 2013, 50 per cent by the end of 2016, 70 per cent by the end of 2019 and 80 per cent from 1 January 2020.[47] It does note, however, that alternative control technologies may be emissions tested periodically to verify compliance, inclusive of selective catalytic reduction and shore-based systems.[48]

The 2010 CAAP update further explains that alternative technologies can include exhaust gas scrubbers, including in combination with selective catalytic reduction, dockside portable systems that utilize LNG as the power source, and shore-based electrical pumps to reduce on-board pumping loads for tankers.[49] There may be grounds to question the efficacy, or at least maturity, of some alternative technologies, however; with a proposed second phase of CARB regulations for vessels not currently regulated, cancelled, due to the lack of cost-effective or commercially-available alternative technology options.[50]

The second CARB regulation applies to harbour craft.[51] Although 'harbour craft' is defined widely, the regulation itself applies primarily to tugboats and towboats, and to ferries and excursion boats; but all harbour craft operating in regulated Californian waters and within 24 nautical miles of the Californian baseline are required to meter engine use. In order to reduce NO_x and PM emissions regulated harbour craft are required to adopt federal EPA marine diesel engine standards, applied variously both to new and in-use vessels, and may require engine replacement with a compliant unit and/or the adoption of a diesel emission control strategy. Such a strategy may include the application of technologies or devices such as diesel oxidation catalysts, selective catalytic reduction or PM filters.[52] Operators of harbour craft also have the option of applying alternative control of emissions methods as long as those alternatives meet equivalent emissions reduction standards, and could employ a range of measures, including unspecified technology applications, *inter alia*, to modify engines or for exhaust treatment.[53] As guidance, CARB has produced a list of U.S. EPA-compliant engine solutions that also comply with the Californian regulation.[54]

The CAAP also initiated a Technology Advancement Plan in 2007 to evaluate new technologies that may be applied to fulfil existing measures or meet future regulatory standards.[55]

MARPOL Annex VI

Revised regulations in the *International Convention for the Prevention of Pollution from Ships (MARPOL), Regulations for the Prevention of Air Pollution from Ships* (Annex VI),[56] which impose stricter NO_x and SO_x controls, including fuel sulphur limits, also provide for the application of unspecified technologies as alternatives to the regulated solutions to reducing emissions from ships. The specific provisions are regulation 3.2, *Exceptions and Exemptions* (Trials for Ship Emission Reduction and Control Technology Research), and regulation 4, *Equivalents*.

Under regulation 3.2 the Administration of a State Party to Annex VI may issue an exemption from specific provisions of the Annex, which allows a particular ship to conduct trials of emissions reduction and control technologies and new engine designs. Such an exemption is only supposed to be approved if the application of parts of the Annex or the revised NO_x Technical Code 2008 could impede such research and development programmes. Exemption permits are only to be provided to 'the minimum number of ships necessary,' albeit without specifying what would constitute a minimum number, and they are to be time limited depending on the ship's engine cylinder displacement. Permits may be renewed, however.[57]

As one example of regulation 3.2 in action, in 2013 the U.S. Coast Guard and EPA approved a request from the American cruise ship company, Carnival Corporation, to undertake a trial programme for 32 ships which would exempt them from the fuel sulphur requirements of the North American and Caribbean Emission Control Areas (ECAs).[58] The ECA concept is built into Annex VI, whereby Parties may propose the designation of an ECA to further limit the impact of NO_x, SO_x and PM emissions on the populations of cities and coastal areas.[59] The IMO Marine Environmental Protection Committee (MEPC) has designated four ECAs: the North American area, which applies to specific parts of U.S., Canadian and French waters adjacent to both the Pacific and Atlantic/Gulf coasts of North America and the eight main Hawaiian islands, designated in March 2010; the United States Caribbean Sea area, around Puerto Rico and the U.S. Virgin Islands, designated in July 2011[60]; the Baltic Sea; and the North Sea. The North American ECA encompasses waters up to 200 nautical miles from relevant U.S., Canadian and French territory coasts,[61] while the Caribbean ECA extends approximately 50 nautical miles from the Puerto Rican and U.S. Virgin Island territorial sea baselines.[62] Neither ECA extends into the jurisdiction of any other State.

The American ECAs' fuel sulphur standard from January 2015 is 0.1 per cent sulphur (1000 ppm), compared to the current global standard of 3.5 per cent. The Carnival exemption requires the company to meet or exceed the 2015 standard by the use of its proposed technological solution of the installation of advanced exhaust gas cleaning systems for the 32 specified ships.[63] The company has developed and trademarked the first technology solution to apply shore-based applications to ships, named ECO Exhaust Gas Cleaning (ECO-EGC™), which combines the use of filters to reduce PM, with the use of sea water in a scrubbing process which removes sulphur compounds from ships' exhaust gases. The system is operable in any ship operating mode. The company has indicated that it will spend up to US$400 million to equip its ships with ECO-EGC™ including retrofitting some existing ships, as well as the system's integration into new builds. Carnival has extended its programme from that agreed with US authorities for 32 ships, to encompass over 70 vessels, or more than 70 per cent of their entire fleet.[64]

Under regulation 4 the Administration of a Party to Annex VI may allow alternatives to compliance methods required by the Annex as long as such alternatives are no less effective in attaining the required emissions reductions.[65] Technological solutions are likely to be a major focus in the search for alternatives. In the case of Annex VI regulation 14 on SO_x and PM, guidelines have been adopted by the MEPC on standards for exhaust gas cleaning systems, which could be employed as alternatives to the normal compliance methods under regulation 4.[66] In order to do so, under regulation 4.2, an Administration must communicate details of such arrangements to the IMO for further circulation. As an example of how this works in practice, The Bahamas Maritime Authority, as the flag State, notified the IMO Secretary-General in 2012 that *Liberty of the Seas*, a cruise ship owned by Royal Caribbean International, had been fitted with an exhaust gas cleaning system approved under the 2009 guidelines (MEPC.184(59)), with attached Certificate of Conformity issued by classification society, Det Norske Veritas.[67]

Technology and enforcement

Technology is an important enabler for maritime enforcement. The focus of this section is on those technologies used for at-sea enforcement of suspected offending vessels, although enforcement doesn't necessarily need to be carried out at sea. For example, in the hypothetical case of a pollution incident caused by a ship only discovered long after the ship has departed the scene of the offence, different vessel tracking and surveillance technologies can be used retrospectively in an attempt to analyze historical data to pinpoint which ship or ships were situated in a particular location at a particular time as the basis for further investigation. Historical vessel track data is collected by many authorities and vessel tracking service providers. In the case of LRIT, the Data Centre of each flag State is expected to store all LRIT information transmitted to them by ships flying their flag.[68] Investigations based on historical data may not be easy, however, due to the need to provide evidence sufficient for a successful prosecution, or if the suspect ship has left the jurisdiction of the coastal State in question.

This section will provide an overview of a number of vessel tracking and surveillance technologies that can be employed to enable enforcement actions. Such technologies are essential unless an offence serendipitously occurs in the presence of an enforcement asset, which generally would be unusual; for the oceans are vast, and enforcement vessels limited in number and geographical coverage. Therefore, tracking and surveillance are usually essential in identifying potential offenders for the tasking of surface enforcement assets. The technological solutions used for this purpose may be prescribed by regulation, especially vessel tracking solutions such as the VMS, AIS and LRIT requirements described above. Such systems are often referred to as 'cooperative' as monitoring only applies to 'participating' vessels,[69] although regulation requires 'participation' of certain classes of vessels or vessels carrying out certain activities, such as fishing in waters so regulated by a coastal State or RFMO. In other words, 'participation' often is mandatory; or in the case of fishing vessels, a matter of choice only in so far as a fishing vessel can choose not to seek a licence to fish in a particular fishery or it may simply choose to fish illegally. However, there are a number of ways for uncooperative vessel operators to circumvent such requirements, from switching tracking systems off, to covering or otherwise interfering with antennae or cameras, power supplies and the like, entering false information or spoofing vessel positions, or even damaging systems. Such possibilities mean that States also need to supplement cooperative information sources with 'non-cooperative' surveillance means, which, on the other hand, are a discretionary matter for the State using them and do not require participation by vessel operators.

The most common types of surveillance technologies involve radar or electro-optical sensors, as well, potentially, as electronic and signals intelligence collection methods, either situated on land or mounted on a variety of platforms. Platforms can include surface assets such as warships and smaller patrol craft, satellites and, most commonly, airborne assets. The coverage of surface platform sensors tends to be quite limited without aerial or space-based surveillance support. The best known surveillance platforms are maritime patrol aircraft. These have been supplemented by space-based assets, particularly satellites equipped with synthetic aperture radar (SAR), which has the ability to 'see' through cloud or other visual environmental impediments, whilst the less effective optical imagery satellites provide another option. In both cases their coverage is limited and their use expensive.[70] Increasingly, robotic,[71] unmanned platforms are being used to carry sensors for ocean surveillance due to their generally lower operating costs and greater endurance characteristics. In particular, unmanned aerial vehicles (UAVs) already are in widespread, and rapidly increasing, use for maritime surveillance,[72] although unmanned surface (USVs) and underwater vehicles (UUVs) have also been developed, as well as small surface (wave) and submersible 'gliders.'[73] In addition, buoys,[74] aerostats and airships,[75] represent other platform options, as do potentially also passive acoustic surveillance systems such as underwater arrays.[76]

One emerging application of technology is being developed for the detection of nuclear materials or weapons being smuggled by sea, which would involve the use of sensors based on surface ships, UAVs or UUVs to detect smuggled nuclear or radiological materials on-board a suspect vessel.[77]

Technology, enforcement and the *LOSC*

The last example above, however, also suggests potential limitations with the lawful application of such technologies in the context of the *LOSC*, if not necessarily the technologies themselves. For example, under the *LOSC*, a warship has the right of visit to board a foreign ship on the high seas only in a very limited number of circumstances.[78] Suspicion of carrying nuclear materials is not one of those grounds. Instead, jurisdiction on the high seas remains with the ship's flag State.[79] To overcome this dilemma, in most circumstances the only realistic interdiction option for the investigating warship would be if the suspect ship's flag State were to grant it permission to undertake a boarding; in the mould of the bilateral ship boarding agreements that the United States has negotiated with eleven flag States under the Proliferation Security Initiative, or which can be arranged under the 2005 Protocol to the *SUA Convention*.[80]

An issue that may arise in the context of the *LOSC* doctrine of hot pursuit,[81] is the extent to which enforcement authorities must follow strictly 'procedural means' of exercising that right. Craig Allen made the persuasive case over 25 years ago that a 'functional' approach would be more appropriate in order to take into account the then new and emerging technologies for maritime surveillance, particularly in regard to the implied need to maintain positive contact with the pursued vessel during the pursuit.[82] Since that time technology has marched on relentlessly, but *LOSC* interpretations have not kept pace to the extent that it could be argued that new customary international law has been settled which accepts unreservedly the role that new means of maintaining contact with the target offender satisfy the requirement for uninterrupted pursuit.[83] Instead, the issue remains at the ad hoc mercy of court decisions on individual cases. In the case of the MV *Saiga*, the International Tribunal for the Law of the Sea (ITLOS) took a strongly procedural position, determining that a patrol boat of the enforcing State, Guinea, had not maintained an uninterrupted pursuit of the suspect vessel.[84] It is interesting to note, however, that Australia's *Maritime Powers Act 2013* establishes that a pursuit 'is not interrupted only because . . . the [suspect] vessel is out of sight,' and implies that 'remote means, including radio, radar, satellite or sonar,' could legitimately be used to conduct an uninterrupted chase.[85] This provision has yet to be tested in a court, however, let alone in an international tribunal such as ITLOS.

Another technology-related issue that arose during LRIT negotiations led to the exclusion of vessel position reports, except for the ship's flag State, whenever a ship is located in the internal or archipelagic waters of another State, or in the territorial sea of the ship's flag State when the requesting party is a coastal State. The latter situation would apply when the targeted ship has not indicated an intent to enter the coastal State's port.[86] This reflected the misplaced fears of some States that their sovereignty would be infringed if ship positions were made available when the ship is 'located within the waters landward of the baselines.'[87] But this exchange of information, for which there are many precedents and which is a 'passive activity,' does not interfere at all with a ship's navigational or other rights under the *LOSC*; nor does it alter enforcement powers in any way.[88] Indeed, *SOLAS* is explicit that LRIT cannot modify in any way the maritime jurisdictional regimes established in the *LOSC*.[89]

Thus, despite the growing importance of technology applications both in regulation and enforcement, the extent to which technology can be utilized for enforcement purposes is still limited in certain circumstances by relatively narrow *LOSC* interpretations based on a decades-old technological context. The scope of what is technologically possible nonetheless influences States to continually push the boundaries of what is permissible under international law. It can be asserted with some assurance that this trend will continue.

Notes

1. *United Nations Convention on the Law of the Sea*, opened for signature 10 December 1982, 1833 UNTS 3 (entered into force 16 November 1994) ('*LOSC*').
2. See Stuart Kaye's Chapter 1 in this volume for elaboration on the enforcement implications of maritime zones of jurisdiction under the *LOSC*.
3. *International Convention for the Safety of Life at Sea, as amended*, opened for signature 1 November 1974, 1184 UNTS 2 (entered into force 25 May 1980) ('*SOLAS*').
4. On the concept of good order at sea, see Geoffrey Till, *Seapower: A Guide for the Twenty-First Century* (Routledge, 3rd revised ed, 2013) ch 12.
5. For further elaboration of the MDA concept, see Chris Rahman, 'Maritime Domain Awareness in Australia and New Zealand' in Natalie Klein, Joanna Mossop and Donald R. Rothwell (eds), *Maritime Security: International Law and Policy Perspectives from Australia and New Zealand* (Routledge, 2010) 202–207.
6. For analysis of the legal basis for, and limitations of, the carriage and use of VMS, see Erik Jaap Molenaar and Martin Tsamenyi, *Satellite-Based Vessel Monitoring Systems: International Legal Aspects and Developments in State Practice*, FAO Legal Papers No. 7 (FAO, 2000) 11–30.
7. On this issue see High Seas Task Force (HSTF), *Closing the Net: Stopping Illegal Fishing on the High Seas. Final Report of the Ministerially-Led Task Force on IUU Fishing on the High Seas* (HSTF, 2006).
8. Western and Central Pacific Fisheries Commission (WCPFC), *Commission Vessel Monitoring System, Commission Eleventh Regular Session 1–5 December 2014*, Conservation and Management Measure 2014-02.

9 Robert Gallagher, 'Current Status of Vessel Monitoring Systems, Satellites and other Technologies for Fisheries Monitoring, Control and Surveillance' in *Report of the Expert Consultation on the Use of Vessel Monitoring Systems and Satellites for Fisheries Monitoring, Control and Surveillance, Rome, 24–26 October 2006*, Food and Agriculture Organization of the United Nations (FAO) Fisheries Report No. 815, FAO Doc FIEL/R815(En) (2007) 39.
10 Ibid.
11 For detail on the technical basis for VMS, see FAO, *Fishing Operations. 1. Vessel Monitoring Systems*, FAO Technical Guidelines for Responsible Fisheries No. 1 Suppl. 1 (FAO, 1998).
12 The MTU acronym has sometimes also been defined as mobile transmitting unit.
13 See, for example, WCPFC, *MTU/ALC Type Approval List as Provided by CCMs*, 16 August 2013, which lists the satellite service provider, unit brand and model, approved by individual Commission member States.
14 *Fisheries (Satellite Vessel Monitoring) Regulations 1993, Reprint as of 1 July 2013* (NZ) SR 1993/354, reg 3.
15 *Fisheries (Vessel Monitoring Systems – Minimum Standards for Automatic Location Communicators) Circular 2014* (NZ) schedule 1.
16 *Vessel Monitoring Systems: Requirements for Enhanced Mobile Transceiver Unit and Mobile Communication Service Type-Approval*, 79 Fed Reg 77 399, 77 405 § 600.1500 (24 December 2014).
17 Pacific Fishery Management Council, *Regional Electronic Technologies Implementation Plan for West Coast Marine Fisheries*, draft (27 January 2015) 1.
18 Ibid.
19 National Marine Fisheries Service (NMFS), NMFS Policy Directive 30–133, *Policy on Electronic Technologies and Fishery-Dependent Data Collection* (3 May 2013) 1.
20 Australian Fisheries Management Authority, Fisheries Research and Development Corporation Project 2009/048, *Electronic Onboard Monitoring Pilot Project for the Eastern Tuna and Billfish Fishery* (2012).
21 Ibid, 17–22, 87.
22 Ibid, 17, 66.
23 Ibid, 68–70.
24 *SOLAS* Chapter V, reg 19, *Carriage Requirements for Shipborne Navigational Systems and Equipment* ('SOLAS V/19').
25 International Maritime Organization (IMO) Maritime Safety Committee ('MSC'), *Recommendation on Performance Standards for a Universal Shipborne Automatic Identification System (AIS)*, MSC.74(69) Annex 3.1.2, *Report of the Maritime Safety Committee on Its Sixty-Ninth Session*, 69th sess, Agenda Item 22, MSC Doc MSC 69/22/Add.1, Annex 12 (1 June 1998).
26 *SOLAS* V/19.2.4.
27 *Vessel Requirements for Notices of Arrival and Departure, and Automatic Identification System*, 80 Fed Reg 5 281, 5 307–5 308 (30 January 2015).
28 For basic comparisons between Class A and Class B AIS capabilities, see U.S. Coast Guard Navigation Center, *Types of Automatic Identification Systems (per ITU-R M1371 and IEC Standards)*, particularly the documents *AIS Comparison by Class* and *Data Broadcasted from Each AIS Station Type (ITU-R M.1371-5 Message Nr.)* <http://www.navcen.uscg.gov/?pageName=typesAIS>. For detailed technical information see International Telecommunication Union, Radiocommunication Sector (ITU-R), *Technical Characteristics for an Automatic Identification System Using Time Division Multiple Access in the VHF Maritime Mobile Frequency Band*, Recommendation ITU-R M.1371–5 (ITU-R, 2014).
29 Pacific Islands Forum Fisheries Agency (FFA), *FFA Vessel Register Requirements for AIS from 1-Jul-2015*, FFA circ SO/6 (15 December 2014).
30 *SOLAS* V/19.2.4.5.
31 *Recommendation on Performance Standards for a Universal Shipborne Automatic Identification System (AIS)* Annex 3.2.1.
32 Ibid Annex 3.6.1; and IMO Assembly Res. A.917(22) adopted on 29 November 2001, *Guidelines for the Onboard Operational Use of Shipborne Automatic Identification Systems (AIS)*, 22nd sess, Agenda Item 9, annex para 12, Assembly Doc A 22/Res.917 (25 January 2002).
33 *Guidelines for the Onboard Operational Use of Shipborne Automatic Identification Systems (AIS)* annex para 12.
34 Ibid, annex 1 para 1.
35 *SOLAS* V/19.2.4.7.
36 MSC, *Measures to Enhance Maritime Security. Freely available AIS generated ship data and the attendant security risks. Submitted by BIMCO, International Chamber of Shipping (ICS), International Association of Dry*

Cargo Shipowners (INTERCARGO) and International Association of Independent Tanker Owners (INTERTANKO), 79th sess, Agenda Item 5, MSC Doc MSC 79/5/10 (23 September 2004).
37 UK Maritime Trade Operations (UKMTO), *BMP 4 Best Management Practices for Protection against Somali Based Piracy*, version 4 (August 2011) section 7.3.
38 *SOLAS V/19–1, Long-range identification and tracking of ships*.
39 The complex LRIT system architecture and functional requirements are set out in Res MSC.263(84) adopted 16 May 2008, *Revised Performance Standards and Functional Requirements for the Long-Range Identification and Tracking of Ships, Report of the Maritime Safety Committee on Its Eighty-Fourth Session*, 84th sess, Agenda Item 24, MSC Doc MSC 84/24/Add.2, Annex 9 (6 June 2008).
40 See Jillian Carson-Jackson, 'Satellite AIS – Developing Technology or Existing Capability?' (2012) 65(2) *The Journal of Navigation* 303–321.
41 Port of Los Angeles and Port of Long Beach, *San Pedro Bay Ports Clean Air Action Plan Final 2006 Overview* (San Pedro Bay Ports, 2006) 7, 11.
42 Ibid, 9.
43 Ibid, 8.
44 Port of Los Angeles and Port of Long Beach, *San Pedro Bay Ports Clean Air Action Plan 2010 Update* (San Pedro Bay Ports, 2010) 83–88.
45 Ibid, 89–102. The regulation is *Airborne Toxic Control Measure for Auxiliary Diesel Engines Operated on Ocean-Going Vessels At-Berth in a California Port*, 17 CCR § 93118.3 (2008).
46 *Airborne Toxic Control Measure for Auxiliary Diesel Engines Operated on Ocean-Going Vessels At-Berth in a California Port* § 93118.3 (c)(1).
47 Ibid, § 93118.3 (d)(2)(A).
48 Ibid, § 93118.3 (e)(4)(D).
49 *San Pedro Bay Ports Clean Air Action Plan 2010 Update*, above n 44, 90.
50 Ibid, 91.
51 Ibid, 134–139.
52 *Airborne Toxic Control Measure for Commercial Harbor Craft*, 17 CCR § 93118.5 (d)(30), (e)(6)(F) (2008).
53 Ibid, § 93118.5 (f)(1).
54 California Air Resources Board, *Alternative Technologies for Complying with the Commercial Harbor Craft Regulation* (15 February 2012).
55 *San Pedro Bay Ports Clean Air Action Plan 2010 Update*, above n 44, 123–124.
56 IMO Marine Environmental Protection Committee (MEPC), *Amendments to the Annex of the Protocol of 1997 to Amend the International Convention for the Prevention of Pollution from Ships, 1973, as Modified by the Protocol of 1978 Relating Thereto (Revised MARPOL Annex VI)*, Res MEPC.176(58) adopted 10 October 2008, *Report of the Marine Environmental Protection Committee on Its Fifty-Eight Session*, 58th sess, Agenda Item 23, MEPC Doc MEPC 58/23/Add.1, Annex 13 (17 October 2008).
57 Ibid, reg 3.2.
58 U.S. Coast Guard, letter to Michael Kaczmarek, Vice President, Shipbuilding, Carnival Corporation & plc (8 August 2013).
59 *Revised MARPOL Annex VI Appendix III, Criteria and Procedures for Designation of Emission Control Areas (Regulation 13.6 and regulation 14.3)*.
60 MEPC, *Amendments to the Annex of the Protocol of 1997 to Amend the International Convention for the Prevention of Pollution from Ships, 1973, as Modified by the Protocol of 1978 Relating Thereto (Designation of the United States Caribbean Sea Emission Control Area and exemption of certain ships operating in the North American Emission Control Area and the United States Caribbean Sea Emission Control Area under regulations 13 and 14 and Appendix VII of MARPOL Annex VI)*, Res MEPC.202(62) adopted 15 July 2011, *Report of the Marine Environmental Protection Committee on Its Sixty-Sixth Session*, 62nd sess, Agenda Item 24, MEPC Doc MEPC 62/24, Annex 14 (26 July 2011).
61 U.S. Environmental Protection Agency (EPA), *Designation of North American Emission Control Area to Reduce Emissions from Ships*, Office of Transportation and Air Quality, EPA-420-F-10-015 (March 2010) 2.
62 U.S. EPA, *Designation of Emission Control Area to Reduce Emissions from Ships in the U.S. Caribbean*, Office of Transportation and Air Quality, EPA-420-F-11-024 (July 2011) 1.
63 U.S. Coast Guard, letter, above n 58.
64 Carnival Corporation & plc, *Sustainability Report FY2013* (c.2013) 46–47.
65 *Revised MARPOL Annex VI* reg 4.1.

66 MEPC, *2009 Guidelines for Exhaust Gas Cleaning Systems*, Res MEPC.184(59) adopted 17 July 2009, *Report of the Marine Environmental Protection Committee on Its Fifty-Ninth Session*, 59th sess, Agenda Item 24, MEPC Doc MEPC 59/24/Add.1, Annex 9 (28 July 2009).
67 MEPC, *Application of Regulation 4 of MARPOL Annex VI. Communication received from the Administration of the Bahamas*, MEPC.1/Circ.978 (27 November 2012).
68 MSC, *Long-range Identification and Tracking System Technical Documentation (Part 1). Interim Revised Technical Specifications for the LRIT System (Version 5)*, Annex 1.2.2.5, MSC Doc MSC.1/Circ.1259/Rev.4 (15 February 2011).
69 Sandra Brooke, Tse Yang Lim and Jeff Ardron, Marine Conservation Biology Institute, *Surveillance and Enforcement of Remote Maritime Areas (SERMA): Surveillance Technical Options* (2010) 2.
70 Ibid, 9–12, 15.
71 P.W. Singer, *Wired for War: The Robotics Revolution and Conflict in the 21st Century* (The Penguin Press, 2009).
72 *Surveillance and Enforcement of Remote Maritime Areas*, above note 69, 20–23; and for detailed analysis of maritime UAV options, see Norman Friedman, *Unmanned Combat Air Systems: A New Kind of Carrier Aviation* (Naval Institute Press, 2010) Appendix 2.
73 *Surveillance and Enforcement of Remote Maritime Areas*, above note 69, 29–30.
74 Ibid, 18–20.
75 Ibid, 24–26; and Martin Streetly, 'Eyes Down: At Last a Viable Role for Airships?' (November 2010) *Jane's International Defence Review* 52–55.
76 *Surveillance and Enforcement of Remote Maritime Areas*, above note 69, 12–13.
77 Liam Stoker, 'New Navy Technology to Net WMDs' (19 September 2012) *Naval Technology* <http://www.naval-technology.com/features/featurenew-navy-technology-wmds-nuclear/>; and for technical detail of recent research, see Thomas M. Miller et al, 'Investigations of Active Interrogation Techniques to Detect Special Nuclear Material in Maritime Environments: Standoff Interrogation of Small- and Medium-sized Cargo Ships' (2013) 316 *Nuclear Instruments and Methods in Physics Research B* 94–104.
78 *LOSC* art 110.
79 Ibid, art 92.
80 See the State Department website <http://www.state.gov/t/isn/c27733.htm>; and *Protocol of 2005 to the Convention for the Suppression of Unlawful Acts against the Safety of Maritime Navigation (SUA Convention)*, opened for signature 14 October 2005 (entered into force 28 July 2010) art 8*bis*.
81 *LOSC* art 111.
82 Craig H. Allen, 'Doctrine of Hot Pursuit: A Functional Interpretation Adaptable to Emerging Maritime Law Enforcement Technologies and Practices' (1989) 20 *Ocean Development and International Law* 309, 322–325.
83 *LOSC* art 111.1.
84 *The M/V "Saiga" (No. 2) Case (Saint Vincent and the Grenadines v Guinea) (Judgement)* (International Tribunal for the Law of the Sea, Case No 2, 1 July 1999) [147].
85 *Maritime Powers Act 2013* (Cth) ss 42(2)(d)–(e).
86 *SOLAS* V/19–1.8.1.
87 Ibid.
88 Martin Tsamenyi and Mary Ann Palma, 'Legal Considerations in the Implementation of Long-Range Identification and Tracking Systems for Vessels' (2007) 13 *Journal of International Maritime Law* 42, 50–55.
89 *SOLAS* V/19–1.1.

22
Cooperative Maritime Surveillance and Enforcement

Warwick Gullett and Yubing Shi

Introduction

States which enjoy maritime domains face the constant threat of illegal activity within their waters. Threats range from modern versions of ancient pursuits such as piracy and illegal fishing through to sophisticated operations of globalised criminal networks illegally moving drugs or involved in people smuggling or wildlife trafficking, as well as marine pollution or biosecurity security incidents. The nature and extent of threats will vary from region to region, and the degree to which a State is exposed to them will depend on the size and characteristics of its maritime zones and its capacity to identify and respond to specific and imminent security challenges. Developments in the international law of the sea since the 1970s have enabled some coastal States to exercise maritime jurisdiction vast distances from their shores, notably out to 200 nautical miles for the exclusive economic zone (EEZ) and even beyond in some circumstances for seabed resources of the continental shelf. The extension of maritime jurisdiction has resulted in intensification of human activities far offshore, such as fishing and hydrocarbon exploration, coupled with an ever increasing volume of international shipping, which all leads to more opportunities for unlawful activities. An important strategy for States to increase their ability to deter illegal activity in their maritime zones is to cooperate with other States in potentially all aspects of law enforcement, from intelligence gathering and security patrols through to arrest and prosecution activities.

There are two general scenarios in which coastal States could benefit from a high level of bilateral or multilateral maritime security cooperation. The first is in circumstances where it would endeavour to enforce its laws regarding conduct aboard a foreign vessel which attempts to escape arrest by fleeing to waters of another State or the high seas. International cooperation is needed because the jurisdictional rights and protections of neighbouring States must be respected. The second scenario is where a coastal State has insufficient surveillance and enforcement assets to police its maritime zone and would benefit from sharing resources with its neighbours. The benefits to be derived from cooperation with neighbouring States in the conduct of surveillance and enforcement operations are reduction in the cost of law enforcement and deterrence and more prosecutions of illegal activities. This can result in greater effectiveness of at-sea operations by, for example, enabling enhanced coordination of sea, air and land based enforcement procedures.

This chapter highlights the need for States to develop cooperative maritime surveillance and enforcement arrangements to combat illegal activities at sea. It reviews the nature and scope of maritime law enforcement challenges and examples of cooperative surveillance and enforcement arrangements in Europe, the South Pacific, the Southern Ocean and East Asia. It is argued that States which share threats of maritime crime can adopt a 'scaffold' approach to surveillance and enforcement cooperation, from initial activities focused on building understanding and trust between counterpart government officers, through to the sharing of intelligence data, and then joint operations at sea.

Transboundary illegal activities at sea

Transboundary illegal activities at sea are a pressing international maritime problem. The term 'transboundary' may refer to the crossing of jurisdictional boundaries at different administrative levels, including intrastate. Here we refer to it as the crossing of an interstate jurisdictional boundary.[1] Depending on the specific jurisdiction of a State, this boundary may be that of its territorial sea, EEZ, or any other maritime zones under national jurisdiction. Transboundary illegal activities take various forms. They include crimes at sea such as piracy, drugs and wildlife trafficking, illegal fishing and people smuggling. The forms of these offences have also evolved with technological advancements and many factors have contributed to their occurrence. Examples are weak and underdeveloped governance structures, corruption, a lack of law enforcement capacity, and disadvantageous geographic characteristics of certain States.[2] In practice, different forms of transboundary illegal activities connect with each other. They not only represent security or environmental threats to States, but also lead to significant economic loss for States.[3]

Illegal fishing

Illegal fishing refers to fishing activities conducted in violation of international and national laws, and agreed regional fisheries management and conservation measures.[4] Examples are fishing beyond allowable catch limits, the taking of juvenile fish and prohibited fish species, and fishing during closed seasons or in closed areas.[5] Illegal fishing is often associated with Illegal, Unreported, Unregulated Fishing (IUU fishing) which is a term first adopted by the UN Food and Agriculture Organization (FAO) in 2001.[6] In practice, IUU fishing is often transboundary in nature. It may occur in the high seas, or in maritime zones of coastal States by national and foreign vessels and in river and inland fisheries. IUU fishing has many negative impacts on States' economic development, environmental protection, and ecological and social balance. For example, it has been recognised as a major threat to fisheries and marine biodiversity. It is estimated that the annual global losses of illegal fishing have reached $23.5 billion.[7] Sometimes fishing vessels are used to conceal transnational organised crimes such as drug running, wildlife trafficking, and people smuggling.[8] This characteristic makes illegal fishing a security threat for many coastal States.[9] In practice, catches of illegal fishing are often transported to their final market via sophisticated routes which may involve transhipments at sea, landing in 'ports of convenience' and processing in a State that is neither a flag State nor a market State. It is difficult in these circumstances to identify the origin of illegal fishing without effective maritime surveillance and enforcement. In view of the negative impacts of illegal fishing, many coastal

States have taken action, such as strengthening coastal State control over EEZs.[10] However, more needs to be done. The 2011 United Nations Convention against Transnational Organized Crime (UNTOC) report on *Transnational Organised Crime in the Fishing Industry* identified four main challenges concerning illegal fishing. These are: (1) the global reach of fishing vessels; (2) a lack of governance and rule of law in the fishing industry (in particular there is a lack of at-sea surveillance of vessel movements and transhipments, and a lack of ability or willingness of some flag States to enforce their criminal law jurisdiction); (3) quota restrictions and declining fish stocks in many regions may make fishers and fishing communities vulnerable to recruitment into criminal activities; and (4) social acceptance.[11] These findings reveal that of these four categories of challenges in addressing illegal fishing, a lack of effective at-sea surveillance and enforcement is a prominent issue to address.

Customs offences – drug running, wildlife trafficking

Drug running and wildlife trafficking are two serious customs offences which can be conducted through international shipping. Indeed, shipping has become the most popular means of transportation for illicit trafficking of narcotic drugs and psychotropic substances due to its high volume and low cost.[12] For instance, the vast majority of marijuana and cocaine arrives in the United States by ship; in Central America drug-traffickers even utilise semi-submersible vessels to ship drugs.[13] The utilisation of advanced technologies facilitates the growth of drug trafficking in size, complexity and organisation.[14] This characteristic, together with the use of drug trafficking as a means of financing terrorist organisations, means that drug trafficking constitutes a major maritime security threat.[15]

Wildlife trafficking refers to any illegal sale or exchange of wild animal and plant resources, which may involve live animals, plants and derived products.[16] A large volume of wildlife and its products are transported internationally by ship every year. For example, in 2003 during a routine inspection Australian Customs officers seized 160kg of illegally imported wildlife products and body parts of endangered tiger, snake, rhinoceros, pangolin and an endangered plant from two shipping containers.[17] Wildlife trafficking may alter the livelihoods of local people, lead to extinction of species and pose a significant biosecurity risk due to the introduction of invasive species.[18] Given the negative impacts of drug running and wildlife trafficking, many coastal States have taken prescriptive and enforcement responses. However, high market demand and gaps in protection continue to present challenges to judicial and enforcement systems.[19]

Immigration offences – people smuggling

People smuggling, also referred to as migrant smuggling, is defined by the Protocol against the Smuggling of Migrants by Land, Sea and Air, supplementing the United Nations Convention against Transnational Organized Crime (Smuggling Protocol) as the:

> 'procurement, in order to obtain, directly or indirectly a financial or other material benefit, of the illegal entry of a person into a State Party of which the person is not a national or a permanent resident.'[20]

Movements of refugees, asylum seekers, stateless persons and migrants from one State to another all constitute people smuggling. Compared with smuggling by land and air, people smuggling by sea is the 'most dangerous' type of smuggling for migrants.[21] This is because this kind of activity involves the frequent use of overcrowded and unseaworthy vessels. For example, during the Arab Spring (since January 2011) more than 1,500 people in migrant boats departing from North Africa died on their voyage crossing the Mediterranean.[22] Sometimes smugglers might abandon their vessels at sea, and it is challenging for those required to conduct rescues at sea. This difficulty was apparent in the 2001 *M/V Tampa* incident where Australia forbade the Norwegian vessel which rescued 430 Afghan asylum seekers from a sinking migrant boat, to enter its territorial sea on the basis that the passengers were asylum seekers.[23] Australia threatened to charge the Norwegian Master with people smuggling if he attempted to offload rescued asylum seekers in Australia.[24] Although the Smuggling Protocol requests States Parties to cooperate 'to the fullest extent possible' to prevent and combat smuggling of migrants by sea in accordance with the international law of the sea,[25] in practice it is not straightforward to achieve effective cooperation between States for this purpose. This is because migration routes are transboundary which involves different jurisdictions, and the smuggled people might be nationals from different States. In these circumstances, maritime authorities need to cooperate in the collection of evidence, prosecution of offenders, mutual legal assistance, extradition and prisoner transfer.[26]

Maritime security including piracy

Piracy has attracted the most extensive media coverage of current maritime security threats, and has received a multipronged international response. This is partially attributed to rampant piracy off the coast of Somalia and the Gulf of Guinea. According to the United Nations Convention on the Law of the Sea (LOSC), piracy consists of 'illegal acts of violence or detention, or any act of depredation, committed for private ends' by the crew or passengers of a private ship directed against another ship on the high seas or outside the jurisdiction of any State.[27] In contrast to piracy, armed robbery refers to the same acts in maritime zones within the sovereignty of the coastal State.[28] In other words, sea piracy may occur on the high seas, EEZs and the contiguous zones of any States, whereas armed robbery may only occur within the territorial sea, archipelagic waters, or internal waters of States. Piracy not only exposes seafarers to personal physical harm and disturbs the normal navigation of ships, but also leads to financial losses to ship owners and insurance companies, and may endanger regional and international economy security.[29] An IMO report identified that in 2013, the overall number of reported acts or attempted acts of piracy and armed robbery decreased by 12.6 per cent with 298 cases reported.[30] This decrease primarily resulted from the reduction of attacks by Somali pirates, as well as those in South America and the Caribbean.[31] Nevertheless, in 2013 there was a significant increase in the number of reported piratical attacks in the South China Sea.[32] It is arguable that the lack of cooperation in maritime surveillance and enforcement in the South China Sea maritime zones, due to numerous disputes in the region, contributed to this increase.[33] Meanwhile, the efforts in jointly combating piracy off Somalia by sea power States contributed to the reduction of piracy in the region.

Pollution incidents/regional environmental protection

Vessel-source pollution accounts for 12 per cent of marine pollution[34] and has been comprehensively regulated. Based on the forms that pollution takes, vessel-source pollution constitutes illegal dumping of waste and illegal emission or discharge of substances. Pollution from ships may also be classified as operational pollution and accidental pollution. Operational discharge of oil and other substances constitutes the majority of vessel-source pollution; accidental pollution emanates from marine casualties and often leads to spillage of pollutants. Examples of accidental pollution are the *Erika* (France, 1999), *Slops* (Greece, 2000), *Prestige* (Spain, 2002), *No7 Kwang Min* (Republic of Korea, 2005), *Solar 1* (Philippines, 2006), *Shosei Maru* (Japan, 2006), *Volgoneft 139* (Strait of Kerch, 2007), *Heibei Spirit* (Republic of Korea, 2007) and *MOL Comfort* (Yemen, 2013). Pollution from ships often causes transboundary environmental harm. While operational pollution is usually a cumulative process, accidental pollution often leads to immediate significant harm including damage to coastal communities, fisheries, wildlife and local ecology.[35] This damage is often long-lasting and difficult to rectify, especially in extra sensitive areas such as the Arctic or Antarctic.[36] The prevention, detection and measurement of these harms is difficult to achieve without cooperation between State authorities. Further, in practice some ship operators intentionally dump their oily waste under cover of night outside any port, flag or coastal States' territorial seas or in an area of recent oil pollution incidents.[37] In this way they seek to avoid detection and punishment by coastal States. Close cooperation between coastal States, flag States and the IMO will be important for addressing this challenge.

Marine biodiversity and biosecurity

Many transboundary illegal activities at sea directly or indirectly lead to the loss of marine biodiversity and thus present a biosecurity threat to States. For example, IUU fishing may render the world's fish stocks fully exploited or overexploited which may further threaten or endanger marine species. Exotic species that are smuggled into a State may also bring significant biosecurity risks once they become pests.[38] Illegal dumping of oily waste may pose a threat to the biodiversity of the global ecosystem.[39] It is predicted that by the year 2100 over half of the world's marine species will be in danger of extinction.[40] Further, a UN report points out that the continued loss in marine biodiversity would make it difficult to achieve development goals, in particular those relating to poverty eradication, food security and health.[41] It is thus important for the international community to combat transboundary illegal activities at sea so that marine biodiversity and biosecurity can be protected.

Jurisdictional framework for maritime surveillance and enforcement

A State has greater ability to take action against a domestic vessel engaged in illegal activity in waters under its jurisdiction in comparison with a foreign-flagged vessel. This is because the State enjoys jurisdiction over the vessel derived from its rights as a coastal State together with its jurisdictional rights as a flag State. More regulatory and enforcement challenges arise in respect of foreign-flagged vessels, and many of the incidents of illegal activity are conducted by these vessels because their operators rely on the protections afforded by the primacy of flag State jurisdiction. The range of options available to a State which wishes to take action against a foreign vessel suspected of engaging in illegal activity in waters under its jurisdiction can depend on the maritime zone in which the vessel is located. The international law of the sea has developed through according States different maritime zones of jurisdiction (see Chapter 1). As a general rule, a coastal State has greater powers of regulation and enforcement the closer the foreign vessel is to its land. The two most critical zones in terms of incidence of illegal foreign activity and the need for bilateral or multilateral cooperation are the territorial sea and the EEZ, although enforcement activity may also be needed while the vessel is in port, where in most cases it will be located in internal waters. The principal distinction is between the full sovereignty rights coastal States enjoy in internal waters and the territorial sea, and the somewhat lesser 'sovereign rights' related to resources they enjoy in the EEZ further out to sea, in which the flag States of foreign vessels enjoy internationally protected navigational freedoms.

Internal waters

The regime of 'internal waters' applies to coastal sea areas landwards of the territorial sea. These waters are subject to the full sovereignty of the coastal State, just as if they were areas of its land.[42] Coastal bays, river mouths and ports are typically included in internal waters. In principle, a foreign vessel in internal waters is fully subject to the sovereignty of the coastal State. In practice, coastal States do not exercise full administrative, civil and criminal jurisdiction over conduct and conditions on board foreign vessels. This is a discretionary non-exercise of powers in the interest of commerce, efficiency and international comity. However, a coastal State is likely to assert its powers if events on a vessel threaten the peace and good order of its internal waters. As all ships must dock somewhere, ports can use entry conditions to ensure that international safety, fisheries conservation and environmental protection standards are being observed at sea. Treaties have been adopted to coordinate port State controls for these purposes (see Chapter 6). A port State can detain a vessel that is in violation of international or national standards and require that it undertake repairs before sailing again.[43] It can also institute legal proceedings against a ship that has discharged pollutants in breach of international standards, even when that breach occurred outside its internal waters, territorial sea or EEZ.[44]

Territorial sea

The territorial sea is a band of ocean (and its airspace above and seabed below) seaward of the baseline along the coast. The coastal State has full sovereignty over it[45] equivalent to that over land territory, except that it must respect the right of 'innocent passage' enjoyed by foreign vessels. The maximum permissible breadth of the territorial sea is 12 nautical miles from the baseline.[46] The right of innocent passage through a coastal State's territorial sea is allowed to merchant ships of all States.[47] Passage means navigation for the purpose of traversing the territorial sea or proceeding to or from a destination such as a port facility, and it must be 'continuous and expeditious'. This means that a ship may anchor only if this is incidental to ordinary navigation or it is necessary as a result of the ship being in distress or rendering assistance to other vessels in distress. Innocence is defined as not being prejudicial to the coastal State's 'peace, good order or security'.[48] LOSC provides a list of non-innocent activities, including: threatening the use of force, illegal fishing or pollution, carrying out research, and loading or unloading currency, contraband or persons.[49] Although coastal States can impose regulations for foreign shipping in the territorial sea, including for navigation safety, environment protection and living resources conservation, these regulations cannot have the practical effect of denying or impairing the right of innocent passage.[50] Accordingly, the regulations cannot be stricter than international standards for the design, construction, manning or equipment of ships.

Exclusive economic zone

The EEZ is a special regime that is neither sovereign territory nor high seas. It begins at the seaward limit of the territorial sea and extends, where this is possible considering the proximity of neighbouring States, out to 200 nautical miles from the baselines. This means that the maximum width of the EEZ is 188 nautical miles, extending from the 12 nautical mile limit of the territorial sea.[51] The EEZ encompasses the water column and the seabed and subsoil. Coastal States have in the EEZ sovereign rights to explore, exploit, conserve and manage all the living resources as well as other economic resources, such as offshore energy available from oil, gas, currents, winds and temperatures.[52] The coastal State does not have full sovereignty in the zone; other States retain their high seas freedoms. These include rights of navigation, overflight, the laying of submarine cables and pipelines and potentially conducting more controversial activities, such as certain military activities.

Legal regime for maritime surveillance and enforcement

A coastal State wishing to deter illegal activity of foreign vessels in its maritime zones will need to develop surveillance procedures and capacity to determine the location and scale of threats it faces from foreign vessels. This will inform its determination of which enforcement operations against foreign vessels are appropriate, and which assets should be deployed. Thus, data gathering and analysis will be critical for the success of coastal State enforcement operations. Surveillance can be achieved by a range of methods, from utilising land-based technology and radar tracking from government vessels or aircraft at sea through to satellite monitoring of all ship movements (see Chapter 21). Various regimes have been established to assist with the monitoring of certain types of commercial vessels, such as transponders on fishing vessels, automatic tracking of large commercial vessels and ship reporting requirements for vessels entering ports. All these activities are passive, involve voluntary acceptance by ship masters or flag States and do not of themselves interfere with the otherwise freedom of the foreign vessels to navigate as they choose, either under the international protections of freedom of navigation within EEZs or of innocent passage in territorial seas. As such, the only legal issues would relate to developing domestic regulatory processes for information collection and dissemination. However, a range of legal issues will arise where such information is likely to be distributed internationally, as would be necessary for sophisticated surveillance and enforcement cooperative arrangements. Yet such data gathering can also be beneficial for the majority of ship owners involved in international shipping. For example, it can assist in the avoidance of navigational hazards and reduce anchoring times ahead of port visits. The main issue of concern is where officials wish to share data that is considered commercially confidential, such as the location of successful fishing operations and cargo manifests. In these circumstances protocols can be developed to ensure that sensitive data is not released to the public or competitors.

A critical issue for coastal States is to ensure that they have appropriate regulations to enable enforcement activities to take place. This is where there is a link between domestic and international law. In circumstances in which enforcement operations will take place against a foreign vessel, the coastal State must ensure that its exercise of jurisdiction is consistent with its rights under international law in the maritime zone or zones in question. As such, it must ensure that its domestic regulations, under which its government officials act, give effect to its jurisdictional rights under international law. Coastal States have both prescriptive and enforcement jurisdiction in the territorial sea and EEZ. It is inevitable that there may be textual disparity between domestic laws and LOSC articles. This is because of the way in which international treaties are developed as consensus documents, especially LOSC which is a global framework convention. Many of its provisions were deliberately constructed in a vague or ambiguous manner, and it is therefore necessary for coastal States when they develop their implementing legislation to clarify their interpretation of the international law provisions to aid in their implementation. The fact that there may be textual disjunction between domestic provisions and international provisions does not necessarily mean they are inconsistent.[53] However, for cooperative arrangements it will be necessary for States to share understanding of how their different domestic provisions operate.

Arguably the most critical maritime security scenario in which high level cooperation between neighbouring or nearby States is needed is where a foreign vessel is suspected of committing an offence within coastal waters, but then flees to the high seas or to waters of a nearby State in order to escape arrest. International law has long accepted the idea that a coastal State can make an arrest of a foreign vessel outside the waters of the coastal State where the foreign vessel has been continuously chased from the coastal State's waters. The ancient doctrine of 'hot pursuit' is enshrined in LOSC. This treaty provides that where a vessel flees to the high seas or to the EEZ of another State, pursuit may be undertaken when there is 'good reason' to believe that a vessel has violated the laws and regulations of a coastal State.[54] With respect to suspected fisheries offences, the pursuit must be commenced while the foreign vessel is in the internal waters, territorial sea or the EEZ of the coastal State.[55] A hot pursuit may only be commenced after a 'visual or auditory signal to stop' has been given 'at a distance which enables it to be seen or heard' by the foreign vessel. The pursuit of a vessel to the high seas may only be continued 'if the pursuit has not been interrupted'.[56] As discussed below, cooperation with neighbouring States can be helpful in effecting arrests.

A scaffold of cooperation

States that share maritime threats in a region can adopt a 'scaffold' approach to cooperation. This can be achieved by developing cooperation in a staged approach, from initial activities aimed at building understanding between counterpart government agencies through to high-level operational cooperation through joint enforcement and prosecution activities. This section outlines examples of successful maritime cooperation, from information sharing and surveillance through to enforcement operations.

Information sharing and surveillance

The benefits of maritime cooperation for neighbouring States or States sharing access to a regional sea is that more effective enforcement operations can be planned. This is because the sharing of information, in particular intelligence about the movements of and risk presented by suspicious foreign vessels, will enable a coastal State to have more accurate information about suspect vessels (especially where surveillance information is shared in real time). In these circumstances, States can better coordinate the deployment of assets to intercept the vessel, such as for boarding, inspection and possibly arrest. The sharing of intelligence data between counterpart agencies in nearby States is the obvious first step in a scaffold of cooperative endeavours. Yet to get to this point it will be necessary to develop relationships between counterpart government agencies and personnel, including though informal and formal meetings, site visits and secondments. This section briefly reviews a success example of regional information sharing.

Baltic Sea: Sea Surveillance Cooperation Baltic Sea (SUCBAS)

The Sea Surveillance Cooperation Baltic Sea (SUCBAS) was established in March 2009. It provides for multilateral cooperation of Baltic Sea navies from Finland, Sweden, Denmark, Germany,

Estonia, Lithuania, Latvia and Poland, and aims to enhance maritime safety and security through exchange of information and cooperation. Its practice has been regarded as effective in countering illegal activities in the maritime environment.[57] This success can be attributed to the following three factors. Firstly, the States in the Baltic region share many common resources and are increasingly interdependent. This provides a strong basis for these States to jointly combat illegal transboundary activities at sea. Accordingly, there is a long tradition of cooperation between governmental organisations and maritime authorities in this region.[58] Secondly, SUCBAS has adopted a phased approach in developing its information sharing mechanism. Information sharing was initially confined to manual exchange of reports and this exchange only took place using diplomatic channels.[59] This meant that cooperation was time consuming and inefficient. However, in 2012 all eight SUCBAS States moved to a higher level of cooperation due to the adoption of automated exchange of information. SUCBAS member States now share data automatically in real time so that potential risks in the Baltic Sea can be easily detected.[60] Further, SUCBAS adopts consensus and federated mechanisms in its decision-making, and this approach has proved to be an effective way to build trust.[61] This approach maintains a balance between efficiency of cooperation and respecting member States' sovereignty.

It remains a challenge to attract the participation of more States in SUCBAS. The Baltic region consists of ten States, namely Belarus, Denmark, Estonia, Finland, Germany, Latvia, Lithuania, Poland, Russia and Sweden. However, only eight States have joined SUCBAS while the other two non-EU States (Belarus and Russia) have remained outside. While it is preferable for all stakeholders in the Baltic Sea to participate in regional maritime cooperation, the absence of two non-EU States from SUCBAS reduces the effectiveness of this initiative. It has even been suggested that Norway, as a State adjacent to the outlet of the Baltic Sea, should be treated as an observer to facilitate the work of SUCBAS.[62]

Enforcement activities

Maritime security cooperation will be at its highest where neighbouring or regional States cooperate in the conduct of enforcement activities at sea. Such arrangements, which must build upon institutional good will and respect, and are legitimated through bilateral or multilateral information sharing, will enable the most efficient use of scarce enforcement assets and will enable the selection of enforcement operations based on the most sophisticated data knowledge possible. Yet arriving at this point is dependent on the gradual build up of trust between partner States, and shared maritime threats. This section reviews four examples of such cooperation.

Mediterranean, Atlantic and European waters: Frontex

The European Agency for the Management of Operational Cooperation at the External Borders of the Member States of the European Union (Frontex) was established in 2004 in accordance with the Treaty establishing the European Community. In contrast to SUCBAS, Frontex provides an institutionalised mechanism to facilitate operational or enforcement cooperation in protecting three types of borders of the European Union (EU), namely sea, land and air. Regarding maritime borders, Frontex has conducted regular joint maritime border control and surveillance operations in European, Atlantic and Mediterranean waters. These operations have been regarded as successful.[63] For example, in 2007 joint Frontex operations contributed to a 60 per cent reduction in illegal migrant flows from the territorial waters of Senegal, Cape Verde,

Mauritania, and Guinea to the EU via the Canary Islands.[64] In January 2015, the Icelandic coast guard vessel ICGV *Týr*, under a Frontex-coordinated joint operation, intercepted the cargo vessel *Ezadeen* with 360 unlawful migrants on board and escorted it to the southern Italian port of Corigliano Calabro.[65]

Three factors have contributed to the success of Frontex in combating transboundary illegal activities at sea. Firstly, bordering EU States understand the need to support joint Frontex operations in order to tackle ever increasing transboundary illegal maritime activities. In 2014 detected illegal border crossing activities totalled 278,000 which is twice as many as in 2011.[66] This increase is largely owing to conflict in Syria and its spread to Iraq. As a result, many refugees and displaced people have been entering the EU (especially through Italian coastal areas) from States such as Turkey, organised by smugglers. This imposes security threats on EU States. Secondly, all Frontex operations have a standard working procedure that is triggered by recommendations based on risk analyses.[67] Thirdly, joint Frontex operations share common rules of engagement and are provided with shared information about illicit at-sea activities by means of the European Border Surveillance System (Eurosur) and various international, regional and national bodies.[68] As a part of this cooperation, Frontex is able to conduct maritime surveillance and enforcement operations in the territorial waters of EU member States and participating non-EU States. Nevertheless, Frontex also faces challenges. For example, its joint operations are sometimes regarded as inefficient and some border protection officers are reported to have violated human rights in their work.[69] In 2011 the EU Parliament authorised additional powers to Frontex to make its work 'more efficient and independent [from the member States of the EU]'.[70]

Southern ocean: Australia and France cooperate

Australia and France have achieved a high degree of cooperation to combat the shared threat of illegal fishing in their maritime zones around their adjacent sub-Antarctic island territories. Joint operational responses are underpinned by two bilateral treaties on cooperative surveillance and enforcement. The second treaty was concluded in 2007. It enables cooperative surveillance and enforcement of domestic fisheries laws against illegal foreign fishing vessels operating off their respective island territories in the sub-Antarctic.[71] The treaty implements a previous treaty concluded between Australia and France in 2003 which contains innovative measures designed to facilitate pursuit and apprehension of suspected illegally operating foreign fishing vessels.[72] The cornerstone of the bilateral arrangements is the cooperation between Australia and France in terms of information sharing, and surveillance and enforcement operations. The impetus for the development of these measures was the shared threat both States face in the remote region from illegal fishing, and the limited resources available to deploy to arrest foreign vessels. This was demonstrated emphatically with two remarkably long hot pursuits conducted by Australia in 2001 and 2003 traversing thousands of nautical miles. The pursuits were only brought to a successful conclusion by cooperation with South Africa in the Togo-registered *South Tomi* pursuit and with South Africa and the United Kingdom with the Uruguayan-registered *Viarsa 1* pursuit.[73]

The 2003 treaty provides for the exchange of information about the location, movements and other details of vessels suspected of fishing illegally in order to facilitate operational responses,[74] logistical support in the conduct of hot pursuits,[75] and the undertaking of cooperative research on marine living resources.[76] There is also provision for surveillance of the parties' maritime zones by the other State with the consent of the coastal State.[77] Of particular note is the innovative provision establishing a consent regime allowing for the continuation of hot pursuit into the other State's territorial sea. This is permitted provided the other State is informed and no physical law enforcement or coercive action is taken against the vessel during this phase of the hot pursuit.[78] The 2007 Treaty gives further effect to the 2003 Treaty by formalising cooperative enforcement of the two States' fishing laws through, for example, boarding, inspection, apprehension, seizure and investigation of fishing vessels suspected of operating illegally within Australia's and France's sub-Antarctic marine jurisdictions.

It was anticipated that the treaty would facilitate 'year-round patrol coverage of the Australian and French Southern Ocean EEZs' and act as a further deterrent to illegal fishers.[79] Pursuant to the terms of the treaty, practical cooperation among enforcement authorities takes place with Australian Customs and Fisheries officers participating in French patrols and *vice-versa*. For example, Australian Customs officers travel on board French patrol vessels when they conduct surveillance in Australian waters. Officers enjoy immunity from the other party's criminal, civil and administrative proceedings where cooperative enforcement actions are taken in the other party's maritime zone, although legal proceedings may be taken against them in their own State.[80] The treaty shares similarities with the Niue Treaty (below). Cooperative activities also include exchanges of information concerning the movements and related details of fishing vessels, especially those suspected of fishing illegally, cooperative surveillance activities and the establishment of a shared register of fishing vessels licensed to operate in French and Australian waters.

The 2003 Treaty anticipated the negotiation of further agreements on cooperative surveillance.[81] The parties envisaged the conclusion of agreements or arrangements 'that may also provide for law enforcement operations possibly accompanied by forcible measures.'[82] This was achieved with the 2007 treaty entitled Agreement on Cooperative Enforcement of Fisheries Laws between the Government of Australia and the Government of the French Republic in the Maritime Areas Adjacent to the French Southern and Antarctic Territories, Heard Island and the McDonald Islands.[83] The Preamble notes Australia and France's concern over 'the continued problem' of IUU fishing 'within and adjacent to the Parties' maritime areas', the 'practical difficulties' the parties face in enforcing their fisheries laws in these areas, and emphasises their determination 'to enhance their ability to enforce effectively their fisheries laws and deter breaches of such laws.'[84]

South Pacific: NIUE Treaty

The Niue Treaty on Cooperation in Fisheries Surveillance and Law Enforcement in the South Pacific Region (Niue Treaty) is a multilateral agreement of members of the Pacific Islands Forum Fisheries Agency on monitoring, control and surveillance of fishing. It provides flexible arrangements for cooperation in fisheries surveillance among Pacific Island States. The purpose of the Treaty is to enable the most efficient use of scarce surveillance equipment by giving vessels and personnel of one State the authority to enforce the laws of another State. Article VI enables the cross-authorisation of officers and the adoption of subsidiary agreements to enable one State to extend its fisheries surveillance and law enforcement activities to the territorial sea and archipelagic waters of another Party. This provision mandates subsidiary agreements to implement the Treaty. The methods that subsidiary agreements adopt to facilitate maritime surveillance and enforcement include the sharing of surveillance and enforcement equipment, the enhancement of extradition procedures and evidentiary procedures, and the empowerment of each other's officers to perform enforcement duties.[85] Articles V, VII and VIII of the Niue Treaty provide that exchange of information, cooperation in prosecutions and cooperation in enforcement of penalties can be achieved by way of provisions in a subsidiary agreement. Article VI of the Treaty has been criticised due to its ambiguities and possible inconsistency with Article 111(3) of LOSC. For example, Aqorau asserts that the requisite location of fisheries violations is not specified under Article VI(1) of the Niue Treaty and the violations do not appear to cover those in the EEZ of Parties to this treaty.[86]

Only a few subsidiary agreements have been concluded to give effect to the Niue Treaty. The first subsidiary agreement was concluded in 2002 between the Federated States of Micronesia, Palau and the Marshall Islands. The second agreement is between Samoa and the Cook Islands, concluded in 2005. Based on these agreements, various Pacific Island States cooperate in joint surveillance operations. For example, the Federated States of Micronesia, Palau and the Marshall Islands conducted Operation 'Island Chief' in 2004.[87] Compared with these bilateral efforts, a breakthrough was achieved when a comprehensive Multilateral Subsidiary Agreement (NTMSA) was signed in November 2012. This agreement adopts a series of measures to strengthen the implementation of the Niue Treaty. In particular, it specifies a National Authority for each Party to administer the agreement, regulates a Niue Treaty Information System to share information, and provides concrete procedures for hot pursuit, and the sharing and use of fisheries data and intelligence. Further, this agreement encourages Parties to cooperate with non-Parties in accordance with international law. Multi-State fisheries surveillance operations are also conducted in the region facilitated by the Forum Fisheries Agency. For over 10 years the annual operation 'Kuru Kuru' has enabled compliance checks across vast areas of EEZs and high seas areas. Many South Pacific Island States participate as well as Australia, France, New Zealand and the United States. In 2014 the operation achieved the boarding of 114 fishing vessels and the detection of 12 vessels in potential breach of licence conditions.[88]

East Asia: coast guard cooperation

Energy security and growing trade in Asia depends extensively on maritime security in critical sea lanes through the South China Sea, the Malacca Straits and the Indian Ocean. However, this region has suffered from increasingly rampant transboundary illegal activities at sea. In particular, in the period 1995 to 2006 more than half of the world's piratical attacks occurred in this region.[89] Accordingly, Asian States have taken various means to strengthen maritime cooperation to address this problem. A highlight is coast guard cooperation. It is arguable that cooperation through coast guards in Asia is more feasible and effective than cooperation through navies because of particular sensitivities about sovereignty and maritime claims.

The overlapping sovereignty claims in this region, particularly in the South China Sea results in cooperation through navies being too 'sovereignty sensitive'. Ruijie He has argued that this concern can be relieved if maritime cooperation is conducted through coast guards.[90] Although navigating in the same geographic waters, coast guards and navies have differing priorities, capabilities and political implications. Generally, navies deal with conflicts and military threats and have more powerful ships with better weapon systems, whereas coast guards often respond to civil and commercial incidents and are less threatening. Meanwhile, the presence of naval vessels from neighbouring States is often misinterpreted as a signal that the neighbouring States wish to exert their territorial claims over disputed areas, and may more easily cause political or military tensions.[91] Comparatively, coast guards as paramilitary organisations have a lower political profile than navies, and thus their activities are less confronting to neighbouring States.[92] A prominent example of the concern about foreign navy activity is Malaysia and Indonesia's fierce opposition to the United States' 2003 Regional Maritime Security Initiative.

Coast guard cooperation between extra-regional powers and coastal States has been increasingly utilised and has proven to be successful in Southeast Asia. This model may provide a reference for maritime cooperation in other parts of this region. To date coast guard cooperation regimes in Southeast Asia, led by Japan and including India and the United States, have been established to tackle piracy threats.[93] There have been regular meetings of Heads of Asian Coast Guard Agencies since 2004. This cooperation is supported by all Association of Southeast Asian Nations (ASEAN) States due to the lack of sovereignty sensitivities it produces. In practice, this cooperation may be conducted by means of technical training, joint exercises and patrols, multilateral meetings, and the transfer of coast guard equipment. China historically has been reluctant to participate in military cooperation in this region. Nevertheless, driven by its concern about energy security, in recent years it has expressed its interest in regional maritime cooperation in non-traditional security areas, including coast guard cooperation that aims to tackle transboundary illegal activities at sea.[94]

Conclusion

It is axiomatic that States can benefit from cooperation when addressing maritime security challenges. This is evident in the examples of successful cooperation reviewed in this chapter. Willingness among States to engage in active cooperation will be most evident where there is a shared threat to be addressed, for example in a regional sea such as the Baltic, or a remote shared region such as Australia and France's adjacent sub-Antarctic marine jurisdictions. More regions around the world can benefit from greater cooperation, either developed at a bilateral level or among a handful of neighbouring States. It is argued here that the best approach to achieve successful cooperation is to build up joint activities gradually. Trust and good will is critical to the success of cooperative endeavours. This means that approaches must recognise the personal dimension of cooperation, with counterpart government officers needing to work effectively together. The development of formal arrangements can be done in a staged and scaffolded step-by-step process. It could commence with joint training programmes and sharing of intelligence data, and subsequently build to authorise joint enforcement operations and cooperation in prosecution activities. Challenges to address include reaching agreement on the maritime areas to be included in cooperative arrangements, determining whether arrangements will apply to all or just some illegal activity, establishing equitable sharing of resources across States with differing levels of capacity, harmonising domestic legislation and enabling cross-vesting authority of officers. There are examples of successful cooperation that have overcome all these challenges, and there are promising signs of further development of cooperation in maritime surveillance and enforcement in many areas.

Notes

1 The term 'transnational' is a broader concept than the term 'transboundary'. Article 3 of the United Nations Convention against Transnational Organized Crime (UNTOC) provides that an offence is 'transnational' in nature if: 'a) it is committed in more than one State; b) it is committed in one State but a substantial part of its preparation, planning, direction or control takes place in another State; c) it

1. is committed in one State but involves an organized criminal group that engages in criminal activities in more than one State; or d) it is committed in one State but has substantial effects in another State'.
2. Robin Warner, 'Joining Forces to Combat Crime in the Maritime Domain: Cooperative Maritime Surveillance and Enforcement in the South Pacific Region' (2008) 8 *New Zealand Armed Forces Law Review* 1, 2.
3. UN Report of the Secretary-General, 'Oceans and the Law of the Sea' (1 September 2014) UN Doc A/69/71/Add.1, para 28.
4. United Nations Office on Drugs and Crime (UNODC), 'Combating Transnational Organized Crime Committed at Sea' (New York, 2013), available at <http://www.unodc.org/documents/organized-crime/GPTOC/Issue_Paper_-_TOC_at_Sea.pdf> accessed 22 January 2015, pp 39–40.
5. Ibid.
6. Food and Agriculture Organization (FAO), *International Plan of Action to Prevent, Deter, and Eliminate Illegal, Unreported, and Unregulated Fishing* (IPOA-IUU), adopted at 24th Session of COFI, Rome, Italy (February 2001) para 3.
7. World Wildlife Fund (WWF), 'Impacts of Illegal Fishing', available at <http://www.worldwildlife.org/threats/illegal-fishing> accessed 22 January 2015.
8. UNODC, above n 4, 40.
9. It is now open to debate whether illegal fishing is a maritime security threat. Natalie Klein, *Maritime Security and the Law of the Sea* (Oxford University Press, 2011) 314.
10. Warner, above n 2.
11. UNODC, *Transnational Organised Crime in the Fishing Industry* (Vienna, 2011), p 5.
12. UNODC, above n 4, 40.
13. Ibid.
14. Klein, above n 9, 311.
15. Ibid.
16. TRAFFIC, 'Wildlife Trade: What Is It?', available at <http://www.traffic.org/trade/> accessed 25 January 2015.
17. Erika Alacs and Arthur Georges, 'Wildlife across Our Borders: A Review of the Illegal Trade in Australia' (2008) 40 (2) *Australian Journal of Forensic Sciences* 147, 153.
18. WWF, 'Illegal Wildlife Trade', < http://www.worldwildlife.org/threats/illegal-wildlife-trade> accessed 25 January 2015.
19. Ibid.
20. Protocol against the Smuggling of Migrants by Land, Sea and Air, supplementing the United Nations Convention against Transnational Organized Crime, GA Res. 55/25, annex III, UN GAOR, 55th Sess., Supp. No. 49, at 65, UN Doc A/45/49 (Vol.1) (2001); 40 ILM 384 (2001). ('*Smuggling Protocol*') art 3(a).
21. UNODC, above n 4, 17.
22. Ibid.
23. See Donald R. Rothwell, 'The Law of the Sea and the MV Tampa Incident: Reconciling Maritime Principles with Coastal State Sovereignty' (2002) 13 *Public Law Review* 118, 118.
24. Ibid.
25. Smuggling Protocol, art 7.
26. UNODC, above n 4, 25.
27. *United Nations Convention on the Law of the Sea*, opened for signature 10 December 1982, 1833 UNTS 3 (entered into force 16 November 1994) ('LOSC'), art 101.
28. IMO, *Code of Practice for the Investigation of the Crimes of Piracy and Armed Robbery against Ships*, adopted 29 November 2001, Res A.922(22), art 2(2).
29. Klein, above n 9, 303.
30. IMO, *Reports on Acts of Piracy and Armed Robbery against Ships* (Annual Report, 2013), IMO Doc MSC.4/Circ.208, para 5.
31. IMO, *Code of Practice for the Investigation of the Crimes of Piracy and Armed Robbery against Ships*, adopted 29 November 2001, Res A.922(22), art 2(2).
32. Ibid, para 7.
33. See, for example, Tomáš Vlček, 'The South China Sea and the Threat of Piracy' (18 June 2009), *Global Politics*, available at <http://www.globalpolitics.cz/clanky/the-south-china-sea-and-the-threat-of-piracy> accessed 28 January 2015.
34. UNODC, above n 4, 45.

35 Patricia Birnie, Alan Boyle and Catherine Redgwell, *International Law & the Environment* (Oxford University Press, 3rd edn, 2009) 400.
36 Ibid.
37 UNODC, above n 4, 45.
38 Alacs and Georges, above n 17, 147.
39 UNODC, above n 4, 45.
40 UNESCO, 'Facts and Figures on Marine Biodiversity', available at <http://www.unesco.org/new/en/natural-sciences/ioc-oceans/priority-areas/rio-20-ocean/blueprint-for-the-future-we-want/marine-biodiversity/facts-and-figures-on-marine-biodiversity/> accessed 30 January 2015.
41 UN Report of the Secretary-General, above n 3, para 47.
42 There is only one minor qualification relating to the continued existence of the right of innocent passage in areas of internal waters enclosed by straight baselines where those waters were not previously considered to be internal waters: LOSC art 8.
43 LOSC art 219.
44 LOSC arts 218(1), 220(1).
45 LOSC art 2.
46 LOSC art 3.
47 LOSC art 17.
48 LOSC art 19(1).
49 LOSC art 19(2).
50 LOSC art 21.
51 LOSC arts 55, 57.
52 LOSC art 56.
53 Warwick Gullett, 'Legislative Implementation of the Law of the Sea Convention in Australia' (2013) 32 *University of Tasmania Law Review* 184–207.
54 LOSC art 111(2).
55 LOSC art 111(4).
56 LOSC art 111(1).
57 See, for example, Koh Swee Lean Collin, 'Pan-ASEAN Maritime Security Cooperation: Prospects for Pooling Resources', *RSIS Commentaries*, No 096/2013 dated 17 May 2013, p 2.
58 MNE7, 'Regional Analysis: Baltic Sea Region (BSR) and SUCBAS' (Draft Version 2, 9 February 2012), p 2.
59 Pekka Visuri, Timo Hellenberg and Hellenberg International Oy, 'Regional Organization Report: Baltic Sea Maritime Cooperation' (July 2013), p 5; MNE 4, above n 58, 18.
60 Visuri, Hellenbery and Hellenberg International Oy, above n 59, 6.
61 MNE 7, above n 58, 19.
62 Christina Gestrin, 'Regional Cooperation in the Baltic Sea Region-Recommendations to Foster a Joint Understanding and Take Action against Common Risks and Threats', 8 (2010) *Asia Europe Journal* 267, 269.
63 See, for example, Collin Koh Swee Lean, 'Boosting Maritime Security Cooperation', *The Straits Time* (18 May 2013).
64 EIU Views Wire, 'Guinea-Bissau Politics: Guinea-Bissau joins Frontex' (4 April 2008).
65 Frontex, 'Update: ICGV Týr conducts search and rescue of 450 migrants' (3 January 2015), available at <http://frontex.europa.eu/news/update-icgv-tyr-conducts-search-and-rescue-of-450-migrants-9zLoW0> accessed 10 February 2015.
66 Frontex, 'Latest Trends at External Borders of the EU' (2 February 2015), available at <http://frontex.europa.eu/news/latest-trends-at-external-borders-of-the-eu-6Z3kpC> accessed 10 February 2015.
67 Frontex, 'How Joint Operations Work', available at <http://frontex.europa.eu/operations/types-of-operations/general> accessed 10 February 2015.
68 Frontex, 'Legal Basis', available at < http://frontex.europa.eu/about-frontex/legal-basis > accessed 10 February 2015; 'Partners', available at <http://frontex.europa.eu/partners/national-authorities/> accessed 10 February 2015. Bodies which have established cooperation relations with the Frontex include the EUROPOL, CeCLAD-M (vessels relating to drug trafficking), EMSA, EFCA and MAOC-N (vessels relating to drug trafficking).

69 For example, based on the authorisation of the EU Parliament, Frontex has the ability to acquire its own helicopters and cars to patrol the borders of the EU. Deutsche Welle, 'EU to Beef up Border Agency Frontex' (13 September 2011).
70 Ibid.
71 Agreement on Cooperative Enforcement of Fisheries Laws between the Government of Australia and the Government of the French Republic in the Maritime Areas Adjacent to the French Southern and Antarctic Territories, Heard Island and the McDonald Islands, Paris, 8 January 2007. Treaty text available at [2007] ATNIF 1.
72 Treaty between the Government of Australia and the Government of the French Republic on Cooperation in the Maritime Areas adjacent to the French Southern and Antarctic Territories (TAAF), Heard Island and the McDonald Islands, Canberra, 24 November 2003. In force 1 February 2005. [Hereafter, "2003 Treaty."] Treaty text available at [2005] ATS 6, and (2004) 19 *International Journal of Marine and Coastal Law* 545–553.
73 See Erik Jaap Molenaar, 'Multilateral hot pursuit and illegal fishing in the Southern Ocean: The Pursuits of the *Viarsa 1* and the *South Tomi*' (2004) 19 *International Journal of Marine and Coastal Law* 19–42.
74 Art 5(1)(a).
75 Art 3(3).
76 Art 3(5), Annex II.
77 Arts 1 and 3.
78 Art 4. The issue of whether this is compatible with LOSC hot pursuit provisions is discussed in Warwick Gullett and Clive Schofield, 'Pushing the limits of the Law of the Sea Convention: Australian and French cooperative surveillance and enforcement in the Southern Ocean' (2007) 22 *International Journal of Marine and Coastal Law* 545–583.
79 Australian Customs Service, 'Enforcement Operations in the Southern Ocean', <http://www.customs.gov.au/webdata/resources/files/FS_Enforcement_Operations_in_the_SOI.pdf>.
80 Art 5.
81 Annex III.
82 Annex II, Art 2.
83 Note 1 above.
84 Preamble.
85 Warner, above n 2, 6.
86 Transform Aqorau, 'Illegal Fishing and Fisheries Law Enforcement in Small Island Developing States: The Pacific Islands Experience' (2000) 15(1) *International Journal of Marine and Coastal Law* 37, 55.
87 See Pio Manoa, 'Fisheries Monitoring, Control and Surveillance in the Pacific Island Region', 18(1) (2006) *PIMRIS Newsletter*, (Pacific Islands Marine Resources Information System), 5–7, 6; <www.usp.ac.fj/fileadmin/files/services/library/PIMRIS/Newsletter/pimris_newsletter_mar2006.pdf>. See also Aqorau, above n 86, 54–58.
88 Australian Fisheries Management Authority, 'Operation Kuru Kuru tackles illegal fishing in the Pacific' at < http://www.afma.gov.au/operation-kuru-kuru-tackles-illegal-fishing-in-the-pacific-2/>.
89 Ruijie He, 'Coast Guards and Maritime Piracy: Sailing past the Impediments to Cooperation in Asia' (2009) 22 (5) *The Pacific Review* 667, 668.
90 Ibid 675.
91 Ibid 672.
92 Ibid 677.
93 Ibid 670.
94 Mingjiang Li, 'China and Maritime Cooperation in East Asia: Recent Developments and Future Prospects' (2010) 19 (64) *Journal of Contemporary China* 291, 293, 297.

23

Developing New Regulatory Paradigms for the Conservation and Sustainable Use of Marine Biodiversity in Areas beyond National Jurisdiction

Robin Warner

Introduction

As international shipping steadily rises and technological advances provide more opportunities to access the resources of marine areas beyond national jurisdiction (ABNJ)[1], the scope of threats to the marine environment and its biodiversity increases exponentially.[2] Seaborne trade and passenger cruises are rapidly expanding and are expected to double over the next two decades.[3] The impacts to the marine environment and its biodiversity from intentional and accidental vessel source discharges including from oil and other hazardous substances, noise and ship strikes on marine mammals, are likely to be compounded with more prevalent high seas traffic.[4] The fishing industry is now supported by a wide array of technology including global positioning systems, multi-beam sonar, and stronger and more powerful cables and winches. Fishing nets and lines are composed of virtually indestructible synthetic material and may be laid over vast areas of ocean. Heavy bottom trawling gear has already caused substantial damage to vulnerable marine ecosystems (VMEs).[5] Beyond these existing risks, new and emerging uses of ABNJ such as more intrusive marine scientific research, bio-prospecting for marine genetic resources, deep seabed mining and marine geo-engineering activities to mitigate the effects of climate change have the potential to harm the fragile and highly interlinked ecosystems of the open ocean and the deep seabed, if not sustainably managed now and into the future.[6]

The 1982 UN Convention on the Law of the Sea (LOSC) establishes an overarching framework for protection and preservation of the marine environment in Part XII which obliges States Parties to protect and preserve the whole of the marine environment including ABNJ. The fairly general and aspirational provisions of Part XII envisage a collaborative system of maritime regulation in which global and regional organisations of States cooperate to craft the international rules, standards and recommended practices and procedures needed to protect and preserve the marine environment both within and beyond national jurisdiction. The LOSC also recognised that regulatory developments around marine environmental protection were already taking place in other international law fora and that this complementary development of international marine environmental law principles would continue to evolve in parallel with the law of the sea. Article 237 highlights this complementary relationship between the LOSC and other conventions on protection and preservation of the marine environment, anticipating and encouraging an ongoing reconciliation between the LOSC and other relevant conventions. In practice, reconciling regulatory developments to support an integrated system of environmental protection for ABNJ, including conservation and sustainable use of marine resources and biodiversity, presents considerable challenges in terms of scale and consistency between the two separate trajectories of law of the sea and international marine environmental law. Modern conservation measures and tools such as environmental impact assessment (EIA), marine protected areas (MPAs), marine spatial planning and development mechanisms such as technology transfer and capacity building are particularly underdeveloped in the legal and institutional framework for ABNJ.[7]

This chapter will explore key features of the maritime regulation framework for ABNJ and its applicability to the conservation and sustainable use of marine biodiversity, gaps and disconnects in that framework and ongoing global efforts to develop more effective regulation systems for these vast areas of the ocean. It will discuss some of the options which have been considered in the UN Ad Hoc Informal Open-ended Working Group to study issues related to the conservation and sustainable use of marine biodiversity in areas beyond national jurisdiction (BBNJ Working Group) to evolve the legal and institutional framework for conservation and sustainable use of marine biodiversity in ABNJ and their current and future relevance for maritime regulation in ABNJ.

Key features of the maritime regulation framework for ABNJ

The high seas provisions of the LOSC, discussed in Chapter 2, specify that freedom of the high seas may be exercised by all States whether coastal or landlocked.[8] The freedom of the high seas encompasses freedoms of navigation and overflight, freedom to lay submarine cables and pipelines, freedom to construct artificial islands and installations, freedom of fishing and freedom of scientific research.[9] High seas freedoms are not unqualified and the LOSC provides that the freedoms of the high seas are exercised under the conditions laid in the LOSC and by other rules of international law.[10] In particular, high seas freedoms must be exercised subject to the general obligation to protect and preserve the marine environment in Article 192 of the LOSC. Additionally, a core high seas freedom, the freedom of fishing, is subject to the duty to cooperate in conserving and managing the living resources of the high seas codified in Article 118 of the LOSC. This obligation has been progressively implemented through the UN Fish Stocks Agreement and the many conservation and management measures adopted by regional fisheries management organisations that are binding on their member States.[11]

Juxtaposed with the high seas regime applicable to the water column in ABNJ, is Part XI of the LOSC which designates the non-living resources of the deep seabed beyond national jurisdiction as the common heritage of mankind and subjects them to a supranational management regime administered by the International Seabed Authority (ISA).[12] The ISA has a circumscribed responsibility under Article 145 of the LOSC to ensure the effective protection of the marine environment from the harmful effects which may arise from activities in the deep seabed beyond national jurisdiction, known as the Area rather than a comprehensive responsibility to protect the deep sea environment from all threats. For this purpose, it is required to adopt appropriate rules, regulations, and procedures for the prevention, reduction and control of pollution from activities such as drilling, excavation, disposal of waste, construction and operation or maintenance of installations pipelines and other devices associated with activities in the Area and for the protection and conservation of the natural resources of the Area and flora and fauna of the marine environment.[13] States have a complementary obligation to adopt laws and regulations no less effective than those adopted by the ISA, to prevent, reduce and control pollution of the marine environment from activities in the Area undertaken by their flag vessels, installations, structures and other devices under their control.[14] The ISA has so far adopted binding codes for the prospecting and exploration phases of deep seabed mining for three mineral resources, polymetallic nodules, polymetallic sulphides and cobalt rich crusts which include detailed environmental safeguards.[15] At every stage of their activities, prospectors and exploration contractors have substantial responsibilities to assess and monitor the effects of their operations on the marine environment. As deep seabed mining activities enter the exploitation phase, further development of the ISA's regulatory framework will be necessary to address the more intrusive impacts of commercial scale mining on the marine environment beyond national jurisdiction.[16]

A substantial body of international law instruments have been developed since the adoption of the LOSC which complement and extend the LOSC framework for protection of the marine environment. Of most importance for the conservation and sustainable use of marine biodiversity, is the Convention on Biological Diversity (CBD) adopted in 1992. The CBD introduced the concept of biodiversity in international law, with Article 2 of the Convention defining biodiversity as 'the variability among living organisms from all sources, including, *inter alia*, terrestrial, marine and other aquatic ecosystems and the ecological complexes of which they are part' and including 'diversity within species, between species and of ecosystems.' This comprehensive approach added new regulatory dimensions to marine environmental protection which had previously focused on prevention reduction and control of marine pollution and the protection of single species.[17]

The three broad objectives of the CBD are the conservation of biodiversity, the sustainable use of its components and the fair and equitable sharing of the benefits arising out of the utilisation of genetic resources.[18] For the purpose of allocating substantive rights and obligations under the CBD, however, the components of biodiversity were divided between those within and beyond national jurisdiction. The jurisdictional scope provision in Article 4 of the CBD limits its application to components of biodiversity in areas within the limits of national jurisdiction and to processes and activities related to biodiversity carried out under the jurisdiction or control of Contracting Parties both within and beyond national jurisdiction. Article 5 of the CBD limits the obligations of Contracting Parties in relation to conservation and sustainable use of biodiversity in ABNJ to a duty to co-operate directly or through competent international organisations. There is therefore no direct obligation on Contracting Parties to conserve or sustainably use the components of marine biodiversity in ABNJ.

The 1979 Convention on the Conservation of Migratory Species of Wild Animals (CMS) also plays a role in conserving marine species across ABNJ. The objective of the CMS is to conserve migratory species of wild animals, including certain marine species that migrate through marine areas within and beyond national jurisdiction. Its provisions have direct relevance to many of the seabirds and marine mammals migrating through ABNJ and measures taken by States Parties within their national jurisdictions can have a beneficial effect on the relevant species throughout their range. It provides a framework for range States to cooperate in protecting species that migrate across national boundaries through undertaking scientific research, restoring the habitat and removing impediments to the migration of species listed in Appendix I to the Convention as endangered. Agreements may also be concluded between range States to protect migratory species listed in Appendix II to CMS as having unfavourable conservation status. Under the Agreement on the Conservation of African-Eurasian Migratory Waterbirds (AEWA) States Parties are obliged to take coordinated measures to maintain migratory waterbird species in a favourable conservation status or to restore them to such a status within the limits of their national jurisdiction.[19] Another key CMS agreement for ABNJ is the 2006 Agreement on the Conservation of Albatross and Petrels (ACAP) which obliges States Parties to take a variety of conservation measures to enhance the conservation status of albatrosses and petrels including restoring their habitats and developing and implementing measures to prevent, remove, minimise or mitigate the adverse effects of activities that may influence the conservation status of albatrosses and petrels.[20]

When viewed together, these disparate features of the ABNJ regulatory framework represent a fundamentally fractured system for the conservation and sustainable use of marine biodiversity in ABNJ. The different legal status of the high seas water column and the deep seabed beyond national jurisdiction complicates the development of a coherent approach to the conservation and sustainable use of biodiversity in ABNJ. Variable compliance standards among flag States with marine pollution obligations and the lack of monitoring and enforcement mechanisms in ABNJ compound the obstacles to achieving an integrated system for conservation and sustainable use of marine biodiversity in these vast areas of the ocean. The separate trajectory of international environmental law instruments such as the CBD has introduced a range of modern conservation principles, measures and tools which have yet to be properly incorporated in the law of the sea framework for protection and preservation of the marine environment.

Gaps in the regulatory framework for conservation and sustainable use of marine biodiversity in ABNJ

Responsibility for implementing international law obligations to conserve the marine biodiversity of ABNJ is dispersed among a variety of global and regional regimes with no overarching global instrument or institutional focal point to develop best practice standards or to adopt conservation measures for unregulated activities in ABNJ. There are multiple gaps in the geographic coverage of the relevant regulatory instruments and institutions, their incorporation of biodiversity conservation objectives, the effectiveness of their decision making structures and the systems in place to monitor and enforce compliance biodiversity conservation measures in ABNJ. These deficiencies are compounded by a lack of coordination and cooperation between the global, regional and sectoral organisations which regulate human uses of ABNJ. This section will discuss selected examples from key sectors with responsibility for regulating activities in ABNJ.

Fisheries

There are 20 existing and prospective RFMOs with mandates to establish fisheries conservation and management measures.[21] Although tuna and tuna-like species are managed by RFMOs in virtually all the relevant areas of ocean beyond national jurisdiction, there are still significant gaps in the coverage of non-tuna fisheries even though regional collaboration is an essential component in conserving and managing the full range of highly migratory and straddling fish stocks as well as discrete high seas fish stocks. The North East Atlantic Fisheries Commission (NEAFC) and the North-West Atlantic Fisheries Organization (NAFO) cover the North East and North West Atlantic but there is no multilateral body regulating fisheries in the Arctic. The Atlantic south of the NEAFC/NAFO areas of responsibility is only partially covered by the South East Atlantic Fisheries Organization and the Commission for Conservation of Antarctic Marine Living Resources area south of the Antarctic convergence. Until the end of 2009, there were no general fisheries commissions in the Pacific to manage non-highly migratory species. The treaty establishing the South Pacific Regional Fisheries Management Organization (SPRFMO) was concluded in November 2009 and entered into force in 2012. Negotiations are still ongoing for a North Pacific RFMO. In the Indian Ocean, the Regional Commission for Fisheries (RECOFI) covers the Gulf area and the Southern Indian Ocean Fisheries Agreement (SIOFA), concluded in July 2006, entered into force in June 2012.[22]

Fisheries governance arrangements exhibit considerable diversity and varying rates of progress in their approaches to incorporating environmental protection principles and biodiversity conservation objectives into their management regimes. Recent reviews of RFMO practice at the global level reveal several factors that have limited the effectiveness of RFMOs in implementing fisheries conservation and management measures in an ecologically sustainable manner.[23] These include:

- **Absence of environmental protection principles in the RFMO Conventions.** The absence of modern environmental protection principles or guidelines such as the precautionary approach and ecosystem based management in some RFMO conventions concluded prior to the Fish Stocks Agreement means that unless all RFMO members agree, they are not obliged to consider principles of sustainability when adopting conservation and management measures although this is slowly altering with the emerging customary international law status of such principles.
- **Ineffective decision-making frameworks.** It is the established practice of RFMOs to take decisions on their conservation and management measures by consensus, even when their instruments may not require it and to allow for individual objections to conservation and management measures agreed by the majority of member States.[24] This allows objecting RFMO members to take advantage of uncertainties in scientific advice and can lead to a dilution of conservation and management measures even where the precautionary approach and ecosystem based management requirements exist. Many of the RFMOs that were established prior to the conclusion of the UN Fish Stocks Agreement allow for States to opt out or object to implementing conservation and management measures that have been agreed within the RFMO.
- **Lack of a formal global coordination mechanism.** There is no overarching global coordination mechanism to oversee the conservation and management activities of RFMOs in ABNJ and monitor their performance against best practice standards and ensure cross-sectoral exchange of information. This makes it difficult to address global problems such as the conservation of highly migratory marine species or Illegal, Unregulated and Unreported (IUU) fishing as fishing vessels may move between regions concentrating their fishing effort in areas where conservation and management measures are lax or non-existent. At the regional level there has been very little consultation and collaboration between RFMOs. The first meeting between the tuna RFMOs, the 'Kobe Process' occurred in 2007.[25]

- **Participation levels.** In many regions developing States lack the resources and capacity to participate fully in RFMOs and implement their obligations effectively.
- **Failure to deal effectively with non-Parties.** Few RFMOs include all the participants in a regional fishery among their members. An RFMO may have agreed on environmentally sound conservation and management measures for fisheries in high seas areas but only those States which have agreed to be bound by its agreement are obliged to apply its measures. The failure to deal effectively with non-Parties or 'free riders' undermines the incentives for fishing vessels of RFMO members to adopt restrictive conservation and management measures.

Regional seas arrangements

Since the early 1970s, a diverse array of binding and non-binding regional arrangements has been negotiated around the globe to engage States in the collaborative protection of their offshore marine environments. Many of the binding regional seas arrangements were initiated through the UN Environment Programme (UNEP) Regional Seas Programme while others are the result of independent agreements between regional partners.[26] They now cover 18 maritime regions which differ markedly in their character and extent.[27] The UNEP regional seas arrangements, together with the non-UNEP regional marine environmental protection arrangements, involve 149 States, approximately 95.5 per cent of the world's States.[28] Currently the areas of responsibility of many of these arrangements are limited to waters within national jurisdiction and very few of them make provision for consensual environmental protection measures in high seas enclaves and high seas areas adjacent to waters within national jurisdiction.[29] The geographic scope of these arrangements has been determined by political opportunity rather than any systematic scheme to encompass all the oceanic regions of the world.[30] No legally binding conventions have yet been developed for the regional arrangements in the East Asian Seas, South Asian Seas, North-West Pacific, North-East Pacific, or for the Arctic. Moreover, these conventions are primarily groupings of coastal States, and their jurisdiction is generally restricted to their coastal zones, or out to 200 nautical miles. The exceptions are the following: the OSPAR Convention area, which has high-seas areas within its remit; the Mediterranean, where most coastal States have for various reasons not yet claimed EEZs; the South Pacific, which includes within its mandate the 'donut' holes between the EEZs of its members;[31] and the Antarctic Treaty System, consisting of both the Antarctic Treaty and its Protocol on Environmental Protection as well as the CCAMLR Convention.[32]

The spread of regional arrangements for marine environmental protection has paralleled the negotiation and entry into force of the LOSC and has both reflected and advanced the development of modern environmental protection principles.[33] The early focus of most regional arrangements such as the OSPAR Convention[34] and the Barcelona Convention[35] in the Mediterranean was the control of marine pollution but many have since adopted a more integrated approach to the protection of the marine environment including conservation of its biodiversity and the development of systems of marine protected areas.[36]

The broadening of their scope in relation to approaches to conservation and targets for conservation intervention has enabled many regional arrangements to assimilate new developments in international environmental law and policy through mechanisms such as protocols and non-binding documents such as action programmes and strategic plans.[37] The majority of regional agreements are based on framework conventions which depend on implementation by States Parties in waters within national jurisdiction. These conventions have been supplemented by Protocols, ministerial level agreements and strategy documents which regulate different sources of marine pollution, provide for the protection of threatened and endangered species and the establishment of marine protected areas to preserve, *inter alia*, rare or fragile ecosystems.[38] In most regions these binding legal instruments and soft law accords are accompanied by planning documents which define regional priorities for marine environmental protection.[39]

Key factors that have limited the effectiveness of RSAs in implementing biodiversity conservation in ABNJ include:

- The limiting of their areas of responsibility to waters under national jurisdiction;
- The lack of reference to sustainable development and use of marine biodiversity in their mandates; and
- The absence of specific collaboration provisions or arrangements and mechanisms between RSAs and RFMOs.

Shipping

Maritime transport particularly seaborne trade and passenger cruises constitute one of the most intensive uses of ABNJ and poses ongoing threats to marine biodiversity through the intentional and accidental discharge of pollutants into the sea. The IMO as the focal point for technical expertise and stakeholder interests in international shipping has developed a variety of instruments to reduce and mitigate vessel source pollution across all areas of the ocean including ABNJ. The principal vessel source pollution conventions, including MARPOL 73/78, the 1972 London Convention and its 1996 Protocol[40] and the 2001 Anti Fouling Convention,[41] apply to the flag vessels of member States both within and beyond national jurisdiction. With such a detailed regulatory framework in place, the key gap which arises in connection with conservation and sustainable use of biodiversity in ABNJ is the need to monitor and enforce compliance with the wide array of instruments which have entered into force. This function is still largely the responsibility of individual flag States particularly in ABNJ with very little reporting of vessel source pollution and negligible follow up action by flag or port States of high seas pollution incidents.

Deep seabed mining

The ISA has established a strong framework of environmental safeguards for exploration contractors in the Area. A contractor must submit an assessment of the potential environmental impacts of proposed activities with an application for approval of a plan of work together with a description of proposed measures for the prevention, reduction and control of possible impacts on the marine environment.[42] The ISA has also issued and revised the 2010 Recommendations for the Guidance of Contractors for the Assessment of the Possible Environmental Impacts Arising from Exploration for Polymetallic Nodules in the Area which specify the particular activities of exploration contractors that are subject to EIA.[43] The sponsoring state of an exploration contractor is under a due diligence obligation to ensure that an exploration contractor fulfils all their responsibilities under the ISA's Mining Code.[44] An important element missing from the deep seabed mining environmental protection framework, however, is a collaborative mechanism for monitoring and enforcing compliance involving exploration contractors and

ISA representatives. In addition, a code for the exploitation phase of deep seabed mining in the Area has not yet been developed and it may prove more challenging to maintain best practice environmental safeguards once commercial scale activities begin.

Global and regional initiatives to develop the regulatory framework for conservation and sustainable use of marine biodiversity in ABNJ

A number of global and regional initiatives have been taken over the last decade to address some of the gaps and disconnects in the regulatory framework for conservation and sustainable use of marine biodiversity in ABNJ. The focal point for these efforts has been the BBNJ Working Group established by the UNGA in 2004. The CBD has supported the discussions in the BBNJ Working Group with some technical and scientific initiatives related to environmental impact assessment (EIA) and the designation of ecologically and biologically significant areas (EBSAs) in the world's oceans including in ABNJ. At the regional level, steps have been taken to designate marine protected areas and fisheries closure areas with biodiversity conservation components in ABNJ by regional seas organisations (RSAs) and regional fisheries management organisations (RFMOs). Governments and non-government organisations with interests in the unique ecosystem of the Sargasso Sea have also launched a special initiative to conserve biodiversity in this ocean area which is largely composed of high seas.

BBNJ Working Group

The main impetus for considering new approaches to strengthen the regulatory framework for conservation and sustainable use of biodiversity in ABNJ originated from the UN Informal Consultative Process on Oceans and the Law of the Sea (UNICPOLOS) which has discussed a wide range of oceans issues since its inception in 1999. The fifth meeting of UNICPOLOS in 2004 canvassed new and emerging uses of the oceans highlighting the risks these uses posed to conservation and sustainable use of biodiversity in ABNJ in the absence of environmental protection measures agreed and implemented by the international community.[45] Recommendations from that meeting to the UNGA resulted in the establishment of the BBNJ Working Group which has now met nine times. Some consistent themes have characterised the discussions of the BBNJ Working Group. It has endorsed the fundamental importance of basing decisions on activities in ABNJ on precautionary and ecosystem based approaches and using the best available science and prior environmental impact assessment to inform such decisions.[46] Participating States have agreed on the need for improved implementation of global and regional agreements relevant to conservation and sustainable use of biodiversity in ABNJ including the LOSC and the CBD.[47] The integral role of sectoral and regional organisations in implementing such agreements has been recognised as has the need to improve the management of these bodies and to develop and strengthen mechanisms for their accountability.[48] Destructive fishing practices have been singled out as one of the major threats to marine biodiversity in ABNJ and it has been agreed that these practices should be addressed on an urgent basis by the UNGA, FAO and RFMOs.[49] IUU fishing was also considered to be a major obstacle to the conservation and sustainable use of marine biodiversity in ABNJ requiring an integrated and accelerated approach across all relevant fora to address this issue through measures such as enhanced flag State responsibility, port State measures, and more collaborative monitoring and enforcement of compliance with fisheries conservation and management measures.[50] A lack of consensus among participating States on the legal status of marine genetic resources in ABNJ has been a contentious issue throughout the BBNJ meetings. In particular there has been no consensus on rights of access to and the sharing of benefits derived from these resources.[51]

In 2011, the BBNJ Working Group recommended to the UNGA that 'a process be initiated [. . .] with a view to ensuring that the legal framework for the conservation and sustainable use of marine biodiversity in areas beyond national jurisdiction effectively addresses those issues by identifying gaps and ways forward, including through the implementation of existing instruments and the possible development of a multilateral agreement under UNCLOS.'[52] This process would address 'together and as a whole, marine genetic resources, including questions on the sharing of benefits, measures such as area-based management tools, including marine protected areas, and environmental impact assessments, capacity-building and the transfer of marine technology.'[53]

At Rio+20, States committed themselves 'to address, on an urgent basis, building on the work of the Ad Hoc Open-ended Informal Working Group and before the end of the 69th session of the General Assembly, the issue of the conservation and sustainable use of marine biological diversity of areas beyond national jurisdiction, including by taking a decision on the development of an international instrument under the United Nations Convention on the Law of the Sea.'[54] This commitment was recalled by the UNGA in its 67th session,[55] and reaffirmed in the recommendations to the UNGA developed at the sixth meeting of the BBNJ Working Group in 2013.[56] At the same meeting, the Working Group also proposed to establish a process to make recommendations to the UNGA 'on the scope, parameters and feasibility of an international instrument under the Convention' in order to prepare for the decision to be taken at the 69th session of the UNGA in 2015, whether to start the negotiation of an international instrument on the conservation and sustainable use of biodiversity in ABNJ.[57] The final BBNJ Working Group meeting in January 2015 recommended that the UNGA decide to *'develop an international legally-binding instrument under the Convention [UNCLOS] addressing the conservation and sustainable use of marine biological diversity beyond national jurisdiction'*.[58] The Working Group also recommended that the negotiations should address marine genetic resources, including questions on the sharing of benefits, measures such as area-based management tools, including marine protected areas, environmental impact assessments and capacity building and the transfer of marine technology and that the prospective treaty should not undermine existing relevant legal instruments and frameworks and relevant global, regional and sectoral bodies. The UNGA has now decided to develop an international legally-binding instrument under the Convention on the conservation and sustainable use of marine biological diversity of areas beyond national jurisdiction.[59] A Preparatory Committee will commence discussions in 2016 with a mandate to make substantive recommendations to UNGA, by the end of 2017, on the elements of a draft text of an international legally-binding instrument. On the basis of these recommendations from the Preparatory Committee, UNGA will take a decision in 2018 on the timing of an intergovernmental conference which will have a mandate to finalise and adopt the treaty text.

Some potential ramifications of such an instrument for the regulatory framework in ABNJ will be discussed in the next section.

CBD initiatives

The CBD has laid some of the groundwork for area based management in ABNJ at the regional level through the provision of expert advice on describing marine areas of ecological or biological significance (EBSAs) and in addressing biodiversity concerns in sustainable fisheries. In 2008, the Ninth Meeting of the Conference of Parties (COP 9) of the CBD adopted the following scientific criteria for identifying 'ecologically or biologically significant areas in need of protection in open ocean waters and deep sea habitats':

- Uniqueness/rarity;
- Special importance for life history stages of species;
- Importance for threatened, endangered or declining species and/or habitats;
- Vulnerability, fragility, sensitivity or slow recovery;
- Biological productivity;
- Biological diversity; and
- Naturalness.[60]

This decision also provided scientific guidance for selecting areas to establish a representative network of marine protected areas including in open ocean waters and deep sea habitats.[61] The tenth CBD COP in 2010 agreed on a process of regional workshops for the description of EBSAs.[62] The workshop outcomes were designed to inform relevant regional and global organisations. The work was premised on recognition that the application of the EBSA criteria is a scientific and technical exercise, that areas found to meet the criteria may require enhanced conservation and management measures, and that this can be achieved through a variety of means, including marine protected areas and impact assessments. The CBD also recognised that the identification of EBSAs and the selection of conservation and management measures is a matter for States and competent intergovernmental organisations, in accordance with international law, including the LOSC.[63] Regional workshops on describing EBSAs have been organised covering the North-East Atlantic, the Western South Pacific, the Wider Caribbean and Western Mid-Atlantic, the Western Indian Ocean and the Eastern Tropical, Temperate Pacific, North Pacific Region and the South-East Atlantic region, among others.[64] In addition, areas meeting EBSA compatible criteria have been described in the Mediterranean. At the CBD COP 11 in Hyderabad in October 2012, it was agreed that the areas described as EBSAs by these workshops and processes, after review by CBD SBSTTA, should be sent to the UN and relevant international organisations.[65]

The Conference of the Parties of the CBD (COP CBD) has also been proactive in investigating the scientific and technical aspects of EIA for activities in ABNJ. It convened an Expert Workshop on Scientific and Technical Elements of the CBD EIA Guidelines which focused on ABNJ in November 2009.[66] This highlighted some of the governance and practical challenges related to the implementation of EIA for activities in ABNJ. Some of the practical difficulties associated with conducting EIAs in ABNJ included:

- The industry proposing the activity and the national flag State jurisdiction are often far from the marine area affected;
- The conduct of EIA and management, control, monitoring, surveillance and follow-up activity were likely to be more costly and may be less effective for a given budget; and
- Capacity building needs for EIA in ABNJ would be greater as customs of practice are less established, methodologies less mature, and multiple assessment cultures may converge in the same area.[67]

The complex and fragmentary nature of the law and institutions governing ABNJ were accentuated including:

- The split legal framework for ABNJ – high seas (LOSC Part VII) and deep seabed beyond national jurisdiction – the Area (LOSC Part XI and Part XI Implementation Agreement);
- The diverse institutional framework for ABNJ including States, non-State actors and global and regional organisations and the need for cooperation between all these actors to conserve biodiversity;
- The fact that stakeholders are harder to define for ABNJ because communities do not have immediate proximity to these areas; and
- The variable standards of compliance among States with environmental assessment obligations in international conventions.[68]

The Workshop's Report was considered by the tenth meeting of the COP CBD in 2010 which endorsed the development of voluntary guidelines for the consideration of biodiversity in EIAs for marine and coastal areas drawing on the guidance from the Workshop.[69] The Guidelines were developed for all marine and coastal areas rather than simply for ABNJ emphasising the interconnections between ocean ecosystems across jurisdictional boundaries and endorsed by the 11th COP CBD in 2012.[70]

Regional initiatives

The OSPAR Convention, the non UNEP regional seas agreement for the North-East Atlantic includes in its area of responsibility waters within and beyond national jurisdiction.[71] At the OSPAR Ministerial meeting in 2010, six MPAs were established in ABNJ.[72] They cover a total area of 287,065 square kms, protecting a series of seamounts and sections of the Mid-Atlantic Ridge and host a range of vulnerable deep-sea habitats and species.[73] A seventh pelagic high Seas MPA, Charlie-Gibbs North (178,094 square kms), was designated in 2012 in waters superjacent to an area of the deep seabed included within an Icelandic submission to the Commission on the Limits of the Continental Shelf.[74] Some management provisions are contained in OSPAR Recommendations for each of these areas; however, to date no cross-sectoral management plans have been put in place.

The NEAFC has regulatory competence over three large maritime areas beyond national jurisdiction in the North East Atlantic Ocean and may recommend conservation and management measures for all fisheries resources within its Convention Area with the exception of sea mammals and sedentary species and tuna or tuna-like species.[75] These measures include regulation of fishing gear and size limits for fish, the establishment of closed seasons and closed areas, the establishment of total allowable catches and their allocation to Contracting Parties and the regulation of the amount of fishing effort and its allocation to Contracting Parties.[76] NEAFC recognised the vulnerability of some of the deep water habitats within its Regulatory Area by closing five seamount areas and a section of the Reykjanes Ridge on the high seas for three years to bottom trawling and static fishing gear from 2005 to 2007.[77] It also agreed to reduce fishing pressures on a large range of vulnerable species in deep water habitats within the Regulatory Area by 30 per cent from 2005 onwards following advice from the International Council for the Exploration of the Sea (ICES).[78] The initial ban on fishing on the Reykjanes Ridge was extended beyond the three year period until new closure measures were adopted based on scientific advice from ICES taking into account FAO's vulnerable marine ecosystem (VME) criteria and consideration by NEAFC's Permanent Committee on Management and Science.

NEAFC's incorporation of biodiversity considerations into its fisheries conservation and management measures has also been facilitated by its close working relationship with OSPAR. OSPAR and NEAFC signed a memorandum of understanding in 2008 and both organisations use ICES as their scientific advisory body.[79] ICES has recommended that a coordinated approach be taken between the two organisations to the protection of VMEs[80] and there has been considerable overlap between areas proposed for protection by OSPAR and those considered for closure to bottom fishing by NEAFC.[81]

A further initiative under the current regulatory framework for conservation and sustainable use of marine biodiversity in ABNJ is an environmental protection programme which was proposed by the Government of Bermuda together with intergovernmental and non-governmental organisations, to introduce conservation and management measures for the Sargasso Sea. The Sargasso Sea, named for the accumulations of holopelagic algae contained within the North Atlantic Subtropical Gyre, is a two million square nautical mile ecosystem that is primarily high seas. The OSPAR Secretariat and the Sargasso Sea Alliance have established informal research and information exchange systems and have concluded a Collaboration Arrangement.[82] The Alliance is using existing sectoral organisations with responsibilities for ABNJ areas – such as ICCAT, IMO and ISA – to put protection measures in place and has convened an inter-governmental meeting to establish a collaborative but non-legally binding protection regime for the Sargasso Sea.[83]

Developing the regulatory framework for conservation and sustainable use of marine biodiversity in ABNJ

Efforts by global and regional organisations to evolve and implement the regulatory framework for conservation and sustainable use of marine biodiversity in ABNJ have so far been unsystematic and geographically limited. In addition, the validity under international law of some initiatives such as the OSPAR designation of high seas MPAs has been questioned. A binding agreement under the LOSC on the conservation and sustainable use of biodiversity in ABNJ could provide the basis for a more integrated regulatory framework to further implement key provisions of Part XII of the LOSC on the protection and preservation of the marine environment.

Conclusion

The biodiversity conservation elements of any multilateral agreement adopted under the LOSC to conserve and sustainably use biodiversity in ABNJ should be designed to implement the spirit and intent of Part XII provisions of the LOSC, rather than radically changing the basic principles and inherent balance of the law of the sea. Part XII of the LOSC has many open-ended provisions suitable for further evolution and implementation. Given the growing threats and pressures on the marine environment of ABNJ and its biodiversity, it is timely to reconcile the modern conservation principles, measures and tools developed under international marine environmental law with the law of the sea. The discussions in the BBNJ process and related initiatives in the CBD and at regional level have demonstrated that a more integrated regulatory framework rather than the existing fragmentary collection of hard and soft law provisions and disparate institutions is needed to achieve this end. The rationale and objectives for incorporating the biodiversity conservation elements of area based management tools and EIA in such a legal and institutional structure have been extensively canvassed in the BBNJ Working Group over almost a decade. The time has now arrived to determine the objectives and content of a potential agreement under the LOSC for conservation and sustainable use of marine biodiversity in ABNJ. These objectives should include the development of an effectively managed, ecologically representative and well-connected system of MPAs in ABNJ and the promulgation of standards and a default system of EIA for all activities not already subject to EIA in ABNJ. The political process taking place in the UNGA will ultimately decide the shape of any new instrument under the law of the sea and its long term contribution to conservation and sustainable use of the marine biodiversity of ABNJ.

Notes

1 Marine areas beyond national jurisdiction (ABNJ) include both the high seas and the deep seabed beyond national jurisdiction.
2 H Scheiber 'Economic Uses of the Oceans and the Impacts on Marine Environments: Past Trends and Challenges Ahead' in D Vidas and PJ Schei (eds) *The World Ocean in Globalisation* (Martinus Nijhoff Publishers, Leiden, 2011) 65, 65–66.
3 Ibid, 87–90.
4 Ibid, 91–92.
5 Ibid, 86.
6 L Reeve, A Rulska-Domino and K Gjerde 'The Future of High Seas Marine Protected Areas' (2012) 26 *Ocean Yearbook* 265, 268.
7 D Freestone, 'Modern Principles of High Seas Governance: The Legal Underpinnings' (2009) 39 *International Environmental Policy and Law* 44.
8 LOSC, Arts 89, 87.
9 Ibid, Art 87(1).
10 Ibid, Art 87(2).
11 1995 Agreement for the Implementation of the Provisions of the United Nations Convention on the Law of the Sea of 10 December 1982 relating to the Conservation and Management of Straddling Fish Stocks and Highly Migratory Fish Stocks, Art 6.
12 LOSC, Arts 136, 137(2).
13 Ibid, Art 145.
14 Ibid, Art 209(2).
15 International Seabed Authority (ISBA), Council of the ISBA, *Decision relating to amendments to the Regulations for Prospecting and Exploration of Polymetallic Nodules* (2013), available at <http://www.isa.org.jm/files/documents/EN/19Sess/Council/ISBA-19C-17.pdf>; ISBA, Assembly of the ISBA, *Decision relating to the Regulations for Prospecting and Exploration of Polymetallic Sulphides in the Area* (2010) available at <http://www.isa.org.jm/files/documents/EN/16Sess/Assembly/ISBA-16A-12Rev1.pdf>; ISBA, Assembly of the ISBA, *Decision relating to the Regulations for Prospecting and Exploration of Cobalt-rich Ferromanganese Crusts in the Area* (2012), available at <http://www.isa.org.jm/files/documents/EN/18Sess/Assembly/ISBA-18A-11.pdf>.
16 The deep seabed regime is addressed in Chapter 15 of this volume.
17 C Joyner, 'Biodiversity in the Marine Environment: Resource Implications for the Law of the Sea' (1995) 28 *Vanderbilt Journal of Transnational Law* 644.
18 CBD, Art 1.
19 See also A Trouwbost, 'Migratory Species Conservation in Warming Polar Oceans, With Particular Reference to Seabirds' in E Molenaar, A Oude Elferink and D Rothwell (eds), *The Law of the Sea and the Polar Regions* (Martinus Nijhoff Publishers, Leiden, 2013) 163.
20 Ibid.
21 Food and Agricultural Organization (FAO), Fisheries and Aquaculture Department, *Regional Fishery Bodies – Fishery Governance Fact Sheets*, available at <http://www.fao.org/fishery/rfb/search/en>.
22 D Freestone, 'Fisheries Commissions and Organizations' in R Wolfrum (ed), *The Max Planck Encyclopedia of Public International Law* online ed (Oxford University Press, Oxford, 2008).
23 OECD, Task Force on IUU Fishing on the High Seas, *Closing the Net: Stopping Illegal Fishing on the High Seas* (2006), available at <http://www.oecd.org/sd-roundtable/papersandpublications/39375316.pdf>;

MW Lodge et al, *Recommended Best Practices for Regional Fisheries Management Organization* (Chatham House London 2007), x.
24 T McDorman, 'Implementing Existing Tools: Turning Words into Action – Decision-Making Processes of Regional Fisheries Management Organizations' (2005) 20 *International Journal of Marine and Coastal Law* 428.
25 See Tuna-org, *Meetings Past* (2012), available at <http://www.tuna-org.org/meetingspast.htm>.
26 A Vallega, 'The Regional Seas in the 21st Century: An Overview' (2002) 45 *Ocean and Coastal Management* 926.
27 UNEP, Regional Seas Programme, *About Regional Seas*, available at <http://www.unep.org/regional seas/About/default.asp>: 'Today more than 143 countries participate in 13 Regional Seas programmes established under the auspices of UNEP: the Black Sea, Wider Caribbean, East Africa, South East Asia, ROPME Sea Area, Mediterranean, North-East Pacific, North-West Pacific, Red Sea and Gulf of Aden, South Asia, South-East Pacific, Pacific and West and Central Africa. Six of these programmes are directly administered by UNEP. The Regional Seas Programmes function through an Action Plan. In most cases the Action Plan is underpinned with a strong legal framework in the form of a Regional Convention and associated Protocols on specific problems. Furthermore, five partner programmes for the Antarctic, Arctic, Baltic Sea, Caspian Sea and North-East Atlantic Regions are members of the regional seas family'; D Freestone, 'International Governance, Responsibility and Management of Areas beyond National Jurisdiction' (2012) 27 *International Journal of Marine and Coastal Law* 196.
28 Vallega, n 26, 926.
29 Freestone, n 27, 196–197.
30 P Sand, 'The Rise of Regional Agreements for Marine Environment Protection' in P Sand, *Transnational Environmental Law: Lessons in Global Change* (Kluwer Law International, The Hague, 1999) 178 and 183; A Boyle, 'Globalism and Regionalism' in D Vidas (ed), *Protecting the Polar Marine Environment* (Cambridge University Press, Cambridge, 2000) 27.
31 1986 Convention for the Protection of the Natural Resources and Environment of the South Pacific Region.
32 1959 Antarctic Treaty; 1980 Convention on the Conservation of Antarctic Marine Living Resources; 1991 Protocol on Environmental Protection to the Antarctic Treaty.
33 T Treves, 'Regional Approaches to the Protection of the Marine Environment' in M H Nordquist, J N Moore and S Mahmoudi (eds), *The Stockholm Declaration and the Law of the Marine Environment* (Kluwer Law International, The Hague, 2003) 137–138.
34 1992 Convention for the Protection of the Marine Environment of the North-East Atlantic.
35 1995 Convention for the Protection for the Marine Environment and the Coastal Region of the Mediterranean.
36 Sand, n 30, 181.
37 Ibid, 181–182.
38 Ibid, 178–182.
39 Ibid, 181.
40 1972 Convention on the Prevention of Marine Pollution by Dumping of Wastes and Other Matter; 1996 Protocol to the Convention on the Prevention of Marine Pollution by Dumping of Wastes and Other Matter.
41 2001 International Convention on the Control of Harmful Anti Fouling Systems.
42 1994 Agreement Relating to the Implementation of Part XI of the United Nations Convention on the Law of the Sea, Annex, [7]; ISBA, *Polymetallic Nodules*, n 19, Regs 18 (c), (d).
43 ISBA, Legal and Technical Commission, *Recommendations for the Guidance of Contractors for the Assessment of the Possible Environmental Impacts Arising from Exploration for Polymetallic Nodules in the Area* (2010) available at <http://www.isa.org.jm/files/documents/EN/16Sess/LTC/ISBA-16LTC-7.pdf>, [10].
44 *Responsibilities and Obligations of States Sponsoring Persons and Entities with Respect to Activities in the Area*, Advisory Opinion of the Seabed Disputes Chamber of the International Tribunal for the Law of the Sea (1 February 2011), 43–44 [141]–[143]; ISBA, *Polymetallic Sulphides*, n 19, Reg 33(6).
45 UNGA, *Report on the Work of the United Nations Open-ended Informal Consultative Process on Oceans and the Law of the Sea*, 5th Meeting, UN Doc A/59/122 (2004).
46 UNGA, *Report of the Ad Hoc Open-ended Informal Working Group to study issues relating to the conservation and sustainable use of marine biological diversity beyond areas of national jurisdiction*, UN Doc A/63/79 (2008), Annex I [5].

47 Ibid, [50], Annex I [4].
48 Ibid, Annex I [6].
49 Ibid, Annex I [7].
50 Ibid, Annex I [8].
51 Ibid, Annex I, [71], [72].
52 UNGA, *Letter from the Co-Chairs of the Ad Hoc Open-ended Informal Working Group to the President of the General Assembly*, 66th session, UN Doc A/66/119 (2011), Annex, Section 1.
53 Ibid.
54 UNGA Res 66/288, UN doc A/RES/66/288 (2012), [162].
55 UNGA Res 67/78, UN doc A/RES/67/78 (2012), [181].
56 UNGA, *Letter from the Co-Chairs of the Ad Hoc Open-ended Informal Working Group to the President of the General Assembly*, 68th session, UN Doc A/68/399 (2013), Annex.
57 Ibid.
58 *Outcome of the Ad Hoc Open-ended Informal Working Group to study issues relating to the conservation and sustainable use of marine biological diversity beyond areas of national jurisdiction and Co-Chairs' summary of discussions*, 20–23 January 2015 (Advance Unedited Copy), http://www.un.org/Depts/los/biodiversityworkinggroup/biodiversityworkinggroup.htm
59 UNGA Resolution, "Development of an international legally-binding instrument under the United Nations Convention on the Law of the Sea on the conservation and sustainable use of marine biological diversity in areas beyond national jurisdiction", UN Doc A/69/L.65, 22 June 2015
60 CBD, COP Decision IX/20, UNEP/CBD/COP/DEC/IX/20 (2008), Annex I.
61 Ibid, Annex II.
62 CBD, COP Decision X/29, UNEP/CBD/COP?DEC/X/29 (2010), [36].
63 Ibid, [26].
64 UNEP, CBD Secretariat. *EBSA Briefing: Organizing Regional Workshops to Describe Ecologically or Biologically Significant Marine Areas (EBSAs)* (2012).
65 CBD, *Report of the Eleventh Meeting of the Conference of the Parties to the Convention on Biological Diversity*, UNEP/CBD/COP/11/27 (2012), Annex, Decision XI/17.
66 CBD, *Report of the Expert Workshop on Scientific and Technical Aspects relevant to Environmental Impact Assessment in Marine Areas beyond National Jurisdiction*, UNEP/CBD/EW-EIAMA/2 (2009).
67 Ibid, Annex II, [10]–[14].
68 Ibid, Annex II, [7]–[9].
69 CBD, *Report of the Tenth Meeting of the Conference of the Parties to the Convention on Biological Diversity*, UNEP/CBD/COP/10/27 (2011), Annex, Decision X/29, [50].
70 CBD, n 69, Annex, Decision XI/18, 7.
71 OSPAR Convention, Art 1(a)(i)–(ii).
72 OSPAR, OSPAR Commission, *OSPAR Ministerial Meeting 2010* (2014), available at <http://www.ospar.org/content/content.asp?menu=01441000000000_000000_000000>.
73 Ibid.
74 OSPAR, *Charlie Gibbs Marine Protected Area*, available at <http://www.charlie-gibbs.org/>.
75 1980 Convention on Future Multilateral Cooperation in North East Atlantic Fisheries, Arts 1(1), (2).
76 Ibid, Art 7(a)–(c), (e), (f).
77 NEAFC, *Media Release on 2004 NEAFC Annual Meeting* (2004), available at <www.neafc.org/news/docs/2004press_release_final.pdf>.
78 Ibid.
79 Ibid.
80 The topic of vulnerable marine ecosystems (VMEs) is addressed in Chapter 10 of this volume.
81 NEAFC, n 76.
82 OSPAR Commission, Sargasso Sea Alliance, *Collaboration Arrangement between the Secretariats of the OSPAR Commission and the Sargasso Sea Alliance and OSPAR* available at <http://www.sargassoalliance.org/storage/documents/Collaboration_Arrangement_-_OSPAR__Sargasso_Sea.pdf>.
83 D Freestone and K Killerlain Morrison, 'The Sargasso Sea Alliance' (2012) 27 *International Journal of Marine and Coastal Law* 647; OSPAR Commission, *Sargasso Sea Alliance* (2014), available at <www.sargassoalliance.org>. The CBD COP11 agreed that the Sargasso Sea, among other areas, is to be entered into the CBD Secretariat's repository of EBSAs and transmitted to the UN and other relevant competent organisations.

INDEX

ABNJ 394–408; CBD initiatives 402–4; deep seabed mining 400–1; developing regulatory framework 405–6; fisheries 397–9; gaps in regulatory framework 397–401; global and regional initiatives 401–5; key features 395–7; marine biodiversity, and 394–409; regional initiatives 404–5; regional seas arrangements 399–400; shipping 400
Aircraft: destruction in flight 35–6
AIS 367–9
Antarctic bioprospecting 330–3; Antarctic treaty 331; policy position of treaty consultative parties 332–3; scientific activity 331–2; strengths 333; weaknesses 333
Antarctic Treaty system 218–19
archipelagic waters 12; coastal state 62–3
armed robbery 277–92 *see also* piracy
asylum seekers 161–2
audits: flag state 51–2
Australia: courts 131–3; marine renewable energy 307–8

BBNJ Working Group 401–2
biodiversity, conservation of 115

cannon-shot rule 6
CCAMLR 333–6; policy position of members 335; scientific activity 334; Southern Ocean resources 334; strengths 335–6; weaknesses 335–6
coastal states 59–70; archipelagic waters 62–3; central role 59; contemporary challenges 65–6; contiguous zone 63; enforcement and regulatory powers 60–5; enforcement issues 65–6; exclusive economic zone 63–4; flag state, and 59–60; high seas 64–5; internal waters 60–1; jurisdictional competence 60; territorial sea 61–2
conservation measures: duty to accept 55
contiguous zone 8; coastal state 63; fisheries enforcement 147
continental shelf 10–12; definition 11–12; EEZ, and 12; fisheries enforcement 146–7; rights of coastal state 11; Truman proclamation 10–11

courts 122–36
crimes of violence at sea 265–8
criminal jurisdiction: territorial sea 7
cooperative maritime surveillance and enforcement 378–93; bio-security 382; customs offences 380; drug running 380; East Asia 389–90; EEZ 383–4; enforcement activities 386–90; Frontex 386–7; illegal fishing 379–80; immigration offences 380–1; information sharing 385–6; internal waters 383; jurisdictional framework 382–3; legal regime 384–5; marine biodiversity 382; maritime security 381; NIUE Treaty 388–9; people smuggling 380–1; piracy 381; pollution incidents 381–2; regional environmental protection 381–2; scaffold of cooperation 385; Southern Ocean 387–8; SUCBAS 385–6; territorial sea 383; transboundary illegal activities at sea 379; wildlife trafficking 380
Corfu Channel case 124–5
customs laws: enforcement 128–9

deep sea mining 95, 231–61; advisory opinion's key obligations 238–41; best environmental practices 240–1; Chamber's Advisory Opinion 233–8; continental shelf 242–3; EEZ 242–3; emerging regulation 241–7; environmental impact assessment 241; key obligations in New Zealand's EEZ 247–52; liability for failure to comply with obligations 237–8; LOSC 233; Nauru's request for advisory opinion 233–4; necessary and appropriate measures to fulfil obligations 237–8; obligations of state parties 234–6; Pacific 231–61; precautionary approach 238–40; regional measures 243–5; regulation in Pacific Island countries 245–7; seabed minerals within national jurisdiction 241–2
destruction of vessels 35–6
discharging flag state responsibilities 47–8
dispute resolution 122–36
dumping: pollution by 92
duty to render assistance 54

409

Index

exclusive economic zone (EEZ) 8–10; coastal state 63–4; continental shelf, and 12; environmental matters 9–10; fisheries enforcement 142–6; jurisdiction 9; regulatory duties 9; resources 9
exhaustion of local remedies 130

fish stocks: conservation and management 106–12; LOSC 106–7; United Nations Fish Stocks Agreement 108–12
fisheries: port state control 76; use of force, and 33–4
fisheries enforcement 139–60; areas under sovereign rights 142; areas under sovereignty 141–2; compliance 139–60; contiguous zone 147; continental shelf 146–7; control 139–60; EEZ 142–6; enforcement of laws and regulations of coastal state 143; flag state 148–50; high seas 147–8; high seas boarding and inspection 148–50; humanity, considerations of 146; imprisonment 146; international legal framework 140–1; monitoring 139–60; offences covered 144–5; port state enforcement 151–2; prompt release of vessels 145–6; sedentary species in extended continental shelf 147; surveillance 139–60; vessels which can be boarded 143–4; who can board fishing vessels 145
fisheries management: flag state, and 52–3
fishing: port state control 80–1
flag state jurisdiction: high seas 20–2
flag states 43–58; assessing performance 49–51; audits 51–2; discharging responsibilities 47–8; duties 54; duty to adopt conservation measures 55; duty to render assistance 54; effectiveness of regime 48–51; enforcement by 55; fisheries enforcement 148–50; fisheries management, and 52–3; improving effectiveness 51–2; limitations on jurisdiction 47; LOSC Articles 54–5; pollution from vessels 55; regime 45–8; sub-standard ships 48–9; vetting regimes 51
flag vessel: genuine link 20–1; recognition 20–1
flags with greater than 10 per cent detention rate 50
Food and Agricultural Organization 87

Germany: renewable energy 308–9
global organisations 86–105
Grotius, Hugo: *Mare Liberum* 16
Gulf of Guinea: piracy 282–5

high seas 16–26; coastal state 64–5; codification of regime 17; conservation of living resources 22–3; enforcement jurisdiction over activities 23; fisheries 19; fisheries enforcement 147–8; flag state jurisdiction 20–2; freedoms of 18–20; invalidity of sovereign claims over 17; origin of doctrine 16; regulation of activities 19

Horn of Africa: piracy 278–9
hot pursuit 13, 129–30
human rights 34–5

I'm Alone case 28–9
innocent passage 7
internal waters 5–6; coastal state 60–1
international law enforcement instruments 30–4
International Civil Aviation Organization 88
International Court of Justice 90, 124–5
International Labour Organization 87
International Maritime Organization 86–7
International Organization for Standardization 88
International Seabed Authority 87
international shipping: flag states 44–5
International Tribunal for the Law of the Sea 90, 125–6
International Whaling Commission 88
INTERPOL 155–6
invasive species 200
island: meaning 4
ITLOS themes 130–1
IUU fishing: emerging issues 155–6

largest flags of registration 1 January 2013 46
Law of the Sea Convention (LOSC) 90–9; conservation and management of fish stocks 106–7; deep sea mining 95; dispute resolution architecture 123–4; fisheries 97–8; fishing 94–5; land-based sources of marine pollution 93–4; liability and compensation 94; marine environment, and 112–14; marine living resources 94–5; marine mammals 95; marine pollution 91; maritime security 95–6; maritime safety 90–1; narcotics 96; piracy 97; pollution by dumping 92; pollution from activities in area 93; pollution from or through atmosphere 93; pollution from seabed activities subject to national jurisdiction 92; pollution from vessels 93; settlement of disputes 98–9; smuggling of migrants 96–7; submarine cables and pipelines 95; underwater cultural heritage 98
limitations on flag state jurisdiction 47

major ship-owning countries 1 January 2013 44
marine areas beyond national jurisdiction *see* ABNJ
marine-based pollution: land-based sources 93–4
marine biodiversity 324–41; Antarctic bioprospecting 330–3; CCAMLR 333–6 *see also* CCAMLR; desirability 327–8; knowledge about 327; measurement 328; vulnerability 328–9
marine environment 18; independent regional seas organisations 115; LOSC, and 112–14; regional seas organizations 112–15; UNEPRSP 114–15

marine genetic resources 324–41; evaluation of knowledge 329–30; no convention 325–7
marine mammals 95
marine protected areas 116
marine renewable energy 295–232; abandonment 305–7; Australia 307–8; decommissioning 305–7; drivers 295–6; electrical connection 304–5; elements of consenting 302–7; enforcement 314–16; environmental impacts 303–4; gaps 316–17; Germany 308–9; health and safety 314–15; international legal instruments 300–1; LOSC 299–300; navigational safety 315–16; occupation of sea space 302–3; ocean currents 298; offshore wind 296; opportunities 316–17; OSPAR Convention 302; OTEC 298; regional seas conventions 301–2; regulatory aspects 299–302; responsibility 314; salinity gradient power 298–9; Scotland 309–11; terminology 296; territorial planning 303; tidal energy 296–7; USA 311–13; wave energy 297–8
marine scientific research 212–30; advancing knowledge through 212–15; Antarctic Treaty system 218–19; areas beyond national jurisdiction 217; areas within national jurisdiction n215–16; capacity building 217–18; consent regimes 216; defining 212–13; duty to provide coastal state with information 216–17; emerging challenges for regulation 219–24; equipment 218; implementation 218; importance of 214–15; installations 218; international cooperation 217–18; investigating oceans 213–14; LOSC 215; marine genetic resources 223–4; marine technology 217–18; minimising environmental impacts 220–1; ocean fertilisation 221–2; profiling floats and drifting buoys 222–3; regulatory framework 215–19; self-regulation and voluntary measures 219
maritime law enforcement: use of force 126–7
maritime safety 90–1
maritime security 95–6
maritime zones 4–5
migrants: smuggling 268–72
monitoring, control and surveillance 153–5

narcotics 96; smuggling 268–72; use of force, and 30–2
nationality of ships 54, 128
naval warfare 27–40
New Zealand: deep sea mining obligations 247–52
noise pollution 202–3

obligation to permit disembarkation 169–71
ocean acidification 342–62; 1996 Protocol to London Convention 352; biological effects 346; CBD 353–4; climate change regime 350–1; direct effects 346–8; ecosystem-level responses 348–9; future directions 355–6; General Assembly resolutions and processes 354–5; GPA 353; key questions 355–6; lagging law and policy responses 349–50; LOSC 349–50; marine pollution control instruments 351–2; MARPOL 352–3; ocean chemistry 343–6; surging science 343–6
ocean currents 298
offshore hydrocarbon exploration and exploitation 193–211; accidental pollution 203–4; air pollution 204; cables and pipelines 194–5; carbon sequestration 204; decommissioning 201; decommissioning scenarios 201–2; discharge of oil 199; disposal of pollutants 199–200; dumping, rules on 201; framework provisions in LOSC and international law 194–8; IMO, role played by 197–8; incorporation by reference of global rules and standards 196–7; invasive species 200; issue specific rules 198–202; lack of implementation of LOSC Articles 208 and 214 197; marine surveys 195–6; noise pollution 202–3; obligation to establish global rules against pollution 197–8; obligation to restore natural environment 202; operating discharges 203; pollution of marine environment 196–7; post-development phase 201; preparedness and response planning for oil spill 198–9; protection against unlawful acts 200; removal, obligation of 201; site restoration 201; states' responsibilities 194–7; structures 194; treaties applicable to activities 198
offshore wind 296
OTEC 298
ownership of world shipping fleet 44

people smuggling: use of force, and 33
piracy 97, 277–292; concept 277–8; effective legal regime 286–7; enforcement 286; golden age 277; governance, and 285–6; Gulf of Guinea 282–5; Horn of Africa 278–0; legal and capacity challenges 280; lessons for combating 285–7; multilateral efforts to counter 279–80; multilateral engagement 287; patrols 286; regional cooperation 287; shipping industry responses 281–2
pollution from vessels 55
pollution offences: port-state control 75
port state control 74–9; development of concept 74–6; effectiveness 78–9; fisheries 76; fishing 80–1; pollution offences 75; port state enforcement, and 77–8; treaty obligations 74–5
port state enforcement 77–8
port states 71–85; concerns 72; contested jurisdiction 74; fisheries enforcement 151–2; internationally agreed standards 73–4; jurisdiction 72–4; policies 73; shipping 79; unilateralism 74; vessel in port 72

Index

Red Crusader case 29
refugee and humanitarian law 171
regional fisheries management organizations (RFMOs) 106–12
regional organizations 106–21; conservation of biodiversity 115; environmental concerns 115; fish stocks, and 106–12; marine environment, and 12–15
right of access to ports 167–9
rock; meaning 4

safety of life at sea 161–75; asylum seekers 161–2; conventions dealing with preservation of life *per se* 164–5; conventions dealing with safety of shipping 166–7; custom 161, 162–3; international conventions 164–7; international law 162–7; obligation to permit disembarkation 169–71; problems with implementing 167–71; refugee and humanitarian law 171; right of access to ports 167–9
safety of shipping: conventions dealing with 166–7
safety zones 12
Saiga principles 28–30, 126–8
salinity gradient power 298–9
Scotland: marine renewable energy 309–11
Sea-Bed Committee 18
settlement of disputes 98–9
shipping: port state control 79
smuggling of migrants 96–7, 268–72
smuggling of narcotics 268–72
Somalia:piracy and armed robbery 37
status of ships 54
SUA Convention 265–6; effectiveness 267–8
sub-standard ships 48–9
submarine cables and pipelines 95

technology 363–77; Californian vessel emission controls 369–71; electronic for fisheries MCS 366–7; enforcement, and 372–3; LOSC, and 373–4; MARPOL Annex VI 371–2; non-specific 369–72; regulation 369–72; regulation versus enforcement 363–4; specific, regulation of 364–9; use in maritime regulation and enforcement 363–77
territorial sea 6–8; coastal state 61–2; criminal jurisdiction 7
terrorism 265–8

tidal energy 296–7
transit passage 8
transnational crime 262–76; concept 262; LOSC: coastal states 262–3; general principles of international law 265; jurisdiction 262–5; LOSC: high seas 263–5
tribunals 122–36

UN Division for Ocean Affairs and the Law of the Sea 89
UN Educational, Scientific and Cultural Organization 88
UN Environment Programme 89
UN Fish Stocks Agreement 108–12
UN Interregional Crime and Justice Research Institute 89
UN Office of Drugs and Crime 89
UNEPRSP 114–15
underwater cultural heritage 98
United States of America: marine renewable energy 311–13
use of force 27–40; LOSC, and 34; maritime law enforcement 126–7; UN Security Council resolutions 36–7

vessel-source pollution 176–92; AFS Convention 181–2; BWM Convention 182; global regulation 178–80; Hong Kong Convention 182; IMO 179–80; IMO compliance mechanisms 185–6; IMO instruments 183; instruments on liability, insurance and compensation 180; international enforcement 184–7; international regulation 178–84; Intervention Convention 180; LOSC 178–9; MARPOL 73/78 180–1; OPRC 90 181; Regional PSC Arrangements 186; regional compliance mechanisms 186–7; regional regulation 183–4; Salvage Convention 181; scope 177–8
vetting regimes: flag states 51
violence against ships and platforms 33
VMS 365–6
Volga cases 131–2

weapons of mass destruction: use of force, and 32

zonal approach 3–15